THE
ESSENTIAL
HANDBOOK OF

DENOMINATIONS
AND MINISTRIES

THE ESSENTIAL HANDBOOK OF

DENOMINATIONS AND MINISTRIES

GEORGE THOMAS KURIAN AND
SARAH CLAUDINE DAY, EDITORS

BakerBooks
a division of Baker Publishing Group
Grand Rapids, Michigan

Published by Baker Books
a division of Baker Publishing Group
P.O. Box 6287, Grand Rapids, MI 49516-6287
http://www.bakerbooks.com

Printed in the United States of America

Library of Congress Cataloging-in-Publication Data
Names: Kurian, George Thomas, editor.
Title: The essential handbook of denominations and ministries / George Thomas Kurian and Sarah Claudine Day, editors.
Description: Grand Rapids : Baker Books, 2017.
Identifiers: LCCN 2016012033 | ISBN 9780801013249 (cloth)
Subjects: LCSH: Christian sects.
Classification: LCC BR157 .E87 2017 | DDC 280.0973—dc23
LC record available at http://lccn.loc.gov/2016012033

Scripture quotations labeled ASV are from the American Standard Version of the Bible.

Scripture quotations labeled KJV are from the King James Version of the Bible.

Scripture quotations labeled NASB are from the New American Standard Bible®, copyright © 1960, 1962, 1963, 1968, 1971, 1972, 1973, 1975, 1977, 1995 by The Lockman Foundation. Used by permission.

Scripture quotations labeled NIV are from the Holy Bible, New International Version®. NIV®. Copyright © 1973, 1978, 1984, 2011 by Biblica, Inc.™ Used by permission of Zondervan. All rights reserved worldwide. www.zondervan.com

Scripture quotations labeled NIV 1984 are from the Holy Bible, New International Version®. NIV®. Copyright © 1973, 1978, 1984 by Biblica, Inc.™ Used by permission of Zondervan. All rights reserved worldwide. www.zondervan.com

Scripture quotations labeled NKJV are from the New King James Version. Copyright © 1982 by Thomas Nelson, Inc. Used by permission. All rights reserved.

Scripture quotations labeled NRSV are from the New Revised Standard Version of the Bible, copyright © 1989, by the Division of Christian Education of the National Council of the Churches of Christ in the United States of America. Used by permission. All rights reserved.

Scripture quotations labeled RSV are from the Revised Standard Version of the Bible, copyright 1952 [2nd edition, 1971] by the Division of Christian Education of the National Council of the Churches of Christ in the United States of America. Used by permission. All rights reserved.

Scripture quotations labeled TNIV are from the Holy Bible, Today's New International Version®. TNIV®. Copyright © 2001, 2005 by Biblica, Inc.™ Used by permission of Zondervan. All rights reserved worldwide. www.zondervan.com

17   18   19   20   21   22   23   7   6   5   4   3   2   1

Contents

Contents

Part 2   Ministries

Preface

The Essential Handbook of Denominations and Ministries is a guide and road map of the religious landscape of the United States. It profiles 200 denominations, with a combined membership of over 150 million people, and 140 ministries that serve not merely in the United States but also in over 190 other countries. The entries in *The Essential Handbook of Denominations and Ministries* provide a narrative profile as well as statistical information. But by themselves they do not provide an overview of Christian America or its strengths and weaknesses. Christianity is more than a set of numbers or raw information. The real strength of the church is from the Lord who watches over it.

"Denomination" is the term most commonly used to denote families of churches that share the same doctrines or dogmas and thus share fellowship. There are over 22,000 denominations in the world today, not counting sects and cults, and there are nearly 5,000 in the United States alone. We have profiled 200 of the largest and most active. The denominations' traditions and confessions vary, as do their organizations, authority structures, practices, and worship modes, and we have sought to illumine these differences, even as we also note the broad agreement on the essentials of the Christian faith.

A ministry can be an outreach of a church, denomination, or fellowship, or it can originate with the passion and call of an individual or small group. These ministries are a means by which the faithful engage with the world around them and participate in the mission of God by serving the community (locally or globally). The ministries section profiles prominent ministries in the United States.

The Essential Handbook of Denominations and Ministries tries as faithfully as possible to inventory and profile the major denominations and ministries in the United States so that Christians have a better understanding of the nature of the church as it operates in America. The entries draw as much as possible on information directly from the denominations or ministries themselves, and often particularly from the organization's website, listed at the end of each entry.

Special thanks are due to Phil Stoner for his commitment to this project. I would also like to acknowledge the prayers and support of my wife, Annie Kurian, during the gestation of this book.

George Thomas Kurian
Yorktown Heights, New York

Part 1

Denominations

Adventist/Sabbatarian

Advent Christian General Conference

History

Following the failed prediction of Christ's visible return in 1844 by William Miller, evangelical Adventist-minded followers formed the American Evangelical Advent Conference. Out of this group the Advent Christian General Conference (ACGC) officially organized in 1860. Two primary doctrinal positions formed the core of this new denomination: belief in the imminent, personal, and visible return of Christ to earth to raise the dead, punish the wicked, and usher in a new heaven and a new earth; and belief in "conditional immortality"—that eternal life is a gift of God given only to those who trust in Christ alone for salvation. Conditional immortality led Advent Christians to deny natural immortality of the soul and that unbelievers will be justly punished for their sin in the lake of fire. Similar to other groups of the Second Great Awakening era, Advent Christians made use of prophecy charts, conferences, and evangelistic camp meetings.

Headquarters

146011 Albemarle Road
Charlotte, NC 28227

Core Beliefs

The watchword of early Advent Christians was "no creed but the Bible." Advent Christians share with other Christians the beliefs set forth in the Apostles' Creed and "make Christian character the only test of fellowship and communion" (*2010 Advent Christian Manual*, 11).

Their beliefs span Reformed and Arminian doctrines as well as a variety of eschatological views. The ACGC website publishes a doctrinal statement.

Website

http://www.adventchristian.org/

Bibliography

Advent Christian General Conference of America. *The 2010 Advent Christian Manual.* Charlotte, NC: Advent Christian General Conference, 2010.

William J. Monroe and Philip G. Monroe

Church of God, Seventh Day

History

The Church of God (Adventist) grew out of William Miller's Great Disappointment (1844), when the church remained independent of the leading Adventist churches. Their independence was characterized by the rejection of Ellen G. White's visions, which in 1863 led to the formation of independent sabbatarian congregations comprised of devout advent believers located in Michigan and Iowa. These believers conducted conferences and camp meetings and were inspired by the periodicals (*The Hope of Israel*) and leadership of Enos Easton, Samuel Davison, and Gilbert Cranmer.

By 1866, the name Church of God was common and in use, and, as the assemblies coalesced, the Church of God, Seventh Day was formally organized in 1884. It was incorporated in Missouri in 1899. Headquartered in Stanberry, Missouri, the church adopted the name Church of God (Adventist) Unattached Congregations in 1906. In 1933, the affiliated congregations of the Church of God met at a general conference to discuss the reorganization of church polity and structure, namely, whether to leave the congregational system for what was perceived as an "apostolic" structure of "apostles" and "prophets."

Though the reorganization move was not adopted, many of its supporters resigned from the general conference and called a second meeting later in the same year in Salem, West Virginia, to discuss the issue. At that meeting, the supporters quickly adopted the reorganization of church polity and distinguished themselves from the other churches as the true Church of God, Seventh Day, Salem, West Virginia. By the late 1940s, calls for the congregations affiliated with Salem to merge with the general conference of the Church of God were heard, and the merger was finalized before the end of the decade. Soon after, however, there arose opposition to the merger among those affiliated with Salem due to charges that the church in Salem did not correctly follow proper church guidelines, and the merger was rejected.

In the end, those in Salem who rejected the merger continued with the Church of God in Salem, West Virginia, and used the designation "7th day" to distinguish themselves from the general conference designation "Seventh Day." The vast majority of the congregations affiliated with Salem accepted the merger and continued on with the general conference. In 1950, headquarters were moved to Denver, and today the official name of the Church of God (Adventist) is the General Conference of the Church of God (Seventh Day).

Headquarters

PO Box 33677
Denver, CO 80233
Telephone: 303-752-7973

Leadership

President: Whaid Rose

Core Beliefs

The Church of God is doctrinally sabbatarian and Adventist (though rejecting Ellen G. White's visions), with a focus on the Old Testament.

The church believes in the authoritativeness of the Bible; the divinity of God the Father, Jesus Christ, and the Holy Spirit; the inevitable presence of sin in all people; and forgiveness of sin and salvation by repentance and faith in Christ's death and resurrection, made possible by God's grace. Through the Holy Spirit, the redeemed must obey God and bear the fruit of good works, although these good works do not earn salvation. The church has a responsibility to evangelize and to perform charitable works. The sacraments are baptism and the Lord's Supper, symbolic in nature and followed by foot washing. Although Communion is practiced annually, allowances are made for those who practice it more frequently. Baptism is by immersion and

must be preceded by a confession of faith and repentance. Marriage is strictly heterosexual, and divorce is allowed only on the grounds of sexual immorality.

A distinguishing doctrine of the church is the teaching that the seventh-day Sabbath must still be observed as part of holy conduct, along with the observance of the other rules of the Ten Commandments. Church members are commanded to "avoid intermixing Christianity with extrabiblical practices, as in the common observances of Sunday, Christmas, Easter, Lent, and Halloween" (www.cog7.org, "Statement of Faith"). Other teachings condemn warfare, limit meat eating to foods called "clean" in the Bible, and require tithing. Prophetic teachings regarding the second advent occupy a central place in the church's doctrine; the reestablishment of the nation of Israel is viewed as an indication of Christ's imminent return. The kingdom of God will see two phases beyond the present time: the millennial kingdom of Christ, culminating with the resurrection of the unrighteous to suffer annihilation, and the eternal kingdom of God, in which Christ turns his kingdom over to the Father as a new heaven and a new earth begin.

Website

http://www.cog7.org/

Bibliography

"Church of God (Seventh Day), Denver, Colorado." The Association of Religion Data Archives. http://www.thearda.com/Denoms/D_1232.asp.

Melton, J. Gordon. *Melton's Encyclopedia of American Religions*. 8th ed. Detroit: Cengage, 2009.

Joseph M. Holden

Primitive Advent Christian Church

History

The Primitive Advent Christian Church is a small denomination in West Virginia. It was formed when some Adventist Christians separated from the Adventist Christian Church because of the teachings of Rev. Whitman, a minister of the Advent Christian Church who rejected foot washing and rebaptism of backsliders and apostates. The use of the word "primitive" refers to a return to the pristine teachings of the church. Like the Adventist Christian Church, the Primitive Advent Christian Church adheres to the views of Charles F. Hudson and George Storrs, who put forth a doctrine of "conditional immortality," meaning that the unredeemed are not immortal but will be unconscious until judgment and extinct afterward. Primitive Adventists are pacifists.

Headquarters

1971 Grapevine Road
Sissonville, WV 25320
Telephone: 304-988-2668

George Thomas Kurian

Seventh-Day Adventist Church

History

The Seventh-Day Adventist Church originated as a denomination in the United States as a consequence of the nineteenth-century Millerite movement. From his studies of the prophecies of Daniel, Baptist preacher William Miller (1782–1849) predicted that the second coming of Jesus Christ would occur within a year subsequent to March 21, 1843. Many thousands believed his teaching and made preparations for the second coming but were devastated as midnight passed on March 21, 1844, and Christ did not return to earth. A similar experience occurred on a revised date of October 22, 1844.

A small group still insisted that a significant event did occur on the prophesied day but not in the earthly manner Miller had prophesied. Through a radical reinterpretation of Miller's teachings, primarily through the explanation of Hiram Edson (1806–82), this small group (the "little flock") believed something significant did occur on October 22, 1844: the cleansing of the sanctuary in heaven, when the ministry of Christ moved from the Holy Place to the Most Holy Place and the investigative (pre-advent) judgment began. Despite several false prophecies, a core group of believers still affirmed the basic theology of Miller (without the predictions of the Lord's return). The core group met in Albany, New York, in April 1845 to clarify their doctrines of the second coming, the resurrection, and the beginning of the millennium. They agreed that the second coming of Christ would be personal and visible but that the date could not be predicted. Believers would be resurrected when Christ returned, but unbelievers would not be resurrected until after the millennium. The group also affirmed belief in the seventh-day Sabbath (Saturday) and "conditional immortality" (i.e., immortality is conditioned upon faith in Christ; thus, those who reject the Savior remain mortal and are subject to death).

Joseph Bates, one of the leaders of the second-generation Millerites, wrote a forty-six-page pamphlet in 1846 that reaffirmed the importance of observing the Sabbath on the seventh day as a perpetual sign of God's eternal covenant between him and his people. In addition to those of Bates, the efforts of Ellen G. Harmon (1827–1915) and her future husband, James White (1821–81), helped to organize a small group in New England that coalesced regarding the doctrines of the Sabbath and the second coming.

The name Seventh-Day was chosen based on the doctrine of the Sabbath, and Adventist was chosen to reflect the urgency to obey the Sabbath in anticipation of the advent of the Lord. The group's name thereby incorporated the two distinguishing doctrines of the Adventist movement, the seventh-day Sabbath and emphasis on the second coming of Christ.

Ellen G. White eventually succeeded Miller as the leader of the movement, and, by the early 1850s, the group had affirmed the spirit of prophecy as manifested through her. The group initially developed slowly, as a consequence of the Great Disappointment (i.e., the failed expectation of the Lord's return in 1844), but prospered and stabilized enough numerically that in 1855 headquarters were established in Battle Creek, Michigan. By 1860, those in the Millerite-Adventist movement had experienced persecution within mainline Protestant denominations for their emphasis on the second coming (as opposed to any particular Protestant belief system), which compelled them to organize themselves into a denomination. On October 1, 1860, the name Seventh-Day Adventist was adopted officially. The headquarters were moved in 1903 to Washington, DC; however, to accommodate the growing needs of the church, its world headquarters were relocated to Maryland in 1989.

Headquarters

12501 Old Columbia Pike
Silver Spring, MD 20904
Telephone: 301-680-6000

Leadership

The Michigan Conference was organized in 1861 (only six months after the start of the American Civil War). The first general conference session was held on May 20, 1863. By that time, there were six state conferences and approximately thirty-five hundred members worldwide. Subsequent to 1900, the current administrative structure was established, which is expressed in a polity that is Presbyterial (i.e., modified

Presbyterian). The organization of the constituent bodies is based on a representative form of church government. The local churches are organized into local (state) conferences, which consist of local churches in a province, state, or territory. All pastors are delegates to their local conference, and all local churches are permitted to commission delegates to their local conference (based on church membership). The primary reason for the local conferences is for evangelistic work in the local church territories and to achieve support for missionary work. Local churches elect the officers of the church, but their local conference supervises all local pastoral and evangelistic work and supports all pastors and workers of the local churches within its territory from a central fund and therefore has the authority to assign or dismiss pastoral workers. The local churches pay tithes to the local conferences. All ministry support of the Adventist churches is based on the tithe.

Local (state) conferences are organized into union conferences, which are made up of local conferences within a larger territory (e.g., an alliance of states or an entire country). The presidents of the local conferences are delegates to their union conference, with additional delegates elected by the local congregations according to membership. A union conference is administered by an executive board, which primarily promotes and supervises work in the local conferences in a manner consistent with the recommendations and resolutions of the general conference.

Union conferences are organized into division conferences, which consist of an indefinite number of union conferences. As a worldwide community of churches, the Adventist church consists of thirteen divisions administratively. The presidents of the union conferences and workers of the division conferences are delegates to their division conference. The presidents of the division conferences are vice presidents of the general conference. A division conference is responsible for church work in its territory in a manner consistent with the policies of the general conference. A division conference is governed by the policies of the general conference.

As the international legislative body, the general conference is the worldwide expression of Seventh-Day Adventists. The constituent membership of the conference is defined in the constitution of the general conference. The general conference consists of divisional offices, which by action of the executive committee at annual councils are assigned general administrative supervision for specific groups of unions and other church constituents within designated geographical areas.

Core Beliefs

Adventists affirm the infallibility of Scripture. They believe in the doctrine of the Trinity and the full deity (and humanity) of Jesus Christ. Although differences exist among Adventist denominations, the majority affirm Saturday as the Sabbath day of rest and worship. Adventists believe Sabbath observance is essential for awaiting the return of Jesus Christ.

The second coming of Christ is one of the core doctrines of the Adventist faith; consequently, it receives much prominence in the denomination's belief. Although Adventists deny that anyone currently possesses the mark of the beast (Rev. 13), there will come a "time of testing" wherein the counterfeit Sabbath will be enforced, and all those who continue in disobedience to the seventh-day Sabbath will receive the mark of the beast. The majority believe the wicked will not suffer eternally but will be annihilated and that the dead are not conscious between death and the resurrection (soul sleep).

Baptism is by immersion of adults. There is strict abstention from alcohol, caffeinated beverages, and tobacco.

Worship

The typical service includes worship music, personal and public prayers, a sermon based on the Bible, and an opportunity to tithe and give thank offerings. Worship styles vary from formal (anthem and hymn singing with organ and piano accompaniment) to contemporary (praise songs with the accompaniment of a guitar or a small band).

Divisions and Splits

The Seventh-Day Adventist Reform Movement was founded in 1925 in reaction against the church's position regarding participation in war. As a consequence of World War I, the Reform Movement believed military service should not be forbidden, but attempts at reconciliation with the mainline Adventists failed. The Branch Davidian groups emerged from 1959 factions among the Davidian Seventh-Day Adventists, who had separated from the Seventh-Day Adventist Church in the late 1920s. The Seventh-Day Adventist Church has been criticized by counter-cult ministries for affirming an extrabiblical authority of Ellen G. White's writings and for communicating an unbiblical gospel by means of the doctrine of the investigative judgment and seventh-day Sabbath obedience.

Statistics

Worldwide church membership is 16,307,880 in 68,225 churches, and by the end of 2009, there was a daily average of approximately 3,000 baptisms (with that average being surpassed for the first time in Adventist history with 3,032 daily baptisms in 2006). By the end of 2009, there was one Adventist for every 418 persons worldwide.

Largest Churches

Loma Linda University Church of Seventh-Day Adventists (Loma Linda, CA)
Sligo Seventh-Day Adventist Church (Takoma Park, MD)

Missionary and Evangelistic Work

Adventist missions began in 1874. The Secretariat Department of the General Conference oversees the worldwide missionary work of Seventh-Day Adventists. Adventist Mission provides coordination and funding for mission work, which currently impacts more than two hundred countries. The outreach of Adventist Mission workers includes community development, disaster relief, education, and medical care.

Academic Institutions

More than one hundred colleges and academic institutions are affiliated with the Seventh-Day Adventist Church. Ellen G. White founded Battle Creek College in Michigan (now Andrews University) in 1874 as the first higher education facility for Adventists. She also founded the College of Medical Evangelists in California (now Loma Linda University and Medical Center) in 1905. The church operates a worldwide system of nearly 6,000 schools with more than 1,065,000 students ranging from kindergarten to graduate level (approximately 4,800 primary schools, 1,000 secondary schools, 100 hundred colleges and universities, and 100 tertiary programs and worker training institutions).

Parachurch Organizations

The church worldwide operates 393 clinics (dispensaries), 174 hospitals, and 158 nursing homes, retirement centers, orphanages, and children's homes. The Adventist Development and Relief Agency works with victims of human-made and natural disasters (e.g., earthquakes, famine, floods, and wars). The Geoscience Research Institute was founded in 1958 to address the alleged conflict between religion and science. The Biblical Research Institute was established officially in 1975 to promote the study and practice of Adventist theology and lifestyle.

Electronic Media

Adventist World Radio is the international broadcast ministry of the church and the only ministry of the church that focuses on local international languages (particularly those in the 10/40 Window) by broadcasting in nearly seventy languages. Adventist Media Production (AMP) is the electronic media ministry of the church. AMP produces some of the programming for Adventist Communication Network, the satellite media distribution service for the church in North America, and Hope Channel, broadcaster of satellite Bible seminars. Adventist Television Network is the global satellite service of the general conference of the Seventh-Day Adventists. Three Angels Broadcasting Network is a private organization primarily consisting of Adventists.

Publications

The Adventist church operates a worldwide publishing ministry of more than fifty publishing houses in addition to printing countless magazines and other publications in 327 dialects and languages. The primary publishing agencies include Pacific Press (Idaho) and Review and Herald (Maryland), which publish a combined total of nearly fifty periodicals in addition to books for distribution in Adventist Book Centers.

Website

http://www.adventist.org/

Bibliography

Bates, Joseph. *The Autobiography of Elder Joseph Bates.* Battle Creek, MI: Battle Creek Steam Press, 1868.

Knight, George R., comp. and ed. *1844 and the Rise of Sabbatarian Adventism: Reproductions of Original Historical Documents.* Hagerstown, MD: Review and Herald, 1994.

———. *Joseph Bates: The Real Founder of Seventh-Day Adventism.* Hagerstown, MD: Review and Herald, 2004.

Maxwell, C. Mervyn. *Magnificent Disappointment: What Really Happened in 1844 and Its Meaning for Today.* Boise, ID: Pacific Press, 1994.

———. *Tell It to the World: The Story of Seventh-Day Adventists.* Nampa, ID: Pacific Press, 1976.

Moore, A. Leroy. *Adventism in Conflict: Resolving the Issues That Divide Us.* Hagerstown, MD: Review and Herald, 1995.

Numbers, Ronald L., and Jonathan M. Butler, eds. *The Disappointed: Millerism and Millenarianism in the Nineteenth Century*. Bloomington: Indiana University Press, 1987.

Ratzlaff, Dale. *The Cultic Doctrine of Seventh-Day Adventists*. Sedona, AZ: Life Assurance Ministries, 1996.

Schwarz, Richard W., and Floyd Greenleaf. *Light Bearers: A History of the Seventh-Day Adventist Church*. Nampa, ID: Pacific Press, 2000.

White, Arthur L. *Ellen G. White*. 6 vols. Hagerstown, MD: Review and Herald, 1981–86.

White, Ellen G. *The Great Controversy*. Oakland: Pacific Press, 1911.

Ron J. Bigalke

Anglican/Episcopal

Anglican Church in North America

History

The Anglican Church in North America (ACNA) began in the first decade of the twenty-first century as large numbers of orthodox believers disaffiliated from the Episcopal Church and the Anglican Church of Canada over doctrinal issues.

Headquarters

800 Maplewood Avenue
Ambridge, PA 15003
Telephone: 724-266-9400

Core Beliefs

The ACNA is in the mainstream of historical Christianity, seeing itself as part of the one holy catholic and apostolic church as handed down by the apostles. Characteristic of Anglicanism and essential for membership are recognition of the canonical books of the Old and New Testaments; observing the sacraments of baptism and the Lord's Supper (additional sacraments are allowed but not agreed on as either major or minor); belief in the godly historic episcopate as the inherent part of the apostolic faith and practice; adherence to three historic catholic creeds—Apostles', Nicene, and Athanasian; following the seven councils of the undivided church defining the person of Christ; receiving the Book of Common Prayer as set forth by the Church of England in 1662 as standard for Anglican doctrine and discipline; and adherence to the Thirty-Nine Articles of Religion of 1571 as expressing the Anglican response to controversial issues of the day.

In addition, the ACNA endorses the Jerusalem Declaration, which is the founding declaration of the global Fellowship of Confessing Anglicans.

Website

http://www.anglicanchurch.net/

Dee Renner

Apostolic Episcopal Church/Order of Corporate Reunion

History

The Apostolic Episcopal Church (AEC) was founded in New York City in 1925 by a former priest of the Episcopal Church, Fr. Arthur Wolfort Brooks. The Order of Corporate Reunion (OCR) became an integral part of the AEC in 1933.

The Order of Corporate Reunion, a quasi-secret society of Anglican origin, was founded in London in 1874 by Frederick George Lee. In the nineteenth century, disputes in Anglicanism that gave rise to the Oxford movement also initiated a debate over the validity of Anglican orders, producing a desire among some for orders that Rome would acknowledge as valid. As a result, three priests were consecrated in a clandestine service: Lee, Thomas Wimberley Mossman, and John Thomas Seccombe. The event was not sanctioned by the Church of England nor officially recognized. The line of succession of the OCR is extant today and is protected by the clergy of the OCR. The OCR is not a religious order in the true sense but rather an ecumenical and interdenominational association of clergy and laity that sees itself as representing a valid apostolic line of succession. The OCR is recognized by neither the Roman Catholic Church nor the Anglican Communion but survives in its original mission to provide apostolic succession to all (men and women) who seek orders in the hopes of restoration of unity among Reformation churches. Bishop William A. Nichols introduced the OCR to the United States in 1933 and in the same year passed succession to Bishop Arthur W. Brooks (founder of the Apostolic Episcopal Church). In the twentieth century, the OCR became associated with various theologies and lacked leadership, bringing it to near extinction. As a result, the Apostolic Episcopal Church and the Order of Corporate Reunion were reorganized, merged, and incorporated into a religious corporation in the state of New York in 1995. The AEC/OCR contains many denominations and clergy worldwide affiliated through apostolic lineage provided by the OCR. The primacy of the OCR passed in 1998 to Bertil Persson and in 2005 to the present primate, Peter Paul Brennan. The current primate of the AEC is Archbishop Francis Spataro.

Headquarters

80-46 234th Street
Queens Village, NY 11427

Core Beliefs

The Apostolic Episcopal Church/Order of Corporate Reunion models itself on pre-Nicene Christianity by teaching and adhering to the Holy Scriptures as expressed in apostolic teachings. The church recognizes the first three ecumenical councils of the early Christian church and the sacraments of baptism and the Eucharist. The ministry reflects an unusual understanding of apostolic succession: the physical or outer lines of succession defined by the original twelve apostles and an inner succession as reflected in the ministry of the apostle Paul; therefore, the AEC holds that the full ministry of apostolic succession includes not only the offices of bishop, presbyter, and deacon but also that of pastor, evangelist, reader, minister of music, and the priesthood of *all* people.

Website

http://innerchurch.wordpress.com/

Bibliography

Ollard, Sidney Leslie. *A Short History of the Oxford Movement.* 2nd ed. London: Mowbray, 1983.

Persson, Bertil. *The Order of Corporate Reunion.* Solna: St. Ephrem's Institute, 2000.

"A Statement of the Society of the Holy Cross Concerning the Order of Corporate Reunion, Printed for the Society by W. Knott, 26, Brooke Street, Holborn, EC, 1879." http://anglicanhistory.org/ssc/ocr.html.

Walsh, Walter. *The Secret History of the Oxford Movement.* 4th ed. New York: AMS Press, 1973.

Barbara Wyman

Communion of Evangelical Episcopal Churches

History

The Communion of Evangelical Episcopal Churches (CEEC) is a product of the Convergence movement (or "convergence of streams"), which sought renewal and unity in the church by envisioning the church as one body with many parts, or one river with many streams. The movement originated in the 1940s with Bishop Leslie Newbigin's *The Household of God*, which asserts that Catholic, Protestant, and Orthodox/Pentecostal/charismatic groups each fulfill a unique and necessary role in the church. Bishop Newbigin's Church of South India was recognized by the Anglican Communion, and his views gained popularity in the 1970s, in part because of Robert Webber's *Common Roots* (1978), which urged contemporary believers to adopt the spirit of unity and other practices that characterized the early church.

An Oklahoma City conference in 1993 gave cohesion to the visions of a growing number of prominent individuals who embraced the one-river-with-many-streams view of the church. The following year, the Evangelical Episcopal Church was formed, and it was instrumental in joining together members of diverse denominational backgrounds. The group has experienced impressive growth. In 1997, the name was changed to the Communion of Evangelical Episcopal Churches.

Leadership

Presiding bishop: Archbishop Duraisingh James

Core Beliefs

The CEEC states that it embraces both Protestant and Catholic traditions as well as various forms of worship. It upholds the significance of evangelical, charismatic, liturgical, and sacramental components to the Christian experience. The Scriptures are believed to contain all the things necessary for salvation, and the Apostles' and Nicene Creeds are accepted as critical statements of faith. Baptism and the Supper of the Lord are the recognized sacraments. The historic episcopate is seen to have a key role in the development of the Christian church.

Website

http://www.theceec.org/

Sarah Claudine Day

Episcopal Church

History

Today part of the worldwide Anglican Communion, the Episcopal Church was known as the Church of England when the colonists first arrived in 1607. British explorers such as Francis Drake, Martin Frobisher, Sir Walter Raleigh, and John Smith all came with Anglican chaplains who read their services from the Book of Common Prayer. Although Puritans were dominant in New England, the Church of England became the largest church in the South. Public taxes and contributions from the Society for the Propagation of the Gospel paid a clergyman's salary, which was fixed in Virginia at fifteen hundred pounds of tobacco and sixteen barrels of corn. Colonies were under the jurisdiction of the bishop of London, and clergymen could only be ordained in England.

With membership rapidly expanding, new institutions were created—William and Mary College in 1693, King's Chapel in Boston in 1689, and Trinity Church in New York City in 1698—and there were more than fifty pastors at work from Maine to the Carolinas by 1702. During and after the American Revolution, the Church of England became stigmatized as the church of an oppressive government, and William White suggested the formation of a new national church in his 1782 pamphlet *The Case of the Episcopal Churches in the United States Considered*. The church leaders changed the name of the church to the Protestant Episcopal Church (shortened to Episcopal Church in 1967) and elected Samuel Seabury of Connecticut as the first bishop. He was ordained by the bishops of the Scottish Episcopal Church in 1784, as the archbishop of Canterbury refused to ordain him. Three years later, Parliament and the Church of England relented, and the archbishop of Canterbury consecrated two more bishops in 1787. The church adopted its constitution and Americanized the Book of Common Prayer during the first meeting of the House of Bishops in Philadelphia in 1789. Eventually, dioceses replaced states as the primary organizational units.

Since much of the clergy and laity were loyalist, there were membership losses that were not recovered for a generation. The church sent missionaries to newly settled areas and, despite competition from Methodists and Baptists, established dioceses across the continent. Contributing to the church's growth were noted leaders such as Bishops J. H. Hobart in New York, A. V.

Griswold in New England, Richard Channing Moore in Virginia, Philander Chase in Ohio, and especially W. A. Muhlenberg. Among Muhlenberg's accomplishments were the introduction of the first male choir, the establishment of sisterhoods, the Fresh-Air movement, and the founding of the first church-run hospital in the country, St. Luke's Hospital in New York. He sponsored the second revision of the Book of Common Prayer in 1892, and his ecumenical vision led to the organization of the Chicago-Lambeth Quadrilateral on church unity.

Unlike most other churches, the Episcopal Church did not suffer division during the Civil War. The church enjoyed a period of growth in the aftermath of the war, with the creation of new seminaries and dioceses. In 1893, the Reformed Episcopal Church declared its separation from the main body, conceived as a reaction to the Oxford movement in England.

Episcopalians have supplied a disproportionately large number of the country's business leaders and political figures, including more than a dozen presidents.

Headquarters

815 Second Avenue
New York, NY 10017
Telephone: 800-334-7626
Email: gcoffice@episcopalchurch.org

Leadership

Presiding bishop: the Most Reverend Dr. Katharine Jefferts Schori

The Episcopal Church consists of dioceses that are autonomous except in doctrine, worship, and discipline. Each diocese is headed by a bishop who is elected locally with the approval of the episcopate and representatives of the clergy and laity of the entire church. The diocesan legislature meets annually and is comprised of clergy and representatives of the local congregations; between sessions, a standing committee of clergy and laity conducts the affairs of the church. The minister (rector or pastor) of each parish is assisted by the wardens and representatives of the vestry. All church property is property of the Episcopal Church as a whole, so parishes cannot secede without losing their assets.

Major policies are decided at the triennial general convention, which is bicameral. The House of Bishops and the House of Deputies meet separately. The delegates in the House of Deputies include clergy and elected laypeople of each parish and district (also called "chapel" or "mission"), as in the annual diocesan convention. The presiding bishop carries on work between sessions. The bishop is elected for a twelve-year term by the House of Bishops, with the concurrence of the House of Deputies. The bishop is assisted by an executive council of forty-three members, of whom twenty are elected by the general convention and eighteen by the provinces, and five are church officials. The council is responsible for the main program areas: national missions, world missions, education, communication, administration, finance, and stewardship.

Core Beliefs

The preface to the Book of Common Prayer states that "this church is far from intending to depart from the Church of England in any essential point of doctrine, discipline or worship." Episcopalians accept the Apostles' and Nicene Creeds as well as the Articles of the Church of England, with some exceptions. Upon ordination the clergy make the following vow: "I do believe the Holy Scriptures of the Old and New Testaments to be the Word of God and to contain all things necessary to salvation; and I do solemnly engage to conform to the doctrine, discipline, and worship of the Episcopal Church" (bcponline .org, "The Ordination of a Priest").

The church permits considerable individual variation on nonessentials. The sacraments of baptism and the Eucharist are seen as "certain sure witnesses, and effectual signs of grace, and God's good will towards us" (churchofengland .org, "Articles of Religion"). The church believes in the real presence of Christ in the elements of the Eucharist, although it does not attempt to specifically define the manner. Infant and adult baptism are performed by immersion, pouring, or sprinkling in the name of the Trinity, and adults are confirmed by the laying on of hands. While the church does not formally acknowledge them as sacraments, confirmation, penance, orders, matrimony, and unction are recognized for their sacramental nature.

Worship

Many Episcopal Churches are "high," that is, distinguished by the majesty of their liturgy, borrowed from the Church of England. Other churches are "low," with less elaborate ceremonies. The Book of Common Prayer is utilized by all Episcopalians and appreciated for its rich cadences. In 1976, it was revised for the third time to present the Eucharist, Morning and Evening Prayers, the service for the burial of the dead, and all the collects (short prayers) in both traditional and modern language while preserving much of the Tudor idiom and Archbishop Cranmer's language for the Great Litany. Other features included an expanded lectionary and two daily offices and complete rites for Ash Wednesday and Holy Week. In 1982, a new hymnal was issued, the first since 1940.

Controversies

In recent decades, the church has suffered from major rifts, the first in 1976 resulting from the authorization to ordain women to the priesthood. The first woman bishop was ordained in 1986 despite opposition from a conservative minority who believed that the general council did not have the right to decide the issue. (Today more than one-quarter of Episcopal clergy are women.) The second rift was created as a result of the ordination of Eugene Robinson, a practicing homosexual, as bishop of New Hampshire; although supported or at least tolerated by the majority of the church leadership and members, the action further enraged the conservative minority and generated opposition from many third world bishops of the worldwide Anglican Communion, who established a rival Anglican Mission in America and ordained bishops in breach of church protocol. The Continuing Church movement was created by opponents of the Episcopal Church leadership; in their Affirmation of St. Louis (1977), they asserted that the Episcopal Church had abandoned the Anglican tradition.

Statistics

In 2010, the Episcopal Church had 110 dioceses and 2,400,000 members.

Missionary and Evangelistic Work

The Episcopal Church operates an extensive range of ministries. These include urban ministries, support for ethnic communities, vocational programs, service opportunities for youth, outreaches to college students, nursery schools, agencies for childcare, elder-care facilities, hospitals, and clinics. Overseas ministries are maintained in Mexico, the Dominican Republic, Haiti, Brazil, Central America, the Philippines, India, Taiwan, Japan, the Middle East, and Liberia. There are nine communities for monks and eleven for nuns.

Among the church's most notable ministries are the following.

Episcopal Relief and Development is an international relief agency established in 1940 and until 2000 called the Presiding Bishop's Fund for World Relief. Originally created to assist refugees, the ministry shifted its focus to emergency relief work as well as long-term development. It operates several funds such as the Disaster Response Fund, Global Needs Fund, Pakistan Fund, Clean Water Fund, Malaria Fund, Women's Development Fund, Hunger Fund, Health Fund, and Economic Opportunities Fund. Together these funds annually help two million people in forty countries.

Episcopal Migration Ministries is one of nine agencies working with the State Department to assist refugees with their adjustment to life in the United States.

Global Mission Networks includes faith-based charities in the worldwide Anglican Communion. Among these are African Palms, African Team Ministries, Kyosato Educational Experiment Project, Church Periodicals Club, El Hogar Projects for orphans, Five Talents International, Friends of Cuttington College in Liberia, Global Episcopal Mission Network, Global Outreach for Addiction Leadership and Learning, Haiti Connection, Matthew 25 Ministries, Miami Valley Episcopal Russian Network, Partners-in-Ministry-in-Liberia, Seaman's Church Institute, Society for Promoting Christian Knowledge, South American Missionary Society, and Uganda Christian University Partners.

Missionary activity has been an essential part of the life of the Episcopal Church since its founding. The new churches that have resulted from Episcopal initiatives maintain a close bond with their parent bodies. To sustain these initiatives, the church has created these funds: Congregational Development, Global Ministry, Communications, Leadership in Ministry, and Spiritual Enrichment. The Fund for Archives and Mission Research Center seeks to develop an archival facility that will promote the study of the church's rich history and traditions.

The church is also engaged in advocacy in numerous ways, including its environmental ministries; Jubilee Network, which works to fight poverty and strengthen communities; ONE Episcopalian campaign, which seeks to fulfill United Nations development goals; Episcopal Public Policy Network, which encourages activism on public policy; and Episcopal Intercultural Network, which facilitates communication between cultural groups. Programs such as Anti-Racism Training combat prejudice, and the Office of Intercultural Ministries strengthens the voices of Native Americans, African Americans, and Asians and works to increase cultural sensitivity. There are also ministries targeted at people with disabilities and prisoners. Federal Ministries serves the needs of military personnel, their families, and the chaplains who minister to them. Campus Ministries assists college students, professors, and chaplains.

The Council of Episcopal Women's Organizations includes the Commission of the Status of Women, which works with the United Nations to advance gender equality; Anglican Women's Empowerment, which fosters collaboration between the United Nations and the Anglican Communion in the furthering of women's rights; Daughters of the King; Episcopal Women's History Project; Episcopal Women's Caucus, which has worked for the political and spiritual goals of women since 1971; and Girls' Friendly Society.

The Episcopal Council for Christian Education is a network of Christian educators working with children and adults.

Ecumenism

Seeing Jesus's prayer for his disciples to "all be one" (John 17:21 ESV) as a mandate for respect and cooperativeness, the Episcopal Church participates in dialogues with many Christian communions around the world.

Affiliations

The Episcopal Church seeks to strengthen the bond between itself and the rest of the Anglican Communion, which has 80 million members, 44 regional and national churches, 38 provinces, and 110 dioceses distributed in 160 nations.

The church's Partnerships Office encourages contact with members of the Communion, who share support in finances, education, missions, and other areas.

Academic Institutions

The church sponsors the following colleges, universities, and seminaries:

Bard College (Annandale-on-Hudson, NY)
Berkeley Divinity School at Yale (New Haven, CT)
Bexley Hall (Bexley, OH)
Church Divinity School of the Pacific (Berkeley, CA)
Episcopal Divinity School (Cambridge, MA)

Episcopal Theological Seminary of the Southwest (Austin, TX)

General Theological Seminary (New York, NY)

Hobart and William Smith Colleges (Geneva, NY)

Kenyon College (Gambier, OH)

Nashotah House (Nashotah, WI)

Saint Paul's College (Lawrenceville, VA)

School of Theology at the University of the South (Sewanee, TN)

Seabury-Western Theological Seminary (Chicago, IL)

Sewanee: The University of the South (Sewanee, TN)

St. Augustine College (Chicago, IL)

St. Augustine's University (Raleigh, NC)

Trinity Episcopal School for Ministry (Ambridge, PA)

Virginia Theological Seminary (Alexandria, VA)

Voorhees College (Denmark, SC)

Publications

Episcopal Life

Episcopal Life Online

Website

http://www.episcopalchurch.org/

George Thomas Kurian

International Communion of the Charismatic Episcopal Church

History

The International Communion of the Charismatic Episcopal Church (ICCEC) grew out of the Convergence movement of the 1970s and later. The purpose of the movement was to bring Christians together under one church with a synthesis of worship styles and patterns. This was accomplished by both recalling the roots of the New Testament church and blending Roman Catholic, Protestant (mainly evangelical and Anglican), and Orthodox sensibilities. Initially, these Christians formed house churches with some later developing into freestanding churches. On June 26, 1992, four congregations banded together to form the Charismatic Episcopal Church (CEC) (it would alter its name after its scope became international). The first convention of the CEC was held in 1994 and was attended by three hundred people. The International Development Agency was formed as well as St. Michael's School for Ministry (later St. Michael's Seminary). The denomination experienced rapid growth from 1995 to 2001 as churches and parishes joined the CEC. In 1996, the ICCEC held its first international convention, which was attended by one thousand people. In

1997, the ICCEC clergy were consecrated and ordained by the Brazilian Catholic Apostolic Church, thus ensuring an unbroken apostolic line of succession.

The ICCEC has over one thousand parishes and congregations in eighteen countries. Being Episcopal, the ICCEC uses the titles "bishop" and "archbishop" as well as the titles "primate" and "patriarch."

Headquarters

122 Broadway

Malverne, NY 11565

Telephone: 516-612-4027

Core Beliefs

The ICCEC accepts the first seven ecumenical councils, apostolic succession, seven sacraments, transubstantiation, the sixty-six books of the Old and New Testaments, and the charismatic revival as an authentic expression of God's actions. The ICCEC proudly professes that it originated independently. The statement "The ICCEC is not and has never been affiliated with the Episcopal Church USA or the Anglican Communion" is frequently found on official websites of the ICCEC and its churches.

Website

http://www.iccec.org/

Mark Nickens

Orthodox Anglican Church

History

The Orthodox Anglican Church (formerly the Episcopal Orthodox Christian Archdiocese of America) is the American branch of the Orthodox Anglican Communion, which is a worldwide movement of Christians committed to the historic faith in the Anglican tradition.

The Orthodox Anglican Church (OAC) was incorporated on March 6, 1964, by Episcopalians concerned with the liberal trajectory of the Episcopal Church. The Orthodox Anglican Communion is part of a growing number of churches considered to be part of the Continuing Anglican movement. The Continuing Anglican movement consists of churches worldwide formed outside the Anglican Communion, that is, no longer in communion with the archbishop of Canterbury. These churches believe they are continuing the traditional forms of Anglicanism, since traditional Anglican belief and worship have been revised or abandoned in recent decades. The

14

OAC was founded as a conservative alternative to the Episcopal Church, with apostolic succession traced through Old Catholic and Eastern Orthodox lines.

Headquarters

14 West Main Street
PO Box 1980
Thomasville, NC 27361-1980

Leadership

The bishop of the OAC is the Reverend Canon T. Creighton Jones, consecrated July 21, 2012. He followed the now retired first primate of the Orthodox Anglican Communion and archbishop of the Orthodox Anglican Church: the Most Reverend Scott McLaughlin, ASF.

Core Beliefs

"We believe and confess the three ancient Creeds of the Church: the Apostles' Creed, the Nicene Creed, and the Athanasian Creed. We believe Holy Scripture is God's written word. We believe in the genuine spiritual power of the sacraments. We believe in the power of God to heal the sick and broken-hearted. We believe that loyalty to our Lord is expressed by service to our fellowmen. We believe in the necessity of inward spiritual development and the outward amendment of life of every Christian. We stand for biblical faith and morality. Thus, we ordain only Godly men to Holy Orders and affirm that marriage is a sacred bond between a man and a woman" (orthodoxanglican.net, "Welcome: OAC-USA").

Defining Statement

"Our purpose is to present our Lord Jesus Christ in Word and Sacrament, and to perpetuate and promote, with the help of Almighty God, the biblical Faith and Anglican doctrine, discipline, and worship as directed by the Book of Common Prayer" (orthodoxanglican.net, "Welcome: OAC-USA").

Core Practices

"As Anglicans, we worship God using the traditional Book of Common Prayer and the Authorized Version of the Bible. We are led by Bishops who trace their Apostolic Succession through the Apostles of our Lord Jesus Christ and enjoy the same Episcopal Succession as the See of Canterbury, among others" (orthodoxanglican .net, "Welcome: OAC-USA").

Largest Churches

Anglican Uka Ndi Igbo (Bronx, NY)
Christ the Pantocrator Ministry (Hartford City, IN)
St. Augustine's Anglican Church (Bryson City, NC)
St. Barnabas' Orthodox Anglican Mission (Le Mars, IA)
St. Philip the Evangelist Anglican Church (Charlotte, NC)
St. Timothy's Anglican Church (Poquoson, VA)

Academic Institution

St. Andrew's Theological College and Seminary

Websites

http://www.orthodoxanglican.net/
http://www.anglicansonline.org/

Barbara Wyman

Reformed Episcopal Church

History

The Reformed Episcopal Church was founded in New York City in 1873 by Bishop George David Cummins (1822–76), eight clergymen, and twenty laypersons. Those who organized the formation of the church had been priests and members of the Protestant Episcopal Church.

The evangelical group separated from the Episcopal Church in reaction to the influence of Tractarian movement, which had resulted in a long debate in England and the United States with regard to the authority and ritualism of the Protestant Episcopal Church. Cummins was the leader of the evangelical party within the Protestant Episcopal Church and protested against the movement from the Protestant character of the Anglican Church toward Anglo-Catholicism. Cummins also protested against the exclusive attitude of other Protestant churches toward different denominations. The influence of the Oxford movement within the Anglican Church was to restore non-Reformational and more medieval doctrines and practices.

The difficulties between the low-church evangelical party and the high-church group climaxed in October 1873 when Cummins was censured by other bishops for his participation in an ecumenical, evangelical Communion service in New York City under the aegis of the Evangelical Alliance. Cummins was convinced that the public criticism against him was uncharitable and unwarranted. He resigned his office a month later on November 10, 1873, and transferred his episcopate to the new jurisdiction of the Reformed Episcopal Church.

15

Headquarters

4142 Dayflower Drive
Katy, TX 77449
Telephone: 800-732-3433

Leadership

Church leadership includes three offices: bishop, elder, and deacon. The majority of authority prevails within the diocesan and parish units. There are seven dioceses, with national headquarters in Blue Bell, Pennsylvania. The presiding bishop is elected by the general council and acts as executive head of the church. A triennial general council governs the Reformed Episcopal Church; her bishops, however, do not constitute a separate house.

Core Beliefs

Doctrine and organization are similar to those of the Episcopal Church, with some important exceptions. The Declaration of Principles, which is regarded as an evangelical response to nineteenth-century liberalism in the Anglican Church, forms the essential convictions of the Reformed Episcopal Church. Since Reformed Episcopalians see the Eucharist and baptism as symbolic, the declaration rejects the high-church doctrines with regard to transubstantiation in the Eucharist and baptism as necessary for regeneration. Reformed Episcopalians affirm the priesthood of all believers. A literal understanding of the Anglican Church's Thirty-Nine Articles of Religion is preserved, as is the Prayer Book of Archbishop Thomas Cranmer, who was martyred for denouncing medieval doctrines of Roman Catholicism. The church confesses three ecumenical creeds: the Apostles' Creed, the Nicene Creed, and the Athanasian Creed.

Reformed Episcopalians vigorously affirm the sanctity of human life. The general council affirmed traditional sexual ethics, condoning intercourse solely between a married man and woman, and therefore opposed adultery, fornication, and homosexual practice in all circumstances.

Defining Statement

"Scriptural, Traditional, Liturgical, Evangelical" (rechurch.org).

Worship

Worship is liturgical, as based on the Anglican 1662 Book of Common Prayer, in addition to components of the 1928 American Book of Common Prayer. The Eucharist and Lord's Supper are sacramental, as outward and visible signs of inward and spiritual grace.

Statistics

The Reformed Episcopal Church has approximately 13,000 members in 154 parishes in the United States and Canada. The largest parishes are located in Maryland, South Carolina, and Texas. The largest parish is Redeemer Reformed Episcopal Church in Pineville, South Carolina, with approximately 250 members (the parish had nearly 500 members but declined numerically as the result of deaths and families moving north).

Missionary and Evangelistic Work

The Reformed Episcopal Church is committed to evangelistic work as the beginning—not the end—of her God-given vocation. Reformed Episcopalians are committed to discipleship as a visible communion. The Board of Foreign Missions promotes mission endeavors for the Reformed Episcopal Church, with missionary support currently in Brazil and Germany. The goal of the mission board is to equip indigenous people to fulfill the Great Commission. The Board of Foreign Missions partners with other missionary and evangelistic endeavors throughout the Anglican community and maintains an alliance with ministries serving in Africa and the Middle East. The Order of Deaconesses was established to assist in institutional, mission, and parish work. The Reformed Episcopalian Church endorses chaplains for a variety of ministries. The Reformed Episcopal Church joined the National Association of Evangelicals in 1990.

Academic Institutions

Cranmer Theological House (Houston, TX)
Cummins Theological Seminary (Charleston, SC)
Reformed Episcopal Seminary (Philadelphia, PA)

Publications

The Episcopal Reader is the distribution and publication agency of Reformed Episcopalians.

Website

http://www.rechurch.org/

Bibliography

Aycrigg, Benjamin. *Memoirs of the Reformed Episcopal Church, and of the Protestant Episcopal Church*. New York: Jenkins, 1877.

Cheney, Charles Edward. *What Do Reformed Episcopalians Believe? Eight Sermons Preached in Christ Church,*

Chicago. Philadelphia: Reformed Episcopal Publication Society, 1888.

Cummins, Alexandrine M. *Memoir of George David Cummins, D.D., First Bishop of the Reformed Episcopal Church*. New York: Dodd, Mead & Company, 1878.

Dator, James Allen, with Jan Nunley. *Many Parts, One Body: How the Episcopal Church Works*. New York: Church Publishing Incorporated, 2010.

Guelzo, Allen C. *For the Union of Evangelical Christendom: The Irony of the Reformed Episcopalians*. University Park: Pennsylvania State University Press, 1994.

Price, Annie Darling. *A History of the Formation and Growth of the Reformed Episcopal Church, 1873–1902*. Philadelphia: James M. Armstrong, 1902.

Sachs, William, and Thomas Holland. *Restoring the Ties That Bind: The Grassroots Transformation of the Episcopal Church*. New York: Church Publishing, 2003.

Vaughan, Frank. *A History of the Free Church of England, Otherwise Called the Reformed Episcopal Church*. Bath, UK: H. Sharp & Sons, 1938.

Ron J. Bigalke

Baptist

Alliance of Baptists

History

The Alliance of Baptists is an organization of progressive Baptists that grew out of the 1980–90 fundamentalist-moderate controversy in the Southern Baptist Convention. Originally named the Southern Baptist Alliance when moderates organized it in 1987, the group adopted its current name in 1992. The alliance has moved beyond its original goal of providing a home for disenfranchised Southern Baptist moderates and has become an association of progressive Baptist churches and individuals committed to an ecumenical stance. For many years, the alliance was led by Stan Hastey, former executive head of the Baptist Joint Committee on Public Affairs, who retired as executive director in 2009. The alliance is noted for its strong stance on the rights of homosexuals to marry and for its advocacy of liberation movements.

The Alliance of Baptists was instrumental in the founding of the Baptist Theological Seminary in Richmond, Virginia, in 1991, and it has continued to form partnerships with theological schools. One of the most significant ministries of the alliance is to provide endorsements for progressive Baptist ministers wishing to serve as chaplains or in other positions where denominational sponsorship is required. This has been particularly important for Southern Baptist women, whom the Southern Baptist Convention does not endorse under its current policies.

In April 2004, the alliance went on record at its annual meeting as opposing all laws that would restrict marriage to a man and a woman, and in 2005, the alliance invited Alison Baker, the openly lesbian copastor of Glendale Baptist Church in Nashville, to speak at its annual convocation. Some of the largest churches affiliated with the alliance, including Wake Forest Baptist Church (located on the campus of Wake Forest University), Binkley Memorial Church, and Pullen Memorial Baptist Church, have been leaders in the battle for marriage equality among Baptists and have had same-sex services of union in their congregations. Alliance churches supporting homosexual persons in ministry or same-sex marriage have been disfellowshipped by the Southern Baptist Convention, and some tensions exist between some alliance congregations and the Cooperative Baptist Fellowship, whose policies prohibit the hiring of homosexuals.

Headquarters

3939 LaVista Road
Atlanta, GA 30084

Finances

The Alliance of Baptists has a budget of roughly $400,000. Membership in the alliance is dependent on financial contributions to the alliance.

Statistics

The Alliance of Baptists has remained small. It currently has 127 churches and approximately 65,000 members, many of whom are also affiliated with the American Baptist Churches in the USA, the Cooperative Baptist Fellowship, or the Southern Baptist Convention.

Largest Churches

Most Alliance of Baptists churches are relatively large. Among the largest are:

First Baptist Church (Washington, DC)
Myers Park Baptist Church (Charlotte, NC)
Northside Drive Baptist (Atlanta, GA)

Ecumenism

Although the alliance is not a denomination, it relates to the National Council of Churches as a participating church. Since 2003, the Alliance of Baptists has had close relations with the United

Church of Christ and the Disciples of Christ (Christian Church), permitting the exchange of ministers, and with the Fraternity of Baptist Churches in Cuba. It is also a partner with the Interfaith Alliance, an interreligious group, and is an active participant in the Baptist-Islamic Dialogue Task-Force, a discussion between six Baptist groups and the Islamic Association of North America.

Website

http://www.allianceofbaptists.org/

Bibliography

Graves, Thomas. "The History of the Baptist Seminary at Richmond." In *The Struggle for the Soul of the SBC: Moderate Responses to the Fundamentalist Movement*, edited by Walter B. Shurden, 187–200. Macon, GA: Mercer University Press, 1993.

Leonard, Bill J. *Baptist Ways: A History*. Valley Forge, PA: Judson, 2003.

———. *God's Last and Only Hope: The Fragmentation of the Southern Baptist Convention*. Grand Rapids: Eerdmans, 1990.

Neely, Alan. "The History of the Alliance of Baptists." In *The Struggle for the Soul of the SBC: Moderate Responses to the Fundamentalist Movement*, edited by Walter B. Shurden, 101–28. Macon, GA: Mercer University Press, 1993.

Shurden, Walter B. *Not an Easy Journey: Some Transitions in Southern Baptist Life*. Macon, GA: Mercer University Press, 2005.

Glenn Miller

American Baptist Association

History

The American Baptist Association is a missionary-coordinating body of Landmark Baptist Churches located largely in the southwestern United States. These churches are better known by their informal name of Missionary Baptists.

Landmarkism was a movement among Baptist churches in the South that antedated the formation of the Southern Baptist Convention. Originally inspired by the work of J. R. Graves (the influential editor of the *Tennessee Baptist*), James Madison Pendleton, and Amos Cooper Dayton, Landmarkism was an ecclesiology that stressed the local church as the only authentic form of New Testament Christianity. Other Christian bodies were religious societies. Naturally, Landmarkist churches prohibited intercommunion, even among Baptist churches, and pulpit exchange with other denominations. Strict Landmarkists held to the equality of all churches in any cooperative action between churches, a view that appealed to the smaller, rural congregations, which were often uncomfortable in larger Baptist groups that weighed participation by contributions.

The Landmark view of history naturally followed from their ecclesiology. If the only true churches were local bodies that practiced immersion, such churches must have always existed. The English Baptist G. H. Orchard in his *Concise History of Foreign Baptists* traced the history of Baptists through various groups of the patristic and medieval periods. His work was reprinted by J. R. Graves and sold throughout the Southwest. J. M. Carroll's 1931 *Trail of Blood* was the most popular exposition of this position.

Two controversies among Southern Baptists led the founders of the American Baptist Association to secede from that body. The first was the dispute over Gospel Missionism. Gospel Missionism, a movement in the Southern Baptist Convention sparked by J. R. Graves and T. P. Crawford, a missionary to China, demanded that the Southern Baptist Convention repudiate its commitment to managing its missionary activity through a centralized agency, the Foreign Mission Board, and return to what they believed was a more authentic system in which local churches and associations appointed and supervised the missionaries. The missionaries would be responsible only to those who appointed them. The task of the convention was primarily to raise funds for the work. The controversy over William H. Whitsitt also troubled Southern Baptist life. Whitsitt, president of Southern Baptist Theological Seminary and a German-trained church historian, published an article in 1893 that argued that Baptists had not practiced immersion before 1641 and that Baptists were part of the radical fringe of the English Reformation. The Landmarkists forced Whitsitt to resign his seminary presidency in 1899, but many of his opponents were not satisfied with the outcome.

Two primary groups left the Southern Baptist Convention in the wake of these controversies. The Baptist Missionary Association of Texas formed in 1900, and the Baptist General Association of the United States formed in 1905 in Texarkana, Texas/Arkansas. Both bodies were similar in faith and practice, and in 1924, they voted to join together as the American Baptist Association. The first meeting of the new organization was in 1925 in Texarkana. The American Baptist Association was primarily interested in foreign missions, although historically it has published Sunday school and other literature for the denomination.

The fundamentalist movement of the 1920s and 1930s deeply influenced the American Baptist Association. Its churches affirm the inerrancy of Scripture, the historicity of Genesis, and a dispensationalist understanding of eschatology.

Headquarters

4605 N State Line Avenue
Texarkana, TX 75503

Core Beliefs

Theologically, the only doctrines distinguishing American Baptist Association churches from other conservative Baptist churches are an insistence on the radical autonomy of the local church and an insistence on the historic Landmark understanding of Baptist history. The name American Baptist Association reflects the organization's understanding of itself as a voluntary cooperative body. The association does not consider itself a denomination or a church. American Baptist Association theology does not permit ecumenical relationships, although there are some ties to convention Baptists.

Although each church affiliated with the American Baptist Association determines it own practices and policies, the churches are distinguished by such practices as "closed" Communion—the restriction of the Lord's Supper to members of the church—and their insistence on baptism by the immersion of believers. Members coming from non-Baptist churches must be baptized again. Local churches are governed democratically.

Worship

Worship services are plain and generally include hymns, an offering, and a Bible-based sermon. The Lord's Supper is celebrated either quarterly or monthly, depending on local practice.

Divisions and Splits

In 1950, a substantial group of churches withdrew from the American Baptist Association to form the North American Baptist Missionary Association. That group was renamed the Baptist Missionary Association of America in 1969. The Interstate and Foreign Baptist Landmark Missionary Association, formed in 1951 by churches earlier associated with the American Baptist Association, is composed of churches that support their pastors through free will offerings and not through budgetary allotments.

Statistics

The American Baptist Association has approximately 250,000 members organized in 1,705 churches. Most churches are small, with the largest churches in Arkansas and Texas.

Publications

The association, through Bogard Press, publishes a full Sunday school curriculum and maintains a bookstore in Texarkana. In addition, Bogard Press publishes volumes of special interest to Landmark Baptists.

Website

http://www.abaptist.org/

Bibliography

Ashcraft, Robert, ed. *History of the American Baptist Association: Commemorating the Seventy-Fifth Meeting.* Texarkana, TX: Baptist Sunday School Committee of the American Baptist Association, 2000.

Glover, Conrad N., and Austin T. Powers. *The American Baptist Association, 1924–1974.* Texarkana, TX: Bogard Press, 1979.

Parrish, Terry. "History of Landmark Baptists." In *Baptist History Celebration, 2007: A Symposium on Our History, Theology, and Hymnody,* edited by the Baptist History Celebration Steering Committee, 372–96. Springfield, MO: Particular Baptist Press, 2008.

Glenn Miller

American Baptist Churches in the USA

History

The American Baptist Churches in the USA, formerly the American Baptist Convention and, prior to that, the Northern Baptist Convention, is the direct successor of the early Baptists who settled in Pennsylvania and Rhode Island. During the Great Awakening, the number of Baptists, in both the North and the South, grew dramatically, although these churches only cooperated with each other informally, if at all. Following English Baptist precedent and often encouraged by the Philadelphia Association, these churches gradually formed associations—voluntary groups of cooperative churches for common action. The Warren Baptist Association in Massachusetts and Rhode Island took the lead in the establishment of the College of Rhode Island, later Brown University, in 1764. The second wave of revival excitement following the Revolutionary War also encouraged the growth of Baptist churches throughout the new nation, with new congregations stretching across the ever-moving frontier.

The Second Great Awakening encouraged all American Protestants to enter actively into the Foreign Missionary movement. Sparked by the work of Adoniram Judson (1788–1859), his former associate in the Burma mission, Luther Rice (1783–1836), toured the nation popularizing his colleague's ministry and urging his fellow Baptists to cooperate together to support the work. As a result of his labor, the general convention of the Baptist Denomination in the United States (the Triennial Convention) met in 1814 in Philadelphia. Although the original plan called for this body to sponsor many types of missions, the convention came to focus on foreign missions, and subsequently, Baptists established societies for home missions, publications, and education.

In many ways, the theological disputes of the nineteenth and twentieth centuries were not kind to these early attempts at Baptist unity. In 1844, Southerners formed the Southern Baptist Convention, protesting the Foreign and Home Missionary Societies' "neutrality" on the slavery issue. In the North, the Free Will Baptists, originally united around a more Arminian theology, became passionately antislavery and drew many abolitionist Baptists to their side. After the Civil War, the American Baptist Home Missionary Society and the American Baptist Education Society were strong supporters of African American education in the South, establishing many schools and colleges. In addition, a few African American churches were planted under the society's leadership.

Financial and other problems convinced many Baptists in the North that they needed to consolidate their efforts in a body more analogous to the Southern Baptist Convention, and in 1907, they formed the Northern Baptist Convention. In 1911, the Northern Free Will Baptists joined the convention, and in 1950, it became the American Baptist Convention. In the 1970s, the American Baptist Convention adopted a major restructuring, granting increased authority to its general secretary, its various regions, and its general board. Faced with declining membership and widespread dissatisfaction with the convention's governance, American Baptists debated yet another restructuring in the twenty-first century's initial decade.

The intense theological controversies of the twentieth century were a challenge to American Baptist churches. The original fundamentalist controversy deeply affected the denomination, which lost many churches and a substantial part of its membership in the 1930s and the 1940s. During those decades, conservatives formed two new Baptist conventions: the General Association of Regular Baptists and the Conservative Baptist Convention. A larger number of Baptist churches either became independent or were founded as independent congregations. In 2005, the Pacific Southwest region left the denomination over the issue of whether churches that tolerated homosexual behavior should be expelled from the denomination (the Pacific Southwest region held to a more traditional stance), and separation was debated in four other regions. Most churches that left the denomination, however, became fully independent congregations.

Headquarters

Mailing Address
PO Box 851
Valley Forge, PA 19482-0851

Street Address
588 North Gulph Road
King of Prussia, PA 19406

Leadership

General secretary: A. Roy Medlin

Core Beliefs

American Baptists have no official creed or confession but maintain that the Bible, interpreted by the Holy Spirit, is the final authority for faith and practice. An identity statement, adopted in 2005, locates American Baptists in the broad stream of orthodox trinitarian Christianity and commits the denomination to missionary work, religious liberty, and an inclusive stance toward race, gender, and ethnic origin. American Baptist theologians were among the founders of the Social Gospel movement, which has influenced the convictions and practices of many American Baptist churches.

American Baptists practice believer's baptism by immersion, celebrate the Lord's Supper, usually monthly, and stress participation in the local church.

Worship

American Baptist churches are diverse in their style of worship, with most churches favoring a simple service that combines prayer, the singing of hymns, and a sermon. Although Judson Press, the denomination's publishing arm, still publishes the Baptist Hymnal (not to be confused with the Southern Baptist publication of the same name), local churches often use interdenominational hymnals from a variety of publishers. Because the denomination has become more diverse, many congregations worship in Spanish, while others follow traditional African American worship patterns. Many congregations have adopted evangelical practices such as using praise bands in worship, lifting hands during singing and prayer, and singing popular Christian music.

Controversies

In many ways, division remains among American Baptists over the issues in the fundamentalist-modernist controversies of the 1920s and the 1930s. In today's denomination, congregations often reflect these disputes' differing stances on the authority of the Bible, the various Christian responses to gay and lesbian persons, and the role of women in Christian ministry and leadership.

Statistics

American Baptist Churches in the USA reports 1.3 million members.

Largest Churches

Most American Baptists belong to small and medium-sized congregations. Among the larger churches are:

First Baptist Church (Elk Grove, CA)
Hillside Community Church (Rancho Cucamonga, CA)
Montgomery Community Church (Cincinnati, OH)
Mount Olive Baptist Church (Arlington, TX)
Shiloh Baptist Church (Washington, DC)
Union Baptist Temple (Bridgeton, NJ)

Growth

Since the 1960s, American Baptist churches have become more diverse and today include many Euro-American, African American, Hispanic American, and Puerto Rican congregations.

Ecumenism

The American Baptist Churches in the USA is a member of the National and World Councils of Churches and the Baptist World Alliance.

Academic Institutions

American Baptist Seminary of the West (Berkeley, CA)
Alderson Broaddus University (Philippi, WV)
Andover-Newton Theological Seminary (Newton Center, MA)
Bacone College (Muskogee, OK)
Benedict College (Colombia, SC)
Central Baptist Theological Seminary (Shawnee, KS)
Colgate Rochester Crozer Divinity School (Rochester, NY)
Eastern University (St. Davids, PA)
Evangelical Seminary of Puerto Rico (San Juan, Puerto Rico)
Florida Memorial University (Miami, FL)
Franklin College (Franklin, IN)
Judson University (Elgin, IL)
Kalamazoo College (Kalamazoo, MI)
Keuka College (New York, NY)
Linfield College (McMinnville, OR)
Morehouse School of Religion (Atlanta, GA)
Northern Seminary (Lombard, IL)
Ottawa University (Ottawa, KS)
Palmer Theological Seminary (King of Prussia, PA)
Samuel DeWitt Proctor School of Theology (Richmond, VA)
Shaw University (Raleigh, NC)
Shaw University Divinity School (Raleigh, NC)
University of Redlands (Redlands, CA)
University of Sioux Falls (Sioux Falls, SD)
Virginia Union University (Richmond, VA)
William Jewell College (Liberty, MO)

Publications

The American Baptist Churches in the USA continues to publish a variety of materials through Judson Press. In addition, the denomination supports the *American Baptist Quarterly*, published by the American Baptist Historical Society, and *The Secret Place*, a popular devotional guide. Much of the work previously done by American Baptist magazines is now done by regular newsletters sent by email to supporting members, churches, and friends. In addition, the Home Mission Society publishes *Mission in America*, a bimonthly newsletter, and International Ministries publishes a quarterly newsletter, *On Location*. The American Baptist News Service provides regular press releases.

Website

http://www.abc-usa.org/

Archives

The American Baptist Historical Society has consolidated its own holdings—the holdings of the American Baptist Archive Center, formerly at Valley Forge, Pennsylvania, and the American Baptist–Samuel Colgate Historical Collection, formerly at Rochester, New York—at its headquarters on the Atlanta Campus of Mercer

University. The mailing address is American Baptist Historical Society, 3001 Mercer University Drive, Atlanta, GA 30341. Researchers should request an appointment.

Bibliography

Baptist History Celebration, 2007: A Symposium on Our History, Theology, and Hymnody. Springfield, MO: Particular Baptist Press, 2008.

Brackley, William. *Baptist Life and Thought, 1600–1980.* Valley Forge, PA: Judson, 1983.

Leonard, William J. *Baptist Ways: A History.* Valley Forge, PA: Judson, 2003.

McBeth, Leon. *The Baptist Heritage.* Nashville: Broadman, 1987.

Torbet, Robert G. *A History of Baptists.* 3rd ed. Philadelphia: Judson, 1973.

Glenn Miller

Baptist Bible Fellowship International

History

The Baptist Bible Fellowship International (BBFI) formed on May 20, 1950, with a meeting comprised of approximately 120 pastors and supporters in a Texas hotel. They had been involved in the World Fundamental Baptist Missionary Fellowship (FBMF) led by J. Frank Norris. The FBMF began in 1928, partly under Norris's leadership, as a breakaway group from the Southern Baptist Convention (SBC), largely due to perceived liberalism in the SBC.

Norris dismissed George Vick, president of the Bible Baptist Institute of Fort Worth, Texas, in 1950. Vick's removal precipitated the May 20, 1950, meeting and the subsequent organization of two new institutions: Baptist Bible College, Springfield, Missouri, with Vick as its president, and the publication the *Baptist Bible Tribune.* These two entities formed the core institutions of the BBFI. The initial decade of the BBFI was a period of consolidation and reorganization as pastors and churches sought to give the new fellowship direction.

In 1975, the fellowship structure was reviewed and underwent several alterations. A new openness created opportunities for missionary training for BBFI missionaries by other independent Baptist colleges. Currently, the BBFI continues its fellowship of pastors committed to fundamental Christian doctrines and the inspiration of Scripture. It is perhaps the best known of the independent Baptist organizations, and several of its churches are among the nation's largest and have exerted a significant influence for evangelism and global missions.

Headquarters

Baptist Bible Fellowship Missions Building
720 E Kearney Street
Springfield, MO 65803
Telephone: 417-862-5001

Leadership

President: Mark Hodges

Core Beliefs

The BBFI is not a denomination, despite its appearance as such in structure and organization. BBFI churches reject any denominational-type control and are completely independent churches agreeing to cooperate together in a loosely framed fellowship. Therefore, each church's doctrine is specific to that congregation. However, uniformity exists in the following areas: trinitarian theology; emphasis on the incarnation, virgin birth, vicarious atoning death, resurrection, and second coming of Jesus; premillennial eschatology; salvation only through faith in Christ's atoning death; strong commitment to local church autonomy; belief in the inerrancy and literal interpretation of the Bible; and zeal for evangelism and world missions.

Website

http://www.bbfi.org/

Bibliography

Hillerbrand, Hans J. *The Encyclopedia of Protestantism.* Vol. 1. New York: Routledge, 2004.

Leonard, Bill J. *Baptists in America.* New York: Columbia University Press, 2005.

Linder, Eileen W., ed. *Yearbook of American and Canadian Churches 2010.* Nashville: Abingdon, 2010.

Randall, Mike. "A Brief History of the BBFI." *Baptist Bible Tribune,* January 1996.

Wardin, Albert W., ed. *Baptists around the World: A Comprehensive Handbook.* Nashville: Broadman & Holman, 1995.

R. Philip Roberts

Baptist General Conference/ Converge

History

The Pietist roots of the Baptist General Conference/Converge lie in the Swedish Baptist movement of the mid-nineteenth century. Sea captain Gustavus Schroeder, a nominal Lutheran, professed personal faith in Christ and was baptized in America in 1844. A year later, in Sweden, he discussed baptism with Fredrik O. Nilsson, who subsequently became a Baptist and was exiled by the state church. Anders Wiberg remained in Sweden, first as a critic and then as a convert and influential apologist for believer's baptism. In 1852, Gustaf Palmquist planted the movement's first American church in Rock Island, Illinois, where the initial plenary meeting of churches was held in 1856. By welcoming immigrants, the group saw remarkable "home missions" growth in America from 1870 to the eve of World War I. The American Baptists long supported the young denomination in education (since 1871) and world missions (since 1888). Moving toward sustainability, however, Bethel Seminary left Chicago for Minnesota and by 1914 had its own St. Paul campus. Subsequently, a 1945 "Advance" established a self-supporting conference foreign missions program as well. Sunday school, Christian camping, and youth work were dynamic contributors in outreach. By the 1930s, the movement from Swedish to English services created a new, expanded fellowship. A generation later, church-planting efforts beginning in the 1960s brought sustained growth geographically, numerically, and in cultural diversity.

Headquarters

Mail Code 200
11002 Lake Hart Drive
Orlando, FL 32832
Telephone: 800-323-4215

Leadership

Reflecting its free-church, congregational polity, the BGC/Converge has a president and elected overseer board, facilitating the mission of autonomous local churches. Biennial June meetings are held concurrently with the historic denominational school, Bethel University. At these meetings, resolutions may be introduced by motion as expressions of conviction.

Core Beliefs

Delegates to the 1951 meeting adopted "An Affirmation of Our Faith," since amended in 1987 and 1998. This twelve-paragraph guideline presents historic evangelical positions on major doctrinal points. The irenic spirit of BGC/Converge offers fellowship to both Particular (Calvinist) and General (Arminian) believers. Most recently, its "Gospel Declaration: A Call to Gospel-Informed Ministry" has expressed the common cause in Christ.

Defining Statement

"Connect, Ignite, Transform: *Connecting* God's people around God's purposes... that he might *ignite* movements of reproduction... for the purpose of *transforming* lives and communities with Christ's love and truth" (convergeworldwide.org, "Mission and Values").

Worship

Worship is seen as proclaiming God's glory and seeking his kingdom, individually and as a people. Historically, corporate worship has centered on the proclamation of the Word, engaged also through music, prayer, and stewardship. Within the denomination, styles range from classical and traditional to contemporary and emergent. Many have sensed that the increasing representation of global and ethnic voices has enhanced a Christ-honoring diversity in the fellowship.

Statistics

There are approximately 1,167 US churches and church plants in 11 districts, over 200,000 in membership, with over 100 additional churches in Canada. Seventeen ethnic groups enjoy recognized ministries, and global outreach includes 27 nations. The 2012–13 combined ministry budget was $15,466,839.

Largest Churches

Bethlehem Baptist (Minneapolis, MN)
Cornerstone Church (Chandler, AZ)
Eaglebrook Church (Lino Lakes, MN)
First Baptist Church (Glenarden, MD)
Golden Hills Community Church (Antioch, CA)
Whittier Area Community Church (CA)
Wooddale Church (Eden Prairie, MN)

Growth

The decades 1960–80 saw the denomination mushroom from 75,000 to 134,000 members and quadruple its $600,000 world mission commitment. Today's figures indicate continued growth.

Trends

After becoming BGC president in 2004, Dr. Jerry Sheveland led several initiatives to inspire and resource Christian transformation. His "Fire and Reign" studies focused on the power and provision of the Lord in spiritual recommitment and church growth. The "Salt and Light" sequel resourced witness. Building on earlier movements valuing prayer and ethnic ministries, missional emphases led the BGC to minister as Converge Worldwide, with headquarters moving from the Chicago area to Orlando.

Ecumenism

The church is a member of the National Association of Evangelicals, the Evangelical Council for Financial Accountability, the Baptist World Alliance, and the Baptist Joint Committee on Public Affairs. Warm connections continue with family services and retirement homes with which BGC/Converge enjoys historic ties. The recent transfer of many denominational functions from Arlington Heights, Illinois, to Orlando, Florida—into a shared facility (with Vision 360 and CrossPointe)—has underlined wider strategic alliances.

Academic Institution

Bethel University (founded in 1871 by John Alexis Edgren) has its main campus in St. Paul, Minnesota, with additional seminary campuses in San Diego, California, and satellites in Maryland and Massachusetts. The BGC/Converge president is an ex officio member of the university trustees, with moderate financial support expressing legal and institutional independence.

Publications

Converge Point magazine (previous longtime BGC magazine was *The Standard*)
Newsline Converge Worldwide

Website

http://www.convergeworldwide.org/

Bibliography

Johnson, Gordon G. *My Church: The Baptist Faith and Lifestyle*. Evanston, IL: Harvest, 1963.

Magnuson, Norris. *How We Grew: Highlights of the First 150 Years of Baptist General Conference History*. Arlington Heights, IL: Harvest, 1995.

Olson, Adolph. *A Centenary History*. Chicago: Baptist Conference Press, 1952.

Spickelmeier, James, and Carole Spickelmeier. *Five Decades of Growth and Change, 1952–2002: The Baptist General Conference and Bethel College and Seminary*. St. Paul, MN: The History Center, 2010.

James D. Smith III

Baptist General Convention

History

Messengers from the Baptist General Association of Texas and the Baptist State Convention of Texas adopted a resolution on December 9, 1885, that dissolved both organizations and consolidated the churches from each one into the Baptist General Convention of Texas (BGCT). The BGCT was received as a state convention of the Southern Baptist Convention.

The BGCT would weather several doctrinal storms and splits during the twentieth century. Movement toward becoming an independent denomination while maintaining ties with the Southern Baptist Convention (SBC) as a state convention began in the 1990s in reaction against the conservative resurgence in the SBC. While continuing to contribute to the Cooperative Program of the SBC, the BGCT took steps that clearly set it apart as a separate denomination. One of these was joining the Baptist World Alliance (BWA), an organization from which the SBC would later withdraw. In response to the BGCT's opposition to the SBC, the Southern Baptists of Texas Convention was formed in 1998 with 183 churches in support of the SBC. This convention contains churches that are dually aligned, supporting both denominations, and singularly aligned in opposition to the BGCT. Other state conventions, such as those in Missouri and Oklahoma, have followed the example of the BGCT by organizing their own Baptist General Conventions. In these cases, however, the convention split from the main body and took measures to become a self-supporting entity. The Texas convention is by far the largest and most established of the BGC conventions, and there is no national organization of the BGC state conventions. The Texas convention was renamed the Texas Baptists in 2012.

Leadership

BGC Texas executive director: Dr. David Hardage
BGC Missouri executive director: Dr. Jim Hill
BGC Oklahoma executive director: Dr. Anthony Jordan

Core Beliefs

The BGCT's strong doctrinal commitment to "soul competency" or "soul freedom"—that is, the individual's freedom to determine their own theological positions apart from denominational confessions or creeds—led to its staunch rejection of the Southern Baptist Convention's edition of the *Baptist Faith and Message 2000*. The denomination does, however, accept the *Baptist Faith and Message 1963*. The argument is that the earlier document allows more doctrinal freedom, while the later document is dangerously creedal.

In 1982, in response to some BGCT churches maintaining homosexual members, the church created a statement of faith that clarified its position by stating that "the homosexual lifestyle is not normal or acceptable in God's sight and is indeed called sin" (old.texasbaptists.org, "What We Believe"). The BGCT's statement regarding its doctrine of the Bible does not declare it to be inerrant but rather that it is the product of "divinely inspired authors and is the record of God's revelation of Himself to humankind" (old.texasbaptists.org, "What We Believe"). The BGCT lists the following as part of its position and posture for practice and ministry: the Bible as God's written Word, transformational churches, spiritual formation and discipleship, servant leadership, the worth of all persons, Baptist distinctives, integrity, and inclusiveness.

Worship

Worship styles among Baptist General Convention churches vary from traditional to highly contemporary. However, many churches strive to fall somewhere in between, blending traditional and contemporary styles of worship.

Divisions and Splits

In the twentieth century, the BGCT encountered three major controversies that resulted in the formation of three new Baptist organizations. In 1894, S. A. Hayden, a member of the executive board and the editor of the *Baptist Standard*, publically accused the denominational leadership of taking excessive salaries. The controversy went on for six years, and in 1900, the East Texas Baptist Convention (now the Baptist Missionary Association of Texas) was organized.

In 1928, J. Frank Norris led a group of Baptist churches in breaking away from the BGCT and the SBC. This split came as a reaction against encroaching liberalism in many areas of mainline Baptist life. The new organization was called the World Fundamental Baptist Missionary Fellowship (now the World Baptist Fellowship) and would spawn the later departure of the Baptist Bible Fellowship International.

In 1979, Adrian Rogers was elected president of the Southern Baptist Convention, inaugurating a theological redirection in the SBC toward a more conservative posture on biblical authority and inerrancy as well as other doctrines. The BGCT responded by deciding to remain in the Southern Baptist Convention but to initiate its own mission efforts apart from the national SBC as well as to support unilaterally other non-SBC ventures. Among the entities sponsored by the BGCT was the Cooperative Baptist Fellowship (CBF). Opposition to the SBC peaked in the late 1990s and was extenuated by the BGTC's desire to be admitted to the BWA as a separate member. Since then, there has been some continued controversy related to the more independent nature of the convention.

Statistics

Members: 2.3 million
Churches: 5,600

Largest Churches

Brookhollow Baptist Church (Houston, TX), with 31,050 members
Prestonwood Baptist Church (Plano, TX), with 28,266 members

Trends

The wave of conservative-liberal conflict that began in the 1990s carried over into the twenty-first century with the publication of the *Baptist Faith and Message 2000* by the SBC. Accusations of creedalism and fundamentalism kept relationships between the BGCT and SBC cool.

Missionary and Evangelistic Work

The BGCT strongly supports evangelism throughout the state and the world. The convention supports numerous outreach organizations that strive to share the gospel with people from Spanish-speaking border towns to big-city suburbs. Twenty-one percent of all financial support given to the BGCT goes to national and worldwide ministry through the SBC and the CBF.

Ecumenism

State Baptist General Conventions are cooperative with other denominations and associations. The BGCT cooperates with and financially supports the SBC, the CBF, and the BWA. However, each local church chooses its own partners and budget percentages.

Academic Institutions

Self-described as a volunteer fellowship of sovereign, autonomous, independent, and Bible-believing Baptist churches, the association is self-supportive and encouraging in terms of its institutional commitment to various seminaries and other academic institutions. These schools include:

Baptist University of the Americas (San Antonio, TX)
Baylor University (Waco, TX)

Dallas Baptist University (Dallas, TX)
East Texas Baptist University (Marshall, TX)
Hardins-Simmons University (Abilene, TX)
Houston Baptist University (Houston, TX)
Howard Payne University (Bronnwood, TX)
University of Mary Hardin-Baylor (Belton, TX)
Wayland Baptist University (Plainview, TX)

Parachurch Organizations

The BGCT operates five retirement and aging care facilities, as well as four centers devoted to children and family care. The convention maintains an advocacy care center that addresses issues such as community development, prison ministry, world hunger, ethical issues, and public policy.

Electronic Media

The Texas and Oklahoma Conventions make their magazines available in a web-based format (baptiststandard.com and baptistmessenger .com). Numerous churches in the conventions, especially the larger ones, make sermons available for free download on their websites.

Publications

Baptist Way Press, the publishing house for BGCT materials and curricula
The Baptist Messenger, BGC Oklahoma magazine
The Baptist Standard, BGC Texas magazine
Word and Way, BGC Missouri magazine

Websites

http://www.bgct.org/
http://www.bgco.org/
http://www.baptistgcm.org/

Bibliography

Alford, Deann. "Cracks in the Convention." *Christianity Today*, December 4, 2000, 17–18.
Baker, Robert A. *The Blossoming Desert: A Concise History of Texas Baptists*. Waco: Word, 1970.
"Seminary Sermon May Signal Thaw among Texas Baptists." *Christian Century*, November 18, 2008, 18.

R. Philip Roberts

Baptist Missionary Association of America

History

The Baptist Missionary Association of America was formed in 1949 as a protest against the American Baptist Association (ABA). The ABA had seated messengers in the associational meetings who were not members of the churches who had appointed them. In 1950, this issue, as reported, was repeatedly ignored. Subsequently, a meeting of "church equality" was held at Temple Baptist Church in Little Rock, Arkansas. During that session, the North American Baptist Association was created in response to the stated concerns regarding ABA messengers and their credentials. In 1969, the association's name was changed to the Baptist Missionary Association of America (BMAA). Headquarters were later established in Little Rock, Arkansas, and a publication board for the BMAA was created. Sunday school materials were produced in Spanish and English, and a vigorous mission program was inaugurated.

Headquarters

9219 Sibly Hole Road
Little Rock, AR
Telephone: 501-455-4977
Email: bmaam@bmaam.com

Leadership

Acting president: Paul Bullock

Core Beliefs

The Baptist Missionary Association's statement of faith is largely fashioned after the historic New Hampshire Confession. It is trinitarian and proclaims Jesus Christ as the Savior of the world, affirming among other issues his virgin birth. The statement also affirms what appears to be the pretribulation rapture of the church. The Scriptures are held to be inerrant and divinely inspired. The statement notes the depraving nature of sin and its impact on human beings. And while the way of salvation is thoroughly elucidated as resting solely on the saving work of Christ, the statement does affirm a complementarian view of divine sovereignty and human freedom. According to the statement, a person's freedom "enables him to make a personal choice in time, either to receive this salvation and be saved, or to reject it and be damned." The church is seen as a local congregation comprised of baptized believers "who are united by covenant in belief of what God has revealed" (bmatexas.org, "Doctrinal Statement"). Believer's baptism and the Lord's Supper are affirmed as the proper ordinances of the church, with pastors and deacons affirmed as permanent divinely ordained leaders of the church.

Website

http://www.bmaamissions.org/

Bibliography

Leonard, Bill J., ed. *Dictionary of Baptists in America*. Downers Grove, IL: InterVarsity, 1994.

Wardin, Albert W., ed. *Baptists around the World: A Comprehensive Handbook*. Nashville: Broadman & Holman, 1995.

R. Philip Roberts

Conservative Baptist Association of America

History

The Conservative Baptist Association of America (CBAmerica) originally began as the Conservative Baptist Foreign Mission Society (now World Venture) in protest of the Northern Baptist Convention's (now the American Baptist Churches/USA) perceived less-rigorous mission society policies. Generally, the Northern Baptist Convention (NBC) was believed to be drifting in a leftward theological direction. Subsequently, the mission agency was organized in Chicago, Illinois, on December 15, 1943, with the desire to maintain consistently conservative doctrinal standards among its mission appointments. Three years later, the NBC made a pivotal decision not to allow any competing missionary agencies within the denominational framework. Consequently, in 1947, the Conservative Baptists convened in Atlantic City, New Jersey, and institutionalized themselves as an alternative to the NBC.

Headquarters

3686 Stagecoach Road
Suite F
Longmont, CO 80504-5660
Telephone: 720-283-3030

Leadership

National executive director: Dr. Stephen LeBar

Core Beliefs

The core beliefs of CBAmerica include a high view of verbal-plenary inspiration, including the statement that the Bible is "without error in the original manuscripts" (cbamerica.org, "What We Believe"); belief in the Trinity, with a clear emphasis on the historical christological elements of the virgin birth of Christ, his bodily resurrection, and his personal return; emphasis on the substitutionary atonement in the saving work of Christ; faith in Christ as essential for salvation; regeneration as simultaneous with conversion, hence being less Calvinistic (while adhering to the doctrine of the perseverance of the saints,

CBAmerica does not endorse a strong Calvinistic soteriology); baptism by immersion upon profession of faith in Christ; and local churches as autonomous, with an emphasis on the body as a group of confessing baptized believers.

Worship

Worship styles—contemporary, traditional, or blended—vary widely depending on the local spirit and nature of the congregation. Preaching is generally Bible-based and is the essential worship component for the association as a whole.

Divisions and Splits

In the late 1950s, internal conflict arose over issues surrounding outside affiliations. The majority of Conservative Baptist churches co-operated with organizations such as the National Association of Evangelicals and the Billy Graham Evangelistic Association, but a vocal minority believed such actions to be dangerous. After seven years of debate, the conflict was resolved in the 1960s with the "militant minority" of two hundred churches leaving for more fundamentalist groups.

Statistics

Associations: 9
Churches: 1,200
Members: approximately 200,000

Largest Churches

Bethany Baptist (Peoria, IL)
Calvary Church (Muscatine, IA)
Washington Heights Baptist Church (Ogden, UT)
Waterstone Community Church (Littleton, CO)

Growth

Despite organization struggles, CBAmerica has grown steadily since its inception. The most rapid growth was seen during the early independent years of ministry in the early 1950s. A nationwide evangelical resurgence in the 1970s served to strengthen Conservative Baptist schools and mission agencies.

Trends

The 1960s and the 1970s were decades of growth for both local churches and educational institutions. But the growth of the 1970s quickly became growing pains in the 1980s. There was a long-term struggle in trying to determine the best relationship between CBAmerica, the Conservative Baptist Foreign Mission Board, and the Conservative Baptist Home Mission Board. Should they be consolidated or remain three separately governed organizations? A resolution was never truly reached as the church issued a "Call for Change among the Conservative Baptist Family" in 2002. The ensuing report stated that future spiritual and relational challenges would not be solved by mere structural changes. Consequently, there was a new resolve to focus ministry and educational resources toward the regional associations.

Missionary and Evangelistic Work

CBAmerica supports approximately one thousand short-term and career missionaries on all five major continents through World Venture, Missions Door, and other similar agencies. Missions and evangelism are at the heart of CBAmerica.

Ecumenism

While remaining firm in maintaining a high view of the inspiration of the Bible and conservative doctrine, CBAmerica cooperates with many evangelical churches and parachurch ministries worldwide. A number of congregations are part of the National Association of Evangelicals.

Academic Institutions

Bethel University and Seminary (Dresher, PA)
Denver Seminary (Littleton, CO)
New England Bible College (South Portland, ME)
Southwestern College (Phoenix, AZ)
Western Seminary (Portland, OR)

Parachurch Organizations

CBAmerica partners with organizations such as Indigenous Ministries International (IMI) to minister around the world through medical missions, micro-business loans, theological training, and church planting. Delta Ministries International, an interdenominational organization that specializes in short- to mid-term mission projects, has partnered with CBAmerica to provide disaster relief assistance, such as hurricane relief throughout the Gulf Coast.

Website

http://www.cbamerica.org/

Bibliography

LeBar, Stephen. "Conservative Baptist Association of America: Historical Perspective." http://www.cbamerica.org/documents/history_CBA/CBA%20Historical%20Perspective.pdf.

Leonard, Bill J., ed. *Dictionary of Baptists in America.* Downers Grove, IL: InterVarsity, 1994.

Shelley, Bruce L. *A History of Conservative Baptists.* 3rd ed. Wheaton, IL: Conservative Baptist Press, 1981.

Wardin, Albert W., ed. *Baptists around the World: A Comprehensive Handbook.* Nashville: Broadman & Holman, 1995.

R. Philip Roberts

Cooperative Baptist Fellowship

History

The Cooperative Baptist Fellowship is an organization for funding and fellowship that supports missions and education. The fellowship grew out of the bitter Southern Baptist Controversy of the 1980s, in which conservatives and moderates battled to take over the machinery of the Southern Baptist Convention. Many moderates shared much, if not all, of the same conservative theology as their opponents; at the same time, they had some commitments that they dared not compromise: a strong belief in Baptist missionary work abroad, a dedication to theological education, a firm belief in women in ordained ministry, and a commitment to such Baptist enterprises as the Baptist Joint Committee on Public Affairs and the Baptist World Alliance. The Cooperative Baptist Fellowship was created to offer moderates a way to merge their theological conservatism with other objectives.

Using the older Baptist model of a "society," the fellowship allows both individuals and churches to join. At the heart of the Cooperative Baptist Fellowship is the idea of covenant partners. In its core values, the fellowship affirms, "We prefer to cooperate in mutually beneficial ways with other organizations rather than to establish, own, and control our own institutions" (thefellowship.info, "Core Values"). The Cooperative Baptist Fellowship is one of a number of loosely related moderate Baptist enterprises, including Baptist Press, Mercer University Press, and a significant number of new Baptist seminaries. The concept of partnership enables the fellowship to be selective in what it elects to fund and, at the same time, to cap or limit funding of any particular entity. Thus, the fellowship can help to fund more ministries than it can sustain on its own.

Headquarters

Atlanta Resource Center
2930 Flowers Road South
Suite 133
Atlanta, GA 30341

Leadership

Executive coordinator: Daniel Vestal

Core Beliefs

The Cooperative Baptist Fellowship shares most of its theology with other Baptists. Perhaps due to its origin in theological controversy, it emphasizes four central Baptist affirmations: soul liberty, the right of each believer to interpret the Bible, religious freedom including the separation of church and state, and the freedom of each congregation to act as it chooses. The fellowship stresses the right of women, under the leadership of the Holy Spirit, to participate in ministry.

Website

http://www.thefellowship.info/

Bibliography

Leonard, Bill J. *Baptist Ways: A History.* Valley Forge, PA: Judson, 2003.

———. *God's Last and Only Hope: The Fragmentation of the Southern Baptist Convention.* Grand Rapids: Eerdmans, 1990.

Shurden, Walter B. *Not an Easy Journey: Some Transitions in Southern Baptist Life.* Macon, GA: Mercer University Press, 2005.

———, ed. *The Struggle for the Soul of the SBC: Moderate Responses to the Fundamentalist Movement.* Macon, GA: Mercer University Press, 1993.

Glenn Miller

General Association of General Baptists

History

The General Association of General Baptists (GAGB) began in the nineteenth century under the leadership of Benoni Stinson (1789–1869). He was a United Baptist minister who originally served in Kentucky and later moved to Indiana. Stinson rejected the Calvinism of many of his colleagues and instead emphasized a general atonement view of the death of Christ, noting Hebrews 2:9, which states that Jesus tasted "death for every man" (KJV).

In 1823, Stinson became the pastor of Liberty Baptist Church in Howell, Indiana, now in greater Evansville, Indiana. This congregation had endorsed an Arminian view of the atonement. Stinson then became an active church planter and formed three other affiliated churches. In 1824, along with Liberty Baptist Church, these four churches formed the Liberty Association of General Baptists.

The movement spread to the neighboring states of Ohio, Kentucky, and Illinois. Eventually, two churches were organized in Tennessee and Missouri as well. By 1870, delegates from three associations formed what became known as the General Association of General Baptists. Several ministries were encouraged by the association. These included the General Mission Board in 1871 and the Foreign Mission Board in 1903. In 1891, Oakland City College, a liberal arts college that now includes a graduate school of theology, was also organized by the GAGB.

General Baptists currently have approximately 60 associations with 816 churches and more than 75,000 members. These churches may be found throughout the Midwest, the South, and parts of the Pacific Coast.

Headquarters

General Baptist Ministries
100 Stinson Drive
Poplar Bluff, MO 63910
Telephone: 573-785-7746

Core Beliefs

The GAGB is an association of Baptist churches that practice traditional Baptist polity, including believer's baptism, congregational church government, and loose-knit denominational organization for missions, evangelism, and discipleship.

The denomination is committed to the principles of Arminian thought and theology, the foremost being the doctrine of a general atonement. This theological position was a reaction against early nineteenth-century Calvinism.

The 1970 revised statement of faith affirms the doctrine of apostasy, that is, the possibility of a believer losing their salvation.

The GAGB adheres to a Baptistic view of ecclesiology, evangelism, church membership, congregational worship, and baptism. The other ordinance of the church besides baptism is the Lord's Supper. Several associations and local churches practice foot washing as an ordinance, but this matter is left up to the discretion of the local leadership.

Worship

Worship services among GAGB churches tend to be more traditional, but contemporary and blended services are sometimes utilized in select congregations. Only a few churches have moved toward a more dramatic contemporary style.

Controversies

To date, no major divisions have occurred within the GAGB. However, in the 1970s, conflict arose over the practice of the charismatic gift of tongues. After struggle and debate, the GAGB concluded that the practice of speaking in tongues is not normative for the church today. The denomination reached this position without a major fissure or disruption.

Statistics

Members: 75,000–80,000
Churches: 816
Associations: 60

Largest Churches

New Walk General Baptist Church (Zephyrhills, FL)
Real Life Church (Springfield, IL)

Growth

The greatest time of growth experienced by the GAGB was the 1970s. This surge may be explained by an emphasis on crusades and outreach that characterized much of the decade. It appears that the denomination is again stressing the importance of evangelism.

Trends

In 2007, the GAGB made a significant shift in focus by changing its annual General Association meeting to the Missions and Ministry Summit. The change signified a desire within the denomination to focus more on missions and ministry than traditional denominational politics. The number of churches that have plateaued, membership-growth-wise, within the GAGB is rising.

Missionary and Evangelistic Work

The denomination conducted a five-year thrust for evangelism on the local church level from 2011 to 2015 titled Mission 1. The program was designed to refocus individual churches on outreach and evangelism. Personal work as well as evangelistic preaching are stressed in most congregations.

Ecumenism

The GAGB is a member of the National Association of Evangelicals and the Baptist World Alliance.

Academic Institutions

Bible College of Davou (Davou, Philippines)
Oakland City University (Oakland City, IN)

Parachurch Organizations

The Missions Department of the GAGB operates a children's home in Honduras and also sends frequent medical teams. The GAGB has also established a medical clinic in the Philippines.

Publications

The *Messenger* is the official publication of the GAGB. However, the denomination is transitioning away from the printed format and redesigning the periodical for online publication that will be freely accessible. Stinson Press is the publishing department for the denomination.

Website

http://www.generalbaptist.com/

Bibliography

General Association of General Baptists. "2010 Report to the Local Associations." http://storage.cloversites.com/generalbaptistministries/documents/2010%20Report%20to%20the%20Local%20Associations.pdf.

Leonard, Bill J. *Baptists in America.* New York: Columbia University Press, 2005.

———, ed. *Dictionary of Baptists in America.* Downers Grove, IL: InterVarsity, 1994.

Mead, Frank S., Samuel S. Hill, and Craig D. Atwood. "General Association of General Baptists." In *Handbook of Denominations in the United States.* 13th ed. Nashville: Abingdon, 2010.

Sloan, John. Unpublished interview conducted by William R. Osborne. September 2, 2010.

Wardin, Albert W., ed. *Baptists around the World: A Comprehensive Handbook.* Nashville: Broadman & Holman, 1995.

R. Philip Roberts

General Association of Regular Baptist Churches

History

The General Association of Regular Baptist Churches (GARBC) was organized and commenced formally as a new Baptist body in May 1932. Doctrinal differences compelled several churches to withdraw from the Northern Baptist Convention (currently the American Baptist Churches in the USA). Twenty-two Baptist churches protested that the convention had embraced modernism, denied the autonomy and independence of the local congregation, and no longer upheld the New Hampshire Confession of Faith (1833), which was affirmed widely by Baptists in the northern and western United States. The churches agreed regarding the need for a new fellowship, and having departed from the convention, these churches founded the General Association of Regular Baptist Churches. The new association agreed to develop a national and international network, as opposed to a convention, denomination, or monolithic body. The churches adopted the New Hampshire Confession of Faith, with a revised premillennial statement in the last article on eschatology. Baptist pastor and leader of separatist fundamentalism Robert T. Ketcham (1889–1978) was the leading founder of the association. Ketcham was elected vice president in 1933, president in 1934, and editor of the *Baptist Bulletin* in 1938.

Headquarters

1300 North Meacham Road
Schaumburg, IL 60173
Telephone: 888-588-1600

Core Beliefs

The association affirms biblical fundamentals of the faith, as opposed to the "irregular" doctrines of theological liberalism. The GARBC is distinguished by its commitment to the "regular" Baptist conviction regarding biblical authority. The churches affirm local church autonomy, public immersion, regenerate church membership, individual soul liberty, and separation of church and state.

The GARBC has an informative literature list that discusses the issues that led to the formation of the association and defines its beliefs, practices, and policies. There are currently fifteen literature items that address the following issues: constitution and articles of faith; formational necessity; identity; operational method; missionary, educational, and social polity; separation; the local church; Baptist bodies and the sovereignty of the local church; Baptist individualism and cooperative fellowship; limited message and fellowship; Baptist heritage; biblical separation; ecumenism and Roman Catholicism; GARBC benefits; and evangelical sectarianism. These defining documents indicate associational actions and positions approved by the Publications Committee of the Council of Eighteen.

Churches cooperate with each other for fellowship, ministry, and witness. The GARBC separates from compromising accommodation and theological liberalism. The churches embrace a fourfold mission: defend biblical truth; impact the world with the gospel, in obedience to the Great Commission; faithfully perpetuate a Baptist heritage; and strengthen existing association churches and begin new ministries.

Worship

Worship services are typically traditional. Baptism is by immersion and only for believers. The Lord's Supper is only for believers, as it commemorates the substitutionary death of Christ and is preceded by solemn self-examination.

Statistics

Membership: 133,000
Churches: 1,415 churches

Largest Churches

The majority of churches are located in Michigan, Ohio, New York, California, Iowa, and Indiana. The largest affiliated congregations include:

Blackhawk Baptist Church (Fort Wayne, IN)
Central Baptist Church (Hobart, IN)
First Baptist Church (New York, NY)

Missionary and Evangelistic Work

The intent of the Baptist Builders Club is to "rechurch" America by providing grants and loans for church plants, mission churches, and emergency and traditional needs. Chaplaincy Ministries communicates biblical truths to the armed forces, hospital patients, law enforcement agencies, prison inmates, and professional athletes. The International Partnership of Fundamental Baptist Ministries facilitates global networking for Baptist ministries.

Academic Institutions

Because the focus of the GARBC is to develop relationships, the GARBC no longer approves colleges and seminaries. Colleges and academic institutions that are consistent with the doctrinal affinity of the association and are identified clearly as Baptist may advertise in the *Baptist Bulletin*. Colleges and academic institutions are affiliated only within the independent Baptist fellowship.

Electronic Media

Joseph M. Stowell II (1911–2007), a pastor who served as the national representative for the GARBC, was a Christian radio pioneer and initiated the nationally syndicated program *Living Reality* in 1970, but it is no longer broadcast.

Publications

The Regular Baptist Press is the publishing agency of the GARBC. The annual catalog includes Sunday school and church-related resources. The official magazine of the GARBC is the *Baptist Bulletin*, which is published monthly by Regular Baptist Press. The *Baptist Bulletin* has been published since January 1933 for the purpose of maintaining "a testimony to the supernaturalism of Christianity as opposed to the antisupernaturalism of modernism" (baptistbulletin.org, "About Us"). Gospel Literature Services provides resources for Regular Baptist missionaries. The *GARBC Church Directory* contains information relevant to the association. *Synergy* is an electronic resource for pastors, wives, and ministry leaders. E-Info is a newsletter communicating information regarding updates pertinent to the association.

Website

http://www.garbc.org/

Bibliography

Brackney, William H. *Baptists in North America: An Historical Perspective*. Malden, MA: Blackwell, 2006.

Brown, L. Duane, et al. *What Happened to the GARBC at Niagara Falls?* Sellersville, PA: Bethel Baptist Press, n.d.

Cohen, Gary G. *Biblical Separation Defended: A Biblical Critique of Ten New Evangelical Arguments*. Philadelphia: P & R, 1966.

Falwell, Jerry, Ed Dobson, and Ed Hindson, eds. *The Fundamentalist Phenomenon: The Resurgence of Conservative Christianity*. Garden City, NY: Doubleday, 1981.

Hull, Merle R. *What a Fellowship! The First Fifty Years of the GARBC*. Schaumburg, IL: Regular Baptist Press, 1981.

Jackson, Paul R. *The Doctrine and Administration of the Church*. Rev. ed. Schaumburg, IL: Regular Baptist Press, 1980.

Jonas, W. Glenn, Jr., ed. *The Baptist River: Essays on Many Tributaries of a Diverse Tradition*. Macon, GA: Mercer University Press, 2006.

Lightner, Robert P. *Neoevangelicalism Today*. Schaumburg, IL: Regular Baptist Press, 1978.

Matthew, Reginald L. *The Ordination of Men Called of God to the Ministry of the Word*. Schaumburg, IL: Regular Baptist Press, 1973.

Murdoch, J. Murray. *Portrait of Obedience: The Biography of Robert T. Ketcham*. Schaumburg, IL: Regular Baptist Press, 1979.

Pickering, Ernest. *Biblical Separation: The Struggle for a Pure Church*. Schaumburg, IL: Regular Baptist Press, 1979.

Ron J. Bigalke

National Association of Free Will Baptists

History

Contemporary Free Will Baptists come from two broad streams. Most derive from the southern movement, commonly known as the Palmer movement of Free Will Baptists. They either descended directly from the eighteenth-century movement in the Carolinas associated with the ministry of Paul Palmer or later identified themselves with that movement. Some contemporary Free Will Baptists, however—probably about 20 to 25 percent of the National Association of Free Will Baptists (NAFWB) and about 10 to 15 percent of all Free Will Baptists, including groups unaffiliated with the National Association—can trace themselves to the Randall movement of northern Free Will Baptists (later Free Baptists). The NAFWB originated in the 1935 merger of the General Conference in the Southeast, a group with Palmer origins, and the Cooperative General Association west of the Mississippi, a group with a mixture of Palmer and Randall origins.

The Palmer movement traces its origin to the seventeenth-century General Baptists who arose in England with the ministry of the English lawyer and churchman Thomas Helwys. In 1727, in Chowan County, North Carolina, Paul Palmer gathered the earliest known church to which Free Will Baptists in the American South can trace themselves. Palmer and those early churches consisted of English General Baptists who had migrated to the colonies of the American South in the late seventeenth century.

The Randall movement originated with Benjamin Randall of New Durham, New Hampshire, who by 1780 had moved from Congregationalism to an Arminian Baptist posture and began gathering Free Will Baptist churches. In the fervor of the Second Great Awakening, the Randall churches exploded with evangelistic and organizational growth. As a result of ecumenism, the Free Baptists merged with the Northern Baptist Convention in 1911. A small remnant remained in the Midwest and the Southwest, helping to organize the Cooperative General Association.

Headquarters

5233 Mount View Road
Antioch, TN 37013
Telephone: 615-731-6812

Leadership

Executive secretary: Keith Burden

Core Beliefs

Free Will Baptists are orthodox Protestants who are Arminian but pre-Wesleyan in their core doctrinal beliefs. They adhere more to the teachings on salvation of Dutch theologian Jacobus Arminius. As Arminians, they believe that human beings are naturally alienated from God and unable to reach out to him. Thus, only through divine grace can human beings come to know God. God mysteriously and graciously convicts and calls all people by means of divine revelation, Christ's universal atonement, and the Spirit's work. Yet he gives them freedom to resist his grace. This freedom to resist persists even after conversion: believers can cease to believe and thus fall from grace.

With regard to the church, Free Will Baptists, like their General Baptist forebears, place more emphasis than other Baptists on the obligation of local congregations to maintain fellowship and accountability in local conferences or associations. Ministerial ordination is facilitated through the conference's presbytery or ordaining council, to which ministers are accountable. Local churches, however, are self-governing, calling their own pastors, holding title to their own property, and maintaining governance of all other internal matters. Free Will Baptists believe the washing of the saints' feet is a divinely ordained liturgical practice.

Divisions and Splits

Between the Free Baptist merger with the Northern Baptists in 1911 and the 1960s, the only major schism among Free Will Baptists occurred when a small group of Free Will Baptists, primarily in the Carolinas, adopted Pentecostalism and withdrew from the Free Will Baptist movement in the 1920s.

In 1962, the North Carolina State Convention (NCSC) and several churches in the Southeast withdrew from the NAFWB. Skirmishes over fundamentalism, philosophy of higher education, and control of Sunday school publishing dominated the debate between the NCSC and the NAFWB. Yet church polity was the issue that resulted in the schism. The NCSC asserted connectional church government, which, among other things, gave conferences the right to arbitrate disputes over ownership of local church property. The NAFWB called on the NCSC to disavow connectionalism. Instead, the NCSC separated from the larger body and later became known as the Convention of Original Free Will Baptists (COFWB). Headquartered in Ayden, North Carolina, it sponsors a Sunday school ministry and publishing house, Free Will Baptist Press, as well as home and foreign missions, a children's home, a conference center, and Mount Olive College in Mount Olive, North Carolina. Several conferences of unaffiliated African American Free Will Baptists in the United States owe their origin to the formation of the United American Free Will Baptist denomination in 1867 after the close of the Civil War. By 1901, they had formed a general conference. Yet most denominational activity today occurs in various regional conferences. The largest conference, the United American Free Will Baptist Church, is headquartered in Kinston, North Carolina. It publishes the *Free Will Baptist Advocate* and sponsors United American Free Will Baptist Bible College. There are also scattered Free Will Baptist churches and associations in the South that are unaffiliated with the NAFWB.

Finances

Budget (2011): $25 million

Statistics

Membership statistics are unreliable due to the loose governance structure of the NAFWB. The most recent official statistics indicate a communicant membership of 186,021 in 2,375 churches. However, officials state that membership is well over the 200,000 mark, given the number of churches not reporting in the most recent reporting period. It is estimated that there are more than 100,000 Free Will Baptists in conventions and associations unaffiliated with the NAFWB, the largest of these being the COFWB.

Free Will Baptist International Missions employs 94 missionaries in 10 foreign countries. Free Will Baptist Home Missions employs 118 church planters in 25 states as well as the US Virgin Islands, Puerto Rico, Canada, and Mexico.

Academic Institution

The NAFWB owns and operates Welch College, a comprehensive, regionally accredited, four-year institution in Nashville, Tennessee.

Parachurch Organizations

The NAFWB sponsors a number of national ministries, including men's and women's ministries (Master's Men, Women Nationally Active for Christ), a charitable foundation (Free Will Baptist Foundation), domestic and international missions (Home Missions Department, International Missions Department), and a retirement board.

Publications

The executive office of the NAFWB publishes *ONE Magazine* and *Rejoice: The Free Will Baptist Hymn Book*. The denomination's publishing house is under the auspices of Randall House Publications, which also oversees its youth convention.

Website

http://www.nafwb.org/

Bibliography

Davidson, William F. *The Free Will Baptists in History*. Nashville: Randall House, 2001.

Pelt, Michael R. *A History of Original Free Will Baptists*. Mount Olive, NC: Mount Olive College Press, 1996.

Pinson, J. Matthew. *A Free Will Baptist Handbook: Heritage, Beliefs, and Ministries*. Nashville: Randall House, 1998.

J. Matthew Pinson

National Baptist Convention

History

Independent black Baptist churches did not emerge until the latter half of the eighteenth century. Prior to emancipation, such churches in the South were virtually nonexistent, and even in the North only a small number enjoyed complete independence. During this time, black Baptists were largely dependent on the patronage of white Baptists, which created tension with regard to the sharing of equal membership and the possibility of independent black churches.

The majority of black Baptists were congregationally minded with regard to church polity and became joined together through regional associations, which were naturally abolitionist and exceptionally active in the Underground Railroad. Local black Baptist churches began organizing local associations, which also functioned as antislavery societies, in response to the distinctive issues they encountered. Associations were voluntary to promote local congregational autonomy, became a primary structural component among black Baptists, and often encompassed significant geographical areas.

As black Baptists developed these associations, regional and statewide conventions were organized to function anonymously during the middle of the nineteenth century. The success of these efforts led to larger associational structures. State conventions became a primary structural component among black Baptists, and the regional conventions stimulated the desire for a national convention.

The Baptist Foreign Mission Convention was organized on November 22, 1880, in Montgomery, Alabama, through the efforts of 151 individuals from 11 states. The goal of the mission organization was the evangelization of Africa. The American National Baptist Convention was organized in 1886 by 600 delegates from 17 states at First Baptist Church in St. Louis, Missouri. The National Baptist Education Convention was founded in 1893. None of the three societies experienced much success as separate organizations. The National Baptist Convention was organized at Friendship Baptist Church in Atlanta, Georgia, on September 28, 1895, as a merger of the educational, missionary, and publishing societies.

Headquarters

1700 Baptist World Center Drive
Nashville, TN 37207
Telephone: 615-228-6292; 866-531-3054

Core Beliefs

The doctrinal consensus is the Articles of Faith, which is embraced by National Baptists and was adopted by the convention. Scripture is divinely inspired and without error with regard to all that it addresses. God, whose name is Jehovah, is three Persons: the Father, the Son, and the Holy Spirit. Adam and Eve were created in holiness but fell voluntarily from that happy and holy state into condemnation unto eternal ruin and were without defense or excuse. Salvation is entirely of grace through the mediatorial offices of Jesus Christ. Christ secures the justification of sinners which includes the pardon of sin and the promise of eternal life for those who believe in him. Baptism is by immersion of a believer in water. Jesus Christ will return personally and visibly at the last day, which is approaching, to resurrect all humanity; the wicked will be punished endlessly, and the righteous will experience endless joy.

Worship

The first day of the week is the Lord's Day, or Christian Sabbath. The Lord's Supper commemorates the death and shed blood of Jesus Christ by the sacred use of bread and wine. Worship is characterized by an open expression of emotion in which singing and active contribution from worshipers are expected. Although services are more spontaneous than among white Baptists, worship is patterned in a manner familiar to regular participants.

Divisions and Splits

The name National Baptist encompasses a larger black Baptist community that includes the following: National Baptist Convention USA; National Baptist Convention of America; National Missionary Baptist Convention; and Progressive National Baptist Convention. The National Baptist Convention has been regarded popularly as the "incorporated" convention since its founding, with the National Baptist Convention of America known as the "unincorporated" convention since its split from the original body in 1917 with regard to ownership of the National Baptist Publishing Board. Debate between Joseph H. Jackson and Martin Luther King Jr. with regard to the former's opposition to the Social Gospel resulted in a split from the "incorporated" convention and the founding of the Progressive National Baptist Convention in 1961. Issues regarding denominational control of publications emerged again, with the result that the National Missionary Baptist Convention of America was founded in 1988.

Statistics

The National Baptist Convention is the largest and oldest black Baptist denomination, with an estimated membership of 7.5 million in 30,000 churches (only 100,000 members exist outside the United States), which demonstrates consistent growth from 1958 membership of 5.5 million. Membership encompasses nearly one-fourth of the entire black population in the United States and approximately one-third of the black religious membership. Late in the twentieth century, membership was approximately 8.5 million; however, such statistics may have been inflated when Henry J. Lyons was president (prior to his 1998 indictment on federal charges). There are 4,700 associations and 59 state conventions.

Largest Churches

Church membership is fairly even throughout the nation. The largest churches are:

Antioch Baptist Church North (Atlanta, GA)
Salem Baptist Church (Omaha, NE)

Missionary and Evangelistic Work

The National Baptist Convention maintains many ministries and outreach programs, including arts (music, poetry, publication), education ministries (teaching, training), disaster relief, foreign missions and travels, health and wellness, housing ministry, ministerial and missionary pensions, prayer ministry, prison ministry, social justice ministry, young ministers ministry

(Spirit of Timothy), and technology ministry (Turned On, Plugged in for Christ).

Ten auxiliaries and boards maintain the active status of the convention's missionary and evangelistic work, including Congress of Christian Education, Evangelism Commission, Foreign Mission Board, Home Mission Board, Laymen's Movement, Moderators Auxiliary, Music Auxiliary, Sunday School Publishing, Ushers and Nurses Auxiliary, and Woman's Auxiliary.

Academic Institutions

American Baptist College (Nashville, TN)
Shaw University (Raleigh, NC)
Virginia Union University (Richmond, VA)

Publications

National Baptist churches publish and distribute Sunday school and other Christian literature, music, and other works of art and religious expression.

Website

http://www.nationalbaptist.com/

Bibliography

Fulop, Timothy E., and Albert J. Raboteau, eds. *African-American Religion: Interpretive Essays in History and Culture.* New York: Routledge, 1997.

Hill, Samuel S., and Charles H. Lippy, eds. *Encyclopedia of Religion in the South.* 2nd ed. Macon, GA: Mercer University Press, 2005.

Jackson, Joseph H. *A Story of Christian Activism: The History of the National Baptist Convention, USA, Inc.* Nashville: Townsend, 1980.

Jaynes, Gerald D., and Robin M. Williams Jr., eds. *A Common Destiny: Blacks and American Society.* Washington, DC: National Academy Press, 1989.

Lincoln, C. Eric, and Lawrence H. Mamiya. *The Black Church in the African American Experience.* Durham, NC: Duke University Press, 1990.

Pelt, Owen D., and Ralph Lee Smith. *The Story of the National Baptists.* New York: Vantage, 1960.

Thomas, E. L. *A History of the National Baptist Convention: The Programs, Personalities, and Power Base.* Nashville: Townsend, 1999.

Wagner, Clarence M. *History of the National Baptist Convention, USA, Inc.* Decatur, GA: Tru-Faith, 1993.

Ron J. Bigalke

National Missionary Baptist Convention of America

History

The National Missionary Baptist Convention of America (NMBCA) was organized on November 14–15, 1988, in Dallas, Texas. It was formed under the direction of several leaders and former members of the National Baptist Convention of America Inc., including the chief conveners Dr. S. J. Gilbert Sr. and Dr. S. M. Wright. A disagreement related to the relationships among the National Baptist Convention, the National Baptist Publishing Board (now the R. H. Boyd Publishing Corporation), the National Baptist Sunday School Board, and the Baptist Training Union Congress generated the separation. The new organization found support in various states such as California, Arizona, Indiana, Oklahoma, and Texas. The NMBCA considers the 1988 organization a restoration of the Foreign Mission Baptist Convention of 1880.

The first president of the NMBCA was pastor S. M. Lockridge of San Diego. Dr. Lockridge served in the capacity of president until his retirement in 1994. Dr. H. J. Johnson of Dallas, Texas, led a movement out of the convention and formed the Institutional Missionary Baptist Conference of America in 1998. This convention holds a winter board meeting, a summer board meeting, and a five-day meeting in September that is considered the annual session.

Headquarters

The convention does not maintain a national headquarters. Unofficially, the presiding president's church functions as the headquarters for the convention. The current president is Dr. C. C. Robertson, pastor of the Bexar Street Missionary Baptist Church.

Bexar Street Missionary Baptist Church
2018 South Marsalis Avenue
Dallas, TX 75216
Telephone: 214-943-3579

Core Beliefs

The NMBCA considers itself Baptistic, evangelical, and conservative. Membership is open to those who have had a conversion experience with Jesus Christ as Savior and who have subsequently made a profession of faith. They must also have been baptized by immersion. The other regularly practiced ordinance is the Lord's Supper. While the denomination does not hold to a strict confessional statement, it is generically evangelical and endorses the Bible as the inspired Word of God, a substitutionary view of the atonement, and the necessity of faith in Christ and conversion for salvation. The denomination's vision "is to edify our member churches, the nation, and the world through the wise use of our spiritual gifts, intellectual ability, and financial resources for the glory of God" (nmbca.org, "About Us"). There is an emphasis on the importance of education and missionary activity as well as women's service and ministry.

Worship

Worship services are traditional, and formal dress is common. Singing and preaching are typically Bible focused as well as energetic and spiritual.

Controversies

The NMBCA is currently discussing the issue of women in ministry. The convention encourages women to serve in various ministries, but it does not recognize women as ordained pastors. Some local churches within the convention, however, are actively ordaining women to pastoral roles.

Statistics

Churches: approximately 500
Membership: 700,000–800,000

Largest Churches

Mount Moriah Baptist Church (Los Angeles, CA)
St. John Baptist Church (Grand Prairie, TX)

Missionary and Evangelistic Work

The convention supports two boards dedicated to missions, relief work, and evangelism. The Foreign Mission Board and the Home Mission Board respond to disasters that occur both in the United States and internationally. These boards also devise and oversee evangelism strategies for spreading the gospel. The Foreign Mission Board sends missionaries through the Lott Carey Foreign Mission Convention.

Ecumenism

The NMBCA cooperates with other denominations and is a member of the Baptist World Alliance and the National Council of Churches USA.

Parachurch Organizations

The NMBCA uses the Lott Carey Foreign Mission Convention (LCFMC) to send missionaries. The LCFMC mobilizes missionaries from several denominations and conventions to provide ministries such as HIV/AIDS prevention education, leadership training, theological education, and disaster relief around the world.

Electronic Media

The denomination does not officially offer any electronic media, but individual NMBCA churches offer sermons, streamed video, and church documents online. They include congregations such as Spring Chapel Baptist Church (springchapel.org) and St. John Baptist Church (sjbcfamily.com).

Website

http://www.nmbca.com/

Bibliography

Burton, W. T. Unpublished interview with William R. Osborne. September 17, 2010.

Leonard, Bill J. *Baptists in America*. New York: Columbia University Press, 2005.

———, ed. *Dictionary of Baptists in America*. Downers Grove, IL: InterVarsity, 1994.

Lindner, Eileen W., ed. *Yearbook of American and Canadian Churches 2010*. Nashville: Abingdon, 2010.

Mead, Frank S., Samuel S. Hill, and Craig D. Atwood. "National Missionary Baptist Convention of America." In *Handbook of Denominations in the United States*. 13th ed. Nashville: Abingdon, 2010.

Wardin, Albert W. *Baptists around the World: A Comprehensive Handbook*. Nashville: Broadman & Holman, 1995.

R. Philip Roberts

National Primitive Baptist Convention, USA

History

The National Primitive Baptist Convention, USA (NPBC) is an African American group of Primitive Baptists who formed in 1907. The first Baptist denomination in the United States was convened at the Triennial Convention in 1814. This convention was formed to promote overseas mission work; it also promoted education through association with seminaries and Sunday schools. In the 1820s and 1830s, some Baptists began to withdraw because of a belief that missions and education should take place at the local church level and not at the larger level of a convention. These views originated in the understanding that the local ministers controlled missions instead of a mission board, families should be in control of education for their children, and young preachers should be discipled by an older minister instead of at a seminary.

These Baptists became known as Primitive Baptists. These Baptists were the least institutionally organized of all Baptist groups. In the late 1800s, though, some black Primitive Baptists began to organize their churches for greater effectiveness. Clarence F. Sams, pastor of Zion Primitive Baptist Church in Key West, Florida, was one of the leading proponents of this movement. A number of black Primitive Baptists gathered at S. Bartley's Primitive Baptist Church in Huntsville, Alabama, in 1907 and formed the National Primitive Baptist Convention. This convention quickly decided to support an existing academy and to create a college and seminary, Sunday school literature, and a publishing board, presently located in Tallahassee, Florida.

Core Beliefs

In contrast to most Primitive Baptists, the NPBC does not teach strict Calvinism. Also, the NPBC differs from Primitive Baptists in that the NPBC holds national conventions, which is a practice not germane to most Primitive Baptists. Along with baptism by immersion and Communion, the NPBC practices foot washing.

Statistics

The NPBC has 1,000 churches in 18 states (mainly in the South) and 250,000 members.

Website

http://natlprimbaptconv.org/

Bibliography

Discipline of the Primitive Baptist Church. Tallahassee, FL: National Primitive Baptist Publishing House, 1997.

Mark Nickens

North American Baptist Conference

History

The North American Baptist General Conference began as a Baptist movement of German-speaking immigrants in North America. Their first session, in 1851, was held at the First German Baptist Church of Philadelphia, and the conference was titled "The First Conference of Pastors and Co-Workers of the German Churches of Baptized Christians (usually called Baptists)." Konrad A. Fleischmann was the pastor of the church as well as the major founder of the movement. Fleischmann had become disillusioned with the Lutheran church he had grown up in and was drawn to the spiritual vitality of many of the Baptists he had met in Philadelphia.

The large number of German immigrants, together with the evangelistic activity of many German preachers and evangelists, created significant initial growth among the German-speaking Baptist churches. In 1851, the conference started with 8 churches and 405 members, but by 1859, it had grown to approximately 2,600 members in 61 churches. While the movement originally saw growth in the major metropolitan areas of Philadelphia, Chicago, and New York, it later expanded into the Midwest along with large numbers of German Baptists and other German immigrants to that region. Churches were organized in Wisconsin, Missouri, Illinois, and parts of Canada by the early 1850s. Consequently, the first general conference of German Baptists occurred in Wilmot, Ontario, on September 14–20, 1865.

During World War I, patriotism and prejudice rapidly increased the number of English services among the churches, and in 1944, the present title of the North American Baptist Conference (NABC) was adopted. Presently, the conference is comprised of twenty associations made up of over four hundred churches, which are predominantly English speaking.

Headquarters

1 S 210 Summit Avenue
Oakbrook Terrace, IL 60181
Telephone: 630-495-2000

Leadership

Executive director: Dr. Rob McCleland

Core Beliefs

The denomination adopted a statement of faith in 1982 and amended it in 2009. The statement affirms that the Bible is God's revealed Word without error, God is triune in nature, mankind is sinful and salvation is available only through repentance and faith in Jesus Christ, all people are endowed with "soul liberty," Christians are to live as salt and light in the world, Christ will return personally and will establish new heavens and a new earth, and the ordinances of the church are believer's baptism by immersion and the observance of the Lord's Supper as a memorial.

Worship

Worship style varies with each congregation, but it is common for churches to hold two worship services—one traditional and one contemporary. Twenty-five percent of the conference is comprised of ethnic churches (e.g., Russian, Romanian, Chinese, and Hispanic).

Controversies

The role of women in ministry was a significant issue for the conference in the past. However, resolution has been reached, and the suggested guidelines presented by the conference are that women can exercise their gifts in pastoral ministry but are encouraged not to serve in senior pastor or lead pastor positions.

Finances

Total Contributions (2006): $72,279,470

Statistics

Members: 75,000
Churches: 400 (75 percent in the United States)
Missionaries: 65

Largest Churches

First Baptist Church Elk Grove (Elk Grove, CA)
Temple Baptist Church (Lodi, CA)

Trends

A recent development among local churches and denominational leaders is a desire for "missional" living (i.e., becoming more culturally sensitive and outreach oriented in everyday life). This evangelistic desire may help the church address two other deficiencies it is currently addressing: leadership development and church planting.

Missionary and Evangelistic Work

The Church Multiplication Resource Team is a designated group within the NABC focused on church planting and evangelism. The mission department supports approximately sixty-five missionaries in seven countries; however, the NABC helped begin a Baptist convention in Cameroon in the 1950s, and it has continued to focus much of its attention on that country. Currently, there are reportedly more NABC-sponsored churches in Cameroon than there are NABC churches in America.

Ecumenism

The conference is a long-standing member of the Baptist World Alliance and has submitted an application to join the National Association of Evangelicals.

Academic Institutions

Sioux Falls Seminary (Sioux Falls, SD)
Taylor College and Seminary (Edmonton, Alberta, Canada)
University of Sioux Falls (Sioux Falls, SD)

Parachurch Organizations

The NABC mission department has worked extensively alongside the Cameroon Baptist Convention in establishing and supporting Baptist hospitals throughout the country of Cameroon. The conference also supports seven Baptist senior homes and twelve camps.

Publications

The NABC has made numerous documents available on its website such as its revised constitution, statement of faith, and denominational profile.

Website

http://www.nabconference.org/

Bibliography

Leonard, Bill J. *Baptists in America*. New York: Columbia University Press, 2005.

————, ed. *Dictionary of Baptists in America*. Downers Grove, IL: InterVarsity, 1994.

Linder, Eileen W., ed. *Yearbook of American and Canadian Churches 2010*. Nashville: Abingdon, 2010.

Norman, Ron. Unpublished interview with William R. Osborne. September 9, 2010.

Wardin, Albert W. *Baptists around the World: A Comprehensive Handbook*. Nashville: Broadman & Holman, 1995.

Woyke, Frank H. *Heritage and Ministry of the North American Baptist Conference*. Oakbrook Terrace, IL: NABC, 1979.

R. Philip Roberts

Primitive Baptists

History

The Primitive Baptists originated as a reaction against the missionary work of the early nineteenth century; as strict Calvinists, they opposed financially based missionary organizations. The name "primitive" was first used in the early 1830s to convey the notion of originality (simplicity) as opposed to backwardness. Primitive Baptists claim the doctrines and practices of Particular Baptist confessions. The three traditional Primitive Baptist groups include the Absoluters, the Old Liners, and the Universalists. In 1826 North Carolina, the Kehukee Association condemned all financially based and centralized societies as contrary to Scripture. Divisions among Baptists intensified with the 1832 "Black Rock Address" in Maryland (a general address in which conservative Baptists announced and explained their intent to withdraw fellowship from liberal doctrines and practices among Baptist churches in America). Within a decade, several other antimissionary Baptists proclaimed that such societies were human

inventions and unwarranted from Scripture. Missionary organizations were opposed for promoting nonecclesial methodology, nonpredestinarian theology, and salaried missionaries.

Leadership

Churches are grouped exclusively in various associations wherein there is fellowship and correspondence through letters and messengers (as opposed to being formed for church government). Individual congregations choose church leaders from among male members. Each church is autonomous; thus, no association has authority over it. Articles of faith, constitutions, and rules of order are printed in the minutes from associational meetings and are examined and approved by other associations. Any association not approved by the minutes is removed from fellowship.

Core Beliefs

The Bible is the infallibly and verbally inspired Word of God. The 1611 King James Version is regarded as the superior English translation. Calvinism is a major emphasis of Primitive Baptist doctrine, as is a rigid predestinarianism. The ordinances are Communion (using wine and unleavened bread), believer's baptism by immersion, and foot washing.

The churches attempt to preserve or restore original patterns of the New Testament church such as a cappella singing, unsalaried ministers, and wine in Communion. They regard themselves as the original Particular Baptists. The Primitive Baptists tend to be hyper-Calvinists, as represented by the Kehukee Association in North Carolina, which was entirely antimissionary.

Worship

Worship is simple. The name Primitive Baptist itself describes the worship style. Primitive Baptists distinguish between aids to worship (e.g., air-conditioning, electrical lighting, songbooks) and additions to worship (e.g., musical instruments). Although worship in the Old Testament did involve a variety of musical instruments, such procedure is not allowed (by most Primitive Baptist groups) to amend the New Testament precedent for worship. Some preachers use a dramatic, singsong voice for the sermon (similar to the Roman Catholic use of Latin). The majority of Primitive Baptists do not have Sunday school classes (because none are mentioned in the New

Testament), though there are exceptions, such as the Progressive Primitive Baptists. Entertainment is not condemned when it is moral and in moderation; however, there are no organized congregational programs for entertaining youth, such as providing games or anything recreational during corporate worship times, since such practice is regarded as neglecting discipleship of all worshipers, irrespective of age. Primitive Baptists do not have crucifixes or pictures of Jesus in their church buildings because Scripture forbids any images of God.

Divisions and Splits

Primitive Baptists today are divided into six groups. The largest and most notable group is the Old Liners, who allow personal responsibility in predestination and active obedience in Christian living. The Absoluters affirm the absolute predestination of all things, including good and evil, which in contrast to the view of the Old Liners designates God as the author of sin. The second largest group is the Progressive Primitive Baptists, who originated in Georgia during the early 1900s. They do allow ministerial salaries, musical instruments in worship, Sunday school, and weekly meetings (as opposed to others who have monthly worship meetings). The Two-Seed-in-the-Spirit Predestinarian Baptists originated from the preaching of Daniel Parker, specifically with his 1826 publication titled *Views on the Two Seeds*. The phrase "two seed" indicates one seed of good, which emanates from God, and one seed of evil, which is from the devil. Consequently, both seeds are spiritual and not of the flesh, which means that neither seed can change its character and both reproduce after their kind. The Primitive Baptist Universalists are known as "No-Hellers" for their belief that God predestined all humanity as beneficiaries of Christ's atonement. The National Primitive Baptists USA represents a black congregation that is less rigid in doctrine.

Statistics

Membership of the various Primitive Baptist groups is approximately 72,000 in approximately 1,000 churches in the United States and overseas. The National Primitive Baptists USA (an African American body) is exceptional in membership (as compared with the other five Primitive Baptist groups), with an estimated membership of more than 50,000 in more than 500 churches; headquarters are located in Huntsville, Alabama.

Trends

Old Liner churches are found throughout the Midwest and the South. The majority of Absoluters are found in Alabama, North Carolina, Texas, Virginia, and the Northeast. Progressive Primitive Baptists are found predominantly in Georgia. Two-Seed-in-the-Spirit Predestinarian Baptists are found in Louisiana and Texas. Universalist churches are small and declining, with associations primarily in the Northeast (Appalachia). The majority of black Primitive Baptists are located in the South. There are ongoing church-planting works in East Africa and the Philippines.

Missionary and Evangelistic Work

Primitive Baptists are generally characterized by a rigid Calvinism that undermines a theology of missions. They are known for opposing all organizations of human effort and favor local churches and associations. Primitive Baptist churches are generally small and have worship services only on a monthly basis (as opposed to Progressive Baptists, who meet weekly).

Academic Institutions

The majority of Primitive Baptists oppose theological schools. Although there are no affiliated colleges and academic institutions among Primitive Baptists, they do not object to collegiate education but cheerfully encourage such an education for their children. Elder E. J. Berry developed the Primitive Baptist Library in Elon College, North Carolina.

Electronic Media

Elder Lasserre Bradley Jr. broadcasts the *Baptist Bible Hour* in California, the Midwest, and the South. Elder Ronaldo L. Lopez maintains the PBC Internet Broadcast Service (pbcradio.net).

Publications

Old Liner publications include the *Advocate and Messenger, Baptist Witness, Christian Pathway,* and *Primitive Baptist.* Absoluter publications include the *Old Faith Contender, Signs of the Times,* and *Zion's Landmark.* Progressive Primitive Baptist publications include the *Banner Herald* and the *Donetsk Report.*

Websites

http://www.primitivebaptistchurches.com/
http://www.primitivebaptist.org/

Bibliography

Berry, W. J., ed. *The Kehukee Declaration and Black Rock Address: With Other Writings Relative to the Baptist Separation between 1825–1840.* Elon College, NC: Primitive Publications, n.d.

Dorgan, Howard. *In the Hands of a Happy God: The "No Hellers" of Central Appalachia.* Knoxville: University of Tennessee Press, 1997.

Hassell, Cushing Biggs. *History of the Church of God, from the Creation to AD 1885; Including Especially the History of the Kehukee Primitive Baptist Association.* Middletown, NY: Gilbert Beebe's Sons, 1886.

Hughes, Richard T., ed. *The American Quest for the Primitive Church.* Urbana: University of Illinois Press, 1988.

Jonas, W. Glenn, Jr., ed. *The Baptist River: Essays on Many Tributaries of a Diverse Tradition.* Macon, GA: Mercer University Press, 2006.

Marsden, George. *The Evangelical Mind and the New School Presbyterian Experience.* New Haven, CT: Yale University Press, 1970.

Mathis, James R. *The Making of the Primitive Baptists: A Cultural and Intellectual History of the Antimission Movement, 1800–1840.* New York: Routledge, 2004.

McBeth, H. Leon. *The Baptist Heritage.* Nashville: Broadman, 1987.

Ron J. Bigalke

Progressive National Baptist Convention

History

Founded in November 1961 by thirty-three delegates of the National Baptist Convention (NBC), the Progressive National Baptist Convention (PNBC) began as a movement to "transform the traditional African American Baptist Convention as well as society" (pnbc.org, "History"). The roots of the split with the NBC included a reaction to the leadership's approach to civil rights activism and the overturning of a term-limit amendment by NBC president Joseph H. Jackson. Rev. L. Venchael Booth sent out a letter to NBC members in September 1961 giving notification of a meeting in Cincinnati "devoted to discussion of How to Build a Democratic Convention Dedicated to Christian Objectives." This was to be an "entirely new movement under new leadership" and open to all those "concerned with redeeming the Baptist initiative and restoring a democratic thrust" (pnbcinc.com, "Original News Release").

The PNBC held its first annual meeting in Philadelphia in 1962 and elected T. M. Chambers as its first president. It supported the civil rights movement; the Rev. Martin Luther King Jr., for whom it provided a "denominational home"; and the Black Power movement. It opposed the Vietnam War. More recently, the PNBC has supported relief to Haiti and has advocated for action in local churches to encourage increased African American participation in the census.

Headquarters

601 50th Street NE
Washington, DC 20019
Telephone: 202-396-0558; 800-876-7622

Core Beliefs

The PNBC identifies itself as an association of Baptist churches and a Christian movement concerned with making disciples of Christ. Since its creation, it has advocated for "progressive" issues such as civil and human rights and "an array of social and political concerns embodied in its founding principles of Fellowship, Progress, Peace and Service" (pnbc.org, "History").

Controversies

The PNBC was born out of the controversy surrounding the policies of the National Baptist Convention during the tenure of Joseph H. Jackson. Beginning in 1956, attempts to remove Jackson from office or to challenge his reelections, including two lawsuits and the nomination (by Martin Luther King Jr.) and roll call election of Gardner C. Taylor at the 1960 convention, were all unsuccessful. During the 1961 convention in Kansas City, a Detroit member was killed after being knocked from the stage during a shouting and shoving match between King and Jackson supporters.

Statistics

Members: over 2.5 million (1.5 million in the US)
Churches: 2,000

Largest Churches

The largest PNBC churches are located in urban areas such as Washington, DC; Oakland, California; and Dallas, Texas.

Growth

The PNBC has shown steady growth in membership since its founding. The convention had more than 500,000 members in 487 churches in the late 1970s and 1 million members by 1984. Today it has over 2.5 million members in 2,000 churches.

Trends

Since the 1970s, the PNBC and its affiliated churches have partnered in various capacities with other Baptist and African American groups (including the Southern Baptist Convention, the National Coalition on Black Civic Participation, American Baptist Churches USA, and the Baptist Joint Committee on Public Affairs).

Parachurch Organizations

African-American Baptist Mission Collaboration
Baptist Global Mission Bureau
Haiti Support Project

Publications

The *Worker*, a "Missionary and Educational Quarterly Magazine," provides Bible study topics for various age levels.

Website

http://www.pnbc.org/

Bibliography

Avant, Albert A., Jr. *The Social Teachings of the Progressive National Baptist Convention, Inc., Since 1961.* New York: Routledge, 2004.

Leonard, Bill J. *Baptist Ways: A History.* Valley Forge, PA: Judson, 2003.

———, ed. *Dictionary of Baptists in America.* Downers Grove, IL: InterVarsity, 1994.

Lincoln, C. Eric, and Lawrence H. Mamiya. *The Black Church in the African-American Experience.* Durham, NC: Duke University Press, 1990.

Mead, Frank S., Samuel S. Hill, and Craig D. Atwood. *Handbook of Denominations in the United States.* 13th ed. Nashville: Abingdon, 2010.

"Progressive National Baptist Convention." http://www.pnbc.org. "History."

Williams, Lawrence H. "The Progressive National Baptist Convention." *Baptist History and Heritage* 40, no. 1 (Winter 2005): 24–33.

David M. Wilmington

Separate Baptists in Christ

History

The Separate Baptists sprang from the New Light movement of the Great Awakening. This movement, which began in New England, was to have a more lasting impact on the South than on New England. This was in large part due to the move of Shubael Stearns (1706–71) and his brother-in-law Daniel Marshall (1706–84) from Connecticut to North Carolina. From there they embarked on a church-planting movement of Separate Baptist congregations.

The present-day Separate Baptists in Christ descended from a split within the Separate Baptist movement over the Arminian/Calvinist debate. Those who supported the Arminian

system moved west into Kentucky and Tennessee. From this group the present associations of the Separate Baptists in Christ were formed. There are currently seven local associations within the Separate Baptists in Christ fellowship: Central Indiana (thirteen congregations), Christian Unity (six congregations), Mt. Olive (two congregations), Nolynn (eighteen congregations), Northeast Florida (one congregation), South Kentucky (thirty-five congregations), and West Virginia (one congregation).

Many of the congregations in the various associations do not have a pastor currently appointed. In 1991, the Ambraw association withdrew from the general association over the adoption of an article of faith that excluded the possibility of a premillennial return of Christ. In 1992, the Northern Indiana association followed suit and also withdrew.

Core Beliefs

Separate Baptists hold to the orthodox beliefs of the Christian faith, including the Trinity, the authority of Scripture, the resurrection, and the exclusivity of Christ for salvation. They also hold to three ordinances: baptism, the Lord's Supper, and foot washing.

They believe that the King James Bible is the only valid English translation of the Scriptures. They reject a literal millennial reign of Christ on the earth.

The defining documents for the Separate Baptists in Christ are the King James Bible and the Articles of Doctrine for All Associations.

Website

http://www.separatebaptist.org/

Bibliography

"Separate Baptists in Christ." http://www.separatebaptist.org. "Association at a Glance," "Our Beliefs," and "Symbol Summary."

Garrett, James Leo. *Baptist Theology: A Four Century Study.* Macon, GA: Mercer University Press, 2009.

Lumpkin, William L. *Baptist Foundations in the South: Tracing through the Separates the Influence of the Great Awakening, 1754–1787.* Nashville: Broadman, 1961.

Rustin J. Umstattd

Seventh Day Baptists

History

Seventh Day Baptists (SDB) trace their roots to the mid-seventeenth-century establishment of several small Sabbatarian Baptist groups in the greater London area during the English

43

Reformation that had earlier given birth to the larger Baptist movement. The first church in the United States was founded in late 1671 (old-style calendar) in Newport, Rhode Island. After more than a century of circular letters and informal relationships between local churches, the Seventh Day Baptist General Conference was founded in 1802. Since then, it has promoted the total work of Seventh Day Baptists and united the churches as they attempt to fulfill the Great Commission (Matt. 28:19–20).

Headquarters

3120 Kennedy Road
PO Box 1678
Janesville, WI 53547

Core Beliefs

Seventh Day Baptists are not creedal. Local churches fashion covenants that bind members according to self-determined standards. Seventh Day Baptists acknowledge the priesthood of all believers and the responsibility of individuals in their relationship with God. All Seventh Day Baptist beliefs are undergirded by belief in the freedom of individual conscience under the guidance of the Holy Spirit. As a result, there is variance within the conference and within local congregations on matters that are deemed to be of secondary importance.

The distinguishing belief of Seventh Day Baptists is that the seventh day of the week, the Sabbath (Saturday), is a day sanctified by God and set apart for worship of God and fellowship with him (with a prohibition from labor). Sabbath observance is not considered salvific but is deemed a blessed opportunity for fellowship with God and his church. The statement of belief adopted in 1987 includes statements on God the Father, the Son, and the Holy Spirit; on the Bible as the inspired Word of God and the final authority in matters of faith and practice; and on salvation from sin and death as the gift of God by redeeming love accomplished by Christ's death and resurrection and received only by repentance and faith in him. Believer's baptism is by immersion, and there is regular observance of the Lord's Supper.

Website

http://www.seventhdaybaptist.org/

Bibliography

Sanford, Don A. *A Choosing People: The History of Seventh Day Baptists*. Nashville: Broadman, 1990.

———. *Greater Than Its Parts: A Study of Seventh Day Baptist Polity and Organization*. 2nd ed. Janesville, WI: SDB Historical Society, 2007.

Nicholas J. Kersten

Southern Baptist Convention

History

The history of the Southern Baptist Convention began with the Triennial Convention of 1814 (also known as the General Missionary Convention of the Baptist Denomination in the United States of America for Foreign Missions), which was organized to provide resources for the financial support of Baptist foreign missionaries Luther Rice and Adoniram Judson. Believing in the autonomy of the local church, the Triennial Convention was an entirely voluntary organization. Supporters were located throughout Northern and Southern state associations. Toward the end of the 1830s, other Baptist societies were created to meet the needs of home missions, Bible and tract distribution, and Baptist publications. Although the societies were headquartered in northern cities, both Northern and Southern Baptists supported them.

In February 1824, Luther Rice and other Baptists formed the Baptist General Tract Society in Washington, DC, which moved to Philadelphia in 1827 and became the American Baptist Publication and Sunday School Society in 1840. The intent for forming the Tract Society was educational. The constitution indicated "its sole object shall be to disseminate evangelical truth, and to inculcate sound morals, by the distribution of tracts" (McBeth, *Baptist Heritage*, 361). The work of the Tract Society eventually developed into publishing books and curricula. The educational outreach began in many regions of the United States in the nineteenth century. The Baptist General Tract Society was formed independent not only from the Triennial Convention but also from the American Baptist Home Mission Society. The "Three Great Societies" flourished and achieved wide acceptance by Baptist churches and individuals. Nevertheless, the characteristic diversity of autonomous congregations resulted in divisions and separations regarding doctrinal matters, such as the antimissionary movement and the disciples movement. The doctrinal disagreements intensified cultural distinctions and resulted in the formation of the Southern Baptist Convention.

The Southern Baptist Convention has an inseparable heritage from the Separate Baptists, who exerted tremendous influence on Baptist doctrines and practices in the South and began in New England as a consequence of the Great Awakening. Separate Baptists were known to preach anywhere, and their passion had a lasting effect on the Southern Baptist Convention. Because of the union between Separate Baptists and Regular Baptists, church distinctives from both groups helped enhance Southern Baptist practices.

In 1845, divisions arose within the General Missionary Convention. William Bullein Johnson was the president of the convention during the years 1841–44, and he became instrumental in the historical development of the new organization for Baptists in the South. Johnson was elected president of the delegation of Southern Baptists in 1845 to discuss the formation of separate mission agencies for Baptists in the South. The Southern Baptist Convention was formed in 1845 in Augusta, Georgia. Johnson was elected as the first president of the Southern Baptist Convention; he served in the role until 1851. One outcome of the convention was the formation of the International Mission Board and the North American Mission Board, focusing on foreign and national issues, respectively. One of the immediate reasons for the division between Northern and Southern Baptists was controversy regarding slavery within the Triennial Convention and the Home Mission Society. There were also disagreements concerning organizational methods for societies and conventions, and home mission work. (In 1995, the Southern Baptist Convention—with nineteen hundred African American congregations—voted to adopt a resolution that would condemn and renounce its past defense of slavery.)

The Landmark movement arose in the decade following the formation of the Southern Baptist Convention and has done more to form the self-identity and denominational loyalty of Southern Baptists than any other movement. Throughout the 1880s and 1890s, the influence of the movement within the Southern Baptist Convention was evident in several controversies, such as the Gospel Missionism of Tarleton Perry Crawford, the Whitsitt Controversy, the Hayden-Cranfill Controversy, and the 1905 separation guided by Ben Marquis Bogard. Landmarkers intended to institute definite landmarks of the faith and taught that people who did not affirm those landmarks were not worthy of administering baptism, preaching in churches, or sharing in Communion.

On a sociological level, the Landmark movement was a challenge and development that helped Southern Baptists gain a separate identity from Northern Baptists. The Landmarkers did argue for the autonomy of local churches, since they believed any organization that was authoritative in regard to local churches was unbiblical. As a result of this argument, many churches did not contribute to the cause of the Southern Baptist Convention. The Civil War prevented the Landmark movement from achieving notable influence in the North, as Northern Baptists gave little attention to its doctrine.

Following the Reconstruction of the South, the Southern Baptists flourished greatly. Home Mission Board head Dr. Isaac Taylor Tichenor persuaded Baptists in the South to reject any partnership with Northern boards and to support only Southern Baptist causes. In 1894, in Fort Monroe, Virginia, both Northern and Southern Baptists approved a territorial agreement that would establish southern states as exclusive territory for the Southern Baptist Convention.

Headquarters

901 Commerce Street
Nashville, TN 37203
Telephone: 615-244-2355

Leadership

There are 41 state conventions and 1,186 associations but no centralized ecclesiastical authority. Southern Baptists are wholly committed to the autonomy of the local church as the highest judicature. The relationship to the state conventions and other local associations is voluntary. Polity is congregational. The pastoral office is restricted to men who are qualified by Scripture (e.g., 1 Tim. 3:1–11; Titus 1:5–9).

Core Beliefs

The New Hampshire Confession (1833) is the basis for the Baptist Faith and Message first adopted in 1925 and revised in 1963 and 2000. Most Southern Baptist churches are conservative theologically, affirming the authority and trustworthiness of Scripture. The convention does not openly endorse charismatics. Although the convention was founded on Calvinist theology, there is no official stance on either Calvinism or Arminianism. (The Building Bridges Conference, sponsored by Founders Ministries and Southeastern Baptist Theological Seminary and hosted by LifeWay Christian Resources near Asheville,

North Carolina, in 2007, sought to address these issues through mutual debate.) The Baptist Faith and Message (2000) affirms the necessity of the grace of God in regeneration and the impossibility of believers ever falling from the state of grace. The convention does not have an official stance regarding millennial views but does affirm the everlasting reward of the godly and judgment of the ungodly.

Southern Baptists affirm believer's baptism by immersion and deny sacramental grace as conveyed through observance of baptism and the Lord's Supper (the two ordinances are symbolic, as opposed to being sacraments). The calling and gifting of both men and women for ministry is affirmed, but the pastoral office is restricted to men. Marriage is identified as only between one man and one woman, and both husband and wife have distinct roles and responsibilities from God (i.e., complementarianism). Children are identified as a blessing and heritage from God. Although each local church is autonomous, Southern Baptists affiliate intentionally for education, evangelism, missions, and stewardship. Southern Baptists affirm that God alone is "Lord of the conscience" (Baptist Faith and Message 2000).

Worship

Sunday is regarded as the Sabbath day. Bible preaching/teaching is primary, as is an emphasis on conversion. An offering is received, often prior to the teaching. Worship services are generally nonliturgical. Singing is congregational, generally with the accompaniment of a choir. Music may be blended, contemporary, or traditional.

Statistics

Membership: over 16 million
Primary worship attendance: approximately 6 million
Churches: 44,000

The Southern Baptist Convention is the largest Protestant denomination in the United States. Approximately half of Baptists in the United States are members of affiliated churches within the convention. Southern Baptist churches are located in all fifty states; therefore, the term "Southern" is a misnomer to some extent. Delegates to the annual convention have suggested the name Great Commission Baptists, since the name Southern Baptist can be a discouragement to potential believers. The new name would plausibly help church planters and missionaries in their efforts to go and make disciples of all nations.

Largest Churches

The largest churches are located (primarily) in Alabama, Georgia, North Carolina, Tennessee, and Texas. The largest congregations are:

Second Baptist Church (Houston, TX), with more than 23,000 members
Saddleback Church (Lake Forest, CA), with more than 19,000 members

Missionary and Evangelistic Work

The North American Mission Board (NAMB) was established as the Board of Domestic Missions in 1845. The NAMB assists Southern Baptists in obedience to the Great Commission in the United States and Canada through a national strategy for proclaiming the gospel, planting churches, and sending missionaries, in cooperation with Acts 1:8 partners. The Acts 1:8 Challenge is a comprehensive and cooperative mission strategy. The International Mission Board was established in 1845 (as the Foreign Mission Board) to appoint missionaries worldwide. The Woman's Missionary Union was founded in 1888, and since that time it has become the largest worldwide Protestant mission organization for women, with membership of approximately one million. As an auxiliary to the Southern Baptist Convention, it is self-governing and self-supporting.

Academic Institutions

There are 56 colleges and universities affiliated with the Southern Baptist Convention, and there are over 13,400 students in 6 seminaries:

Golden Gate Theological Seminary (Mill Valley, CA)
Midwestern Baptist Theological Seminary (Kansas City, MO)
New Orleans Baptist Theological Seminary (New Orleans, LA)
Southeastern Baptist Theological Seminary (Wake Forest, NC)
Southern Baptist Theological Seminary (Louisville, KY)
Southwestern Baptist Theological Seminary (Fort Worth, TX)

Parachurch Organizations

Baptist Men on Mission encourages the spiritual transformation of churchmen so they can live as godly fathers, husbands, and mentors. Guidestone Financial Resources was founded in 1918 as a financial partner of the Southern Baptist Convention. Disaster Relief is a partnership ministry of the state Baptist conventions and the North American Mission Board.

Electronic Media

Beginning in 1941, the Radio and Television Commission (RTVC) operated five radio stations and both FamilyNet and the American Christian Television System network. Southern Baptist radio and television efforts ceased with the sale of the RTVC building in Fort Worth, Texas. The North American Mission Board continued video production and thirty minutes of programming on FamilyNet.

Publications

The *Baptist Press* is a weekday international newswire service that was established in 1946. Supported by Cooperative Program funds, the *Baptist Press* is distributed to 40 state Baptist newspapers with a combined circulation of 1.16 million. Established in Nashville in 1891, LifeWay Christian Resources, which is owned and operated by the Southern Baptist Convention, is one of the largest Christian retail distributors. LifeWay is also the world's largest publisher of religious materials, producing approximately 180 monthly and quarterly resources and 1,500 annually updated products.

Website

http://www.sbc.net/

Bibliography

Ammerman, Nancy Tatom. *Baptist Battles: Social Change and Religious Conflict in the Southern Baptist Convention*. New Brunswick, NJ: Rutgers University Press, 1990.

Baker, Robert Andrew. *The Southern Baptist Convention and Its People, 1607–1972*. Nashville: Broadman, 1974.

Barnes, William Wright. *The Southern Baptist Convention, 1845–1953*. Nashville: Broadman, 1954.

Bush, L. Russ, and Tom J. Nettles. *Baptists and the Bible*. Rev. ed. Nashville: Broadman & Holman, 1999.

Draper, James T., Jr. *Bridges to the Future: A Challenge to Southern Baptists*. Nashville: Convention Press, 1994.

Duncan, Pope A. *Our Baptist Story*. Nashville: Convention Press, 1958.

Fletcher, Jesse C. *The Southern Baptist Convention: A Sesquicentennial History*. Nashville: Broadman & Holman, 1994.

Harvey, Paul. *Redeeming the South: Religious Cultures and Racial Identities*. Chapel Hill: University of North Carolina Press, 1997.

Humphrey, Fisher. *The Way We Were: How Southern Baptist Theology Has Changed and What It Means to Us All*. Macon, GA: Smyth & Helwys, 2002.

Leonard, Bill J. *God's Last and Only Hope: The Fragmentation of the Southern Baptist Convention*. Grand Rapids: Eerdmans, 1990.

McBeth, H. Leon. *The Baptist Heritage*. Nashville: Broadman, 1987.

Nettles, Tom. *Ready for Reformation? Bringing Authentic Reform to Southern Baptist Churches*. Nashville: Broadman & Holman, 2005.

Sutton, Jerry. *The Baptist Reformation: The Conservative Resurgence in the Southern Baptist Convention*. Nashville: Broadman & Holman, 2000.

Waggoner, Brad J., and E. Ray Clendenen. *Calvinism: A Southern Baptist Dialogue*. Nashville: Broadman & Holman, 2008.

Ron J. Bigalke

Sovereign Grace Churches

History

People of Destiny began in 1982 as a network of churches started by C. J. Mahaney and Larry Tomczak, who were involved in the Catholic charismatic renewal of the 1970s. Both Mahaney and Tomczak were founding pastors of Covenant Life Church (originally Gathering of Believers) in April 1977 in Gaithersburg, Maryland. Restorationist Bryn Jones in Britain influenced the network informally. Tomczak left the movement primarily due to doctrinal refocusing by the leadership in 1997. People of Destiny changed its name to PDI Ministries in 1998; and, in 2003, it changed its name to Sovereign Grace Ministries. In 2012, a civil lawsuit was filed against Mahaney and Sovereign Grace Ministries, regarding the alleged concealment of sexual abuse at Covenant Life Church by a former youth pastor. The lawsuit was dismissed and Mahaney denied all the claims against him (as defendant) in the civil suit. Mahaney resigned the presidency of Sovereign Grace Ministries, in 2013, for the purpose of founding Sovereign Grace Church in Louisville, Kentucky, which is now the headquarters of Sovereign Grace Ministries. In 2014, the group adopted the name Sovereign Grace Churches.

Headquarters

303 N Hurstbourne Parkway
Suite 160
Louisville, KY 40222
Telephone: 502-855-7700; 800-736-2202

Leadership

Executive director: Patrick Ennis

Core Beliefs

Sovereign Grace believers are evangelical. Foundational beliefs and doctrinal emphases are identified as essentially Reformed and charismatic (continuationist). Believers affirm a Reformed soteriology; however, they do not follow some Reformed traditions, such as cessationism (the belief that some miraculous spiritual gifts have ceased to exist), infant baptism, or traditionally Reformed models of church polity. The foundational belief and passion is the gospel of Jesus Christ, that is, his death and resurrection for the reconciliation of sinners to God.

Sovereign Grace believers affirm experiencing the active presence of God, as consistent with the sovereignty of God. They believe in Scripture as authoritative, inerrant, and inspired, while insisting that all spiritual gifts are available and vital for the contemporary mission of the church. The supernatural gifts of the Holy Spirit are necessary for the edification of the believer and the ministry of the church and are therefore solemnly desired and practiced. Only followers of Jesus Christ are to observe the ordinances of baptism and the Lord's Supper.

Worship

Believers see worship not just as music but as a way of living. Music is one aspect of expressing devotion to God. They have published hundreds of songs written by men and women in their family of churches. The Come and Worship series was created in 1997 (under the previous name PDI Music). Sovereign Grace continues to produce special worship projects and singles.

Divisions and Splits

Sovereign Grace Ministries was previously known as People of Destiny, which was co-founded by C. J. Mahaney and Larry Tomczak. Tomczak left People of Destiny due to doctrinal and directional changes.

Statistics

Members: 27,000

Churches: 77, primarily in the United States but also in Canada, England, Mexico, and Wales; other congregations can be found in Bolivia, Ethiopia, Germany, India, the Philippines, Sri Lanka, and Uganda

Largest Churches

The largest churches are found in the United States.

Missionary and Evangelistic Work

Sovereign Grace believers have tremendous respect for the classical missions approach. Their primary intent, however, is for the local church to first establish a biblical model (based upon their understanding of such a definition

in Scripture) and then to send forth the model by reproducing gifts, maturity, and values in another location. Leaders seek indigenous leaders who have expressed interest in the vision of Sovereign Grace. The mission strategy includes inviting leaders from other countries to the Pastors College and sending teams of believers to serve cross-culturally. The evangelistic desire of Sovereign Grace believers to proclaim the gospel and witness conversions is equal to their desire to preserve the gospel and make mature disciples.

Academic Institutions

The Pastors College provides academic and practical training for men for ministry within the family of Sovereign Grace Churches. The Pastors College is a ten-month training program, which is a series of nonaccredited, weeklong classes. The Pastors College also provides continual training for current Sovereign Grace pastors. As a consequence of the economic recession in the United States, the Ministries Board decided to relocate the Pastors College and the Gaithersburg, Maryland, office to Louisville, Kentucky, in 2012.

Parachurch Organizations

Parachurch ministries are regarded as subordinate to the local church and thus should not be entirely disassociated from the local church. Sovereign Grace Churches does not regard the local church and the parachurch as functioning in opposition, but it does believe that the latter is not the ultimate benefit for God's people.

Mark Dever, Ligon Duncan, C. J. Mahaney, and Albert Mohler began Together for the Gospel (T4G) as a friendship between four pastors. A biennial conference is held to encourage other pastors to stand together for the gospel. A mission presentation is produced annually that provides information regarding the family of churches.

Publications

People of Destiny magazine was published for nearly two decades (publication ceased in 2002). Joshua Harris published *New Attitude* magazine from 1993 to 1996. The books in the Pursuit of Godliness series are written by Sovereign Grace pastors. The Perspectives series is written to address various issues of doctrine and practice in the local church. Sovereign Grace produces audio series on various topics for personal and small group application.

Website

http://www.sovereigngrace.com/

Bibliography

Harvey, Dave. *Polity: Serving and Leading the Local Church.* Gaithersburg, MD: Sovereign Grace Ministries, 2004.

Mahaney, C. J. *The Cross Centered Life: Keeping the Gospel the Main Thing.* Sisters, OR: Multnomah, 2002.

————. *Living the Cross Centered Life.* Sisters, OR: Multnomah, 2006.

————, ed. *Why Small Groups? Together toward Maturity.* Gaithersburg, MD: Sovereign Grace Ministries.

Tomczak, Larry. *Clap Your Hands!* Plainfield, NJ: Logos, 1973.

Virgo, Terry. *No Well-Worn Paths.* Eastbourne: Kingsway, 2001.

Ron J. Bigalke

Brethren

Brethren Church, Ashland, Ohio

History

The Brethren Church was formally organized in 1883 in Dayton, Ohio, a year after Henry Holsinger and six thousand of his followers were expelled from the German Baptist Brethren Church. They were called "Progressive Dunkers" because of their progressive views and their practice of baptizing by immersion. (Another group of four thousand Old Order Brethren had withdrawn from the German Baptist Brethren Church between 1880 and 1881, becoming the Old German Baptist Brethren Church.) The German Baptists held more conservative views and adopted the name Church of the Brethren in 1908. The progressives stressed education, the ordination of women, and foreign missions and gained more and more mainstream acceptance.

A controversy threatened the church between 1913 and 1920 after the Ministerial Association issued a conservative doctrinal statement and most of the liberals left the church. The church saw growth of home and foreign missions during the interwar years, when there was also an expansion of minister training as the Ashland College Theological Seminary began to offer graduate-level degrees. Nonetheless, another controversy erupted in 1939 between traditional and fundamentalist Brethren regarding the conversion of Ashland College into a liberal arts institution. It resulted in another schism in which the dispensational fundamentalists formed the Grace Brethren (or the National Fellowship of Brethren Churches, now the Fellowship of Grace Brethren Churches), named after Grace Theological Seminary, and the traditionalists formed the Ashland Brethren, signifying their support of Ashland College. Since the Grace Brethren took over almost all the mission and youth outreaches, the Ashland Brethren were forced to rebuild their entire home and foreign mission effort.

The church was back on solid footing by the 1960s, with help from Ashland Theological Seminary, which had an enrollment of close to seven hundred. Since the 1960s, relations with other evangelicals have improved considerably. The Ashland Brethren continue to be active in domestic and foreign evangelism.

Headquarters

524 College Avenue
Ashland, OH 44805
Telephone: 419-289-1708
Email: brethren@brethrenchurch.org

Leadership

Executive director: Kenn Hunn

Core Beliefs

The Ashland Brethren represent the Arminian wing of the Progressive Dunker movement. The Brethren never had a formal creed, fearing that would hinder the work of the Holy Spirit in illuminating Scripture. The Dayton Convention stated the church's doctrinal position as follows: "The Bible and Bible alone is our all-sufficient creed and rule of practice" (brethrenchurch.org, "Belief Statement"). Brethren also maintain that their adherence to Christ's teaching must be evident to all. Christ's death is viewed as the cause of renewed fellowship with the Father. Scripture and the church together provide all the necessary tools to the Brethren's walk of faith, in which they strive to follow Christ's example and to utilize the power made available through Christ's resurrection. The Brethren rely on the enabling of the Holy Spirit to obey God and mature spiritually. The church is viewed simply as a gathered community that nurtures believers as their faith leads to faithfulness to the Lord.

Seeing salvation as both an event and a process, the Brethren believe it is witnessed through water baptism. They believe all people are sinners as a result of original sin, and they believe in the divine inspiration and authoritativeness of all Scripture. The New Testament church is regarded as an extension of Christ's own ministry, composed of all those who accept Christ as Lord and who act as his faithful disciples. The church works collectively to evangelize, nurture believers, be of service to the community, and worship the Lord. The Brethren Church believes that spiritual gifts have been given to Christians by God to equip them for ministry and that certain symbolic rites established by Jesus and the apostles can demonstrate faithfulness and obedience to the gospel. These rites include water baptism through immersion in the name of the Father, Son, and Holy Ghost; the laying on of hands; Communion; the washing of feet; and the anointing of the sick with oil.

The priorities of the Brethren Church include missions, building new churches, evangelism, and service to the community.

Website

http://www.brethrenchurch.org/

George Thomas Kurian

Brethren in Christ Church

History

The Brethren in Christ Church was born in Lancaster County, Pennsylvania, near what is today the town of Marietta, between 1775 and 1788. The founders were Anabaptists who were influenced by the Pietism of the Moravians and the German Baptists as well as by Wesleyan eighteenth-century revivals. While they originally called themselves "Brethren," their location by the Susquehanna River prompted outsiders to call them "River Brethren." They distanced themselves from many activities they regarded as worldly, including politics, games such as card playing, and the wearing of colorful or ostentatious clothing. Their evident distinctness from surrounding communities, including their German tongue, reinforced their desire for isolation and doctrinal simplicity.

True to their name, the Brethren were a brotherhood in Christ and until the late 1800s met in one another's homes. Meetinghouses that were eventually constructed were simple with an unelevated pulpit. Renamed Brethren of Christ in 1863, the Brethren had spread to Ohio, Indiana, Michigan, Iowa, Kansas, Oklahoma, California, and Canada, where their practice of immersion baptism led to the name "Tunkers" or "Dunkers" after the German word for "dipping." The formation of the general conference in 1879 facilitated the expansion of the church. By the end of the eighteenth century, it had launched urban missions, starting with the Chicago mission in 1894. Today the Brethren in Christ Church is present throughout the United States, Canada, and twenty-one other nations.

Headquarters

431 Grantham Road
Grantham, PA 17027-0901
Email: dwinger@messiah.edu

Core Beliefs

The Brethren in Christ Church adheres to basic Christian teachings embodied in the Apostles' Creed and the Nicene Creed. It believes in the authoritativeness of the Bible, with the Old Testament to be interpreted in light of the New; the existence of three Persons of the Godhead—Father, Son, and Holy Spirit; the sinfulness of all people and their accountability for their conduct; the death and bodily resurrection of Christ to redeem those who have faith in him and to give them eternal life; the work of the Holy Spirit since Pentecost to guide individuals to Christ; and the role of the church as the community of God that facilitates worship, fellowship, discipleship, missions, and evangelism.

The unique theology of the Brethren in Christ Church represents the merger of the Anabaptist, Pietist, and Wesleyan traditions. The Anabaptists placed great importance on personal responsibility, obedience to God, and separation from political affairs; Pietism stressed simplicity and genuineness in spiritual matters; Wesleyan teachings urged believers to live holy lives. The Brethren in Christ are pacifists and discourage any political involvement that could conflict with loyalty to the church. They oppose abortion and homosexuality. Recognized ordinances are baptism and the Lord's Supper, both symbolizing identification with Christ's death and resurrection. Infants are dedicated rather than baptized, and foot washing is practiced as a sign of humility. Prayers are offered for the sick, with laying on of hands and anointing with oil. Doctrinal statements have been revised four times since the first one was adopted in 1780.

51

Statistics

Year	Clergy	Churches	Members
1935	75	90	4,426
2001	295	232	20,739

Missionary and Evangelistic Work

The Brethren in Christ extend support beyond local congregations through the office of Co-operative Ministries. Its activities include sending missionaries, planting churches, teaching effective ministry, and providing care for pastors.

Global evangelistic goals of the Brethren in Christ began in 1884 with an impassioned plea by a participant at the general conference. The first foreign mission was started in Rhodesia (today Zimbabwe) in 1898. By 1900, there were twenty thousand Brethren in Christ members outside the United States; international membership grew to 120,000 in 2010, with three overseas congregations for each one in North America.

The World Hunger Fund was founded more than thirty years ago to address the problem of hunger in countries around the globe. In 2009, it offered more than $250,000 for hunger relief and other charitable purposes, including flood recovery, school supplies, and housing.

The Brethren in Christ Foundation assists with practical needs of ministry by offering low-interest loans. The church also has ministries that deal specifically with the needs of students, youth, and urban communities.

Affiliations

Denominational organizations include the International Brethren in Christ Association and the Mennonite and Brethren in Christ Resource Center.

Academic Institutions

Messiah College in Grantham, Pennsylvania, is home to the Sider Institute for Anabaptist, Pietist, and Wesleyan Studies. Niagara Christian Community of Schools is in Fort Erie, Ontario. The Commission on Ministry and Doctrine operates Equipping for Ministry, a program to further theological education of clergy and lay ministers.

Parachurch Organizations

Missions and charities include Circle Thrift, a network of thrift shops in Philadelphia; Council for Women in Ministry and Leadership; Lifeline Ministries Women's Shelter Inc. in Upland, California; Mennonite Disaster Service in Akron, Pennsylvania; Navajo Brethren in Christ Mission in Bloomfield, New Mexico; Pacific Christian Center in Upland, California; Paxton Ministries in Harrisburg, Pennsylvania, providing food and housing to the poor and those with mental health problems; and Priority 1 Ministries, based in Chambersburg, Pennsylvania, providing short-term mission opportunities in urban areas and overseas.

The church supports retirement communities in Mechanicsburg, Pennsylvania (Messiah Village); Mount Joy, Pennsylvania (Mount Joy Country Homes); and Upland, California (Upland Manor).

Other organizations include:

Camp Freedom (St. Petersburg, FL)
Camp Kahquah (Ontario, Canada)
Christian Retreat Center (East Waterford, PA)
Kenbrook Bible Camp (Lebanon, PA)
Memorial Holiness Camp (West Milton, OH)
Mile High Pines Camp (Angelus Oaks, CA)
Roxbury Holiness Camp (Roxbury, PA)
West Milton Christian Center (West Milton, OH)

Publications

Evangel Press and Evangel Publishing (Nappanee, IN)
In Part, an online magazine
Momentum, Invest, and *Share* newsletters
Shalom! A Journal for the Practice of Reconciliation, a quarterly that examines Christian perspectives on current issues

Archives

Brethren in Christ Historical Library and Archives (Grantham, PA)
Brethren in Christ Historical Society (Grantham, PA)
Ringgold Meeting House (Smithsburg, MD), restored in the 1970s and built in 1871 (making it one of the oldest Brethren in Christ Church meetinghouses)

Website

http://www.bic-church.org/

George Thomas Kurian

Christian Brethren/ Plymouth Brethren

History

The Plymouth Brethren is an evangelical, independent, and nondenominational Christian body that originated in early nineteenth-century England. (The history of the Plymouth Brethren is distinct from that of the Brethren churches of the Pietist movement.) Irishman John Nelson Darby (1800–1882), a lawyer who became a clergyman in the Church of Ireland (Anglican), was one of the primary preachers among the Brethren. Soon after his ordination as deacon in the Anglican Church in 1825, he became dissatisfied with what he viewed as unrestrained clericalism (the authority and influence of clergy in political and secular matters) and Erastianism (the doctrine that the state has authority over the church in ecclesiastical matters). Darby sought fellowship and ministry outside the Anglican Church and began meeting with a group of like-minded believers, who were members of the Anglican Church in Dublin, for Bible study and worship without ecclesiastical hierarchy or formalism. This was the group that later became known as the Plymouth Brethren.

In 1831, Darby resigned from Anglicanism and joined those he had been meeting with for several years; thus, the first congregation was established in Plymouth, England. The Powerscourt Conferences (1831–33) would have an enduring influence on Darby, as his ecclesiology and eschatology would be systematized. (Darby was not present at the Albury Conferences, which were held in the late 1820s for the purpose of studying the prophetic portions of Scripture. When the Albury Conferences ended, Lady Theodosia Powerscourt [Lord Powerscourt's widow] sponsored subsequent conferences at her estate in Ireland. Darby and the Dublin Brethren were present in addition to some of the Plymouth and Bristol Brethren.) Although neither Darby nor the Brethren originated the interpretation of Scripture known as dispensationalism (a premillennial theology that affirms a transition from the present church era to the millennial kingdom, in which Israel is a regenerate and restored nation, thus indicating a distinction between promises for the church and for regenerate Israel), Darby did promote the system widely through his travels and writings from 1832 to 1845. Through conferences, founding of schools, literature, and preaching, dispensationalism became a leading influence on evangelicalism and fundamentalism, especially in the formation of independent churches and mission boards. By the beginning of the twentieth century, dispensationalism had become well respected and the dominant evangelical system of theology.

Early Plymouth Brethren were known for their great emphasis on expository preaching. Brethren Bible conferences in Great Britain and North America impacted leading evangelical church leaders such as James Hall Brookes, Arno C. Gaebelein, H. Gratton Guinness, Dwight L.

Moody, and C. I. Scofield. Scofield was tutored by Brookes, who was evidently influenced significantly by Darby (at least in a simpler form), and was also a close friend of Gaebelein in addition to others in the Bible conference movement who communicated Darby's teachings. Scofield would publish his reference Bible with the encouragement of the Brethren.

Core Beliefs

Plymouth Brethren affirm the fundamentals of conservative Christianity, including the plenary and verbal inspiration of Scripture. Brethren are trinitarian and affirm the eternal Sonship of Jesus Christ. The majority of Exclusive Brethren are Calvinistic with regard to their soteriology, although they deny particular (limited) redemption. Open Brethren have tended to oscillate between Arminianism and Calvinism and seek to maintain the doctrine of eternal security. They are cessationists with respect to the "sign gifts" and strongly opposed the charismatic developments among Edward Irving (1792–1834) and the Irvingites. Brethren affirm premillennial dispensationalism, as characterized by a consistent, literal interpretation of Scripture; a distinction between Israel and the church; and a doxological purpose of history.

Plymouth Brethren are earnest students of Scripture and are characterized by a practical piety in their lives. Some Exclusive Brethren practice child baptism of members, whereas Open Brethren practice believer's baptism.

Worship

Worship services are informal, nonliturgical, and participatory. Communion is celebrated weekly on Sundays. An extensive variety of hymnbooks is used among assemblies.

Divisions and Splits

Disagreement with B. W. Newton regarding the doctrine of the rapture and his alleged clericalism resulted in the 1845 Great Schism. Once the majority of the Brethren divided from Newton, some from the Ebbrington Street meeting in Plymouth visited the Bethesda meeting in Bristol and were welcomed to Communion. George Müller (1805–98) did not believe these Brethren affirmed Newton's teachings. Thus, he did not refuse them from fellowship. In addition to this Bethesda Question, there were other disagreements between Darby and Müller regarding the interrelationship of Brethren assemblies in response to matters of church discipline. The Brethren split into two dominant groups. The Exclusive Brethren, who were represented by Darby and against the actions at Bethesda, believed Communion should be restricted to members of their own churches. Those Brethren who agreed that Bethesda was justified in receiving the visitors from the Ebbrington Street meeting became known as the Open Brethren because they believed all Christians should be welcome to Communion.

Statistics

A lack of central headquarters increases the difficulty in maintaining records. The majority of large cities in North America and Europe have Brethren assemblies. There are assemblies in Africa, Asia, Australia, the Caribbean, Great Britain, and Latin America. Recent estimates suggest total membership is approximately one million worldwide.

Missionary and Evangelistic Work

The early history of the Brethren evidences a strong commitment to evangelistic work and church planting. Churches were established throughout the British Isles, Europe, and North America. Plymouth Brethren serve actively in foreign missionary work, primarily in Central Africa, India, and Latin America. Exclusive Brethren have tended to be more concerned with doctrinal affirmation, whereas Open Brethren have been more zealous evangelistically. Brethren churches in Australia, New Zealand, North America, and the United Kingdom have commissioned more than twelve hundred foreign missionaries in addition to several thousand missionaries serving locally, indigenously, and with other evangelistic ministries.

Academic Institutions

The Plymouth Brethren maintains Emmaus Bible College in Dubuque, Iowa. Emmaus Bible College offers either two- or four-year degrees and has a correspondence school division with courses available in 105 countries and 125 languages. Emmaus Bible College is regionally accredited by the Higher Learning Commission and is a member of the North Central Association.

Publications

Most assemblies publish regular magazines or newsletters. The *Emmaus Journal* is published semiannually by Emmaus Bible College. The prominent Brethren publishing houses include Believer's Bookshelf (Sunbury, PA), Bible Truth Publishers (Addison, IL), Brockhaus Verlag Wuppertal (Germany), Chapter Two (London), Gospel Folio Press (Ontario), Gospel Tract Publications (Scotland), Loizeaux Brothers (Neptune, NJ), and Present Truth Publishers (Jackson, NJ). The John Rylands University Library at the University of Manchester hosts a unique collection of Christian Brethren books, manuscripts, and periodicals.

Websites

http://www.theexclusivebrethren.com/
http://www.plymouthbrethren.com/

Bibliography

Arnott, Anne. *The Brethren: An Autobiography of a Plymouth Brethren Childhood*. London: Mowbray, 1969.

Baylis, Robert H. *My People: The Story of Those Christians Sometimes Called Plymouth Brethren*. Wheaton: Shaw, 1995.

Coad, F. Roy. *A History of the Brethren Movement: Its Origins, Its Worldwide Development, and Its Significance for the Present Day*. Exeter: Paternoster, 1968.

Geldbach, Erich. *Christliche Versammlung und Heilsgeschichte bei John Nelson Darby*. Wuppertal: Brockhaus, 1971.

Ischebeck, Gustav. *John Nelson Darby: Seine Zeit und sein Werk*. Witten: Bundes-Verlag, 1929.

Neatby, William Blair. *A History of the Plymouth Brethren*. London: Hodder & Stoughton, 1901.

Rowdon, Harold H. *The Origins of the Brethren, 1825–1850*. London: Pickering and Inglis, 1967.

Smith, Nathan DeLynn. *Roots, Renewal, and the Brethren*. Pasadena, CA: Hope Publishing, 1986.

Teulon, Josiah S. *The History and Teaching of the Plymouth Brethren*. New York: E. & J. B. Young & Co., 1883.

Turner, W. G. *John Nelson Darby*. London: C. A. Hammond, 1944.

Weremchuk, Max S. *John Nelson Darby*. Neptune, NJ: Loizeaux Brothers, 1992.

Ron J. Bigalke

Churches of God, General Conference (Winebrenner)

History

The Churches of God, General Conference (CGGC) is an evangelical denomination that is Arminian in theology with a combination of Baptist doctrines and presbyterian ecclesiastical structures. The origin of the denomination can be traced to John Winebrenner (1797–1860). Winebrenner, originally from Maryland and trained at Dickinson College and then under Rev. Samuel Helffenstein in Philadelphia, was

54

initially a pastor in Harrisburg, Pennsylvania, in the German Reformed Church. He was ordained in 1820, locked out of his congregation in 1823, and expelled from the denomination in 1825 for his approval of and participation in revivals and camp meetings as well as his affiliation with Methodists.

In 1825, Winebrenner formed an independent Church of God in Harrisburg. Winebrenner's name for the new church exemplified his aversion to denominations as well as his belief that he was not really starting a new one. But inevitably his activity in camp meetings and revivals in nearby towns led to additional churches being formed in the following years. A general conference (originally called an "Eldership") of six pastors was formed in 1830, and the denomination quickly spread westward from central Pennsylvania to the Midwest and beyond due to the efforts of Winebrenner and several dedicated ministers. Since then the denomination has spread to all parts of the country (and to some countries outside the United States), although it is strongest in Pennsylvania and the Midwest.

The name of the denomination changed several times over the years. It was first called Church of God (in 1825), then Church of God in North America (in 1845), then Churches of God in North America (in 1896), and finally Churches of God, General Conference, its current name (in 1975).

Headquarters

700 East Melrose Avenue
Findlay, OH 45840-4417
Telephone: 419-424-1961

Core Beliefs

The Churches of God, General Conference is similar to many other American evangelical denominations in its belief in the Trinity, the inspiration of Scripture, and salvation by faith in Christ. Some of the distinctives of the denomination include belief in regeneration or the new birth, in which each believer is born again spiritually at the moment of his or her conversion to the gospel; the view that humans are free moral agents who can either choose to accept Christ or to reject him; three ordinances rather than two sacraments (baptism by immersion, Communion as memorial, and foot washing in conjunction with Communion); and belief in the second coming of Christ in either its premillennial or amillennial forms.

Worship

There is a mixture of traditional and contemporary worship in the Churches of God, General Conference churches. Traditionally, however, the church used hymns and psalms for worship.

Statistics

Members: 35,000
Churches: around 350, mostly in Pennsylvania and the Midwest

Growth

The denomination seems to have hit its largest number of members in the early 1990s but has declined over the past decade.

Missionary and Evangelistic Work

Evangelistic work is focused on a few key areas outside the United States. Missionary work began in India in 1898, Bangladesh in 1905, Haiti in 1967, and to the Navajo in the southwestern United States in 1976.

Academic Institutions

University of Findlay and Winebrenner Theological Seminary are on the same campus in Findlay, Ohio, and share resources but are officially separate institutions.

Publications

The *Gospel Publisher* (1835–43) was the denomination's first periodical and was published weekly, but it ceased publication within ten years. The *Church Advocate* (1846–) is essentially the continuation of the *Gospel Publisher*, and it is the denomination's bimonthly periodical. The *Gem* (1867–) is the denomination's weekly Sunday take-home paper. The *Workman* (1890–) is a lesson booklet that is published quarterly. Although the denomination formerly operated its own publishing press called Central Publishing House (1901–79), with headquarters in Harrisburg, Pennsylvania, it eventually ceased operations.

Website

http://www.cggc.org/

Bibliography

Kern, Richard. *Time for Review: Facts about the Founding of the Churches of God, General Conference.* Harrisburg, PA: Central Publishing House, 1975.

Mead, Frank S., Samuel S. Hill, and Craig D. Atwood. "Brethren and Pietist Churches." In *Handbook of Denominations in the United States.* 13th ed. Nashville: Abingdon, 2010.

O'Brien, T. C., ed. *Corpus Dictionary of Western Churches.* Washington: Corpus, 1970.

Rayle, F. D. *The Church: Nature and Organization.* Harrisburg, PA: Central Publishing House, 1975.

Yahn, S. G. *History of the Churches of God in North America.* Harrisburg, PA: Central Publishing House, 1926.

Derek Cooper

Church of the Brethren

History

Alexander Mack and seven German Anabaptists/Pietists in Schwarzenau, Germany, founded the Church of the Brethren in 1708. The church was formed in reaction to a perceived spiritual lethargy within state churches and from the desire for religious freedom. As a consequence of persecution, the Brethren migrated to the American colonies between 1719 and 1729, settling in Germantown, Pennsylvania, and then moving westward and southward for the next two hundred years. By its bicentennial year, the church was commonly known as the German Baptist Brethren or the "Dunkers" ("Dunkards"). In 1908, the name Brethren was adopted with regard to church members to be indicative of the brotherhood and kinship that existed among the first-century church.

Headquarters

1451 Dundee Avenue
Elgin, IL 60120
Telephone: 800-323-8039

Leadership

Brethren combine congregational and presbyterian polity with an authoritative annual conference of elected delegates. The leadership team of the church consists of the general secretary and the annual conference moderator, moderator elect, and secretary. The team provides guidance and leadership for committees and general oversight of the annual conference and serves as a connection between the annual conference and the mission and ministry board.

Core Beliefs

Brethren reject creedal statements and affirm basic Protestant doctrines, including the inspiration of Scripture (however, some discount plenary, verbal inspiration, believing instead that the biblical writers had a broader spiritual awareness when they wrote); the virgin birth and deity of Christ; the personality of the Holy Spirit; the sacrifice of Christ for sinners; the resurrection, ascension, and personal and visible return of Jesus Christ; and the resurrection of both the just and the unjust.

The Brethren Revival Fellowship was organized in 1959 at the annual conference due to a concern that New Testament beliefs and practices were being disregarded and neglected.

Similar to the Mennonites and the Quakers, the Church of the Brethren is a historic peace church and therefore conscientiously opposes military service and is intentional with regard to involvement in peacemaking and reconciliation. Churches oppose taking any oaths (preferring affirmation instead) and use of force in religion. They practice anointing for healing, believer's baptism by trine immersion (immersion three times in the name of the three Persons of the Trinity), biblical salutation (the holy kiss in Rom. 16:16), church discipline, Communion, foot washing, head coverings, the laying on of hands, and the love feast (John 13). Churches promote service and simplicity and emphasize separation from all secular influences. During the early years of the movement, church leaders were not salaried or formally trained. The Brethren adopted several changes during the twentieth century, including the modernization of the dress code (but continue to oppose extravagance and immodesty), ordination of women, and both salaries and formal training for church leaders.

Worship

With a heritage in Anabaptism and Pietism, the Church of the Brethren amalgamates practicality and spirituality. Consequently, the Brethren understand the church as a covenanted and mutually accountable community of believers (the Anabaptist heritage). The heritage of the Pietist movement is evident through an emphasis on personal conversion and the consequent experience of salvation. Churches prioritize orthopraxis (right living) over orthodoxy (right doctrine). Emphasis is placed on the faith community being in service. The model for church life is the early Christians. Thus, the Brethren have a nonconforming and simple manner of worship.

Statistics

Members: 122,810

Churches: 994 (with 53 fellowships) in the United States (mostly Illinois, Indiana, Maryland, Ohio, Pennsylvania, and Virginia) and Puerto Rico

Largest Church

Frederick Church of the Brethren (Frederick, MD), with 1,176 members and an average attendance of 992

Missionary and Evangelistic Work

The life and work of the Brethren begin with the local churches (Congregational Life Ministries) and extend to the district and the church universally. Outdoor ministries provide a directory of Brethren camps and facilities, an outdoor ministry association, and resources for the outdoors curriculum (*New Earth*). The Global Mission Partnerships office includes the denominational witness, food security, service ministries, and overseas missions. The efforts of this office encompass advocacy for the voiceless, church planting and evangelism, peacemaking, and response to human need. The pension board established a benefit trust in 1943 for missionaries and pastors. The Brethren Volunteer Service was formed in 1948 as the result of an emphasis on religion in daily life. M. R. Ziglar organized a group of people in 1974 to strengthen the peace witness of the Brethren (On Earth Peace).

Ecumenism

Evangelism Connections is an ecumenical association that strives to support church vitality, evangelism, and hospitality in a modern context and to provide resources for communicating that message. The general secretary serves as the church's ecumenical officer and represents the denomination to Christian Churches Together in the USA, the Council of Moderators and Secretaries of Anabaptist Churches, the National Council of Churches of Christ in the USA, US Religions for Peace, and the World Council of Churches.

Academic Institutions

Bridgewater College (Bridgewater, VA)
Elizabethtown College (Elizabethtown, PA)
Juniata College (Huntingdon, PA)
Manchester College (North Manchester, IN)
McPherson College (McPherson, KS)
University of La Verne (La Verne, CA)

Bethany Theological Seminary, founded in Chicago in 1905, is the Church of the Brethren graduate school and academy for theological education. In 1994, the seminary moved to Richmond, Indiana, and affiliated with Earlham School of Religion, a graduate theological school in the Quaker tradition.

Parachurch Organizations

Children's Aid Society
COBYS Family Services
Fellowship of Brethren Genealogists
Global Women's Project
Mutual Aid Association
Voices for an Open Spirit
Women's Caucus

Publications

Brethren Press is the publishing ministry of the denomination. Publications include books that illuminate Brethren identity, a denominational magazine (*Messenger*), Sunday school curricula, a website and news service, worship resources, and a variety of other resources to equip Brethren to mature in discipleship, faith, and understanding. Bethany Theological Seminary and the Brethren Journal Association cooperatively publish *Brethren Life and Thought*. Brethren Revival Fellowship publishes *BRF Witness* bimonthly in addition to an Old Testament and New Testament commentary series and books articulating Brethren beliefs, heritage, and practices. *Dunker Journal* is an ongoing independent commentary from the fellowship. Congregational Life Ministries publishes *Basin and Towel* three times a year.

Websites

http://www.brfwitness.org/
http://www.brethren.org/

Bibliography

Durnbaugh, Donald F. *Church of the Brethren: Yesterday and Today*. Elgin, IL: Brethren Press, 1986.

——, ed. *The Church of the Brethren: Past and Present*. Elgin, IL: Brethren Press, 1971.

Durnbaugh, Donald F., and Dale V. Ulrich, eds. *The Brethren Encyclopedia*. 4 vols. Philadelphia: Brethren Encyclopedia Inc., 1983–84, 2005.

Eller, David B., ed. *Servants of the Word*. Elgin, IL: Brethren Press, 1990.

Fisher, Virginia S. *The Story of the Brethren*. Elgin, IL: Brethren Publishing House, 1957.

Wieand, David J. *Visions of Glory*. Elgin, IL: Brethren Press, 1979.

Winger, Otho. *History and Doctrines of the Church of the Brethren*. Elgin, IL: Brethren Publishing House, 1919.

Ron J. Bigalke

Church of the United Brethren in Christ

History

The Church of the United Brethren in Christ (UB) claims to be the first denomination to begin in the United States as opposed to being transplanted. In May 1767, an interdenominational revival meeting was held at a barn in Lancaster, Pennsylvania. Martin Boehm (1725–1812), a Mennonite preacher, spoke of becoming a Christian through crying out to God while plowing in a field. William Otterbein (1726–1813), a Reformed pastor in York, Pennsylvania, left his seat, embraced Boehm, and said, "Wir sind bruder" (We are brethren). The followers of Boehm and Otterbein formed a loose movement that spread to include German-speaking churches in Pennsylvania, Virginia, Maryland, and Ohio. In 1800, they began a yearly conference, and at that first conference, they adopted the name United Brethren in Christ. Boehm and Otterbein were elected bishops. In subsequent years, a confession of faith (1815) and a constitution (1841) were adopted.

The United Brethren took a stand against slavery around 1820. After 1837, slave owners were no longer allowed to remain as members. Expansion occurred into the western United States, but the church's stance against slavery limited expansion into the South.

Due to various splits over the years, two factions operated under the name Church of the United Brethren in Christ. The present church is descended from the minority who organized under the leadership of Bishop Milton Wright. They eventually adopted two of the changes that led to the division of 1889: local conferences have proportional representation at the general conference, and half of the delegates are laypersons. In 1897, a denominational headquarters, a college, and a publishing house were established in Huntington, Indiana. In 1946, the larger United Brethren group merged with the Evangelical Association to form the Evangelical United Brethren Church. That body in turn merged with the Methodist Church in 1968 to form the United Methodist Church. William Otterbein retained a connection with the Reformed Church, pastoring a Reformed Church in Baltimore, Maryland, from 1774 until his death in 1813. Martin Boehm was excluded by the Mennonites in 1775. He joined the Methodist Church in 1802 while remaining bishop of the United Brethren until his death in 1812.

Leadership

Bishop: Phil Whipple

Core Beliefs

The Church of the United Brethren in Christ, its longer official name, is a conservative trinitarian denomination that believes in the deity, humanity, and atonement of Jesus Christ; sees the Bible, in both the Old and New Testaments, as the inspired Word of God; and believes salvation is through faith, repentance, and following after Christ. The church holds two ordinances: baptism and the Lord's Supper. The church takes a neutral position on the observance of foot washing, stating, "The example of washing feet is left to the judgment of every one to practice or not" (ub.org, "Doctrinal Beliefs"). The UB Confession of Faith, spelling out fundamental doctrines, was adopted in 1815 and has never been changed. The constitution, adopted in 1841, has been amended only a few times. The Discipline details membership standards and church organization. At the international level, four documents bind the various national conferences together: the Confession of Faith of 1815, the Core Values, the International Constitution, and the International By-Laws.

Statistics

Churches: 500 (US: 200; elsewhere: 300)
Attendance: 41,500 (US: 25,150; elsewhere: 16,350)

Of the 200 UB churches in the United States, 180 are located in Pennsylvania, Ohio, northern Indiana, and Michigan. The remainder are scattered in Florida, California, Washington, Idaho, and New York.

With the number of churches, membership, and weekly attendance declining for decades, in 2003, the executive leadership team voted to pursue joining with the Missionary Church. The merger was scheduled to occur in 2005, but the national lay members voted against it.

The UB has national conferences in nine other countries: Sierra Leone, Honduras, Jamaica, Mexico, Nicaragua, the Philippines, Guatemala, Canada, and Hong Kong. All of those national conferences, as in the United States, are self-governing. There are also churches in countries that have not yet organized an official conference: India, Macau, Thailand, Myanmar, El Salvador, Haiti, Germany, and Costa Rica.

Academic Institution

Huntington University, a Christian liberal arts school with 1,200 students (Huntington, IN)

Website

http://www.ub.org/

58

Bibliography

"Church of the United Brethren in Christ." http://www.ub.org. "Doctrinal Beliefs" and "Our History."

Fetters, P. *Trials and Triumphs: A History of the Church of the United Brethren in Christ.* Huntington, IN: Church of the United Brethren in Christ, Dept. of Church Services, 1984.

Mead, Frank S., Samuel S. Hill, and Craig D. Atwood. "Church of the United Brethren in Christ." In *Handbook of Denominations in the United States.* 13th ed. Nashville: Abingdon, 2010.

Thompson, H. *Our Bishops: A Sketch of the Origin and Growth of the Church of the United Brethren in Christ, As Shown in the Lives of Its Distinguished Leaders.* Dayton, OH: U. B. Publishing House, 1906.

Mark A. Lamport

Fellowship of Grace Brethren Churches

History

The Fellowship of Grace Brethren Churches is a theologically conservative denomination that developed from the eighteenth-century Pietists and the Schwarzenau Brethren in Wittgenstein, Germany, led by Alexander Mack, the founder of the Brethren movement. In 1719, the Brethren emigrated to America under the leadership of Peter Becker. The majority settled near Germantown, Pennsylvania, but were not formally organized. In 1723, the first Brethren church in America was founded when it held its first baptisms and love feast. As descendants of the early German Protestants, the Brethren are authentic Pietists.

Headquarters

PO Box 384
Winona Lake, IN 46590
Telephone: 574-269-1269

Core Beliefs

Grace Brethren churches are conservative among the Brethren denomination. The Bible is the authority in all matters of faith and practice. The statement of faith for the fellowship includes belief in the verbal and plenary inspiration of Scripture; the Trinity; the person and work of Jesus Christ; the person and work of the Holy Spirit; the direct creation of man and his fall into sin and need for the new birth; salvation by God's grace alone through personal faith in Jesus Christ; the church as the body and bride of Christ and composed of believers of the present age; the Christian life as that of righteousness, good works, and separation unto God; ordinances of baptism and Communion; the personality and existence of Satan; the second coming as pretribulational and premillennial; and the resurrection and judgment of all people.

Grace Brethren differ from other evangelicals and fundamentalists in their particular observance of baptism of believers by triune immersion (in the name of the Father, the Son, and the Holy Spirit) and a threefold Communion service that includes washing the feet of the saints, observance of the Lord's Supper, and the love feast. Other distinctives include calling for the church elders to pray and anoint the sick with oil (in accordance with James 5:13–18) and refraining from worldly amusements (as is common among Pietistic groups). Continuing resolutions include affirmations of the sanctity of human life, religious freedom, and personal commitment as the church and as individuals. A resolution opposing homosexuality as unbiblical clarifies matters of fundamental rights and respect, ethical and religious issues, and governmental and corporate coercion.

Worship

Worship services are relevant in style and biblical in substance.

Statistics

Membership: 750,000
Churches: over 2,000 worldwide, with 260 in the United States and Canada

Largest Churches

The largest churches are found in California, Ohio, and Pennsylvania.

Missionary and Evangelistic Work

In addition to relief efforts, the churches support home and international missions. Grace Brethren International Missions is a cross-cultural mission organization associated with the churches for the purpose of mobilizing men and women in evangelism and discipleship through church multiplication movements. CE National assists churches and individuals in effective ministry training and opportunities. Women of Grace USA was formed to challenge women to grow in their relationship with Christ. A life of service to God in active Christian work is continually prioritized among young people.

Academic Institution

Grace College and Theological Seminary (Winona Lake, IN)

Publications

Since 1940, the Brethren Missionary Herald Company has been the communication and publication agency of the fellowship. *FGBC World* began publication in 2004 for the purpose of connecting people and churches of the Fellowship of Grace Brethren Churches.

Website

http://www.fgbc.org/

Bibliography

Durnbaugh, Donald F., and Dale V. Ulrich, eds. *The Brethren Encyclopedia.* 4 vols. Philadelphia: Brethren Encyclopedia Inc., 1983–84, 2005.

Etling, Harold H. *Our Heritage: Brethren Beliefs and Practices.* Winona Lake, IN: BMH Books, 1975.

Kent, Homer A. *250 Years Conquering Frontiers: A History of the Brethren Church.* Winona Lake, IN: BMH Books, 1958.

Plaster, David R. *Finding Our Focus: A History of the Grace Brethren Church.* Winona Lake, IN: BMH Books, 2003.

Rohrer, Norman B. *A Saint in Glory Stands: The Story of Alva J. McClain, Founder of Grace Theological Seminary.* Winona Lake, IN: BMH Books, 1986.

Ron J. Bigalke

Old German Baptist Brethren Church

History

In 1881, the Old German Baptist Brethren Church, a conservative, "old order" group, withdrew from the German Baptist Brethren (Church of the Brethren). Grievances included protracted meetings, Sunday schools, prayer meetings, mission boards, musical instruments in worship, and paid ministers. In addition, the Old German Baptist Brethren appealed for uniformity in teaching and dress, and they desired to be of one mind in other aspects of thought and practice. Samuel Kinsey (1832–83) was among the early leaders of the movement.

Headquarters

6952 N Montgomery County Line Road
Englewood, OH 45322
Telephone: 937-884-7531

Core Beliefs

Stemming from both Pietists and Anabaptists, Old German Baptist Brethren emphasize the depravity of humanity and the transformation of individuals through Jesus Christ. Repentance with public confession is expected as well as a subsequent yielding of spirit and acceptance of

practice; however, salvation is by divine grace through faith. Scripture is central in all matters. Ordinances include believer's baptism by forward, trine immersion; double-mode foot washing (that is, two people washing the feet of each participant); the love feast; closed Communion; the holy kiss; and anointing the sick with oil.

Defining documents include *Resolutions Passed at the Special Conference* (1881), *The Brethren's Reasons for Producing and Adopting the Resolutions of August 24th [1881] with a Brief Account of How Things Worked Thereafter* (1883), *Doctrinal Treatise* (1991, 5th ed.), and *Polity Statement by the Old German Baptist Brethren New Conference* (July 3, 2009).

Old German Baptist Brethren refrain from making oaths, filing lawsuits, entering military service, participating in politics, and consuming alcohol. Plain dress after baptism is one overt manifestation of their nonconformity to the world. They uphold the sanctity of marriage. They do not seek to grow the church through missionary or evangelistic outreach.

Website

http://ogbbc.org/

Bibliography

Benedict, Fred W. "Brethren's Reasons, The." In *The Brethren Encyclopedia,* edited by Donald F. Durnbaugh and Dale V. Ulrich, vol. 1, 205–6. Philadelphia: Brethren Encyclopedia Inc., 1983.

Filbrun, Jerry A. "Kinsey, Samuel." In *The Brethren Encyclopedia,* edited by Donald F. Durnbaugh and Dale V. Ulrich, vol. 2, 696. Philadelphia: Brethren Encyclopedia Inc., 1983.

Kraybill, Donald B., and Carl Desportes Bowman. *On the Backroad to Heaven: Old Order Hutterites, Mennonites, Amish, and Brethren.* Baltimore: Johns Hopkins University Press, 2001.

Linder, Eileen W., ed. *Yearbook of American and Canadian Churches 2011.* Nashville: Abingdon, 2011.

Miller, Marcus. "Old German Baptist Brethren." In *The Brethren Encyclopedia,* edited by Donald F. Durnbaugh and Dale V. Ulrich, vol. 2, 966–70. Philadelphia: Brethren Encyclopedia Inc., 1983.

"Old German Baptist Brethren Church: New Conference Fellowship." http://www.ogbbc.org. "Polity Statement."

Warren C. Robertson

United Christian Church

History

The United Christian Church is a small evangelical body headquartered in Pennsylvania. It separated from the Church of the United Brethren in Christ in 1864 because of doctrinal differences. Its theological origin can be found in the Pietist movement of Martin Boehm and William Otterbein. Originally its adherents were known as Hoffmanites, after George W. Hoffman, who led the group for many years along with his friends John Stamn and Thomas Lesher. Hoffman was strongly opposed to practices such as infant baptism, slavery, secret societies, and military enrollment as well as the doctrine of total depravity. The church formally organized and endorsed a statement of faith in Campbelltown, Pennsylvania, in 1877. The following year the group took its present name.

Headquarters

523 West Walnut Street
Cleona, PA 17042
Telephone: 717-273-9629

Core Beliefs

Trinitarian in faith, the United Christian Church stresses inspiration of the Scriptures, justification by faith, regeneration, and sanctification. Baptism, the Lord's Supper, and foot washing are regarded as established rites.

George Thomas Kurian

United Zion Church

History

The United Zion Church is a small denomination related to Mennonite Pietism. The River Brethren, who lived near the Susquehanna River in Pennsylvania, formed in the late 1770s, and many of their churches evolved into the Brethren in Christ. In 1853, the River Brethren, who met only in believers' homes, expelled Matthias Brinser for his support of the use of meetinghouses. He and his followers organized the United Zion's Children, later United Zion Church, and continued to adhere to the majority of the River Brethren's beliefs. The church's congregations are all concentrated in three counties in eastern Pennsylvania.

Headquarters

4041 Shanamantown Road
Annville, PA 17003
Telephone: 717-867-1133

Website

http://www.unitedzionchurch.org/

Bibliography

Martin, J. Paul. "United Zion Church." *Global Anabaptist Mennonite Encyclopedia Online.* 1989. http://www.gameo.org/encyclopedia/contents/U569.html.

Wittlinger, Carlton O. *Quest for Piety and Obedience: The Story of the Brethren in Christ.* Nappanee, IN: Evangel Press, 1979.

George Thomas Kurian

Catholic

Greek Catholic Church

History

The Greek Catholic Church is a convenient yet partially inaccurate label for several churches that follow the Byzantine (Constantinopolitan) liturgical tradition but are also in full communion with Rome and therefore technically part of the Roman Catholic Church. They are also called Eastern Rite Catholic Churches. "Rite" signifies the liturgical, theological, spiritual, and legal inheritance. They are, in part, Albanian, Belarusian, Bulgarian, Croatian, Greek Byzantine, Hungarian, Italo-Albanian, Macedonian, Melkite, Russian, Ruthenian, Slovak, and Ukrainian Greek Catholic Churches.

These churches emerged in the sixteenth and eighteenth centuries as a part of the Counter-Reformation to curb the spread of Protestantism into Eastern Europe. They were proscribed during the Socialist period, often forced to merge with Orthodox communities. However, they retained their unique religious identity and are viewed by some as a cultural and ecclesiastical bridge between the East and the West.

Headquarters

Vatican City State
00120, Italy

Leadership

The Greek Catholic Church is under the authority of the pope of the Roman Catholic Church.

Core Beliefs

The Greek Catholic Church follows in the nearly two-millennia-long Byzantine tradition, despite the East/West schism in 1054. It is a trinitarian, creedal group, emphasizing growth without change and apostolic succession.

Bibliography

Mahieu, Stéphanie, and Vlad Naumescy, eds. *Churches In-between: Greek Catholic Churches in Postsocialist Europe.* Piscataway, NJ: Transaction Publishers, 2009.
"Unici.pl." http://www.unici.pl.

John DelHousaye

Roman Catholic Church

History

The Roman Catholic Church officially dates its origin to Jesus Christ's granting of "ecclesiastical primogeniture" to the apostle Peter as the "rock" on which the church is built and therefore possessing the keys of heaven as chief of the apostles (Matt. 16:18–19). The history of Roman Catholicism is traced through the successors of Peter in the bishopric of Rome. Thus, it would be best to understand Catholicism as originating with the structure of papal supremacy, which regards the bishop of Rome as pope (earthly vicar of Christ) and visible head of the church.

Roman Catholicism affirms the concept of a single leader of a city-church based on the following historical emphases: the teaching of Ignatius with regard to the monarchical bishop and the emphasis of Clement of Rome on apostolic succession (resulting in an episcopal ecclesiology ca. 100); Cyprian's concept of the federation of bishops and apostolic succession; the Novatian controversy (250); Augustine's confirmation of Cyprian's federationism and concept of apostolic succession; the Donatist controversy (430); and the accession of Leo I to the episcopal throne (440). After Gregory I ended the federation of bishops, the early seventh century was distinguished by a significant change to singularity of the bishop's office. The Old Catholic Church became the Roman Catholic Church between 313 and 590, with the growth of the dominance of the bishopric of Rome. In an absence of power, which was occasioned when the capital of the

Roman Empire was moved to Constantinople, the bishop of Rome assumed authority. Widespread acceptance of the Petrine theory of apostolic succession and formal recognition of the primary of Peter were also contributing factors. The bishopric of Rome extended influence and prestige by loyal missionaries. Moreover, continued institutionalization of the Romanist faith influenced the dominance of the bishopric of Rome. Once the doctrine of apostolic succession was accepted, one bishop in each church was elevated as a monarchical bishop above his fellow elders. The Roman bishop was recognized as the first among his equals by virtue of his see (the papal court).

In 590, Gregory the Great (540–604) accepted election as pope reluctantly but exercised all the power and prerogative of the later popes. He greatly enhanced the papacy through the creation of an ecclesiastical mosaic: papal episcopacy, apostolic succession, impossibility of salvation outside the Roman Church, veneration of Mary, baptismal regeneration, penance, Gregorian chant, and the doctrine of purgatory. During the latter seventh to eleventh centuries, the Roman Empire declined in power. As a result, the authority of the bishopric of Rome also experienced general decline.

The bishop of Rome and the bishop of Constantinople served respectively as the heads of the Eastern and Western Churches until 1054, with neither bishop asserting absolute authority over the other. The influence of the Roman Catholic Church increased greatly between 1054 and 1305 as a consequence of events such as the Carolingian Reform and the Cluny Reform and the influence of individuals such as Gregory VII (1076), Innocent III (1200), and Boniface VIII (1300).

Innocent III is probably the most important of the popes during this period since he brought the papacy to the zenith of its influence in the spiritual and temporal realms. He made papal claims in the political realm and used the papal weapon of excommunication. Gregory VII should also be distinguished for enlarging the power of the papacy. One of Pope Gregory VII's outstanding contributions prior to becoming pope was his part in the creation of the College of Cardinals at the Lateran Council in 1059. This body assumed the responsibility of nominating the pope, thereby eliminating nonecclesiastical interference. Essentially, the action eliminated lay control of the election of the pope. Pope Gregory

VII's contribution to the history of the papacy can best be described as the exercise of papal sovereignty over the temporal, in addition to the spiritual, which paved the way for the extensive use of power by Innocent III. Gregory was in sympathy with the reforms of the Cluny order, and he opposed clerical marriage, lay investiture, and simony. Boniface VIII was significant for the rise of papal power because of his papal bull *Unum Sanctum* (1302). This document claimed that no salvation was possible outside the Roman Church, the pope had spiritual and temporal authority, and submission to the pope was necessary for salvation.

Although a reform papacy was able to restore episcopal power by the late eleventh century, divisions between the Western Catholic Church and the Eastern (Greek) Orthodox Church culminated in the Great Schism in 1054. When Constantine moved his capital to Constantinople in 330, he laid the foundation for administrative differences that would lead to political separation of the empire. Theodosius I placed the separate areas of the church (West and East) under separate heads (a bishop in the Western capital and a patriarch in the Eastern capital). Intellectual factors also contributed to the schism since the Latin West tended to be more concerned with practical matters of polity and had little difficulty formulating orthodox dogma; by contrast, the Greek East tended to resolve theological disagreements philosophically. Disagreement over practices such as celibacy, language, marriage, and the shaving of beards were also important matters. Theological disagreements included the West being charged with heresy for believing in the procession of the Holy Spirit from the Son and the focus and motif of the celebration of the Easter event (West—resurrection and hope; East—death and sacrifice). The iconoclast controversy within the Eastern Church in the eighth and ninth centuries resulted in an embittered relationship between the East and the West. The pope in the West (and even the emperor Charlemagne) favored the use of visible symbols of divine reality. The church in the West used pictures and statues in worship, whereas the church in the East eventually eliminated statues while keeping icons to be accorded reverence but not worship. Papal interference was also a contributing factor since the East did not think the pope should interfere with the appointment of the patriarch.

The disagreements intensified on July 16, 1054, when the Roman legate Humbert excommunicated the patriarch for his views. Not to be outdone, the patriarch anathematized the pope on the following day. Michael Caerularius, the bishop of Constantinople, assumed power in 1058 when the Eastern Church split from the Western Church. The separation between the Eastern and Western sections distinguishes the Eastern Orthodox (Catholic) Church and the Roman Catholic Church.

Headquarters

The Holy See
00120 Via del Pellegrino
Vatican City, Italy
Telephone: 39-06-698-99-390

United States Conference of Catholic Bishops
3211 Fourth Street NE
Washington, DC 20017
Telephone: 202-541-3000

Leadership

The bishop of Rome as pope is the supreme authority in matters of faith and conduct of the church. Members of the College of Cardinals serve as advisors to the pope in the governance of the church and elect his successor should he die or resign (authority is vested in the college until there is a successor). The three orders of approximately two hundred cardinals are bishop, priest, and deacon. Cardinal bishops serve the seven sees around Rome (Albano, Frascati, Ostia, Palestrina, Porto and Santa Rufina, Sabina and Poggio Mirteto, and Velletri) and Eastern-Rite patriarchs. The cardinal bishop of Ostia is the dean (president) of the college; the subdean (vice president) is the cardinal bishop of Porto. Cardinal priests are primarily archbishops beyond the Roman province (often they are regarded as cardinal archbishops to indicate the two dignities). Cardinal deacons have various functions in the papal government and may become cardinal priests after ten years of service; there are few exceptions when a cardinal priest is not an archbishop or bishop (i.e., "lay cardinals" who have not been granted major orders). As successors of the apostles, the bishops are true guardians of the deposit of faith but inherit the gift only collectively (individual bishops might abandon their calling and embrace heresy). The apostolic delegate consists of archbishops, bishops, cardinals, and priests. Provinces are geographic areas that include many dioceses and are governed by an archbishop (metropolitan) whose own province is designated as the archdiocese. The dioceses are geographic areas that

are governed by bishops. The local congregation is a parish, which is the responsibility of a priest (pastor) who is subject to the bishop. The orders of tonsured clergy consist of minor orders, deacons, subdeacons, and priests.

Core Beliefs

The doctrinal foundation of the Roman Catholic Church is the Old and New Testaments, which are supplemented by tradition that is expressed in written doctrines. The "magisterium" is the authoritative teaching office of the church. The extraordinary magisterium is the special exercise of this teaching office by both the pope and the ecumenical councils of bishops (approved by the pope) or by the pope alone; the purpose is to provide a definitive judgment. A solemn definition by a general council is the exercise of the extraordinary magisterium and is thus an *ex cathedra* definition by the pope (i.e., a definitive decision with regard to a matter in question). By contrast, the ordinary magisterium is the exercise of the teaching office of the church without a solemn definition.

Roman Catholicism affirms four fundamentals of the Christian faith: the Triune God; the deity of Jesus Christ; the virgin birth of Christ; and the bodily resurrection and return of Christ. The Roman Catholic Church teaches that justification establishes cooperation between the grace of God and the freedom of human beings. According to the Council of Trent, anyone who affirms faith alone for justification is anathema (accursed). This doctrine was reaffirmed by Vatican II and also the *Catechism of the Catholic Church*.

Catholicism affirms the Apostles' Creed, the Nicene Creed, and the Athanasian Creed as expressing the core beliefs of the church. The Profession of Faith within the *Catechism of the Catholic Church* is a helpful summary of the Catholic faith. The Catholic Church affirms matters of faith as defined and declared by the sacred canons, the general councils, and particularly the Council of Trent (as a consequence of the ecumenical council's comprehensive decrees and authoritative definitions that clarified every doctrine disputed by the Protestant Reformers). These matters of faith have been delivered, defined, and declared by the general council of the Vatican, especially those concerning the infallible teaching authority and primacy of the Roman pontiff.

Roman Catholic traditions (and year decreed) include regeneration of the soul through infant baptism (431), Mass as a reenactment of Jesus's sacrifice (500), Mass as mandatory attendance (1000), celibacy of the priesthood (1079), praying the rosary (1090), indulgences granted to reduce time in purgatory (1190), transubstantiation and confession of sins to priests (1215), the doctrine of purgatory (1438), tradition and Scripture as equal in authority (1545), the immaculate conception of Mary (1854), papal infallibility (1870), the Virgin Mary as co-redeemer with Jesus (1922), and the Virgin Mary's assumption into heaven (1950).

The core practices expected of Catholics include observing Sunday Mass and holidays of obligation, fasting and abstaining from meat on appointed days, a general confession annually or more often, receiving Communion (the Eucharist) during the Easter season, contributing to the support of the church and clergy, and observing marital regulations. The Second Vatican Council (1962–65), which was called by Pope John XXIII and closed under the pontificate of Pope Paul VI, considered several issues that resulted in extensive change in core practices of the church. The announced purpose of the council was renewal and reunion.

Vatican II permitted the vernacularization of the liturgy and encouraged greater participation of the laity in parish life. The decree on ecumenism allowed Roman Catholics to engage in ecumenical and interfaith dialogue. The Declaration on the Relationship of the Church to Non-Christian Religions of Vatican II concluded that Muslims "worship God" and "highly esteem an upright life." Protestants ("Communities") and Churches ("Orthodox") were considered parts of Christ's mystical body if "Christian" but "separated brethren" from the visible body of Christ on earth. The council concluded, "The Church knows that she is joined in many ways to the baptized who are honored by the name of Christian, but who do not however profess the Catholic faith in its entirety or have not preserved unity or communion under the successor of Peter" (*Vatican Council II*, 1:366). Minor schisms developed among Catholics who were critical of changes made by Vatican II. Traditional Catholics are critical of liberalism and modernism within the church but identify with the ideological spectrum of Vatican II. Nevertheless, there is unity in parish diversity as a consequence of the basic doctrine, liturgy, and organization of the Catholic Church. In the latter 1960s, the Roman Catholic Church expressed significant interest in modern methods of Bible study and interpretation, charismatic theology, and family and parish renewal. The seven sacraments of the church are baptism, confirmation, Communion (the Eucharist), penance, marriage, anointing of the sick, and holy orders. It is believed that each sacrament produces sanctifying grace and a special actual grace (sacramental grace). The veneration of the Virgin Mary and other saints is expressed by approaching them in prayer and with efficacy.

Worship

The influx of "barbarians" into the church meant the liturgy needed to be materialized through the veneration of angels, saints, relics, pictures, and statues to make worship more palpable. As large numbers of pagans converted to Christianity, the church struggled to disciple them. Many of the converts still practiced former customs and lifestyles. Thus, the worship of saints, for example, replaced the barbarian worship of heroes. The liturgy also created a sharp distinction between the clergy and the laity, especially as related to the sacraments of the church. Gregory I was profoundly influenced by the teachings of Augustine as he developed medieval ecclesiology. One example of Augustine's influence is the consideration of marriage as a sacrament. Cyprian stressed the need for penance in sanctification.

As the gap widened between clergy and laity, ordination was considered a sacrament. Approximately AD 400, confirmation and extreme unction were sacramentalized. The doctrine of original sin led to the importance of infant baptism. The Lord's Supper was primary in the thinking of the worshiper and the order of the liturgy. The Catholic Eucharist is currently regarded as "the source and summit of the Christian life," "the efficacious sign," "the heavenly liturgy and [anticipation of] eternal life," and "the sum and summary of our [the Roman Catholic] faith" (*Catholic Catechism*, 368–96).

The growth of liturgy occurred in the midst of a period of intellectual and political decline. Augustine's theology was accommodated into the church during the early Middle Ages by diminishing the characteristics of the doctrines of grace and predestination and by replacing them with spurious doctrines and practices, as evident in the rise of sacramentalism. The sacramentalization of the church led to the dominance of Cassian soteriology. As opposed to the unmerited grace of God, the sacraments were seen as necessary to save the soul of man since they were believed to produce grace. The sacraments were regarded as instrumental causes of God's grace and thus the sacred signs and means of grace for Catholic worshipers.

Divisions and Splits

The Great Schism of 1054 and the Protestant Reformation were the two most significant splits from the Roman Catholic Church. The former resulted in the formal separation of the Roman Catholic Church from the Eastern Orthodox Church (as explained earlier), and the latter resulted in a pivotal period in church history as the gospel of justification by faith alone was promulgated. By the mid-fifteenth century, the lack of success in securing effective reform from within the Roman Catholic Church by mystics, reformers, and councils made the Reformation inevitable. The church was not only struggling with dissent and unrest within but also facing direct and indirect opposition from without. External opposition came from the cultural, political, and religious realms.

Cultural opposition included the Renaissance spirit that undermined the church by stressing that man (in contrast to the glory of God) was the measure of all things. During a period of affluence, leisure, and security, existence in the present was assumed to be of primary importance. The Renaissance resulted in the cultural reorientation primarily of the upper classes, which were deemed more important than the old rural agrarian society of the feudal era.

Political opposition was evident in nationalism, which manifested itself through the emergence of strong nation-states after the period of the Crusades, the opposition of England and France to the papacy during and after the Hundred Years' War, the voting by nations at the Council of Constance, and the Pragmatic Sanction of Bourges. After the fall of Constantinople to the Turks in 1453, the religious influence of that city diminished greatly.

In the religious realm, Russian patriarchs progressively assumed greater control of the church in the East (the last bastion of classical Christian antiquity) as a result of the invasion of Russia by the Mongols, who isolated the church from the leadership of the patriarch of Constantinople. The result was the development of native leadership and a popularization of religion in a time of crisis. When Constantinople succumbed to

the Turks, numerous Greek scholars fled to the West with invaluable manuscripts and knowledge of the language in which the New Testament was written. The metropolitan archbishop was moved to the city of Moscow, which separated the leadership of the Russian church from the influence of Constantinople.

Between 1305 and 1517, the church also experienced abuse of power, agonizing attempts at reform, dangers of Islam, heresy, loss of purpose, paganizing influences, and secularism. The Protestant Reformation became official on October 31, 1517, when Martin Luther tacked his *Ninety-Five Theses* on the church door of Wittenberg, protesting the unbiblical teachings and practices that were prevalent in his day and calling an obstinate Roman Catholic Church back to the essential truth of the gospel that sinners are justified by grace through faith alone, on the Word alone, because of Christ alone, and this to the glory of God alone. In response to the Protestant Reformation, there have been several attempts at reform within the Roman Catholic Church, and new standards for the Catholic Church were accomplished by the Council of Trent and by the Jesuits.

Statistics

Membership exceeds 69 million people in more than 19,000 parishes in 195 archdioceses or dioceses, with approximately 45,000 priests, 5,250 brothers, and nearly 68,000 sisters.

Nations with the largest population of Roman Catholics (and where Roman Catholics make up at least 90 percent of the population) include Italy, Mexico, Poland, Spain, Colombia, and Argentina.

Nations with the highest percentage (at least 95 percent) of Roman Catholics include Vatican City, San Marino, Saint Pierre and Miquelon, Wallis and Futuna Islands, Italy, Cape Verde, Poland, Mexico, Republic of Ireland, and Guadeloupe.

States with the largest population of Roman Catholics include Connecticut, Illinois, Louisiana, Maine, New Jersey, New Mexico, New York, Pennsylvania, Rhode Island, and Wisconsin.

Massachusetts has the highest percentage (approximately 50 percent) of Roman Catholics. United States counties with the highest proportion (at least 90 percent) of Roman Catholics include Kenedy (Texas), Mora (New Mexico), Reeves (Texas), and Guadalupe (New Mexico).

Missionary and Evangelistic Work

Independent missions have been operated by more than five hundred religious orders in the United States. Pope Benedict XVI's message for the celebration of the XLIV World Day of Peace on January 1, 2011, urged Roman Catholics to make converts, as opposed to restricting efforts to humanitarian good works, but rejected conversion by force. The Real Presence of Christ in the Eucharist is the focus of the new evangelization of the Roman Catholic Church, which was the challenge of Pope Benedict XVI at the International Eucharistic Congress in Rome on June 18–25, 2000.

Academic Institutions

The number of Catholic colleges and universities exceeds two hundred with approximately eight hundred thousand students. Vatican II was instrumental in providing a vision for all Catholic education and higher education specifically. The most well-known Catholic colleges and universities include Boston College (Chestnut Hill, MA), College of the Holy Cross (Worchester, MA), Georgetown University (Washington, DC), Santa Clara University (Santa Clara, CA), St. John's University (Collegeville, MN), and University of Notre Dame (Notre Dame, IN). The only institution sponsored and partially funded directly by the church is the Catholic University of America in Washington, DC.

Parachurch Organizations

The Catholic Church operates more than 600 hospitals. Catholic health care systems and hospitals have been founded in every American state. The Catholic Charity Network provides assistance to more than 1,600 local agencies and institutions worldwide. Disaster relief in the United States is mobilized by Catholic Charities. Humanitarian aid is provided overseas through Catholic Relief Services. Founded in 1882, the Knights of Columbus is a men's fraternal benefit society. More than 2.5 million students are enrolled in approximately 6,500 elementary schools and 1,350 secondary schools.

Electronic Media

Prominent radio programs are broadcast by Ave Maria Radio, Catholic Answers, Catholic Radio (Toronto), Holy Spirit Radio (WISP), Vatican Radio, and EWTN Radio. The primary broadcasters of Catholic television are the Eternal World Television Network (EWTN) and the Vatican Television Center (CTV).

Publications

Nearly all dioceses publish a weekly newspaper that provides general parish information or addresses special ministries within the parish, such as liturgical or parish education. Some of the primary periodicals include *Catholic Digest, Catholic World Report, Ligourian, National Catholic Register, Our Sunday Visitor, St. Anthony Messenger, This Rock,* and the *Wanderer.*

The Catholic Periodical and Literature Index Online is the consequence of a partnership between the American Theological Library Association (ATLA) and the Catholic Library Association. Some of the primary Catholic publishers include Ascension Press, Catholic Answers, Franciscan University Press, Ignatius Press, Liturgical Press, Liturgy Training Publications, Paulist Press, Sophia Institute Press, and University of Notre Dame Press.

Websites

http://www.vatican.va/
http://www.usccb.org/

Bibliography

Abbott, Walter M., ed. *The Documents of Vatican II.* New York: Guild Press, 1966.

Akin, Jimmy. *The Fathers Know Best: Your Essential Guide to the Teachings of the Early Church.* San Diego: Catholic Answers, 2010.

Broderick, Robert C., ed. *The Catholic Encyclopedia.* Nashville: Nelson, 1987.

Catechism of the Catholic Church. New York: Doubleday, 1994.

Congregation for Institutes of Consecrated Life and Societies of Apostolic Life. *Starting Afresh from Christ: A Renewed Commitment to Consecrated Life in the Third Millennium.* Vatican City, Italy: Libreria editrice Vaticana, 2002.

Flannery, Austin, gen. ed. *Vatican Council II: The Conciliar and Post Conciliar Documents.* Rev. ed. Northport, NY: Costello Publishing, 1975.

Fremantle, Anne. *The Papal Encyclicals in Their Historical Context: The Teachings of the Popes.* New York: New American Library, 1956.

Hardon, John. *The Catholic Catechism: The Contemporary Catechism of the Teachings of the Catholic Church.* Garden City, NY: Doubleday, 1975.

Hasler, August Bernard. *How the Pope Became Infallible: Pius IX and the Politics of Persuasion.* Garden City, NY: Doubleday, 1981.

Keating, Karl. *Catholicism and Fundamentalism: The Attack on "Romanism" by "Bible Christians."* San Francisco: Ignatius Press, 1988.

McLoughlin, Emmett. *Crime and Immorality in the Catholic Church.* New York: Lyle Stuart, 1964.

Mullett, Michael A. *The Catholic Reformation.* New York: Routledge, 1999.

O'Brien, John A. *The Faith of Millions.* Huntington, IN: Our Sunday Visitor, 1974.

Ott, Ludwig. *Fundamentals of Catholic Dogma*. Rockford, IL: Tan Books, 1974.

Plummer, Robert L., gen. ed. *Journeys of Faith*. Grand Rapids: Zondervan, 2012.

Puglisi, James F., ed. *Petrine Ministry and the Unity of the Church*. Collegeville, MN: Liturgical Press, 1999.

Schroeder, H. J., trans. *The Canons and Decrees of the Council of Trent*. Rockford, IL: Tan Books, 1978.

Schrotenboer, Paul G., ed. *Roman Catholicism: A Contemporary Evangelical Perspective*. Grand Rapids: Baker, 1988.

Stravinskas, Peter M. J. *The Catholic Response*. Huntington, IN: Our Sunday Visitor, 1985.

Ron J. Bigalke

Churches of Christ/ Christian Churches

Christian Church (Disciples of Christ)

History

The Christian Church (Disciples of Christ) is one of the three primary bodies that formed as a result of the Stone-Campbell movement (or Restoration movement). The Disciples is the only one of the three religious bodies that willingly accepts classification as a denomination. The congregations are known as Christian Churches (and sometimes derogatorily as "Campbellites"), but the members claim the New Testament name of Christians or Disciples.

The Disciples emerged from the historic 1832 union between the followers of Barton W. Stone (1772–1844) and those of Alexander (1788–1866) and Thomas Campbell (1763–1854). However, a conflict between the Churches of Christ (strict restorationists) and the Disciples of Christ (progressive restorationists) developed in the latter nineteenth century. The Churches of Christ separated from the Disciples in protest against missionary societies, which were thought to weaken local church autonomy, and the use of instrumental music in worship services. The progressives allowed missionary societies and instrumental music, and in 1968, they reorganized as the Disciples of Christ.

The original intent of the movement was to restore a primitive Christianity and to unite Christian churches and denominations, which resulted in tremendous development and growth subsequent to the Civil War.

Headquarters

130 East Washington Street
Indianapolis, IN 46204
Telephone: 317-635-3100

Leadership

The government of the Disciples was originally congregational in form, but the church now functions under a representative government. Church officers include pastors, elders, and deacons. Elders primarily address spiritual matters in the congregations, and deacons focus on temporal matters such as financial affairs and benevolence.

Core Beliefs

The Bible is the answer to all matters of faith and practice, but many doctrines are defined in the context of modern biblical criticism. Although Disciples do not teach the doctrine of original sin, they do teach the necessity of redemption by the sacrifice of Christ. The red chalice with the cross of St. Andrew is the logo of the Disciples, representing the centrality of the Lord's Supper in the life of the church.

Congregations possess local autonomy. Church membership is generally based on the "Good Confession" of Matthew 16:16 and baptism by immersion for the remission of sins. Congregations do not practice infant baptism, although there is debate as to the validity of the custom. The Lord's Supper is celebrated weekly as a memorial feast. The majority of congregations practice open membership, which means they receive—as full members—those who transfer membership from another denomination, even if those individuals were not baptized by immersion. Some congregations insist that any who seek full membership must have received baptism by immersion. The ecumenical nature of the denomination is evident in its founding of the Federal Council of Churches and the World Council of Churches as well as its membership in Churches Uniting in Christ.

Statistics

Membership: 700,000 (representing a steady decline over the past twenty-five years)

Congregations: 3,800

Largest Churches

The largest churches are located in the Southwest and the West. Mississippi Boulevard Christian Church (Memphis, TN) is the largest of the Disciples of Christ congregations.

Academic Institutions

Barton College (Wilson, NC)
Bethany College (Bethany, WV)
Brite Divinity School (Fort Worth, TX)
Chapman University (Orange, CA)
Christian Theological Seminary (Indianapolis, IN)
Culver-Stockton College (Canton, MO)
Disciples Divinity House at Vanderbilt University Divinity School (Nashville, TN)
Disciples Divinity House of the University of Chicago (Chicago, IL)
Disciples Seminary Foundation (Claremont, CA)
Drake University (Des Moines, IA)
Drury University (Springfield, MO)
Eureka College (Eureka, IL)
Hiram College (Hiram, OH)
Lexington Theological Seminary (Lexington, KY)
Lynchburg College (Lynchburg, VA)
Midway College (Midway, KY)
Northwest Christian University (Eugene, OR)
Phillips Theological Seminary (Tulsa, OK)
Texas Christian University (Fort Worth, TX)
Tougaloo College (Tougaloo, MS)
Transylvania University (Lexington, KY)
William Woods University (Fulton, MO)

Parachurch Organizations

The Regional Ministries of the Christian Church provides resources for congregational growth and leadership development. Upon recommendation of the general board, the general assembly establishes or recognizes the General Ministries of the Christian Church. The services addressed by the General Ministries include central administrative functions, general work, and specialized research and services to fulfill congregational responsibilities. Controversy regarding whether missionary efforts should be cooperative or independent has further divided the Restoration movement.

Electronic Media

Disciples have not invested significantly in evangelistic and missionary programming in recent years. The Disciples Amateur Radio Fellowship is located in Indianapolis, Indiana, and sponsored by the Division of Overseas Ministries.

Publications

The Office of Communications is located in Indianapolis, Indiana, and the Christian Board of Publications is located in St. Louis, Missouri.

Website

http://www.disciples.org/

Bibliography

Baker, William R., ed. *Evangelicalism and the Stone-Campbell Movement*. Downers Grove, IL: InterVarsity, 2002.

Foster, Douglas A., Paul M. Blowers, Anthony L. Dunnavant, and D. Newell Williams, eds. *The Encyclopedia of the Stone-Campbell Movement*. Grand Rapids: Eerdmans, 2004.

Garrett, Leroy. *The Stone-Campbell Movement: An Anecdotal History of Three Churches*. Rev. ed. Joplin, MO: College Press, 1994.

Garrison, W. E., and A. T. DeGroot. *The Disciples of Christ: A History*. St. Louis: Bethany Press, 1948.

Harrell, David Edwin, Jr. *A Social History of the Disciples of Christ*. 2 vols. Nashville: Disciples of Christ Historical Society, 1966, 1973. Reprint, Tuscaloosa: University of Alabama Press, 2003.

Tucker, William E., and Lester G. McAllister. *Journey in Faith: A History of the Christian Church (Disciples of Christ)*. St. Louis: Bethany Press, 1975.

Ron J. Bigalke

Christian Union

History

The Christian Union is an evangelical denomination founded in 1864 in Columbus, Ohio, by Rev. James Given, who had been ejected from the Methodist Church for his failure to support military action against slavery. He objected to all political stands taken by various churches during the Civil War. In 1909, some its adherents broke away to form the Churches of Christ in Christian Union.

Headquarters

PO Box 361
Greenfield, Ohio 45123-0361
Telephone: 937-981-2760
Email: joecuw@gmail.com

Leadership

President: Rev. Marion Hunerdosse

Core Beliefs

At the time of its founding, the Christian Union stated its adherence to certain beliefs, including the unity of the church with Christ as its only head; the Bible as the source of all teachings; the fellowship of all believers bearing good fruit, regardless of their views on nonessential matters; the self-governance of the local church; and the shunning of political partisanship in the church. Over time, additional conservative, fundamental principles were added. These include the Father, Son, and Holy Spirit as the three persons of the Godhead; the deity of Christ and his virgin birth, atoning death, bodily resurrection, and return in glory; the sinfulness of all men; and salvation by grace based on repentance and faith in Christ and leading to a regenerated life. Also, the Holy Spirit dwells in believers, gives them guidance, and equips them for service with spiritual gifts; all believers receive the baptism of the Holy Spirit at the time of salvation and should continuously be filled with the Spirit; believers are not free of the capacity to sin until death; and ordinances are symbolic of salvation and include water baptism, preferably by immersion, and the Lord's Supper, which is available to true believers of all denominations.

Divorce is permitted only for adultery, and only the innocent are allowed to remarry. Believers are expected to tithe to finance the work of the church.

George Thomas Kurian

Churches of Christ

History

The Churches of Christ developed during the religious fervor of the early nineteenth century and is the largest religious body that grew out of the Restoration movement led by Alexander Campbell and Barton W. Stone. It emphasized a biblical primitivism and a desire for Christian unity that resonated with many during the antebellum period. The two other branches of the Restoration movement, the Disciples of Christ and the Christian Churches, were united by the end of the nineteenth century. However, class, sectional, theological, and ecclesiological issues created fissures in the movement, leading David Lipscomb, a leader of the movement, to openly acknowledge a split in the 1906 census. At issue were controversies over a commitment to biblical literalism, the formation of missionary societies, the use of instrumental music in worship services, and political activism. The conservative side of the debate began to use churches (with a small c) of Christ to demonstrate their claim that they were not a new denomination but rather a first-century church.

Headquarters

Although congregations are essentially autonomous, the magazine *Gospel Advocate* does serve as a central clearinghouse for information for many churches.

1006 Elm Hill Pike
Nashville, TN 37102
Telephone: 800-251-8446

Core Beliefs

The Churches of Christ is a trinitarian group that believes in salvation through the sacrificial death of Christ available to all who come to him through repentance and faith expressed through confession of faith and baptism by immersion.

The Churches of Christ also believes in the inerrancy and sufficiency of Scripture—the Bible is the "beginning place," and members recognize no other written creed or confession of faith; the incarnation, virgin birth, and bodily resurrection of Christ; the universality of sin; the church as the body and bride of Christ; premillennial and dispensationalist eschatology; strict adherence to the New Testament model of worship and church organization; observance of baptism by immersion, tithing, and weekly observance of the Lord's Supper; and rejection of any role for women in public worship (women are not allowed to teach, preach, lead congregational singing, or even participate in the distribution of Communion elements in many traditional congregations, although this is changing among some churches).

Worship

Worship services are often traditional, though some congregations favor more contemporary services. Singing is predominantly a cappella.

Divisions and Splits

There was a strong conservative wing whose disciplining methods were sometimes regarded as cultish. Part of the Crossroads movement or the Boston movement, these conservative congregations grew by emphasizing total commitment. Many among the Churches of Christ, however, became concerned that the discipling tactics in the movement were too stringent. Eventually, some of these churches left to become International Churches of Christ.

Controversies

The history of the Churches of Christ has included several controversies, including the

71

premillennial or dispensationalist view of eschatology, whether baptism is essential for salvation, the use of instrumental music in worship, whether membership in the Churches of Christ is essential for going to heaven, biblical literalism, whether only one cup should be used in Communion, and whether Sunday schools are unbiblical.

Statistics

Because each congregation within the denomination is autonomous, no central records are kept of congregational size or financial status. Unofficial data indicate that there are 2 million members of the Churches of Christ in 13,500 churches in the United States. The group has remained stronger and larger in the South.

Largest Churches

The largest churches are found in Tennessee and Texas. The largest congregation is Richland Hills Church in Richland, Texas.

Growth

The Churches of Christ experienced strong growth in the immediate aftermath of World War II. A strong evangelistic campaign at that time identified the Churches of Christ as "Neither Protestant, Catholic, nor Jew" but as a nondenominational first-century church restored in the contemporary age. Evangelistic campaigns were led by "cottage meetings" that met in houses and represented the Churches of Christ as the only true church.

Trends

In the early twenty-first century, some churches have attempted to erase the perception that Churches of Christ are exclusivist and combative. Some have identified the congregation as the community church of Christ or removed "of Christ" from the name altogether. Some churches still maintain the doctrinal positions traditionally associated with the Churches of Christ, whereas others have abandoned them. The use of instrumental music, historically opposed by the church, has become part of the worship service in some churches. Some congregations permit women to assume minor teaching or leadership roles.

Missionary and Evangelistic Work

The Churches of Christ does extensive missionary work in Africa and India and more recently in Russia. African membership is estimated at four hundred thousand, but hard numbers are difficult to come by. Eastern European

Missions provides Bibles and biblical literature to Russian public schools.

Ecumenism

Ecumenism is limited to the progressive wing of the Churches of Christ. Some overtures have been made to Baptists, and reunification is discussed occasionally with the Disciples of Christ and the Christian Churches.

Academic Institutions

The Churches of Christ runs twenty-one colleges, including one in Japan and several in Europe, and seventy secondary and elementary schools. Among them are:

Abilene Christian University (Abilene, TX)
Freed-Hardeman University (Henderson, TN)
Harding University (Searcy, AR)
Lipscomb University (Nashville, TN)
Ohio Valley University (Parkersburg, WV)
Oklahoma Christian University (Edmond, OK)
Pepperdine University (Malibu, CA)
Southwestern Christian College (Terrell, TX)

Because the word "theology" does not occur in the Bible, theological departments are called Bible (or biblical studies) departments. In addition, there are several preaching schools focused on training ministers for service in local churches. Most of the preaching schools are conservative and traditional in their doctrinal stance.

Parachurch Organizations

Churches of Christ Disaster Relief mobilizes supplies and assistance in the wake of natural disasters. The Churches of Christ runs eighty-three childcare facilities and forty-six senior citizens' facilities.

Electronic Media

The Churches of Christ sponsors radio and television programs, such as the *Herald of Truth* (the oldest such program, sponsored by the Highland Church of Christ in Abilene), *Truth for the World*, and *In Search of the Lord's Way*. The Gospel Broadcasting Network is a twenty-four-hour satellite network. The "Amazing Grace Bible Class" is conducted by Steve Flatt.

Publications

The journal with the widest circulation is the *Christian Chronicle*, which provides news on all church-related activities. The *Gospel Advocate* is the oldest publication with a biblical focus.

Restoration Quarterly and the *Stone-Campbell Journal* have a more academic slant. The latter is a joint venture of scholars from the three branches of the Stone-Campbell movement: the Churches of Christ, the Christian Church (Disciples of Christ), and the Christian Churches/Churches of Christ.

Other journals published by the Churches of Christ are *Action, Christian Woman, Christian Bible Teacher, Firm Foundation, Guardian of Truth, 21st Century Christian, Rocky Mountain Christian, Spiritual Sword,* and *Word and Work.*

Website

http://www.church-of-christ.org/

Bibliography

"Churches of Christ." http://www.church-of-christ.org. "Who Are the Churches of Christ?"

Foster, Douglas A., Paul M. Blowers, Anthony L. Dunnavant, and D. Newell Williams. *The Encyclopedia of the Stone-Campbell Movement.* Grand Rapids: Eerdmans, 2004.

Harrell, David Edwin, Jr. *A Social History of the Disciples of Christ.* 2 vols. Nashville: Disciples of Christ Historical Society, 1966, 1973. Reprint, Tuscaloosa: University of Alabama Press, 2003.

Hughes, Richard T. *Reviving the Ancient Faith: The Story of the Churches of Christ in America.* Grand Rapids: Eerdmans, 1996.

West, Earl. *The Search for the Ancient Order.* 4 vols. Germantown, TN: Religious Book Service, 1950–94.

Todd M. Brenneman

Churches of Christ in Christian Union

History

The Churches of Christ in Christian Union (CCCU) was formed in 1909 by ministers and laypeople whose embrace of teachings of the Holiness movement was rejected by the Ohio-based Christian Union. James McKibban was the denomination's first leader. The group advocated female suffrage and abstinence from alcohol and founded Circleville Bible College, today known as Ohio Christian University, in 1948.

Headquarters

Churches of Christ in Christian Union
Global Ministry Center
1553 Lancaster Pike
Circleville, OH 43113
Telephone: 740-474-8856

Core Beliefs

Evangelical in nature, the CCCU teaches biblical inerrancy, the deity of Christ, and ordinances of the Lord's Supper and water baptism (of any mode). A statement of beliefs appears on the denomination website.

Website

http://www.cccuhq.org/

Bibliography

Brown, Kenneth, and P. Lewis Brevard, *A Goodly Heritage: History of the Churches of Christ in Christian Union.* Circleville, OH: Circle Press, 1980.

"The Churches of Christ in Christian Union." http://www.cccuhq.org. "Contact" and "What We Teach."

Melton, J. Gordon. *Encyclopedia of American Religions.* 6th ed. Detroit: Gale, 1999.

George Thomas Kurian

Congregational

Conservative Congregational Christian Conference

History

The Conservative Congregational Christian Conference (CCCC) originated with a 1935 plea by Pastor H. B. Sandine for a reinstatement of Congregationalism's founding beliefs. In 1939, he started a mimeographed publication called *Congregational Beacon*, which evolved into *Congregational Christian* and later *Foresee*; with the vocal support of these publications, a Conservative Congregational Christian Fellowship was organized in 1945 in Chicago. Comprised of churches and ministers who disagreed with liberal theological positions held by other Congregationalists, the fellowship became the Conservative Congregational Christian Conference in 1948 and refused to join Congregational Christian churches merging with the Evangelical and Reformed Church to form the United Church of Christ.

Headquarters

8941 Highway 5
Lake Elmo, MN 55042-8900
Telephone: 651-739-1474
Email: dmjohnson@ccccusa.com

Leadership

Executive director: Rev. Steve Gammon

Core Beliefs

The statement of faith expresses belief in biblical inerrancy, the Trinity, the deity of Christ and his bodily resurrection, man's need for salvation and regeneration, damnation of the lost, and the unity of believers. The CCCC opposes abortion, homosexuality, and nonmarital sexual activities and is ardently evangelical.

While its statement of faith embodies tenets that are universal among conservative evangelicals, the CCCC accommodates varying opinions on subjects not addressed in the statement. It sees this diversity as consistent with the scriptural principle of Christ's headship of the church and his guidance of the believer's conscience through Scripture, principles that Congregational forefathers promoted. Congregational polity gives each church autonomy and the opportunity to act on its own convictions in many areas, including the ordination of women, predestination, and Reformed perspectives.

Finances

The CCCC has been a member of the Evangelical Council for Financial Accountability since 1990. Its revenue for 2008 was more than $800,000.

Statistics

In 1990, the CCCC had 177 congregations and 35,600 members. In 2000, it had 250 congregations and 50,940 members.

Missionary and Evangelistic Work

The CCCC started a new initiative in 2007 to dedicate major resources to its priorities of Conference Care, Church Redevelopment, and Church Multiplication. Conference Care provides mentoring for individual members and support of their needs. It includes special programs dealing with ministry students, crisis intervention, review of pastoral credentials, and intracongregational conflict. Church Redevelopment seeks to reintroduce many American churches to the New Testament vision of spiritual training that changes lives and is not limited to Sunday as well as to evangelism that is not prepackaged but rather an outgrowth of the enthusiasm of believers. A related goal is to revitalize church attendance. The objective of Church Multiplication is to create new congregations that are in turn able to develop new ones themselves, especially by training pastors in church planting.

The CCCC actively attempts to recruit seminarians to work in urban and minority communities, to build new churches in urban areas, to invite unaffiliated urban churches to join the conference, and to invite those churches to avail themselves of CCCC services. Urban multicultural ministry workshops are scheduled for the CCCC annual meetings.

The conference honors the biblical command to equip the saints for the work of the church through its Lay Ministries Committee. The committee encourages and facilitates lay participation in ministry, thereby contributing to the maturity of the church as defined in the New Testament.

The CCCC Missions Committee fosters interest in missionary activity on the part of local churches. Congregational missionaries have had a commitment to the Federated States of Micronesia since the 1850s, when they were first sent there by the American Board of Foreign Missions. The CCCC is working with the Morning Star Institute to provide US-trained pastors to teach Bible classes and develop leaders in Micronesian churches.

Affiliations

The CCCC belongs to the National Association of Evangelicals (NAE), including its World Relief Organization. Members of the NAE participate in the World Evangelical Alliance. The CCCC also belongs to the Mission America Coalition, which works for global evangelization, and the National Religious Pro-Life Council. It has partnerships with Interim Ministry Network, Interim Pastor Ministries, and Titus Ministries, which all promote congregational health. Itself conceived as an effort at congregational renewal, the CCCC offers its support of renewal movements in related traditions, including Biblical Witness Fellowship in the United Church of Christ, Disciple Heritage Fellowship in the Disciples of Christ Churches, and Evangelical Association of Reformed and Congregational Churches, which promotes Reformed teaching within Congregationalism.

The conference helps to put churches in touch with evangelical pastors via the Pastor Referral Network.

Academic Institutions

The CCCC does not operate a seminary but rather has formed partnerships with institutions that maintain a CCCC presence on their campuses and offer its Congregational Standards course. These include Gordon-Conwell Theological Seminary, with full participation at its South Hamilton, Massachusetts, location; Westminster Theological Seminary in Philadelphia, which also offers online programs from the Reformed perspective; and Trinity Evangelical Divinity School in Deerfield, Illinois.

The CCCC's IMPACT Distance Education Program provides theological education without offering degrees.

Publications

Foresee is a monthly periodical that keeps members informed of ministry news. *PrayerPoints* is an electronic prayer bulletin. The CCCC has partnered with the publications department of the Evangelical Free Church in America, Next-Step Resources.

Website

http://www.ccccusa.com/

George Thomas Kurian

Evangelical Association of Reformed and Congregational Christian Churches

History

The Evangelical Association of Reformed and Congregational Christian Churches came to formation in 1998 when a group of pastors met in New Braunfels, Texas, to discuss their dissatisfaction with the United Church of Christ (UCC). The association, or fellowship, is comprised mostly of former UCC churches, pastors, and laypersons who desired to form not a new denomination but a fellowship of evangelical-minded Christians who could support and encourage one another. This desire seems to be the main purpose of the association. Two additional goals are worth noting: guiding churches with clergy life insurance and retirement planning, and supporting churches in finding clergy.

Headquarters

The Evangelical Association of Reformed and Congregational Christian Churches has no headquarters but offers the following contact address:

9051 Watson Road #241
St. Louis, MO 63126

Core Beliefs

The Evangelical Association of Reformed and Congregational Christian Churches adheres to no traditional creed or confessional statement, but members do believe in a few core evangelical doctrines. Jesus Christ is the only head of the church both universal and local. The association delineates between the universal, historical, and global church and the local church. The local church is the body of Christ and is believed to be autonomous as it is led by the Holy Spirit through the Holy Scriptures. The local church is not governed by or accountable to any higher governing body other than Jesus Christ.

Under their statement of faith, they affirm the trinitarian name of God (Father, Son, and Holy Spirit). Furthermore, they affirm that God reveals himself fully and decisively in Scripture, but there is no mention of how (or to whom) God has revealed himself to humanity. Rejecting notions of universal salvation, the association adheres to *sola Christus*, salvation though Jesus Christ alone.

Also in its statement of faith, the Evangelical Association of Reformed and Congregational Christian Churches lists two social ethical concerns: the belief that humans are created in the image of God, which causes members to affirm the sanctity of every stage of human life; and with regard to human sexuality, advocacy of chastity for those living outside the bounds of marriage and fidelity for those living within the bounds of marriage. However, the statement of faith contains no definition of marriage.

In terms of missions, the association believes the purpose of the church (universal) is to promulgate the gospel—the atoning death and resurrection of Jesus Christ—to every person and to bring them into a life of faith in and submission to the lordship of Jesus Christ, which includes individual discipleship.

Website

http://www.evangelicalassociation.org/

Robert Leach

National Association of Congregational Christian Churches

History

The National Association of Congregational Christian Churches (NACCC) was founded in 1955 by some two hundred members of the Congregational Christian Churches who opposed the entry of that church into the United Church of Christ. It is a voluntary association united by its dedication to the Congregational tradition, with the objective of providing service to member churches and opportunities for fellowship among congregations. Since its founding, the NACCC

has doubled in size and welcomes new congregations every year.

Historically, Congregational churches have been eager to join forces with other bodies. They entered into a Plan of Union with Presbyterians to conduct combined missionary efforts on the western frontier, until it became evident that Presbyterian churches benefited disproportionately. The National Council of Congregational Churches was formed in the early 1900s and merged with the General Convention of the Christian Church in 1931 to create the General Council of Congregational Christian Churches. Congregationalists and Christians had similar beliefs, with the latter group stressing the use of the name Christian. Years later, the United Church of Christ was born when the General Council of Congregational Christian Churches united with the ethnically German Evangelical and Reformed Church, which accepted the principal Congregational beliefs except for local autonomy. It was this issue of congregational independence that prompted the formation of the National Association of Congregational Christian Churches.

The NACCC assists in minister education and placement, promotes mission work, and works to build new churches. It offers more than eighty services to member congregations, including help with many practical matters, such as church signs, background checks, web hosting, and clergy benefits, as well as consulting about various aspects of church work. It also enters into relationships with independent groups.

Headquarters

PO Box 288
8473 South Howell Avenue
Oak Creek, WI 53154
Telephone: 800-262-1620

Core Beliefs

As part of their dedication to church freedom and rejection of legalism, Congregationalists do not endorse a specific creed but instead insist on the direct leading of the Holy Spirit, prayer, Bible study, and love for other believers. Nonetheless, the early Congregationalists adhered to Calvinist views of covenantal theology; when those beliefs fell out of favor, their popularity was renewed for a time by Jonathan Edwards and the Great Awakening. Eventually, liberal doctrines such as Unitarianism began to exert influence over the Congregationalists and their interpretation of

Scripture, which became less literal. Liturgy in worship became more acceptable as well.

Statistics

Year	Clergy	Churches	Membership
1962		230	100,000
2002	650	432	65,392

Missionary and Evangelistic Work

Congregationalists have an illustrious history of mission work. Among their earliest successes was the work of John Elliot, a church teacher from Roxbury, Massachusetts, who learned Indian languages and started fourteen praying Indian communities. The 1806 Haystack Meeting, in which seminarians hid from a thunderstorm in a haystack and discussed and pledged support for foreign missions, led to the 1810 establishment of the American Board of Commissioners for Foreign Missions. This body became the Missionary Society in 1954 and seven years later a division of the NACCC. The Missionary Society's objectives reflect Congregational beliefs and address physical as well as spiritual needs. Overseas, the society utilizes the talents of indigenous missionaries. It is currently providing support to missionaries in ten countries as well as to projects in the United States, including some intercultural ones.

Social activism has historically been a part of the Congregationalist mission. Congregationalists were instrumental in the abolition of slavery and in women's rights, and Washington Gladden's promotion of the Social Gospel movement resulted in Christian support for urban workers.

Affiliations

The NACCC is affiliated with certain recognized ministries to which it has a historical bond or to which its member churches offer support. These include the American Bible Society, Habitat for Humanity International, Heifer International, and the Congregational Library.

Academic Institutions

Congregationalists have a long-standing tradition of respect for education, especially ministerial education, as evidenced by their founding of many of America's first colleges and universities, among them Harvard, Yale, Dartmouth, Williams, Bowdoin, Middlebury, and Amherst. At the same time, they have never formally sponsored any of the institutions they founded. Since there are no officially Congregational colleges or seminaries, ministry students are able to enroll at various institutions sponsored by other denominations in addition to availing themselves of programs offered by the NACCC's Congregational Foundation for Theological Studies, founded in 1961. The foundation, along with its sister Lay Ministry Training Program, is operated by the NACCC's Center for Congregational Leadership, which trains church leaders and is located at Olivet College in Olivet, Michigan. The college was founded in 1844 by Congregationalists and maintains an affiliation with the NACCC as well as with the United Church of Christ. Olivet has a history of embracing diversity, civic-mindedness, and real-world educational experiences. Another popular college choice among Congregationalist students is Piedmont College in Demorest, Georgia, which stresses human conduct and individual responsibility as part of the Judeo-Christian tradition.

Parachurch Organizations

The Commission on Youth Ministries promotes the spiritual and character development of youth through fellowship, public service, and conferences and is run by the National Association of Pilgrim Fellowship (for high school students) and the Heritage of Pilgrim Endeavor (for young adults). The World Christian Relations Commission promotes interfaith and ecumenical objectives. The Institute for Congregational Studies is an NACCC think tank. The Washington Gladden Society raises awareness of ethical issues among member congregations.

Publications

Congregational Communicator newsletter

The Congregationalist, providing inspirational articles since 1818

NACCC News, a monthly publication for member churches

News and Needs, *describing projects of the Missionary Society*

Website

http://www.naccc.org/

George Thomas Kurian

Reformed Congregational Fellowship

History

Begun in the mid-1990s, the Reformed Congregational Fellowship is not a formal denomination. It is a fellowship of individuals and congregationally governed churches of various denominations who affirm a high view of Scripture as well as the Savoy Declaration in matters of doctrine; the Cambridge Platform in matters of ecclesiology; and biblical, theological preaching as a matter of revitalized worship and doctrinal teaching.

Core Beliefs

Teaching at recent conferences has focused on articles from the Savoy Declaration. Defining documents include the Cambridge Platform (1648), the Savoy Declaration (1658), and the congregational revision of the Westminster Confession. Members also acknowledge the 1689 Baptist Confession of Faith, which was influenced by the Savoy Declaration.

Website

http://www.reformedcongregational.org/

Bibliography

"Reformed Congregational Fellowship." http://www.reformedcongregational.org. "Conferences."

Warren C. Robertson

Eastern Orthodox

American Carpatho-Russian Orthodox Diocese

History

The American Carpatho-Russian Orthodox Diocese was founded in 1938 by thirty-seven formerly Roman Catholic parishes that returned to the Eastern Orthodox faith. These parishes consisted largely of immigrants from the Carpatho-Russian regions of present-day Slovakia, Poland, and Western Ukraine who since 1935 had been objecting to Roman Catholic efforts at latinization. Their discontent led to a call for a congress of Carpatho-Russian churches to decide their status, and a council (sobor) was held in Pittsburgh in 1937 to plan the formation of the new diocese with Father Orestes P. Chornock as administrator. The council rejected the three-hundred-year union with Catholicism as superficial, reinstated the Orthodox faith among the Carpatho-Russians, and petitioned the ecumenical patriarch of Constantinople to rejoin his jurisdiction. (Their ancestors were first converted to Christianity by Sts. Cyril and Methodius from Constantinople.) In 1938, His All-Holiness, the late Benjamin I, ecumenical patriarch of Constantinople, accepted the request and canonically created the American Carpatho-Russian Orthodox Diocese as a new self-governing diocese, which was canonized in the name of the Holy Orthodox Church of Christ. Father Chornock was consecrated as bishop, and the diocese was incorporated in Pennsylvania in 1950 with the seat of the diocese, Christ the Saviour Cathedral, located in Johnstown.

The use of English liturgy books was phased in beginning in 1966, and today the diocese includes converts from various ethnic backgrounds. Since 1985, attempts have been made to foster greater closeness with the Carpatho-Russian Orthodox in Europe. In 2007, the sixteen hundredth anniversary of the repose of St. John Chrysostom was jointly honored by the diocese and the ecumenical patriarch of Constantinople.

Headquarters

312 Garfield Street
Johnstown, PA 15906
Telephone: 814-539-9143

Leadership

Metropolitan: His Eminence, Metropolitan Nicholas

Website

http://www.acrod.org/

George Thomas Kurian

Antiochian Orthodox Christian Archdiocese of North America

History

The Antiochian Orthodox Christian Archdiocese of North America is the offshoot of the Syrian Orthodox Church, which was located in Antioch, Syria, from the first century. When Syrian Orthodox Christian immigrants came to the United States to flee Turkish and Druze persecutions in the late nineteenth century, the Syro-Arabian Mission of the Russian Orthodox Church was set up in 1895 as a place for them to worship, and the Syrian Orthodox Benevolent Society was organized in New York City.

In the same year, the first Arab ethnic parish in North America was established by Raphael Hawaweeny. Hawaweeny was a young clergyman from Damascus who had been working as a professor of Arabic language at the Orthodox Theological Seminary in Kazan, Russia, before emigrating to the United States and receiving the omophorion of the head of the Russian Orthodox Church. St. Nicholas Cathedral in Brooklyn is considered the mother parish of the archdiocese. In 1904, Hawaweeny was ordained as the first Orthodox bishop in North America and proceeded to establish several other parishes to serve the growing Arab Christian community. His death in 1915 pushed the church into a period of apathy, which was followed by the devastation of the 1917 Russian Revolution. The diocese split into two branches, one in New York and the other in Toledo, and it was only in 1975 that they were reunited. Metropolitan Philip Saliba of New York and Michael Shaheen of Toledo signed the Articles of Reconciliation with the Holy Synod; Saliba was installed as the metropolitan and Shaheen as the auxiliary. Two more bishops were added to the episcopate by 1994.

Headquarters

358 Mountain Road
Englewood, NJ 07631
Telephone: 201-871-1355
Email: FrJoseph@antiochian.org

Leadership

Metropolitan: His Eminence, Metropolitan Philip Saliba

Core Beliefs

The Antiochian Orthodix Christian Archdiocese of North America mirrors the mother church in doctrine.

Statistics

There are nine dioceses, including Charleston, Oakland, and the Mid-Atlantic; Eagle River and the Northwest; Los Angeles and the West; Miami and the Southeast; New York and Washington, DC; Ottawa, Eastern Canada, and Upstate New York; Toledo and the Midwest; Wichita and Mid-America; and Worcester and New England. There are more than two hundred churches and missions throughout the United States and Canada.

Year	Clergy	Churches	Members
1925	21	23	26,000
2006	517	252	425,000

Missionary and Evangelistic Work

The Department of Missions and Evangelism was founded in 1988 to fulfill Metropolitan Philip's campaign to "Make America Orthodox." Among its objectives were the founding of new missions in North American cities with populations of more than one hundred thousand and no Orthodox churches, providing English-speaking parishes to Orthodox Christians who had requested them, responding to the interest of other Christian (often Protestant) laypeople and ministers to convert to the Orthodox Church, and encouraging the Orthodox to evangelize and start new missions in nearby communities. It established 108 missions, of which 55 became full parishes.

The Department of College Ministry keeps students close to the faith during their college years by helping to create mission parishes near major college campuses with no English-speaking Orthodox Church in the area.

Ecumenism

The Antiochian Archdiocese participates in ecumenical activities within the Orthodox Church as well as with other Christian churches. While it upholds the biblical call to show love to all humanity, it does not seek to achieve unity by accommodating views that are inconsistent with the Orthodox faith.

Affiliations

The Antiochian Orthodox Christian Archdiocese of North America is in full communion with believers in various other Orthodox Christian jurisdictions, such as the Greek Orthodox Archdiocese of America and the Orthodox Church in America. All the churches are affiliated through the Standing Conference of Canonical Orthodox Bishops in the Americas.

Electronic Media

The Conciliar Media Ministries runs Ancient Faith Radio (ancientfaith.com).

Publications

Conciliar Press has been a source of Orthodox Christian books for more than thirty years. Among its publications are the *Orthodox Study Bible* and the *Word* magazine, the official publication of the archdiocese. Founded in 1905 by St. Raphael of Brooklyn, the *Word* was an Arabic-language publication until Metropolitan Antony Bashir converted it into English in 1957. It contains news and articles about the Orthodox faith and is a member of the Associated Press, Ecumenical News International, and the Orthodox Press Service. Back issues are available at antiochian.org. The Publications Department is located in Englewood, New Jersey.

Website

http://www.antiochian.org/

George Thomas Kurian

Greek Orthodox Archdiocese

History

The Greek Orthodox Archdiocese was incorporated in 1921 and recognized officially by the state of New York in 1922. Founded under the jurisdiction of the ecumenical patriarch of Constantinople, it is the largest Orthodox body in the United States. During the early 1800s, the first recorded Greek colonists immigrated to the United States, followed by an expansive immigration from Asia Minor and Greece between 1880 and 1920. The first Greek colony was established in St. Augustine, Florida, in 1768. A small community of Greek merchants in New Orleans founded the first parish, Holy Trinity Cathedral, in 1864.

Headquarters

8 East 79th Street
New York, NY 10075
Telephone: 212-570-3500

Leadership

The Greek Orthodox Archdiocese is an eparchy of the ecumenical patriarch of Constantinople.

Core Beliefs

The core beliefs and practices of the Greek Orthodox Archdiocese are consistent with those of the Eastern Orthodox Church. Fundamentals can be identified within four main correlated divisions: "principles of belief and faith; the worship of God, in Whom lies belief and hope for salvation; the living of life so as to serve one's neighbor and especially the 'least of them' as well as oneself; and the enforcing of a system of order of discipline and administration for the members of this Church" (goarch.org, "The Fundamental Teachings of the Eastern Orthodox Church").

Worship

Worship services are often elaborate, lengthy, solemn, and involve the whole person. Worship is the focus of congregational life and has two dimensions: the manifestation of God's presence among his people and the congregational response of praise and thanksgiving that affirms God's presence and action.

Worship is expressed in the daily offices (matins and vespers), Eucharist (Divine Liturgy), sacraments (anointing of the sick, baptism, chrismation, confession, holy orders, and marriage), and special services and blessings.

Divisions and Splits

For composite purposes, the church was under the jurisdiction of the Church of Greece between 1908 and 1922. The Patriarchal Tome of 1922 restored jurisdiction to the patriarch of Constantinople.

Statistics

Members: approximately 1,500,000
Parishes: 560
Priests: 840

Largest Churches

The Greek Orthodox Diocese of Denver is the largest. Other large parishes are located in Illinois, New York, and Utah.

Missionary and Evangelistic Work

The church supports several ministry outreaches through the Department of Marriage and Family, Department of Outreach and Evangelism, Department of Philanthropy, Department of Religious Education, and Department of Youth and Young Adult Ministries.

The Philoptochos Society promotes the benevolent and philanthropic purposes of the church. Saint Basil Academy is a home for Orthodox children in need. St. Michael's Home is for the aged. The Trinity Children's Foundation helps children who have experienced abandonment, abuse, or neglect. The International Orthodox Christian Charities organizes humanitarian activities. The Orthodox Christian Mission Center, as the official international mission agency of the Standing Conference of Canonical Orthodox Bishops in the Americas (SCOBA), assists Orthodox communities throughout the world in proclaiming and practicing the Great Commission. The Orthodox Christian Fellowship is the official campus ministry of SCOBA.

Academic Institutions

The Greek Archdiocese operates Hellenic College and Holy Cross School of Theology, both located in Brookline, Massachusetts.

Electronic Media

Radio programs include *Ancient Faith Radio*, *Church of Greece*, and *For the Life of the World*. The ministry of *For the Life of the World*, which was broadcast from 1994 until 2004, defended the Orthodox faith and served as an apologia to the Christian Research Institute. Founded by Christopher T. Metropulos, the Orthodox Christian

Network (OCN) maintains an effective media witness for the Orthodox Christian Church in North America. *Come Receive the Light* is a nationally syndicated weekly radio program of the OCN. Since 1998, the Department of Internet Ministries has provided live weekly broadcasts of church services, and the Department of Religious Education broadcast the Internet School of Orthodox Studies through the fall of 2005.

Publications

Founded as a monthly publication in 1934 to communicate the message and work of the church by Archbishop Athenagoras, the *Orthodox Observer* has a current readership exceeding five hundred thousand. The Department of Religious Education serves parishes with the publication of catechetical and educational resources. The department publishes a biennial *Orthodox Christian Resource Catalog*, the latest of which included over seven hundred resources for equipping parishioners, including interactive multimedia. *PRAXIS* magazine focuses on parish education.

Website

http://www.goarch.org/

Bibliography

Bulgakov, Sergius. *The Orthodox Church.* London: Centenary Press, 1935.

The Divine Liturgy of Saint John Chrysostom. Brookline, MA: Holy Cross Orthodox Press, 1985.

Lossky, Vladimir. *The Mystical Theology of the Eastern Church.* Greenwood, SC: Attic Press, 1973.

Meyendorff, John. *Catholicity and the Church.* Crestwood, NY: St. Vladimir's Seminary Press, 1983.

Ouspensky, Leonid, and Vladimir Lossky. *The Meaning of Icons.* Rev. ed. Translated by G. E. H. Palmer and E. Kadlousbovsky. Crestwood, NY: St. Vladimir's Seminary Press, 1982.

Schmemann, Alexander. *Sacraments and Orthodoxy.* New York: Herder & Herder, 1965.

Stavropoulos, Christoforos. *Partakers of Divine Nature.* Translated by Stanley Harakas. Minneapolis: Light and Life, 1976.

Ugolnik, Anthony. *The Illuminating Icon.* Grand Rapids: Eerdmans, 1989.

Ware, Timothy. *The Orthodox Church.* New York: Penguin, 1963.

Ron J. Bigalke

Macedonian Orthodox Church

History

Macedonians in the United States and Canada created their own parishes in North America as the Macedonian Orthodox Church began to distance itself from the Serbian Orthodox Church, into which it had been incorporated in the mid-1300s. The first parish in the United States began in Gary, Indiana, in 1963. A year later, the Macedonian faithful in Toronto completed their church, which would become the diocesan see for the Macedonian Orthodox Church in the United States and Canada.

Headquarters

Diocese of America and Canada
St. Clement of Ohrid Macedonian Orthodox Cathedral
76 Overlea Boulevard
Toronto, Ontario, Canada M4H 1C5
Telephone: 416-421-7451
Email: info@stclementofohrid.com

The patriarchate of the Macedonian Orthodox Church is located in Ohrid, Macedonia.

Leadership

Archbishop Stefan (Veljanovski), the patriarch and the archbishop of Ohrid and Macedonia, is the leader of the church. In North America, the Most Reverend Metropolitan Methodij directs the church.

Core Beliefs

The theological beliefs of the Macedonian Orthodox Church are typical of Orthodoxy in general. The church has a trinitarian faith and accepts the authority of the Bible and the first seven ecumenical councils. It practices the veneration of saints and icons and emphasizes mystical theology (experience of God beyond human understanding) and the importance of the Holy Spirit. There is an emphasis on the sacraments, especially the Eucharist (Divine Liturgy); asceticism, including fasting and frequent prayer; and the veneration of icons and saints, including the Virgin Mary.

Worship

The highlight of worship is the Divine Liturgy (Eucharist), which is celebrated by a priest using the Liturgy of John Chrysostom. Worship is typically conducted in English, Macedonian, or Church Slavonic.

Divisions and Splits

Partially at the instigation of the communist Yugoslav government, the Orthodox Church leaders in Macedonia began in the 1940s to organize with the intent of separating from the Serbian Orthodox Church. The separation was effected in 1967 when the Macedonian Orthodox Church declared itself autocephalous. This action was not accepted by the Serbian Church or by the ecumenical patriarch of Constantinople. Although talks occur between the Macedonian Church and the Serbian Orthodox Church as well as with the ecumenical patriarch, the Macedonian Church is currently considered to have irregular status by Orthodoxy in general.

Statistics

There are about seventeen parishes and missions in the United States and eight in Canada, with five new parishes in the process of forming in North America. There are also two monasteries, one in Toronto and one in New Jersey. Adherents in the United States and Canada number around 22,000 to 25,000. In North America, the areas with the highest concentration of Macedonian Orthodox adherents are Ontario, Michigan, New Jersey, New York, Ohio, and Indiana. Worldwide there are around 1.5 million adherents.

Largest Churches

St. Clement of Ohrid Cathedral in Toronto is the diocesan see of North America. Other large churches in North America are in Detroit; Passaic, New Jersey; and Rochester, New York.

Growth

The church has experienced moderate growth in the last two decades. Reasons for the increase in numbers include immigration and the growth of families. Five new churches have recently formed or are in the process of forming. New geographic areas that the church is reaching are Montreal, Missouri, and Arizona.

Trends

In the United States, the church focuses on education of the youth and preservation of the Macedonian heritage, such as the use of the Macedonian language and the performance of traditional music.

Missionary and Evangelistic Work

The Macedonian Orthodox Church has a strong ethnic character, and evangelism is not currently a major focus. The church endeavors to strengthen its position in North America first by appealing to believers of Macedonian heritage.

The church in North America is particularly interested in meeting the spiritual and material needs of Macedonian immigrants.

Ecumenism

Because its announcement of complete independence (autocephaly) was perceived as breaking canon law, the Macedonian Orthodox Church is not in communion with the ecumenical patriarch of Constantinople or Orthodoxy as a whole. The ecumenical patriarch contends that the Macedonian Church's break from the Serbian Church was mostly a matter of nationalism and cannot be accepted by the Orthodox Church. Efforts to solve the disagreement continue.

Academic Institution

St. Clement of Ohrid Theological School (Skopje, Macedonia)

Parachurch Organizations

Although there are no major Macedonian Orthodox parachurch organizations in North America, many individual parishes have men's and women's auxiliaries, youth groups, and groups for traditional music or dancing.

Electronic Media

The metropolitanate and many individual parishes host websites. Ancient Faith Radio (an online station) has programs and podcasts of Orthodox liturgies, music, and theological discussions.

Publication

Duhovna Iskra (Spiritual Spark; circulation of about five thousand in North America)

Websites

http://www.akmpe.org/
http://www.mpc.org.mk/

Bibliography

Krindatch, Alexei D. "Orthodox (Eastern Christian) Churches in the United States at the Beginning of a New Millennium: Questions of Nature, Identity, and Mission." Journal for the Scientific Study of Religion 41, no. 3 (2002): 533–63.

Obolensky, Dimitri. The Byzantine Commonwealth: Eastern Europe, 500–1453. London: Phoenix, 1971.

Roberson, Ronald. The Eastern Christian Churches: A Brief Survey. 6th ed. Rome: Edizioni Orientalia Christiana, 1999.

"St. Clement of Ohrid Cathedral." http://www.stclementofohrid.com. "About St. Clement Cathedral" and "Links."

Scott Goins

Orthodox Church in America

History

The Orthodox Church in America is the oldest of the Orthodox churches on the North American continent. It entered the New World in 1741, when the Russian Orthodox Church established a mission in Russian Alaska. In 1792, the first Orthodox church was built by eight Russian monks who settled in Kodiak, Alaska, and in two years, more than twelve thousand people were baptized there. A second church was built in Paul's Harbor in 1794, and a seminary followed in the 1840s.

As part of their outreach to the native people, Orthodox monks and bishops created an alphabet in the Aleutian language, printed a grammar, translated portions of the Bible, and built a cathedral at Sitka. The purchase of Alaska by the United States in 1867 brought changes for the Orthodox mission, including the moving of the newly created diocese to a Russian trading post in San Francisco. Although the episcopal see was also transferred to that city in 1872, it moved to New York City in 1905. Since it was the first Orthodox diocese in the United States, it soon was granted primacy, and newer Orthodox groups generally formed their first parishes as branches of the diocese.

By the early twentieth century, Orthodox communities were, with few exceptions, united under the Russian Orthodox Church in a single jurisdiction, even though some of the newer ethnic parishes, such as the Serb, Rumanian, Bulgarian, Arab, and Ukrainian, were quick to leave the Russian orbit. As a result of divisions created by the Russian Revolution of 1917, the diocese became an independent church in 1970 under a charter of autocephaly from the Moscow patriarchate. The dream of a united Orthodox denomination in the United States has not been realized, but the Orthodox Church in America is a member of the Standing Conference of Canonical Orthodox Bishops in the Americas, whose members regularly concelebrate the liturgy, especially on the Triumph of Orthodoxy on the first Sunday in the Great Lent.

The Orthodox Church in America gains strength from being part of a worldwide communion, with over 150 million Orthodox Christians in the world, including 100 million in Russia, Ukraine, Belarus, Georgia, Moldova, and the Baltic States. The Orthodox also form a majority in the Balkans (Greece, Romania, Bulgaria, Serbia, Montenegro, and Cyprus) and the largest body of Christians in the Middle East. They represent significant minorities in Finland, Australia, New Zealand, South America, Ghana, and Nigeria.

Celebrating its bicentennial in 1993–94, the Orthodox Church in America was an ethnic church until the end of World War II. This is no longer the case, as there are many American converts in every congregation. Five of the ten bishops of the Holy Synod are converts from other denominations, and almost one-half of the students at St. Herman's, St. Tikhon's, and St. Vladimir's Seminaries joined the Orthodox Church as adults.

Headquarters

PO Box 675
6850 N Hempstead Turnpike
Syosset, NY 11791
Telephone: 516-922-0550
Email: info@oca.org

Leadership

Metropolitan of all America and Canada: the Most Blessed Jonah, Archbishop of Washington

The metropolitan is the primate of the Orthodox Church in America in addition to being the diocesan bishop of one of the dioceses of the church. He oversees the church's internal affairs and represents it in its dealings with religious groups, other churches, and secular authorities. Orthodox tradition views the primate not only as an archbishop but also as the ethnarch, that is, the head of the entire Orthodox community and its principal spokesman. The election of the primate by the clergy does not require the approval of the Moscow patriarchate.

The highest-ranking legislative and administrative authority in the church is the All-American Council, which includes the metropolitan, all the bishops of the church, the priests of each parish, and an equal number of lay delegates. Decisions of the All-American Council are implemented by the Metropolitan Council, which is the executive body of the church administration. The metropolitan is chairman, and there are priests and laymen from each diocese. The Holy Synod of Bishops, also headed by the metropolitan, is the supreme canonical authority and includes all the diocesan bishops of the church as voting members. Each jurisdiction in the United States is incorporated.

The three orders in the ministry are deacons, priests, and bishops. Deacons and priests may be either secular or monastic, and candidates for those positions may marry before ordination but not after. Bishops are chosen from the monastic community following the ancient Rule of St. Basil the Great and uphold lifelong vows of poverty, chastity, and obedience.

Core Beliefs

The Orthodox faith is defined by the seven ecumenical councils, starting with Nicea, and by later Eastern councils. The Nicene Creed is recited in its original form (without the Filioque clause) in all liturgies. The Virgin Mary is honored as the *Theotokos* (bearer of God), but the church does not adhere to the doctrines of immaculate conception and assumption. The Orthodox reverence the cross, the saints, and nine orders of angels but do not subscribe to the teaching of the surplus merits of the saints or the doctrine of indulgences. Described as windows to heaven representing Christ's human nature, icons are a historic feature of Orthodoxy, but images are banned, and iconoclasm is condemned as a heresy.

Worship

Worship for the Orthodox is preparation for sanctification with the goal of *theosis*, meaning "perfection" or "deification," that is, living in harmony with God not just in eternity but also here and now. With God-centered and mystical services, the liturgy is perhaps the fullest expression of the Orthodox faith. The "mysteries"—as the Orthodox call the sacraments—are essential to Orthodox worship, with the Eucharist or Communion, in which the bread and wine are accepted as the body and blood of Christ, regarded as "the mystery of mysteries." As in the Catholic Church, the other six sacraments— baptism, confirmation, penance, holy orders, marriage, and anointing of the sick—are also important. Prayers are offered for the dead, though there is no belief in purgatory. Evocative of paradise, Orthodox church services are among the most resplendent in the Christian church.

A unique feature of Orthodox church architecture is the "royal doors" leading up to the sanctuary that contain icons of the four evangelists and the annunciation. Colorful vestments are intended not so much to adorn the priest as to hide his own garments and signal his role as a shepherd. Liturgical music is diverse, including not only the slow, elaborate Italianate harmonies popular in nineteenth-century Russia but also quicker and simpler melodies derived from monastic chants. Since the 1980s, congregational singing has become more common. Orthodoxy, unlike Roman Catholicism, does not have a sacred language and conducts services in the vernacular of each congregation.

Statistics

In 2010, the church had 700 parishes, 737 churches, and 1,064,000 members.

Missionary and Evangelistic Work

Numerous departments and organizations oversee the work of the church's ministries. Offices include Canonization; Canons and Statutes; Christian Education; Christian Service and Humanitarian Aid; Development and Stewardship; Evangelization; External Affairs and Interchurch Relations; History and Archives; Institutional Chaplaincies; Liturgical Music and Translations; Military Chaplaincies; Pastoral Life and Ministry; Theological Education; and Youth, Young Adult, and Campus Ministry.

Through its affiliation with International Orthodox Christian Charities, the church has helped to raise tens of millions of dollars to fight problems such as hunger around the world, especially in Eastern Europe, the Caribbean, and Central Africa. The Orthodox Church in America's annual charity appeal raises over $100,000 to be used around the United States. There are also appeals to raise money for missions work, including the Church Planting Grant Program, and the seminaries. The Orthodox Church in America Endowments include the Theological Education Endowment, to offer grants to seminarians; the Mission Endowment, to support missions; the General Purpose Endowment, to assist all church ministries as well as daily operation of the church; the Clergy Care Endowment, to provide medical care to retired clergy; the Charity Endowment, to provide assistance to a variety of charities; and the Fellowship of Orthodox Stewards Endowment, to supply additional support to several church ministries.

Affiliations

Alumni Association of St. Herman's Seminary
Alumni Association of St. Tikhon's Seminary
Alumni Association of St. Vladimir's Seminary
International Orthodox Christian Charities
Orthodox Charismatic Renewal
Orthodox Christian Education Commission

Orthodox Christian Laity
Orthodox Christian Mission Center
Orthodox Christians for Life
Orthodox Fellowship of the Transfiguration
Orthodox Inter-Seminary Movement
Orthodox Peace Fellowship
Orthodox People Together
Orthodox Theological Society in America
Religious Books for Russia
Russian Orthodox Theological Fund
Standing Conference of Canonical Orthodox Bishops in the Americas
St. John of Damascus Association of Iconographers, Iconologists, and Architects

Academic Institutions

St. Herman's Seminary (Kodiak, AK)
St. Tikhon's Seminary (South Canaan, PA)
St. Vladimir's Seminary (Crestwood, NY)

Parachurch Organizations

Orthodox spirituality has a strong tradition of monasticism, and twenty Orthodox monasteries have been established in the United States and Canada since the 1970s. The first monastic community, St. Tikhon's in South Canaan, Pennsylvania, was founded in 1905.

Electronic Media

The *Voice of Orthodoxy* radio program is directed at former Soviet Union countries.

Publications

The *Orthodox Church*, a bimonthly newspaper, has been the official publication of the Orthodox Church in America since 1965. The *Steward* is the official newsletter of the Fellowship of Orthodox Stewards, which assists the Outreach Ministries of the Orthodox Church in America. The Orthodox Christian Publications Center (Brooklyn, OH) was established in 1989 by former primate His Beatitude, Metropolitan Theodosius.

Website

http://www.oca.org/

Archives

The Department of History and Archives (Crestwood, NY) maintains the records of the history of the church from its beginning in the eighteenth century and publishes periodic monographs on the history of the church. It offers its assistance to researchers and makes its members available for lectures.

George Thomas Kurian

Patriarchal Parishes of the Russian Orthodox Church

History

The Patriarchal Parishes of the Russian Orthodox Church remained under the direct jurisdiction of the patriarch of Moscow and all Russia even as most United States groups within the Russian Orthodox Church joined the Orthodox Church in America when that group was formed as an independent body in 1970. The church had been incorporated in 1898 under the name Russian Orthodox Greek Catholic Three Saints Society in Passaic, New Jersey, but was reincorporated in 1952 as Russian Orthodox Greek Catholic Three Saints Society in Garfield, New Jersey. In 1959, the name was changed to the present one. The group is commonly known as the Three Saints Church or the Three Saints Russian Orthodox Church (referring to three fourth-century church leaders). The membership is predominantly Eastern European. In 1951, John Chrysostom More-Moreno encouraged some members to separate and form the Eastern Orthodox Catholic Church in America.

The original Three Saints Church was a wooden building decorated with traditional murals and a bell from Russia. The church, completed in 1916, was built with five domes, since the dome is a symbol of Christ and the apostles. In 1984, a newly constructed Three Saints Church was dedicated. A small number of the Three Saints Church left the parish to create the Eastern Church of the Holy Apostles.

Headquarters

St. Nicholas Cathedral
15 East 97th Street
New York, NY 10029
Telephone: 212-831-6294

Leadership

Archpriest George Konev

Website

http://www.3saints.com/

George Thomas Kurian

Romanian Orthodox Church

History

Large numbers of Romanian Orthodox Christians began arriving in the United States after 1895, prompted by cultural and religious persecution under the Hapsburg Empire's Hungariza-tion policies. By 1920, Romanians in the United States numbered fifty thousand, many of them coming from Banat, Moldova, and other adjoining regions. They had all been served by itinerant priests from the homeland until 1904, when the first Romanian parish was established under the diocese of Sibiu in Transylvania. Another twelve parishes were established from 1904 to 1920, and collectively they were also home to Orthodox Christian Gypsies called "Rom."

The archdiocese of the Romanian Orthodox Church in America was formally established in 1929; it was authorized by the Holy Synod of the Romanian Orthodox Church in Romania in 1934 and granted autonomy in 1950. In 1947, the communist government abolished the Romanian Orthodox Episcopate in America as part of its campaign against the Christian church, but defiant Americans refused to disband. Bucharest created the Romanian Orthodox Missionary Episcopate in America as a new diocesan structure, and all but two Romanian parishes severed ties with Bucharest and elected their own bishop after lengthy and expensive court cases. In 1951, roughly forty parishes broke off to eventually (in 1960) join the Orthodox Church of America metropolia as the Romanian Orthodox Episcopate of America, headquartered in Jackson, Michigan. In 1973, the head of the church, the bishop, was made archbishop by the patriarch of the Romanian Orthodox Church in Romania.

Headquarters

5410 North Newland Avenue
Chicago, IL 60656-2026
Email: romarch67@aol.com

Leadership

Archbishop: His Eminence Nicolae Condrea

Core Beliefs

The Orthodox Church sees itself as part of the apostolic community established by Christ and sees the institution of the Christian church as inseparable from the faith itself. In addition to upholding the teachings of Scripture, Orthodoxy teaches that God's revelation can be found in church tradition. The components of that tradition include celebration of the Eucharist, prayers, hymns, icons, the work of the seven ecumenical councils, and the Nicene Creed. Social concern is also seen as an essential part of the church's teaching. Every aspect of church life is viewed as a reflection of God the Father, Son, and Holy Ghost, and the church is viewed as the guardian of the authentic faith.

Website

http://www.romarch.org/

George Thomas Kurian

Romanian Orthodox Episcopate

History

Romanian Orthodox parishes have existed in the United States since the early 1900s, but the Romanian Orthodox Episcopate of America was established only in 1929 at a general church conference in Detroit. It rejected ties to the Romanian Orthodox Church in Bucharest when the communist government came to exert influence there. Seeking to promote unity among Orthodox Christians, the episcopate is under the canonical jurisdiction of the Orthodox Church in America, based on a December 1970 agreement.

Headquarters

Mailing Address
PO Box 309
Grass Lake, MI 49240

Street Address
255 Grey Tower Road
Jackson, MI 49201-9120
Telephone: 517-522-4800
Email: doancea@roea.org

The diocesan cathedral is St. George Cathedral, built in 1912 and located outside Detroit in Southfield, Michigan.

Leadership

Hierarchs: the Most Reverend Dr. Nathaniel Popp, archbishop of Detroit and the Romanian Orthodox Episcopate of America; the Right Reverend Irineu Duvlea, bishop of Dearborn Heights and auxiliary bishop of the Romanian Orthodox Episcopate of America
Chancellor: Archdeacon David Oancea

Website

http://www.sgroc.org/

George Thomas Kurian

Russian Orthodox Church Outside Russia

History

Russian Orthodox missionaries began traveling to North America in the eighteenth century.

In 1794, the first Orthodox Christian Mission to America arrived on Kodiak Island in Alaska. One of the missionaries was Herman, later canonized as St. Herman of Alaska. He led the way in converting many of the native Aleuts and helped to protect them from exploitation by colonizers. (He was canonized in 1970 and is considered by Orthodox Christians to be the patron saint of the Americas.)

As a result of the Russian Revolution, émigré communities were cut off from the Moscow patriarchate of the Russian Orthodox Church. In 1920, Tikhon, patriarch of Moscow, issued an *ukase* (decree) authorizing Russian Orthodox Christians abroad to govern and organize themselves independently of the patriarchate. Two years later, exiled Russian Orthodox bishops met in Serbia. At this synod, the Russian Orthodox Church Outside Russia (ROCOR) was founded to fulfill Patriarch Tikhon's *ukase*. Metropolitan Platon Rozhdestvensky was elected as primate of the Russian archdiocese in North America.

Controversy marked the decade of the 1920s in the American diocese. Metropolitan Platon declared the North American diocese autonomous and labeled the ROCOR uncanonical. The Synod of Bishops of the Russian Church Abroad, the ruling body of the ROCOR, dismissed Metropolitan Platon, replacing him with Archbishop Apollinary Koshevoy. Also during this period, a schism took place among Russian Orthodox churches, with some churches identifying themselves with the ROCOR and others identifying themselves with the Russian Orthodox Greek Catholic Church in America, more popularly known as the Metropolia and known today as the Orthodox Church in America.

A temporary reconciliation marked the next decade until the Cleveland Sobor (Synod) in 1946, when the Metropolia separated itself completely from the church abroad. The Metropolia declared its loyalty to the Moscow patriarchate. The ROCOR rejected this decision, claiming that the patriarchate was compromised by its association with the Soviet government.

On May 17, 2007, the ROCOR was fully restored to communion with the Moscow patriarchate. The Act of Canonical Communion reestablished the canonical connection between the churches.

Headquarters

The Synod of Bishops of the Russian Orthodox Church Outside Russia
75 East 93rd Street
New York, NY 10128

Leadership

Eastern America and New York Diocese ruling bishop: Metropolitan Hilarion Kapral (first hierarch of the ROCOR)
Chicago and Mid-America Diocese ruling bishop: Archbishop Alypy (Gramanovich)
San Francisco and Western America Diocese ruling bishop: Archbishop Kyrill (Dmitrieff)

Core Beliefs

Jesus Christ came to earth to found his church through the apostles for the salvation of humanity. The teachings of the church derive from Holy Scripture and sacred tradition. The members of the church comprise the body of Christ because in the Eucharist they partake of the body and blood of Christ. The many Orthodox churches are united in faith and worship by the partaking of the "mysteries" (sacraments).

Worship

Russian Orthodox churches do not provide instrumental accompaniment to the traditional chant of the congregational voices. Many of the churches provide liturgy in both Slavonic languages and the vernacular.

Russian Orthodox churches celebrate three liturgies: Liturgy of John Chrysostom, Liturgy of Basil the Great, and Liturgy of the Presanctified Gifts. The Divine Liturgy can be celebrated only by a bishop or a priest. The Liturgy of the Presanctified Gifts is celebrated only during the season of Lent.

Academic Institution

Holy Trinity Orthodox Seminary (Jordanville, NY)

Publications

Church Life is the official publication of the Synod of Bishops of the ROCOR. *Orthodox Russia* is issued twice monthly through Holy Trinity Seminary Press, while *Orthodox Life* is a monthly companion to *Orthodox Russia*. *Orthodox America* is a missionary periodical published eight times per year.

Websites

http://www.roca.org/
http://www.russianorthodoxchurch.ws/english/

Bibliography

Fiftieth Anniversary of the Russian Orthodox Church Outside of Russia. Montreal: Monastery Press in Canada, 1974.
Rodzianko, M. *The Truth about the Russian Church Abroad.* Jordanville, NY: Holy Trinity Monastery, 1975.

Young, Alexey. *The Russian Orthodox Church Outside Russia: A History and Chronology.* San Bernardino, CA: St. Willibrord's Press, 1993.

Scott Rushing

Serbian Orthodox Church

History

The origin of Christianity among the Serbs is usually attributed to the missionary work of Sts. Cyril and Methodius or their followers during the last half of the ninth century, although there is some evidence that Roman missionaries evangelized the Serbs as early as the seventh century. Around 870, Serbian Prince Mutimir brought his nation under the authority of the Byzantine Church. By 1219, St. Sava, the brother of the Serbian king, had negotiated with the Byzantine Church for independence for the church in Serbia. In 1346, at the urging of Emperor Dushan, the Serbian Church declared itself a patriarchate, and by 1375, the Byzantine Church had agreed to this status, thus making the Serbian Church fully independent (autocephalous). Around this time, the Ottoman Empire began successful attacks on Serbia, and by the end of the fifteenth century, both Serbia and Montenegro were under Turkish control. It was not until 1879 that the Serbian Church was restored and again recognized as independent by Constantinople. The twentieth century saw times of great difficulty for the Serbian Orthodox Church, including severe persecution by the fascist Croatian state during World War II and by the communists after the war. Additionally, the bloodshed and dislocations resulting from the war in Bosnia-Herzegovina left many challenges for the church in Serbia.

For both economic and political reasons, many Serbian Orthodox immigrated to the United States and Canada starting in the 1860s. The 1890s saw the establishment of the first parish in Jackson, California. Initially under the jurisdiction of the Russian Orthodox Church in America, the Serbian Church in the United States was granted independence in 1921. During and after World War II, the church experienced growth as many Serbians migrated to North America. In 1963, the Serbian Church in the USA and Canada was divided into three dioceses, the Eastern (including Canada), Midwestern, and Western. In the same year, because of disagreements over the Serbian patriarchate's relationship with the communist government in Yugoslavia, a Free Serbian Orthodox Church split from the Serbian Orthodox Church in America. The rift was healed in 1991. In 1983, the Canadian parishes were granted separate status.

Headquarters

St. Sava Monastery
32377 N Milwaukee Avenue
PO Box 519
Libertyville, IL 60048
Telephone: 847-362-2440

The patriarchate of the Serbian Orthodox Church is located in Belgrade, Serbia.

Leadership

The Serbian Orthodox Church in North America is governed independently but falls under the jurisdiction of the patriarch of the Serbian Orthodox Church. The dioceses in the United States are led by His Grace Longin (Krco), bishop of America and Canada.

Core Beliefs

The Serbian Orthodox Church is a canonical Eastern Orthodox Church, and its beliefs are those of Orthodoxy in general. Tenets of faith include trinitarianism, acceptance of the Bible and the first seven ecumenical councils, an emphasis on mystical theology (the experience of God beyond human understanding) and the Holy Spirit, the veneration of saints and icons, the transformation of the individual into the likeness of God (*theosis*), and the role of the church in healing human beings wounded by sin. There is an emphasis on the sacraments, especially the Divine Liturgy (Eucharist); the practice of asceticism; monasticism as a source of vitality for the church; and veneration of icons and saints, including the Virgin Mary.

Worship

The highlight of worship is the Divine Liturgy (Eucharist), which is celebrated by a priest using the Liturgy of John Chrysostom. In the United States and Canada, worship normally takes place in English or Serbian. Particularly at monasteries and cathedrals there are daily services, including the Divine Liturgy and various prayer services.

Divisions and Splits

In 1967, partially at the instigation of the communist Yugoslav government, the Macedonian Orthodox Church formed and separated itself from the Serbian Orthodox Church. The Macedonian and the Serbian churches have not been fully reconciled. Because of this split, there are around thirty Macedonian Orthodox parishes in the United States and Canada that share the heritage of the Serbian Orthodox Church but are not in communion with it or with Constantinople. There is also a Montenegrin Orthodox Church that has declared its independence in Montenegro. During the period of communist control of Yugoslavia, some churches in the United States broke with the Serbian patriarchate because of conflicts over church-state relations and formed the Free Serbian Orthodox Church. In 1991, the rift was healed and communion restored.

Statistics

There are about 130 parishes and missions in the United States and 36 in Canada. There are also over a dozen monasteries and hermitages in the United States and one in Canada. Serbian Orthodox faithful number about 100,000–110,000 in the United States and about 35,000–40,000 in Canada. Worldwide membership in the Serbian Orthodox Church is difficult to establish, especially because of recent dislocations in the Balkans; a good estimate is probably 10 to 11 million.

Largest Churches

Holy Resurrection Cathedral in Chicago is the largest church in North America. Other large churches in the United States are located in Alhambra, California; Detroit; New York City; and Pittsburgh. In Canada, there are large Serbian Orthodox populations in Toronto; Hamilton, Ontario; Montreal; and Vancouver. In Serbia, the Temple of St. Sava in Belgrade, the interior of which is still being finished, will be the largest Orthodox church in the world, holding about ten thousand worshipers. In Serbia and Montenegro, there are many famous monasteries and churches dating back as far as the Middle Ages.

Growth

The church has experienced substantial growth in the last two decades. Reasons for the growth include immigration, growth of families, and conversions to the church.

Trends

As the Serbian Church in North America continues to embrace its ethnic heritage, it also endeavors to be open to the diverse communities in the United States and Canada. The church effectively uses modern media to increase awareness of its rich heritage. In recent years, the church has stressed the need to disciple young persons. In 2006, an annual youth conference was initiated, and in 2007, an annual young adult conference was begun. There are also several youth camps.

Missionary and Evangelistic Work

Because of recent wars, the Serbian Orthodox Church worldwide has focused on easing suffering in the Balkans. This desire led to creation of the International Orthodox Christian Charities, which has provided aid not only to the Balkans but also to other areas throughout the world. In North America, the church publishes several journals and maintains numerous websites in an effort to disciple and evangelize. The Serbian Orthodox Church is part of a consortium of Orthodox churches that cooperate in a mission training center in Jacksonville, Florida. Monasteries in the United States and Canada seek to help the needy and provide spiritual support for the faithful.

Ecumenism

The Serbian Orthodox Church in North America is in full communion with the ecumenical patriarch of Constantinople and with all canonical Eastern Orthodox churches. It is a member of the National Council of the Churches of Christ, the World Council of Churches, and the Joint Committee of Orthodox and Catholic Bishops. In 2010, the newly elected patriarch Irinej invited Pope Benedict XVI to visit Serbia to discuss closer relations with the Roman Catholic Church.

Academic Institution

St. Sava Theological School (Libertyville, IL)

Parachurch Organizations

The Brotherhood of the Serbian Orthodox Clergy in the USA and Canada is an association of Serbian Orthodox Church clergy members. The Circle of Serbian Sisters is an association for laywomen in the church. There is also a Serbian Singing Federation.

Electronic Media

The metropolitanate and all of the four dioceses of the church host websites, as do many churches and some monasteries. Ancient Faith Radio (http://www.ancientfaith.com) has some programs with liturgies and music from Serbian Orthodox churches and monasteries. Podcasts are also available from Ancient Faith Radio and from the website of the Western Diocese.

Publications

The *Path of Orthodoxy* is the official publication of the Serbian Orthodox Church in the United States and Canada. Other publications include the *Diocesan Observer* (US), *Istocnik* (Canada), *Little Falcons* (for children, US), the *Clergy Messenger* (US), and *Orthodox Word* (US).

Websites

Serbian Orthodox Church in North and South America: http://www.serborth.org/

Eastern American Diocese: http://www.eastern diocese.org/

Metropolitanate and Midwestern Diocese: http://midwestmetropolitanate.org/

Western American Diocese: http://westsrbdio.org/

Serbian Orthodox Church (worldwide): http://www.spc.rs/

Bibliography

Ivanovic, Filip. "Ancient Glory and New Mission: The Serbian Orthodox Church." *Studies in World Christianity* 14, no. 3 (2008): 220–32.

Krindatch, Alexei D. "Orthodox (Eastern Christian) Churches in the United States at the Beginning of a New Millennium: Questions of Nature, Identity, and Mission." *Journal for the Scientific Study of Religion* 41, no. 3 (2002): 533–63.

Obolensky, Dimitri. *The Byzantine Commonwealth: Eastern Europe, 500–1453*. London: Phoenix, 1971.

Pavlovich, Paul. *The History of the Serbian Orthodox Church*. Toronto: Serbian Heritage Books, 1989.

Roberson, Ronald. *The Eastern Christian Churches: A Brief Survey*. 7th ed. Rome: Edizioni Orientalia Christiana, 2007.

Scott Goins

Syriac Antiochian Orthodox Catholic Church

History

The Syriac Antiochian Orthodox Catholic Church has also been known as the Eastern Orthodox Catholic Archdiocese, the American Orthodox Catholic Archdiocese, and the Syro-Russian Orthodox Church. The church's origin can be traced to 1892, when an American priest, Father Joseph Vilathi (Vilatte), was ordained as archbishop in Ceylon (Sri Lanka) by Indian Malabar bishops under the auspices of the Syrian Orthodox patriarch of Antioch. Father Vilathi was thereafter known as Mar Timotheos I.

Mar Timotheos returned to the United States and founded several churches, mostly in the Midwest. After the death of Mar Timotheos in 1929, the church experienced a period of slower growth, with some parishes falling into disuse or being sold, although some parishes were also added. In 1966, the church consecrated an archbishop from the Russian Orthodox tradition. Thus, the church claims apostolic succession from the Syrian, Greek, and Russian lines. The church recently experienced a change in leadership and moved its location from Duluth, Minnesota, to Canfield, Ohio.

Headquarters

Metropolis Headquarters
7815 Akron Canfield Road
Canfield, OH 44406
Telephone: 330-286-0274

Leadership

Metropolitan Archbishop Timothy

Core Beliefs

The church recognizes Scripture, tradition, and the tenets of Orthodoxy, including the seven ecumenical councils, the Apostles' Creed, the Athanasian Creed, and the Nicene Creed. It accepts seven sacraments (baptism, chrismation, confession, holy orders, holy matrimony, holy unction, and the Eucharist—with the real presence of Jesus being seen in the Eucharistic elements). Members venerate icons, saints, and the Virgin Mary as well as practice asceticism, especially prayer and fasting.

Worship

The church is Eastern Rite, thus generally following the worship of the Eastern Orthodox Church. The Divine Liturgy (Eucharist) is usually celebrated using the Liturgy of St. John Chrysostom and is generally in the vernacular. Some parishes use a Western Rite adapted from Roman Catholicism.

Divisions and Splits

The church has suffered many divisions. During the early twentieth century, the church broke official ties with the Syrian Orthodox Church over political issues. There have been many schisms and separations by individual churches, bishops, and priests. Some of these separations have occurred because of financial exigencies or personal disagreements.

Controversies

Controversies in the early part of the twentieth century were generally between the Syro-Russian

Church and the patriarchate in Antioch over the authority of the Council of Chalcedon and over political matters pertaining to World War I. These disagreements caused the Syro-Russian Church to proclaim its autonomy in 1910. Other disagreements have tended to be more localized, centering around individual priests, bishops, or parishes.

Statistics

A few sources list the church as having twenty thousand to twenty-five thousand members in the United States, but a few thousand seems much more likely. There are four archdioceses: the United States (with dependencies outside the United States), Cuba, India, and the United Kingdom. The church's website lists several parishes in the United States. Independent confirmation of these parishes is difficult.

Trends

The headquarters of the church recently moved from Duluth, Minnesota, to Canfield, Ohio. A church and monastery are located there. The church's website mentions monasteries in the Congo and in the United Kingdom. At its new location, the church plans to expand and to have a homeless shelter and a retreat center. The church continues to reach out to other Orthodox churches as well as to churches of the Western traditions. The church also continues to emphasize holistic healing.

Missionary and Evangelistic Work

The church continues to open missions within the United States and reports activities in Africa, India, and Bangladesh.

Ecumenism

The church is not a canonical Orthodox Church and is not recognized by the ecumenical patriarch of Constantinople. It continues to seek dialogue with various Orthodox churches.

Academic Institution

St. Mark Seminary and College (distance education only) (Sharon, PA)

Parachurch Organizations

The Commission on Religious Counseling and Healing is dedicated to holistic healing and the healing ministry of the church. The Canon Law Society of the Syro-Russian Metropolia is dedicated to the study and practice of canon law. The Sovereign Order of Chivalry is dedicated to

promoting harmony among the nations, pursuing the corporal and spiritual works of mercy, and promoting ethics and morals.

Electronic Media

The church offers a comprehensive website and advertises distance education through St. Mark Seminary and College.

Publications

The Orthodox Christian Herald

Website

http://www.rbsocc.org/

Scott Goins

True Orthodox Church of Greece (Synod of Metropolitan Cyprian)

History

The True Orthodox Church of Greece (Synod of Metropolitan Cyprian) is part of the reaction—hence the adjective "True"—to the introduction of the Western (Gregorian) calendar into the life of the Orthodox Church in 1924. It instead holds that the Julian calendar corresponds with the worship in the heavenly court and is especially important for determining the timing of the moveable feasts, such as Easter. About a decade later (1935), three metropolitans—Germanos of Demetrius, Chrysostom, and Chrysostomos of Zakynthos—declared the archbishop of Athens to be schismatic, appealing to the sixteenth-century anathemas against the Gregorian calendar issued by three Patriarchal and Pan-Orthodox Synods in Constantinople. Members are also called "Old Calendarists" and are in communion with the Old Calendar Orthodox Churches of Romania and Bulgaria.

Headquarters

Holy Monastery of St. Cyprian
PO Box 46006
133 10 Ano Liosia, Greece

Leadership

The True Orthodox Church of Greece follows the episcopal leadership structure of the Orthodox tradition but with opposing metropolitans. Metropolitan Cyprian (b. 1935) was consecrated bishop on February 7, 1979, and was elected president of the Holy Synod in Resistance on April 5, 1985 (old style).

Core Beliefs

The True Orthodox Church of Greece follows in the nearly two-millennia-long Byzantine tradition. It is a trinitarian, creedal group, emphasizing the preservation of truth and apostolic succession. The only deviating core belief or practice from the Greek Orthodox Church is adherence to the old calendar.

Following baptism (which is understood as being sealed by the Holy Spirit), the goal is to draw near to God throughout life. To this end, God channels grace through the "mysteries"— baptism, *charismation* (anointing), Holy Communion, confession, holy orders, marriage, and *euchelaion* (oil of prayer).

Websites

http://www.hotca.org/
http://www.synodinresistance.org/

Bibliography

"The Church of the GOC in America." http://www.hotca .org. "The True Orthodox Church of Greece."

"Old Calendar Orthodox Church." http://www.synodin resistance.org. "Publication" and "Theology."

Piepkorn, Arthur Carl. *Profiles in Belief: The Religious Bodies of the United States and Canada.* Vol. 1. San Francisco: Harper & Row, 1977.

John DelHousaye

Ukrainian National Autocephalic Orthodox Church in Exile

History

The Ukrainian National Autocephalic Orthodox Church in Exile (UNAOCIE; formerly the Holy Ukrainian Autocephalic Orthodox Church in Exile) was organized in 1951 in New York by Ukrainian immigrants. In 1960, the UNAOCIE was incorporated as a member of the Standing Conference of Canonical Orthodox Bishops in the Americas, but it now exists as an independent jurisdiction. Leadership was provided by Archbishop Palladios Rudenko, a former bishop of Krakiv, Lviv, and Lemkenland, and Archbishop Ihor Huba, a former bishop of Poltava and Kremenchuk.

In 1978, Nikolaus Ilnyckyj (d. 1998) was consecrated as metropolitan by Archbishop Peter Zhurawetsky. During this period, the jurisdiction of the church experienced decline. By 1997, the church had eight bishops and a total membership of approximately one thousand. In that same year, Nikolaus elevated Bishop Haralambos Bouchlas to the rank of archbishop. Upon the death of

Metropolitan Nikolaus, Archbishop Haralambos was elevated to the office of metropolitan. Haralambos has sought to reaffirm the documented canonical position of the church within Orthodox Christianity.

The archdiocese established Saint Michael Academy in 1985 and sponsors the Holy Theotokos Monastery.

Headquarters

PO Box 7007
West Palm Beach, FL 33405

Core Beliefs

The UNAOCIE affirms apostolic succession, tracing its heritage to the apostle Andrew. The church also affirms the seven sacraments of the Orthodox Church.

Bibliography

Agadjanian, Alexander, Jerry Pankhurst, and Victor Roudometof, eds. *Eastern Orthodoxy in a Global Age: Tradition Faces the Twenty-First Century.* Lanham, MD: Rowman & Littlefield, 2005.

Davis, Nathaniel. *A Long Walk to Church: A Contemporary History of Russian Orthodoxy.* Boulder, CO: Westview, 2003.

Pospielovsky, Dimitry. *The Orthodox Church in the History of Russia.* Crestwood, NY: St. Vladimir's Seminary Press, 1998.

Scott Rushing

Ukrainian Orthodox Church

History

By the early twentieth century, Ukrainian Christians had begun to immigrate to the United States. These immigrants included both Orthodox and Roman Catholic followers of the Eastern Rite. In 1915, a number of parishes determined that the Ukrainian population should have its own jurisdiction. Bishop Germanos Shehadi of the Syrian Orthodox Church in the USA provided spiritual leadership during this time. In 1921, the Ukrainian Autocephalous Orthodox Church (UAOC) was formed in response to Ukraine's newly declared independence from Russia.

Archbishop John Theodorovich was appointed by the UAOC in 1924 to lead the American-Canadian diocese, which was named the Ukrainian Orthodox Church of the USA. One of the initial problems faced by the new diocese was that the UAOC had not received canonical recognition by mainstream Orthodoxy. In 1929, a second group of Ukrainian Orthodox Christians met in Allentown, Pennsylvania, and established itself as the Ukrainian Orthodox Church in America (UOCA). This group was formed primarily by Greek Catholics who disagreed with the Vatican about parish property ownership and enforced clerical celibacy. Joseph Zuk was initially elected as the administrator of the diocese, and in 1932, he was consecrated as bishop. Bishop Joseph died two years later, to be succeeded by Bohdan Spylka. Under Bishop Bohdan's leadership, the UOCA was received into the ecumenical patriarchate. At this time, the Ukrainian Orthodox Church of the USA and the Ukrainian Orthodox Church in America coexisted separately.

In 1948, Bishop Mstyslav Skrypnk emigrated from Ukraine to lead the Ukrainian Orthodox Church of Canada. The next year he moved to the United States, seeking to unify the rival Ukrainian Orthodox dioceses. As part of the agreement to unite the two existing jurisdictions, Archbishop John was reconsecrated by Bishop Mstyslav. In 1950, the two churches held separate synods at St. Volodymyr Cathedral in New York City. Unification was approved by both jurisdictions, and on October 13, a combined synod of unification took place. Archbishop John was elected metropolitan of the new church, while Bishop Mstyslav headed the consistory. While a number of Bishop Bohdan's parishes did join the new union, some of them rejected unification. The Ukrainian Orthodox Church in America, led by Bohdan, continued to exist separately.

Metropolitan John died in 1971 and was succeeded by Archbishop Mstyslav, who served as head of the church until his death in 1993. Under Mstyslav's leadership, the church dedicated the Ukrainian Cultural Center, the St. Andrew the First-Called Memorial Center, and St. Sophia Ukrainian Orthodox Theological Seminary.

In 1996, the Ukrainian Orthodox Church of the USA and the Ukrainian Orthodox Church in America were united under Metropolitan Constantine.

Leadership

Eastern Eparchy (Connecticut, Delaware, Massachusetts, Maryland, New Jersey, New York, Pennsylvania, Rhode Island): Archbishop Antony
Central Eparchy (Florida, Georgia, Ohio, western Pennsylvania): Metropolitan Constantine
Western Eparchy (Arizona, California, Colorado, Illinois, Indiana, Michigan, Minnesota, Oregon, Washington, Wisconsin, Ontario Province): Bishop Daniel

Core Beliefs

The Ukrainian Orthodox Church is united in faith and practice with world Orthodoxy. Ukrainian Orthodox churches affirm the authority of the seven ecumenical councils and the sacraments of baptism, Holy Communion, charismation, holy repentance, holy unction, holy matrimony, and holy orders. The Orthodox churches continue apostolic succession and pass on the apostolic tradition by written and spoken word.

Worship

Ukrainian Orthodox churches allow vocal, but not instrumental, music in worship.

Academic Institutions

St. Andrews College (Winnipeg, Manitoba, Canada)
St. Sophia Seminary (South Bound Brook, NJ)

Parachurch Organizations

St. Herman's House of Hospitality is a monastery located in Cleveland, Ohio. It has been in existence for over twenty years. The monastery primarily helps indigent men by feeding and clothing them as well as by providing emotional support and access to health and social services. The monastery averages eighty-four thousand meals and seventeen thousand showers per year.

Publications

Ukrainian Orthodox Word
Visynk

Websites

http://www.uocofusa.org/
http://www.uocc.ca/

Bibliography

Bilon, Peter. *Ukrainians and Their Church*. Johnstown, PA: Western Pennsylvania Branch of the UOL, 1953.

Krawchenko, Oleh. "Yesterday, Today, and Tomorrow." Orthodox Research Institute. http://www.orthodoxresearch institute.org/articles/church_history/oleh_krawchenko _yesterday.htm.

Serafim, Archimandrite. *The Quest for Orthodox Church Unity in America: A History of the Orthodox Church in North America in the Twentieth Century*. New York: Saints Boris and Gleb Press, 1973.

Scott Rushing

Friends

Evangelical Friends Church International

History

The Evangelical Friends Church International is one of the three largest Friends (Quaker) denominations, and it is the most conservative (regarding the importance of Jesus for salvation, moral issues, etc.) of the three main Friends groups (the other two are the Friends United Meeting and the Friends General Conference). The Friends originated with George Fox (1624–91) and began as the Religious Society of Friends in the 1640s in England. They migrated to the American colonies, where they were persecuted but eventually accepted; up to 50 percent of Rhode Island colonists were Friends. The colony of Pennsylvania was founded by William Penn in 1682 in part as a safe place where Friends could live. The Friends were eventually present in many of the colonies, with two signing the Declaration of Independence of the United States and three signing the United States Constitution. In 1877, ninety-five Friends met in Richmond, Indiana, and drafted the Richmond Declaration. As with the Friends United Meeting, this declaration defines the beliefs of the Evangelical Friends Church International in the absence of a creed.

In the early part of the twentieth century, the conflict between modernist and traditional ideologies affected the Friends as it did many churches. In 1926, some Friends withdrew from what today is known as the Friends United Meeting because they did not want to embrace many of the modernist ideas that were being accepted in the Friends United Meeting. This group went through several name changes, from the Association of Evangelical Friends in 1947 to the Evangelical Friends Association in 1965 to the Evangelical Friends Church International in 1989. Today the Evangelical Friends number approximately 140,000 members in 1,100 churches spread over 24 countries.

Headquarters

EFC/NA co EFC-ER
5350 Broadmoor Circle NW
Canton, OH 44709
Telephone: 330-493-1660

Core Beliefs

George Fox believed in a direct experience of God, sometimes known as the Inner Light. Many Friends accept this doctrine. Basic Quaker ideals of peace and pacifism are upheld. The mission of the Evangelical Friends Church International is "to help local Friends churches around the world meet the spiritual needs of their communities" (evangelicalfriends.org, "Home").

Website

http://www.evangelicalfriends.org/

Mark Nickens

Friends General Conference

History

One of the three largest Friends (Quaker) denominations, the Friends General Conference (FGC) is the most liberal of the three main Friends groups (the other two are the Evangelical Friends Church International and the Friends United Meeting). The Friends originated with George Fox (1624–91) and began as the Religious Society of Friends in the 1640s in England. They migrated to the American colonies, where they were persecuted but eventually accepted; up to 50 percent of Rhode Island colonists were Friends. The colony of Pennsylvania was founded by William Penn in 1682 in part as a safe place where Friends could live. The Friends were eventually present in many of the colonies, with two signing the Declaration of Independence of the United States and three signing the United States Constitution. A number of Quaker Friends gathered in Chautauqua, New York, in 1900 to form the FGC.

The FGC developed from the union of seven yearly meetings (a collection of churches in a region), which were all aligned with the Hicksite Friends. Elias Hicks (1748–1830) was a Friend who led a divisive movement within the Friends of the early nineteenth century. He held beliefs that centered on the Inner Light of each Christian giving guidance and repudiated certain biblical doctrines that other Friends held, such as the divinity of Christ and the need for everyone to receive salvation through Christ. By the late nineteenth century, the internal division transformed into an outward division and resulted in the development of the Friends General Conference in 1900.

Headquarters

Friends General Conference
1216 Arch Street #2B
Philadelphia, PA 19107
Telephone: 215-561-1700

Core Beliefs

George Fox believed in a direct experience of God, sometimes known as the Inner Light. Many Friends accept this doctrine. Basic Quaker ideals of peace and pacifism are upheld. The FGC does not visibly practice the rites of baptism and Communion nor accept religious symbolism.

Worship

FGC churches often follow what is known as "unprogrammed worship." This is the traditional Friends-style worship service and involves periods of silence in which Friends practice "expectant waiting." The congregation sits in silence, and individual members can speak what they believe God has told them. Sometimes no one speaks, and sometimes many people speak. FGC churches do not use paid leadership.

Statistics

Members: 32,000
Meetings (churches): 832

Website

http://www.fgcquaker.org/

Mark Nickens

Friends United Meeting

History

The Friends United Meeting (FUM) is one of the three largest Friends (Quaker) denominations (the other two are the Evangelical Friends Church International and the Friends General Conference) and of the three most resembles mainline Protestant denominations in theology and practices. The Friends originated with George Fox (1624–91) and began as the Religious Society of Friends in the 1640s in England. They migrated to the American colonies, where they were persecuted but eventually accepted; up to 50 percent of Rhode Island colonists were Friends. The colony of Pennsylvania was founded by William Penn in 1682 in part as a safe place where Friends could live. The Friends were eventually present in many of the colonies, with two signing the Declaration of Independence of the United States and three signing the United States Constitution. In 1887, ninety-five Friends met in Richmond, Indiana, and drafted the Richmond Declaration. While the FUM does not have a creed, this declaration came to define their beliefs.

The nineteenth and early twentieth centuries produced many modernist tensions that affected churches. The Friends were affected as several groups broke ties with other Friends. In 1902, a group of Friends gathered in Indianapolis, Indiana, and formed the Five Years Meeting of Friends in America. In 1966, this name was changed to the Friends United Meeting (FUM). The FUM is an association of twenty-six yearly meetings of like-minded Friends.

Headquarters

Friends United Meeting
101 Quaker Hill Drive
Richmond, IN 47374-1926
Telephone: 765-962-7573

Core Beliefs

The FUM holds to the Richmond Declaration of 1887, which was endorsed in 1902 at the organizational meeting of the FUM. George Fox believed in a direct experience of God, sometimes known as the Inner Light. Many Friends accept this doctrine. Basic Quaker ideals of peace and pacifism are upheld.

FUM churches do not visibly practice the rites of Communion and baptism nor accept religious symbolism. Many FUM meetings (churches) have pastors.

Worship

Many FUM meetings follow what adherents describe as "programmed worship," which follows a typical Protestant worship service. These meetings include regular readings from the Bible, songs, and a sermon. Some FUM churches include a period of silence.

Statistics

Members: 42,000
Meetings (churches): 425

Academic Institutions

Earlham College (Richmond, IN)
Earlham School of Religion (Richmond, IN)

Publication

Quaker Life magazine

Website

http://www.fum.org/

Mark Nickens

Philadelphia Yearly Meeting of the Friends

History

The Religious Society of Friends, or Quakers, meets in three types of settings: monthly, quarterly, and yearly meetings. The "monthly" meetings are weekly worship meetings at which members discuss concerns in the local organization. The quarterly meetings gather a designated region of local meetings. The yearly meetings are annual events that gather by specific region but also allow visitors from other yearly meetings to attend. Each meeting is wholly independent of the others, yet each contributes resources interdependently. The Philadelphia Yearly Meeting (PYM) of the Friends includes the areas of eastern Pennsylvania, southern New Jersey, all of Delaware, and eastern Maryland.

The PYM is among the oldest yearly meetings of the Friends. The origin of the PYM coincides with the establishment of Pennsylvania after the introduction of the Quaker faith to New England in the late seventeenth century by William Penn. On this territory, given to the estate of his father, William Penn sought to create the "Holy Experiment," where New Testament principles and freedom of conscience reigned.

The PYM started as one meeting, but the Hicksite/Orthodox schism of 1827 separated the meetings, although both were called PYM and met during the summer. In 1955, the two factions reunited to form the PYM that exists today. The PYM is staffed by both paid employees and volunteers.

Headquarters

1501 Cherry Street
Philadelphia, PA 19102

Core Beliefs

The Society of Friends, in general, is non-creedal. The PYM follows a guideline as expressed in *Faith and Practice*, which is revised per the belief in continuing revelation. *Faith and Practice* is a book of Christian discipline that details the beliefs and practices particular to the PYM. It was first adopted in 1955 and has since been revised in 1972, 1997, and 2002.

Website

http://www.pym.org/

Bibliography

Dandelion, Pink. *The Quakers: A Very Short Introduction.* Oxford: Oxford University Press, 2008.

Hamm, Thomas D. *The Quakers in America.* New York: Columbia University Press, 2003.

Philadelphia Yearly Meeting of the Religious Society of Friends. *Faith and Practice: A Book of Christian Discipline.* Philadelphia: Philadelphia Yearly Meeting, 1998.

Philadelphia Yearly Meeting of the Religious Society of Friends. *Vital and Growing: 2009 Annual Report.* Philadelphia: Philadelphia Yearly Meeting of the Religious Society of Friends, 2009.

Phuc Luu

Religious Society of Friends

History

The Religious Society of Friends (Quakers) emerged in seventeenth-century England, in addition to other religious groups, as a consequence of the Puritan Revolution (1625–60). The Society of Friends began with a vision. George Fox (1624–91) climbed Pendle Hill in Lancashire in June 1652 and received a vision of "a great people to be gathered" (Fox, *Autobiography*, 150). Robert Barclay (1648–90), Isaac Penington (1616–79), and William Penn (1644–1718) were among others who were attracted to the charismatic preaching of Fox. Margaret Fell, the wife of the deeply respected judge Thomas Fell, vice-chancellor of the duchy of Lancaster, attended several of Fox's meetings and was convicted by his challenge of an inward experience with God. Judge Fell never became a Quaker but did allow his wife to let the movement meet in their home at Swarthmoor Hall in Cumbria, near Ulverston. (Fox married Margaret some years following the death of Judge Fell.) Through the Kendal Fund, Margaret was able to finance the activities of Fox and assist those families who had been imprisoned during the Commonwealth period.

Although Fox never intended for the movement to be more than a plain and simple Christian fellowship and to encourage response to the Christ within every heart, the need for organization was soon apparent. Swarthmoor Hall became the headquarters of the movement, which spread throughout the country to the American colonies and continental Europe prior to the end of the seventeenth century. Throughout the 1660s, Fox encouraged local and county meetings to discuss issues and conduct business. He established an annual national meeting in 1668. Fox labored to convince people that every person possesses a divine Inner Light and that every heart is an altar or shrine of God. The nickname "Quaker" was first applied to Fox with derision by a prosecuting judge at Darby, England. The name was given to other groups who allegedly quaked (shivered and shook) with the power of God. Consequently, the preferred name is Friends based on Jesus's words in John 15:14.

Core Beliefs

The absence of a formal creed does not mean Quakers do not have core beliefs. The majority of yearly meetings adopt a book of discipline, frequently called *Faith and Practice*. Although there are differences within the Religious Society of Friends, most generally affirm belief in direct and immediate communion with God and commitment to living a life that demonstrates response to this Inner Light. Testimonies (principles) guide beliefs. Obedience to the Inner Light is the means of receiving more light and growing in knowledge of God.

Worship

Worship services vary as "programmed" (pastoral) or "unprogrammed."

Divisions and Splits

The distinct branches of Quakers in the United States include the Evangelical Friends Church International; the Friends General Conference; the Friends United Meeting; the Religious Society of Friends; and the Religious Society of Friends, Conservative. There is also the Committee of Latin American Friends. Although there is significant agreement among the groups, the differences primarily include manner of worship, missionary and evangelistic work, organizational affiliation, and theological emphasis.

Statistics

Approximate membership includes 1,700 Conservative Friends, 36,000 Evangelical Friends Church International, 32,000 Friends General Conference, 40,000 Friends United Meeting, and 6,700 Independent Friends. With all the groups included, there are approximately 1,000 Quaker congregations in the United States. Worldwide membership is approximately 360,000.

Largest Church

The largest congregation is Friends Church (Evangelical Friends Church International) in Yorba Linda, California.

Missionary and Evangelistic Work

Some branches do extensive missionary and evangelistic work in addition to social service, whereas others are primarily engaged in service work.

Academic Institutions

Azusa Pacific University (Azusa, CA)
Barclay College (Haviland, KS)
Bryn Mawr College (Bryn Mawr, PA)
Carolina Evangelical Divinity School (High Point, NC)
Cornell University (Ithaca, NY)
Earlham College and School of Religion (Richmond, IN)
Friends University (Wichita, KS)
George Fox University (Newberg, OR)
Global College, Long Island University (formerly Friends World) (Brooklyn, NY)
Guilford College (Greensboro, NC)
Haverford College (Haverford, PA)
Johns Hopkins University (Baltimore, MD)
Malone College (Canton, OH)
Swarthmore College (Swarthmore, PA)
Whittier College (Whittier, CA)
William Penn University (Oskaloosa, IA)
Wilmington College (Wilmington, OH)

Publications

Friends Journal, which is published by the liberal, unprogrammed tradition, serves the Quaker community and the wider community of spiritual seekers. The Friends United Meeting publishes *Quaker Life* magazine. Quaker Books is an imprint of Friends General Conference. Barclay

Press serves the Quaker community through various publications.

Websites

http://www.quaker.org/
http://www.religioussocietyoffriends.org/

Bibliography

Barbour, Hugh, and J. William Frost. *The Quakers.* Westport, CT: Greenwood, 1988.

Birkel, Michael L. *Silence and Witness: The Quaker Tradition.* Maryknoll, NY: Orbis, 2004.

Cooper, Wilmer A. *A Living Faith: An Historical and Comparative Study of Quaker Beliefs.* Richmond, IN: Friends United Press, 1990.

Fox, George. *An Autobiography.* Edited by Rufus M. Jones. Philadelphia: Ferris & Leach, 1903.

Gillman, Harvey. *A Light That Is Shining: An Introduction to the Quakers.* London: Quaker Home Service, 1988.

Ingle, H. Larry. *First among Friends: George Fox and the Creation of Quakerism.* New York: Oxford University Press, 1994.

———. *Quakers in Conflict: The Hicksite Reformation.* Knoxville: University of Tennessee Press, 1986.

Moretta, John A. *William Penn and the Quaker Legacy.* New York: Pearson Longman, 2007.

Oliver, John W., Jr., Charles L. Cherry, and Caroline L. Cherry, eds. *Founded by Friends: The Quaker Heritage of Fifteen American Colleges and Universities.* Lanham, MD: Scarecrow, 2007.

Penny, Norman, ed. *The Journal of George Fox.* London: J. M. Dent and Sons, 1924.

Wildes, Harry Emerson. *Voice of the Lord: A Biography of George Fox.* Philadelphia: University of Pennsylvania Press, 1965.

Ron J. Bigalke

Religious Society of Friends, Conservative

History

The Religious Society of Friends, Conservative was formed in the early nineteenth century in response to several divisions among Quakers. Conservative Quakers adhered to the traditional Quakerism of John Wilber (1774–1856). They are regarded as conservative not in regard to theology but as an indication of their intention to preserve historical Quakerism (as opposed to liberal Hicksite Quakerism and pastoral Gurneyite Quakerism).

Leadership

The Conservative Quakers belong to three yearly meetings: Iowa Yearly Meeting, North Carolina Yearly Meeting, and Ohio Yearly Meeting.

Core Beliefs

The core beliefs and practices of Conservative Quakers are diverse. Therefore, only representative statements are possible.

God is accessible to all people, whether Quaker or not. Jesus Christ is the Inner Light who will teach believers individually. Therefore, the Bible is secondary to the Inner Light of Jesus Christ, who is the primary authority of truth. Scripture is regarded as helpful but subordinate to experiencing the Inner Light. The Inner Light is the means of salvation and convicts of sin, even if Scripture is absent. Conservative Quakers reject the doctrine of original sin. Humanity is born innocent with a tendency to sin. Physical sacraments are shadows and incapable of providing the recipient with grace. Water baptism is an ineffectual shadow that may accompany genuine baptism of the Holy Spirit. The grace of God to overcome sin is available to all people. A holy and obedient life is evidence of the justifying and sanctifying Inner Light of Jesus Christ. Salvation can be lost if the Inner Light is rejected.

Conservative Quakers are characterized by "waiting worship" and "free gospel ministry" as an understanding of the immediate presence of Jesus Christ as head of the church. They stress the importance of speaking plainly and simply, which means using not only the plain speech of "thee" and "thou" but also other peculiarities of language. They refuse to take oaths in accordance with the plain and simple truth. As they seek to withdraw from the world in certain significant aspects, plainness is applied to dress and manners, an act that is thought to conform to the simplicity of the gospel. The teaching of Christ is interpreted as opposition to war; accordingly, Conservative Quakers seek to be peacemakers. They are cautious of affiliation with others of the Religious Society of Friends.

Worship

Conservative Quakers reject programmed (preplanned) worship. The service is characterized by the practice of waiting worship. Experiencing the Holy Spirit may sometimes result in a message, prayer, song, or even complete silence. All people are regarded as able to commune directly and immediately with God. Unplanned and voluntary ministry is worship in Spirit and in Truth. The manner of daily living is sacramental and an expression of worship. Quaker actions have included peace and social witness, prison reform, prohibition, the Underground Railroad, the United Nations, and women's suffrage.

Divisions and Splits

John Joseph Gurney (1788–1847) influenced Quakers in England to affirm evangelical doctrines, such as the authority of the Bible. Elias Hicks (1748–1830) opposed Gurney, which resulted in the first schism of the Quakers. The Hicksite Quakers believed the Inner Light was more authoritative than the Bible. In 1827, the Gurneyite and Hicksite groups divided. The Gurneyite Quakers emigrated to the United States and experienced another division with the followers of John Wilbur. The Wilburite Quakers did not deny the authority of the Bible but believed Gurney did not give enough emphasis to the Inner Light. The Evangelical Friends Alliance was formed in 1965 by members of the Gurneyite Friends United Meeting who desired a more evangelical emphasis and denominational unity. The Evangelical Friends Church International remains more conservative and evangelical than other liberal and non-evangelical Quaker churches.

Statistics

There are no central records available. Most statistics demonstrate decreasing numbers of members, who now total approximately seventeen hundred. The Iowa Yearly Meeting seemed to create a revived interest in Conservative Quakerism throughout the past two decades. The largest Conservative Quaker Meetings are in Iowa, North Carolina, and Ohio. Meetings can also be found in Canada and Greece.

Publications

Members of Glenside Friends Meeting began Quaker Heritage Press to publish early historical Quaker writings. The *Journal of the North Carolina Yearly Meeting (Conservative)* is an occasional publication of historical and present circumstances. The *Conservative Friend* is an official quarterly newsletter of the Wider Fellowship of Conservative Friends of Ohio Yearly Meeting of Friends.

Websites

Iowa Yearly Meeting: http://www.iymc.org/
North Carolina Yearly Meeting: http://www.ncymc.org/
Ohio Yearly Meeting: http://www.ohioyearlymeeting.org/

Bibliography

Cooper, Wilmer A. *Growing Up Plain: The Journey of a Public Friend*. Richmond, IN: Friends United Press, 1999.

Hamm, Thomas D. *The Transformation of American Quakerism: Orthodox Friends, 1800–1907*. Bloomington: Indiana University Press, 1992.

Heiss, Willard C. *A Brief History of Western Yearly Meeting of Conservative Friends and the Separation of 1877*. Indianapolis: Woolman, 1963.

Hinshaw, Seth B. *The Carolina Quaker Experience, 1665–1985: An Interpretation*. Greensboro: North Carolina Yearly Meeting, North Carolina Friends Historical Society, 1984.

Holden, David E. W. *Friends Divided: Conflict and Division in the Society of Friends*. Richmond, IN: Friends United Press, 1988.

Morlan, Charles P. *A Brief History of Ohio Yearly Meeting of the Religious Society of Friends (Conservative)*. Barnesville, OH: Representative Meeting, 1959.

Morse, Kenneth S. P. *A History of Conservative Friends*. Barnesville, OH: self-published, 1962.

Wilbur, John. *Journal of the Life of John Wilbur, a Minister of the Gospel in the Society of Friends; with Selections from His Correspondence, &c.* Providence: Whitney, 1859.

Ron J. Bigalke

Fundamentalist

Berean Fellowship of Churches

History

The Berean Fellowship of Churches is a small, Bible-focused, vigorously evangelistic denomination located mainly in the Midwest. In 1935, Dr. Ivan E. Olsen, a graduate of Denver Bible Institute, became the first pastor of the Berean Fundamental Church (known as the Church of the Open Bible until January 5, 1935), an independent congregation in North Platte, Nebraska. Olsen then assisted in planting sixteen other churches in surrounding communities, and in 1947, the churches officially formed the Berean Fundamental Church Council Inc. At present, the Berean Fellowship is comprised of about sixty churches in ten states. Nebraska holds over half of the denomination's churches at thirty-three congregations. There are also assemblies in Alabama, California, Colorado, Kansas, Minnesota, Oregon, South Dakota, Tennessee, Wyoming, and Canada. The fellowship has maintained strong ties with Maranatha Bible Camp since its formation in the 1930s and supports several independent faith missions, such as CRU (Campus Crusade for Christ).

Headquarters

Berean Fellowship of Churches
PO Box 234
Broken Bow, NE 68820
Telephone: 1-855-OUR-BEREAN or 308-381-5964
Email: office@BFCnetwork.org

Core Beliefs

The vision of the Berean Fellowship of Churches is "to glorify Christ in our generation through aggressively establishing churches worldwide, training believers in Christ-likeness, and reaching the lost with the hope of the Gospel" (*Constitution of the Berean Fundamental Church Council*). A strong component of the denomination is an emphasis on advancing the gospel through evangelism, church planting, and world missions.

The Berean Fellowship is a trinitarian group that places a strong emphasis on the authority of Scripture and asserts the verbal, plenary inspiration and inerrancy of the original manuscripts. Members also hold to the incarnation and deity of Christ, the virgin birth, substitutionary atonement, and the bodily resurrection of Christ. Salvation occurs solely by the grace of God through faith in Christ alone. They are unambiguous regarding the actual existence of Satan and the eternal punishment of the unbeliever. They believe that the return of Christ will follow the rapture and precede the millennial kingdom (premillennialism). They understand the sign gifts to have ceased (cessationism) and should not be expected in the church today.

Overall, the local Berean churches enjoy flexibility in methodology while agreeing on a clearly defined doctrinal statement (*10 Articles of Faith*), a common constitution (*Constitution of the Berean Fundamental Church Council* and the *Local Berean Church Constitution*), and a shared vision for worldwide impact.

Website

http://www.weareberan.org/

Bibliography

Mead, Frank S., Samuel S. Hill, and Craig D. Atwood. "Berean Fundamental Church." *Handbook of Denominations in the United States.* 13th ed. Nashville: Abingdon, 2010.

Alyssa Lehr Evans

Fellowship of Fundamental Bible Churches

History

The Fellowship of Fundamental Bible Churches (FFBC) is a group of independent churches that share the same foundational Christian beliefs. Because the fellowship is not a denomination, the churches in the FFBC operate independently and have no financial obligations to the fellowship. The churches are expected to teach fundamental Christians beliefs, but the FFBC does not have control over the churches in the fellowship.

The FFBC began in Atlantic City, New Jersey, in 1939 during a period when several Methodist denominations sought to merge into one denomination, the United Methodist Church. A number of Methodist Protestant Church pastors opposed this merge because they believed there was apostasy and liberal leadership in the emerging denomination. Thus, these pastors and church delegates walked out of the group and formed their own coalition to stand united for fundamental biblical truths and to support and serve one another. From 1939 to 1985, this fellowship was known as the Methodist Protestant Church and the Bible Protestant Church, but in 1985, it changed its name to the Fellowship of Fundamental Bible Churches, a name members deemed described their common beliefs more accurately and distinctly separated them from the Methodist denomination.

Headquarters

284 Whig Lane Road
Monroeville, NJ 08343
Telephone: 856-881-0057

Leadership

President: Dan Boyce

Core Beliefs

The Fellowship of Fundamental Bible Churches firmly stands against apostasy, false teaching, ungodliness, and fanatical cults. The FFBC holds to the following core beliefs (fellowshipoffundamentalbiblechurches.wordpress.com, "FFBC Distinctives" and "FFBC Positions"):

Literal interpretation of Scripture: the Bible is inerrant, infallible, and the final authority for faith and practice.

Essential doctrines of the Christian faith: the Bible is the inspired Word of God, Christ was born of the Virgin Mary and is also divine, Christ's death was an atonement for human sin, Christ physically rose from the dead, and Christ is coming again.

Dispensational (not covenantal) theology: there will be "a pretribulational rapture of the church and a premillennial return of Christ to establish his thousand-year reign."

Separatism: the FFBC should not be associated with organizations or individuals that oppose biblical fundamentals or that support the National or World Council of Churches, the National Association of Evangelicals, or other similar organizations.

Evangelism: evangelism and mission-oriented outreach is important.

Baptism: baptism is by immersion only and is for believers only.

Spiritual gifts: spiritual gifts (e.g., speaking in tongues) ceased after the New Testament was written.

Marriage: marriage is a divine and sacred institution that unites one man and one woman in a lifelong bond.

Based on the FFBC's core beliefs, pastors in FFBC churches preach from the Bible, do not perform infant baptisms, and do not recommend ministry candidates who have been divorced and remarried.

Website

https://fellowshipoffundamentalbiblechurches.wordpress.com/

Bibliography

Conant, Newton. *How God Delivered Thirty-Four Churches.* Camden, NJ: Bible Protestant Press, 1964.

"Fellowship of Fundamental Bible Churches." The Association of Religion Data Archives. http://www.thearda.com/denoms/D_1433.asp.

"Fellowship of Fundamental Bible Churches." https://fellowshipoffundamentalbiblechurches.wordpress.com. "FFBC Distinctives" and "FFBC Positions."

Linda Gray

Grace Gospel Fellowship

History

Founded in Evansville, Indiana, in 1944 by John Cowan O'Hair, Charles Baker, and Cornelius Stam, Grace Gospel Fellowship is a fundamentalist association of churches. O'Hair was a pastor, radio minister, and author of *The Unsearchable Riches of Christ*, a collection of Bible studies published in 1941. He and Baker were prominent figures in the dispensationalist movement (which taught that historical periods reflected different covenants with God), as was Stam, who had been a pastor and was Baker's cofounder of the Milwaukee Bible Institute.

At a gathering of O'Hair, Baker, and other dispensationalist pastors in 1943, the idea for the fellowship was born; the following year, the time of its formal organization, the constitution was adopted.

Headquarters

1011 Aldon SW
Grand Rapids, MI 49509

Leadership

President: Frosty Hansen

Core Beliefs

The Grace Gospel Fellowship views all those with true faith in Christ, regardless of denomination, as part of the true church. The fellowship believes in the divine inspiration of Scripture, the doctrine of the Trinity, the deity of Christ and of the Holy Spirit, the sinfulness of all people, redemption by grace through faith in Christ's shed blood and finished work, the physical resurrection of the dead, and eternal punishment of the unredeemed and eternal blessedness for the redeemed. Doctrines about the end-times are premillennial and pretribulational.

The fellowship not only teaches the centrality of the apostle Paul's teachings on grace but also asserts that the church began with Paul, prior to his earliest writings.

Finances

The Grace Gospel Fellowship is a member of the Ethics and Financial Integrity Commission, which seeks to ensure good stewardship of financial resources. Financial records are public record, with the exception of names of donors and amounts of their gifts.

Missionary and Evangelistic Work

The founders of the fellowship helped to launch Worldwide Grace Testimony in 1939 (five years before the fellowship's formation), which started its missionary work in Zaire, then Belgian Congo. Grace Gospel News began publication in 1946, and in 1951, the newly formed Bethesda Mission of the Bethesda Free Church in Minneapolis sent missionaries to Bolivia.

The creation of Grace Ministries International (GMI) resulted from the merger of Grace Mission and Bethesda Mission in 1984. Its missionary endeavors currently involve Australia, Bolivia, Congo, Costa Rica, India, Puerto Rico, Tanzania, the United States, and Zambia and offer assistance to daughter churches in Brazil, Uruguay, and Curacao. Establishment of indigenous churches, training of church workers, medical work, education, and community development are all within the scope of its activities. GMI has a fifteen-member board and publishes a newsletter, *Grace Ministries around the World*.

Church Missions Link has fostered interest in world missions on the part of local congregations since 1997. The Sharbuilders Programs offers financial assistance to groups needing facilities in which to worship. The Pastoral Subsidy Program assists smaller churches in hiring pastors.

Academic Institution

Grace Bible College was established in 1939 as Milwaukee Bible Institute by Rev. Charles F. Baker of the Fundamental Bible Church, later a founder of Grace Gospel Fellowship. Originally created to train laity and Sunday school teachers, the institute came to be known for its promotion of dispensationalism and the centrality of the Pauline revelation as the fellowship's official educational institution. It was renamed Milwaukee Bible College in 1953 and adopted its present name in 1961, when it moved to suburban Grand Rapids, Michigan. In 1991, the college was accredited to grant professional degrees. Today Grace Bible College offers not only three-year programs but also two-, four-, and five-year offerings that train students in ministry and Christian service. Working in conjunction with the fellowship, the college formed the Vernon Schutz Chair of Pastoral Ministries to encourage students to become pastors.

Publications

Truth magazine is a quarterly publication offering news about the denomination and its organizations as well as Bible studies pertaining to the dispensation of grace. It was started in 1950 as a joint venture of the Milwaukee Bible Institute (later Grace Bible College) and Worldwide Grace Testimony, a foreign mission board established in 1939.

Grace Publications, formerly operated by Grace Mission and today directly operated by the fellowship, produces literature reflecting the fellowship's point of view.

Website

http://www.ggfusa.org/

Sarah Claudine Day

House of God, which is the Church of the Living God, Pillar and Ground of the Truth

History

The House of God, which is the Church of the Living God, Pillar and Ground of the Truth is a predominantly black Pentecostal church founded in 1919 by Mary Magdalena Lewis L. Tate, who was called an apostle and elder of Jesus Christ. She started work in the Church of the Living God in 1903 in Steel Springs, Tennessee, and in Paducah, Kentucky. Her ministry stressed a call to holiness, by which she meant clean living, sanctification, and perfection. She later moved to Paris, Tennessee, where she continued to preach boldly to both blacks and whites. Her work then carried her to Alabama, where she converted over nine hundred people.

She and her followers, who were called "Do Rights," promoted a teaching based on John 15:3 that they described as "the Cleanliness of the Word." After her own baptism of the Holy Ghost, she baptized numerous converts and organized them into "bands" instead of churches. These bands were united as the Church of the Living God, Pillar and Ground of the Truth. Mother Tate was named the first overseer of the church, and she traveled and preached the gospel with her two sons in Tennessee. She presided over the first general assembly of the church in Greenville, Alabama. Churches were established in Georgia, and an assembly was held in Waycross in 1911. By 1914, elders and bishops had been appointed. By 1916, churches had been established in twenty states, including Tennessee, Kentucky, Florida, and Mississippi, as well as the District of Columbia and some foreign countries; they had been established in every state of the union by 1924.

In 1929, Mother Tate appointed Bishop A. H. White as her successor. The general assembly elected him senior bishop of all churches connected with House of God, which is the Church of the Living God, Pillar and Ground of the Truth, which had been incorporated in Pennsylvania. Bishop White expanded the church's efforts to include Church of the Living God Publishing House, a convalescent home, White's Theological Bible School and Business Institute, and a radio broadcast. The name Church of the Living God is used by many branches of the denomination.

Headquarters

PO Box 331169
Philadelphia, PA 19142-9998
Email: information@houseofgodclg.org

Leadership

President general: Bishop David E. Drone

Core Beliefs

The Church of the Living God believes in biblical infallibility, the virgin birth of Christ, repentance from sin, the atonement by the substitutionary death and the shed blood of Jesus Christ, salvation by grace, baptism by immersion in water, sanctification, the filling and indwelling of the Holy Spirit in the believer's life, the church as the body and bride of Christ, the operations of gifts in the church, the Great Commission, and the imminent return of Jesus Christ.

Website

http://www.houseofgodclg.org/

George Thomas Kurian

Independent Fundamental Churches of America

History

The Independent Fundamental Churches of America (IFCA) organized in 1930 in Cicero, Illinois, as a group of independent churches, pastors, organizations, and laymen with the common interests and goals of proclaiming the gospel of Christ and teaching believers. The association was created in opposition to modernism and in support of orthodox biblical ministry and evangelism. The IFCA exists to equip, partner with, and strengthen local churches in their work toward fulfilling the Great Commission.

Headquarters

PO Box 810
3520 Fairlanes
Grandville, MI 49468-0810
Telephone: 616-531-1840

Leadership

Executive director: Les Lofquist

Core Beliefs

The Independent Fundamental Churches of America holds to the following core beliefs: the Old and New Testaments are the inspired Word of God; God is one in three persons; Christ was fully God and fully man, born of the Virgin Mary, and redeemed humanity through his death on the cross and physical resurrection; mankind is totally depraved; salvation is received by personal faith in Jesus and is permanent; Christians should distance themselves from religious apostasy and all worldly sin; the gift of miracles ceased at the close of the New Testament canon; local churches should be autonomous; water baptism and the Lord's Supper are scriptural and serve as a testimony to the church; and the unsaved will receive everlasting punishment.

The IFCA opposes the following religious movements: ecumenism, which seeks to unify all religions and potentially threatens to alter core beliefs; neo-orthodoxy, which while adhering to some orthodox beliefs (e.g., the transcendence of God) departs from orthodoxy by denying biblical inerrancy and by elevating religious experience over biblical revelation; and finally, neoevangelicalism/neoconservatism, which emphasizes the social application of the gospel, moderates Christian beliefs to make Christianity more acceptable to nonbelievers, and is inconsistent with Scripture.

Core Practices

Core practices include separation from religious apostasy and worldly pleasures, practices, and associations; expository preaching and a commitment to proclaiming the historic and fundamental teachings of Scripture; holy living and personal integrity based on biblical morality; raising up and mentoring subsequent generations of biblical leaders; establishing local churches and proclaiming the gospel worldwide; responding to physical and emotional needs through God's love; fervent prayer; generous financial stewardship; and facilitating ministry skills to reach people from all generations and diversities.

Controversies

In 1947, the IFCA discussed "scriptural options regarding divorce, remarriage, and qualifications for local church leaders and IFCA membership in light of 1 Timothy 3:2," but no decision was made (ifca.org, "Committee on Divorce and IFCA"). The topic has been brought up at several IFCA conventions since, and in 2006, a decision was finally made clarifying that church pastors and leaders could not serve if they were divorced.

In 1997, the IFCA adopted a resolution reiterating its view on the inerrancy of Scripture and rejecting certain translations of the Bible (e.g., NIV) that "strive for political correctness" because such translations "have great potential for either obscuring or distorting the doctrines of Scripture resulting in grave error" (ifca

.org, "Proposed Resolution on the Cambridge Resolution"). In 2002, the IFCA rejected the TNIV translation on the same basis.

Finances

The Independent Fundamental Churches of America is an organization of autonomous local churches; therefore, financial accountability is done at the local church level.

Section 3 from the IFCA constitution (1930) states that "a qualified independent accountant shall conduct an annual review of the financial records and the financial procedures of this organization. A report of the findings shall be included as part of the financial report to the annual convention."

Growth

The IFCA believes that church growth is most effective when it involves building smaller churches instead of expanding ones already planted. It is believed that numerous small churches are more stable and fit the mission model of church planting. A recent IFCA statement explains the commitment "to aggressive involvement in planting, establishing, and nurturing biblical, local churches in the United States of America" (ifca.org, "Vital Signs for Healthy Churches").

Missionary and Evangelistic Work

The IFCA views missionary and evangelistic work as important and commanded in Scripture. To this end, the IFCA has established two evangelistic programs: Vision America and Vision World.

Publication

Voice, an online magazine, http://www.ifca.org/site/default.asp?sec_id=140001509

Website

http://www.ifca.org/

Bibliography

"The Independent Fundamental Churches of America." http://www.ifca.org/. "Committee on Divorce and IFCA," "An Old Paradigm," "Proposed Resolution on the Cambridge Resolution," and "Vital Signs for Healthy Churches."

LePeau, Andrew. "As Different as We Think." *Books & Culture* (March/April 2010). http://www.ctlibrary.com/bc/2010/marapr/asdifferentwethink.html.

Mead, Frank S., Samuel S. Hill, and Craig D. Atwood. *Handbook of Denominations in the United States*. 13th ed. Nashville: Abingdon, 2010.

Linda Gray

Holiness

American Rescue Workers

History

The American Rescue Workers is a national organization and socially active Holiness Church founded in 1884 by Thomas E. Moore, formerly of the Salvation Army. Including former members of the Gospel Mission Corps as well as former members of the Salvation Army, the group was known as the Salvation Army until 1890 and from 1890 to 1913 as the American Salvation Army. It is operated on a quasi-military pattern similar to that of the Salvation Army. Its membership includes officers (clergy), soldiers/adherents (laity), members of activity groups, and volunteers who serve as advisors and associates. The American Rescue Workers stresses its role as an evangelical church, not merely as a social service organization.

Headquarters

25 Ross Street
Williamsport, PA 17701
Telephone: 570-323-8694
Email: amersewk@pespower.net

Leadership

Commander in chief: General Claude S. Astin Jr.

Core Beliefs

The mission of the American Rescue Workers is based on Matthew 25:36–46. The organization is orthodox and trinitarian. Members believe in the deity of Jesus Christ and the redeeming work of the Holy Spirit. Its social work is rooted in its view that faith in Christ is the solution to all social ills. Practical assistance to the needy is deeply intertwined with evangelistic work.

Website

http://www.arwus.com/

George Thomas Kurian

Christian and Missionary Alliance

History

Founded in 1887 by Canadian Presbyterian minister Albert Benjamin (A. B.) Simpson (1843–1919) as two interdenominational parachurch organizations headquartered in New York City, the Christian Alliance and the Evangelical Missionary Alliance merged together as the Christian and Missionary Alliance (C&MA) in 1897, officially becoming a denomination in 1974.

Simpson's purpose was to unite people from all denominations with a common bond emphasizing holiness, faith, healing, and missionary vision in what he called "the higher Christian life." Simpson outlined a fourfold gospel of presenting Jesus Christ as Savior, Sanctifier, Healer, and Coming King.

In 1883, Simpson founded Berachah Healing Home and the Missionary Training Institute, the first Bible institute in America, now a fully accredited four-year liberal arts college known as Nyack College.

Headquarters

PO Box 35000
8595 Explorer Drive
Colorado Springs, CO 80920
Telephone: 719-599-5999

Leadership

C&MA church polity blends presbyterial and congregational models. A biannual general council is the decision-making body. A president and board of directors constitute the executive branch. The C&MA is divided into geographical and ethnic districts, led by district superintendents. Women can be licensed and/or consecrated (similar to ordination) and may serve in a wide variety of ministry roles, except for elder and pastor.

Core Beliefs

The C&MA is an evangelical denomination that affirms the doctrines of the Trinity, virgin birth, deity of Christ, inerrancy of Scripture, salvation by grace through faith, believer's baptism by immersion, and premillennial second coming of Christ. The two main distinctives of the C&MA are a belief in a sanctifying filling of the Spirit subsequent to conversion (believing all spiritual gifts are operative today) and a rejection of the Pentecostal belief in tongues as the evidence of Spirit filling.

Statistics

United States membership: over 420,000

United States churches: over 2,000

Worldwide membership: over 4 million in more than 80 nations (indigenous churches often take a different name). It is the largest evangelical denomination in countries such as the Philippines, Syria, and Vietnam.

Four retirement centers

Missionary and Evangelistic Work

The C&MA in the United States has 888 missionaries in 81 mission fields worldwide and has one of the highest mission per capita giving of any denomination.

Academic Institutions

The C&MA has five colleges and two seminaries in the United States and Canada:

Alliance Theological Seminary (Nyack, NY)
Ambrose University College (Calgary, Alberta, Canada)
A. W. Tozer Theological Seminary (Redding, CA)
Crown College (St. Bonafacius, MN)
Nyack College (Nyack, NY)
Simpson University (Redding, CA)
Toccoa Falls College (Toccoa, GA)

It also has seminaries in Southeast Asia, South America, and Africa.

Parachurch Organization

CAMA Services

Publication

Alliance Life, published monthly

Website

http://www.cmalliance.org/

Bibliography

King, Paul L. *Genuine Gold: The Cautiously Charismatic Story of the Early Christian and Missionary Alliance.* Tulsa: Word and Spirit Press, 2006.

Nicholas, Robert L., John S. Sawin, and Samuel J. Stoesz. *All for Jesus.* Camp Hill, PA: Christian Publications, 1986.

Simpson, A. B. *The Fourfold Gospel.* Harrisburg: Christian Publications, n.d.

Tozer, A. W. *Wingspread.* Camp Hill, PA: Christian Publications, 1943.

Paul L. King

Church of Christ (Holiness) U.S.A.

History

The Church of Christ (Holiness) U.S.A., like its sister denomination, the Church of God in Christ, traces its origin to the work of Charles Price Jones. Jones was an African American missionary Baptist pastor, first in Alabama and later in Mississippi, who expounded a teaching of Holiness in 1896. Joined by W. S. Pleasant, J. A. Jeter, Charles Harrison Mason, and others, Jones conducted a Holiness convention in 1897 at his church, Mt. Helm Baptist Church, which was renamed Church of Christ the following year. When Jones and the others were expelled from the Jackson Baptist Association, the group took the name Christ Association of Mississippi of Baptized Believers in Christ in 1900; six years later, the leadership of the Holiness movement agreed to recognize the group by a name suggested by C. H. Mason, Church of God in Christ.

Later in 1906, an assembly of Holiness clergy sent two of Jones's early associates, Jeter and Mason, along with D. J. Young, to William Seymour's revival on Azusa Street in Los Angeles, where the Pentecostal movement was born. Mason and Young embraced Seymour's doctrine of the baptism of the Holy Spirit and won over a large enough contingent of followers to create a significant rift at the 1907 Holiness convention: Mason and Young adopted the Pentecostal positions of Azusa Street, stressing supernatural manifestations of baptism in the Holy Spirit, such as speaking in tongues; Jones retained his original Holiness perspective. For several years, both factions laid claim to the name Church of God in Christ, until Mason's Pentecostals incorporated as COGIC. The Holiness faction then adopted the name Church of Christ Holiness and was chartered as Church of Christ (Holiness) U.S.A. in 1920.

Headquarters

329 East Monument Street
PO Box 3622
Jackson, MS 39207
Telephone: 601-353-0222
Email: everything@cochusa.com

Leadership

National president: Bishop Vernon Kennebrew

Core Beliefs

The Church of Christ (Holiness) U.S.A. accepts the doctrine of the Trinity. It believes that sin is present in all people and that those who repent and have faith in Christ's atonement will be pardoned and resurrected in glory. The unjust will be resurrected to experience eternal punishment. The church stresses the need for holiness in personal conduct. Its sacraments are baptism (by immersion) and the Lord's Supper, which is seen as symbolic and utilizes unfermented wine. Although not a sacrament, foot washing is practiced. Members see the gift of the Holy Spirit as universally present among believers. While glossolalia (speaking in tongues) is not rejected, it is not seen as a necessary corollary to the gift of the Holy Spirit. The church believes that the Bible teaches that divine healing is available to believers who are sick.

Website

http://www.cochusa.com/

Sarah Claudine Day

Church of God (Anderson, Indiana)

History

The Church of God (Anderson, Indiana) was established in 1881 as an outgrowth of a movement seeking to promote Christian unity as well as personal holiness. Its leading figure was Daniel S. Warner, who rejected the hierarchies and creeds of existing denominations. Arguing that the church should be guided only by the Holy Spirit and Scripture, Warner and his followers did not seek to create a new denomination but rather to stress dedication to Christ across denominational lines.

Headquarters

PO Box 2420
Anderson, IN 46018
Telephone: 765-642-0256

Leadership

General director: Ronald V. Duncan, DMin, DD

Congregational in government, the Church of God (Anderson, Indiana) offers autonomy to local congregations. There are voluntary associations of ministers at the state, regional, and national levels. There is an annual North American Convention in Anderson, Indiana, including ministers as well as lay delegates.

Core Beliefs

The Church of God (Anderson, Indiana) has embraced teachings in the Wesleyan and Pietist traditions, including the divine inspiration of Scripture, forgiveness of sin achieved through Christ's atonement and individual repentance, and the personal return of Christ. Baptism is by immersion and, like the Lord's Supper, is viewed as symbolic and not mandatory. Foot washing is performed to represent the Christian's dedication to service. Unlike similarly named Holiness groups in Tennessee and the Carolinas, the Church of God headquartered in Anderson, Indiana, does not emphasize Pentecostal practices such as speaking in tongues. There are no formal requirements for membership; rather, conduct consistent with the conversion experience is regarded as evidence of membership.

Statistics

Congregations in the United States and Canada: 2,200
Average weekend attendance in US and Canadian congregations: approximately 250,000, largely in the Midwest, in western Pennsylvania, and along the Pacific Coast
Worldwide presence: approximately 7,500 churches with more than 1.1 million adherents in 89 countries and territories

Missionary and Evangelistic Work

Specific areas of ministry include those dealing with education, children and youth, seniors, Hispanics, Native Americans, social justice and relief work, pastoral health, leadership development, church multiplication, and chaplain ministries. Christian Women Connection encourages fellowship, service, and support for missions; Churchmen of the Church of God sponsors study groups and recruits participants for other Christian groups and social service projects. Church of God Ministries was created by the general assembly in 1997 to coordinate various ministry efforts in the United States and to partner with similar bodies in Canada. (There are similar organizations in Kenya, Argentina, Japan, and other countries.) Its objectives are established by the grassroots church. Fundraising for Church of God Ministries is coordinated by World Ministry Advance, which offers donors guidance in the stewardship process to ensure funding of the World Ministries budget. The North American Convention (formerly the Anderson Camp Meeting or the International Convention) conducts evangelistic meetings, conferences, and workshops.

The Church of God (Anderson, Indiana) launched its foreign mission efforts in 1891 with the sending of a missionary to Mexico. Today three programs exist to further missionary activity: Living Link offers career missionaries the support of specific congregations and individuals; Project Link directs churches and members to mission projects needing support; and Eye on the World offers individuals and groups the opportunity to participate in trips that expose them to global mission work.

Affiliations

Partners in Ministry of the Church of God (Anderson, Indiana) is made up of independent ministries that reflect the church's values and teachings. They include the American Indian Council Inc. (Sanders, AZ), the Hispanic Council of the Church of God (conciliocog.org), and the National Association of the Church of God (West Middlesex, PA).

Academic Institutions

Anderson University and School of Theology (Anderson, IN)
Gardner College (Camrose, Alberta, Canada)
Mid-America Christian University (Oklahoma City, OK)
Warner Pacific College (Portland, OR)
Warner University (Lake Wales, FL)

Parachurch Organizations

The general assembly of the Church of God (Anderson, Indiana) recognizes endorsed agencies as co-workers in the pursuit of its ministry objectives. An endorsed agency is autonomous and has responsibilities not addressed by Church of God Ministries; at the same time, it agrees to adopt the principles of the Church of God and to seek approval of its officials from the general assembly. Endorsed agencies may receive financial support from the church. They include the church's academic institutions as well as its board of pensions.

Electronic Media

Christians Broadcasting Hope offers radio broadcasts in many parts of the United States and around the globe.

Publications

CHOGnews is an e-newsletter providing monthly news. Communion Together contains inspiration for ministry leadership and is published six times a year. Multiplication Moments, an e-letter, discusses the health and growth of the church. The Church of God (Anderson, Indiana) is associated with Warner Press, also of Anderson, Indiana.

Website

http://www.jesusisthesubject.org/

Sarah Claudine Day

Church of God, Holiness

History

The Church of God, Holiness began in 1886 with the founding of a congregation in Centralia, Missouri. The people involved were part of the "come-outer" movement from the Methodist Church and were active in the Southwest Holiness Association, which was organized by Kansas and Missouri ministers in 1876. They departed from the association because they believed the doctrine of entire sanctification was neglected.

Headquarters

7407 Metcalf
PO Box 4244
Overland Park, KS 66204
Telephone: 913-432-0331

Core Beliefs

Wesleyan in faith and practice, the Church of God, Holiness believes in the plenary inspiration of Scripture and that God's Word contains all truth necessary for faith and practice. Members believe in the Trinity, the fallen nature of humanity, and the hopeless and eternal destiny of unbelievers. The atonement of Jesus Christ was for all humanity; therefore, whoever repents and believes in him will be justified, regenerated, and saved from the power of sin. Believers are to be wholly sanctified following the new birth. The Holy Spirit gives witness to the new birth and to the entire sanctification of believers. As a second work of grace and preceded by definite conviction of the inherited, continuing effects of original (inbred) sin, entire sanctification means a believer is delivered from inbred sin and is entirely consecrated to the Holy Spirit, with a perfect love for God and humanity. There are no accompanying signs (i.e., tongues speaking) of this occurrence. Jesus Christ will return to raise the dead, after which the final judgment will occur. Water baptism and the Lord's Supper are the two ordinances taught and observed.

Website

http://www.cogh.net/

Bibliography

Cowan, Clarence Eugene. *A History of the Church of God (Holiness)*. Overland Park, KS: Herald and Banner Press, 1949.

Dieter, Melvin E. *The Holiness Revival of the Nineteenth Century*. Metuchen, NJ: Scarecrow, 1980.

Jones, Charles Edwin. *A Guide to the Study of the Holiness Movement*. Metuchen, NJ: Scarecrow, 1974.

Purkiser, Westlake Taylor. *Sanctification and Its Synonyms: Studies in the Biblical Theology of Holiness*. Kansas City, MO: Beacon Hill, 1961.

Scott, Noel Wayne. "The Schools of the Church of God (Holiness): A Historical Study." PhD diss., University of Missouri–Columbia, 1973.

Synan, Vinson. *The Holiness-Pentecostal Tradition*. Grand Rapids: Eerdmans, 1997.

Ron J. Bigalke

Church of the Nazarene

History

The Church of the Nazarene emerged from the nineteenth-century Holiness movement. In an event considered the birth date of the church, three groups united in Pilot Point, Texas, on October 13, 1908. They were the Association of Pentecostal Churches of America centered in Brooklyn and Boston; the Church of the Nazarene (from which the denomination received its name), which began in Los Angeles in 1895 under former Methodist minister Phineas Bresee (1838–1915); and the Holiness Church of Christ, which included small, rural congregations scattered in Texas and Tennessee. Other groups followed. During the 1920s and 1930s, because of the influx of Midwestern Methodists, the church's strength shifted from urban to rural areas. By the 1960s, it was suburban in orientation.

The reason for the church's founding was the doctrine and experience of entire sanctification. This teaching had come to be neglected, Holiness people thought, in Methodist churches.

Missions began in India, near Bombay, where the Association of Pentecostal Churches had missionaries by 1898. Policy architects such as Hiram F. Reynolds (1854–1938) determined not to establish national churches but to allow districts around the world full participation in the church's governmental processes proportional to membership.

Headquarters

Global Ministry Center
17001 Prairie Star Parkway
Lenexa, KS 66220
Telephone: 913-577-0500

Core Beliefs

The Articles of Faith of the Church of the Nazarene, indebted to the Methodist Articles, ground the church in the historic teachings of Christianity. Broad in its understanding of essentials, the church takes no hard line on eschatological timetables and centers the inerrancy of the Bible on "all things necessary to our salvation" (nazarene.org, "Articles of Faith"). The church retains a place for infant as well as believer's baptism, and membership is open to those who testify to conversion. Entire sanctification, one of the articles of faith, is a cleansing and Spirit-infilling grace subsequent to new birth.

The church identifies the fruit of the Spirit—love—with entire sanctification. This impels the church's involvement in various forms of compassionate ministries around the world. Since the beginning of the church, Nazarenes have been committed to the ordination and full participation of women at all levels.

The church's *Manual* includes a section titled "The Covenant of Christian Conduct." Nazarenes avoid entertainment "subversive of the Christian ethic"; lotteries and other forms of gambling; membership in "oath-bound secret orders or societies"; forms of dancing that "break down proper moral inhibitions and reserve"; and using, selling, or in any way lending approval to either liquor or drugs (nazarene.org, "Church of the Nazarene Manual, 2013–2017"). Further statements permit membership for divorced persons, disapprove abortion, and disavow the practice of homosexuality.

Worship

Nazarene churches reflect typical evangelical forms, though worship varies greatly around the world. The sermon occupies the center of worship. Some churches use choruses, musical bands, and worship teams. A few churches have recovered formal liturgy.

Divisions and Splits

During the 1950s and 1960s, certain Nazarenes believed that the church was drifting away from Holiness standards. Two conservative splits occurred: the Bible Missionary Church formed in 1955 and the Church of the Bible Covenant in 1967.

Controversies

A controversy revolved around whether it was appropriate to continue to identify Pentecost and baptism with the Holy Spirit with entire sanctification. Recently, concerned Nazarenes have objected to worship styles, spiritual formation, and perceived emerging church trends in the church.

Largest Churches

The largest congregations of the Church of the Nazarene are in South America: the Casa De Oracion Paso Ancho Church in Cali, Colombia, has 7,500 in worship and 5,600 members, and Central Church in Campinas, Brazil, has over 6,000 in worship and 8,700 members. In the United States, the largest churches are in Grove City, Ohio, which has 3,200 attendees and 2,500 members, and Bethany, Oklahoma, with 2,475 attendees and 4,750 members.

Growth

Recent growth has been strong outside North America. By the 2000 general assembly, just more than half of Nazarenes lived outside North America. In 2010, when Nazarene membership stood at more than two million, two-thirds were from outside North America. Twenty percent resided in Africa, and more than 20 percent spoke Spanish as their first language.

Missionary and Evangelistic Work

The Church of the Nazarene is in 160 countries around the world. In the United States, it is among the most evenly distributed denominations. Methods of evangelism reflect the church's revival heritage. The church increasingly emphasizes small groups and discipleship as means of making and growing Christians.

Ecumenism

In the United States, the Church of the Nazarene is a member of the Christian Holiness Partnership and (since 1984) the National Association of Evangelicals. It joins similar organizations in other countries. In 1999, the Church of the Nazarene joined the World Methodist Council.

Academic Institutions

There are fifty-six educational institutions around the world under the church's International Board of Education. The largest is Korea Nazarene University. There are other Nazarene universities in Nairobi, Kenya, and Sao Paulo, Brazil. In North America, Nazarene colleges include Eastern Nazarene College, MidAmerica Nazarene University, Mount Vernon Nazarene University, Northwest Nazarene University, Olivet Nazarene University, Point Loma Nazarene University, Southern Nazarene University, and Trevecca Nazarene University.

The church maintains a Bible college in Colorado Springs and, in partnership with the Christian and Missionary Alliance, Ambrose University College in Calgary, Alberta. Graduate theological seminaries are in Kansas City and the Philippines. Nazarene Theological College in England offers doctoral degrees through Manchester University. Several other schools, including ones in Costa Rica, Australia, and Trinidad, offer master's degrees. There are nursing and Bible colleges in Papua New Guinea, India, and Swaziland. Swaziland also has a teachers' college. European Nazarene College in Busingen, Switzerland, is multinational.

Parachurch Organizations

Nazarene Compassionate Ministries undertakes worldwide relief efforts and aids children in crisis. Heart to Heart International has close connections to the church.

Publications

Holiness Today is the church's main publication. The *NCM Magazine* is published by Nazarene Compassionate Ministries. The *Preacher's Magazine* is published online. There is also an online *Nazarene News*.

Website

http://www.nazarene.org/

Bibliography

Cunningham, Floyd, et al. *Our Watchword and Song: The Centennial History of the Church of the Nazarene.* Kansas City, MO: Nazarene Publishing House, 2009.

Smith, Timothy L. *Called Unto Holiness: The Story of the Nazarenes: The Formative Years.* Kansas City, MO: Nazarene Publishing House, 1962.

Tracy, Wes, and Stan Ingersol. *Here We Stand: Where Nazarenes Fit in the Religious Marketplace.* Kansas City, MO: Beacon Hill Press of Kansas City, 1999.

Floyd Cunningham

Evangelical Church

History

The Evangelical Church was founded in June 1968 in Portland, Oregon. Its roots extend back to John Wesley in England, and its North American history traces back to York County, Pennsylvania, in 1789. Since then, many individuals in a dozen or more states have initiated congregations, denominations, and mergers.

The most recent composition of the Evangelical Church is the result of an incomplete merger between the Evangelical United Brethren Church and the Methodist Church, which joined to become the newly formed United Methodist Church. A group of churches and ministers from the Evangelical United Brethren Church determined, based on theological emphasis and social philosophy, not to join the new denomination, and the Evangelical Church was born. Since its creation in 1968, the Holiness Methodist Church (in 1969) and the Wesleyan Covenant Church (in 1977) have joined to expand the reach and ministry of the Evangelical Church.

Headquarters

9421 West River Road
Minneapolis, MN 55444
Telephone: 763-424-2589
Evangelical Church email: ecdenom@usfamily.net
Evangelical Church missions email: ecmissions
@usfamily.net

Leadership

General superintendent: Rev. Brian Eckhardt

Core Beliefs

As declared on the official website, "The Evangelical Church is a denomination committed to living as the body of Christ so people might be transformed into the likeness of Jesus Christ and mobilized on his mission" (theevangelicalchurch .org, "Home").

The central document, titled *The Discipline of the Evangelical Church*, contains a variety of categories, including the church's declaration of faith, the church's view of society and morality, and its own church history. Its nineteen articles largely contain orthodox, Protestant views. The church subscribes to a variety of historical Christian beliefs ranging from the doctrine of the Trinity to an eternal state after death of either reward or punishment. The Bible is believed to be inspired and inerrant and to describe the will of God for the purpose of salvation. Humanity is, due to the sin of Adam, inclined to evil, but God through the Holy Spirit and prevenient grace makes it possible for humanity to do good. Regarding the scope of Christ's work on the cross, members affirm that Christ died for the sins of the whole world, "both original and actual" (theevangelical church.org, "What We Believe").

The article on sanctification sets the Evangelical Church apart from other Protestant groups. Sanctification begins with justification but has two additional stages beyond justification: total consecration and entire sanctification. The former refers to a "more or less gradual process of devoting oneself wholly to God, consummating in the crucifixion of the old self or death to the Adamic nature, by the help of the Holy Spirit which comes to a completion at a point in time" (theevangelicalchurch.org, "What We Believe"). Total consecration prepares the way for entire sanctification, which "is that second definite, instantaneous work of God, wrought in the heart of the believer, subsequent to regeneration, by which God cleanses the heart from all inherited sin and fills the soul and spirit with the person of the Holy Spirit, thus enabling us to love God with all our heart, soul, mind, and strength and to love our neighbor as ourselves" (theevangelical church.org, "What We Believe").

In addition to its theological statements, the Evangelical Church has provided moral standards that promote economic justice and abstinence from alcohol and gambling. The church allows divorce only in the case of adultery. Homosexual behavior is a sin. Abortion is a social evil and forbidden unless a threat to the life of the mother can be proven.

Statistics

The Evangelical Church has congregations in 120 cities, with a high concentration in the Pacific Northwest.

Missionary and Evangelistic Work

The Evangelical Church Missions office supervises and coordinates the stateside and foreign activities of the mission. It is a ministry of the Evangelical Church. The office currently has missionaries involved in projects in Bolivia, Brazil, Germany, India, Japan, Fiji Islands, and the southwestern United States, especially Texas. The focus of the mission is evangelism, church planting, and training of pastors and local leaders.

Dr. Bruce Moyer was elected at the 2010 general conference of the Evangelical Church to serve as the next executive director. He began his duties in September 2010.

Publication

The Evangelical Church publishes the *Evangelical Challenge*, a denominational periodical, four times a year. It includes feature articles along designated themes, news from across the church, and updates from Evangelical Church mission fields.

Website

http://www.theevangelicalchurch.org/

Bibliography

"The Evangelical Church." http://www.theevangelicalchurch.org. "Home" and "What We Believe."

"Evangelical Church of North America." The Association of Religion Data Archives. http://www.thearda.com/Denoms/D_1474.asp.

Evangelical Church of North America. *The Discipline of the Evangelical Church.* A publication of the Evangelical Church, by Order of the Annual Conferences of the Evangelical Church of North America, Minneapolis, MN.

Hotrum, Brian. *The Evangelical Story: The History of the Evangelical Church.* Self-published, 2006.

Ryan A. Neal

Evangelical Congregational Church

History

The Evangelical Congregational Church traces its roots to the movement founded by Jacob Albright, who organized Bible classes for German Americans in 1800. Albright's three existing classes organized themselves in 1803 with Albright as elder, eventually taking the name Evangelical Association in 1816.

The United Evangelical Church officially splintered away between 1891 and 1894, a secession that was decades in the works and would take decades longer to culminate. Principal issues included cultural tension between German- and English-speaking congregants, Wesleyan doctrinal disagreements, and bitter personal rivalries. The primary issue was a yearning to incorporate more democracy while limiting centralized church polity. The newly formed denomination was seen as a voluntary association of like-minded believers, not an autocracy, with local congregations owning their own buildings.

In 1922, the United Evangelical Church reunited with the Evangelical Association under a new Evangelical Church (which is now part of the United Methodist Church), but a large portion of the United Evangelical Church was not satisfied with the merger. In east Pennsylvania, the Evangelical Congregational Church was formed in 1928.

Headquarters

100 West Park Avenue
Myerstown, PA 17067
Telephone: 717-866-7581; 800-866-7581
Email: eccenter@eccenter.com

Core Beliefs

The Evangelical Congregational Church is Arminian and Wesleyan. Affirming free will, grace is available to all who accept it. At the inception of the United Evangelical Church, the Twenty-Five Articles of Religion were adopted, which were taken largely from Milton Terry's "Doctrines of Arminian Methodism." There is a strong emphasis on Christian perfection, with reference to Genesis 17:1, Colossians 1:28, and Wesley's 1746 treatise *A Plain Account of Christian Perfection*.

Website

http://www.eccenter.com/

Bibliography

Albright, Raymond W. *A History of the Evangelical Church.* Harrisburg, PA: The Evangelical Press, 1942.

Heisey, Terry M., ed. *Evangelical from the Beginning: A History of the Evangelical Congregational Church and Its Predecessors.* Lexington, KY: Emeth Press, 2006.

Spreng, Rev. Samuel P. *American Church History, Vol. XII: A History of . . . The Evangelical Association.* New York: The Christian Literature Co., 1894.

Strege, M. D. "Albright, Jacob." In *Dictionary of Christianity in America,* edited by Daniel G. Reid, Robert Deal Linder, Bruce L. Shelley, and Harry S. Stout, 32–33. Downers Grove, IL: InterVarsity, 1990.

Wilson, Robert Sherer. *A Brief History of the Evangelical Congregational Church for the Enlightenment of Her Pastors and People.* Myerstown, PA: Church Center Press, 1963.

———. *Jacob Albright: The Evangelical Pioneer.* Myerstown, PA: Church Center Press, 1940. http://www.eccenter.com/files/ECC/Historical%20Society/Wilson-Albright%20gray.pdf.

T. C. Porter

Free Methodist Church USA

History

The Free Methodist Church USA (FMC) emerged out of the Methodist Episcopal Church (MEC) in 1860 as a call to uphold Wesleyan Holiness and proclaim the gospel to the poor. Cofounder B. T. Roberts had been seeking reform within the MEC for years, calling for spiritual renewal and free—not rented—pews. Roberts and others were expelled from the MEC in 1858 but were widely supported by those who shared their views. A group of MEC outcasts in Illinois and Missouri, organized under John Wesley Redfield,

113

joined the launch of the new denomination. The name "Free" symbolized a call for free pews, free worship, and free persons. The FMC fought for freedom and equality for African Americans and was an early proponent of women in ministry.

Headquarters

Free Methodist World Ministries Center
PO Box 535002
Indianapolis, IN 46253-5002
Telephone: 317-244-3660; 800-342-5531

Core Beliefs

The Free Methodist Church USA is a staunchly Wesleyan Holiness denomination. From the beginning, it has followed versions of the Twenty-Five Articles of Religion, John Wesley's treatise adopted in 1808 by its parent denomination.

At inception, the FMC was known for giving preferential kindness to marginalized people and setting up urban ministries to African Americans. Today the FMC leads the push in such organizations as Help Haiti Heal, Eden Reforestation Projects, and Heavenly Treasures.

Worship

For years, the standard was the denomination's *Hymns of the Living Faith* (1968). Today styles are as diverse as the churches themselves. The FMC baptizes infants and adults and practices the Lord's Supper.

Division and Splits

Schisms occurred in 1955 (resulting in the United Holiness Church) and 1962 (resulting in the Midwest Holiness Association and the Evangelical Wesleyan Church of North America).

Controversies

The doctrine of entire sanctification has drawn much scholarly debate. It was often a point of confusion for congregants who erroneously thought they were without sin.

Statistics

As of 2009, the Free Methodist Church had 967 churches, average worship attendance of 105,520, and a membership of 76,620. Worldwide Free Methodist worship attendance each week is about 800,000.

Largest Churches

Cross Roads Community Church (Ottawa Lake, MI)
Free Methodist Church (Spring Arbor, MI)

Free Methodist Church (Wenatchee, WA)
New Life Ministries (Endicott, NY)
NewPointe Community Church (Dover, OH)
Timberlake Christian Fellowship (Redmond, WA)
Pearce Memorial (North Chili, NY)

Growth

Membership in the Free Methodist Church USA rose slowly and steadily throughout the twentieth century, from under forty thousand in 1925 to over seventy thousand by the 1980s.

Trends

The church is becoming comparatively less episcopal and more networked. Churches pursue local agendas while coming alongside neighbors with shared values. Church planting is more creative and organic. Collaboration is visible locally and institutionally. The FMC is looking for ways to gauge and celebrate more than just membership numbers and baptisms, instead aiming to measure holiness, transformation, and kingdom success in urban ministries, which do not always translate into dollars.

Academic Institutions

Azusa Pacific University (Azusa, CA), a partnership with other denominations
Central Christian College of Kansas (McPherson, KS)
Greenville College (Greenville, IL)
Roberts Wesleyan College (Rochester, NY)
Seattle Pacific University (Seattle, WA)
Spring Arbor University (Spring Arbor, MI)

Parachurch Organizations

Central Africa Healthcare Organization
Clear Blue Global Water Project
Eden Reforestation Projects
Heavenly Treasures
Help Chile Heal
Help Haiti Heal
International Child Care Ministries
Seed
VISA Ministries

Electronic Media

Mission resources for local churches: http://www.fmwm.org/resources/index.php
Bible quizzing: http://www.fmquizzing.org/

Publications

Evangel
Light and Life
World Mission People

Website

http://www.freemethodistchurch.org/

Bibliography

Bates, Gerald E., and Howard A. Snyder, eds. *Soul Searching the Church: Free Methodism at 150 Years*. Indianapolis: Light and Life Communications, 2007.

Kostlevy, William C. *Historical Dictionary of the Holiness Movement*. Lanham, MD: Scarecrow, 2001.

Marston, Leslie R. *From Age to Age: A Living Witness: A Historical Interpretation of Free Methodism's First Century*. Indianapolis: Light and Life Communications, 1960.

McKenna, David L. *A Future with a History: The Wesleyan Witness of the Free Methodist Church: 1960 to 1995 and Forward*. Indianapolis: Light and Life Communications, 1997.

Snyder, Howard A. *Populist Saints: R. T. and Ellen Roberts and the First Free Methodists*. Grand Rapids: Eerdmans, 2006.

T. C. Porter

Salvation Army

History

The Salvation Army (SA) began as the East London Christian Mission (later called simply the Christian Mission) in London's East End in 1865 through the work of William and Catherine Booth. The original intent of the Booths was not to establish a separate denomination but to channel those ministered to by the Christian Mission into the established churches. The Booths' ministry targeted saloons and advocated abstinence from alcohol, tobacco, and gambling, which William Booth saw as contributing directly to the conditions his congregants were coming from. Those changed by the work of the Christian Mission did not feel welcome in established venues, however, resulting in the emergence of the Christian Mission as a distinct Christian group early in its existence.

The appellation Salvation Army was not applied to the group until 1878, after Bramwell Booth, son of William and Catherine, objected to the group's slogan "The Christian Mission is a Volunteer Army," replacing "volunteer" with "salvation" to emphasize the compulsory nature of the Christian life. Soon after this, the group internalized the army motif into its structures, organizing itself into corps led by generals and other officers who directed the day-to-day activities of the Salvation Army. Members of the Salvation Army are known as Salvationists.

By 1888, the Salvation Army was reportedly the fastest-growing Christian sect and firmly involved in social reform movements globally, from temperance movements in the United States to educational reform in India.

Headquarters

The Salvation Army National Headquarters
615 Slaters Lane
PO Box 269
Alexandria, VA 22313

Core Beliefs

The SA operates as a distinct Christian group, abiding by eleven central doctrines, including perseverance of the saints and regeneration of believers. The Army's founders, William and Catherine Booth, were affiliated with a branch of Wesleyanism known as the Methodist Reform movement, theologically influenced by the work of American evangelists Charles Finney and Phoebe Palmer. Finney's book *Lectures on Revivals of Religion* (1873) was required reading for the Booths' earliest recruits. Consequently, the SA still bears a strong Wesleyan/Holiness emphasis in its doctrines and theology. William Booth's approach in particular placed little emphasis on the use of sacraments, as he felt that the outward forms of religion had replaced inward regeneration. This view continues to the present, with the emphasis of SA doctrine placed on personal behaviors rather than on sacraments.

Social reform and social services have always been a hallmark of the SA, initially as a means to win a hearing for the evangelistic message. William Booth was initially opposed to social services that could be described as social reform, remarking that such endeavors tended to siphon energy from evangelism. Social reform and services have remained at the heart of the Salvation Army's efforts, however. Social needs are seen as barriers to the Salvation Army's primary purpose of evangelization and thus are addressed.

One joins the SA either as an adherent, by which one identifies with the Salvation Army's doctrines and mission, or by soldiership, by which one becomes a full member of the Salvation Army.

The doctrines of the SA are summed up in two documents available on the SA website: the Doctrines of the Salvation Army and the Soldier's Covenant (formerly known as the Articles of War).

Worship services are held in citadels (worship halls), where each local corps (congregation) meets for preaching and worship. There is not a uniform liturgy for each meeting, but worship typically involves a number of hymns or music by the local Salvation Army band/choir. Meetings are led by a resident officer (clergy) who provides an address (sermon).

Controversies

The SA continues to encounter difficulties with governmental entities for the religious nature of its social reforms. In 2001, Russia expelled the SA on the grounds that it was a "paramilitary entity" and thus subject to expulsion under a 1997 law forbidding conversion by parachurch organizations. More recently, in 2004, the Salvation Army came under fire in New York for refusing to compromise its stance on same-sex marriage and refusing to extend benefits to same-sex partners, citing religious grounds for its stance.

Growth

Originating in England, the Salvation Army expanded first to Wales in 1874 and then to Scotland, Australia, and the United States by 1880. The SA currently operates in 115 countries through over 15,000 corps and churches. In the United States, there are approximately 120,000 soldiers and officers, 500,000 adherents, and over 3.5 million volunteers. Globally, the Salvation Army claims over 1.8 million soldiers and adherents, not counting those who participate in various Salvation Army services or who volunteer for the Salvation Army.

Although initially working alongside broad-based national reform movements, in the late nineteenth century, the Army began to take on its own identity apart from such movements, establishing a naval ministry (1885), a family tracing and reunion service (1881), and the first homeless crisis shelters in Greenwich Village in New York (1891). The global view of the SA began to change following the Galveston hurricane in 1900 and the San Francisco earthquake in 1906, in which the SA was involved with relief efforts.

Missionary and Evangelistic Work

Evangelism remains central to the Salvation Army. To this end, it maintains a strong emphasis on verbal evangelism and preaching but sees these activities going hand in hand with social ministry. It thus understands its various social ministry enterprises as part of its ongoing evangelism.

The form of evangelism, however, has changed throughout Salvation Army history. Initial preaching by William Booth was done in open-air forums, while most contemporary preaching by Salvationists takes place in their services and evangelistic crusades.

In the twentieth century, the Salvation Army's work expanded from the original soup kitchens to a variety of social endeavors, including HIV awareness, opposition to sex trafficking, the establishment of numerous hospitals and clinics, tsunami and hurricane relief, and community development.

Academic Institutions

Education for Salvation Army officers (clergy) takes place at any number of officer training schools. Education is for a two-year term. Four schools are present in the United States: Suffern, New York; Chicago; Atlanta; and Rancho Palo Verdes, California.

Globally, the SA is involved in numerous education initiatives, with over seventeen hundred schools established for the education of the blind, disabled, and marginalized.

Publications

The oldest publications of the Salvation Army are the *Salvationist*, a biweekly internal publication, and the *War Cry*, a biweekly magazine geared toward a more general readership. Both publications were established in 1879. Other publications of the SA include *All the World*, *Battle Cry*, *Global Exchange Revive*, *Word and Deed* (journal of theology), and *Young Salvationist*.

Websites

American Salvation Army: http://www.salvationarmyusa.org/

International Salvation Army: http://www.salvationarmy.org/

Salvationists (Salvation Army volunteers): http://www.salvationist.org/

Bibliography

McKinley, E. H. *Marching to Glory: The History of the Salvation Army in the United States, 1880–1992.* Grand Rapids: Eerdmans, 1995.

Rithmire, R. David. *Sacraments and the Salvation Army: Pneumatological Foundations.* Metuchen, NJ: Scarecrow, 1990.

Sandall, Robert. *The History of the Salvation Army: 1865–1946.* 6 vols. New York: Salvation Army, 1979.

Winston, Diane H. *Red-Hot and Righteous: The Urban Religion of the Salvation Army.* Cambridge, MA: Harvard University Press, 1999.

Myles Werntz

Volunteers of America

History

The Volunteers of America is a social ministry organization that began in 1896 as a splinter movement of the Salvation Army. Ballington (son of Salvation Army founder William) and Maud Booth were appointed joint commanders of the American branch of the Salvation Army. Numerous issues, however, created a division between the Booths and the Salvation Army. In January 1896, Ballington and Maud were ordered to leave their post in the United States and accept a position elsewhere in the Salvation Army. Ballington and Maud, however, choose to resign their post in the Salvation Army, and in March 1896, they announced at a rally the formation of a new organization that would become known as the Volunteers of America. Since its formation, the Volunteers of America has focused on social ministry, including the development of affordable housing and professional long-term nursing care.

Headquarters

660 Duke Street
Alexandria, VA 22314
Telephone: 703-341-5000; 800-899-0089

Core Beliefs

Central to the Volunteers of America is social ministry. The Volunteers of America provides services in the areas of long-term nursing care, homelessness, employment and job training, affordable housing, community enhancement, emergency support, intellectual disabilities, community corrections, veteran services, substance abuse, mental health, and senior services.

Statistics

In 2009, the Volunteers of America provided service to more than 2 million people through more than 16,000 employees, 70,738 volunteers, 935,747 hours volunteered, and 38 local offices.

Ecumenism

The Volunteers of America views itself as an interdenominational church and as a parachurch with a special ministry of service. From its inception, it has been ecumenical, encouraging its ministers to be involved in local churches for worship, ministry of service, and personal spiritual growth.

Publication

The Volunteers of America publishes a biyearly magazine titled *Spirit Magazine*.

Website

http://www.voa.org/

Bibliography

Platt, Warren C. "The Volunteers of America: The Origins and Development of Its Ideology." *Journal of Religious History* 16, no. 1 (June 1990): 35–50.

"Volunteers of America." http://www.voa.org. "About Us," "Our History," "Our Mission," "Our Ministry of Service," and "National Network of Services."

Bryan C. Maine

Wesleyan Church

History

The Wesleyan Church is an evangelical, Protestant denomination. The Wesleyan Methodist Church was founded in 1843 at an organizing conference in Utica, New York, as a group of ministers and worshipers who divided from the Methodist Episcopal Church primarily in support of the abolitionist movement. The Pilgrim Holiness Church was founded in 1897 in Cincinnati, Ohio, as a consequence of the Holiness revival movement, which prioritized evangelism, healing, holiness, and premillennialism. The Wesleyan Church was formed on June 26, 1968, through the union of the Wesleyan Methodist Church and the Pilgrim Holiness Church. Both bodies have a theological heritage in the abolitionist and Holiness revival movements of the nineteenth century and share mutual belief in the doctrines of Holiness taught by John Wesley.

Headquarters

13300 Olio Road
Fishers, IN 46037
Telephone: 317-774-7900

Core Beliefs

The church is Wesleyan-Arminian in doctrine. Wesleyans believe the Bible is the foundation for faith and seek to establish actions based on its teachings. They believe in the one Triune God, who is the Savior of all those who trust in him alone for eternal life. God's prevenient grace has made salvation from sin possible, but it necessitates a voluntary response through repentance and faith. It is God's will for all people to know him. Those who receive new life in Christ are called to be holy in character and conduct, which is possible only through the filling of the Holy Spirit. It is possible to fall into sin subsequent to regeneration, but the grace of God may bring forgiveness and restoration through genuine repentance and faith. The purpose of the church is to be a witness with regard to Christ through its loving actions, witness, and worship. Water baptism and the Lord's Supper are the sacraments of the church. The second coming of Christ is personal and imminent.

The denomination consists of those members within district conferences and local churches who affirm the Articles of Religion and acknowledge the ecclesiastical authority of its governing bodies. The Wesleyan Church periodically adopts official statements with regard to cultural and public policy issues for the purpose of providing a Wesleyan-Arminian position that will encourage ministers and worshipers to integrate faith and life and to respond appropriately and responsibly to such issues. Recent statements have been issued with regard to creation care, domestic violence, global human trafficking, global poverty, and immigration. The board of general superintendents may also release additional statements that define the faith and practice of the Wesleyan Church, such as the Pastoral Letter on the Economy. The official press of the Wesleyan Church has compiled official statements with regard to various public moral and social concerns in a publication titled *Standing Firm: The Wesleyan Church Speaks on Contemporary Issues.*

The soul of the Wesleyan Church is expressed in its core values. The primary motivation for all Wesleyan practices includes biblical authority, Christlikeness, disciple-making, local church centeredness, servant leadership, unity in diversity, and cultural relevance.

Similar to other Holiness churches, the church emphasizes the doctrine of entire sanctification.

Worship

Worship is a variant of emphases and styles. Most churches incorporate singing, praying, giving, and studying Scripture.

Statistics

United States and Canadian membership: 124,000
United States and Canadian churches: 1,700
Worldwide worshipers: 400,000
Worldwide churches and missions: 5,000 in 90 countries

Largest Churches

The largest congregations include Central Wesleyan Church (Holland, MI) and Skyline Wesleyan Church (La Mesa, CA), with both having approximately three thousand members and average attendance of more than two thousand.

Missionary and Evangelistic Work

The Wesleyan Church is intent to exalt Christ through compassion ministries, worldwide missions, and social justice concerns for all people. The broader scope of the church's compassion ministries includes counseling services, free clinics, global human trafficking prevention and recovery, global poverty and disaster relief, HIV/AIDS relief programs, hospitals, inner-city daycare and relief ministries, job training, online education, orphanages, parenting groups, and second career ministerial training and schools.

Global Partners is the mission department, which serves more than 90 countries with 230 missionaries.

Academic Institutions

Asbury Seminary (Wilmore, KY)
Azusa Pacific University (Azusa, CA)
Bethany Bible College (Sussex, New Brunswick, Canada)
Evangelical Theological Seminary (Myerstown, PA)
George Fox Seminary (Portland, OR)
Houghton College (Houghton, NY)
Indiana Wesleyan University (Marion, IN)
Nazarene Theological Seminary (Kansas City, MO)
Oklahoma Wesleyan University (Bartlesville, OK)
Southern Wesleyan University (Central, SC)
Tyndale Seminary (Toronto, Ontario, Canada)
Wesley Biblical Seminary (Jackson, MS)
Wesley Seminary (Marion, IN)

Parachurch Organizations

The Wesleyan Church has several affiliations, including the Center for Women in Ministry, International Bible Society, National Association of Evangelicals, Wesleyan Holiness Clergy, Wesleyan Holiness Consortium, Wesleyan Leader Summit, World Hope International, and World Methodist Council.

Electronic Media

The church broadcasted a weekly international radio program known as the *Wesleyan Hour,* which featured Dr. Norman G. Wilson as director and speaker, for thirty-two years. The award-winning broadcast was heard in English, Russian, and Spanish. The last broadcast was aired on June 29, 2008. The WesleyanHQ's channel is available on YouTube.

Publications

Wesleyan Life is the official quarterly magazine. The Wesleyan Publishing House communicates the distinctive message of Holiness through the publication of quality resources for local churches and ministries around the world.

Website

http://www.wesleyan.org/

Bibliography

Carter, Charles W., gen. ed. *A Contemporary Wesleyan Theology: Biblical, Systematic, and Practical.* 2 vols. Grand Rapids: Zondervan, 1983.

Haines, Lee M., and Paul William Thomas. *An Outline History of the Wesleyan Church.* Marion, IN: Wesley Press, 1985.

Kostlevy, William, ed. *Historical Dictionary of the Holiness Movement.* Lanham, MD: Scarecrow, 2001.

———. *Holiness Manuscripts: A Guide to Sources Documenting the Wesleyan Holiness Movement in the United States and Canada.* Metuchen, NJ: American Theological Library Association, 1994.

Stanley, Susie C. *Holy Boldness: Women Preachers' Autobiographies and the Sanctified Self.* Knoxville: University of Tennessee Press, 2004.

Ron J. Bigalke

Lutheran

American Association of Lutheran Churches

History

The American Association of Lutheran Churches (AALC) was formed in 1987 by twelve congregations of the American Lutheran Church that rejected the plan to become part of the Evangelical Lutheran Church in America, which was seen as being ambivalent about biblical inerrancy. Although not partisan or sectarian, the AALC continues to be staunchly conservative. Member congregations collectively train Lutheran pastors, jointly develop strategies to successfully present the gospel, and assist in one another's ministries.

Headquarters

921 East Dupont Road, #920
Fort Wayne, IN 46825-1551
Telephone: 260-452-3213

Leadership

Presiding pastor: Rev. Franklin Hays

Core Beliefs

The AALC teaches that salvation is available to all people who believe in Christ. It insists on maintaining strict adherence to the Scriptures while presenting its message in a relevant way. It does not recognize tradition as a legitimate origin for church doctrines and requires acceptance of the explanation of doctrines in the Lutheran Book of Concord. The church universal is seen as one body of which the AALC considers itself a part.

The AALC views the ordination of women as pastors and their appointment as elders as unscriptural and contrary to its confessional perspective. At the same time, it encourages women to participate in church life by serving as deaconesses and in other roles. Women may serve as voting delegates on the Joint Council.

Statistics

Year	Clergy	Churches	Membership
1988	80	78	15,150
2006	187	73	26,537

Ecumenism

Although Lutheran churches have historically cooperated in terms of social ministry, divisions in the 1970s over the ordination of women impeded many joint ventures. The founding of the AALC reopened interest in altar and pulpit fellowship, at one time established by the American Lutheran Church and the Lutheran Church—Missouri Synod to welcome one another's pastors and commune at one another's altars. After eighteen years of discussions, the AALC and the Lutheran Church—Missouri Synod found a large enough area of doctrinal agreement to re-create the altar and pulpit fellowship.

The AALC practices a Communion that is neither open nor closed but rather "responsible," meaning that the church discloses its beliefs about the practice and individuals must ensure that those beliefs are consistent with their own.

Academic Institution

The American Lutheran Theological Seminary (ALTS), on the campus of Concordia Theological Seminary in Fort Wayne, Indiana, is supported and operated by the AALC. The ALTS supplements Concordia's theological training with practical training, including field work and vicarages at local AALC churches.

Parachurch Organization

Women of L.I.F.E. (Lutherans in Fellowship and Evangelism), with at least one clergy member on its commission, conducts Bible studies that are consistent with AALC teachings.

Publication

The Evangel

Website

http://www.taalc.org/

George Thomas Kurian

Apostolic Lutheran Church of America

History

The Apostolic Lutheran Church of America is a Finnish-American group established in 1872 as the Solomon Korteniemi Lutheran Society. It was incorporated as the Finnish Apostolic Lutheran Church in America in 1929 and took its present name in 1962. The Apostolic Lutheran Church of America is the largest body of Apostolic Lutherans, whose roots are in Pietism.

Headquarters

124 Binney Hill Road
New Ipswich, NH 03071

Leadership

Chairman of the central board: Wilfred Sikkila

Core Beliefs

The Apostolic Lutheran Church of America believes in the divine inspiration of the Bible; the unity of the Father, Son, and Holy Spirit; and the universal need for repentance and for salvation and spiritual new birth through faith in Jesus Christ.

God's grace is an unmerited gift. Christians are still capable of sin; confession of sin should be made not merely to God but also to trusted confessors. Individuals can fall from grace by disregard of Christ's teachings but with repentance will be welcomed back by God. Believers are commanded to nourish themselves and their children spiritually, to faithfully endure their suffering, and to preach the gospel so that faith can be created in those who hear its message. On the day of Pentecost, the power of the Holy Ghost came to empower believers. The Holy Ghost gives assurance of salvation, guides and comforts Christians in the truth through God's Word, and prompts believers to act in a Christian manner and to bear the fruit of good conduct. Christ is the only leader of the church, which is his body unified by love, and all those who reject him are condemned to destruction.

Water baptism is a necessary token of union with Christ's death and of the New Testament covenant, replacing circumcision in the Abrahamic covenant of the Old Testament. A proper baptism cannot be invalidated by any future actions of the individual. Infants should be baptized not as a means of joining the family of God but because as humans they possess original sin and are eligible to participate in Christ's redemptive work since they have no unbelief in their hearts. (Faith is not intellectual in nature but rather instilled by God in the heart.) The laying on of hands is used for healing and other purposes. The Lord's Supper stands in place of the Feast of the Passover and is a symbolic event that shows unity with Christ's sacrifice and strengthens faith. Foot washing is a custom that shows believers' responsibility to be humble and to encourage one another. There must be complete abstention from alcoholic beverages.

Website

http://www.apostoliclutheran.org/

George Thomas Kurian

Association of Free Lutheran Congregations

History

The Association of Free Lutheran Congregations (AFLC) traces its roots to the Lutheran Pietist revivals of the late 1600s. With the arrival of thousands of Scandinavian Pietists in the United States in the 1800s came their dedication to learning and to Lutheran educational institutions.

Minneapolis's Augsburg College, a preparatory academy and seminary, was introduced to a revolutionary view of the simplicity of Christian teaching by two young Norwegian scholars in the 1870s. Professors Georg Sverdrup and Sven Oftedal came from prominent families and were well acquainted with the hostility of the church hierarchy to revival. Sverdrup and Oftedal taught that the New Testament never made mention of bishoprics, church councils, or synods, and that although congregations may have elders and bishops, their true leadership should come from the Holy Spirit. Their teaching represented a new style of church government as well as the view that congregations should be led rather than dominated and should utilize their spiritual gifts. The free congregation was seen as both a cause and an effect of the nurturing of believers.

In the 1890s, the formation of the United Norwegian Lutheran Church in America by three Norwegian Lutheran groups led to disappointment on the part of followers of the Augsburg professors, who called themselves the "Friends of Augsburg" and who felt that their views were being shunned. Sverdrup and Oftedal refused to surrender control of Augsburg College to the new denomination and were subsequently refused delegate status at the United Norwegian Conference in 1895. Twelve congregations were expelled from the United Norwegian Lutheran Church in 1897 for continuing their support of the Augsburg principles, and the same year Augsburg supporters from one hundred congregations formed the Lutheran Free Church. They articulated a series of fundamental principles and welcomed participants in the Norwegian revival movement of the time, many of whom came to study at Augsburg College. Graduates of Augsburg College assisted in the expansion of the Lutheran Free Church beyond eastern North Dakota and northwestern Minnesota.

By 1962, a need for revitalization led to a merger with other Lutherans to form the American Lutheran Church. In October of that year, some seventy congregations objecting to the merger formed the Association of Free Lutheran Congregations in Thief River Falls, Minnesota, under the leadership of Rev. John P. Strand. They stated their dedication to the original principles of the Lutheran Free Church, including its conservatism, rejection of formality and ritual, desire for simple services focused on preaching, and support of free congregations led only by the Holy Spirit. Accordingly, the AFLC is not an incorporated synod but rather a free association or fellowship of local congregations that are separate corporations.

Because it seeks to enhance the ministry potential of its members through joint efforts, the AFLC sponsors five ministry corporations to promote the work of the association, which includes training pastors, distributing Bibles and other literature, assisting with missions in the United States and abroad, offering conferences and other intercongregational fellowship opportunities, and operating charitable endeavors such as children's homes. Most of the association's congregations can be found in the upper Midwest.

Headquarters

3110 East Medicine Lake Boulevard
Plymouth, MN 55441

Telephone: 763-545-5631
Email: webmaster@aflc.org

Leadership

President: Pastor Elden K. Nelson

Core Beliefs

The AFLC accepts biblical inerrancy without endorsing a particular translation and rejects any church practices that are not rooted in Scripture. It adheres to the Apostles', Nicene, and Athanasian Creeds; Luther's Small Catechism; and the original Augsburg Confession. Christ is seen as the only Savior, but all believers who accept Christ's saving work and are baptized are viewed as children of God, regardless of denomination. Believers are expected to guide their conduct by studying Scripture and considering the advice of other believers. They must distance themselves from negative worldly influences. While spiritual gifts are valued, the AFLC is not charismatic and has been wary of potential abuses of the charismatic movement.

Worship

There are no guidelines regarding liturgy or vestments, but simplicity in worship is preferred. Church services should be centered on preaching. Sacraments carry value only when participants act in genuine faith.

Finances

The AFLC does not impose financial goals on its member congregations. The annual conference budget is met by voluntary contributions.

Statistics

Year	Clergy	Churches	Membership
1974	77	125	13,471
2006	234	267	43,360

The AFLC is the fourth largest US Lutheran denomination, present in twenty-seven states.

Missionary and Evangelistic Work

There is a strong tradition of evangelism in the AFLC, furthered by its Commission on Evangelism, World Missions Department, and Missions Corporation. The corporation, consisting of one hundred individuals from AFLC congregations, includes a World Missions Committee and a Home Missions Committee, which plants new churches in the United States. At the present time, the World Missions outreach extends to Brazil, Mexico, India, and Uganda.

The Missions Department offers FLAPS (Free Lutheran Association of Pilot Supporters), a nonprofit corporation started in 1999 to provide aviation services for AFLC staff, sometimes in remote areas. The Women's Missionary Federation is an auxiliary organization that encourages women's participation in missions as well as the study of Scripture.

Youth outreach is a high priority for the AFLC and includes its Youth Ministries Department, Youth Workers Retreat, Student Missions, and the blog *Grounded 3.17*, which offers young adults guidance about social and family issues. The auxiliary FLY (Free Lutheran Youth; previously the Luther League Federation) runs FLY Boot Camp, holds a biennial convention, and supports local youth programs.

The AFLC encourages lay ministry and charitable work both inside and outside the congregation.

Ecumenism

Seeing unity among believers as entirely spiritual and unrelated to man-made institutions, the AFLC does not participate in organizations such as the World Council of Churches or the National Council of Churches. At the same time, it urges cooperation with doctrinally similar Lutheran groups for the purposes of evangelization. Cooperation with other Protestant groups is permissible when Lutheran beliefs are safeguarded.

Academic Institutions

The AFLC has bodies dedicated to educational needs, including the Parish Education Department and the Schools Corporation. The fifty members of the corporation come from AFLC congregations and elect trustees to oversee the Association Free Lutheran Bible School and the Association Free Lutheran Theological Seminary, both located at denomination headquarters. The Bible School, established in 1966, offers a unique two-year college-level Bible program for high school graduates that equips students with spiritual skills that they can use in real-life situations in ministry or secular environments. Since 1964, the seminary has offered postgraduate training for pastors in the orthodox Lutheran and Pietist traditions. Its program consists of three years of academics and a one-year internship. The schools are expanding their current housing capacity of 145 students to accommodate the considerable growth of recent years.

Parachurch Organization

The Association Retreat Center in Osceola, Wisconsin, was formerly a United States Air Force Radar Base. The property was purchased by the AFLC in 1979 to be operated as a Christian retreat center and Bible camp serving scholastic groups and various other Christian youth and adult groups.

Publications

The *Lutheran Ambassador* is a monthly magazine that provides inspiration, evangelizes non-Christians, and describes the work of the AFLC. The publications arm of the denomination, Ambassador Publications, produces the Ambassador Series of instruction for Sunday schools and new members as well as *The Ambassador Hymnal*, which contains over six hundred hymns.

Website

http://www.aflc.org/

George Thomas Kurian

Church of the Lutheran Brethren

History

The Church of the Lutheran Brethren (CLB) began in 1900 in Milwaukee, Wisconsin, when five independent Lutheran congregations made a decision to form a new denomination. The founders of this new denomination were ethnically Norwegian, and their concern was that many of the Norwegian immigrants entering the United States were Lutheran church members but not necessarily active believers in Jesus. They also felt that there were some aspects of the existing Lutheran churches that were not conducive to spiritual vitality, specifically, church membership practices, the form of worship, and the leadership structure of these churches. These areas of concern became the primary distinctives of the new denomination.

A Bible school was organized, and soon thereafter the CLB sent its first missionaries to carry the gospel of Christ overseas. In the 1950s, a home mission department was organized to more intentionally plant new churches in North America.

Headquarters

1020 W Alcott Avenue
Fergus Falls, MN 56537
Telephone: 218-739-3336

Leadership

The Church of the Lutheran Brethren is led at the denominational level by a president and a council of directors, who are elected by delegates of local congregations at the biennial convention. The denomination is subdivided into five regions, each led by a regional pastor.

Locally, congregations are autonomous, led by a board of elders, and choose to call their own pastors. The pastors are ordained by the denomination and generally have been trained through the Lutheran Brethren Seminary.

Core Beliefs

The Bible . . . is the verbally and plenarily inspired Word of God . . . and therefore is the final authoritative guide for faith and conduct.

There is one God eternally existent in three distinct persons in one divine essence, Father, Son, and Holy Spirit. . . .

Through [Adam and Eve's] disobedience the entire human race became totally depraved. . . . They are . . . under the eternal wrath of God.

Jesus Christ, who is true God and true man, by His perfect obedience and substitutionary death on the cross, has purchased our redemption. . . .

The Holy Spirit, . . . through the Word of God . . . convicts people of sin, persuades them to confess their sinfulness to God, and calls them to faith through the gospel. . . .

The knowledge and benefit of Christ's redemption from sin is brought to the human race through the means of grace, namely the Word and the sacraments.

Through the Word of the Law God brings sinners to know their lost condition and to repent. Through the Word of the Gospel He brings sinners to believe in Jesus Christ, to be justified, to enter the process of sanctification, and to have eternal life. . . .

The Church Universal consists of all those who truly believe on Jesus Christ as Savior. The local congregation is an assembly of believers in a certain locality among whom the Gospel is purely taught and the sacraments are rightly administered. . . .

The Lutheran confessions are a summary of Bible doctrines. We adhere to the following confessional writings: The Apostles' Creed, Nicene and Athanasian Creeds, unaltered Augsburg Confession, and Luther's Small Catechism. (clba.org, "Statement of Faith")

The Bible is central in our congregations and in our households.

The Gospel is our treasure and our joy.

We revere God's Law.

The Word and the Sacraments are God's precious means of grace.

We cherish the love and fellowship of God's people.

We long for people to trust in Jesus Christ as Savior and Lord, to come to know Him in a personal way.

We seek to be people of prayer. (clba.org, "Core Values")

Core Practices

The CLB practices believers membership, which means that it attempts to have all of the members of its congregations confessing believers in Christ and actively engaged in the life of the church.

In the local CLB church leadership structure, congregations are led by elders but with the congregational membership still retaining the final decision-making authority.

Each congregation owns its own property, calls its own pastors, and functions autonomously.

Worship

Historically, the CLB's form of worship has been informal as opposed to the typically more formal Lutheran liturgy. Today many CLB congregations incorporate contemporary aspects of worship into their services.

Statistics

There are approximately 115 churches in 21 states and 2 Canadian provinces. The largest pockets of churches are in metro New York, the upper Midwest, and the Pacific Northwest.

Growth

In the 1950s, the CLB began a more intentional effort at starting new churches in the United States and Canada when the home mission arm of the denomination was begun. Since that time, the denomination has more than doubled in size.

Evangelistic Work

The original founders of the denomination had a deep commitment to international mission efforts, a focus illustrated by the fact that the denomination sent its first missionaries just two years after it formed and that the CLB in Africa (Cameroon and Chad) is well over ten times as large as the North American church body. The CLB also conducts mission work in Taiwan and Japan.

Academic Institutions

Hillcrest Lutheran Academy (Fergus Falls, MN)
Lutheran Brethren Seminary (Fergus Falls, MN)

Publication

The CLB provides a bimonthly magazine, *Faith & Fellowship*, for members and parishioners of all CLB congregations.

Website

http://www.clba.org/

Bibliography

Levang, Joseph H. *The Church of the Lutheran Brethren 1900–1975: A Believers Fellowship—A Lutheran Alternative*. Fergus Falls, MN: Faith and Fellowship Press, 1980.

Varberg, Dale E. *Faith and Fellowship: A Look at Lutheran Brethren Theology 1900–2000*. Fergus Falls, MN: Faith and Fellowship Press, 2000.

Brent Juliot

Church of the Lutheran Confession

History

The Church of the Lutheran Confession (CLC) considers itself "the true spiritual descendant of the Evangelical Lutheran Synodical Conference" of North America (clclutheran.org, "Our History"), an association of conservative Lutheran Midwestern church bodies formed in 1872 and dissolved in 1967. Growing conflict beginning in the late 1930s among Synodical Conference member bodies, notably the Lutheran Church—Missouri Synod (LCMS), the Wisconsin Evangelical Lutheran Synod (WELS), and the Evangelical Lutheran Synod (ELS), led Wisconsin to declare itself in "protesting fellowship" with the Missouri Synod in 1953 and the ELS to suspend fellowship with Missouri in 1955. Wisconsin marked Missouri as a persistently erring church body but postponed the decision to terminate fellowship with Missouri until 1957, when a vote to suspend fellowship failed narrowly. At that, some Wisconsin pastors accused their synod of "marking" Missouri as causing divisions and offenses in the church but failing to "avoid" Missouri without delay. They began to withdraw from the Wisconsin Synod, as did some pastors from the ELS and the LCMS, and in 1960 at Watertown, South Dakota, formed the Church of the Lutheran Confession. Meetings between WELS and CLC representatives, particularly during the late 1980s, failed to bring about a resolution of differences required to reestablish formal church fellowship between the two bodies.

Headquarters

501 Grover Road
Eau Claire, WI 54701
Telephone: 715-836-6623

Core Beliefs

According to its website, the CLC holds the principle, "If it is not in Scripture, it is not Lutheran!" (clclutheran.org, "Home").

The CLC is "eager to testify to the truths that had been held by the Synodical Conference in the days when it had been faithful to the doctrines of Scripture and the Lutheran Confessions, as found in the Book of Concord of 1580; thus the name that was chosen: Church of the Lutheran Confession" (clclutheran.org, "Our History").

The CLC rejects "as sacrilegious and destructive every effort by which the intellect or science of man would modify or set aside a single inspired word [of Scripture]." It deplores "the wide-spread apostasy" which "reduces the Bible to the status of a human document containing errors and myths" (clclutheran.org, "Our History").

Website

http://www.clclutheran.org/

Bibliography

Braun, Mark E. *A Tale of Two Synods: Events That Led to the Split between Wisconsin and Missouri*. Milwaukee: Northwestern Publishing House, 2003.

Brug, John F., Edward C. Fredrich II, and Armin W. Schuetze. *WELS and Other Lutherans: Lutheran Church Bodies in the USA*. Milwaukee: Northwestern Publishing House, 1995.

"Church of the Lutheran Confession." http://www.clclutheran.org. "Home" and "Our History."

Lau, John. *Apologia*. Eau Claire, WI: CLC Book House, 2008.

Nolting, Paul Frederick. "Mark . . . Avoid" (Lest the hearts of the simple be deceived). *Romans 16:17–18: Origin of the CLC*. West Columbia, SC: Coordinating Council of the CLC, 1970.

Mark Braun

Conservative Lutheran Association

History

The Conservative Lutheran Association (CLA) emerged from the struggles over doctrinal orthodoxy that ensued upon the merger of the American Lutheran Church (ALC) with the Evangelical Lutheran Church and the United Evangelical Lutheran Church to form the new American Lutheran Church (ALC) in 1960–61. Reuben H. Redal, pastor of Central Lutheran Church in Tacoma, Washington, from 1955 until 2006, founded the CLA under the name Lutherans Alert-National (LAN) in 1965. The organization, a small fellowship of conservative Lutheran congregations and individuals, initially sought to fight liberalizing tendencies within the American Lutheran Church. To this end, the LAN began to sponsor the publication of *Lutherans Alert*, a magazine founded in 1960 to rally opposition to theological liberalism among Lutherans.

In 1969, moreover, the group founded Faith Evangelical Lutheran Seminary (FELS) in order to supply an alternative to the reputedly unorthodox theological education offered by the ALC's official seminaries. It was controversy over this institution that eventually led to the LAN's transformation from a pressure group into a denomination. In 1972 specifically—the year before FELS graduated its first class of ministerial candidates—the ALC's national convention voted not to recognize ministerial education received at unaccredited institutions. Then as now, the primary accrediting body for seminaries in the United States was the American Association of Theological Schools (AATS), now known simply as the Association of Theological Schools (ATS).

FELS at the time lacked AATS accreditation and enjoyed no realistic prospect of attaining it. The denomination's new educational standards thus rendered the first class of FELS graduates ineligible for ALC ordination. Notwithstanding the ALC's decision not to ordain FELS graduates, Redal's congregation called a FELS graduate to be the church's assistant pastor in 1978. After a judicial process that lasted over a year, the denomination decided to expel Central Lutheran from its fellowship because of this offense.

In 1980, Lutheran Alert-National changed its name to the Conservative Lutheran Association and began to function as a denomination. By 1981, the small denomination contained six member congregations, and by 1984, it had grown to twelve congregations and had joined the National Association of Evangelicals. Subsequently, however, the CLA began to dwindle and now numbers only two congregations: Central Lutheran Church of Tacoma and Trinity Lutheran Church of Anaheim, California. The denomination's school, now known as Faith Evangelical College and Seminary, remains committed to conservative evangelicalism but caters to a broad, interdenominational constituency.

Core Beliefs

CLA churches adhere to the Book of Concord and lay special emphasis on the inerrancy of Scripture.

Bibliography

Redal, Reuben H., and Paul G. Vigness. *The Rape of a Confessional Church: The Story of the Excommunication of Central Lutheran Church, Tacoma, Washington, by the American Lutheran Church.* Tacoma, WA: privately printed, 1981.

Dennis W. Jowers

Evangelical Lutheran Church in America

History

The Evangelical Lutheran Church in America (ELCA) is the largest Lutheran denomination in the United States. It is, ironically, both the youngest and the oldest of the large Lutheran church bodies. It is the youngest because the ELCA was constituted in 1987 and officially began operation on January 1, 1988. However, this new denomination was formed from three separate and already well-established North American church bodies: the American Lutheran Church, the Association of Evangelical Lutheran Churches, and the Lutheran Church in America. These bodies already represented mergers of several smaller, ethnic-heritage Lutheran churches that took place in the early twentieth century and the 1960s.

The ELCA also traces its history back to the eighteenth century and the formation of the first Lutheran synod in North America (the Ministerium of Pennsylvania) as well as to Martin Luther and the German Reformation. Today the denomination is composed of 4.2 million members, 65 synods, 9 regions, and nearly 10,000 local congregations in the United States and Caribbean region.

Headquarters

The ELCA churchwide office is also known as the Lutheran Center.

ELCA Churchwide Ministries
8765 West Higgins Road
Chicago, IL 60631
Telephone: 773-380-2700; 800-638-3522
Email: info@elca.org

Core Beliefs

The ELCA holds to traditional doctrinal beliefs in the Trinity and the incarnation of Jesus Christ. It believes that the canonical Scriptures of the Old and New Testaments are the inspired Word of God and "the authoritative source and norm of its [the church's] proclamation, faith, and life" (*ELCA Confession of Faith*). There is an emphasis on the proclamation of the Word of God through both law and gospel. Its confession of faith declares Romans 1:16: "the gospel as the power of God for the salvation of all who believe."

The ELCA also accepts the Apostles', Nicene, and Athanasian Creeds. Along with these ecumenical creeds, it recognizes the unaltered

Augsburg Confession and other confessional writings in the Book of Concord as a true witness to the gospel.

Worship

The Word proclaimed and the sacraments (baptism and Holy Communion) are together considered the means of grace. The ELCA believes that God is genuinely present in baptism, in preaching, and in the sharing of the bread and wine of Holy Communion.

The basic structure of worship is fourfold: gathering, hearing the Word, sharing the meal, and being sent into the world. Many Lutheran churches follow liturgical patterns of worship traditional to Western Christianity. *Evangelical Lutheran Worship*, published in 2006, is the primary worship resource for the ELCA. The *Revised Common Lectionary* is also used.

Controversies

There have been substantial disagreements between more conservative and liberal sections of the denomination that were emphasized by the mergers that formed the ELCA as well as regional differences. Issues of sexuality, specifically homosexuality, have been an area of intense controversy in the past few years. In 2009, the Churchwide Assembly adopted the tenth social statement of the ELCA titled *Human Sexuality: Gift and Trust*. The assembly recorded a two-thirds vote allowing congregations that choose to do so to call and ordain homosexual clergy in "publicly accountable, lifelong, monogamous, same-gender relationships." This decision led hundreds of congregations to leave the ELCA.

There was also heated debate in the late 1990s concerning the Call to Common Mission and full communion agreement with the Episcopal Church (USA). The disagreement centered largely on the validity and necessity of the historic episcopate.

Statistics

As of December 31, 2012, there were 9,533 organized congregations in the ELCA. This number has reportedly decreased by over 700 since 2009.

The synods that have the greatest number of the larger congregations in the denomination (those of 750 or more average weekly attendance) are the Minneapolis Area Synod, the St. Paul Area Synod, and the Grand Canyon Synod.

Largest Churches

Mount Olivet Lutheran Church (Minneapolis, MN), with 15,239 baptized members

Lutheran Church of Hope (West Des Moines, IA), with 13,557 baptized members

St. Andrew Lutheran Church (Eden Prairie, MN), with 10,662 baptized members

Hope (Fargo, ND), with 10,575 baptized members

Shepherd of the Valley (Apple Valley, MN), with 9,456 baptized members

St. Andrew's Lutheran Church (Mahtomedi, MN), with 8,777 baptized members

Lord of Life (Maple Grove, MN), with 8,399 baptized members

Prince of Peace (Burnsville, MN), with 6,857 baptized members

Ecumenism

The ELCA is an active participant in ecumenical discussion and the global community. This is a strong vision within the denomination. The ELCA maintains close ties and has adopted full communion relationships with six church bodies: the Presbyterian Church (USA), the United Church of Christ, the Episcopal Church (USA), the Moravian Church (USA), the Reformed Church in America, and the United Methodist Church. In addition to Orthodox-Lutheran dialogues, the ELCA has an ongoing dialogue with the Roman Catholic Church. Representatives of the Lutheran World Federation and the Roman Catholic Church signed the Joint Declaration on the Doctrine of Justification in 1999 (the United Methodist Church also signed this declaration in 2006). This represented a historic consensus on key issues of faith and called for further dialogue and study together.

The ELCA office of Ecumenical and Inter-Religious Relations also works in cooperation with the ELCA Global Mission and especially with those of the Jewish and Muslim faith. The church seeks for its ecumenical life to be defined by the characteristics of "cooperation, facilitation, accompaniment and formation" (elca.org, "Ecumenical and Inter-Religious Relations").

Affiliations

The ELCA has many connections with Lutheran, ecumenical, and interfaith partner organizations. These connections are often referred to as the "fourth expression" of the church. The ELCA has a strong relationship with ministries such as the Lutheran World Federation, the World Council of Churches, the National Council of the Churches of Christ in the USA,

Lutheran Services in America, the Lutheran Immigration and Refugee Service, Lutheran World Relief, and many more. For the complete list, see elca.org/organization.

Academic Institutions

There are twenty-six colleges and universities, eight seminaries, and over two thousand grade schools and early childhood education centers related to the ELCA. In addition, the denomination has many campus and outdoor ministries. See elca.org/colleges and elca.org/seminaries for a list of colleges and seminaries.

Parachurch Organizations

The ELCA emphasizes faith in action. This is evident by its many social efforts and its strong endeavor to make a difference in the world in practical, realistic ways. The ELCA supports and shares missions with nearly three hundred Lutheran Social Ministry Organizations in the United States. The Global Mission has a presence in over ninety countries around the world. The ELCA also regularly releases social statements, messages, social policy resolutions, and studies of social issues as a means of participating in society.

Electronic Media

The ELCA is involved with numerous events in the mainstream media. *Grace Matters*, previously hosted by Rev. Peter Marty, is a weekly radio ministry of the ELCA. Its television and video programs include *Davey and Goliath*, *Mosaic Television*, documentaries, and many Christmas and Easter specials. It was also involved in the making of films such as *Amazing Grace* and *The Ten Commandments*.

Publications

The *Lutheran* magazine relates the stories of the people of the Evangelical Lutheran Church in America (thelutheran.org.) The ELCA also publishes the *Journal of Lutheran Ethics* (elca.org /jle). The publishing house of the ELCA is Augsburg Fortress, located in Minneapolis, Minnesota.

Website

http://www.elca.org/

Alyssa Lehr Evans

Evangelical Lutheran Synod

History

The Evangelical Lutheran Synod (ELS) is an outgrowth of Norwegian Lutheran immigration to the United States that began in the 1820s. Lay preacher Elling Eielsen served Norwegian settlements in the Fox River Valley and Muskego, Wisconsin, during the 1830s and 1840s, and in 1853, the Norwegian Synod was organized near Beloit, Wisconsin.

In 1872, the Norwegian Synod became a founding member of the Evangelical Lutheran Synodical Conference of North America, but during the 1880s, about one-third of its membership left the synod as a result of the election controversy. The Madison Agreement of 1912 failed to resolve differences regarding the doctrine of election, but a majority of Norwegian Synod leaders joined various other Norwegian Lutheran groups to form the Norwegian Lutheran Church in America in 1917. The next year, a minority of members at Winnebago County, Iowa, formed the Norwegian Synod of the American Evangelical Lutheran Church, known informally as the Little Norwegian Synod. In 1920, this smaller group joined the Lutheran Synodical Conference and in 1955 adopted its present name, the Evangelical Lutheran Synod.

Headquarters

6 Browns Court
Mankato, MN 56001
Telephone: 507-344-7354

Core Beliefs

The 1992 statement "We Believe, Teach and Confess" summarizes the doctrinal position of the ELS, in accordance with the Lutheran Book of Concord of 1580. Article 8 of "We Believe, Teach and Confess" says that "the pastoral office cannot be conferred on women" and that "it is God's will that only qualified men be called to this office." By the same principle, "women should not exercise authority over men in the congregational decision-making process, such as by holding voting membership in an assembly that makes the final decisions for a church" (els .org, "We Believe, Teach and Confess").

Worship

The ELS worship committee produced the *Evangelical Lutheran Hymnary* in 1996. While containing hymns of German, Scandinavian, Greek, Latin, Czech, French, and other origins, the Norwegian heritage of the ELS is evident throughout. The *Hymnary* contains 602 hymns; texts of the Augsburg Confession, Martin Luther's Small Catechism, and the three ecumenical creeds; and numerous rites of the Divine Service and daily orders.

Divisions and Splits

During the 1930s and 1940s, the ELS became increasingly distressed at perceived theological drift in the Lutheran Church—Missouri Synod (LCMS), chiefly concerning the doctrine of church fellowship. In 1955, the ELS terminated fellowship with the LCMS and in 1963, together with the Wisconsin Evangelical Lutheran Synod (WELS), withdrew from the Synodical Conference. Because of disagreements over admonition and termination of fellowship, some pastors and congregations of the ELS left to form the Church of the Lutheran Confession in 1960. The ELS and the WELS remain in doctrinal fellowship today.

Controversies

Although some Norwegian immigrants practiced the custom of lay preaching, in 1862, the Norwegian Synod adopted a position statement that said ministers needed a divine call for public preaching. The early Norwegian Synod also experienced controversies over the understanding of Sunday, slavery, and absolution.

Statistics

There are 19,945 members worldwide.

Growth

The strongest concentration of ELS congregations is in Minnesota, Wisconsin, and other parts of the upper Midwest. Its greatest expansion has occurred in Florida and along the West Coast of the United States.

Ecumenism

Article 10 of "We Believe, Teach and Confess" rejects "unionism, that is, church fellowship with adherents of false doctrine" as well as participation in "ecumenical endeavors which compromise the pure doctrine of God's Word." The ELS also condemns separatism, "the refusal to acknowledge and practice fellowship where there is agreement in doctrine" (els.org, "We Believe, Teach and Confess").

Academic Institutions

Founded in 1911 as Bethany Ladies College in Mankato, Minnesota, Bethany Lutheran College was reorganized in 1919 and was purchased by the ELS in 1926. It remained a two-year college until 2001, when it became a four-year liberal arts college. Bethany Lutheran Theological Seminary, also in Mankato, opened in 1946.

Parachurch Organization

The ELS works with Thoughts of Faith, a church-related organization with missions in the Czech Republic and Latvia.

Publications

Lutheran Sentinel
Lutheran Synod Quarterly

Website

http://www.evangelicallutheransynod.org/

Bibliography

Aaberg, Theodore A. *A City Set on a Hill: A History of the Evangelical Lutheran Synod (Norwegian Synod) 1918–1968.* Lake Mills, IA: Graphic Publishing Company, 1968.

"Evangelical Lutheran Synod." http://www.els.org. "We Believe, Teach, and Confess."

Larson, Herbert J., and Juul B. Madson. *Built on the Rock.* Mankato, MN: Lutheran Synod Book Company, 1992.

Lillegard, George O., ed. *Faith of Our Fathers.* Mankato, MN: Lutheran Synod Book Company, 1953.

Ylvisaker, S. C. *Grace for Grace.* Mankato, MN: Board of Publications, Evangelical Lutheran Synod, 1943.

Mark Braun

Lutheran Church—Missouri Synod

History

The German Evangelical Lutheran Synod of Missouri, Ohio, and Other States was organized in Chicago in 1847 and joined together several small groupings of confessional or "Old Lutherans." The synod's home base was Perry County, Missouri, where Saxon immigrants had fled to avoid government pressure to compromise their confessional convictions. Under the aggressive leadership of C. F. W. Walther, the Missouri Synod established itself as a strong voice for confessional Lutheranism throughout the United States. The Missouri Synod was a founding partner in the Evangelical Lutheran Synodical Conference of North America in 1872. Upon Walther's death in 1887, synod leadership passed to Franz Pieper, who continued in Walther's confessional Lutheran path until his death in 1931. By World War I, Concordia Seminary in St. Louis had become the largest Protestant seminary in North America and Concordia Publishing House the third largest Protestant publishing house in the United States. The synod adopted its current official name, the Lutheran Church—Missouri Synod (LCMS), in 1947.

Headquarters

LCMS International Center
1333 S Kirkwood Road
St. Louis, MO 63122

Worship

While the synod has adhered to historic Lutheran liturgical worship since its founding, widespread elements of evangelical and charismatic worship are also featured in many LCMS churches.

Divisions and Splits

The Lutheran Synodical Conference suffered doctrinal disagreement and the loss of two of its member synods in the election controversy of the 1880s. Several attempts early in the twentieth century to resolve these differences proved unsuccessful.

Deeper internal conflict arose in the 1930s over the doctrines of church fellowship and the inerrancy of Scripture, resulting in the dissolution of the Synodical Conference in 1967. Tensions demarcated and exacerbated by independent publications of opposing factions within the synod led to a showdown between conservative administrators and an increasingly liberal faculty at Concordia Seminary in St. Louis. Rather than submit to individual doctrinal examinations, a majority of professors, along with sympathetic students, walked off campus in February 1974. Supporters of the striking professors formed the American Evangelical Lutheran Church in 1976 and joined with the Lutheran Church in America and the American Lutheran Church to form the Evangelical Lutheran Church in America in 1988. Since the late 1970s, the LCMS has returned to a more conservative stance similar to its pre-1935 position.

Controversies

Remnants of Missouri's mid-twentieth-century controversies remain. The requirement of full doctrinal agreement as the basis for church fellowship is challenged by the desire to present greater testimony in a world of declining Christian witness and growing religious pluralism. Debates linger over the inerrancy of Scripture. The ordination of women finds sporadic but unsustained support.

Statistics

Baptized members: 2,383,084
Congregations: 6,167

Clergymen: 9,164
Elementary schools: 977
Regional Lutheran high schools: 109

Growth

Riding a massive wave of German migration to the Midwest, the Missouri Synod grew to a baptized membership of 687,334 in 1897, with Missouri congregations in all but three states and in Canada and Mexico. By its centennial in 1947, the synod numbered 1,567,453 baptized members in 4,429 congregations.

Ecumenism

Reception of Holy Communion is "a confession of the unity of Faith," although "there will be instances when sensitive pastoral care needs to be exercised" (lcms.org, "Frequently Asked Questions: Denominations"). By following a practice in which fellowship is practiced only with members of the LCMS or churches with which it is in altar and pulpit fellowship, pastors and churches seek to preserve confessional and gospel integrity.

Academic Institutions

Concordia College (Selma, AL)
Concordia College, New York (Bronxville, NY)
Concordia Seminary (St. Louis, MO)
Concordia Theological Seminary (Fort Wayne, IN)
Concordia University (Ann Arbor, MI)
Concordia University (Irvine, CA)
Concordia University (St. Paul, MN)
Concordia University, Chicago (River Forest, IL)
Concordia University, Nebraska (Seward, NE)
Concordia University, Portland (Portland, OR)
Concordia University, Texas (Austin, TX)
Concordia University, Wisconsin (Mequon, WI)

Publications

Concordia Journal
Concordia Theological Quarterly
The Lutheran Witness

Website

http://www.lcms.org/

Bibliography

Adams, James E. *Preus of Missouri and the Great Lutheran Civil War*. New York: Harper & Row, 1977.

Baepler, Walter A. *A Century of Grace: A History of the Missouri Synod, 1847–1947*. St. Louis: Concordia, 1947.

Braun, Mark E. *A Tale of Two Synods: Events That Led to the Split between Wisconsin and Missouri*. Milwaukee: Northwestern Publishing House, 2003.

Graebner, Alan. *Uncertain Saints: The Laity in the Lutheran Church—Missouri Synod, 1900–1970.* Westport, CT: Greenwood, 1975.

Lueking, F. Dean. *Mission in the Making: The Missionary Enterprise among Missouri Synod Lutherans, 1846–1963.* St. Louis: Concordia, 1964.

Marquart, Kurt E. *Anatomy of an Explosion: Missouri in Lutheran Perspective.* Fort Wayne, IN: Concordia Theological Seminary Press, 1977.

Suelflow, August R. *Servant of the Word: The Life and Ministry of C. F. W. Walther.* St. Louis: Concordia, 2000.

Weisheit, Eldon. *The Zeal of His House: Five Generations of Lutheran Church—Missouri Synod History (1847–1972).* St. Louis: Concordia, 1973.

Zimmerman, Paul A. *A Seminary in Crisis: The Inside Story of the Preus Fact Finding Committee.* St. Louis: Concordia, 2007.

Mark Braun

Wisconsin Evangelical Lutheran Synod

History

The Wisconsin Evangelical Lutheran Synod (WELS) developed amid the vast migration of German immigrants to the upper Midwest of the United States from the early 1840s to the outbreak of World War I. Founded by Milwaukee pastor Johannes Muehlhaeuser and four other Lutheran pastors in 1850, the German Evangelical Ministerium of Wisconsin originally practiced a "mild" confessionalism. Under the leadership of Adolf Hoenecke and Johannes Bading, the synod moved toward a more confessional stance in the 1860s. The Wisconsin Synod formed a federation with Lutheran synods of Minnesota and Michigan in 1892, and the Nebraska Synod was added in 1904. These synods formed the single Joint Evangelical Lutheran Synod of Wisconsin and Other States in 1917. The name Wisconsin Evangelical Lutheran Synod was adopted in 1959.

Headquarters

2929 N Mayfair Road
Milwaukee, WI 53226
Telephone: 414-256-3888

Core Beliefs

The WELS subscribes without reservation to the Lutheran Book of Concord of 1580. Chief among Lutheran beliefs is justification by grace alone through faith alone in the substitutionary atonement of Christ. Lutherans regard baptism and the Lord's Supper as sacraments through which the Holy Spirit works saving faith. The WELS considers the Bible to be the inspired and inerrant Word of God. It is in doctrinal fellowship with the Evangelical Lutheran Synod.

The WELS practices infant baptism and does not ordain women to pastoral ministry but allows them to serve in various public ministries, primarily as elementary and secondary teachers. Church fellowship is practiced only with those whose outward confession demonstrates complete doctrinal agreement with the WELS. The teaching of the "two kingdoms" recognizes both church and state as God's institutions, but each with separate tasks and tools.

Worship

Worship in the synod's early history was simple and unadorned, but with the twentieth century came increasing emphasis on observance of the historic Lutheran liturgy and greater use of Lutheran hymnody. A growing cohort of WELS congregations is adopting a more evangelical style of worship.

Divisions and Splits

In 1872, the Wisconsin Synod became a founding partner in the Evangelical Lutheran Synodical Conference of North America along with the Missouri, Ohio, and other Midwestern Lutheran bodies. Beginning in the 1930s, disagreements chiefly over the teaching and practice of church fellowship led to Wisconsin's break in fellowship with the Lutheran Church—Missouri Synod in 1961 and its exit from the Synodical Conference in 1963.

Controversies

The requirement of complete doctrinal unity as a basis for church fellowship has precluded WELS participation in twentieth-century Lutheran mergers, such as those that formed the United Lutheran Church in America (1918), the American Lutheran Church (1930), and the Evangelical Lutheran Church in America (1988). Church fellowship disputes also led to an exodus of pastors and congregations in the 1950s and 1960s, many of whom formed the Church of the Lutheran Confession in 1960. Fellowship disagreements precipitated the demise of the Lutheran Synodical Conference in 1967.

Statistics

Baptized members: 394,241
Congregations: 1,276
Pastors: 1,300
Elementary schools: 343, with an enrollment of 25,712

Largest Churches

The numerical strength of the WELS remains in Wisconsin, Minnesota, and Michigan, with a significant representation of congregations also in Arizona, California, Texas, Florida, and other parts of the Great Lakes and Northern Plains regions.

Missionary and Evangelistic Work

Organized originally to reclaim German immigrants, the WELS now conducts neighborhood canvasses and has planted new congregations in many metropolitan areas of the United States, particularly where Lutheranism has been historically underrepresented.

Academic Institutions

Luther Preparatory School (Watertown, WI)
Martin Luther College (New Ulm, MN)
Michigan Lutheran Seminary (Saginaw, MI)
Wisconsin Lutheran Seminary (Mequon, WI)

Federations of individuals and congregations maintain Wisconsin Lutheran College in Milwaukee and twenty regional Lutheran high schools.

Publications

Wisconsin Lutheran Quarterly is the oldest continuously published Lutheran theological journal. *Forward in Christ,* formerly the *Northwestern Lutheran,* is the synod's monthly news magazine.

Website

http://www.wels.net/

Bibliography

Braun, Mark E. *A Tale of Two Synods: Events That Led to the Split between Wisconsin and Missouri.* Milwaukee: Northwestern Publishing House, 2003.

———. "The Black Geneva Piety of the Wisconsin Synod: An Analysis of the Changing View of the Relationship of Doctrine and Liturgy within the WELS." *Concordia Historical Institute Quarterly* 79 (Fall 2006): 180–94 (part 1); (Winter 2006): 206–34 (part 2).

Brug, John F., Edward C. Fredrich II, and Armin W. Schuetze. *WELS and Other Lutherans: Lutheran Church Bodies in the USA.* Milwaukee: Northwestern Publishing House, 1995.

Fredrich, Edward C. *The Wisconsin Synod Lutherans: A History of the Single Synod, Federation, and Merger.* Milwaukee: Northwestern Publishing House, 1992.

Koehler, John Philipp. *The History of the Wisconsin Synod.* St. Cloud, MN: FaithLife, 1970.

Schuetze, Armin W. *The Synodical Conference: Ecumenical Endeavor.* Milwaukee: Northwestern Publishing House, 2000.

Mark Braun

Mennonite

Apostolic Christian Church (Nazarean)

History

The Apostolic Christian Church (Nazarean) began in Switzerland in 1830 with the conversion of Samuel H. Froehlich, a young divinity student. Froehlich was shaped largely by the Anabaptist and Pietist movements of the sixteenth century, and he believed his conversion marked the pattern of the New Testament Christian experience. Consequently, he sought to restore the church to its New Testament origin. He formed disciples around him, and his group took the name Evangelical Baptist Church.

By the 1850s, Froehlich had come to America and was ministering to Swiss and German immigrants in the Midwest. A fellow Swiss pastor named Benedict Weyeneth had organized a congregation in upstate New York in 1847 that joined and supported Froehlich's movement. In 1917, to prevent confusion with other similarly named Baptist groups, the group's nomenclature was changed to the Apostolic Christian Church.

The Apostolic Christian Church (Nazarean) separated from the Apostolic Christian Church of America in 1906. The division was due primarily to cultural conflicts that arose with new émigrés from the Balkans who sought to assimilate into the churches of North America. One notable example was the wearing of mustaches, which was not acceptable for those who had been under Amish influence. Some members were subsequently disciplined for their refusal to shave. A significant division followed. Many of the congregations of this Nazarean group retained their Eastern European character, which is reflected in their cultural practices. To date, the Apostolic Christian Church (Nazarean) and the Apostolic Christian Church of America are nearly identical in doctrine yet are completely separate denominations.

Headquarters

Apostolic Christian Church Foundation Inc.
1135 Sholey Road
Richmond, VA 23231
Telephone: 877-662-7905

Core Beliefs

The core beliefs of the church are contained in an eighteen-point statement of faith. Among these are belief in the Bible as the infallible Word of God; an affirmation of the triune nature of God; and an affirmation of the deity and humanity of Christ, his virgin birth, and his bodily resurrection. This document also affirms the fact that all sinners are lost and that every person needs salvation by faith and trust in Christ. The church holds to believer's baptism for those who have articulated a salvation experience. The statement of faith affirms the doctrine of apostasy, or losing one's salvation.

Website

http://accfoundation.org/

Bibliography

Mead, Frank S., Samuel S. Hill, and Craig D. Atwood. "Apostolic Christian Churches of America." In *Handbook of Denominations in the United States*. 13th ed. Nashville: Abingdon, 2010.

R. Philip Roberts

Apostolic Christian Church of America

History

The Apostolic Christian Church of America was founded in the early 1830s by Samuel H. Froehlich (1803–57) in Switzerland. Approximately 110 congregations were formed across Europe in thirty-five years. Froehlich's intent was to organize a church based on a literal interpretation of God's Word. At first, the movement was known as the Evangelical Baptist Church but later became known as the Apostolic Christian Church of America. This name was chosen because the church followed the teachings of Christ and the apostles. The first congregation in America was organized in Lewis County, New York, in 1847. Another church was formed a year later in Sardis, Ohio.

From this beginning in America the church grew, primarily in the fertile farming areas of the Midwest. As immigrants came from Europe (mostly from the Froehlich churches) and new converts were added in the United States, the church grew rapidly. The believers were very evangelistic. From the 1920s on, most of the new churches formed in America were founded in urban areas. The biggest reason for this seems to have been that many in the younger generation wanted to pursue occupational opportunities in areas other than farming. Today the Apostolic Christian Church consists of a blend of city and rural churches.

Headquarters

3420 North Sheridan Road
Peoria, IL 61604

Core Beliefs

The church believes in the Bible as the inspired, infallible, and inerrant Word of God. The New Testament is the foundation of the Apostolic Christian Church. The authorized King James Version is preferred. The church also believes in the Trinity, the atoning death of Christ on the cross as a ransom for all, and the sealing of the Holy Spirit. This is acknowledged and symbolized in a prayer of consecration (following baptism) by the laying on of hands of the elder. The church also believes in the loss of one's salvation.

Governmental authority is respected and obeyed. Members serve in a noncombatant status in the military. Oaths are not taken, but truth is affirmed.

The church's statement of faith consists of a twenty-point biblical-theological statement of belief, which also contains a ten-point statement definition of "Apostolic Christian Church Government" (apostolicchristian.org/faith_state ment.php).

Website

http://www.apostolicchristian.org/

Bibliography

Klopfenstein, P. A. *Marching to Zion: A History of the Apostolic Christian Church in America, 1847–1982.* Eureka, IL: Apostolic Christian Church of America, 1984.

Mead, Frank S., Samuel S. Hill, and Craig D. Atwood. *Handbook of Denominations in the United States.* 13th ed. Nashville: Abingdon, 2010. (See esp. pp. 213–14.)

Michael McMullen

Beachy Amish Mennonite Churches

History

The Amish originated with Jacob Ammann (1644–1725). He lived in Switzerland and led a split of the Mennonites in his area over the issue of shunning. Some Mennonites believed they could have fellowship with like-minded non-Mennonites, whereas Ammann believed all non-Mennonites should be shunned. Ammann's followers eventually formed the group known as the Amish, with a substantial number coming to the colonies, especially to the Lancaster County, Pennsylvania, area.

By 1787, at least seventy communities of Amish lived in Pennsylvania. These Amish became known as the Old Order Amish and today number over one hundred thousand (although they have expanded outside Pennsylvania). Other divisions occurred, with the one producing the Beachy Amish taking place in the early 1900s.

A church known as the Weavertown Amish Mennonite Church in Lancaster County, Pennsylvania, disagreed with the practice of shunning all non-Amish. As members became involved with non-Amish, they began to withdraw from the Old Order Amish community. At first, this small Amish church was known as the Peachey Church, after Amish pastor Samuel W. Peachey. Eventually, this group decided in 1928 to allow some modern conveniences, such as cars and electricity. In 1927, an Amish church in Salisbury, Pennsylvania, broke from the Old Order Amish, also over the matter of shunning. The leader of this church was Bishop Moses M. Beachy (1874–1946). The Salisbury church became linked with the Weavertown Amish Mennonite Church and eventually formed the Beachy Amish.

Headquarters

The Beachy Amish is a fellowship, which is a loose alignment of like-minded churches. While no central headquarters exists, the Beachy Amish does have annual ministers' meetings and youth fellowship meetings.

Core Beliefs

While the Beachy Amish has no central declaration of faith, all churches adhere to the principles of the Dordrecht Confession of Faith of 1632, a central Mennonite confession. Members uphold certain Anabaptist principles, such as nonresistance, congregational rule, noninvolvement in governmental affairs, and adult baptism; certain Amish principles, such as plain dress (although not as plain as Old Order Amish) and avoiding full involvement in modern conveniences; and practices that separate them from Old Order Amish, such as use of automobiles, electricity, telephones, and limited computer/internet services, although television is not utilized.

Website

http://www.beachyam.org/

Bibliography

Nolt, Steven M. *A History of the Amish*. Rev. ed. Intercourse, PA: Good Books, 1992.

Yoder, Elmer S. *The Beachy Amish Mennonite Fellowship Churches*. Hartville, OH: Diaknoia Ministries, 1987.

Mark Nickens

Bible Fellowship Church

History

The Bible Fellowship Church has its roots in the Evangelische Mennoniten Gemeinschaft von Ost-Pennsylvanien (Evangelical Mennonite Society of East Pennsylvania), founded in 1858 as a protest by revivalists against their former bishops in the New Mennonite Association who were seeking to impose unacceptable rules on their churches. The first meetinghouse was dedicated in November 1859.

As a result of revivals, the Evangelical Mennonites joined with other Mennonite groups and became the Evangelical United Mennonites in 1879. Further unions resulted in another name change in 1883 to the Mennonite Brethren in Christ. In 1947, the general conference voted to change the name again, to the United Missionary Church, and dropped all Mennonite connections. The Pennsylvania Conference protested and voted in 1952 to separate themselves, adopting the name Bible Fellowship Church in 1959. They ratified new articles of faith, dropped the practice of foot washing, and subsequently also dropped the position of conference superintendent. Autonomous congregational government was replaced by a modified presbyterian system with each congregation ruled by local elders.

Headquarters

3000 Fellowship Drive
Whitehall, PA 18052
Telephone: 888-724-5325

Core Beliefs

The Bible Fellowship Church is a trinitarian church that believes in eternal salvation through the acceptable sacrifice of Christ for sinful humanity. This salvation comes to individuals by grace through faith and the instrumentality of the Holy Spirit, completely apart from human merit and works. The Bible is verbally inspired and is the only authority for faith and conduct. Christ instituted the local church for the instruction and fellowship of Christians and the evangelization of the world. At the time of his personal, bodily return, he will establish his earthly kingdom.

The Bible Fellowship Church's practices include baptism by immersion, observance of the Lord's Supper, and tithing.

The defining document of the Bible Fellowship Church is *Faith and Order of Bible Fellowship Church*, 2009, revised edition.

Website

http://www.mybfc.org/

Bibliography

Faith and Order of Bible Fellowship Church. Rev. ed. Produced by order of the Annual Conference of the Bible Fellowship Church, 2009. http://www.mybfc.org/downloads/2010FaithAndOrder.pdf.

Mead, Frank S., Samuel S. Hill, and Craig D. Atwood. *Handbook of Denominations in the United States*. 13th ed. Nashville: Abingdon, 2010. (See esp. pp. 278–79.)

Shelly, Harold P. *The Bible Fellowship Church*. Bethlehem, PA: Bible Fellowship Church Historical Society, 1992.

Michael McMullen

Church of God in Christ, Mennonite

History

The Mennonites are descended from the Anabaptists of the sixteenth century, who insisted on believer's baptism and a nonconformed way of life. They were bitterly persecuted for their doctrines.

Desiring religious freedom, Mennonites began to immigrate to America in 1683. Holding to the doctrine of nonresistance, they refused to participate in war, which earned them the reputation of being a peace-loving people.

However, times of testing brought spiritual decline. One who contended for the historic faith was John Holdeman (1832–1900), a member of

135

the Mennonite Church in Ohio. He appealed to church leaders for spiritual revival, but little action was taken. In 1859, he and others began worshiping separately. Eventually, this small group organized as the Church of God in Christ, Mennonite.

Headquarters

420 N Wedel Avenue
PO Box 313
Moundridge, KS 67107
Telephone: 620-345-2532

Core Beliefs

Two historic Mennonite confessions of faith are accepted, the Eighteen Articles of Faith, adopted in 1632 in Dordrecht, Holland, and the Thirty-Three Articles of Faith, as printed in the *Martyrs' Mirror*, a seventeenth-century Dutch martyrology. The writings of Anabaptist leaders Menno Simons and Dirk Philips are held in high regard.

The church is trinitarian and believes in the inerrancy of the Bible, the incarnation, the virgin birth, and the bodily resurrection of Jesus Christ.

Salvation is through grace, beginning with faith in Jesus Christ as Savior, and results in obedience to Christ's teachings. The saving gospel should be shared with mankind. The church is amillennialist in eschatology.

Baptism is administered by pouring and is for born-again believers only. During the annual Communion service, foot washing precedes the Lord's Supper. Communion is for church members only, and each member must first testify of his or her standing with God and fellow man as well as harmony with the doctrines of the church.

Personal service to others is encouraged, especially in times of need or disaster, but members are nonconformed to the world in spirit and manner of life. Being nonresistant, they do not take part in politics, elected government offices, or the military. Men wear a beard and women wear a devotional head covering after baptism. A simple, modest lifestyle is highly advocated, and higher education is discouraged. Church teachings prohibit involvement with modern electronic entertainment except for properly filtered internet.

The church practices excommunication and scriptural avoidance of members who have become willfully disobedient or have resisted brotherly admonition, as described in Matthew 18. Restoration of repentant, errant members is actively sought, and they are welcomed back.

Worship

Most congregations worship twice on Sunday. Sunday school is held prior to the morning preaching service. Singing is a cappella.

Controversies

There have been no major schisms since the beginning of the church. Some members have become dissatisfied and left the church, but few have followed. Those who leave usually do so because they find the doctrines of the church too restrictive. Though some members left the faith during a time of deep revival in the 1970s, the overall effect on the denomination was a strengthening of unity and purpose.

Statistics

The church has congregations in the United States, Canada, and twenty-seven other countries. Brazil, Haiti, Mexico, Nigeria, and the Philippines have the most members outside North America. There are over twenty-two thousand members worldwide.

Missionary and Evangelistic Work

The church expanded its mission program during the 1930s in Mexico. Since then, congregations or mission stations have been established in various countries in Africa, Asia, Central and South America, the Caribbean, and Europe.

Parachurch Organizations

Mission outreach and humanitarian service are under the oversight of various committees. Disaster relief work is accomplished by many volunteers. The church publishes and distributes literature worldwide in fifty-four languages. In several locations, skilled nursing care facilities are operated for the benefit of the aged or handicapped. Emergency shelter homes and hospital aid services are provided in several communities. Youth members often volunteer to staff these voluntary service units.

Publications

The *Messenger of Truth* has been published every two weeks since 1903. This periodical contains doctrinal articles and items of general interest to the church. Numerous other books on doctrine and Christian life and shape note songbooks have been written by church members. This literature is published or distributed by Gospel Publishers.

Website

http://www.churchofgodinchristmennonite.net/

Bibliography

Bible Doctrine and Practice. Moundridge, KS: Gospel Publishers, 1998.

Principles of Faith. Moundridge, KS: Gospel Publishers, 1996.

Douglas Salsbury

Conservative Mennonite Conference

History

The roots of the Conservative Mennonite Conference go back to the sixteenth-century Anabaptist movement in Switzerland, the influence of Menno Simons (1496–1561) of Holland, and a movement among the Swiss-German Anabaptists of the late seventeenth century connected with Jacob Ammann. The more recent history is traced to a meeting in 1910 in Pigeon, Michigan, attended by five Amish Mennonite ministers who focused on the vision and concerns of the churches they represented. They believed strongly in the autonomy of the local congregation and so were concerned that a conference not override the authority of congregational decision making. At the same time, they were concerned about the lack of unity among many Amish Mennonite congregations and desired a conference structure that could help local congregations when unity was threatened. So was born the Conservative Amish Mennonite Conference. In 1954, the name was changed to Conservative Mennonite Conference.

Headquarters

9910 Rosedale Milford Center Road
Irwin, OH 43029
Telephone: 740-857-1234

Core Beliefs

The Conservative Mennonite Conference is an evangelical body that believes in the infallibility and authority of the Bible, the full divinity and full humanity of Jesus Christ, the need of salvation because of human rebelliousness and self-will, salvation by divine grace through faith in the sacrifice of the shed blood of Jesus Christ, the necessity of preaching Jesus Christ as the only way of salvation, and the personal return of Jesus Christ, followed by eternal punishment for the lost and eternal bliss for the saved.

As an Anabaptist fellowship of churches, the conference also believes in the New Testament as fulfilling and succeeding the Old Testament as

the authoritative guide for God's people today; the church as the body of Christ, redeemed by Jesus Christ, and visibly consisting of committed disciples; voluntary baptism and church membership; separation of church and state; the way of love in human relations, including refraining from participation in military and other violent force; and honesty in speech without the use of an oath.

As a conservative affiliation of churches, the conference seeks to interpret and apply the Scriptures in their full literary sense, believing that the available manuscripts and texts emanated from autographs inspired inerrantly by the Holy Spirit.

The Conservative Mennonite Conference practices believer's baptism, seen as an external symbol of internal spiritual purity and performed by immersion or pouring of water on the head; Communion; washing the feet of the saints, following Jesus's example and reminding believers of the need to be washed of pride, rivalry, and selfish motives; anointing the sick with oil—a symbol of the Holy Spirit and of the healing power of God—offered with the prayer of faith; and laying on of hands for ordination, symbolizing the imparting of responsibility and of God's power to fulfill that responsibility.

The defining documents of the denomination include the following: the *Conservative Mennonite Statement of Theology* (1991) and the *Conservative Mennonite Statement of Practice* (2007).

Bibliography

Mead, Frank S., Samuel S. Hill, and Craig D. Atwood. *Handbook of Denominations in the United States.* 13th ed. Nashville: Abingdon, 2010.(See esp. pp. 138, 384.)

Miller, Ivan J. *History of Conservative Mennonite Conference, 1910–1985.* Grantsville, MD: Miller, 1985.

Michael McMullen

Fellowship of Evangelical Bible Churches

History

The Fellowship of Evangelical Bible Churches (FEBC) was organized on October 14, 1889, under the name Conference of the United Mennonite Brethren in North America. It marked the joining of two churches: the Ebenezer Church in Henderson, Nebraska, led by Isaac Peters, and the *Brudertaler* Church in Mountain Lake, Minnesota, led by Aaron Wall. Both Peters and Wall were immigrants from southern Russia who had joined with the Mennonite movement in the midwestern United States. Having become frustrated with the "worldly" practices of the larger Mennonite community, this new group sought to reemphasize the new birth and a changed life as a requirement for baptism. Members also emphasized a Christian life more separated from worldly practices and a more rigid implementation of church discipline. Soon after its beginning, the church changed its name to the Defenseless Mennonite Brethren of Christ in North America. In 1937, the group adopted the name the Evangelical Mennonite Brethren Conference, which was later changed to the Fellowship of Evangelical Bible Churches in July 1987. The fellowship is currently comprised of forty-seven churches spreading up through the Midwest into Canada. Despite being small in size, the church continues to make considerable strides toward international missions and evangelism.

Headquarters

FEBC International Office
11605 W Dodge Road
Suite 3
Omaha, NE 68154-2566
Telephone: 402-965-3860

Leadership

President: Blaine Donaldson

Core Beliefs

The core beliefs of the FEBC are reflected in the Articles of Faith and Ordinances and Practices adopted by the fellowship. In summation, these articles declare that the Bible is the inspired Word of God and without error in the original manuscripts; God is triune in nature—one in essence, three in persons; man is created in the image of God but sinful and in need of redemption; salvation is by divine grace alone through faith that results in assurance, justification, sanctification, and eternal security for all who believe; the return of Christ is personal, imminent, and premillennial; and the ordinances are believer's baptism (no prescribed mode) and the Lord's Supper. The FEBC also has a strong dispensational view of Israel and the church.

Website

http://www.fellowshipforward.org/

Bibliography

Epp, H. F. "Evangelical Mennonite Brethren." In *The Mennonite Encyclopedia: A Comprehensive Reference Work on the Anabaptist-Mennonite Movement*, edited by Harold S. Bender and C. Henry Smith, 4:262–64. Scottdale, PA: Mennonite Publishing House, 1959.

———. "Historical Sketch of the Evangelical Mennonite Brethren Conference." http://www.febcministries.org/pdf/historic_sketch-epp_1953.pdf.

"Fellowship of Evangelical Churches." In *Yearbook of American and Canadian Churches 2010*, edited by Eileen W. Linder. Nashville: Abingdon, 2010.

Smith, Henry C. *The Story of the Mennonites*. 4th ed. Revised by Cornelius Krahn. Newton, KS: Mennonite Publication Office, 1957.

William R. Osborne

Hutterian Brethren

History

Hutterites are Anabaptists who descended from the Radical Reformation of the sixteenth century. They practice a communal form of life and share in a community of goods while practicing absolute pacifism. After the death of their founder, Jakob Hutter, in 1536, the Hutterites experienced a migration through numerous countries due to persecution in the nineteenth century. This oppression eventually brought them to settle in America in the 1800s. Between 1874 and 1879, three groups of Hutterites numbering over twelve hundred individuals migrated to the United States. Once settled in America, the Hutterites followed three distinct leaders and thereby divided into three clear groupings: the Schmiedeleut, the Dariusleut, and the Lehrerleut. Most Hutterites are located in Canada, but the Dakotas, Montana, and other parts of the United States host a number of colonies. By the end of the nineteenth century, the Hutterite movement had decreased significantly.

During the course of World War I, the Hutterites underwent a measure of persecution in the United States due to their commitment to pacifism. Four Hutterite men were imprisoned, later dying in Leavenworth Prison. Consequently, many Hutterites abandoned the United States and moved to the western Canadian provinces. A number of them did return to the Dakotas, however, in the late 1930s when laws were passed to protect conscientious objectors. The Hutterites have expanded to other countries, including Japan, Australia, and Nigeria.

Headquarters

The Hutterites do not have a central organization and therefore have no headquarters.

Core Beliefs

The Apostles' Creed is considered to be a minimal mandatory belief statement for all Hutterites. The creed serves as their confession of faith, and its twelve individual points must be acknowledged as truth. Hutterites practice baptism by immersion for those who have confessed faith and acknowledged the truths of the Apostles' Creed. The Lord's Supper is practiced by believers only and is considered symbolic and nonsacerdotal. Hutterites believe in the essential sharing of goods among the community, practicing their interpretation of the statement "having all things in common" from Acts (2:44–46; 4:32). Hutterites believe in absolute separation of church and state as well as pacifism.

Worship

Daily worship is observed in the Hutterite communities. It generally lasts half an hour and is most often observed before supper. On Sundays and religious holidays, church services are held in the morning, typically lasting about seventy-five to ninety minutes. Services are usually started with a song followed by teaching that focuses on a biblical theme. Sunday morning also includes a sermon that begins with a song and is followed by a short prayer. Special services are held for baptisms and weddings.

Statistics

Members: 42,000

Colony size: 60–160 people

Number of colonies: Alberta, 167; British Columbia, 2; Manitoba, 105; Minnesota, 9; Montana, 50; North Dakota, 6; Saskatchewan, 60; South Dakota, 54; Washington, 5

Trends

Hutterites continue to experience a measure of prosperity due to their disciplined work habits. Their numbers are not increasing, and a growing number of young people seem to be looking for opportunities to assimilate into mainstream society. The movement remains small, although as a whole it is generally free from controversy or schism.

Missionary and Evangelistic Work

In 2006, a Hutterite colony named Palmgrove was started in Uyo, Nigeria. This colony began as an evangelistic effort and currently has three hundred people.

Ecumenism

Hutterites do not communicate or fellowship with other Christian groups. They are generally focused on their own community.

Academic Institution

In 1994, Brandon University in Manitoba, Canada, began teaching Hutterian students in several colonies. The Brandon University Hutterian Education Project was designed to educate and train future Hutterian teachers. However, few colonies have Hutterian teachers. Most hire local educators to serve the colony's needs.

Publication

Hutterite Journal

Website

http://www.hutterites.org/

Bibliography

Bender, Harold S., ed. Hutterite Studies: Essays by Robert Friedmann. Goshen, IN: Mennonite Historical Society, 1961.

Hutterian Brethren, eds. The Chronicle of the Hutterian Brethren. 2 vols. Rifton, NY: Plough, 1987.

Petes, Victor. All Things Common: The Hutterian Way of Life. Minneapolis: University of Minnesota Press, 1965.

University of Cumbria: Philosophy, Theology and Religions. "Overview of World Religions: Hutterites." http://philtar.ucsm.ac.uk/encyclopedia/christ/cep/hutt.html.

R. Philip Roberts

Mennonite Church USA

History

The Mennonite Church USA is an Anabaptist denomination. Mennonites began as a movement first in Switzerland during the Radical Reformation (1525–80). The teachings of Swiss Reformer Ulrich Zwingli (1484–1531), with the Bible as the basis for teaching, encouraged the development of Anabaptist concepts. In the Netherlands, the leadership of Menno Simons (1496–1561) precluded the devastating influence of the Münster chiliasts upon the Anabaptist movement. The Anabaptists in the Westphalian city of Münster were characterized by an extreme and violent apocalypticism, and subsequent to the Münster debacle of apocalyptic speculations, there were few calculations with regard to prophetic events not only among Anabaptists but also among other Christians. Simons embraced Anabaptist concepts based on the Bible and renounced his priesthood in 1536. His moderate leadership and prolific writings helped to unify the "brethren" (a name adopted to avoid the stigma associated with the radical element of the Anabaptist movement). Following the death of Simons, the brethren were soon known as Mennonites.

Although Mennonites were granted freedom of religion in 1676, continual persecution caused many to emigrate to North and South America. Dutch and German Mennonites in the late 1600s settled in Germantown, Pennsylvania, to establish their congregation. On July 5, 2001, the nation's two leading Mennonite denominations, the Mennonite Church ("Old Mennonites") and the General Conference Mennonite Church ("New Mennonites" established in 1860), merged to form the Mennonite Church USA.

Headquarters

National Office, Elkhart
3145 Benham Avenue
Suite 1
Elkhart, IN 46517
Telephone: 574-294-7523

National Office, Newton
718 North Main Street
Newton, KS 67114
Telephone: 316-283-5100

National Office, Harrisonburg
1251 Virginia Avenue
Harrisonburg, VA 22802
Telephone: 540-434-6701

Leadership

Executive director: Ervin Stutzman

Executive leadership exists to oversee the Mennonite Church USA as a missional Anabaptist denomination. The executive director serves as a pastor for each of the churches. Executive leadership focuses efforts on church extension services, communications, convention planning, denominational ministry, the historical committee, interchurch relations, and intercultural relations.

The polity of the individual churches is a modified form of congregationalism. The focus of authority is the congregation, which belongs to a conference that maintains a relationship with the Mennonite Church general board. Conferences send delegates to the biennial general assembly, which is responsible to the general board. The general assembly unites representatives from all area conferences and many North American congregations.

Core Beliefs

The Confession of Faith in a Mennonite Perspective, with twenty-four articles, was adopted at a 1995 joint session of the Mennonite Church USA and the Mennonite Church Canada.

The Mennonite Church USA is often considered liberal in conduct due to its insistence on freedom from traditional regulations on attire. Members continue to affirm the Mennonite commitment to nonviolence and peacemaking.

Worship

Four-part singing, which was only a cappella for many years, is an enduring tradition. Worship styles vary, but the emphasis is on God (as opposed to the congregation) as the "audience." Some congregations use a prayer book for corporate worship. Most worship services are similar to those of evangelical churches.

Statistics

Membership: more than 109,000
Congregations: 939

Largest Churches

The largest churches are found in Pennsylvania and the Midwest. The largest congregation is Calvary Community Church in Hampton, Virginia.

Missionary and Evangelistic Work

The mission agency of the Mennonite Church USA is the Mennonite Mission Network, which supports ministries in more than fifty countries. The Mennonite Mission Network succeeded the mission agencies of the former General Conference Mennonite Church (Commission on Home Ministries and Commission on Overseas Mission) and the former Mennonite Church (Mennonite Board of Missions). The name signifies the intention of the network "to lead, mobilize and equip the church to participate in holistic witness to Jesus Christ in a broken world" (mennonitemission.net, "About Us"). The network accomplishes this goal through several ministries, partnerships, and programs.

Christian service ministries are available for all ages and interests and include those that are community based (Mennonite Voluntary Service and Service Adventure), discipleship and outreach oriented (Radical Journey), short-term group projects (DOOR), and short-term individual projects (SOOP and Youth Venture). International ministries include AIDS education in Africa, agricultural development in Asia, theological training in Latin America, and reconciliation services in Europe. Leadership development is available for Spanish-speaking Mennonite churches through the Instituto Biblico Anabautista. New ministry partnerships are facilitated through the department of Church Relations and Partnership Formation.

Academic Institutions

Associated Mennonite Biblical Seminary (Elkhart, IN)
Bethel College (North Newton, KS)

Bluffton University (Bluffton, OH)
Eastern Mennonite University (Harrisonburg, VA)
Goshen College (Goshen, IN)
Hesston College (Hesston, KS)

Electronic Media

Mennonite Media is responsible for media production such as DVDs, music group recording, newspaper columns, radio PSA, videos, and websites. Several churches broadcast church services locally, nationally, and internationally.

Publications

The publishing agency of the Mennonite Church USA is the Mennonite Publishing Network, which publishes books, church supplies, curriculum (adult Bible study, Gather 'Round, and vacation Bible school), periodicals (*Leader, Purpose, Rejoice!,* and *With*), and recorded music. Church supplies, curriculum, and periodicals are published from an Anabaptist perspective under the name Faith and Life Resources. Books and recorded music are published for churches, families, and schools under the name Herald Press.

Website

http://www.mennoniteusa.org/

Bibliography

Beck, Ervin. *MennoFolk: Mennonite and Amish Folk Traditions.* Scottdale, PA: Herald Press, 2004.

Bender, Harold S. *Two Centuries of American Mennonite Literature: A Bibliography of Mennonitica Americana 1727–1928.* Goshen, IN: Mennonite Historical Society, 1929.

Hartzler, Jonas S., and Daniel Kauffman. *Mennonite Church History.* Scottdale, PA: Mennonite Book and Tract Society, 1905.

Kauffman, Daniel. *Bible Doctrines Briefly Stated.* Scottdale, PA: Mennonite Publishing House, 1951.

"Mennonite Mission Network." http://www.mennonite mission.net. "About Us."

Smith, C. Henry. *The Story of the Mennonites.* Berne, IN: Mennonite Book Concern, 1941.

Wenger, John C. *The Doctrines of the Mennonites.* Scottdale, PA: Mennonite Publishing House, 1950.

Williams, George Huntston. *The Radical Reformation.* Philadelphia: Westminster, 1962.

Ron J. Bigalke

Missionary Church

History

Joseph Ramseyer founded the Missionary Church Association after he was dismissed from his former denomination for wanting to be baptized by immersion as a born-again believer in Christ. Ramseyer continued to preach the message of God's love through Jesus Christ as Savior, Sanctifier, Healer, and Coming King. In 1898, those who shared his convictions adopted the name Missionary Church Association because of their desire to evangelize the world.

The United Missionary Church, known until 1947 as the Mennonite Brethren in Christ, was formed at a meeting near Dayton, Ohio, in 1883. It began, however, in the 1870s when a number of Mennonite ministers were dismissed from their former churches for having prayer meetings, holding revival services, and giving public testimonies. The denomination was organized largely through the leadership of Daniel Brenneman and Solomon Eby. The name Missionary Church was selected following the 1969 merger of the Missionary Church Association and the United Missionary Church.

Headquarters

Missionary Church Inc.
3811 Vanguard Drive
Fort Wayne, IN 46809

Core Beliefs

The Missionary Church is an evangelical body that believes in the Bible as the inspired, only infallible, and authoritative Word of God; in one God, eternally existent in three persons: Father, Son, and Holy Spirit; in the deity of the Lord Jesus Christ, his virgin birth, his sinless life, his miracles, his vicarious and atoning death through his shed blood, his bodily resurrection, his ascension to the right hand of the Father, and his personal return in power and glory; in the necessity of salvation of lost and sinful people and regeneration by the Holy Spirit; in the present ministry of the Holy Spirit by whose indwelling the Christian is enabled to live a godly life; in the resurrection of both the saved and the lost, in which they who are saved are saved unto the resurrection of life and they who are lost are lost unto the resurrection of damnation; in the spiritual unity of believers in our Lord Jesus Christ; in baptism by immersion; and in the observance of the Lord's Supper.

Worship

There is no prescribed form of worship, resulting in a wide range of worship styles from traditional to contemporary.

Statistics

Members: 38,000
Average worship attendance: 61,000
Churches: 450

Largest Churches

There are approximately twenty-five churches with weekly average worship attendance ranging from five hundred to three thousand. Three churches are considered megachurches, with weekly worship attendance in excess of two thousand.

Growth

In the past twenty years, the Missionary Church has grown from 290 to approximately 450 churches. The average weekly worship attendance has grown from 38,000 to 61,000, membership from 27,000 to 38,000, annual conversions from 2,700 to 6,500, annual baptisms from 1,400 to 2,800, and the annual conversion growth rate from 7 percent to 10–11 percent.

In 2009, the Missionary Church approved a five-year Dynamic Vision plan to revitalize its evangelistic efforts.

Trends

Trends include church and district planting, more nationals as part of the missionary arm, an emphasis on conversion growth as opposed to transfer growth, a greater prayer emphasis, and raising up catalytic leaders.

Missionary and Evangelistic Work

In recent years, great emphasis in the United States and abroad has focused on making disciples who make disciples. Missionary work has been a driving factor in the denomination, with major works in India, Nigeria, Guinea, Sierra Leone, Haiti, the Dominican Republic, Jamaica, Ecuador, Brazil, Canada, the United States, Colombia, Venezuela, and Ethiopia.

Ecumenism

The Missionary Church is not in discussion to merge with any other religious body at this time but cooperates freely with like-minded organizations. The Missionary Church is a member of the National Association of Evangelicals.

Academic Institutions

Bethel College (Mishawaka, IN)
Pastoral Leadership Institute (online training for licensing and ordination in the Missionary Church)

Parachurch Organizations

The church has an unofficial partnership with World Relief and Samaritan's Purse.

Publications

Missionary Church Today, a twenty-four-page periodical published three times per year
Reflections: A Publication of the Missionary Church Historical Society
Today's Latest, a news publication sent via email every two weeks

Website

http://www.mcusa.org/

Bibliography

Engbrecht, Dennis. "Merging and Diverging Streams: The Colorful and Complex History of the Missionary Church." http://www.mcusa.org/AboutMC/BecomingaPartofthe MissionaryChurch/ProspectivePastors/HistoryPolity /CourseSyllabus.aspx.

———. "1883–1983, One Hundred Years of Historical Distinctives." http://www.mcusa.org/AboutMC/Becominga PartoftheMissionaryChurch/ProspectivePastors/History Polity/CourseSyllabus.aspx.

———. *The Word, Revival, and Evangelism: Historical Origins of the Missionary Church.* Mishawka, IN: Pilot Productions, Bethel College, 2005. DVD.

Erdel, Timothy Paul. "The Missionary Church: From Radical Outcasts to the Wild Child of Anabaptism." *Illinois Mennonite Heritage*, September 1997. http://www.mcusa .org/AboutMCBecomingaPartoftheMissionaryChurch /ProspectivePastors/HistoryPolity/CourseSyllabus.aspx.

———, and Dennis Engbrecht. "Marriage, Memory, and Mission: Reflections on the 25th Anniversary of the MCA/UMC Merger." http://www.mcusa.org/AboutMC /BecomingaPartoftheMissionaryChurch/Prospective Pastors/HistoryPolity/CourseSyllabus.aspx.

Lageer, Eileen. *Merging Streams.* Elkhart, IN: Bethel, 1979.

Lugibihl, Walter H., and Jared F. Gerig. *The Missionary Church Association.* Berne, IN: Economy Printing Center, 1950.

Storms, Everek R. *History of the United Missionary Church.* Elkhart, IN: Bethel, 1958.

Bill Hossler and Mark A. Lamport

Old Order Amish Church

History

The Amish became a distinct group within Anabaptism at the end of the seventeenth century, after Jakob Ammann introduced innovations in the Swiss Anabaptist congregations. The Amish began immigrating to America in the mid-eighteenth century. In 1865 the conservative faction withdrew from the annual Amish conferences and subsequently became known as the Old Order Amish.

Core Beliefs

The Amish espouse historic Christian beliefs and seek to uphold the teachings of Jesus in everyday life. The Old Order Amish subscribe to the Dordrecht Confession of Faith (1632), written by Dutch Anabaptists. In addition, the majority of Amish practices are dictated by the *Ordnung*, an unwritten guide that is interpreted individually by the leaders of each Amish community. The Amish have a strong doctrine of separation from the kingdom of this world, and that separation results in many distinctive practices: these include using horse-and-buggy transportation, speaking the Pennsylvania German dialect, and insisting on plain dress (including the adoption of a beard for men and a prayer cap for women). They do not proselytize, although ethnic outsiders are permitted to join Amish communities if they agree to adopt the lifestyle, submit to ecclesiastical regulations, and learn Pennsylvania German.

Worship

Amish worship is governed by the *Ausbund*, a collection of hymns written in German. This music is passed from generation to generation (musical notation is not included in the *Ausbund*) and is sung a cappella.

Statistics

The Young Center for Anabaptist and Pietist Studies at Elizabethtown College estimated that the total population of Old Order and New Order Amish in 2011 exceeded 261,000, over 95 percent of whom were likely Old Order. Amish can be found in twenty-eight states (as well as Ontario, Canada), with the largest populations residing in Ohio, Pennsylvania, and Indiana. The last of the European Amish had disappeared by 1937.

Trends

The Amish population has increased by 100 percent over the last twenty years. This is mostly due to fecund families (an average of five children per family) and an 85 percent retention rate among youth.

Publications

Pathway Publishers is the main Old Order publishing house. It distributes *Family Life*, *Young Companion*, and *Blackboard Bulletin*. Other Amish periodicals include *The Budget*, *Die Botschaft*, *The Diary*, *Farming*, and *Plain Communities Business Exchange*.

Websites

The Young Center for Anabaptist and Pietist Studies at Elizabethtown College (http://www.etown.edu/centers/young-center/index.aspx) operates a website dedicated to Amish studies (http://www.groups.etown.edu/amishstudies/).

Bibliography

Amish Studies. The Young Center for Anabaptist and Pietist Studies, Elizabethtown College. http://www.groups.etown.edu/amishstudies/.

Johnson-Weiner, Karen M. *Train Up a Child: Old Order Amish & Mennonite Schools.* Baltimore: Johns Hopkins University Press, 2007.

Kraybill, Donald B., and Carl F. Bowman. *On the Backroad to Heaven: Old Order Hutterites, Mennonites, Amish, and Brethren.* Baltimore: Johns Hopkins University Press, 2001.

Yoder, Paton. *Tradition & Transition: Amish Mennonites and Old Order Amish, 1800–1900.* Scottdale, PA: Herald Press, 1991.

Benjamin J. Wetzel

Old Order (Wisler) Mennonite Church

History

The Old Order (Wisler) Mennonite Church, one of several factions of the Old Order Mennonites, was founded in 1870 by Jacob Wisler. Though Anabaptist in heritage, it has its roots in the Radical Reformation of the sixteenth century. Between 1872 and 1901, four Old Order splits took place in the Mennonite Church, the one led by Jacob Wisler (1808–89) occurred in Indiana and Ohio. The four recognized each other as brother groups and collectively but informally became known as the Old Order Mennonites. As the late nineteenth century saw widespread acceptance of new church activities and agencies, such as Sunday schools and organized evangelistic meetings, the Old Order chose to remain committed to more conservative traditions.

Wisler, a conservative Mennonite bishop, had begun his protests against change in church life by protesting exuberant preaching, nonunison singing, and Sunday schools. As a result, his status as bishop was suspended in 1871. The following year, after rejecting that judgment, Wisler and his followers were finally deprived of their church membership. At that point, Wisler began his own services, and his following grew. Not long after, three affiliated district conferences were organized in Ontario (1889), Pennsylvania (1893), and Virginia (1901). In 1907, the Wisler Mennonites split into two groups, the Old Order or Martin Mennonites, who are the more conservative and who do not permit phones or cars, and the Wisler or Ramer Mennonites. Nevertheless, the Old Order (Wisler) Mennonites remain one of the most conservative in terms of dress, forms of worship, and social customs.

Core Beliefs

The Old Order (Wisler) Mennonites practice the baptism of believers only, the necessity of repentance and conversion for salvation, the administration of discipline within the congregation, simple Communion among the faithful, the refusal to bear arms and to take oaths, the rejection of worldly concerns, simplicity of dress and habits, and a disapproval of marrying outside the church.

Website

http://www.mhsc.ca/

Bibliography

Mead, Frank S., Samuel S. Hill, and Craig D. Atwood. *Handbook of Denominations in the United States*. 13th ed. Nashville: Abingdon, 2010.

"Old Order Mennonites." Global Anabaptist Mennonite Encyclopedia Online. http://www.gameo.org/encyclopedia/contents/O544.html.

"Old Order (Wisler) Mennonite Church." The Association of Religion Data Archives. http://www.thearda.com/denoms/D_1371.asp.

Scott, Stephen. *Introduction to Old Order and Conservative Mennonite Groups*. Intercourse, PA: Good Books, 1969.

Michael McMullen

Reformed Mennonite Church

History

The Reformed Mennonite Church states emphatically that it had its origin with Christ and the apostles. This church is only a modern continuation of the true first-century church. The church traces its history through the Anabaptist groups of Peter Waldo in the thirteenth century (Waldensians) and Menno Simons in the sixteenth century (Mennonites).

The separate organization of the Reformed Mennonite Church formally began on May 30, 1812, in the home of John Herr in Lancaster, Pennsylvania. Herr's father, Francis, left the Mennonite Church because it had reportedly strayed from the teachings of Menno Simons and the New Testament. The Herr family, along with a few others, continued meeting informally until John was appointed as pastor and bishop of the new organization in 1812. John, who had never been a member of the Mennonite Church, was baptized by a fellow dissenter and began leading the new group at the age of thirty.

Through numerous pamphlets and tracts, John Herr accused the "old" Mennonites of practicing carnal behavior such as voting, being involved in politics, foolish talking, attending county fairs, observing races, not practicing the ordinance of foot washing, and failing to greet fellow members with a holy kiss.

The Reformed Mennonite Church has changed very little since its inception in the Herr home.

Headquarters

602 Strasburg Pike
Lancaster, PA 17602
Telephone: 717-697-4623

Core Beliefs

The Reformed Mennonite Church views itself as a reformation movement within the Mennonite Church, reclaiming the true doctrine of the church. The Dordrecht Confession of 1632 is the most agreed-upon Mennonite confession of faith by conservative Mennonites. The informal statements made by the Reformed Mennonite Church reflect much of this earlier document.

The church holds that salvation is by God's grace alone through faith in the gospel and will result in regeneration and repentance. This salvation will bring about unity, love, and peace among all believers, without which it is impossible for the church to obey the commands of Christ. Members strive to maintain regenerate church membership and hold to a strict view of church discipline. Three ordinances are regularly carried out in worship: believer's baptism, closed Communion, and foot washing.

To avoid pride and association with the "world," members practice modesty in dress and home decor, striving for simplicity and humility. Members are prohibited from engaging in lawsuits, voting in elections, running for government office, and serving in the military.

Website

http://www.reformedmennonite.org/

Bibliography

Bender, Harold S., and C. Henry Smith. "Reformed Mennonite Church." In *The Mennonite Encyclopedia: A Comprehensive Reference Work on the Anabaptist-Mennonite Movement*, edited by Harold S. Bender and C. Henry Smith, vol. 4, 267–69. Scottdale, PA: Mennonite Publishing House, 1959.

Musser, Daniel. *The Reformed Mennonite Church: Its Rise and Progress with Its Principles and Doctrines*. Lancaster, PA: Elias Barr, 1873.

"Reformed Mennonite Church." In *Yearbook of American and Canadian Churches 2010*, edited by Eileen W. Linder. Nashville: Abingdon, 2010.

Smith, Henry C. *The Story of the Mennonites*. 4th ed. Revised by Cornelius Krahn. Newton, KS: Mennonite Publication Office, 1957.

Wegner, John Christian. *Glimpses of Mennonite History and Doctrine*. 2nd ed. Scottdale, PA: Herald Press, 1947.

William R. Osborne

African Methodist Episcopal Church

History

The African Methodist Episcopal (AME) Church is among the oldest black denominations in the United States. The origin of the AME Church is normally traced back to Richard Allen (1760–1831). Allen, a former slave, was a prominent member of the Free African Society. The Free African Society was formed in Philadelphia in 1787 and was comprised mostly of African Americans who had left St. George's Methodist Episcopal Church after facing mounting racial discrimination. In 1794, Allen purchased a blacksmith shop and converted it into Bethel Church. Between 1807 and 1815, Allen successfully engaged in legal battles with St. George's over the legal right of Bethel to exist as an independent congregation. The AME Church was formed in 1816 at Bethel Church. The new denomination was initially comprised of Bethel and various black congregations located throughout the mid-Atlantic states that also desired autonomy and to escape racism.

The AME Church was active in the antislavery struggle of the antebellum period. It protested the attempts of the American Colonization Society to establish colonies for freed African Americans in Africa, AME churches and the homes of members provided key stops on the Underground Railroad, and a large number of AME Church clergy volunteered as chaplains for the Union army. In the period following the Civil War, extensive efforts were made to plant churches among and make converts of the freed slaves in the South. Theophilius G. Steward's sermon "I Seek My Brethren" was often read during this time and became akin to a mission statement for the denomination during those years of expansion (ame-church.com, "Our History"). In the twentieth century, the denomination remained active in the struggle for African American civil rights. Rev. Oliver Brown, assistant minister of St. Mark's AME Church in Topeka, Kansas, was the named plaintiff in the important *Brown v. Board of Education* Supreme Court case. Today the denomination remains active in social and global outreach.

Headquarters

Office of the General Secretary
500 8th Avenue South
Nashville, TN 37203
Telephone: 615-254-0911

Core Beliefs

The AME Church is very similar to other Methodist bodies in terms of its basic beliefs. In general, the denomination tends to be moderate to conservative theologically. It adheres to the Apostles' Creed and the Twenty-Five Articles of Religion compiled by Methodism's founder, John Wesley. The official doctrine of the AME Church asserts the standard Protestant beliefs in the Trinity, original sin, the atoning death of Christ, and the sufficiency of Scripture for addressing issues of human salvation and morality. Like other Methodist bodies, the AME Church stresses freedom of will, justification by faith, and the importance of lifelong growth in holiness through cooperation with God's grace (ame-church.com, "Our Beliefs").

Despite this general consistency between the theology of the AME Church and other Methodist bodies, the AME Church stresses the importance of theological praxis, or the living out of Christian convictions in the world. Many contemporary theologians with ties to the AME Church tradition, such as James H. Cone, Jacqueline Grant, and Cecil W. Cone, have even gone so far as to suggest that theology should be rooted in faith and the experience of the oppressed as opposed to classic elements of the

Eurocentric religious heritage (ame-church.com, "Our History").

The most important way the denomination lives out its Christian convictions is through emphasizing the importance of social outreach. Historically, the AME Church has served an important role in helping to provide for both the spiritual and the material needs of the African American community. This role was both thrust on the church by racism and slavery in American society and also a natural extension of the denomination's roots in eighteenth-century British Methodism. After all, Methodism emerged among the poor and working class in industrial Britain. Thus, contemporary AME churches often work very heavily in their local communities, helping to provide health, money management, and job skill education; coordinating food and blood drives; and providing various other means of support.

AME churches practice infant baptism by sprinkling. If a person was not baptized as an infant, they may be baptized as an adult by sprinkling, pouring, or immersion. The Lord's Supper is celebrated regularly in AME churches.

Women and men are viewed as equals in terms of lay and clergy status. The first female bishop was elected to the episcopacy in 2000.

Worship

The majority of AME Church worship services are based on *The AMEC Hymnal* and *The AMEC Book of Worship*. Most AME churches employ a traditional, formal style of worship, though there is some variance depending on the congregation.

Controversies

The AME Church has dealt with a number of controversies in its history. These issues have included the use of spirituals in worship, the right of women to be preachers, and the right of women to serve in the episcopacy. One of the most contentious issues in the denomination today is the use of Pentecostal-infused worship styles. Unlike many of its Methodist counterparts, the AME Church has remained fairly consistent in its rejection of gay marriage and openly gay clergy. However, this is a controversial topic with a small percentage of its membership.

Statistics

Estimates place the AME Church at about two million members and seven thousand congregations worldwide. The leadership consists of approximately eight thousand ministers, twenty bishops, and twelve general officers.

Largest Churches

While continuing to have an impressive presence in the mid-Atlantic and Southern states, one of the largest AME churches is First AME Church in Los Angeles, California, which boasts a membership of over nineteen thousand (fame church.or, "About FAME"). The Greater Allen AME Cathedral in New York City has around twenty-three thousand members (allencathedral .org, "Rev. Dr. Floyd H. Flake"). In Baltimore, the Gen-X focused Empowerment Temple AME Church reports a membership of ten thousand.

Growth

Prior to the Civil War, the AME Church was strong primarily in the northeastern and mid-Atlantic states. In the period following the Civil War, the AME Church launched mission campaigns to the freed slaves in the South. This allowed the denomination to experience tremendous growth in the late nineteenth century. During this time of expansion, Bishop Henry McNeil Turner led the AME Church to Sierra Leone and Liberia in 1891. This began the global expansion of the denomination. Today the AME Church has adherents on five continents.

Missionary and Evangelistic Work

At the present time, the AME Church has ministries in more than thirty nations on four continents, including North America, South America, Europe, and Africa. The expansion into Africa began in 1891 under the leadership of Bishop Henry McNeil Turner. One of the most prolific global ministries of the denomination remains the 15th Episcopal District, which is located in South Africa.

Ecumenism

The AME Church is active in ecumenical dialogues and organizations. The denomination is a member of the National Council of Churches and the World Council of Churches. It is also a participant in the World Methodist Council, which is made up of representatives from most of the major Methodist bodies in the world.

Academic Institutions

The AME Church supports five four-year colleges and universities, one junior college, and three theological seminaries:

Allen University (Columbia, SC)
Edward Waters College (Jacksonville, FL)
Jackson Theological Seminary (North Little Rock, AR)
Morris Brown College (Atlanta, GA)
Paul Quinn College (Dallas, TX)
Payne Theological Seminary (Wilberforce, OH)
Shorter College (Little Rock, AR)
Turner Theological Seminary (Atlanta, GA)
Wilberforce University (Wilberforce, OH)

Parachurch Organizations

The major relief organization of the AME Church is the African Methodist Episcopal Church Service and Development Agency. Its mission is "Helping People Help Themselves," and efforts are spent on health and education programs. Presently, disaster relief is being provided to South Africa and Haiti.

Publications

The *Christian Reporter* is the oldest existing black periodical in the United States. It is a monthly periodical that focuses on providing news and addressing various issues that are pertinent to the black community. The *A.M.E. Church Review* is another important periodical. Frequently containing pieces written by leading academic scholars, it is published quarterly and covers topics related to history, theology, education, and social issues.

Website

http://www.ame-church.com/

Bibliography

"African Methodist Episcopal Church." http://www.ame-church.com. "Directory—Institutions of Higher Education," "Leadership—Bishops of the Church," "Our Beliefs," and "Our History").

"African Methodist Episcopal Church Service and Development Agency." http://www.ame-sada.org. "About AME-SADA."

Campbell, James T. *Songs of Zion: The African Methodist Episcopal Church in the United States and South Africa.* Chapel Hill: University of North Carolina Press, 1998.

Dickerson, Dennis C. *Religion, Race, and Region: Research Notes on A.M.E. Church History.* Nashville: AMEC Sunday School Union, 1995.

"First African Methodist Episcopal Church of Los Angeles." http://www.famechurch.org. "About Fame."

"The Greater Allen A.M.E. Cathedral of New York." http://www.allencathedral.org. "Rev. Dr. Floyd H. Flake."

Melton, J. Gordon. *A Will to Choose: The Origins of African American Methodism.* Lanham, MD: Rowman & Littlefield, 2007.

Newman, Richard. *Freedom's Prophet: Bishop Richard Allen, the AME Church, and the Black Founding Fathers.* New York: New York University Press, 2009.

Michael K. Turner

African Methodist Episcopal Zion Church

History

The African Methodist Episcopal Zion (AMEZ) Church originated with John Street Methodist Church in New York City, which began in 1766 and grew to include a congregation of both whites and blacks. Like all biracial churches in that era, the races were segregated during worship services. The blacks desired to have space in which to worship unimpeded by race. In 1796, after receiving permission from Bishop Frances Asbury, James Varick led a group of about one hundred Christians to a rented building and formed a Methodist congregation. They moved again in 1800 to a small wooden building. It was chartered in 1801 as the African Methodist Episcopal Church of the City of New York and became known as Zion Church.

A similar church, called Asbury Church, formed nearby. Both churches remained under the auspices of the Methodist Episcopal authority. In 1820, the members of the two churches voted to be removed from the white Methodist Episcopal denomination. The next year they, along with other similarly formed black churches in New York, Connecticut, and Pennsylvania, formed the African Methodist Episcopal Church in America; James Varick became the first bishop in that year. Because a group of black Methodists had formed in Philadelphia in 1816 under the name the African Methodist Episcopal (AME) Church, the congregation in New York decided to add "Zion" to its name in 1848 in order to distinguish it from the Philadelphia-based denomination. Members of the AMEZ Church included Sojourner Truth, Frederick Douglass, and Harriet Tubman. After the Civil War, the AMEZ Church spread throughout the South, eventually placing its headquarters in Charlotte, North Carolina.

Headquarters

3225 W Sugar Creek Road
Charlotte, NC 28269
Telephone: 704-599-4630

Core Beliefs

The Doctrines and Discipline is published every four years. The first edition was published in 1820 as *The Doctrines and Discipline of the African Methodist Episcopal [Zion] Church in America.*

The AMEZ Church took an early lead in the ordination of women, with two women ordained as deacons and then as full elders between 1894 and 1900. The AMEZ Church practices Communion and paedobaptism.

Division and Splits

The AMEZ Church did not split from the African Methodist Episcopal (AME) Church or the Christian Methodist Episcopal (CME) Church; all three developed due to different circumstances. Early in the AMEZ Church's history, its future leaders considered joining with the AME Church (led by Richard Allen). This effort was thwarted when the AME Church sent a church planter to New York who began a church linked with the Philadelphia-based AME Church. This move was understood to be an encroachment on the AMEZ Church (which was based in New York), and so the AMEZ Church leaders decided to remain a separate entity. Since the early 1990s, the AMEZ and CME Churches have discussed merging, but this had not occurred as of 2012.

Statistics

Members: 1,400,000
Churches: 6,000

The AMEZ Church is the second largest black Methodist denomination (behind the AME Church).

Academic Institutions

Clinton Junior College (Rock Hill, SC)
Hood Theological Seminary (Salisbury, NC)
Livingstone College (Salisbury, NC)
Lomax-Hannon Junior College (Greenville, AL)

Parachurch Organizations

AME Zion Publishing House
Bureau of Evangelism
Christian Education Department
Department of Church Extension and Home Missions
Department of Church School Literature
Department of Health and Social Concerns
Department of Overseas Missions

Publications

AME Zion Quarterly Review
The Star of Zion

Website

http://www.amez.org/

Bibliography

Bradley, David H., Sr. *A History of the A.M.E. Zion Church.* 2 vols. Nashville: Parthenon, 1956, 1970.

Lincoln, C. Eric, and Lawrence Mamiya. *The Black Church in the African-American Experience.* Durham, NC: Duke University Press, 1990.

Walls, William J. *The African Methodist Episcopal Zion Church: Reality of the Black Church.* Charlotte, NC: AME Zion Publishing House, 1974.

Mark Nickens

Allegheny Wesleyan Methodist Connection

History

The Allegheny Wesleyan Methodist Connection was originally the Allegheny Conference of the Wesleyan Methodist Church, which developed out of the antislavery battles that engulfed the Methodist Episcopal (ME) Church in the decades prior to the Civil War. The success with which the ME Church had evangelized the young nation produced a problem of national proportions: almost half of its membership lived in slave-holding states.

The general conference of 1836 witnessed the introduction of hundreds of resolutions from the New England Conference demanding that the bishops take action to force slave-owning members of the church to either divest themselves of slaves or withdraw as members. The bishops' response was to enforce a gag rule that prohibited any discussion of the matter. Ministers who failed to comply were placed on trial in local churches and annual conferences. Others were relegated to small churches where their path to advancement in the church was effectively ended.

In the winter of 1842–43, Luther Lee, Cyrus Prindle, Lucius Matlack, Jotham Horton, and LaRoy Sunderland, elders in the New England Annual Conference led by Orange Scott, presiding elder of the Springfield, Massachusetts, district of the ME Church, published in the church periodicals their intention to withdraw from the ME Church and to form a new "connection" of churches that would include a representative form of government (presbyterian polity rather than episcopal), prohibit the manufacture or sale of alcohol, prohibit membership in secret societies, and return to an emphasis on the teaching of John Wesley and his stress on the experience and life of Christian perfection.

A call for an organizing conference was announced by these men, who met first in Andover, Massachusetts. In June 1843, in Utica, New York, the new denomination materialized. Initially composed of six annual conferences from New England to the Ohio Valley, its membership increased dramatically as disenchanted members left the ME Church in droves. Its dramatic growth continued until the passage of the Thirteenth and Fourteenth Amendments by Congress.

Other annual conferences were added as the nation expanded, and Wesleyan Methodism enjoyed healthy growth until modern lifestyle issues and proposed mergers with the Free Methodist and Pilgrim Holiness Churches surfaced in the mid-twentieth century. The conservative stance of the Allegheny Conference placed it in opposition to the merger plans of the Wesleyan Methodist Church of America, and in 1966, the parent body refused to seat the delegates of the Allegheny Conference at the general conference held in Houghton, New York. Separation plans were agreed on, and in 1968, the annual conference became the Allegheny Wesleyan Methodist Connection, a denomination in its own right.

Headquarters

2291 Depot Road
PO Box 357
Salem, OH 44460-0357
Telephone: 330-337-9376

Core Beliefs

The Allegheny Wesleyan Methodist Connection is a trinitarian body that believes in salvation through the sacrificial death of Christ—available to all who come to him through repentance and faith expressed through confession of faith—and in Christian perfection as taught by John Wesley as a subsequent work of grace that is wrought in the heart of the believer by faith, purifying the heart from inherited depravity. Other important beliefs include the inerrancy and sufficiency of Scripture; the incarnation, virgin birth, and bodily resurrection of Christ; and the universality of sin—that all are born in sin, all may be saved from sin, and all may know they are saved from sin. Members believe that all may enter into Christian perfection, subsequent to the new birth; the church is the body and bride of Christ; the New Testament model of worship and church organization should be

followed; the Lord's Supper should be observed; adult believers should be baptized; tithing should be practiced; and women may be ordained and participate in worship.

Paul L. Kaufman

Christian Methodist Episcopal Church

History

The Christian Methodist Episcopal (CME) Church was established in 1870 in Jackson, Tennessee, as the Colored Methodist Church by forty-one blacks who had left the Methodist Episcopal Church, South. Its birth reflected the emancipation of blacks from slavery and the corresponding desire to control their own institutions. Some white members of the Methodist Episcopal Church, South, offered assistance with the organization of an African American branch of Methodism. The new church elected two preachers as bishops and maintained use of the Methodist South's Book of Discipline. The church has stressed a message of community values as well as evangelism. The current name was adopted in 1956.

Headquarters

4466 Elvis Presley Boulevard
Memphis, TN 38116-7100
Telephone: 901-345-0580
Email: WHGraves@aol.com

Leadership

Senior bishop: Bishop William H. Graves

Core Beliefs

The Christian Methodist Episcopal Church adheres to traditional Methodist beliefs, including that it is the duty of Christians to strive for spiritual perfection; all people, not merely a handful of elect, are eligible to be saved; service is an expression of faith but does not merit justification, which is by faith in Christ's grace; the Holy Spirit gives each believer certainty about his or her salvation; it is possible for Christians to fall from grace; and the sacraments include baptism and the Lord's Supper, which are external symbols of inner grace.

Statistics

Year	Clergy	Churches	Members
1961	1,914	2,523	444,493
2006	3,548	3,500	850,000

Missionary and Evangelistic Work

Missions and sister churches are present in Haiti, Jamaica, Ghana, Liberia, and Nigeria.

Ecumenism

The Commission on Ecumenicity is responsible for examining the CME Church's dealings with other denominations and religious bodies.

Parachurch Organizations

Departments of the CME Church are classified as Connectional Ministries, which minister directly to congregations, or Connectional Operations, which deal with the practical affairs of the denomination, such as finance, publications, and personnel. The Connectional Ministries include the departments of Christian Education, Lay Evangelism, Mission, and Human Concerns. There is a Commission on Life and Witness as well as a Commission on Social Justice and Human Concerns. More specialized bodies include the Ministers' Spouses Widows/Widowers Department, Department of Ministry to Men, Women's Missionary Society, Women's Missionary Council, Connectional Young Adult Ministry, and One Church One School Community Partnership Program. The Commission on Faith and Order examines theological issues.

Publications

The church runs the CME Church Publishing House (Memphis, TN) and the Miles Bookstore. The official publication of the CME Church is the *Christian Index*, which includes the official announcements and communications of the church, with special issues as needed. Another publication is the *Missionary Messenger* for missionaries.

Website

http://www.c-m-e.org/

George Thomas Kurian

Evangelical Methodist Church

History

The Evangelical Methodist Church (EMC) emerged in 1946 from a growing unease with liberalism—what it termed a "growing apostasy"—in the Methodist Church. In 1945, John Henry Hamblen of Abilene, Texas, began an independent congregation and fielded calls from other theologically conservative churches that wanted to return to historic Wesleyan doctrines. The denomination was born at a conference in Memphis

with Hamblen named first general superintendent. EMC merged with the Mexican Evangelical Mission in 1957, the Evangel Church in 1960, and the People's Methodist Church in 1962. It has congregations in Mexico (since 1946) and Myanmar (since 2003) and missions in many other countries.

Headquarters

Evangelical Methodist Church
PO Box 17070
Indianapolis, IN 46217
Telephone: 317-780-8017
Email: headquarters@emchurch.org

Core Beliefs

The EMC is theologically conservative. It upholds the Wesleyan Articles of Religion of the former Methodist Episcopal Church, South, to which it has added an article upholding perfect love (entire sanctification, or Christian perfection). The EMC adheres to its founding premise that true historic Christianity, what it calls "conservative Christianity," differs greatly from modern and liberal variety.

Website

http://www.emchurch.org/

Bibliography

General Conference of the Evangelical Methodist Church. *Discipline of the Evangelical Methodist Church.* Indianapolis: International Headquarters, 2010. http://emchurch.org/files/2010/06/Draft-Copy-Discipline-of-EMC-2010-Revision-41.pdf.

Kostlevy, William C. *Historical Dictionary of the Holiness Movement.* Lanham, MD: Scarecrow, 2001.

T. C. Porter

Fundamental Methodist Conference

History

The Fundamental Methodist Conference was founded as the Independent Fundamental Methodist Church in 1942 in Ash Grove, Missouri. It sought to join together independent Methodist congregations that had dissented from the 1939 merger of the three principal Methodist conferences—the Methodist Episcopal; the Methodist Episcopal, South; and the Methodist Protestant—to form the Methodist Church. While there were dissenters in all three conferences, the Methodist Protestant body of John's Chapel Church in Lawrence County, Missouri, launched the movement to separate from the Methodist Church. It elected a committee to draft a constitution and bylaws for a new church. Three congregations participated in the first annual conference in 1944 in Greene County, Missouri, and changed the organization's name to the Fundamental Methodist Church. The church was chartered four years later.

The annual conference is held at the Fundamental Methodist Conference Grounds in Ash Grove, Lawrence County, Missouri, since all of the conference's congregations are located in the southwestern area of that state.

Headquarters

1034 North Broadway
Springfield, MO 65802
Telephone: 417-235-3849

Core Beliefs

Fundamental Methodists do not practice infant baptism but rather infant dedication. Although baptism is by immersion only, believers who have been baptized in other fashions are welcomed.

George Thomas Kurian

Primitive Methodist Church in the United States of America

History

The first Primitive Methodists were formed in England in the early 1800s. Two Wesleyans, Hugh Bourne and William Clowes, held an American-style (open air) camp meeting at Mow Cop in 1807 in England, resulting in many people becoming Christians. The Wesleyan Church did not acknowledge this service and so did not allow the new Christians to become Wesleyan; in addition, it reprimanded the two preachers. The two continued to conduct open-air services and so were excommunicated from the Wesleyan Church. They desired to rejoin the denomination, but after waiting two years with no answer, they decided to form a new group. This new group became the Primitive Methodists.

The first Primitive Methodist missionaries arrived in America in 1829 in Brooklyn, New York. Churches, also known as "societies," were formed and were under the auspices of the British Primitive Methodist Conference until 1840. In that year, the American Primitive Methodist Church (APMC) was established. Eventually, the great geographic distance between churches caused two conferences to develop by the 1870s: the Eastern and Western Conferences. The two

conferences met in 1889 and agreed to form one denomination (although retaining the Eastern and Western Conference names) and a discipline. In 1891, the Eastern Conference had grown to the point that it divided into the Eastern Conference and the Pennsylvania Conference. In 1975, the official name was chosen, the Primitive Methodist Church in the United States of America.

Headquarters

730 Preston Lane
Hatboro, PA 19040

Core Beliefs

The APMC does not adhere to historical creeds but instead has a self-produced set of beliefs that includes the inerrancy of Scripture in the original autographs, the Trinity, the fall of man, the second coming of Christ, a final judgment, and a final reward.

The APMC is evangelical. All APMC churches and members follow the Discipline.

Website

http://www.primitivemethodistchurch.org/

Mark Nickens

Reformed Methodist Union Episcopal Church

History

The Reformed Methodist Union Episcopal Church, originally the Independent Methodist Church, was formed as a result of a secession from the African Methodist Episcopal Church in 1885 over disagreements regarding the selection of ministerial delegates to the general conference.

The new group was led by William E. Johnson, who was elected president by a convention of delegates representing churches in South Carolina and Georgia. At first, the church was nonepiscopal, but in 1896, an episcopacy was created to solidify the group's position among Methodist Episcopal churches. At the same time, the group adopted its present name.

The church follows the same doctrines and the same polity as the African Methodist Episcopal Church. It retains the signature practices of love feasts; class meetings; and quarterly, district, church, annual, and general meetings. However, there are no presiding elders, and each pastor has full control over his congregation. The group's strongest presence is in South Carolina, historically in rural areas.

Headquarters

1136 Body Avenue
Charleston, SC 29407

George Thomas Kurian

Reformed Zion Union Apostolic Church

History

The Reformed Zion Union Apostolic Church was formed in Virginia in the aftermath of the Civil War by African Americans who were excluded from white churches. They were largely from Mecklenburg, Brunswick, and Lunenburg Counties and objected to the ecclesiastical organization of the existing black churches. Although they had no educated clergy of their own, they benefited from the efforts of influential former slaves to help them create an organization.

Elder James R. Howell from New York City, a minister from the African Methodist Episcopal Zion Church and former abolitionist, met with the group in Boydton, Virginia, in 1869 to help them form the Zion Union Apostolic Church to evangelize Southern blacks. Its name was indicative of Howell's vision of the body as a stronghold for believers, reminiscent of Zion in the Bible. The group included factions whose views often collided: liberal former Episcopalians, conservatives from the white Methodist churches, and fundamentalists who were former Baptists or new converts.

A few months later in 1869, a constitution was adopted and Howell was elected president; however, this constitution was changed five years later to make Howell bishop for life. Opposition to this move and to a suggested merger with the Episcopal Church threw the church into two years of conflict. Much of it was rooted in personal dislike of Howell, who was particularly strident in his objection to talk of a merger. Elder John M. Bishop, one of the noted founders of the Zion Union Apostolic Church, started the process of reorganization in 1881 by gathering together some followers into a union.

The following year the new church was named the Reformed Zion Union Apostolic Church, with Elder Bishop elected bishop. It accepted most of the doctrines of the Methodist Episcopal Church as well as its organizational style, with conferences and an episcopate. The president of the episcopate was initially elected for four years, but in 1884, the bishop was given life tenure. The general conference would meet annually, and elders were required to be ordained. An informal

home missionary venture would send evangelists into communities that lacked churches.

By 1906, roughly a quarter century after its establishment, the church had 3,059 members and 33 ministers in 45 congregations, of which 39 were in Virginia and 6 in North Carolina. All but two congregations had edifices, and the church's property was valued at $37,000.

Headquarters

Route 1, Box 64D
Dundas, VA 23938
Telephone: 804-676-8509

Leadership

Executive board chairman: Rev. Hilman Wright

Sarah Claudine Day

Southern Methodist Church

History

The Southern Methodist Church finds its deep historical roots in the Methodist Episcopal Church and in the ministerial work of John Wesley. At the general conference in 1844, with racial segregation of local church bodies being the divisive factor, the Methodist Episcopal Church split into Northern and Southern constituents. By a landslide of votes, this plan of separation was adopted, and the Methodist Episcopal Church, South, held its first conference in Louisville, Kentucky, on May 1, 1845.

In May 1938, the general conference held in Birmingham, Alabama, announced a union of the Methodist Episcopal Church with the Methodist Protestant Church. Refusing the modernism of this united church, and with the rise of fear associated with centralized ecclesiastical control, a group of four hundred representatives convened and decided to split from the leadership of the Methodist Episcopal Church, South, on January 14, 1940. There were an estimated seven hundred attendees at the first Southern Methodist Church conference in Turbeville, South Carolina, in June 1940. After several court decisions, this new group lost the rights to the name Methodist Episcopal Church, South, and therefore became the Southern Methodist Church. This led to a total of four regional conferences held every year: the Alabama-Florida-Georgia Conference, the South-Western Conference (Louisiana, Arkansas, and Texas), the Mid-South Conference (Tennessee, Mississippi, and Kentucky), and the Eastern Conference (North Carolina, South Carolina, Virginia, and Maryland).

Currently, the Southern Methodist Church consists of ninety-nine churches in the United States and six churches in India and Haiti with roughly sixty-one hundred members. The church educates its pastors and leaders at Southern Methodist College in Orangeburg, South Carolina.

Headquarters

425 Broughton Street
Orangeburg, SC 29115
Telephone: 803-536-1378

Core Beliefs

The Southern Methodist Church is a conservative Protestant denomination that exists "to spread the message of salvation and Biblical holiness that John Wesley preached" (southern methodistchurch.com, "About Us"). All of its doctrinal essentials are found in *The Doctrines and Discipline of the Southern Methodist Church.* The church adopted the Methodist Episcopal Articles of Religion and added portions on prevenient grace, Satan, the testimony of the Spirit, premillennialism, and Christian perfection. Core beliefs include Wesleyan-Arminian doctrine; a commitment to the divine inspiration of Scripture; premillennialism; that the moral laws found in the Old Testament are binding on the Christian, but the civil and ceremonial laws are not; Christian perfection, wherein the believer's soul is filled with the love of God and experiences the fullness of God's divine presence; and the KJV as a trustworthy standard to preach from the pulpit.

The Southern Methodist Church ascribes to a set of general rules for faith and practice in the Christian life. The triad list is to (1) avoid every kind of evil, (2) be good and do good to all men, and (3) attend the ordinances of God, namely, "the public worship of God; the ministry of the Word, either read or expounded; the Supper of the Lord; family and private prayer; searching the Scriptures; fasting and abstinence" (southernmethodistchurch.com, "General Rules").

Website

http://www.southernmethodistchurch.com/

Bibliography

Briden, Gary, president of Southern Methodist College, personal email conversation.

The Doctrines and Discipline of the Southern Methodist Church. Orangeburg, SC: Foundry Press, 1970.

"The Southern Methodist Church." http://www.southern methodistchurch.com. "About Us," "Doctrine," "General Rules," and "Our History."

"Southern Methodist College." http://www.smcollege.edu. "About Us."

Chad C. Brewer

United Methodist Church

History

The United Methodist Church (UMC) is the largest Methodist denomination in the world and among the largest Protestant bodies in the United States. Methodism first emerged in the middle decades of the eighteenth century as a reform movement within the Church of England. Led by John Wesley, the first Methodists focused on spreading a Pietist message and providing social outreach to the urban working poor of England.

In North America, Irish immigrants in New York and Maryland started the first Methodist society meetings around 1760. While these societies were initially independent, John Wesley sent representatives from England to help organize and link together the various North American societies. In 1784, the Methodist Episcopal Church was formed in Baltimore under the leadership of Bishops Francis Asbury and Thomas Coke. It was the first denomination organized in the United States.

In the time since its organization, Methodism has undergone a number of schisms and unifications. In 1828, a contingent of Methodist Episcopal Church clergy and laity formed the Methodist Protestant Church. This split was the by-product of debates over the rights of laypeople to vote at conferences. The most significant split came in 1844. That year, the Southern contingent of the Methodist Episcopal Church formed the Methodist Episcopal Church, South as a result of significant differences with their Northern counterpart over the issues of slavery and the power of the episcopacy. In 1939, the Methodist Church was formed as a result of the reunification of the Methodist Episcopal Church; the Methodist Episcopal Church, South; and the Methodist Protestant Church. In 1968, the Methodist Church and the Evangelical United Brethren Church joined together, forming the United Methodist Church.

Headquarters

Due to its system of church government, the UMC lacks a central headquarters. The Council of Bishops is located at:

153

100 Maryland Avenue NE
Suite 320
Washington, DC 20002

Leadership

The UMC is organized in a manner similar to the United States government. The major legislative branch is the general conference, the major executive branch is the Council of Bishops, and the judicial branch is the Judicial Council.

Each individual charge, or church, is part of an annual conference. The UMC consists of over sixty annual conferences. At these annual conference meetings, clergy appointments are made and conference-wide issues are discussed and voted on. These annual conferences are further organized into five jurisdictional conferences. These jurisdictions are determined by geographical location and meet every four years. The principle purpose of the jurisdictional conference is the election of new bishops and the leadership of the boards and agencies of the church. Every four years, five hundred laypeople and five hundred clergy representatives elected from the annual conferences come together for the denomination's general conference. The general conference is tasked with creating and passing legislation concerning the governance and doctrine of the denomination. The new rules and revisions passed at the general conference are included in *The Book of Discipline of the United Methodist Church*, which contains the denomination's constitution, doctrines, and laws.

Bishops are elected for life, though they generally serve only two four-year terms. They are assigned to a specific annual conference and are charged with making final decisions regarding clergy appointments and overseeing the direction and affairs of that conference. All bishops meet together in a Council of Bishops at least once a year. The UMC also has a Judicial Council, which is tasked with determining whether or not the actions of the general conference are consistent with the denomination's constitution.

The UMC also contains a number of general agencies, tasked with furthering the mission, spiritual nourishment, and educational goals of the denomination. These agencies are held accountable to the general conference.

Core Beliefs

The UMC is a theologically moderate Protestant body. Due to the denomination's size and polity, United Methodist pastors, theologians, and laity range from very liberal to conservative theologically. However, the core theological teachings of the denomination are drawn from the writings of Methodism's founder, John Wesley.

Consistent with many Protestant groups, the UMC is trinitarian and stresses original sin, the atoning death of Jesus Christ, and the sufficiency of Scripture for addressing issues related to human salvation.

Historically, Methodists have not been biblical literalists. The method for theology employed by the UMC has often been referred to as the "Wesleyan Quadrilateral." The quadrilateral is composed of four methods: Scripture, tradition, reason, and experience. Specifically, the heart of the Christian faith is revealed in Scripture and interpreted through the lens of personal experience, reason, and the Christian tradition.

The most distinctive theological emphasis of the UMC has to do with its theological concept of grace. Following the teachings of John Wesley, Methodists emphasize a threefold understanding of grace. Methodists believe that human beings are born tainted with sin. Through God's prevenient grace, human beings are empowered to respond to God's invitation to salvation. Those individuals who accept God's invitation receive God's justifying grace (often referred to as "conversion"). Justifying grace provides pardon from sinfulness and reconciliation with God. After believers have been justified, they engage in an ongoing relationship with God. With God's sanctifying grace, believers begin the lifelong process of moving toward spiritual perfection, or perfect love for God and others. Sanctifying grace entails not only personal piety but also that a believer engages in good works in the world.

United Methodists practice infant baptism by sprinkling. If a person was not baptized as an infant, they may be baptized as an adult by sprinkling, pouring, or immersion. The Lord's Supper is celebrated in each United Methodist church at least once a month. Women and men are viewed as equals in terms of lay and clergy status; women were given full clergy rites beginning in 1956 and first elected to the episcopacy in 1980.

The denomination has a "social creed" that stresses the need for Methodists to be engaged in issues of social justice.

Worship

The majority of the United Methodist worship services are based on *The United Methodist*

Hymnal and *The Book of Worship of the United Methodist Church*. Most United Methodist churches employ a traditional, formal style of worship, though there is some variance depending on the congregation. Some United Methodist churches embrace (or have select services in) a contemporary, casual worship style. A few United Methodist churches embrace an exceptionally formal, high-church style of worship akin to that practiced in Episcopalian congregations.

Controversies

Historically, the UMC has dealt with a number of controversies. Those included slavery, the rights of women preachers, the rights of laity, and the power of the episcopacy.

In the modern day, the major issue facing the church is homosexuality. At the present time, a majority of the church continues to assert that homosexuality is inconsistent with Christian teachings. However, a vocal minority asserts that gay and lesbian men and women should have full rights to be ordained as clergy and be married in a church. In fact, some United Methodist clergy have been tried for performing same-sex unions (while others have not been tried for similar offenses). This issue continues to be debated at the general conference.

Statistics

According to data collected in 2010 by the General Council on Finance and Administration of the United Methodist Church, there are 7,570,541 professing members in the United States. In addition, there are approximately 3.5 million members in Asia, Africa, and Europe.

Largest Churches

United Methodist congregations are strongest in the US South and Midwest. The largest congregations are Church of the Resurrection in Kansas City, Kansas, and Windsor Village in Houston, Texas.

Growth

Like most other mainline Christian denominations, the UMC has experienced numerical decline in recent decades.

Missionary and Evangelistic Work

The UMC is a member of the World Council of Churches. The denomination has seven central conferences located in Africa, Europe, and Asia. Through the general board of Global Ministries and the United Methodist Committee on Relief, the UMC remains active in providing missionary and relief efforts to countries throughout the world.

Ecumenism

The UMC has been active in ecumenical dialogues. The denomination is a member of the National Council of Churches and the largest financial supporter of the World Council of Churches. The UMC is also a participant in the World Methodist Council, which is comprised of seventy-six Methodist religious bodies and pursues ecumenical dialogue with the Roman Catholic Church, Anglicans, the Lutheran World Federation, the World Alliance of Reformed Churches, Pentecostal churches, the Orthodox Church, and the Salvation Army. At the local level, many UMC clergy regularly engage in ecumenical groups with ministers from other Christian groups and other faith traditions.

Academic Institutions

There are over twelve hundred institutions of higher education founded by or associated with the UMC. At the present time, the UMC supports eight two-year colleges, eighty-two four-year colleges, ten universities, and thirteen theological schools.

Notable universities include:

American University (Washington, DC)
Boston University (Boston, MA)
DePauw University (Greencastle, IN)
Drew University (Madison, NJ)
Duke University (Durham, NC)
Emory University (Atlanta, GA)
Northwestern University (Evanston, IL)
Southern Methodist University (Dallas, TX)

The theological seminaries include:

Boston University School of Theology (Boston, MA)
Candler School of Theology, Emory University (Atlanta, GA)
Claremont School of Theology (Claremont, CA)
Duke University, Divinity School (Durham, NC)
Gammon Theological Seminary (Atlanta, GA)
Garrett-Evangelical Theological Seminary (Evanston, IL)
Iliff School of Theology (Denver, CO)
Methodist Theological School in Ohio (Delaware, OH)
Perkins School of Theology, Southern Methodist University (Dallas, TX)
Saint Paul School of Theology (Kansas City, MO)

Theological School, Drew University (Madison, NJ) United Theological Seminary (Dayton, OH) Wesley Theological Seminary (Washington, DC)

Parachurch Organizations

The major disaster relief organization of the denomination is the United Methodist Committee on Relief (UMCOR), which is currently working to help deal with the repercussions of civil and natural disasters in over eighty countries. In addition, the UMC has a number of designated relief efforts, such as Imagine No Malaria.

Electronic Media

The UMC engages in a number of aggressive television, internet, and radio advertising programs, mostly put together by United Methodist Communications. The United Methodists do not actively sponsor many television programs on a denominational level, but many individual congregations have worship services that appear on either the radio or local television stations.

Publications

The most widely circulated magazine produced by the UMC is the *Upper Room,* with a circulation of over three million in over one hundred countries. In the United States, the *Interpreter* and *Newscope* provide information on denominational activities for both laity and clergy. *Circuit Rider* has a circulation of over thirty-two thousand and addresses the spiritual and intellectual needs of United Methodist pastors. *Weavings* explores topics related to Christian spirituality.

The major academic journal of the UMC is the *Methodist History Journal,* which contains articles written by scholars on topics relevant to the history of the UMC.

Website

http://www.umc.org/

Archives

The archives and the History Center of the United Methodist Church are located in Madison, New Jersey.

Bibliography

The Book of Discipline of the United Methodist Church. Nashville: United Methodist Publishing House, 2008.

Bucke, Emory S., ed. *History of American Methodism.* Nashville: Abingdon, 1964.

"General Board of Higher Education and Ministry." http://www.gbhem.org. "United Methodist Theological Schools."

"General Council on Finance and Administration, the United Methodist Church." http://www.gcfa.org. "Data Services."

"Imagine No Malaria." http://www.imaginenomalaria.org.

McElhenney, John G., et al. *United Methodism in America: A Compact History.* Nashville: Abingdon, 1992.

Norwood, Frederick. *The Story of American Methodism.* Nashville: Abingdon, 1974.

Richey, Russell, et al. *The Methodist Experience in America.* Nashville: Abingdon, 2010.

Tuell, Jack M. *The Organization of the United Methodist Church, 2009–2012.* Nashville: Abingdon, 2010.

"United Methodist Church." http://www.umc.org. "Agency Publications."

"World Methodist Council." http://worldmethodistcouncil .org. "What We Do" and "Who We Are."

Michael K. Turner

Non-Chalcedonian

Armenian Apostolic Church

History

The Armenian Genocide (the "Great Crime") of the twentieth century and related political events shaped the modern Armenian Apostolic Church both in Armenia and in diaspora. An American diocese was established in Worcester, Massachusetts, in 1898. A second diocese was created in 1927 in Fresno, California, thereby formalizing an Eastern Diocese and a Western Diocese.

In 1933, at the annual assembly, the Armenian Church in America split because of strong disagreement regarding communist control of the see of Etchmiadzin. Later that year the assassination of Archbishop Leon Tourian (primate of the Eastern Diocese) by members of the Armenian Revolutionary Federation (a nationalist, anti-Etchmiadzin group) further deepened the schism. Communities, congregations, and even families were divided. The pro-Etchmiadzin faction was recognized by the Supreme Patriarch and Catholicos of All Armenians as the true church, and it retained all legal rights. The anti-Etchmiadzin faction, also claiming to represent the true Armenian Church, established an alternative parallel structure, the Armenian Prelacy, which was recognized by and came under the jurisdiction of the see of the Great House of Cilicia in 1956. The Armenian Prelacy of Canada was created two years later.

In 1973, after years of growth, it was necessary to create an Eastern Prelacy and a Western Prelacy. In 1983, the pro-Etchmiadzin diocesan church formed a separate diocese for Canada, the Diocese of the Armenian Church of Canada, under the authority of Etchmiadzin. In the post-Soviet era, individuals from both the diocesan and the prelacy structure have sought reconciliation, but the church remains divided.

Leadership

The supreme spiritual and administrative head of the Armenian Apostolic Church is the Supreme Patriarch and Catholicos of All Armenians. The current head is His Holiness Karekin II, 132nd successor to St. Gregory and shepherd of the nine million Armenian Christians around the world. The headquarters are located at the ancient mother see of Etchmiadzin in the city of Vagharshapat, Republic of Armenia. Since 1441, for historical reasons, there has been a second catholicossate, the catholicossate of the Great House in Cilicia. Currently, this is held by Aram I and is located in Antelias, Lebanon. Two patriarchates serve the catholicoi, the patriarch of Jerusalem and the patriarch of Constantinople.

The Eastern Diocese of the Armenian Church in America, headquartered in New York City, is headed by His Eminence Archbishop Khajag Barsamian. The Western Diocese, headquartered in Fresno, California, is headed by His Eminence Archbishop Hovnan Derderian. The Canadian Diocese is led by Bishop Bagrat Galstanian. The Eastern Prelacy, headquartered in New York City, is led by His Eminence Archbishop Oshagan Choloyan. The Western Prelacy, headquartered in La Crescenta, California, is led by His Eminence Archbishop Moushegh Mardirossian. The Canadian Prelacy is led by His Eminence Archbishop Khajag Hagopian.

Core Beliefs

The Armenian Apostolic Church, with the five other Oriental Orthodox churches, rejects both dyophysitism (the two natures position of Chalcedon) and monophysitism (the Eutychian view condemned at Chalcedon) in favor of miaphysitism, the position expounded by St. Cyril of Alexandria, who spoke of the one (mia) nature (physis) of God the incarnate logos, arguing that the one nature of Christ was an inward and real union of the divine and human natures. Many theologians from Eastern and Western Christianity regard the resultant schism as the consequence of an unfortunate terminological misunderstanding, and there have been various unsuccessful attempts at reconciliation (e.g., the Henoticon of 482 and the Three Chapters Controversy of the sixth century). Dialogue among theologians of various churches continues to this day, and there have been several unofficial consultations working toward greater communion.

Statistics

The Eastern Diocese of the Armenian Church in America is comprised of sixty-two parishes in twenty-one states. The Western Diocese is comprised of fifty-two parishes in twelve states. The Canadian Diocese is comprised of six main parishes. The Eastern Prelacy is comprised of twenty-three churches in eleven states. The Western Prelacy is comprised of twelve churches in six states.

Academic Institutions

The church established St. Nersess Armenian Seminary (New Rochelle, NY) in 1962 to train men and women for service in the church.

Websites

Etchmiadzin: http://www.armenianchurch.org/
Cilicia: http://www.armenianorthodoxchurch.org/
Eastern Diocese: http://www.armenianchurch.net/
Eastern Prelacy: http://www.armenianprelacy.org/
Western Diocese: http://www.armenianchurchwd.com/
Western Prelacy: http://westernprelacy.org/

Bibliography

Arbery, A. J. *Religion in the Middle East.* Vol. 1. Cambridge: Cambridge University Press, 2009.

Bailey, B. J., and J. M. Bailey. *Who Are the Christians in the Middle East?* Grand Rapids: Eerdmans, 2003.

Lang, David Marshall. *The Armenians: A People in Exile.* London: Allen and Unwin, 1981.

Robert Keay

Assyrian Church of the East

History

In the fourth century, the Persian Church established itself at Seleucia-Ctesiphon. The church and its theology were shaped by the Synods of Isaac (410), Yahballaha (420), and Dadyeshu (424). These established the autocephalic nature of the church and the primacy of the bishop of Seleucia-Ctesiphon. Although the Council of

Ephesus (431 CE) condemned Nestorius, influential teachers (Ibas and Barsauma) at the School of Edessa, a training center for Persian Christians, continued to champion Nestorius and Theodore until 489 CE, when Zeno closed the school. The Persian Church, exercising its independence, welcomed Nestorians fleeing from the Byzantine and Roman persecution. The Synod of Acacius (486), under the leadership of Barsauma, proclaimed a Nestorian Christology. When the School of Edessa was closed by Zeno, Barsauma organized a school at Nisibis. When the Second Council of Constantinople (553 CE) anathematized Theodore of Mopsuestia and Ibas of Edessa in the Three Chapters Controversy, the schism was deepened. The next century brought the church's greatest theologian, Babai the Great, whose christological writings defined the church's teachings on the two natures of Christ.

During the medieval period, the Persian Church evangelized the Far East and Asia and established dioceses from the Mediterranean to China. In the sixteenth century, hereditary succession and corruption in the church led to unrest and ultimately schism. In 1552, rival patriarchs were elected. When Yohannan Sulaqa traveled to Rome, submitted to the Roman pope, and was consecrated patriarch, the church split and the Sulaqa faction became known as the Chaldean Catholic Church. The other group became known as the Assyrian Church of the East. In 1898, a small group in the Urmia region of Iran identified themselves with the Russian Orthodox Church. When Patriarch Mar Simon XXIII adopted the Gregorian calendar in 1964, traditionalists, already wary of his youthful appointment by hereditary principle, responded in 1968 by electing a rival patriarch, Mar Thoma Darmo, in Baghdad, Iraq, and identifying themselves as the genuine church, the Ancient Church of the East. Darmo's death in 1969 was followed by the election of Mar Addai II as patriarch. Immigrants to North America have established five parishes of the Ancient Church of the East (Chicago, IL; Los Angeles, CA; Modesto, CA; Phoenix, AZ; and Ontario, Canada).

Mar Simon XXIII was expelled from Iraq by the government and went into exile in the United States. Starting in 1940, he lived in Chicago, Illinois, and then in San Francisco, California. He resigned as patriarch in 1973. The next and current catholicos and patriarch of the Assyrian Church of the East, Mar Dinkha IV, also living in exile in

Chicago, Illinois, has continued the program of negotiating and seeking reconciliation with other Christian bodies. His first act was to abolish the hereditary principle, significantly easing tension with the Chaldean Catholic Church. In 1996, he and the patriarch of the Chaldean Catholic Church signed a Joint Synodal Decree for Promoting Unity to work toward greater integration and cooperation in several areas. In 2001, this extended to sharing in Holy Communion. Mar Dinkha IV met with the Roman pontiff, Pope John Paul II, in November 1994, and the two signed the Common Christological Declaration between the Catholic Church and the Assyrian Church of the East. In 2001, the Roman Catholic Church approved as valid the Assyrian liturgy of the Eucharist. In 1997, Mar Dinkha IV entered negotiations with the Syriac Orthodox Church, and each has removed from its liturgy anathemata against the other.

Leadership

The catholicos and patriarch of the Assyrian Church of the East, Mar Dinkha IV, resides outside Chicago in Morton Grove, Illinois. He oversees the Eastern Diocese of the USA. The Western Diocese of the USA is served by Bishop Mar Aprim Khamis. The Diocese of California is served by Bishop Mar Awa Royel. The Diocese of Canada is led by Bishop Mar Emmanuel Yosip.

Statistics

The Eastern Diocese of the USA includes nine churches. The Western Diocese of the USA includes six churches. The Diocese of California includes five churches. The Diocese of Canada includes four churches.

Websites

http://www.assyrianchurchnews.com/
http://www.maryosipparish.org/
http://nestorian.org/

Bibliography

Angold, Michael, ed. *The Cambridge History of Christianity*. Vol. 5, *Eastern Christianity*. Cambridge: Cambridge University Press, 2006.

Baum, Wilhelm, and Dietmar Winkler. *The Church of the East: A Concise History*. London: Routledge, 2003.

Baumer, Christoph. *The Church of the East: An Illustrated History of Assyrian Christianity*. London: Taurus, 2006.

Moffett, Samuel Hugh. *Christianity in Asia*. Vol. 1, *Beginnings to 1500*. Maryknoll, NY: Orbis, 1998.

Soro, Mar Bawai. *The Church of the East: Apostolic and Orthodox*. San Jose, CA: Adiabene, 2007.

Robert Keay

Coptic Orthodox Church

History

After 1950, immigration of Copts to North America increased and Coptic immigrants expressed the need for more formal ecclesiastical leadership and structures. In August 1964, Father Marcos A. Marcos became the first priest ordained in North America, in Toronto. St. Mark's Coptic Orthodox Church in Toronto, formed in November 1964, became the first Coptic church in North America, serving thirty-six families. The church spread, and there are now at least forty churches and priests in Canada, primarily in Ontario and Quebec. The late 1960s saw the formation of the first churches in the United States. St. Mark's Coptic Orthodox Church in Jersey City, New Jersey, led by Father Gabriel Abdel-Sayed, is regarded as the first Coptic church in the USA, and St. Mark's Coptic Orthodox Church in Los Angeles, led by Father Bishoy Kamel, is regarded as the second. Both were incorporated in 1970. In 1977, Pope Shenouda III made his first pastoral visit to the churches in the United States and Canada.

Leadership

The highest authority in the church is the Holy Synod, which is headed by His Holiness Pope Shenouda III and is located in Cairo, Egypt. The leader's official title is Pope of Alexandria and Patriarch of All Africa on the Holy See of St. Mark. The Archdiocese of North America is led by His Grace David, general bishop and patriarchal exarch, in Cedar Grove, New Jersey.

Core Beliefs

The first great schism in the Christian church occurred in the fifth century when Egyptian Christianity rejected the dogmatic pronouncement of the Council of Chalcedon (451 CE) that Christ was one person in two natures. Egyptian Christians followed the terminology of St. Cyril, former patriarch of Alexandria (412–44 CE) and champion of orthodoxy in the previous council (Ephesus, 431 CE), who spoke of the one (mia) nature (physis) of God the incarnate logos and argued that the one nature of Christ was an inward and real union of the divine and human natures. Some Greek-speaking Egyptians accepted the Chalcedonian formula and formed the Greek Orthodox Church of Alexandria (Melkites). Thereafter, Christianity was divided by Chalcedonian and non-Chalcedonian churches (Oriental Orthodox churches).

The ecclesiastical language of the Coptic Orthodox Church is Coptic; Arabic is also used. The church uses three liturgies in Coptic (Basil, Cyril, and Gregory) and offers seven sacraments (baptism, confirmation, repentance, Eucharist, unction of the sick, holy matrimony, and priesthood).

Statistics

There are now nearly three hundred churches in the United States and Canada. Of the more than two hundred churches in the United States, most are in New Jersey and New York. The Coptic Orthodox Diocese of the Southern United States, established in 1993, is led by His Grace Bishop Youssef and currently includes eleven states with thirty-four priests serving twenty-nine churches and twenty-five communities. The Coptic Orthodox Diocese of Los Angeles, Southern California, and Hawaii was established in 1995 with His Grace Bishop Serapion as leader and currently serves thirty-two churches with fifty-five priests.

Academic Institutions

Pope Shenouda III Coptic Orthodox Theological Seminary (Cedar Grove, NJ; Los Angeles, CA)
St. Athanasius Theological Seminary (Corpus Christi, TX)

Websites

Coptic Orthodox Church Network: http://copticchurch.net/
Coptic Church in diaspora: http://www.coptic.org/
US Copts Association: http://www.copts.com/
Southern Diocese: http://www.suscopticdiocese.org/
Los Angeles Diocese: http://www.lacopts.org/

Bibliography

Angold, Michael, ed. *The Cambridge History of Christianity.* Vol. 5, *Eastern Christianity.* Cambridge: Cambridge University Press, 2006.

Atiya, Aziz Suryal, ed. *The Coptic Encyclopedia.* 8 vols. New York: Macmillan, 1991.

Chaillot, Christine. *The Coptic Orthodox Church: A Brief Introduction to Its Life and Spirituality.* Geneva: Inter-Orthodox Dialogue, 2005.

DeWit, Puck. "Internet: A Religious Sheepfold. The Coptic Orthodox Religious Regimes in the Diaspora." *Journal of Eastern Christian Studies* 54 (2002): 91–108.

Griggs, C. Wilfred. *Early Egyptian Christianity: From Its Origins to 451 CE.* Leiden: Brill, 1990.

Kamil, Jill. *Christianity in the Land of the Pharaohs: The Coptic Orthodox Church.* London: Routledge, 2002.

Meinardus, Otto F. A. *Two Thousand Years of Coptic Christianity.* New York: American University in Cairo Press, 1999.

Stene Preston, Nora. "The Challenge of the Diaspora as Reflected in a Coptic Sunday School." *Journal of Eastern Christian Studies* 54 (2002): 77–89.

Robert Keay

Malankara Syrian Orthodox Church

History

The Malankara Syrian Orthodox Church is an apostolic church founded by the apostle St. Thomas in AD 52. It is one of the five Oriental Orthodox churches, also known as non-Chalcedonian churches. For most of the first fifteen centuries, the church was under the leadership of the Nestorian catholicos of Babylon, but when the Nestorians were annihilated by the Arabs and the Mongols, the St. Thomas Christians were left without a shepherd. The Portuguese, arriving in India in the 1500s, attempted to Romanize the church but were met with resistance. Roughly one-half of the St. Thomas Christians met at Coonen Cross in 1653 and took an oath to abjure Roman Catholicism. After electing Archdeacon Mar Thoma as their leader, they asked Mar Gregorios, the Jacobite (Syrian Orthodox) archbishop of Jerusalem, to come to India to ordain Mar Thoma as their metropolitan. The church named itself the Malankara Syrian Orthodox Church and has remained Monophysite in its confession.

An Anglican-inspired reformist group split to form the Mar Thoma Church in 1836, but the majority of the St. Thomas Christians continued to be affiliated with the Jacobite patriarchate of Antioch. In the nineteenth century, Patriarch Peter III of Antioch visited Kerala and granted the church a degree of autonomy. Nonetheless, between 1909 and 1911 a dispute arose regarding the control of church property by the patriarch of Antioch (who had moved to Damascus in Syria to escape Turkish persecution). This resulted in decades of legal conflict and a rift in which most church members, despite retaining the Jacobite Orthodox confession, named as their head the catholicos of the East, an ancient title of the Nestorian catholicos of Babylon. The rest continued to acknowledge the authority of the patriarch.

Around 1900, the Malankara Syrian Orthodox Church was introduced in the United States. Bishop Timotheos presided over the exarchate. In 1964, the first service was held in New York; it was soon followed by the establishment of churches in Philadelphia, Chicago, and Washington. The first United States diocese was formed for all parishes in the United States and Canada in 1979, but in 1993, the Canadian parishes separated. The American diocese was divided into the Northeast American Diocese and the Southwest American Diocese in 2009.

Headquarters

80-34 Commonwealth Boulevard
Bellrose, NY 11426
Telephone: 718-470-9844
Email: malankara@malankara.org

Leadership

The primate of the church is the catholicos of the East, residing in Kottayam, Kerala, India.

Core Beliefs

The Malankara Syrian Orthodox Church subscribes to the Nicene Creed and the teachings of the Councils of Nicea, Constantinople, and Ephesus. It follows the traditions of the early church. Monophysite in theology, the church views the Son as consubstantial with the Father and sees his humanity and divinity united in one incarnate nature. He is begotten by the Father; the Holy Spirit proceeds from the Father. Episcopal and conciliar, the church believes that every baptized Christian shares in its kingly, priestly, and prophetic authority.

Statistics

There are 3.5 million members and 24 dioceses worldwide. In America, there are over 75 urban parishes where mass (*qurbana*) is celebrated regularly. The Northeast American Diocese has 10,000 members, with 50 parishes and 40 priests.

Academic Institutions

The church operates the oldest theological seminary in India, the Orthodox Theological Seminary in Kottayam founded in 1835. A second church-run seminary is located in Nagpur, India.

Publication

Diocesan Voice

Website

http://www.malankaraorthodoxchurch.in/

George Thomas Kurian

Syriac Orthodox Church

History

In the late nineteenth century and early twentieth century, religious persecution in Ottoman Turkey forced many Syrian Orthodox Christians to flee their homeland. Many arrived in the United States and Canada. One of the exiles, Hanna Koorie, became their first spiritual leader. He was ordained to the priesthood in Jerusalem in 1907 and served the community in New Jersey. The first Syriac Orthodox Church was established in West Hoboken (now Union City), New Jersey. It was soon followed by the parish of St. Mary's in Worcester, Massachusetts, served by Father Favlos Samuel; the parish of St. Ephraem in Central Falls, Rhode Island, served by Father Ephrem Barsoum; and later the parish of Sts. Peter and Paul in the region of Detroit, Michigan, led by Father Estefan Durghali. In 1957, the Archdiocese of North America was created with Mor Athanasius Yeshue Samuel serving as archbishop. As a result, St. Mark's Cathedral was established in Hackensack, New Jersey. The cathedral parish relocated to Teaneck, New Jersey, in 1994.

In 1995, following the death of Archbishop Mor Athanasius Yeshue Samuel, the Holy Synod divided the Archdiocese of North America into three archdioceses: the Patriarchal Vicariate of Western United States (based in Burbank, CA), the Patriarchal Vicariate of Eastern United States (based in Teaneck, NJ), and the Patriarchal Vicariate of Canada (based in Montreal, Quebec).

Leadership

The supreme head of the universal Syriac Orthodox Church is the patriarch of Antioch and all the East. That office is now held by His Holiness Ignatius Zakka II in Damascus, Syria. The Patriarchal Vicariate of Western United States is led by His Eminence Mor Clemis Eugene Kaplan. The Patriarchal Vicariate of Eastern United States is led by His Eminence Mor Cyril Aphrem Karim.

Core Beliefs

The Syriac Orthodox Church is part of the Oriental Orthodox communion, which accepts the first three ecumenical councils (Nicea, Constantinople, and Ephesus) but rejects the Dyophysite (one person in two natures) Christology of the Council of Chalcedon (451 CE), adhering instead to the Miaphysite Christology of St. Cyril, who argued for one nature in the incarnate logos.

Liturgical language is Syriac Aramaic, and the church uses the oldest surviving liturgy, the Liturgy of St. James.

Websites

http://sor.cua.edu/
http://socdigest.org/

Bibliography

Angold, Michael, ed. *The Cambridge History of Christianity.* Vol. 5, *Eastern Christianity.* Cambridge: Cambridge University Press, 2006.

Chaillot, Christine. *The Syrian Orthodox Church of Antioch and All the East: An Introduction to Its Life and Spirituality.* Geneva: Inter-Orthodox Dialogue, 1998.

O'Mahony, Anthony. *Christianity in the Middle East.* London: Melisende, 2008.

———. *Eastern Christianity.* London: Melisende, 2004.

Teule, H. "Middle Eastern Christians and Migration: Some Reflections." *Journal of Eastern Christian Studies* 54 (2002): 1–23.

Robert Keay

Pentecostal

Apostolic Assembly of the Faith in Christ Jesus

History

The Apostolic Assembly of the Faith in Christ Jesus was formed in California in 1925 as the first Spanish-speaking Oneness Pentecostal denomination in the United States. Today it is the largest such denomination as well as one of the most rapidly growing Hispanic denominations in the world, benefiting from Hispanic immigration to the United States.

The Apostolic Assembly is a product of the Azusa Street, Los Angeles revival that gave birth to the Pentecostal movement. In 1912, Francisco Llorente was baptized by a participant in the revival, Juan Navarro; thirteen years later Llorente was elected bishop president of the newly established Apostolic Assembly. The Apostolic Assembly was incorporated five years later.

Headquarters

10807 Laurel Street
Rancho Cucamonga, CA 91730
Telephone: 909-987-3013
Email: headquarters@apostolicassembly.org

Leadership

Bishop president: Daniel Sanchez

Core Beliefs

The Apostolic Assembly embraces traditional evangelical Pentecostal beliefs pertaining to the virgin birth, deity of Christ, baptism of the Holy Spirit accompanied by speaking in tongues, gifts of the Spirit, and eternal punishment of the unjust. As a Oneness denomination, it rejects the doctrine of the Trinity. Members emphasize holiness, with the caution that "in the practice of holiness we believe that we must avoid all extremes, asceticisms and deprivations" (apostolicassembly.org, "Doctrine"). Baptism is by immersion and in the name of Jesus Christ. The Lord's Supper is observed with unleavened bread and unfermented wine and is seen as a commemorative practice. Participation is limited to faithful church members and is followed by the ceremony of foot washing. Marriage is only to fellow believers, and divorce is not permitted. The assembly teaches tithing and divine healing.

Statistics

Churches in the United States: 700
Worldwide membership: 130,000
Ordained ministers and deacons worldwide: 5,500
Missionary churches: 550 (in 20 countries in Central and South America and Europe)

From 1996 to 2002, the assembly experienced 87 percent growth in membership in the United States.

Missionary and Evangelistic Work

The Department of National Missions, headed by Abel Aguilar, plants churches in the United States and, with the specific vision of the One in a Million initiative, seeks to send a missionary to each city with a population of one million or more. It is also involved in the School of Evangelism and the National Evangelist Training Network. Arthur Espinosa is secretary of the Department of International Missions, which oversees global evangelism. Currently, it is active in twenty countries, including Argentina, Bolivia, Brazil, Canada, Chile, Colombia, Cuba, Costa Rica, the Dominican Republic, Hawaii, Honduras, Italy, Mexico, Panama, Paraguay, Peru, Puerto Rico, Spain, Uruguay, and Venezuela.

Academic Institution

The National Apostolic Bible College has twenty-four branches throughout the country.

Parachurch Organizations

The Apostolic Assembly offers help to needy families, widows, and orphans through the A. C. Nava Trust Fund of its Department of Social Assistance, headed by Joe Prado. The department also awards academic scholarships and deals with practical matters such as pastoral retirement plans and medical and life insurance for denomination members.

A men's auxiliary department, Apostolic Men, raises money for national missions through its Mano a Mano project. Dorcas, the women's auxiliary, funds both foreign and domestic mission work with the Flor Azul project. Messengers of Peace sends youth into foreign and domestic mission fields as assistants to pastors and missionaries, and Juniors4Jesus seeks to involve even younger children in the work of ministry.

The A.D.A.M. Community (Advocating for the Deaf through Apostolic Ministry) includes both deaf and non-deaf members who seek to meet the needs of the deaf. It sponsors a camp for the deaf, three levels of religious signing classes, a convention, and an annual conference and workshop.

The Single Adult Ministry provides moral support to over-thirty single, divorced, and widowed individuals. The Apostolic Assembly also operates two drug rehabilitation facilities in California.

Electronic Media

The assembly has several recording studios and radio programs.

Publications

The Department of Christian Education is an auxiliary organization of the assembly that produces Bible-based literature, including outreach tracts and the Apostolic Biblical Expositor. Its secretary is board member Ismael Martin del Campo. The denomination headquarters has a bookstore that is open to the public.

Website

http://www.apostolicassembly.org/

Archives

An Apostolic Assembly history museum/library is being planned.

Sarah Claudine Day

Apostolic Faith Mission Church of God

History

The Apostolic Faith Mission Church of God is a predominantly black Oneness Pentecostal body founded by F. W. Williams in 1906. Williams was a black man who went to the Azusa Street revival in Los Angeles and was baptized by William Seymour. He returned to the South and converted the entire membership of a Primitive Baptist Church, which gave Williams its church building for use as a meeting place. He later became one of the first to adopt nontrinitarian (Oneness) doctrine. Oneness Pentecostalism describes God not as three distinct persons but rather as one being who manifests himself as the Father, Son, and Holy Ghost. After Williams separated from the main body, the Apostolic Faith Mission Church of God was incorporated in Mobile, Alabama, in 1915.

Headquarters

The Word's Temple
806 Muscogee Road
Cantonment, FL 32533
Telephone: 404-284-7596

Core Beliefs

Core beliefs include an emphasis on faith healing; the ordination of women; foot washing as part of the Communion rite; the refusal to recognize any baptism without the words "the Lord Jesus Christ"; the forbidding of alcohol, drugs, and tobacco; and marriage only with a person who is saved.

George Thomas Kurian

Apostolic Faith Mission of Portland, Oregon

History

The Apostolic Faith Mission of Portland, Oregon (AFP), traces its roots to the Azusa Street revival, which began in 1906 in Los Angeles, California. Florence Crawford was alongside William Seymour as one of the early leaders of the revival, which is believed by many to be the primary impetus for the worldwide Pentecostal movement. After eight months of work at the Azusa Street Mission, Crawford parted with Seymour in December 1906 in order to establish a similar work in the Pacific Northwest. After months of meetings in Northern California and Oregon, she established her headquarters in Portland in early 1908. She began publishing the *Apostolic Faith* newsletter in the summer of 1908 after her colaborer at Azusa Street, Clara Lum, joined her in Portland with the Azusa Street mailing list.

AFP's headquarters have remained in Portland, Oregon, along with the flagship church, which is the center of AFP identity. The practice of summer camp meetings for evangelistic and discipleship purposes has been a constant throughout the church's history.

Headquarters

6615 SE 52nd Avenue
Portland, OR 97206

Leadership

Superintendent general: Darrel D. Lee

Core Beliefs

AFP has steadfastly maintained its Wesleyan Holiness and Pentecostal distinctives, which Florence Crawford adopted at Azusa Street and emphasized throughout the remainder of her ministry. They include the teaching that entire sanctification is to be experienced as the second definite work of grace, subsequent to salvation (John 17:15–21; Heb. 13:12). One can also experience the baptism of the Holy Spirit, which is the enduement of power from on high upon the clean, sanctified life and is evidenced by speaking in tongues (Luke 24:49; Acts 1:5–8; 2:1–4). The movement resisted all urgings from other Pentecostal leaders early in the twentieth century to adopt a Oneness view of the Godhead, and the cover of its 1965 self-published history volume includes the subtitle "A Trinitarian-Fundamental Evangelistic Organization." Other doctrines emphasized in the movement's doctrinal statement include the infallibility of Scripture, divine healing, and the sanctity of marriage for life (neither partner is free to marry again as long as the first companion is alive).

Website

http://www.apostolicfaith.org/

Bibliography

Apostolic Faith Mission. *A Historical Account of the Apostolic Faith: A Trinitarian-Fundamental Evangelistic Organization.* Portland, OR: Apostolic Faith Publishing House, 1965.

Barrett, Karen. "The Apostolic Faith Mission of Portland, Oregon." http://www.apostolicfaith.org.

Blumhofer, Edith L. "Apostolic Faith Mission (Portland, OR)." In *The New International Dictionary of Pentecostal and Charismatic Movements,* edited by Stanley M. Burgess and Eduard M. van der Maas, 327. Grand Rapids: Zondervan, 2002.

Mitchell, R. Bryant. *Heritage and Horizons: The History of Open Bible Standard Churches.* Des Moines, IA: Open Bible Publishers, 1982.

Robeck, Cecil M., Jr. "Florence Crawford: Apostolic Faith Pioneer." In *Portraits of a Generation: Early Pentecostal Leaders,* edited by James R. Goff Jr. and Grant Wacker, 219–35. Fayetteville: University of Arkansas Press, 2002.

David Cole

Apostolic Overcoming Holy Church of God

History

The Apostolic Overcoming Holy Church of God is an African American Oneness Pentecostal church established by Rev. William Thomas Phillips, formerly of the Faith Mission Church of God. The nineteen-year-old Phillips felt a call to promote Christian holiness in 1912 and entered the ministry the following year despite his limited education. He began preaching in Mobile, Alabama, in 1916 and in the same year founded the Ethiopian Overcoming Holy Church of God, incorporated four years later. Although predominantly black, the church changed its name in 1941 to the Apostolic Overcoming Holy Church of God to stress its welcome of all ethnic groups. Over the course of the fifty-seven-year tenure of Bishop Phillips, the church enjoyed expansion throughout the United States and into foreign countries.

Headquarters

2257 St. Stephens Road
Mobile, AL 36617
Telephone: 251-473-8312

Leadership

Presiding prelate: Bishop G. W. Ayers

Core Beliefs

The Apostolic Overcoming Holy Church of God is a Oneness denomination, meaning it rejects the doctrine of the Trinity, that is, the existence of three separate persons of the Godhead. It does not baptize in the name of the Father, the Son, and the Holy Spirit, seeing that as a Catholic practice without a scriptural basis.

Among the thirteen articles that express the church's faith are those that affirm biblical infallibility and teach baptism by immersion, foot washing, divine healing, and the right of women to preach and teach.

Website

http://www.aohchurch.com/

George Thomas Kurian

Assemblies of God

History

The Assemblies of God, a multiethnic Pentecostal denomination with over three million adherents in the United States, was organized in Hot Springs, Arkansas, on April 2–12, 1914. The approximately three hundred participants at the first general council, representing a variety of independent churches and loosely organized networks of ministers, formed the first truly national Pentecostal body in the United States. The Assemblies of God was formed for the purpose of helping congregations and ministers fulfill the Great Commission both by providing accountability on doctrine, morals, and finances and by establishing institutions such as schools, a publishing house, and a missionary agency.

The Assemblies of God located its national headquarters in Findlay, Ohio, in 1914, moved to St. Louis, Missouri, in 1915, and then moved to Springfield, Missouri, in 1918. It established the Missionary Department in 1919 and the Home Missions and Education Department in 1937; other departments followed. Formed in the midst of the emerging worldwide Pentecostal revival, the Assemblies of God quickly took root in other countries and formed indigenous national organizations. The Assemblies of God (USA) is a constituent member of the World Assemblies of God Fellowship. The Assemblies of God maintains close relations with other Pentecostal and evangelical churches and is a member of the Pentecostal/Charismatic Churches of North America, the Pentecostal World Fellowship, and the National Association of Evangelicals.

Headquarters

1445 N Boonville Avenue
Springfield, MO 65802
Telephone: 417-862-2781

Leadership

Church government is hybrid congregational and presbyterian. Each local church operates under both a district and a national structure. There are forty-seven geographical districts and seventeen ethnic districts. The national church is called the General Council of the Assemblies of God. The biennial general council elects the executive leadership team, sets doctrinal standards, and provides for the development of the church. Voting members of the general council include all ordained and licensed ministers and one lay delegate from each church. The executive leadership team includes the general superintendent, assistant general superintendent, general treasurer, general secretary, director of world missions, and director of United States missions. Dr. George O. Wood has served as general superintendent since 2007.

Core Beliefs

The Statement of Fundamental Truths, which provides the basis of fellowship for the Assemblies of God, affirms the historic doctrines of the Christian faith. Of the statement's sixteen tenets, four are deemed cardinal doctrines and identify Christ in four roles: Savior, Baptizer in the Holy Spirit, Healer, and soon-coming King. The statement also affirms the inspiration of Scripture, the trinitarian view of the Godhead, justification by faith, substitutionary atonement, progressive sanctification, speaking in tongues as the initial physical evidence of Spirit baptism, and premillennial eschatology.

Two ordinances—water baptism and Holy Communion—are practiced.

Worship

Worship services are generally informal and allow freedom of expression.

Divisions and Splits

Almost immediately after the Assemblies of God was organized, its leaders were faced with a doctrinal dispute—whether to abandon traditional trinitarian theology in favor of a view of God as one person, whose name, Jesus Christ, is redemptive. Responding to this controversy—also called the New Issue or the Oneness movement—in 1916, the Assemblies of God approved a Statement of Fundamental Truths, which affirmed trinitarian orthodoxy and resulted in the departure of Oneness advocates.

Statistics

In 2011, the Assemblies of God claimed 3,041,957 adherents in the United States served by 12,595 churches and 35,483 ministers. Few major denominations in the US have greater racial diversity than the Assemblies of God: white (61%), Hispanic (20%), black (9%), Asian/Pacific Islander (4%), Native American (2%), other (4%).

The World Assemblies of God Fellowship counted 65,398,796 adherents in 252 countries served by 358,450 churches and 371,427 ministers.

Missionary and Evangelistic Work

Missions has always been central to the identity of the Assemblies of God. The second general council, held in November 1914, resolved to achieve "the greatest evangelism that the world has ever seen" (ifphc.org, "The Assemblies of God: Our Heritage in Perspective"). Within the first year of the church's existence, approximately thirty missionaries became members of the Assemblies of God. Beginning in the 1950s, missionaries focused greater emphasis on training indigenous leaders, which led to dramatic church growth in many places.

The Assemblies of God engages in vigorous evangelism and church planting in the United States and in other nations, and it supports an extensive system of schools, medical missions, orphanages, Teen Challenge drug rehabilitation centers, and works of compassion. In 2011, Assemblies of God World Missions supported 2,708 missionaries and associates, and Assemblies of God US Missions supported 603 endorsed chaplains and 977 appointed missionaries, candidates, and spouses who served in church planting and development, church and school construction teams, Chi Alpha college ministries, Teen Challenge, Youth Alive, and ministries to ethnic and cultural minorities.

Academic Institutions

In 2011, the Assemblies of God endorsed 18 institutions of higher education in the United States that enrolled 15,995 students. In other nations, the Assemblies of God reported 1,976 Bible schools and extension programs that served over 100,000 students.

The largest US schools are:

American Indian College (Phoenix, AZ)
Assemblies of God Theological Seminary (Springfield, MO)
Central Bible College (Springfield, MO)
Evangel University (Springfield, MO)
Global University (Springfield, MO)
North Central University (Minneapolis, MN)
Northwest University (Kirkland, WA)
Southeastern University (Lakeland, FL)
Southwestern Assemblies of God University (Waxahachie, TX)
Trinity Bible College (Ellendale, ND)

Valley Forge Christian College (Phoenixville, PA)
Vanguard University (Costa Mesa, CA)
Zion Bible College (Haverhill, MA)

Publications

Gospel Publishing House produces books, Christian education curriculum, and other religious literature. A weekly periodical, the *Pentecostal Evangel*, has a circulation of approximately 170,000. A Spanish edition, *El Evangelio Pentecostal*, is published quarterly. A quarterly pastoral journal, *Enrichment*, and an annual historical journal, *Assemblies of God Heritage*, are distributed to credentialed ministers and subscribers.

Website

http://www.ag.org/

Archives

Flower Pentecostal Heritage Center, Springfield, Missouri

Bibliography

"Flower Pentecostal Heritage Center." https://ifphc.org. "The Assemblies of God: Our Heritage in Perspective."

Horton, Stanley M., ed. *Systematic Theology: A Pentecostal Perspective*. Springfield, MO: Logion, 2007.

McGee, Gary B. *People of the Spirit: The Assemblies of God*. Springfield, MO: Gospel Publishing House, 2004.

————. *This Gospel Shall Be Preached: A History and Theology of Assemblies of God Foreign Missions*. 2 vols. Springfield, MO: Gospel Publishing House, 1986, 1989.

Menzies, William W., and Stanley M. Horton. *Bible Doctrines: A Pentecostal Perspective*. Springfield, MO: Logion, 1993.

Darrin J. Rodgers

Assemblies of God International Fellowship

History

The Assemblies of God International Fellowship has a Swedish background. In St. Paul, Minnesota, in 1922, Full Gospel ministers held a regional meeting and unanimously voted to recognize themselves as a fellowship of independent churches. The Scandinavian Independent Assemblies coexisted alongside these Full Gospel ministers, and their collected efforts affected the midwestern states of America. This fellowship quickly spread into South America through the work of Gunnar Wingren and now has over 14,500,000 members and a few thousand churches.

In 1935, the Scandinavian Independent Assemblies dissolved its fellowship and joined the Full Gospel ministers to create an interchurch fellowship that continues to this day.

The founder of this movement was the late Rev. T. A. Lanes. In 1986, this fellowship changed its name to the Assemblies of God International Fellowship.

Headquarters

PO Box 22410
San Diego, CA 92192-2410
Telephone: 858-677-9701
Email: info@agifellowship.org

Leadership

The Assemblies of God International Fellowship is governed by a board of elders, and the executive director/chairman is George Ekeroth.

Core Beliefs

The Assemblies of God International Fellowship is a conservative trinitarian fellowship with a Pentecostal view of the present ministry of the Holy Spirit. Core beliefs include the plenary-verbal inspiration of Scripture, which should be the basis of preaching; the vicarious and atoning death of Jesus; baptism of the Holy Spirit as a separate and distinct experience following salvation; water baptism (by immersion) as a requirement for believers; and Communion as a practice for believers only.

Core Practices

The Assemblies of God International Fellowship's main thrust is "its devotion to presenting the Pentecostal message" (agifellowship.org, "Resources: Our History"). Its main purpose is to provide credentials for ministerial candidates, functioning as a clergy registration bureau that has no gender disqualification.

Publications

The Assemblies of God International Fellowship publishes the magazine *Fellowship*. It is found in its entirety on their website for free and is designed to promote the gospel and awareness of the Pentecostal message.

Website

http://www.agifellowship.org/

Bibliography

"The Assemblies of God International Fellowship." http://agifellowship.org. "Home," "Resources: Board of Directors," "Resources: Our History," "Resources: Our Principles," "Resources: Publications," and "Resources: What We Believe."

Chad C. Brewer

Assemblies of the Lord Jesus Christ

History

The Assemblies of the Lord Jesus Christ (ALJC) believes it is part of a continuation of the great revival that began on the day of Pentecost in Jerusalem in AD 30 and that took root in the United States in the twentieth century. At the beginning of the twentieth century, thousands were filled with the Holy Spirit and were baptized in the name of Jesus Christ in the United States. The Acts 2:38 new-birth message began to spread, and many churches were established or converted to these beliefs. From these churches, groups of ministers came together for organization and fellowship. Various groups throughout the country went by different names, trying and striving to promote the gospel of Jesus Christ. At the camp meeting in Urania, Louisiana, in March 1952, three groups known as the Assemblies of the Church of Jesus Christ, Jesus Only Apostolic Church of God, and the Church of the Lord Jesus Christ formulated a merger and adopted the name the Assemblies of the Lord Jesus Christ.

During the early years of the ALJC, the organization did not have a constitution but was governed by a bishop's board. However, because of subsequent growth, the ALJC adopted a constitution in the early 1960s, and the bishop's board was replaced by separate districts with their own duly elected officers. The first general chairman of the ALJC was L. A. Parent (1952–59). Subsequent chairmen/superintendents were J. T. Mayo (1959–61), David Mayo (1961–69), Lester McGruder (1969–73), Raymond Bishop (1973–81), Don Johnson (1981–99), Steve Wilson (1999–2007), and Robert W. Martin (2007–present).

Headquarters

875 North White Station Road
Memphis, TN 38122

Leadership

Currently, the ALJC has an executive board comprised of a general superintendent (changed from chairman during Don Johnson's administration), general secretary, southern region assistant superintendent, northern region assistant superintendent, and western region assistant superintendent. Each district consists of a district superintendent, who serves on the general board, as well as other district offices.

Core Beliefs

The Assemblies of the Lord Jesus Christ is apostolic in doctrine and teachings, with a strict adherence to the Bible as the Word of God. The ALJC teaches that Acts 2:38 is the biblical plan of salvation (repentance, baptism in Jesus's name, the infilling of the Holy Spirit). The ALJC teaches the Oneness of God, meaning there is one God in three manifestations (Father in creation, Son in redemption, and Holy Spirit in regeneration). These three manifestations of God do not reflect three persons in the Godhead; rather, these three are one. The church also teaches the importance of personal holiness and separation.

Statistics

There are 550 churches, 1,200 ministers, and 23 districts throughout the United States, especially in the South and the Midwest. The largest churches are located in Tennessee, Mississippi, Louisiana, Indiana, and Ohio.

Missionary and Evangelistic Work

The ALJC has a strong missionary presence in Chile, Argentina, Brazil, Mexico, Cuba, the Dominican Republic, Haiti, and Venezuela and has grown in recent years in Europe (Russia, Norway, Ireland, Italy, Spain, Germany, Poland, and the Netherlands), Asia (Taiwan, the Philippines, Papua New Guinea, India, and Nepal), Africa (Nigeria, Uganda, Kenya, Zambia, Liberia, Ghana, Rwanda, and the Congo), and the Middle East (Lebanon).

The ALJC has the following departments of ministry: World Missions, Missions America (home missions), Apostolic Crusaders (youth ministry), Women's Esprit (women's ministry), Ministry (men's ministry), KidzQuest (children's ministry), Evangelists, and Christian Schools. The ALJC has developed television commercials for a special advertising campaign (they can be viewed at hopeforyou.org). The ALJC hosts an annual General Ministry Conference, annual National Youth Convention, annual National Christian Church School Competition, biennial Women's Esprit Conference, and biennial Ministry Conference.

Academic Institution

Parkersburg Bible College (Parkersburg, WV)

Publication

Apostolic Witness, a monthly magazine

Website

http://www.aljc.org/

Robert Martin

Bible Church of Christ

History

Roy Bryant founded the nondenominational Bible Church of Christ in 1961 after becoming a pastor in 1959 and holding church meetings in his home. A few years earlier, in his early thirties, Bryant had experienced a miraculous healing while attending an event conducted by revivalist Jack Coe. This led to Bryant's emphasis on healing and the exorcism of demons and later to books on the subject of demonology. In 1966, Bryant was ordained as a bishop, and the church moved to a facility on Morris Avenue in the Bronx, New York, which was destroyed by fire three years later. Rebuilding was accompanied by expansion; currently, beyond two locations in the Bronx, the church has branches in Schenectady and Mount Vernon, New York; Delaware; North Carolina; and India. It also operates a school in Liberia.

Headquarters

1358 Morris Avenue
Bronx, NY 10456
Telephone: 718-588-2284
Email: info@thebiblechurchofchrist.org

The Morris Avenue building, purchased in 1976, houses not only administrative offices but also the Theological Institute, a Christian bookstore, a childcare facility, a gymnasium, and dining facilities.

Leadership

President: Bishop Roy Bryant Sr.

Core Beliefs

The church is trinitarian and teaches biblical inerrancy, baptism of the Holy Spirit, and miraculous healing and deliverance.

Website

http://www.thebiblechurchofchrist.org/

Sarah Claudine Day

Bible Way Church of Our Lord Jesus Christ World-Wide

History

The Bible Way Church of Our Lord Jesus Christ World-Wide Inc. was established in 1957 as an offshoot of the Church of Our Lord Jesus Christ of the Apostolic Faith Inc. (COOLJC).

Predominantly African American, the Bible Way Church of Our Lord Jesus Christ World-Wide is a Oneness Pentecostal denomination. Its founder, Smallwood E. Williams, had been general secretary of the COOLJC and led a Washington, DC, National Pentecostal Ministerial Conference for other former members of that body. The participants objected to COOLJC practices that they viewed as indicative of poor administration and authoritarianism, especially the sole governorship of the COOLJC leader. Some seventy churches withdrew from the COOLJC to form the Bible Way Church of Our Lord Jesus Christ World-Wide. Williams was made presiding bishop of the new church, and four pastors were made bishops, with a bishop from the Pentecostal Assemblies of the World officiating at the ceremonies.

Williams's reputation among his followers as a preacher, orator, modern-day apostle, and civil rights activist contributed to the growth of the denomination during his thirty-four-year tenure. The church has branches throughout the United States and in Canada, Europe, Africa, South America, and the Caribbean. In 1997, a dispute among the membership caused a majority of members to form a new body, the International Bible Way Church of Our Lord Jesus Christ, headquartered in Danville, Virginia. The other group, continuing to utilize the original name, moved to Brooklyn, New York.

Headquarters

Greater Bibleway Temple
261 Rochester Avenue
Brooklyn, NY 11213

Leadership

Chief apostle and presiding bishop: Apostle Huie Lee Rogers

Core Beliefs

The church's doctrinal statement includes belief in the inspiration of Scripture, the necessity of repentance and remission of sins, salvation only through Christ, baptism by immersion and in the name of Christ, baptism of the Holy Ghost accompanied by speaking in tongues, holy living, the imminent premillennial return of Christ, the resurrection and rapture of the true church, the final judgment, and the establishment of the new heaven and new earth.

Website

http://www.biblewaychurch.org/

Sarah Claudine Day

Calvary Ministries International

History

In 1969, the Fort Wayne, Indiana, area experienced a revival among hippies commonly referred to as the Jesus movement. As a result, six hundred people were baptized that summer. Six men asked Dr. Paul Paino to mentor them in the ministry. He met with these men, and the group grew over the next few years, leading Dr. Paino to incorporate the ministry in 1978 as Calvary Ministries International.

The group was a self-described denomination, and prior to the 1980s, it held the deeds to the churches and handled all the finances from its headquarters in Fort Wayne. In the late 1980s, it moved toward a fellowship structure. As charismatic churches left their denominations, they wanted to maintain their own deeds. To adjust to the trend and to entice these new independent churches to join, Calvary Ministries International changed its structure, deeding all properties back to the local churches.

Headquarters

111 E Ludwig Road
Fort Wayne, IN 46856
Telephone: 260-489-1381

Core Beliefs

Calvary Ministries International is an evangelical, classical Pentecostal fellowship. This means it holds to Scripture as the infallible Word of God and believes that Jesus died to pay the penalty for each person's sins. It believes that speaking in tongues is the evidence of the baptism of the Holy Spirit, although this experience does not make a person any more spiritual than one who has not spoken in tongues.

Statistics

Churches: 100 in 20 states
United States clergy: 230
Largest church: Waterloo, Indiana, with 750 attendees

Bibliography

Kutzner, Dennis. Telephone interview. September 17, 2010.

Ray Reid

Christian Congregation in North America

History

The Christian Congregation in North America developed out of a Pentecostal revival meeting in

Chicago in 1907. Under the leadership of Louis Francescon, the group initially focused its efforts on individuals of Italian descent throughout the United States as well as in some foreign countries. Eventually, with the cultural assimilation of Italian-speaking individuals, the group reached out to all ethnicities. The present name was adopted in the 1980s. Today the denomination represents some seventy congregations across North America.

Headquarters

The Christian Congregation does not have a headquarters but rather rotates yearly meetings among Los Angeles, Buffalo, and Chicago.

Core Beliefs

The Twelve Articles of Faith was adopted at a 1927 convention in Niagara Falls. It includes statements pertaining to biblical infallibility, the Trinity, the deity of Christ, baptism by immersion, speaking in tongues, healing, the premillennial return of Christ, and the bodily resurrection of all the dead.

Website

http://www.ccnamerica.org/

Bibliography

Alves, Leonardo M. *Christian Congregation in North America: Its Inception, Doctrine, and Worship.* Dallas: 2006.
"Christian Congregation in North America." http://www.ccnamerica.org. "Articles of Faith," "CCUSA," and "History."

George Thomas Kurian

Church of God (Cleveland, Tennessee)

History

The Church of God, with headquarters in Cleveland, Tennessee, was instituted on August 19, 1886, in Monroe County, Tennessee, under the name Christian Union. The first eight members were under the leadership of ordained Baptist minister Richard G. Spurling (1810–91). As a consequence of the Holiness revival and dissatisfaction with formalism and spiritual lethargy in the churches, they gathered at Barney Creek Meeting House on the Tennessee–North Carolina border desiring a closer relationship with Christ. Their goal was to promote Holiness doctrine, restore biblical doctrines, and unite all denominations.

The church changed its name to the Holiness Church in 1902 and adopted the name Church of God in 1907. The current organizational name was adopted in 1923 due to divisions among the Holiness churches with regard to church polity and the leadership of Ambrose J. Tomlinson (1865–1943). The first congregation in Canada was established in 1919 in Scotland Farm, Manitoba. Paul H. Walker became the first overseer of Canada in 1931.

Headquarters

2490 Keith Street
Cleveland, TN 37320
Telephone: 423-472-3361

Core Beliefs

Core beliefs are based on Scripture (not creeds), particularly the New Testament (or law of Christ) as the binding rule for faith and practice. Church of God churches affirm the inspiration and inerrancy of Scripture, the virgin birth and deity of Christ, the atoning sacrifice of Christ's death, the literal resurrection of the body, and the premillennial return of Christ. They believe in the Trinity, justification by faith, the necessity of regeneration, and spiritual maturity as a Christian. They are distinctively Pentecostal in affirming the baptism of the Holy Spirit subsequent to sanctification, which is evidenced by speaking in tongues. Three ordinances are practiced: baptism by immersion, the Lord's Supper, and foot washing.

Although the Church of God originally disparaged creedal statements, a declaration of faith was formulated in 1948 to affirm belief in the verbal inspiration of Scripture, divine healing, and the premillennial return of Christ.

Churches have sought to restore primitive Christianity and to effect the union of all denominations (hence the original name Christian Union). Churches practice divine healing, condemn the use of alcohol and tobacco, and oppose membership in all secret societies. Practical commitments include behavioral temperance, family responsibility, modest appearance, moral purity, social obligation, and being a spiritual example.

Worship

Churches are committed to Pentecostal worship wherein God is exalted, the soul is engaged, and believers are challenged to great commitment and discipleship. Worship is designed to be authentic and spiritually vibrant. Varying styles and forms of worship may be used. Occasionally, the music may overshadow the traditional Protestant sermons. Emphasis is on the priority of biblical stewardship and the centrality of God's Word as fundamentals of worship. The Pentecostal experience is common in addition to the charismatic gifts of the Spirit (those of revelation, power, and inspiration or utterance).

Statistics

The Church of God (Cleveland, Tennessee) is one of the largest and oldest Pentecostal bodies in the United States (and perhaps worldwide). Worldwide membership in 1986 was 1,650,000, with current membership near 6 million. United States and Canadian membership is 1,068,120 in approximately 7,000 churches. There are local congregations in all 50 states and missionary divisions in 107 countries (with missionaries serving in many of those countries). Countries are divided into 6 general territories: Atlantic and the Caribbean, Central America, South America, Europe and the Middle East, the Far East and Oceania, and Africa.

Largest Churches

Bethel Church, or Gereja Bethel Indonesia (GBI), in Jakarta, Indonesia, which includes 800 satellite churches, is the largest Church of God congregation worldwide with more than 250,000 members.

The majority of churches are located in the southeast United States. One of the largest churches is the Central Church of God in Charlotte, North Carolina, with membership exceeding 7,000. Free Chapel (Gainesville, GA) and Free Chapel OC (California) comprise one church with two campuses, and both are pastored by Jentezen Franklin. The Orange County church has approximately 1,500 members and an average attendance of 5,000. The Gainesville church, which Franklin visited annually as a Church of God evangelist (prior to becoming its senior pastor in 1989), has approximately 5,500 members and an average attendance of 11,000.

Missionary and Evangelistic Work

The Church of God is committed to missionary and evangelistic work through Care Ministries, Chaplains Commission, Evangelism and Home Missions (Black Ministries, Multi-Cultural Ministries, Hispanic Ministries, and Native American Ministries), Family Ministries, Hispanic Educational Ministries, Lay Ministries, Men/Women of Action, Ministry to Israel, Ministry to the Military, Music Ministries, Pentecostal Resource Center, SpiritCare, Women's Ministries, World Missions, and Romanian Ministries.

Academic Institutions

The Church of God has numerous colleges and academic institutions, with the majority functioning as Bible colleges. Educational institutions exist in Argentina, Germany, Indonesia, Korea, Mexico, Panama, the Philippines, Puerto Rico, and South Africa.

Primary academic institutions and colleges located in the US include:

Church of God School of Theology (Cleveland, TN)
East Coast Bible College (Charlotte, NC)
Lee University (Cleveland, TN)
Lee University Charlotte Center (Charlotte, NC)
Northwest Bible College (Minot, ND)
Patten University (Oakland, CA)
West Coast Christian College (Fresno, CA)

Parachurch Organizations

The Church of God maintains extensive ministry activities through several departments: benevolence, evangelism and home missions, higher education, lay ministries, publications, radio and television, stewardship, women's ministries, world missions, and youth and Christian education.

The church is a member of the National Association of Evangelicals.

Electronic Media

Faith News Network is the church's official news source.

Publications

The Church of God Publishing House and Pathway Press are located in Cleveland, Tennessee. Publications include music, Sunday school literature, and a variety of inspirational and religious books. Pathway Bookstore provides a complete inventory of inspirational materials and resources for the local church. Pathway Digital is the on-demand imprint of Pathway Press. Derek Press is also print-on-demand and publishes books for the Christian market. Penman Publishers is the nondenominational imprint for the non–Church of God and secular market. *Church of God Evangel* is the official journal, which has been published since March 1, 1910. Editorial Evangélica provides Sunday school literature and Christian educational materials in Spanish.

Website

http://www.churchofgod.org/

Bibliography

Black, Daniel L. *A Layman's Guide to the Holy Spirit*. Cleveland, TN: Pathway, 1988.

Conn, Charles W. *Like a Mighty Army: A History of the Church of God, 1886–1995*. Cleveland, TN: Pathway, 1996.

———. *Where the Saints Have Trod: A History of Church of God Missions*. Cleveland, TN: Pathway, 1959.

Crews, Mickey. *The Church of God: A Social History*. Knoxville: University of Tennessee Press, 1990.

Morgan, Toby. *An Acts 2 Church in the 21st Century*. Cleveland, TN: Pathway, 2005.

Simmons, Ernest L. *History of the Church of God*. Cleveland, TN: Church of God Publishing House, 1938.

Synan, Vinson. *The Holiness-Pentecostal Tradition*. Grand Rapids: Eerdmans, 1997.

Ron J. Bigalke

Church of God in Christ

History

Charles H. Mason (1866–1961) and Charles P. Jones (1865–1947) were accused of an overemphasis on the doctrine of Holiness and as a result were forced to leave the Baptist groups they belonged to in Arkansas. They founded the Church of Christ (Holiness) in 1895 and began to stress the doctrine of entire sanctification. Mason led a church in Lexington, Mississippi, in 1897, which he called the Church of God in Christ. Mason's turning point in life came in 1906 when he attended the Azusa Street revival in Los Angeles led by William J. Seymour. There he received the baptism of the Holy Spirit with the evidence of speaking in tongues. This significant event brought about a disagreement between Jones and Mason that resulted in Jones choosing to go his own way. Mason and the legally organized Church of God in Christ (COGIC) was one of a few early Pentecostal groups that could ordain ministers who would then be recognized by civil authorities. This period of time saw the COGIC provide guidance to scores of ministers and congregations across the southern part of the United States. Black and white Pentecostals worked, worshiped, and evangelized together in an interracial fellowship that modeled itself after the Azusa Street Mission in Los Angeles.

In 1914, the Pentecostal movement took two directions—the first with a Wesleyan-Holiness emphasis and the second advocating the "finished work" doctrine that favored a more Reformed understanding of sanctification. This separation largely ended the interracial dimensions of early

Pentecostalism, though Mason remained deeply revered by many white Pentecostal leaders, and his leadership was a significant force in the church until his death in 1961.

Following his death, the church experienced difficult and complex struggles in the 1960s, including court-ordered changes. The First Constitutional Convention in January 1968 ushered in the post-Mason era. The church is now structured around seven primary sections: the General Assembly, the General Board, the Board of Bishops, the General Council, the Women's Department, the Jurisdictional Assemblies, and the Local Churches.

Headquarters

930 Mason Street
Memphis, TN 38126

Leadership

Presiding bishop: Bishop Charles E. Blake Sr.

Core Beliefs

The denomination believes in biblical infallibility, the Trinity, the return of Christ, salvation only through repentance and faith in Christ, the necessity of regeneration by the Holy Ghost for salvation, the baptism of the Holy Spirit as an experience subsequent to salvation and available to all Christians who ask for him, and the responsibility of Christians to live holy lives.

The ordinances of the church are water baptism by immersion, the Lord's Supper, and foot washing (an ordinance of humility). The church affirms divine healing but does not advocate it to the exclusion of medical supervision.

Statistics

The COGIC has congregations in sixty countries of the world. As of 2007, its membership was over five million, making it the largest Pentecostal group in the United States and the second largest primarily African American denomination in the United States after the National Baptist Convention.

Academic Institutions

All Saints Bible College (Memphis, TN)

Charles H. Mason Theological Seminary (an affiliate of the Interdenominational Theological Center in Atlanta, GA)

Publication

The Whole Truth, the church magazine

Website

http://www.cogic.org/

Bibliography

Bean, Bobby. *This Is the Church of God in Christ.* Atlanta, GA: Underground Epics Publishing, 2001.

Clemmons, Ithiel C. *Bishop C. H. Mason and the Roots of the Church of God in Christ.* Bakersfield, CA: Pneuma Life Publishing, 1996.

Green, Eugenia. *Mason: The Profiling of a Saint.* Panorama City, CA: Education Plus, 2007.

Mason, Mary. *The History and Life Work of Elder C. H. Mason Chief Apostle and His Co-Laborers.* Memphis: Church of God in Christ, 1987.

Byron D. Klaus

Church of God in Christ International

History

The Church of God was founded in 1895 when C. P. Jones, J. A. Geter, and C. S. Mason were expelled from the Baptist Church for teaching that holy living was essential to achieve salvation. The year 1906 marked the beginning of a rift in the church, as Mason received the baptism of the Holy Ghost and began speaking in tongues after attending a Los Angeles revival. The following year Jones presided over a meeting of the church's general assembly in Jackson, Mississippi, at which the organization withdrew its support of Mason and his teachings regarding speaking in tongues. Mason gathered his supporters, including six other elders, in Memphis to form the first general assembly of the Church of God in Christ. The name Church of God in Christ originated with Mason's examination of various Scripture verses.

With Mason in the role of chief apostle, the church achieved significant growth and established state assemblies with their own overseers, five of whom became bishops in the church in 1933. Mason's death in 1961 left the organization without a leader for one year. Bishop Ozro Thurston Jones Sr. of Philadelphia, the only surviving bishop of the original five, became senior bishop in 1962.

The church experienced division once more in 1969 when a group led by Bishop William David Charles Williams Sr. of Evanston, Illinois, called for a return to previously held doctrines and government under a senior bishop rather than a twelve-member board. Williams's followers included bishops, elders, and other church workers who designated him senior bishop and chief apostle of a new body that described itself as the original church. They used the name Church of God in Christ International and established their headquarters in Evanston, Illinois, in 1970.

As many dioceses were added, a growing National Building Fund helped to facilitate improvements that continued until the tenures of Williams's successors, Bishop Tony Clemon, who led from 1984 to 1988, and Bishop John H. Davis, whose tenure began in 1988. A major objective beginning in the 1980s was the establishment of a new headquarters; it was achieved with the completion of an expansive building in Jonesboro, Arkansas, near the site where Mason first named the original group.

Headquarters

125 N Fisher Street
Jonesboro, AR
Email:info@cogicinternational.com

Leadership

Senior bishop and chief apostle: Bishop Dr. John Henry Davis

Core Beliefs

The Church of God in Christ International adheres to most of the beliefs espoused by its parent denominations, the Church of God and the Church of God in Christ. These include belief that the Bible is divinely inspired; that the Father, Son, and Holy Ghost are the three persons of the Godhead; that Jesus was born of a virgin and was the suffering servant who came to redeem man from sin and now is a mediator between God and man; that all men are sinful and require repentance and faith in Christ to gain salvation; that sanctification is an ongoing work of the Holy Ghost that renews the believer's godlike character and ability to do good works; and that the gift of the Holy Ghost equips the believer for service.

A distinguishing tenet of the Church of God in Christ International is its insistence on baptism of the Holy Ghost, which, although not seen as responsible for salvation, is regarded as necessary for the performance of Christ's work and is believed to result in speaking in tongues. As in other Pentecostal and Holiness denominations, water baptism in the name of the Father, the Son, and the Holy Ghost—demonstrating acceptance of Christ as Savior—is done only by immersion. The Lord's Supper is viewed as symbolic of the believer's sharing in Christ's death, foot washing is an ordinance of the church, prayers are offered for divine healing of the sick, miracles are regarded as still part of the church's present-day activity, the church is seen as a unified body with Christ as its head, and Christ is expected to return bodily to earth.

Missionary and Evangelistic Work

Missionary and evangelistic work includes the New Life Theological Seminary, the Williams-Clemon-Davis Bible Institute, and the Women's Department, with eighteen groups around the country.

Website

http://www.cogicinternational.com/

George Thomas Kurian

Church of God Mountain Assembly

History

When a small group of ministers in southeastern Kentucky embraced the Wesleyan doctrine of entire sanctification just after the turn of the twentieth century, the South Union Baptist Association (United Baptist) excluded them from its fellowship. These ministers and their followers met at Ryan's Creek, Kentucky, on August 24, 1907, to organize a new association of Holiness churches. Ten churches (from Whitley and McCreary Counties in Kentucky and Campbell County in Tennessee) met at the first general assembly in October at Little Wolf Creek, Kentucky, and adopted Church of God as the name of the association.

By 1911, the group had become fully Pentecostal and that year added Mountain Assembly to its name to distinguish itself from the Church of God in Cleveland, Tennessee. For fifteen years, the general assembly convened in a church selected by the general council until it chose Jellico, Tennessee, as a permanent location and constructed a tabernacle for that purpose.

Headquarters

256 N Florence Avenue
Jellico, TN 37762

Core Beliefs

The Church of God Mountain Assembly believes in the infallibility and authority of the Holy Bible, salvation by grace through faith in the blood of Jesus Christ, baptism by immersion (trinitarian formula) upon profession of faith, sanctification, holiness, baptism of the Holy Spirit (with the initial evidence of speaking in tongues), healing for the body, the Lord's Supper,

washing of saints' feet, and the premillennial return of Christ.

Website

http://www.cgmahdq.org/

Bibliography

Gibson, Luther. *The History of the Church of God Mountain Assembly, Inc.* Jellico, TN: Church of God Mountain Assembly Inc., 1970.

Padgett, Michael. *A Goodly Heritage: A History of the Church of God Mountain Assembly.* Middlesboro, KY: Self-published, 1995.

Michael Padgett

Church of God of Prophecy

History

The Church of God of Prophecy (COGOP) has an early history that parallels the Church of God (Cleveland, Tennessee). In 1903, Ambrose Jessup (A. J.) Tomlinson became affiliated with the Holiness Church at Camp Creek, North Carolina. In 1907, when G. B. Cashwell returned from the Los Angeles Azusa Street revival, Tomlinson and the leaders of the Church of God embraced the Pentecostal doctrine of speaking in tongues as the initial physical evidence of the baptism of the Holy Spirit. The Church of God would continue in this vein, led by Tomlinson, until 1922, when the denomination ousted Tomlinson for alleged financial improprieties. Tomlinson, with his sons and a host of followers, began a new movement that in 1952 gained its current name, Church of God of Prophecy. Other leaders who helped him form the new movement were R. G. Spurling and W. F. Bryant.

Leadership of the COGOP was very much a family affair. A. J. Tomlinson died in 1943, and his son Milton was elected leader and served until 1990, when he stepped down. Milton's election led to a split in the denomination as his brother Homer began a new church with a small part of the denomination in 1946.

Headquarters

3720 Keith Street
PO Box 2910
Cleveland, TN 37320-2910
Telephone: 423-559-5100

Core Beliefs

"In contemporary theological terms, the Church of God of Prophecy is a Protestant, evangelical, Wesleyan holiness, Pentecostal movement that believes in man's freewill regarding salvation" (cogop.org, "History"). One is regenerated by receiving Christ and his sacrifice as an atonement for sin. Sanctification is theologically a separate experience. "Sanctification is an experience that can be sought that empowers one to walk in a holy life" (Adrian Varlack, telephone interview, June 2010). Sanctification is the door into the process of spiritual growth. It is not a formula for growth as much as an experience.

The COGOP is a classical Pentecostal denomination in that it believes baptism in the Holy Spirit is necessary for empowered service. The experience is subsequent to salvation and sanctification, and speaking in tongues is the initial evidence. The defining documents of the COGOP include the Church Business Guide, Assembly Minutes, and COGOP International Inc. Bylaws.

Finances

The COGOP encourages support of its ministries with tithing. Each minister pays tithes to the national office. International financial records are kept in Cleveland, Tennessee.

Statistics

United States membership: 89,600 (of which 6,000 are in North Carolina and 3,000 are in Florida)
United States congregations: 6,900

The COGOP boasts 10,000 preaching venues with 1.3 million members worldwide. The COGOP is in 125 nations, and 90 percent of its adherents are outside the United States. In the Congo alone, the COGOP has over 600,000 members. Ukraine has 730 congregations and 138,000 members in a ministry that began in 1992.

Growth

The COGOP is much larger overseas than it is in the United States, as noted above. The church is also growing very quickly overseas. In Africa alone, the church is experiencing about one hundred thousand conversions a year. The challenge is for the church to disciple as fast as it is winning souls. The COGOP emphasizes leadership training due to this explosion in growth.

Affiliations

The COGOP is a member of the Pentecostal/Charismatic Churches of North America.

Academic Institutions

The COGOP has worked with Lee University of the Church of God in Cleveland to operate a college-level academic institution, largely based online, called the Tomlinson Center. The degrees offered through the Tomlinson Center focus on ministerial and biblical materials and include a certificate of ministry. The Center for Biblical Leadership School of Practical and Advanced Studies is nonaccredited. Gordon-Conwell/Church of God of Prophecy Consortium offers a Leader of Leaders Program, which trains potential national leaders to perform their office effectively.

Parachurch Organizations

The Church of God of Prophecy owns and operates a biblically based theme park in North Carolina called Fields of the Woods. Between 200,000 and 250,000 visitors a year come to experience this tribute to the Bible and the history of the Pentecostal movement. The site includes an enlarged copy of the Ten Commandments in a hillside. At the top of the hill is a Bible open to Matthew 22, where Jesus expounds the fulfillment of the law and prophets in Christ. There are also monuments to COGOP departments and its teachings. Today this site houses many activities and especially commemorates Tomlinson's early involvement in the church.

Electronic Media

Voice of Salvation radio and TV programs have been phased out. Because of the international nature of the denomination, the COGOP encourages local governing bodies, national churches, and local churches to operate their own media ministries.

Publications

White Wing Messenger is the monthly denominational magazine and is published in several languages. The English version is published monthly, and issues are published quarterly in Spanish or French. *Connections* is an online publication put out by the general overseer's office. It has no regular release date and targets specific issues. The publishing arm of the COGOP is White Wing Publishing House.

Website

http://www.cogop.org/

Archives

The archives are located at the international headquarters.

Bibliography

"Church of God of Prophecy." http://www.cogop.org. "History."

Hunter, H. D. "Church of God of Prophecy." In *The New International Dictionary of Pentecostal and Charismatic Movements*, edited by Stanley Burgess and Eduard M. van der Maas, 539–42. Grand Rapids: Zondervan, 2002.

———. "Fields of the Woods." In *The New International Dictionary of Pentecostal and Charismatic Movements*, edited by Stanley Burgess and Eduard M. van der Maas, 636–37. Grand Rapids: Zondervan, 2002.

Robins, Roger. "Plainfolk Modernist." In *Portraits of a Generation*, edited by James Goff Jr. and Grant Wacker, 347–68. Fayetteville: University of Arkansas Press, 2002.

Varlack, Adrian. Telephone interview. June 2010.

Ray Reid

Church of God of the Apostolic Faith

History

In 1914, James O. McKinzie, Edwin A. Buckles, Oscar H. Myers, and Joseph P. Rhoades—leaders of a small network of Pentecostal churches in the south central states—expressed concern for the pressing need for organization and church government amid a Pentecostal movement often susceptible to hyper-spiritualized fanaticism. These four men called a meeting at the Cross Roads Mission, near Ozark, Arkansas, to establish the Church of God of the Apostolic Faith (COGAF).

The COGAF leaders held fast to the Wesleyan belief that entire sanctification occurs as a second definite work of grace subsequent to the initial conversion experience. According to this belief, Christians who have a crisis experience of sanctification are enabled to experience perfect love and to live sinless lives. The Wesleyan (also called Holiness) view of sanctification stood as an important doctrine among the earliest American Pentecostal churches, including Charles Parham's Apostolic Faith movement, the Church of God (Cleveland, Tennessee), the Church of God in Christ, and the Pentecostal Holiness Church.

However, a debate within Pentecostal circles over the nature of sanctification set in motion a series of events that would lead to the formation of the COGAF. When the Assemblies of God convened its first meeting in Hot Springs, Arkansas, in April 1914, the opening address delivered by Mack M. Pinson titled "The Finished Work of Calvary" made it clear to advocates of a Wesleyan doctrine of sanctification that their view was not welcome. Therefore, the COGAF and its four pioneers convened their first meeting at the Cross Roads Mission, just months after the Assemblies of God was formed, because they believed a new body was needed that held to entire sanctification.

Headquarters

Mailing Address
PO Box 691745
Tulsa, OK 74169-1745

Street Address
13334 East 14th Street
Tulsa, OK 74169

Core Beliefs

The Church of God of the Apostolic Faith is a trinitarian fellowship that believes in the sacrificial death of Jesus Christ for the atonement of the sins of anyone who comes to him in faith and repentance. Members believe the Bible is the inspired and only infallible and authoritative written Word of God; after conversion, sanctification is the second definitive work of grace; the third work is the baptism of the Holy Spirit, evident by speaking in other tongues; divine healing is ongoing; and baptism is by immersion in the name of the Father, Son, and Holy Spirit. The church also holds to a premillennial rapture eschatology.

Website

http://www.cogaf.org/

Bibliography

Buckles, E. A. *A Brief History: The Church of God of the Apostolic Faith*. Drumright, OK: n.p., 1935.

Melton, Gordon J. *Melton's Encyclopedia of American Religions*. 5th ed. Detroit: Gale Research, 1996.

Monacell, Martin T. "Pioneering the Church of God of the Apostolic Faith: Edwin A. Buckles and Oscar H. Bond." In *Servants of the Spirit: Portraits of Pentecostal/Charismatic Pioneers*, edited by Andrea Johnson, 63–73. Des Moines: OBC Publishing, 2010.

Piepkorn, Arthur Carl. *Profiles in Belief: The Religious Bodies of the United States and Canada*. Vol. 3. San Francisco: Harper & Row, 1979.

Martin Monacell

Church of Our Lord Jesus Christ of the Apostolic Faith

History

The Church of Our Lord Jesus Christ of the Apostolic Faith (COOLJC) was established in 1919 by Bishop Robert Clarence Lawson (1883–1961). This group began as the Churches of Christ of the Apostolic Faith, with the Refuge Church of Christ of the Apostolic Faith serving as its headquarters and mother church in the village of Harlem, New York City.

Lawson was a general elder in the Pentecostal Assemblies of the World (PAW) and was pastoring the Church of Christ of the Apostolic Faith in Columbus, Ohio. While still pastoring the Ohio church, Lawson went to New York City, leaving his assistant pastor, Elder Karl Smith (1892–1972) in charge. In New York, Lawson founded the Refuge Church of Christ of the Apostolic Faith. Between 1919 and 1920, Lawson resigned from the PAW and continued to pastor the Ohio church. Lawson's movement was birthed through the New York church, and his assistant pastor, Smith, served as the first general secretary of the movement, which was known as the Churches of Christ of the Apostolic Faith, named after the Ohio church.

After Lawson returned to Ohio, a schism took place between Smith and Lawson over the issue of divorce and remarriage. Smith brought the Ohio church back into the PAW in 1925. The members who remained loyal to Lawson followed him, and he established the Rehoboth Temple Church of Christ.

Lawson eventually gave Rehoboth to Elder Herbert Spencer (1901–74) and returned to New York. Lawson personally established many of the congregations in his religious organization. Some of the churches he founded included Emanuel Temple, Bridgeport, Connecticut; Bronx Refuge, Bronx, New York; and Greater Refuge Temple, Charleston, South Carolina. Lawson also sent out ministers to pastor churches and establish congregations. In 1931, Lawson incorporated the Churches of Christ of the Apostolic Faith as the Church of Our Lord Jesus Christ of the Apostolic Faith. Incorporators included Sherrod C. Johnson, Smallwood E. Williams, and Charles Michael. Johnson and Williams would later establish their own denominations, and Michael would pioneer the COOLJC Caribbean mission on the British West Indian island of St. Kitts.

The first major schism in the denomination occurred in 1933 over ecumenism and sanctification ideology and was led by Bishop Sherrod C. Johnson (1897–1961). In the COOLJC, Johnson was state bishop of North Carolina and Pennsylvania. Lawson fellowshiped with churches outside the COOLJC, including Baptist, AME, and Church of God in Christ. Johnson felt that if you have the truth you cannot fellowship with what he called false groups. Johnson also held ultraconservative sanctification standards. He taught against African American and Caribbean women using hair-straightening products and believed that women should wear cotton stockings to hide their nakedness. He taught that both men and women should dress in modest apparel and that men should not wear beards. With the defection of Johnson, Lawson lost churches in North Carolina and Pennsylvania. Johnson made his Philadelphia church his headquarters and called his movement the Church of the Lord Jesus Christ of the Apostolic Faith. The only difference in the names of the two groups was "our" and "the."

The second major split occurred in 1957, headed by Elder Smallwood E. Williams (1907–91). Williams was the executive secretary of the COOLJC and left over ecclesiastical polity. Williams believed church government should be a cooperative effort and challenged the sole leadership of Lawson. On September 25, 1957, Williams called the National Pentecostal Ministerial Conference. As a result of this conference, the Bible Way Church of Our Lord Jesus Christ World Wide, also known as the Bible Way Church World Wide, was incorporated on November 1, 1957. With this split, the COOLJC lost seventy of its churches. Williams used his Washington, DC, church as the organization's headquarters.

The Church of Our Lord Jesus Christ of the Apostolic Faith grew to be the third largest Oneness Pentecostal denomination in the United States following the United Pentecostal Church (UPC) and the Pentecostal Assemblies of the World. The COOLJC is unique in that it evolved through the efforts of one man and not through a ministerial association, like the PAW in 1906, or a merger, like the UPC in 1945. It can trace its roots to the Azusa Street revival of 1906 and the Arroyo Seco Pentecostal camp meeting of 1913. It influenced Pentecostalism doctrinally and hymnologically, and it is the parent body of numerous African American Pentecostal and charismatic denominations and ministries. Lawson's Oneness theology and his views on women preachers and divorce and remarriage have caused much discussion within Pentecostal circles, and the songs he wrote are sung by those within and outside his movement. Some of his more popular songs are "His Name Should Be Praised," "Praise Thy Name," and "God Is Great in My Soul."

Headquarters

Greater Refuge Temple
2081 Adam Clayton Powell Jr. Boulevard

New York, NY 10027
Telephone: 212-866-1700

Leadership

Senior prelate: Bishop William L. Bonner

Core Beliefs

Core beliefs include the following: Scripture given by inspiration of the Holy Spirit, Oneness Pentecostal and Arminian theology, the deity and virgin birth of Christ, universal sin, salvation through belief in Christ and repentance, water baptism by total immersion and in the name of the Lord Jesus Christ, and baptism of the Holy Spirit. Members believe the rapture of the church will occur before the tribulation period, the second coming of Christ is premillennial, and only those who are baptized in the Holy Spirit and living a righteous life will make the rapture. Observance of the Lord's Supper consists of bread and kosher wine; women are not ordained to the clergy but are permitted to teach; in public worship, women are to cover their heads and men are to remove their hats; and members are to shun worldliness, including fornication, adultery, gambling, sensual dancing, immodest apparel, and drinking alcoholic beverages.

Worship

Worship services are lively and joyful. Music and preaching are the highlights of the service. There is generally a call and response to the sermon. The laying on of hands is practiced, and an invitation for water baptism is a part of the sinner's invitation to accept Christ as Savior.

Divisions and Splits

The COOLJC serves as the parent body for the following denominations:

Washington, DC	Way of the Cross Church of Christ	1927	Bishop Henry Chauncey Brooks (ca. 1895–1968)
Philadelphia, PA	Church of the Lord Jesus Christ of the Apostolic Faith	1933	Bishop Sherrod C. Johnson (1897–1961)
Washington, DC	Bible Way Church World Wide	1957	Bishop Smallwood E. Williams (1907–91)
Roanoke, VA	Bible Way Pentecostal Apostolic Church of Christ	1960	Bishop Curtis P. Jones (?–1976)
Jackson Heights, NY	Evangelistic Churches of Christ	1974	Bishop Lymus Johnson (1922–2012)
Brooklyn, NY	Beulah Church of God in Christ Jesus	2005	Apostle Wilbur L. Jones

Controversies

Subjects of controversy have included the need for water baptism by immersion in the name of the Lord Jesus Christ, instead of in the name of the Father, Son, and Holy Spirit; the Oneness of the Godhead in contrast to the Trinity; speaking in tongues as the sign of receiving Christ; the use of kosher wine and leavened bread for the Lord's Supper in place of grape juice and unleavened bread; and the interpretation of the Pauline Epistles that led to denying women the right to ordination or to be commissioned as ministers.

Statistics

Estimated adherents worldwide: 100,000
Churches in the United States, England, Africa, and Caribbean: 506
Churches are also located in Canada, Mexico, and India

Largest Churches

Cleveland Church of Christ (Cleveland, OH)
Greater Refuge Temple (Buffalo, NY)
Greater Refuge Temple (New York, NY)
Solomon's Temple (Detroit, MI)

Missionary and Evangelistic Work

Each local congregation is encouraged to have community outreach programs. Foreign works are sponsored by the international body through Global Missions. The Home Missions Department assists in church planting and church construction. At each International Holy Convocation, a mass witnessing campaign is held in the host city.

Academic Institutions

Church of Christ Bible Institute (New York, NY)
W. L. Bonner College (Columbia, SC)

Publications

The Contender for the Faith, the official magazine
Minute Book, published annually
Discipline Book, gives the fundamental creeds of the church with rules, regulations, and governing boards' responsibilities

Website

http://www.cooljc.org/

Bibliography

Dupree, Sherry Sherrod. *African-American Holiness-Pentecostal Movement: An Annotative Bibliography.* New York: Garlanding, 1996.

Payne, Wardell. *Dictionary of African American Religious Bodies.* Washington, DC: Howard University Press, 1991.

Spellman, Robert C., and Mabel Thomas. *The Life, Legend, and Legacy of Bishop R. C. Lawson.* Scotch Plains, NJ: privately printed, 1983.

Stewart, Alexander C. Alexander and Shirlene Stewart Pentecostal Collection. Schomburg Center, New York Public Library.

Williams, Smallwood Edmond. *This Is My Story: A Significant Life Struggle.* Washington, DC: Willoughby, 1981.

Alexander C. Stewart

Church of the Living God

History

In 1888, Rev. William Christian broke away from the Baptist Church to establish Christian's Friendship Work, later the Church of the Living God, in Caine Creek, Arkansas. The first congregation included an elder who served as secretary, two reverends, a lawyer, and a landowner.

The Church of the Living God experienced many schisms, starting with a rift between William Christian and his own brother, Rev. John Christian, in 1895. Although newer groups still utilized the name Church of the Living God, the original group distinguished itself with the phrase "Christian Workers for Fellowship (CWFF) National Brotherhood." Others groups used phrases such as "the Pillar and Ground of Truth" (1895) and "Which He Purchased With His Own Blood" (1953).

The denomination claims the distinction of being America's first predominantly black church that does not trace its roots to an Anglo-Saxon church or white missionaries. Although formally nondenominational and nonsectarian, it clearly reflects Pentecostal Holiness influences.

Headquarters

Church of the Living God
CWFF National Headquarters
430 Forest Avenue
Cincinnati, OH 45229
Telephone: 513-569-5660
Email: national@ctlgcwff.org

Leadership

Presiding bishop: R. D. Tyler

Core Beliefs

The Articles of Faith declare belief in the inerrancy of the Bible; the three persons of the Trinity; the death and resurrection of Christ as the only means for mankind's redemption; the sacraments of baptism, the Lord's Supper, and the washing of feet; and the unity of the church and the brotherhood of man. Members believe that all men are created free and equal and should be treated according to the Golden Rule. Baptism is done by immersion, and unleavened bread is used in the Lord's Supper. The teachings for the Jews of the Old Testament are viewed principally as foreshadowing the appearance of Christ.

Missionary and Evangelistic Work

The W. E. Crumes Ministerial Training Institute, named in honor of a late chief bishop, partners with Moody Bible Institute to offer a three-year curriculum for pastors, evangelists, and some lay workers.

Parachurch Organizations

Several departments focus on specific areas of ministry, including education, health services, and women's concerns.

George Thomas Kurian

Congregational Holiness Church

History

The Congregational Holiness Church (CHC) emerged from the early twentieth-century Pentecostal revival and was organized on January 29, 1921, in High Shoals, Georgia. The CHC was formed for the purpose of helping Christians follow the teachings of the Bible in doctrine, personal conduct, and church government.

The CHC developed ministries to serve its growing constituency. In 1924, one of the founders, Watson Sorrow, began publishing the *Gospel Messenger*, which became the CHC's official monthly magazine. Within several years of its founding, the CHC established campgrounds in Georgia, Alabama, North Carolina, and South Carolina. Rapid growth led to the creation of three regional divisions in 1935 for more effective governance. The CHC began commissioning foreign missionaries in the 1930s. Hugh and Louise Skelton, who went to Cuba as missionaries in 1955, laid the groundwork for much of the church's growth in Central and South America.

The international headquarters was located in Lincolnton, Georgia, from 1925 to 1965, when it moved to Griffin, Georgia. The CHC maintains close relations with other Pentecostal and evangelical churches and is a member of the Pentecostal/Charismatic Churches of North America, the Pentecostal World Fellowship, and the National Association of Evangelicals.

Headquarters

3888 Fayetteville Highway
Griffin, GA 30223
Telephone: 404-228-4833

Core Beliefs

The Congregational Holiness Church is Wesleyan and Pentecostal. Its Articles of Faith affirm the following: a trinitarian understanding of the "One Living and True God"; the inspiration of Scripture; justification by faith; sanctification as "a definite work of Grace, subsequent to Salvation"; baptism of the Holy Spirit, with the initial evidence of speaking in tongues; divine healing as provided for in Christ's atonement; the gifts and the fruit of the Spirit; the imminent rapture of the church and the personal, premillennial second coming of Jesus Christ; the redemption of believers "who are faithful to the end" (rejecting the doctrine of eternal security); eternal punishment for "all who die out of Christ" and eternal life with Christ for "those who die in Him"; the bride of Christ consisting "of the entire Spiritual Church"; the "sacredness of marriage between one man and one woman"; and a "commitment to strong family values" (chchurch.com, "What We Believe").

All members must be in harmony with the Articles of Faith and also abstain from tobacco, alcohol, profane language, abuse of drugs, sexual immorality, and membership in oathbound secret societies. Ordinances include baptism by immersion, the Lord's Supper, and foot washing.

Worship

Worship services are generally informal and allow freedom of expression.

Divisions and Splits

Congregational Holiness Church founders withdrew from the Pentecostal Holiness Church (PHC) because of disagreement over the role of medicine in divine healing. Many early Pentecostals, including PHC leaders, discouraged human remedies (such as physicians and medicine) and instead encouraged believers to seek divine healing, which they taught was provided for in Christ's atonement. This rejection of modern medicine was not universally held in the PHC. When Watson Sorrow and Hugh Bowling disagreed with the PHC on this and other issues, they left the PHC in 1920. They—along with a handful of other ministers and churches—organized the CHC in 1921 along congregational lines, differing from the PHC's episcopal polity, in an attempt to democratize church governance. The Pentecostal Holiness Church (now known as the International Pentecostal Holiness Church) changed its position on divine healing and reconciled with the CHC in 1944, although the two bodies remain separate.

Statistics

The Congregational Holiness Church in the United States grew from 12 churches in 1921 to over 246 churches in 16 states in 2012. The CHC claims 25,000 adherents in the United States and about 1 million adherents in about 9,000 churches outside the United States (primarily in Central and South America).

Largest Churches

The largest congregation is Free Chapel (Gainesville, GA), and the denomination is strong elsewhere in Georgia as well as in Alabama, Florida, North Carolina, South Carolina, Texas, and Virginia.

Missionary and Evangelistic Work

Mission USA encourages vigorous church planting in the United States. The Hispanic constituency is fast growing, fed in part by immigrants who were CHC members in their countries of origin. World Missions works with CHC constituencies in twenty countries and supports orphanages, ministerial training schools, church construction projects, national workers, and works of compassion. Approximately eight thousand churches and missions and over ten thousand ministers serve about one million members outside the United States. Churches are located in Cuba, Haiti, India, Mexico, Nigeria, Zimbabwe, and most Central and South American nations. Fewer than 5 percent of CHC churches and members are located in the United States, demonstrating the growing importance of the emerging Pentecostal movement outside the West.

Academic Institutions

The Congregational Holiness Church partners with Heritage Bible College (Dunn, NC) and Emmanuel College (Franklin Springs, GA) to offer accredited theological training to its ministers. The CHC also offers continuing education courses.

Publications

The Congregational Holiness Church Publishing House publishes a monthly periodical, the *Gospel Messenger,* as well as books and other literature.

Website

http://www.chchurch.com/

Bibliography

"The Congregational Holiness Church Inc." http://www.chchurch.com. "What We Believe".

Cox, B. L. *History and Doctrine of the Congregational Holiness Church.* Greenwood, SC: Congregational Holiness Publishing House, 1958.

Discipline of the Congregational Holiness Church. Griffin, GA: Congregational Holiness Publishing House, 1921–present.

Minutes of the General Conference. Griffin, GA: Congregational Holiness Publishing House, 1921–present.

Sorrow, Watson. *Some of My Experiences.* Franklin Springs, GA: Pentecostal Holiness Church, 1954.

We Believe. 2nd ed. Griffin, GA: Congregational Holiness Publishing House, 2003.

Darrin J. Rodgers

Elim Fellowship

History

Named for the biblical oasis for the children of Israel, the Elim Minister Fellowship was established as a charismatic Pentecostal affiliation of churches in 1932 by Rev. and Mrs. Ivan Q. Spencer. In 1972, it adopted its present name of Elim Fellowship.

Member churches are self-governing but share key beliefs and receive benefits such as access to traveling ministries, publications, seminars, and other services. The fellowship helps those with a call to ministry to receive their credentials. It then makes Elim-trained ministers available to congregations in need of a minister, with preferential treatment given to bodies within its network. Monthly meetings and the annual leadership conference offer training, inspirational teaching, and networking opportunities. Church specialists offer counsel through their vast experience with church growth, launching of campaigns, stewardship, and incorporation issues, and changes in church leadership. Guidance and mediation services are offered in the event of conflict within a congregation. In addition to its role in networking churches, Elim is formally affiliated with numerous ministries that gain recognition through the association. The Home Missionary Program assists with ministry fund-raising.

Headquarters

1703 Dalton Road
Lima, NY 14485-9516
Telephone: 585-582-2790
Email: info@elimfellowship.org

Leadership

President: Ron Burgio

Core Beliefs

The church's statement of faith describes the fifteen cardinal tenets of the fellowship, including belief in biblical infallibility, the deity of Christ, and the mandate to evangelize. Divine healing is seen as part of the atonement. Baptism is by immersion.

The fellowship stresses dedication to prayer, evangelism, sacrificial service to God, and manifestation of spiritual gifts. It embraces diversity, promotes reconciliation and restoration, and seeks to foster Christian conduct.

Finances

Total revenue is more than $4.9 million, of which more than $4.3 million comes from cash donations. Total expenses exceed $4.5 million, of which $340,000 are used for administrative purposes and more than $200,000 for fund-raising.

Missionary and Evangelistic Work

Elim Fellowship has a strong history of involvement in missions, dating back to its work in East Africa in 1938. The Department of International Ministries (formerly called World Missions) seeks to promote awareness of the needs of mission work and actively recruits missionaries to serve as Elim Fellowship International workers. Currently, it is active in Africa, Asia, Latin America, and Europe. The missionaries are sent on long-term assignments as well as short-term assignments of up to two years as part of the Short-Term Enlistment Program (STEP), which provides field support for host ministries. In all cases, the emphasis is on working in conjunction with indigenous bodies. Elim equips its missionaries not only financially but also with expertise, useful contacts, administrative and personal assistance, and prayer support. In addition, it works with churches as they develop mission programs.

Affiliations

Charismatic Leaders' Fellowship
Evangelical Council for Financial Accountability
International Pentecostal Association
National Association of Evangelicals
North American Renewal Services Committee
Pentecostal/Charismatic Churches of North America

Academic Institutions

Elim Bible Institute was founded in 1924 by Ivan Spencer to train believers to conduct revivals. Initially located in Hornell and then Red Creek, New York, the institute moved to Lima, New York, with the purchase of the original campus of Genesee Wesleyan Seminary. Elim Bible Institute has eighteen buildings across its seventy-five-acre campus and stresses the importance of an intimate and invigorated relationship with God.

Parachurch Organizations

Various ministries target the needs of men, women, and youth.

Publication

F.A.M.I.L.Y. magazine features articles describing new and established member churches, home missionaries, leadership principles, and administrative news as well as jokes and quotes. Its content seeks to reinforce the fellowship's goals of spiritual development, productive use of believers' talents, dedication to integrity and leadership, and concern for youth.

Website

http://www.elimfellowship.org/
Sarah Claudine Day and Ernest M. Day Jr.

Full Gospel Fellowship of Churches and Ministers International

History

The Full Gospel Fellowship of Churches and Ministers International is an independent fellowship of ministers, ministries, and churches. Including many illustrious leaders and organizations, it originated from the Voice of Healing formed by Gordon Lindsay and Jack Moore in 1948. It was joined by T. L. Osborn, Jack Coe, Richard Vineyard, F. F. Bosworth, Kenneth Hagin, Gayle Jackson, Raymond T. Richie, W. V. Grant, Louise Nankeville, and others. The success of the healing ministry prompted one hundred evangelists to elect Gordon Lindsay president of their newly formed fellowship.

The evident need for an organization uniting and providing encouragement to those of the Full Gospel perspective prompted Lindsay to hold a ministers conference in Dallas in 1962, at which the Full Gospel Fellowship of Churches and Ministers International was created. The fellowship does not exercise authority over member churches. While it does not license or ordain ministers itself, viewing that as the role of churches and seminaries, the fellowship offers ministers certificates acknowledging their status to give them the added benefit of affiliation with an international organization.

Headquarters

1000 North Belt Line Road
Suite 201
Irving, TX 75061-4000
Telephone: 214-292-1254
Email: fgfcmi@aol.com

Leadership

President: Rev. Gene E. Evans

Core Beliefs

The Articles of Faith states the organization's belief in the following: Scripture is divinely inspired; the one true God is revealed in the Father, Son, and Holy Ghost; all mankind has voluntarily fallen into sin and can only be redeemed through Christ; justification is by grace through faith; baptism, by washing the body in water, is a necessary outward symbol of inner cleansing; the elements of the Lord's Supper—bread and fruit of the vine—are symbolic and indicate participation of Christ's divine nature, tribute to his suffering and death, and expectation of his return; baptism in the Holy Ghost was commanded by Christ to empower believers and to bestow them with spiritual gifts and is evidenced by speaking with other tongues; believers are to be entirely sanctified and live holy lives; the church, as the body of Christ, is responsible to fulfill the Great Commission and edify its members; divine healing from physical sickness is an entitlement of all believers; at the second coming of Christ, sleeping believers will be resurrected; and believers look forward to the millennial reign of Christ, the punishment of the devil and the unredeemed in the lake of fire, and the establishment of a new heaven and earth.

Statistics

Year	Clergy	Churches	Members
1980	931	394	59,100
2006	2,887	902	414,100

Missionary and Evangelistic Work

The Full Gospel Fellowship strives to promote not just evangelism but also discipleship, ethical conduct, pro-family policies, and humanitarian aid. Its agencies include Young Leader's Network; Youth Department; Evangelism—Traveling Ministries; World Missions Department, serving Central America, Mexico/Caribbean, North America, South Asia, and UK/Europe; Fellowship World Missions website (thechristianmissions.net), enabling networking between ministries; Regional Ministries, each covering one of six geographical regions in the United States; and FGFCMI Chaplaincy Program, serving chaplains in all branches of the military as well as other institutions.

Publication

Tidings e-newsletter

Website

http://www.thefellowshiptoday.org/

George Thomas Kurian

International Bible Way Church of Our Lord Jesus Christ Inc.

History

The International Bible Way Church of Our Lord Jesus Christ Inc. formed in 1997 and is an iteration of the Bible Way Church of Our Lord Jesus Christ World Wide, founded in September 1957 under the leadership of Elder Smallwood E. Williams. Williams, who previously served as the general secretary of the Church of Our Lord Jesus Christ (COOLJC), became increasingly discontented with the authoritarian administration of founder and presiding bishop Robert C. Lawson and led several ministers and approximately seventy congregations into the Bible Way Church of Our Lord Jesus Christ World Wide after unsuccessful attempts to reform organizational leadership in the COOLJC.

As prelate of the organization he founded, Williams became a prominent supporter of the civil rights movement and led the Bible Way Church in social and political activism.

Williams died in 1991, and both Lawrence Campbell and Huie Rogers were considered potential successors of the organization's founder. The general assembly decided to allow each to fill respective three-year terms before confirming a permanent successor. At the church's annual convocation in 1997, the body voted to extend Rogers's term by an additional year. The

resolution ultimately divided the church, and Campbell retained the greater following, with the support of thirty-seven of the fellowship's forty-three bishops. Despite Campbell's numerical strength, Rogers retained the charter of the organization founded by Williams. The International Bible Way Church of Our Lord Jesus Christ became a distinct organization led by Campbell, who was succeeded by the current leader, Chief Apostle Cornelius Showell.

Headquarters

27 South Caroline Street
Baltimore, MD 21231

Core Beliefs

The International Bible Way Church of Our Lord Jesus Christ is a Oneness Pentecostal body that rejects the doctrine of the Trinity and teaches that the Father, Son, and Holy Spirit are the manifested economy of the One God. The church also embraces a tripartite conversion experience consisting of repentance, water baptism by immersion in the name of Jesus Christ, and baptism of the Holy Ghost with the evidence of speaking in tongues.

Core beliefs include the virgin birth, death, burial, and bodily resurrection of Christ; the remission of sins through baptism in the name of Jesus Christ; the regenerative power of the Holy Ghost, empowering Christians to live sinless lives and to witness to others; premillennial eschatology, culminating in the translation of both the dead and living saints; and divine healing as a component of Christ's atonement.

Baptism is administered by immersion in the name of Jesus Christ. There is an emphasis on tithing, speaking in tongues and interpretation, and the practice of holiness—with local pastors establishing regulations of modesty and Christian conduct.

Worship

Worship is exuberant and ecstatic and is marked by traditionally Pentecostal practices such as glossolalia, shouting, dancing, and clapping.

Statistics

Membership: estimated at 500,000
United States churches: approximately 300 (with a concentration along the Eastern Seaboard)

Largest Churches

The largest congregations are located in urban areas, including Columbia, South Carolina;

184

Woodbridge, Virginia; Washington, DC; and Baltimore, Maryland. There are also several relatively large congregations in areas of New York and New Jersey.

Trends

Significant trends include the elevation of younger men to the bishopric and innovative worship that uses praise dancing and dramatic interpretations.

Missionary and Evangelistic Work

The church is evangelistic and employs various models of church planting, especially in urban areas. In some cases, an elder will settle in a city to perform evangelistic groundwork, which may include a radio broadcast. A follow-up crusade may be conducted, with converts joining the nascent church.

Ecumenism

The International Bible Way Church is not a broadly ecumenical organization; however, there have been some pulpit exchanges with trinitarian Pentecostal groups such as the Church of God in Christ. While maintaining its message of the Oneness of God, it avoids isolation and uses dialogue to disseminate the message of the church.

Parachurch Organization

International Bible Way Relief mobilizes workers and gathers supplies to offer humanitarian aid during domestic and international crises.

Website

http://www.intlbibleway.com/

Matthew Shaw

International Church of the Foursquare Gospel

History

The International Church of the Foursquare Gospel (ICFG), also known as the Foursquare Church, is an evangelical Pentecostal denomination founded in 1927 by Aimee Semple McPherson (1890–1944). The origin of the ICFG is inseparable from McPherson's life from 1927 to her death in 1944. In 1915, she began preaching in tent revivals; in 1916, she and her mother began traveling on preaching tours; and in 1919, the Baltimore newspaper ran a story on her that produced much public attention. She decided to travel less frequently and settled on Los Angeles as a base for her church. She built the Angelus Temple in 1923 and preached every day. McPherson was one of the first women to preach on the radio and the second woman to be granted a broadcast license when, in 1924, KFSG (a Foursquare radio station) went on the air. The church services drew large crowds, and McPherson frequently made points by acting out scenes from her life on stage. The ICFG was formed in 1927 out of the Angelus Temple and McPherson's ministry.

As McPherson's fame grew, the denomination she founded grew, and by her death, the denomination had grown to four hundred churches throughout the United States. At her death, her son, Rolf McPherson, became the leader of the denomination. During the forty-four years of his leadership, the ICFG grew from a national to an international denomination. After his resignation in 1988, the ICFG continued to grow and expanded into other countries. Today 95 percent of the membership of the ICFG is outside the United States.

The term "Foursquare" originated from a 1922 sermon given by McPherson, who saw the fourfold ministry of Jesus as the Savior, the Baptizer with the Holy Spirit, the Healer, and the Soon-Coming King.

Headquarters

1910 West Boulevard
Suite #200
Los Angeles, CA 90026

Core Beliefs

The ICFG does not accept the opinion of councils and creeds and instead has its own self-generated beliefs. These include acceptance of the Bible as the inspired Word of God, the Trinity, the fall of man, the new birth, evangelism, and involvement in civil affairs.

The two ordinances are believer's baptism (by immersion) and regular—although not weekly—Communion. Other practices include baptism with the Holy Spirit, which includes speaking in tongues, and divine healing. Women are allowed as ministers and church officers.

Worship

The worship style tends toward a contemporary service with a praise band. Speaking in tongues often occurs, both as praying in tongues and as a message given in tongues followed by the interpretation.

Statistics

United States membership: 400,000
United States churches: 1,800 (most in the western US)
United States clergy: 9,000
Worldwide membership: 8 million
Worldwide churches and meeting places: 64,000 in 144 countries

Largest Churches

The Angelus Temple, constructed in 1923 under the guidance of Aimee Semple McPherson, is the founding church and the worship center for the ICFG. At its construction, it could seat fifty-three hundred people. Today it is the largest ICFG church in the United States with a membership of eight thousand.

Growth

The ICFG experienced tremendous growth from its inception but slowed in the 1940s through the 1960s. The charismatic renewal of the late 1960s and 1970s prompted more growth.

Ecumenism

The ICFG was one of the founding members of the Pentecostal/Charismatic Churches of North America. This body was formed in 1948 for the purpose of bringing together like-minded churches and ministries. Today the group has twenty-nine member denominations and church groups and represents approximately five hundred thousand churches with ninety million members.

Academic Institutions

Life Pacific College, formerly L.I.F.E. Bible College (San Dimas, CA)

The church has numerous Bible institutes and ministry training institutes.

Parachurch Organizations

Foursquare Missions International is the missions and aid arm of the ICFG. Urban and Multicultural Ministries focuses on working with ethnic groups in the United States. Its tasks include translating resources, training, and immigration issues.

Publications

Advance, the official journal

Website

http://www.foursquare.org/

Bibliography

Blumhofer, Edith L. *Aimee Semple McPherson: Everybody's Sister*. Grand Rapids: Eerdmans, 1993.

Epstein, Daniel Mark. *Sister Aimee: The Life of Aimee Semple McPherson*. San Diego: Harvest, 1993.

Van Cleave, Nathaniel M. *The Vine and the Branches: A History of the International Church of the Foursquare Gospel*. Los Angeles: Foursquare Publications, 1994.

Mark Nickens

International Fellowship of Christian Assemblies

History

The International Fellowship of Christian Assemblies (formerly the Christian Church of North America or CCNA) is a Pentecostal cooperative fellowship of churches and ministers that began in the Pentecostal revival that took place in Chicago in 1907 among recent Italian immigrant families. Luigi Francescon and Pietro Ottolini heard and received the testimony of William H. Durham at the Azusa Street revival in Los Angeles. On September 15, 1907, they led the Grand Avenue Mission, later named *Assemblea Christiana*, into its own Pentecostal revival. This mission became the center from which the Pentecostal message radiated out to Italian Americans in Los Angeles, New York City, St. Louis, and Philadelphia.

By 1927, there was a network of Italian Pentecostal churches spread from Massachusetts to Arkansas and California. In that year, the need to establish doctrinal unity among their ranks led to a gathering in Niagara Falls, New York. Twelve Articles of Faith were accepted along with a hymnbook, *Nuovo Libro D'Inni e Salmi Spirituali*. In the next ten years, this informal association, the Unorganized Italian Christian Churches of the United States, added a mission fund and committee as well as five overseers. Missionary efforts followed ethnic lines in Europe and South America; fields in Africa and India were opened later.

In the late 1940s, the word "Italian" was dropped, and the mission department incorporated with a mission secretary. Five overseers became part of an executive board along with the missionary committee, general secretary, and general overseer. The 1963 reorganization produced an official incorporation under the name the General Council of the Christian Church of North America. In 2007, a new name was incorporated: International Fellowship of Christian Assemblies (IFCA). The IFCA is a member of the Pentecostal Churches of North America, a networking association of Pentecostal denominations and fellowships.

The transition from an ethnic fellowship to a more diverse one has taken place. Today only 20 to 25 percent of its ministers are of direct Italian descent. More than 75 percent of its members are non-Italian. Few churches maintain an Italian language service. This change has given the fellowship a wide-open posture for outreach and growth within the freedom of local church initiative and organization.

Headquarters

1294 Rutledge Road
Transfer, PA 16154
Telephone: 724-962-3501

Core Beliefs

The twelve Articles of Faith reflect evangelical positions on the Bible, the Trinity, and salvation. Being a Pentecostal fellowship, the IFCA holds to a definite experience of the Spirit's empowerment and the exercise of spiritual gifts such as divine healing. It is premillennial in eschatology. The IFCA teaches the sovereignty of the local congregation in terms of self-government and selection of pastoral leadership.

Website

http://www.ifcaministry.com/

Bibliography

DeCaro, Louis. *Our Heritage: The Christian Church of North America*. Sharon, PA: General Council, Christian Church of North America, 1977.

Galvano, Stephen, ed. *Fiftieth Anniversary: Christian Church of North America*. Sharon, PA: General Council, Christian Church of North America, 1977.

Robinson, E. B. "Christian Church of North America." In *New International Dictionary of Pentecostal and Charismatic Churches*, edited by Stanley M. Burgess and Eduard M. van der Maas, 525–27. Grand Rapids: Zondervan, 2002.

Saggio, Joseph J. "A Brief History of Italian Pentecostalism in America." *Assemblies of God Heritage* 30 (2010): 34–41.

Malcolm R. Brubaker

International Pentecostal Church of Christ

History

Pentecostal pioneer G. B. Cashwell and a small group of believers began the *Bridegroom's Messenger* in 1907. Led by Paul and Hattie Barth, they planted a church in Atlanta, Georgia, and later founded the Association of Pentecostal Assemblies (APA) in 1921.

In 1919, the National and International Pentecostal Missionary Union, later known as the International Pentecostal Church (IPC), was chartered in Ohio for the purposes of missions and encouraging fellowship, with Paul Wittich as the president.

In 1936, the APA and the IPC merged into the International Pentecostal Assemblies (IPA). John W. Pitcher became chairman. The IPA kept its offices in Atlanta and a campground in Lake Odessa, Michigan. Its mission activities were focused in Kenya, India, and Mexico.

John Stroup of the Methodist Protestant Church received the baptism of the Holy Ghost in 1907. In 1913, he was among the first to carry the rediscovered doctrine into southern Ohio and eastern Kentucky. In 1917, he organized the Pentecostal Church of Christ (PCC) and became its first bishop.

The PCC operated Faith Bible Institute from 1941 to 1952 and Ambassador Bible Institute from 1964 to 1977. It focused its mission work in Brazil. The *Pentecostal Witness* was printed from 1923 until it was consolidated with the *Bridegroom's Messenger* in 1974. The PCC's headquarters were maintained in Ashland, Kentucky, from 1943 to 1957, when they were moved to London, Ohio.

In 1976, after a two-year trial consolidation of the IPA and the PCC and with the support of an overwhelming majority from each group, one body came forth out of two with the name International Pentecostal Church of Christ (IPCC). Chester I. Miller of the PCC and Tom G. Grinder of the IPA were elected as general overseer and assistant general overseer. The facilities of the PCC in London, Ohio, were chosen as the site for the international headquarters.

With nearly five hundred congregations in fourteen American states and thirteen nations, the IPCC has expanded its mission outreach to include Argentina, Brazil, French Guiana, India, Israel, Kenya, Mexico, the Philippines, Spain, Suriname, Uruguay, and Venezuela, with ten Bible colleges worldwide.

The IPCC has been a member of the National Association of Evangelicals since 1946 and is a charter member of the Pentecostal/Charismatic Churches of North America, which are members of the World Evangelical Alliance and the Pentecostal World Fellowship, respectively.

Headquarters

2343 US 42 SW
PO Box 439
London, OH 43140

Core Beliefs

The IPCC is strongly in the center of ortho-dox evangelical and classical Pentecostal doctrine, which includes belief in the inspiration of Scripture; inerrancy; the Trinity; the virgin birth; the literal resurrection; Christ as the only way to heaven; special creation; the existence of Satan; a literal heaven and hell; humanity's need for a Savior; the baptism of the Holy Spirit with speaking in tongues as the initial evidence; the nine spiritual gifts for the church today; believer's baptism; open Communion; the universal church as the body of Christ; God-called ministry; divine healing; the pretribulational, premillennial return of Christ; and the threefold mission of the church to worship, evangelize, and make disciples. The church also believes that racism, in all its forms, is a sin against God and humanity. The IPCC is among few denominations that elevate the issue of racism to the highest level of beliefs.

The IPCC has no distinctive requirements beyond the typical classical Pentecostal church. Members are advised to dress in an unspecified but modest fashion and to abstain from alcohol, tobacco, and illicit drugs.

Worship is typically Pentecostal, meaning exuberant and exciting with a variety of music styles used.

Publications

The Pentecostal Leader, the current official magazine

The Constitution and By-Laws of the International Pentecostal Church of Christ

2010 Annual Report Book, International Pentecostal Church of Christ

The Mission and Vision Statement of the International Pentecostal Church of Christ

Website

http://www.ipcc.cc/

Clyde M. Hughes

International Pentecostal Holiness Church

History

The first Holiness group in the United States formed in 1895 in Iowa, calling itself the Fire-Baptized Holiness Association and overseen by Benjamin Hardin Irwin. Because of the ministry of Ambrose B. Crumpler, a Methodist Holiness preacher from North Carolina, the Holiness movement grew greatly, but in 1896, in conflict with the Methodist Church, Crumpler

withdrew and formed the Pentecostal Holiness Church (PHC) in Fayetteville, North Carolina. In 1906, a Pentecostal Holiness minister, Gaston B. Cashwell, attended the Azusa Street revival in Los Angeles and then returned to North Carolina to share his Pentecostal experience, which led to a merger of the Pentecostal Holiness Church and the Fire-Baptized Holiness Association. The group became the International Pentecostal Holiness Church (IPHC) in 1975.

Headquarters

7300 NW 39th Expressway
Oklahoma City, OK 73008
Telephone: 405-787-7110

Leadership

Presiding bishop: Dr. Ronald W. Carpenter Sr.

Core Beliefs

The five tenets of the IPHC are justification by faith, sanctification as a second definite work of grace, baptism in the Holy Spirit as evident by speaking in tongues, divine healing, and the premillennial second coming of Christ. Unlike Oneness Pentecostal churches, the IPHC is trinitarian.

Water baptism (sprinkling or immersion) is in the name of the Father, Son, and Holy Ghost but only after a conscious decision to follow Christ. There is nonalcoholic Communion every quarter, which is open to all believers. Women are ordained in the ministry. Speaking in tongues accompanies baptism in the Spirit.

Worship

Worship is Pentecostal, or a free flow of the Holy Spirit as described in Acts.

Divisions and Splits

In 1920, the church split over divine healing. A faction led by Rev. Watson Sorrow believed that God often heals through medicine and medical knowledge. Subsequently, Sorrow was evicted from the PHC, and he and several other ministers of like mind formed the Congregational Holiness Church in 1921.

Controversies

The IPHC, which is now a racially integrated body, struggled with racism. It also became divisive within and without over the use of tobacco (a particular dispute in the tobacco belt), alcohol, medicine, baptism in the Spirit with tongues, mandatory dress codes, and worldly amusements.

Statistics

Global membership: 1,667,962
United States members: 257,758
Churches: 2,010
Missionary activity: 90 nations

Largest Churches

Cathedral of Praise World (Oklahoma City, OK)
Christian Heritage Church (Tallahassee, FL)
Evangelistic Temple (Tulsa, OK)
Life Christian Center (Oklahoma City, OK)
Northwood Temple (Fayetteville, NC)
Redemption World Outreach Center (Greenville, SC)
World Agape Mission Church (Los Angeles, CA)

Growth

With the divine healing crusades that followed World War II, the attendance in Pentecostal churches soared. In the 1960s, the PHC formed affiliations with the largest national Pentecostal churches in the world, such as the Pentecostal Methodist Church of Chile, the Jotabeche Pentecostal Methodist Church in Chile, and the Brazilian Methodist Church.

Trends

According to the IPHC Manual (2001–5), the church will continue to "maintain a strong biblical position against premarital, extramarital, and deviant sex, including homosexual and lesbian relationships" (97–98). However, in 1989, the general conference did agree that people may be a pastor or an elder if their divorce and/or remarriage occurred before they became a Christian.

Missionary and Evangelistic Work

The best-known PHC evangelist was Oral Roberts, who led tent revivals beginning in 1948. Other powerful evangelists started in the IPHC but launched their careers elsewhere, such as Charles Stanley, former president of the Southern Baptist Convention; C. M. Ward, an Assemblies of God radio preacher for twenty-five years; and T. L. Lowery of the Church of Christ.

Ecumenism

The IPHC works closely with the Pentecostal/Charismatic Churches of North America, the Pentecostal World Fellowship, the National Association of Evangelicals, the Mission America Coalition, the World Pentecostal Holiness Fellowship, and Christian Churches Together in the USA.

Academic Institutions

Advantage College (Sacramento, CA)
Emmanuel College (Franklin Springs, GA)
Homes Bible College (Greenville, SC)
Southwestern Christian University (Oklahoma City, OK)

Parachurch Organizations

Founded in 1909, the Falcon Children's Home has two outreach ministries: the Alternative to Abortion Ministries for crisis pregnancy and the Royal Home, a residential group care facility/maternity home for pregnant girls and women. Other benevolences include NewLife Christian Adoptions in North Carolina; a hospital for children with disabilities, the Children's Center in Bethany, Oklahoma; Disaster Relief, USA; and People to People.

Electronic Media

eNews
online periodicals
podcast channel
videos

Publications

In 1892, there were forty-one Holiness periodicals. Currently, the IPHC prints the monthly *IPHC Experience* and posts three electronic periodicals: *Issachar File*, *Networkings*, and *FYI*.

Website

http://www.iphc.org/

Archives

http://www.iphc.org/archives

Bibliography

Beacham, A. D. *A Brief History of the Pentecostal Holiness Church*. Franklin Springs, GA: Advocate Press, 1983.

Campbell, Joseph. *The Pentecostal Holiness Church, 1898–1948: Its Background and History*. Raleigh, NC: World Outlook, 1981.

Melton, J. Gordon. "White Trinitarian Pentecostal Holiness Church: International Pentecostal Holiness." In *Melton's Encyclopedia of American Religions*, edited by J. Gordon Melton, 344. 8th ed. Detroit: Gale, 2009.

Synan, Vinson. *The Century of the Holy Spirit: 100 Years of Pentecostal and Charismatic Renewal, 1901–2001*. Nashville: Nelson, 2001.

———. *Oldtime Power: A Centennial History of the International Pentecostal Holiness Church*. Franklin Springs, GA: LifeSprings Resources, 1998.

Brenda Ayres

Open Bible Churches

History

Open Bible Churches (OBC) is a Pentecostal organization originally formed by a merger of two smaller groups that were established in conjunction with evangelistic revival meetings in the Pacific Northwest and the midwestern United States, respectively. The Bible Standard Conference (BSC) was founded by evangelist Fred Hornshuh in 1919 in Eugene, Oregon, after he had spent a decade as an evangelist and church planter under the leadership of Florence Crawford and the Apostolic Faith Mission of Portland, Oregon. In 1935, the Bible Standard group joined forces with the Open Bible Evangelistic Association (OBEA), based in Des Moines, Iowa, forming Open Bible Standard Churches (now Open Bible Churches). The OBEA had formed in 1932 under the leadership of John Richey, who organized a number of ministers and churches that had formerly been associated with Aimee Semple McPherson's International Church of the Foursquare Gospel.

Headquarters

From 1919 until the 1935 merger, BSC headquarters were in Eugene, Oregon. Des Moines, Iowa, was home to the OBEA prior to the merger and has been the international headquarters of OBC since then, both to the United States church and to the department of International Ministries, which provides covering and leadership for Open Bible ministries and churches in over forty nations.

Leadership

President: Jeff Farmer

Core Beliefs

Since its founding, OBC has maintained a clearly evangelical and Pentecostal doctrinal stance. Its statement of faith includes a high view of the authority of Scripture, a trinitarian view of the Godhead, and emphases on the person and work of Christ, personal salvation, believer's baptism, baptism in the Holy Spirit, the Spirit-filled life, divine healing, the personal return of Christ, and evangelism and missions.

Statistics

United States churches: over 300
Worldwide churches: over 1,500 in 44 nations

OBC's International Ministries reports that approximately 20,000 people per year receive Christ through the global ministries of Open Bible Churches.

Largest Churches

OBC has historically been characterized by smaller churches, with the largest churches ranging in size from five hundred to twelve hundred. In 2010, the largest churches in the United States included Open Bible Christian Center in Rapid City, South Dakota; the Turning Point in Spokane, Washington; and churches in Hollywood, Florida; Martinez, California; Dayton, Ohio; Springfield, Oregon; and Des Moines, Iowa. One of the largest churches outside the United States is in San Fernando, Trinidad.

Ecumenism

OBC has historically identified with similar church families in the evangelical and Pentecostal movements. It was a charter member of such North American organizations as the National Association of Evangelicals (NAE) and the Pentecostal Fellowship of North America, which was disbanded in 1994 in favor of the Pentecostal/Charismatic Churches of North America (PCCNA), of which OBC is a member. In recent decades, OBC has broadened its ecumenical commitment and activities, joining such organizations as Christian Churches Together in the USA, the Mission America Coalition, and the Sentinal Group, with OBC president Jeff Farmer serving in executive leadership in those groups as well as in the NAE and the PCCNA. In 1998, OBC approved David Cole as an official delegate to the International Dialogue between Pentecostals and the Roman Catholic Church.

Academic Institutions

In recent decades, the primary college for OBC in the United States has been Eugene Bible College in Oregon, especially after its 1986 merger with Dayton Bible College (Ohio) and Open Bible College (Iowa). The college was renamed New Hope Christian College in 2010 and has taken a more interdenominational posture.

The other major ministry training institution for OBC is Inste Bible College, which uses a nontraditional model of training that includes a challenging curriculum and a church-based small-group style of delivery led by trained facilitators.

Publication

OBC's primary communication vehicle is the *Message of the Open Bible*, a monthly publication that updates the constituency on relevant issues, celebrates testimonies related to the movement's mission, and communicates significant policy and personnel changes.

Website

http://www.openbible.org/

Bibliography

Cole, David. "Heritage and Horizons: The Derivation and Destiny of Open Bible Churches." In *The Future of Pentecostalism in the United States*, edited by Eric Patterson and Edmund Rybarczyk, 157–76. Lanham, MD: Lexington Books, 2007.

Farmer, Jeff, and Andrea Johnson. *Heart for the Harvest: A Biographical History of Open Bible Churches, 1982–2007.* Des Moines: Open Bible Publishers, 2009.

Mitchell, Robert Bryant. *Heritage and Horizons: The History of Open Bible Standard Churches.* Des Moines: Open Bible Publishers, 1982.

Mitchell, R. Bryant, and Lucille M. Mitchell. *Heritage and Harvests: The History of International Ministries of Open Bible Standard Churches.* Des Moines: Open Bible Publishers, 1995.

Warner, Wayne E. "Open Bible Standard Churches, Inc." In *The New International Dictionary of Pentecostal and Charismatic Movements*, edited by Stanley M. Burgess and Eduard M. van der Maas, 945–46. Grand Rapids: Zondervan, 2002.

David Cole

Original Church of God

History

In 1886, a revival began in the Great Smoky Mountains of northwest Georgia and eastern Tennessee under the leadership of Baptist Richard G. Spurling and his Methodist son William F. Bryant. They formed the Christian Union in Munroe County, Tennessee, later reforming into the Holiness Church at Camp Creek in North Carolina. Ambrose J. Tomlinson, a mystical Quaker and an agent for the American Bible Society who sold tracts and Bibles, organized the group into a denomination and became its first general overseer.

In 1895, the doctrine of sanctification was taught by a United Baptist pastor, J. H. Parks, in McCreary County, Kentucky. The belief was embraced by three other Baptist pastors who, in 1909, after being excluded from the Baptist denomination, combined five churches to create a general assembly at Jellico Creek Church in Whitley County, Kentucky, and adopted the name Church of God. It was more Holiness than

Pentecostal until supernatural manifestations of the Holy Spirit took place at Camp Creek, Cherokee County, which ignited both revival and violent persecution by neighbors.

In 1917, the Chattanooga congregation, led by Joseph L. Scott, seceded over how tithes were being administered. They added "Original" to the name Church of God to reflect their intention to uphold the original beliefs of the movement. The Original Church of God became incorporated in 1922.

Headquarters

2214 E 17th Street
PO Box 3638
Chattanooga, TN 37404

Contact Address

Trinity Worship Center
128 Chestnut Street
Pulaski, TN 38478
Telephone: 931-363-8200

Leadership

General overseer: Bishop James R. (Randy) Taylor

Core Beliefs

Core beliefs include repentance, justification, regeneration for salvation, and John Wesley's teaching on sanctification.

Water baptism is by immersion, and baptism of the Holy Spirit is believed to be evidenced by speaking in tongues. Other practices include Communion, foot washing, tithing, divine healing, fasting, and total abstinence from alcohol, tobacco, and mood-altering chemical substances.

Members may serve only in noncombatant positions during war. The church ordains women and accepts those who have been divorced and remarried.

Website

http://www.theocogfellowship.org/

Bibliography

Burgess, Stanley M., and Eduard M. van der Maas, eds. *The New International Dictionary of Pentecostal and Charismatic Movements.* Grand Rapids, MI: Zondervan, 2002.

Conn, Charles W. *Like a Mighty Army: A History of the Church of God, 1886–1976.* Cleveland, TN: Pathway Press, 1977.

Hollenwegger, Walter J. *The Pentecostals.* Minneapolis: Augsburg, 1972.

Melton, J. Gordon. "White Trinitarian Pentecostal Holiness Church: International Pentecostal Holiness." In *Melton's Encyclopedia of American Religions*, edited by J. Gordon Melton, 344. 8th ed. Detroit: Gale, 2009.

Synan, Vinson. *The Holiness Pentecostal Movement in the United States*. Grand Rapids: Eerdmans, 1971.

Brenda Ayres

Pentecostal Assemblies of the World

History

The Pentecostal Assemblies of the World (PAW) is Oneness Pentecostal, or Apostolic, in doctrine and predominantly African American. It was founded in 1906–7 in Los Angeles out of the Azusa Street revival. After the Oneness movement began in 1914, the PAW embraced the Oneness view of God under the influence of G. T. Haywood, a prominent member since 1911. When Oneness ministers were forced to leave the fledgling Assemblies of God in 1916, they initially formed a new organization, but in early 1918, this group merged with the PAW, and the united group retained the PAW name. Most Oneness Pentecostal groups today descended directly or indirectly from the PAW.

In 1919, 25 to 30 percent of the ministers were black, 29 percent were female, and the leadership was biracial. In 1924, most of the white ministers left the PAW, citing the inability to hold conferences in the South due to segregation laws, and they formed three regional organizations. In 1925, the PAW adopted a modified form of episcopal church government and elected Haywood as its first presiding bishop. Although the membership was now mostly black, the PAW continued its policy of integration in ministry and leadership.

Two of the white organizations soon merged, and because of the strong desire for interracial unity, this new group merged with the PAW in 1931 to form the Pentecostal Assemblies of Jesus Christ. Some blacks did not believe this merger would be successful, so they renewed the charter of the PAW before it expired and reorganized it in 1932. The same legal and social pressures as before continued to work against the newly merged body. By 1938, almost all the black ministers had withdrawn and returned to the PAW.

Headquarters

3939 N Meadows Drive
Indianapolis, IN 46205
Telephone: 317-547-9541
Email: web_team@pawinc.org

Leadership

Presiding bishop: Charles H. Ellis III

Core Beliefs

The inspiration and authority of the Bible.

The Oneness view of God. God is indivisibly one, and Jesus Christ is the fullness of the Godhead incarnate. God is manifested as Father, in his Son Jesus Christ, and as the Holy Spirit, but these three manifestations do not constitute a trinity of self-conscious persons.

The full deity, full but sinless humanity, virgin birth, atoning death, bodily resurrection, and ascension of Jesus Christ.

The Apostolic message of salvation. Salvation is by grace through faith based on the death, burial, and resurrection of Jesus Christ. The new birth (New Testament experience of salvation) consists of repentance, water baptism by immersion in the name of the Lord Jesus Christ, and the baptism of the Holy Spirit with the initial sign of speaking in tongues.

The translation of saints (rapture), premillennial second coming of Christ, millennial kingdom of Christ, resurrection of the dead, last judgment, lake of fire, new heaven, and new earth.

Communion, foot washing, miraculous gifts of the Spirit, divine healing, heartfelt and demonstrative worship, and the pursuit of holiness in personal lives, relationships, and society (*2011 Organizational Manual*, 111–26).

Divisions and Splits

In 1919, Robert C. Lawson left the PAW in opposition to women pastors and to remarriage after divorce in cases of adultery and founded the Church of Our Lord Jesus Christ of the Apostolic Faith.

In 1957, Samuel N. Hancock left the PAW over leadership issues and founded the Pentecostal Churches of the Apostolic Faith.

In 2007, Arthur Brazier, bishop of Illinois and pastor of a twenty-thousand-member church in Chicago, left the PAW over what he characterized as its nonprogressive nature and its decision to use only apostolic speakers at the annual convention. He was also a longtime advocate of unconditional eternal security, which the PAW does not hold.

Statistics

United States churches: about 1,650
Worldwide churches: 800 in 34 other nations, with an estimated constituency of 1.5 million

Academic Institution

Aenon Bible College (Indianapolis, IN)

Publication

The Christian Outlook

Websites

http://www.pawinc.org/
http://www.pawimd.org/

Bibliography

Bernard, David K. *A History of Christian Doctrine*. Vol. 3, *The Twentieth Century*. Hazelwood, MO: Word Aflame Press, 1999.

Foster, Fred J. *Their Story: 20th Century Pentecostals*. Rev. ed. Hazelwood, MO: Word Aflame Press, 1981.

Golder, Morris E. *History of the Pentecostal Assemblies of the World*. Indianapolis, IN: Self-published, 1973.

Haywood, G. T. *The Life and Writings of Elder G. T. Haywood*. Compiled by Paul Dugas. Portland, OR: Apostolic Book Publishers, 1968.

Pentecostal Assemblies of the World. 2011 Organizational Manual. Indianapolis, IN: PAW, 2011.

Tyson, James L. *The Early Pentecostal Revival: History of Twentieth-Century Pentecostals and the Pentecostal Assemblies of the World, 1901–1930*. Hazelwood, MO: Word Aflame Press, 1992.

David K. Bernard

Pentecostal Churches of the Apostolic Faith Inc.

History

The Pentecostal Churches of the Apostolic Faith Inc. emerged from the Pentecostal Assemblies of the World (PAW) in 1957. The schism was led by Samuel N. Hancock, who joined the Pentecostal movement under the ministry of Garfield Thomas Haywood in 1914. Hancock served as Haywood's assistant pastor at Christ Temple in Indianapolis until 1921, when he assumed the pastorate of a small church in Detroit, Michigan, which grew to become one of the largest churches in the PAW.

Following the death of Haywood in 1931, a sustained power struggle ensued between Samuel Hancock and Samuel Grimes. In 1952, Grimes won another decisive victory against the contending Hancock, who became increasingly dissatisfied with the PAW.

Hancock was also purportedly at variance with the PAW's traditional Oneness view of Jesus Christ as God incarnate. Some of Hancock's detractors claimed that he never embraced the full deity of Jesus Christ, though he signed an affirmation of the organization's Oneness perspective developed by the executive board in December 1955.

In 1957, Hancock made good on repeated threats to leave the PAW. He, along with Heardie Leaston, Willie Lee, and David Collins, signed articles of incorporation for the Pentecostal Churches of the Apostolic Faith (PCAF) on November 20, 1957, and established headquarters in Detroit, Michigan.

In 1964, Lee, one of the original incorporators of the PCAF, withdrew to form the Emmanuel Pentecostal Church of Our Lord, Apostolic Faith. He cited his belief that Jesus was only the Son of God, not God himself. Later in the 1960s, refusing to believe in the deity of Christ, ten churches withdrew to form the True Churches of the Apostolic Faith. In 1970, G. M. Boone exited the PCAF over administrative differences and confusion surrounding the organization's charter to found the Apostolic Assemblies of Christ in Detroit, Michigan.

Today the PCAF does not permit an open fellowship with trinitarian churches or ministries.

Headquarters

723 S 45th Street
Louisville, KY 40211
Telephone: 502-778-7948

Core Beliefs

The Pentecostal Churches of the Apostolic Faith Inc. is a Oneness organization that rejects the doctrine of the Trinity. Rather, the One God is revealed in manifestation as Father, Son, and Holy Ghost. Following the soteriological model of Acts 2:38, members believe that personal conversion consists of repentance, water baptism by immersion in the name of Jesus Christ, and the infilling of the Holy Spirit, evidenced by speaking in tongues. Adherents pursue a holy, consecrated, and sanctified life and believe in the inspiration and inerrancy of Scripture, the foundation of faith and doctrine; the virgin birth, death, burial, and bodily resurrection of Christ; the remission of sins through baptism in the name of Jesus Christ; the regenerative power of the Holy Spirit, empowering Christians to live sinless lives and to witness to others; and the need for holiness.

Members are traditionally encouraged not to wear jewelry or cosmetics. Women wear dresses or skirts and do not cut their hair short. The church teaches modesty and moderation and discourages participation in many worldly activities such as dancing, gambling, and drinking. This has, however, been a topic of recent debate, with some younger pastors electing to remove restrictions related to personal appearance. The PCAF still officially subscribes to these teachings, however, and members attending the annual convocation are expected to observe

193

holiness standards while at the meeting. Other beliefs include tongues and interpretation as a prophetic method of divine communication to the church, performed by inspiration; tithing; and premillennial eschatology, culminating in the translation of both dead and living saints. The church embraces an exuberant and ecstatic worship style marked by shouting, dancing, and clapping.

Statistics

Members: 20,000 (by PCAF leadership estimates)
Congregations: less than 300, with the largest in Jackson, Mississippi, and other large churches in metropolitan areas of the Midwest

Missionary and Evangelistic Work

Temporary missionary workers are sent to help national pastors develop autonomous congregations that may affiliate with the PCAF after formation.

Academic Institution

Midwest Apostolic Bible College, a graduate seminary (Chicago, IL)

Parachurch Organization

Global Ministries supports international relief for natural disasters and has recently participated in efforts in Haiti and the Philippines.

Publication

Voice in the Wilderness is the church's only official publication and is published bimonthly to announce church events and to share news about initiatives and meetings.

Website

http://www.pcaf.net/

Matthew Shaw

Pentecostal Church of God

History

Originally called the Pentecostal Assemblies of the USA, the Pentecostal Church of God (PCG) was founded in December 1919 in Chicago by *Pentecostal Herald* editor George Brinkman. He had feuded with Assemblies of God leaders and suggested a convention that included many members of that denomination. Brinkman served as the new organization's first secretary. In 1922, Brinkman again called for a reorganizational meeting when he felt the

new leaders of the organization were not acting legally.

The denominational headquarters remained in Chicago until 1927, and the *Pentecostal Herald* was adopted as the official publication of the PCG, with Brinkman as its editor. Since 1927, the denomination has been headquartered in the following locations: Ottumwa, Iowa; Kansas City, Missouri (1933); Ft. Worth, Texas (1938); Kansas City again (1939); and Joplin, Missouri (1951). In 2011, the headquarters were moved to Bedford, Texas.

The PCG has gone by several names because of legal issues. First called the Pentecostal Assemblies of the USA, the church became the Pentecostal Church of God in 1922. In 1934, it became the Pentecostal Church of God of America Inc. In 1979, it once again became known by the name Pentecostal Church of God.

Headquarters

PO Box 211866
Bedford TX, 76095
Telephone: 817-554-5900

Core Beliefs

The PCG is trinitarian and views Scripture as inspired by God. Jesus came from God and died for the atonement of the sins of humanity. A person accepts Jesus's saving work by faith and as a subsequent experience receives the baptism of the Holy Spirit, with the initial physical evidence of speaking in tongues. Sanctification is immediate and progressive, meaning that God sanctifies new believers when they accept salvation but that they continue to grow in maturity until death or the second coming.

Besides Scripture, the PCG relies on very few written documents. They include a constitution, bylaws, and doctrinal statement. In addition, the PCG has commissioned one position paper on the family, which was adopted by the convention in 2003. It defined marriage as between one man and one woman and addressed gender roles in family and in ministry, defining the husband/father as the head of the family and asserting that the role of women in ministry is supplementary.

Divisions and Splits

In the late 1940s, as a result of the Latter Rain revival, several churches in the Pacific Northwest left the denomination. Years later the PCG would again grow in this region.

Finances

To provide for the finances of the headquarters, each minister affiliated with the PCG pays monthly dues of $30. In addition, churches are "encouraged to support general and district ministries with Firstfruits (10 percent) of their undesignated income" (*Pentecostal Church of God: General Bylaws 2010*, 48).

The ministries of the PCG are generally supported by offerings taken during services; missionaries and leaders itinerate for their own support and the support of their ministries.

The headquarters' day-to-day operations are run by a business manager who is nominated by the general council and approved by the general board. The business manager may attend any committee meeting but has no vote. The manager reports to the general bishop.

Statistics

United States members: 44,850

Ministers: 2,677 (including ordained and licensed ministers as well as exhorters)

Churches: 1,134 (down 103 in the last decade)

Largest Churches

New Hope International Church (Concord, CA), with 1,500 attendees

Solid Rock Family Church (Jefferson City, MO), with 1,300 attendees

Trends

Largely Caucasian, the PCG seeks to reach out to ethnic minorities within the United States. The PCG is also confronted with the questions of how to challenge ministers to grow in knowledge while not placing on them the burden of academics that mainline denominations have required of their ministers, and of how to exert more of a presence in media and online ministry.

Missionary and Evangelistic Work

Missionaries: 31

Bible schools: 30

Day schools: 43

Orphanages: 1

Countries: 60 (with Ethiopia having the strongest PCG presence overseas)

Affiliations

The PCG belongs to the Pentecostal/Charismatic Churches of North America, a representative body made up of many of the Pentecostal denominations of North America.

Academic Institution

Messenger College (Euless, TX)

Parachurch Organizations

The PCG has specific departments tasked with various areas of ministry, including Women's Ministries, Youth Ministries, and King's Men Fellowship.

The PCG also sponsors Awakening America, a prayer ministry led by Billy Wilson that focuses on county seats.

Eagles Wings Ministries, led by Robert Stearns, enhances Israeli-American relations and has sent 130 leaders to Israel.

Publication

The *Pentecostal Messenger* is the official publication. Each department publishes its own magazine as well.

Website

http://www.pcg.org/

Archives

The PCG archives are located in the headquarters.

Bibliography

Ming, Wayman C. *Report of the General Secretary*. Pentecostal Church of God, 2009.

Pentecostal Church of God: General Bylaws 2010. Joplin, MO: Messenger, 2010.

Ray Reid

Pentecostal Fire-Baptized Holiness Church

History

The Pentecostal Fire Baptized Church of God in the Americas traces its origin to the Pentecostal Holiness Church, founded in 1898 by William Edward Fuller Sr. and today known as the International Pentecostal Holiness Church. Also formed in 1898 was the Fire-Baptized Holiness Association, later the Fire-Baptized Holiness Church, which merged with the Pentecostal Holiness Church in 1911 under the full name of the latter body. (The church did not use "Pentecostal" as part of its name from 1901 to 1909.) The Tabernacle Pentecostal Church joined the merger in 1915. In 1918, a faction formed, urging more conservative dress and stricter conduct in terms of association between men and women, use of tobacco, and recreational activities; this group became the Pentecostal Fire-Baptized Holiness Church. A further split in 1953 created the Emmanuel Holiness Church.

Headquarters

901 Bishop William Edward Fuller Sr. Highway
Greenville, SC 29601

Leadership

The presiding prelates of the first, second, and third episcopal dioceses are, respectively, Bishop W. E. Fuller Jr., Bishop P. L. Frazier, and Bishop N. J. Roach.

Core Beliefs

The Basis of Union states the denomination's central doctrines. These include belief in the shedding of Christ's blood for salvation and regeneration of sinners; justification by faith alone; sanctification as a distinct second work; the availability of the baptism of the Holy Ghost and fire to wholly sanctified believers, with speaking in tongues as its evidence; divine healing as part of the atonement; and the imminent premillennial bodily return of Christ.

The church also condemns certain teachings of several groups by name, including Christian Scientists, Muslims, Spiritualists, Unitarians, Universalists, Mormons, Seventh-Day Adventists, Jehovah's Witnesses, and Roman Catholics.

Citing Galatians 3:28, that in Christ there is neither male nor female, the church has, since its infancy, allowed women to serve as elders and today licenses and appoints women to preach.

Website

http://www.fbhchurch.org/

Sarah Claudine Day

Pentecostal Free Will Baptists

History

As the name of the denomination suggests, the Pentecostal Free Will Baptists (PFWB) has roots in two strains of Protestantism in the United States. The PFWB can trace its origin back to Paul Palmer, who started General Baptist churches in eastern North Carolina in the early eighteenth century.

Palmer did not pastor the churches he founded; Joseph and William Parker, brothers and both pastors, led the churches founded by Palmer and eventually established new General Baptist churches in North Carolina during the middle years of the eighteenth century. These churches would eventually form the core of the Free Will Baptist movement in the state.

In 1812, a small group of General Baptist churches, representing those Baptist congregations that had remained true to an Arminian soteriology and among which were those originally founded and led by the Parker brothers, issued a declaration of faith. This document, titled *An Abstract of the Former Articles of Faith Confessed by the Original Baptist Church Holding the Doctrine of General Provision with a Proper Code of Discipline* (now known simply as the *1812 Former Articles*), was largely based on the Standard Confession of 1660, a General Baptist statement of faith issued in London. From the title, it is clear that the emphasis for this group of churches was "holding the doctrine of general provision." Around this same time, this group of churches started to be known as Free Will Baptists.

During the nineteenth century, other churches were founded in North and South Carolina that would eventually play a role in the formation of the PFWB. In 1831, Reading Moore established a conference of several churches near Marion, South Carolina. In 1855, the Cape Fear Conference of Free Will Baptist churches was founded through the association of seven churches located in the Cape Fear River basin. The relationship between the Cape Fear Conference and the Pentecostal movement was forged during the early years of the twentieth century.

G. W. Cashwell, a Methodist minister, experienced the Azusa Street revival in Los Angeles in 1906. He subsequently organized a revival meeting in Dunn, North Carolina, during January and February 1907. Several pastors from the Cape Fear Conference attended this meeting and testified to receiving the baptism of the Holy Spirit. Thus, in November 1907, baptism of the Holy Spirit was officially adopted as a doctrine of the association. This doctrine would ultimately prove to be divisive, causing several churches to leave the association in 1912 and solidifying the doctrine among those that remained.

In 1943, three conferences in North Carolina and the aforementioned conference in South Carolina discussed the possibility of joining together as one general conference, meeting every three years. Two of the North Carolina conferences thus joined with the South Carolina conference, and they began to work cooperatively in the areas of missions and youth ministry. Finally, in 1959, a charter and bylaws were drafted and accepted by the North Carolina conferences, officially forming the Pentecostal Free Will Baptist denomination.

Headquarters

Pentecostal Free Will Baptist Church Inc.
1200 Bud Hawkins Road
Dunn, NC 28334

Core Beliefs

Doctrines and practices of the PFWB are described in *Faith and Practices of the Pentecostal Free Will Baptist Church, Inc.* Doctrinal emphases are seen in the areas of Arminian soteriology, entire sanctification and the baptism of the Holy Spirit, and eschatology. Salvation is viewed as having been "rendered equally possible to all. ... Therefore if any fail, it is the fault of the individual and not of God" (pfwb.org, "Faith and Practices"). Sanctification is seen as an act of God subsequent to regeneration. The baptism of the Holy Ghost is characterized as a scriptural imperative. One gives evidence of having been baptized in the Spirit through the practice of glossolalia. Regarding eschatology, the PFWB is premillennial.

The PFWB accepts three ordinances: Christian baptism, the Lord's Supper, and foot washing, which is described as an ordinance of humility.

Academic Institutions

Cape Fear Christian Academy (Erwin, NC)
Heritage Bible College (Dunn, NC)

Bibliography

Butts, Elvin. "The Pentecostal Free Will Baptist Church." *Baptist History and Heritage* 40, no. 1 (2005): 65–75.

Davidson, William F. "The National Association of Free Will Baptists." In *The Baptist River: Essays on Many Tributaries of a Diverse Tradition*, edited by W. Glenn Jonas Jr., 129–57. Macon, GA: Mercer University Press, 2006.

Durso, Keith E., and Pamela R. Durso. *The Story of Baptists in the United States.* Brentwood, TN: Baptist History and Heritage Society, 2006.

Leonard, Bill J. *Baptist Ways: A History.* Valley Forge, PA: Judson, 2003.

McBeth, Leon H. *A Sourcebook for Baptist Heritage.* Nashville: Broadman, 1990.

Pelt, Michael R. *A History of Original Free Will Baptists.* Mount Olive, NC: Mount Olive College Press, 1996.

"Pentecostal Free Will Baptist Church." http://www.pfwb.org. "Faith and Practices."

James R. McConnell

Pillar of Fire

History

Pillar of Fire was founded in Denver, Colorado, in 1901 by Alma White. Originally called the Pentecostal Union, the church rejected the Pentecostal label in 1917, instead utilizing the biblical term found in Exodus 13:21–22, where God's people were directed to freedom through the darkness with a pillar of fire. Although Pillar of Fire has origins in the Methodist Episcopal Church, its doctrines are unique to the Holiness branch of Methodism. Today the church has congregations in Los Angeles and Pacifica, California; Denver and Westminster, Colorado; Cincinnati, Ohio; and Zarephath, New Jersey, where the group's international headquarters are located.

Headquarters

Pillar of Fire International
10 Chapel Drive
Zarephath, NJ 08890
Telephone: 732-356-0102
Email: info@pillar.org

Core Beliefs

Pillar of Fire's doctrines are Wesleyan in nature. The central beliefs of the church are the Trinity; biblical inerrancy; universal sin; the virgin birth; the death and bodily resurrection of Christ; the active role of the Holy Spirit in the world; justification by repentance and faith; sanctified, holy lives on the part of believers; assurance of salvation for believers; the biblical mandates to preach the gospel and to work for justice; the church—the body of Christ—as the place where believers hear the Word and receive sacraments; the return of Christ, resurrection of the body, and experience of either eternal reward or eternal punishment; and the establishment of God's kingdom on a new earth.

Website

http://www.pillar.org/

George Thomas Kurian

United Holy Church

History

The United Holy Church is the oldest African American Pentecostal denomination in the United States. It was founded in May 1886 in North Carolina by Rev. Isaac Cheshier. Cheshier and the other early members of the church were part of the widespread revivals in the South and the West in the late 1800s. They did not originally intend to establish a new denomination but were made unwelcome in existing churches because of their teachings of Holiness, the Spirit-filled life, and the need for sanctification in addition to salvation. Cheshier met with three other believers from Raleigh—L. M. Mason, G. A. Mials, and H. C. Snipes—in the nearby town of Method to form the United Holy Church. Over the next two years the group had its first convocation and held a convention to formulate rules of church government. In 1894, C. M. Nathan was elected as the first of the organization's ten presidents to date. Districts formed in various regions, and headquarters were moved to Durham and later to Greensboro, North Carolina. The present name was adopted in 1916.

Headquarters

5104 Dunstan Road
Greensboro, NC 27405
Telephone: 336-621-0669

Leadership

President: Bishop Elijah Williams

Missionary and Evangelistic Work

Hayes Mission School in Bomi County, Liberia, is a private boarding institute that offers Bible-based training.

Parachurch Organization

Triad Christian Academy in Greensboro, North Carolina, is a licensed childcare facility with a capacity for one hundred children. Its teachers are trained in child development, and many possess the North Carolina Child Care Credential or teaching degrees. The academy's programs include one for early childhood, an after-school program for school-age children, and a summer camp.

Website

http://www.uhcoa.org/

Sarah Claudine Day

United Pentecostal Church International

History

The United Pentecostal Church International (UPCI) arose out of the American Pentecostal movements of the early twentieth century, and it is the largest Oneness Pentecostal denomination in the world. The UPCI was formed in 1945 by the merging of the Pentecostal Church, Incorporated, and the Pentecostal Assemblies of Jesus Christ. These earlier groups were formed by Pentecostals who dissented from historic trinitarian theology and rejected the Statement of Fundamental Truths that was issued by the fourth general council of the Assemblies of God in 1916. While maintaining the importance of the baptism of the Holy Spirit with the initial evidence of speaking in tongues like trinitarian Pentecostals, the UPCI has distinguished itself by baptizing only in the name of Jesus Christ, by an adamant defense of a singular understanding of God, and by a strict holiness code expressed through position papers and articles of faith.

Headquarters

8855 Dunn Road
Hazelwood, MO 63042
Telephone: 314-837-7300

Leadership

General superintendent: Dr. David K. Bernard

Core Beliefs

The UPCI is a Oneness Pentecostal group that believes in salvation through faith in Jesus Christ and the integral acts of repentance, believer's baptism in the name of Jesus Christ, the reception of the gift of the Holy Spirit as evidenced through speaking in tongues, and a life lived in obedience to God. The UPCI asserts the full divinity and full humanity of Jesus Christ and that the full expression of God is in Jesus Christ, the one divine person incarnate. Denying the Nicene view of God as three distinct persons, the UPCI refers to God working as the Father in creation, as the Son in the redemption of humanity, and as the Holy Spirit in regeneration.

Repentance, baptism, and a holy life are essential to the Christian. Baptism is by immersion and according to the model found in Acts, that is, in the saving name of Jesus Christ. The UPCI also asserts that the experience of the Holy Spirit by the disciples in Acts 2 is typical for all Christians and that following the initial, observable evidence of the baptism of the Holy Spirit by speaking in tongues, the believer will demonstrate the fruit of the Spirit described in Galatians 5. Holiness in life is expected of adherents, and standards of dress (particularly for women) and sexuality are of paramount importance, as are avoiding any practices or technologies that might lead to worldliness or ungodliness. The UPCI maintains a premillennial eschatology, thus anticipating an imminent return of Jesus in the rapture, and it officially endorses noncombatant military service for its constituents, although the UPCI has military chaplains.

Baptism is by immersion and in the name of Jesus Christ. There are periodic observances of the Lord's Supper. Divine healing and tithing are taught. Women are licensed to preach.

Worship

Worship includes speaking in tongues, open Communion, and instrumental music. Hymnology is shared with other Pentecostal movements.

Divisions and Splits

The UPCI experienced rifts beginning in the twenty-first century over the loosening of regulations regarding the use of technology, particularly television, in UPCI homes and over the utilization of television and internet webcasts by members of the executive leadership. Historically, local churches frequently separated from the UPCI and became independent Pentecostal churches under the leadership of a charismatic minister.

Statistics

Constituents: 250,000 in the United States, approximately 4 million worldwide

Churches: 4,300 in the United States and Canada, more than 24,000 churches or meeting places in 170 countries outside North America

Daughter works (i.e., church plants that are overseen by a mother church): more than 200

Ministers: more than 9,000

Active international missionaries: 800

Largest Churches

Apostolic Church (Auburn Hills, MI)
Calvary Tabernacle (Indianapolis, IN)
Christian Life Center (Stockton, CA)
New Life United Pentecostal Church (Austin, TX)
Pentecostals of Alexandria (Alexandria, LA)

Growth

The UPCI has benefited from the expansion of Pentecostalism in Eastern Europe, Asia, and Central America. Within the United States, the number of adherents has continued to rise since 1990, before which date the movement had experienced a decade of numerical stagnation.

Trends

The UPCI has maintained a base in the South and the Midwest and among predominately white adherents. Although concerned with missions, the UPCI has resisted being designated as evangelical and unlike many Pentecostal groups has not joined the National Association of Evangelicals (NAE). The denomination is gradually engaging the challenges of a dramatically changing global society and modern technological and philosophical shifts.

Ecumenism

The UPCI has resisted integration with predominantly trinitarian organizations and denominations, and it is not a member of the World Council of Churches or the NAE.

Academic Institutions

The UPCI touts its Apostolic Bible Curriculum for primary and secondary students in Christian schools and home schools, and the UPCI encourages its members to attend institutions of higher education endorsed by the UPCI, most of which retain an identity as a Bible college. The UPCI also maintains a seminary, Urshan Graduate School of Theology in Florissant, Missouri. The UPCI endorses the following schools:

Apostolic Bible Institute (St. Paul, MN)
Centro Teológico Ministerial (Houston, TX)
Christian Life College (Stockton, CA)
Indiana Bible College (Indianapolis, IN)
Northeast Christian College (Fredericton, New Brunswick, Canada)
Texas Bible College (Lufkin, TX)
Urshan College (Florissant, MO)

Electronic Media

Historically, the UPCI has resisted the use of visually oriented technology. In the last decade, the church has utilized internet-related media, including a webcast from the general superintendent.

Publications

Established in 1945, the Pentecostal Herald is the official periodical of the UPCI. There are numerous electronic and print publications associated with division ministries. The Pentecostal Publishing House publishes and sells print, electronic, video, and music media associated with the UPCI and its ministries. World Aflame Press was founded in 1968 and is the UPCI's publishing house for books and academic and church curricula.

Website

http://www.upci.org/

Bibliography

Bernard, David K. *A Handbook of Basic Doctrines*. Hazelwood, MO: Word Aflame Press, 1988.

———. *The Oneness of God*. Hazelwood, MO: Word Aflame Press, 1983.

Reed, David A. *"In Jesus' Name": The History and Beliefs of Oneness Pentecostals*. Blandford Forum, Dorset: Deo Publishing, 2008.

"United Pentecostal Church International." http://www.upci .org. "About Us," "Computers and the Internet," "Divine Healing," "Media Technology Position Paper," "Modesty," "Our Doctrinal Foundation," "The Social Media and the Young Church," "Technology," and "What We Believe."

Bracy V. Hill II

Vineyard USA

History

Kenn and Joanie Gulliksen were sent from Calvary Chapel Costa Mesa in 1974 to plant a church in Los Angeles. Kenn chose the name Vineyard for several other church plants.

Carol Wimber began a home Bible study in 1976 that grew to approximately one hundred attendees, and her husband, John, became the leader. The study group held its first public service in May 1977 and was associated with the Calvary Chapel fellowship until 1982. The Wimbers's Calvary Chapel of Yorba Linda joined the Vineyard movement, which was a group of six churches led by Gulliksen. In association with other Vineyard leaders, Wimber incorporated the Association of Vineyard Churches in 1983. The movement began officially in 1983 in Southern California through the leadership of John Wimber, who is the founding pastor of the central church of the association, Vineyard Christian Fellowship in Anaheim, California.

Headquarters

5115 Grove West Boulevard
Stafford, TX 77447
Telephone: 281-313-8463

Leadership

National director: Bert Waggoner

Core Beliefs

Vineyard churches are evangelical with regard to the inspiration and infallibility of Scripture, the Trinity, the fall of Adam and Eve from grace, the sinfulness of the human race, and the necessity of salvation.

Churches also affirm Pentecostal doctrines such as the spiritual gifts of healing and speaking in tongues. Spirit baptism is often taught as a component of an evangelical conversion. The concept of power is a primary emphasis (e.g., power encounters, power evangelism, power healing). Vineyard churches not only proclaim the kingdom of God but also expect it to be manifested as an invasive force with spiritual gifts and demonstrative deeds (signs and wonders). These deeds indicate the power of God's kingdom in the confrontation with Satan's kingdom.

Worship

Vineyard worship is Pentecostal and charismatic. Worship is expectant and relaxed, with a style that attracts and appeals to the young. There are typically five phases to Vineyard worship, which is similar to the Old Testament temple worship experience: invitation, or call to worship; engagement; adoration; intimacy; and closeout.

Expressive worship encourages ecstatic praise, lengthy sermons, prayers for healing, prophecy, speaking in tongues, and words of knowledge. The average Vineyard church devotes thirty to fifty minutes to singing.

Divisions and Splits

Prior to his death in 1997, Wimber attempted to minimize the denominationalism of the movement so that it would not become an institution. His personality, however, was a primary factor in the success of the movement, and his death, in addition to seriously challenging the notion that prayer will always result in healing, resulted in directional, leadership, and organizational issues. Waggoner was appointed as national director in September 2000 in response to potential problems.

Statistics

Members: approximately 188,000
Churches: 1,500 worldwide in 47 countries, with over 550 churches in the United States
Regions actively engaged in church planting: 8

Largest Churches

Vineyard Columbus (Westerville, OH), with more than 8,500 attendees

Missionary and Evangelistic Work

The association has many groups working at the national level to further the Vineyard movement. Some of the groups are internal, while others are focused on outreach. Task forces and ministries include Blessing Muslims, Children's Ministry

Task Force, Church Planting Task Force, Ethnic Diversity Task Force, Mercy Response, Missions Task Force, Society of Vineyard Scholars (SVS), Vineyard Anti-Slavery Team (VAST), Women's Ministry Task Force, and Youth Ministry Task Force.

Academic Institutions

The Vineyard Leadership Institute is a two-year, part-time academic program with courses in biblical studies and theology. The institute is not an educational institution according to the definition of the Council for Higher Education and Accreditation, but it has been able to achieve college credit equivalency through the American Council on Education. Asbury Theological Seminary has partnered with the Vineyard Leadership Institute in Columbus, Ohio.

Parachurch Organizations

Vineyard USA is a member of three organizations: Christian Churches Together in the USA, the National Association of Evangelicals, and the Pentecostal/Charismatic Churches of North America.

Publications

Vineyard International Publishing prints works espousing the theology of the kingdom of God and the values of the Vineyard; it operates under the international board. Vineyard Resources is a nonprofit ministry for equipping the church. The ministry includes a book club (BookSource), download store (DigitalSource), and music club (ClubVineyard). *Cutting Edge* is the church-planting magazine of the Vineyard movement in the United States. Vineyard Music began in 1986 and is dedicated to providing new worship songs to the association. Christians worldwide embrace many of the songs. Vineyard Music has tremendous influence in radio, with industry awards from ASCAP for songs such as "Breathe," "Draw Me Close," and "In the Secret (I Want to Know You)."

Website

http://www.vineyardusa.org/

Bibliography

Albrecht, Daniel E. *Rites in the Spirit: A Ritual Approach to Pentecostal/Charismatic Spirituality*. Sheffield, UK: Sheffield Academic Press, 1999.

Jackson, Bill. *Quest for the Radical Middle: A History of the Vineyard*. Cape Town, South Africa: Vineyard International, 1999.

Nathan, Rich, and Ken Wilson. *Empowered Evangelicals: Bringing Together the Best of the Evangelical and Charismatic Worlds*. Boise, ID: Ampelon Publishing, 2009.

Pytches, David. *John Wimber: His Influence and Legacy*. Guildford, Surrey: Eagle, 1998.

Wagner, C. Peter. *Signs and Wonders Today*. Altamonte Springs, FL: Creation House, 1987.

Wimber, Carol. *John Wimber: The Way It Was*. London: Hodder & Stoughton, 1999.

Wimber, John, and Kevin Springer, eds. *Riding the Third Wave: What Comes after Renewal?* Basingstoke, UK: Marshall Pickering, 1987.

Ron J. Bigalke

Pietist

Evangelical Covenant Church

History

The Evangelical Covenant Church (ECC), originally the Swedish Evangelical Mission Covenant of America, was founded by Swedish immigrants in Chicago in 1885. The denomination was organized by Mission Friends—products of eighteenth- and nineteenth-century Pietistic revivals in Sweden. Disenchanted with what they saw as theological and spiritual formalism in the Lutheran state church, lay readers began to meet in conventicles to read Scripture, pray, and sing spiritual songs.

Upon immigrating to North America, those who formed the ECC rejected the formal confessionalism of the Lutheran Augustana Synod and the radical congregationalism of the "free" contingent. The ECC has been described as "evangelical, but not exclusive; biblical, but not doctrinaire; traditional, but not rigid; and congregational, but not independent" (covchurch.org, "Who We Are"). During the past twenty years, the ECC has grown significantly, most notably among non-European ethnic populations.

Headquarters

8303 W Higgins Road
Chicago, IL 60631
Telephone: 773-784-3000

Core Beliefs

The ECC recognizes Scripture as the final authority, along with the historic creeds of the church—the Apostles' and Nicene. Because of a Pietist heritage that emphasizes lived faith over dogma, the ECC holds that the unity of all Christians comes through Word and Spirit, not through formal creed. As a broadly evangelical denomination, the ECC affirms the Reformation doctrine of justification by grace through faith and six affirmations: the centrality of the Word of God, the necessity of the new birth, a commitment to the whole mission of the church, the church as a fellowship of believers, conscious dependence on the Holy Spirit, and the reality of freedom in Christ.

The ECC's three most significant documents are its constitution and bylaws, its Rules for the Ordered Ministry, and its Covenant Affirmations, a document outlining its six central affirmations of faith and its identity as an orthodox Protestant church with a Reformation heritage. The denomination also publishes an annual yearbook of statistics and reports. The Committee on Christian Action brings to the annual meeting, by way of the Covenant Executive Board, resolutions that the meeting discusses and approves. These are nonbinding and address contemporary cultural, ethical, and political issues from a biblical perspective. Finally, the denomination and the Board of Ordered Ministry provide occasional papers on significant theological issues that are intended to represent ECC positions.

Statistics

North America total membership: 124,082
Average attendance: 178,997
North America member churches: 746 (55 affiliated)

Covenant World Mission includes 2,638 churches in 20 countries with a total of 279,639 members.

Largest Churches

Because of original patterns of Swedish immigration, membership in the ECC has historically been strongest in the Midwest, Pacific Northwest, and East Coast. Recently, church attendance in the Mid-South and Pacific Southwest has grown significantly. This growth is largely because of two megachurches: LifeChurch.tv in Edmond, Oklahoma, and the

Bayside family of churches in California, with its main campus in Roseville. These churches together maintain an average attendance of almost forty thousand people per week and mark clearly the transition of the ECC from a Swedish ethnic denomination to the American evangelical mainstream.

Missionary and Evangelistic Work

The ECC is divided into seven departments, each with an ecclesial and evangelistic function. The departments are Christian Formation; Church Growth and Evangelism; Communications; Compassion, Mercy, and Justice; Covenant World Mission; the Ordered Ministry; and Women Ministries.

Covenant World Mission maintains ministries on 4 continents and 26 countries and supports (as of January 1, 2009) 2,638 churches, 2,215 pastoral workers, 84 career missionaries, and 36 short-term missionaries. World Mission also sponsors the Paul Carlson Fellowship, an international relief and development organization focusing on central Africa. The Department of Church Growth and Evangelism plants new churches, provides resources to strengthen new churches, and develops resources for evangelism and prayer. The Department of Compassion, Mercy, and Justice sponsors Covenant World Relief, a humanitarian aid ministry, and sponsors trips and retreats that emphasize racial righteousness.

Ecumenism

The ECC is a member of the International Federation of Free Evangelical Churches and Christian Churches Together and maintains observer status with the World Council of Churches. While the ECC has never joined American bodies such as the National Council of Churches or the National Association of Evangelicals, several theologians and church leaders have been actively involved in ecumenical activities locally, nationally, and internationally. Individual ECC churches maintain membership in various organizations such as the National Association of Evangelicals, the Willow Creek Association, the Emerging Church Network, and similar institutions.

Academic Institutions

Alaska Christian College (Soldotna, AK) (associate's degrees in biblical studies)
Centro Hispano de Estudios Teologicos (Bell Gardens, CA) (a theological and pastoral training center for Hispanic church planters, pastors, and lay leaders)
Minnehaha Academy (Minneapolis, MN) (K–12)
North Park Theological Seminary (Chicago, IL) (offers MA, MDiv, and DMin degrees)
North Park University (Chicago, IL) (accredited university offering bachelor's and master's degrees)

Parachurch Organizations

In addition to its seven departments, the ECC maintains related institutions to aid the work of the church. Covenant Ministries of Benevolence manages Covenant Retirement Communities, assisted-care residences, Swedish Covenant Hospital, and other related ministries. Covenant Trust Company provides trustee and management services for trusts arranged by Covenant Estate Planning Services. National Covenant Properties lends money to churches for building projects and provides investment opportunities to friends and members of the ECC. The ECC's Association of Covenant Camps and Conference Centers runs twenty-one camps across North America.

Electronic Media

KICY (AM 850) broadcasts from Nome, Alaska, and is owned by Arctic Broadcasting Association, which is a 501(c)(3) nonprofit affiliated corporation of the ECC. KICY serves native Alaskan villages throughout the Seward Peninsula, the Yukon and Kuskokwim Deltas, and the Russian regions of Chukotka, Kamchatka, and Siberia.

Publications

Covenant Press publishes books relevant to denominational heritage. The Department of Communications publishes the Covenant Companion (monthly periodical), the Covenant Home Altar (quarterly devotional guide), and the Covenant Quarterly (quarterly academic journal for ministers).

The Covenant Hymnal includes over 775 hymns and songs as well as significant resources for public worship. The Covenant Book of Worship is a resource designed to help pastors lead public worship. Features include four complete outlines for Sunday worship services, services for the church year, additional services for special occasions, and scriptural resources for ministry.

Website

http://www.covchurch.org/

Archives

The Covenant Archives and Historical Library, along with the North Park University Archives and the Swedish American Archives of Greater Chicago, are housed on the campus of North Park University.

Bibliography

Olsson, Karl. *By One Spirit*. Chicago: Covenant Press, 1962.

———. *Into One Body... by the Cross*. 2 vols. Chicago: Covenant Press, 1985, 1986.

Kurt W. Peterson

Evangelical Free Church of America

History

The Evangelical Free Church of America (EFCA) was formed in Boone, Iowa, in October 1884 from a merger between several independent Protestant congregations and churches of the Swedish Ansgarii Synod and the Mission Synod. The resultant organization was of "free" churches under the name the Swedish Evangelical Free Mission, which later changed its name to the Swedish Evangelical Free Church (SEFC). Also arising from the revivalism of the late nineteenth century, congregations of Norwegian and Danish immigrants began to worship together in 1884 on the northeastern and northwestern coasts of America. This union yielded the Norwegian-Danish Evangelical Free Church Association, which changed its name to the Evangelical Free Church Association.

In 1950, the Swedish Evangelical Free Church united with the Evangelical Free Church Association at Medicine Lake Conference Grounds outside Minneapolis, Minnesota, to form the EFCA, comprising approximately 275 congregations, the majority from the SEFC.

Headquarters

901 East 78th Street
Minneapolis, MN 55420-1300
Telephone: 800-745-2202

Leadership

President: Rev. Kevin Kompelien

Core Beliefs

In 2008, the annual conference adopted a rather flexible statement of faith articulated in ten articles called convictions. Reflecting the inclination of the majority of the clergy to Calvinistic theology and a strong concern about the incursion of open theism, the first article maintained that God has "limitless knowledge and sovereign power" and that he "purposed from eternity to redeem a people for Himself and to make all things new for His own glory." Evincing a strong evangelical orientation, the second article asserted the "verbally inspired Word of God" without error in original texts and fully revealing the divine will for salvation and authority for all human knowledge. Affirming a pessimistic anthropology, the statement of faith contended for a traditional view of the person and salvific work of Jesus Christ ("our representative and substitute") (efca.org, "Statement of Faith").

According to the statement, the visible church is comprised of those who have been justified by faith alone and are gathered in local churches. No definitive comment was made regarding the interpretation or mode of the Lord's Supper. Similarly absent was any comment on the appropriate time of baptism in the life of the believer. "Justifying grace" and "sanctifying power" were believed to be active in the life of the believer and to be expressed in good works toward others and in spreading of the gospel. The final articles, despite considerable debate over their formulation, were explicit in espousing the imminent "personal, bodily, and premillennial return" of Christ and a final judgment (efca.org, "Statement of Faith").

Baptism is not required for membership, nor is there an obligatory mode, although it is always performed with a trinitarian formula and almost always by immersion. Emphasis is on preaching and on evangelization, both foreign and domestic.

Worship

Due to the diverse nature of the church, liturgical practices are varied, generally taking forms congruent with other Protestant, evangelical denominations within the local area. The Lord's Supper may be celebrated in a host of manners and may vary in its frequency of observance. EFCA worship often includes open Communion, instrumental music, contemporary or blended music with hymns and choruses, responsive readings and a lectionary (in some congregations), Bible-based preaching and teaching, and utilization of small groups or "life groups."

Statistics

Adherents: more than 350,000

Congregations: approximately 1,300, with the densest representation in the upper Midwest and with the most local churches in such states as California,

Nebraska, North Dakota, Minnesota, Iowa, and Colorado

Ordained ministers: 1,800

Largest Churches

Blackhawk Church (Madison, WI)

First Evangelical Free Church of Fullerton (Fullerton, CA)

North Coast Church (Vista, CA)

Growth

The EFCA has grown substantially since 1950, when it had fewer than three hundred churches and approximately twenty thousand members. By 1970, the church had more than doubled its original number of churches and congregants. The first decade of the millennium witnessed unprecedented growth in the number of adherents.

Trends

The EFCA has intentionally embraced greater diversity in the theological and demographic makeup of its adherents. Integral to its commitment to adapt the message of the gospel to the new millennium was its refreshing of its statement of faith in 2008. EFCA churches generally take a pragmatic approach to worship and programming, adapting to methods deemed most effective at a given time.

Ecumenism

The EFCA has set a goal to become more racially, ethnically, and socially diverse, better reflecting the demographics of the United States. The EFCA has been a member of the National Association of Evangelicals since 1943.

Academic Institutions

The EFCA supports Trinity International University (TIU) in Deerfield, Illinois, which was founded in 1897. TIU is comprised of Trinity Evangelical Divinity School (TEDS), the graduate school, the law school, and Trinity College. TIU also has regional campuses in the United States. The EFCA is also affiliated with Trinity Western University in Langley, British Columbia.

Publication

EFCA Today, a quarterly publication for clergy and laity

Websites

http://www.efca.org/

http://www.efcatoday.org/

Bibliography

"The Evangelical Free Church of America." http://www.efca .org. "About the EFCA: Our History," "Distinctives of the Evangelical Free Church of America," "Statement of Faith," "Statistics," and "Who We Are."

Olson, Arnold Theodore. *The Significance of Silence.* Minneapolis: Free Church Press, 1981.

———. *This We Believe: The Background and Exposition of the Doctrinal Statement of the Evangelical Free Church of America.* Minneapolis: Free Church Publications, 1961.

Bracy V. Hill II

Moravian Church (Unitas Fratrum)

History

The Moravian Church (Unitas Fratrum) originated in the provinces of Bohemia and Moravia in what is now the Czech Republic. It traces its roots to the work of John Hus (1369–1415), a philosophy professor and rector at the University of Prague who appealed for reforms in the Catholic Church as he gave sermons in the Bethlehem Chapel in Prague. Receiving vast support from students and the common people, Hus was persecuted by the authorities; after a lengthy trial on a charge of heresy, he was burned at the stake. Hus's followers organized a church in Kunvald, one hundred miles from Prague, known since 1457 as Unitas Fratrum (meaning Unity of Brethren). Moravians proudly note that their break from Rome took place several decades before Luther's Reformation activities.

The church launched its own ministry efforts, subsequently categorized in three orders: deacon, presbyter, and bishop. Over the next fifty years, the Unitas Fratrum came to number more than two hundred thousand with more than four hundred parishes. It developed its own hymnal and catechism and created two printing presses to provide Bibles to the people of Bohemia and Moravia in their own language. Persecution starting in 1547 forced the Brethren to move to Poland, where they enjoyed considerable growth until a defeat in 1620 during the course of the Thirty Years' War. The Brethren's noted leader of the time, educational reformer John Amos Comenius, went into exile in Holland and England. In 1722, Moravian families fleeing persecution in Bohemia and Moravia were offered safe haven on the estate of the Pietist count Nicholas Ludwig von Zinzendorf in Saxony. They founded the community of Herrnhut, which welcomed more refugees. With encouragement from the count, the Moravians were revitalized and began their own missionary work in the West Indies in 1732.

The Moravians settled in Pennsylvania on the estate of George Whitefield after failing to establish a settlement in Georgia in 1735–40. In 1741, they purchased five hundred acres and created the settlement of Bethlehem; shortly thereafter they purchased five thousand acres of the Barony of Nazareth from Whitefield's manager and linked the agricultural and industrial activities of Bethlehem and Nazareth.

Moravian settlements in Pennsylvania, New Jersey, and Maryland were all active in ministering to Native Americans. In North Carolina, Bishop Augustus Spangenberg selected a one-hundred-thousand-acre parcel of land, originally named Wachau after an Austrian estate of Count Zinzendorf and later called Wachovia. Wachovia was soon joined by other settlements in North Carolina, such as Bethabara, Bethania, and Salem (today Winston-Salem). It became the headquarters of the South province, with Bethlehem as the headquarters of the North, when the Moravian Church in North America became independent with the Unity Synod of 1848.

The church spread to the Midwest with the growing presence of German immigrants there. As persecution continued in Eastern Europe and even Canada, the church continued to grow in America. The Northern Province was subdivided into Eastern, Western, and Canadian districts. By the mid-twentieth century, the province's reach extended all the way to Southern California, where previously the only Moravian presence was an Indian mission founded in 1890. Meanwhile, the Southern Province expanded to include Florida and Georgia.

Headquarters

PO Box 1245
Bethlehem, PA 18016
Telephone: 610-867-0593
Email: pubs@mcnp.org

Leadership

President, Provincial Elders' Conference, Northern Province: Rev. David L. Wickmann
President, Provincial Elders' Conference, Southern Province: Rt. Rev. Wayne Burkette
President, Provincial Elders' Conference, Alaska Province: Rev. Peter Green

Core Beliefs

The Covenant for Christian Living (formerly the Brotherly Agreement of the Moravian Church) encapsulates Moravian beliefs, including belief in the Trinity. The Moravian Church is characterized by a high degree of tolerance of doctrines of other denominations. The essential beliefs are in the lordship of Christ, salvation not by works but through God's goodness, and God's enabling of the believer to walk in faith. The believer is responsible to develop spiritually through participation in the church, personal prayer and study, and family devotions.

The sacraments are baptism and Communion. Baptism is viewed as a union with Christ's death and resurrection; the individual receives a pledge of forgiveness of sin and enters into a covenant with God through the blood of Christ. It is usually performed by sprinkling and is done in the name of the Father, Son, and Holy Spirit. Baptism of infants is allowed as a symbol of Christ's pledge that theirs "is the kingdom of heaven." Parents and the congregation are responsible to ensure that the child is raised in the faith, and at an appropriate age, youth confirm their baptismal covenant or receive an adult baptism accompanied by a profession of faith. The sacrament of Communion is treated as a mystery, with no attempt to define the nature of Christ's presence in the elements. It represents a covenant with Christ as Savior and also with fellow believers, with the "right hand of fellowship" extended at the start and close of each Communion service. There is also praise, prayer, and singing of hymns as the elements are distributed.

Worship

Moravian worship has a strong musical component, including chorales and hymns from the eighteenth century. Church festivals are usually occasion for trombone choirs or brass bands to perform. The love feast is a service involving music and the sharing of simple foods.

Liturgical traditions reflect the seasons. In the Christmas Eve candle service, the congregation receives candles of pure beeswax, symbolizing the purity of Christ, and a "putz" scene depicts not just the nativity but the entire gospel message starting with Isaiah's prophecy. Another highlight of the calendar is the Easter sunrise service.

Statistics

There are 152 congregations in 16 states, the District of Columbia, and 2 Canadian provinces. In addition, there are 18 fellowships.

Missionary and Evangelistic Work

There is mission activity in the Americas, Europe, Africa, and Asia. The Unity Synod, which meets every seven years, unites mission fields with the mother churches. The Board of World Mission oversees all mission efforts and has created programs to further mission work, including the Adopt-a-Village program; the Antioch Project, which involves youth; Moravian Volunteer Resources, which stimulates interest on the part of individuals, congregations, and other groups to serve on disaster-response mission teams; and numerous AIDS ministries.

Evangelistic work also takes the form of educational and social work. Moravians have established schools in Germany, England, America, and mission fields. Congregations usually offer educational programs that encourage spiritual development, sometimes taking the form of camps, conferences, and retreats for children, youth, and adults. The denomination advocates social reforms where they are necessary to correct injustice.

Congregations offer a variety of programs to the local community, including youth outreaches. Throughout the country there are facilities that provide quality care for the aging, including Sunnyside Ministry, an emergency assistance agency founded in 1978 that helps residents of portions of Forsyth and Davidson Counties in North Carolina. Other programs include Moravian Open Door, located in New York City, which offers housing and other services to the needy; Hope Conference and Renewal Center in Hope, New Jersey; Van-Es Camp and Conference Centre in Edmonton, Alberta; Mt. Morris Camp and Conference Center in Wautoma, Wisconsin; and Laurel Ridge Camp, Conference, and Retreat Center in Laurel Springs, North Carolina.

The Moravian Ministries Foundation works to generate income for various programs through investments, planned giving, financial planning, and capital campaigns.

Ecumenism

A charter member of the World Council of Churches and the National Council of Churches of Christ in the USA, the Moravian Church embraces ecumenical cooperation.

Academic Institutions

Moravian Theological Seminary (Bethlehem, PA) offers a graduate level Christian education in pastoral work and other ministries. It incorporates practical experiences and welcomes students of other denominational backgrounds.

Publications

The Interprovincial Board of Communication oversees denominational publications as well as audiovisual and electronic media resources. The *Moravian* magazine contains daily devotions, provincial elders' news, and a wide range of other articles about faith and the work of the church.

Since 1731, the church has published a guide to personal devotions called the *Daily Texts*. The publication originated with Count von Zinzendorf's practice of distributing a "Losung" (watchword) for the following day to each member of the Herrnhut group. The texts are still selected in Herrnhut but by a different party each month; the English language edition also contains hymns and prayers written by clergy and laity. With a circulation of 1.5 million, of which 1 million copies are in the German language, the *Daily Texts* reach many non-Moravians.

Website

http://www.moravian.org/

Archives

The Moravian Church operates archival facilities in Bethlehem, Pennsylvania, and Winston-Salem, North Carolina.

The Moravian Music Foundation, located in Winston-Salem, North Carolina, has worked since 1956 to preserve and share musical heritage of the Moravian Church and to assist researchers. Its primary archival collection, housed in both Winston-Salem and Bethlehem, Pennsylvania, includes ten thousand pieces, among them music manuscripts, first editions, early imprints, and other materials. Many items are of unique historical significance. A secondary collection, Peter Memorial Library, has six thousand titles. A lending library circulates materials among Moravian and non-Moravian groups.

Sarah Claudine Day

Unity of the Brethren

History

The Unity of the Brethren (not to be confused with Unitas Fratrum), originally the Evangelical Union of Bohemian and Moravian Brethren (Czech Moravian Brethren Church), is an offshoot of the Moravian Church, with congregations located principally in Texas. Once primarily Czech in composition, today the denomination includes members of many other ethnic backgrounds.

The martyred priest John Hus is regarded as the forefather of the Unity of the Brethren denomination. Hus sought reforms in the Catholic Church that would restore its spiritual purity by purging it of secular authority, material possessions, and many of its traditions. He also supported making the Scriptures available in the people's language rather than in Latin. Though popular, Hus's proposed reforms infuriated Catholic authorities, who executed Hus in 1415 but, in doing so, gave his followers reason to create their own church, the Unity of Brethren. The church became the dominant one in the Czech population, influenced Martin Luther and John Calvin, and offered sanctuary to Anabaptists.

In 1620, early in the Thirty Years' War, Protestants experienced a defeat in Czech lands that brought on the Catholic Counter-Reformation there and the exodus of many Protestants who later formed the Moravian Church. The Brethren who stayed in Czech lands concealed their beliefs as they were passed down from one generation to another. Reforms in the late 1700s created limited tolerance for Lutherans and Calvinists, who were joined by some Brethren, as the Brethren faith was still prohibited.

In the 1850s, the promise of cheap farmland in Texas launched a period of immigration that lasted until the start of the First World War. Congregations that were started among the Czech immigrants in Texas formed the Unity of the Brethren in 1903. From the 1940s to the 1970s, the use of English was phased into worship services in the various congregations.

Headquarters

4009 Hunter Creek
College Station, TX 77845

Core Beliefs

The Unity of the Brethren adheres to the Apostles' Creed. Members stress that all doctrines and teachings about Christian conduct must originate in Scripture. At the same time, the church accommodates individual freedom of conscience in some matters, as reflected in its long-standing motto, "In essentials, unity; in nonessentials, liberty; in all things, love."

The essential beliefs include belief in the three persons of the Godhead, Father, Son, and Holy Spirit; belief in Christ as the only means of salvation; belief in the active role of the Holy Spirit in the world, especially in the lives of believers; and belief in the return of Christ in glory to judge the world and reward his followers. The church, as the body of Christ, consists of those who accept the grace of Christ's gift of salvation by faith, and it forms the kingdom of God on earth by implementing God's will.

Although the Unity of the Brethren insists on the presence of Christ in Communion and baptism, disagreement is permitted on the manner in which he is present. Parents are expected to baptize infants, indicating an intention to teach them the faith and a claim for their salvation, which should be reaffirmed by the children once they are old enough to do so. Those not baptized as infants are baptized as adults and select the manner of baptism. There is also freedom for congregations to determine the structure of church government.

The emblem of the Unity of the Brethren, consisting of a cross, an open Bible, and a chalice, demonstrates the denomination's dedication to Christ's resurrection, to the Bible—open to study—as the origin of truth, and to the Lord's Supper. Even before the Reformation, John Hus and his followers insisted on inclusion of the cup in addition to bread in Holy Communion.

Website

http://www.unityofthebrethren.org/

George Thomas Kurian

Reformed

Associate Reformed Presbyterian Church

History

The Associate Reformed Presbyterian (ARP) Church owes its origin to the 1782 union of Scottish Covenanter and Seceder groups in the United States (the terms "Associate" and "Reformed" refer to the Seceder and Covenanter traditions, respectively). A Synod of the South was formed in 1803, which then separated from the Northern Associate Reformed Synods in 1822. Long known as the Associate Reformed Synod of the South, the term "Presbyterian" was added in 1935 in recognition of the church's presbyterian form of government. The church was historically distinguished from other Presbyterian groups not so much by theology as by certain issues of praxis—exclusive psalmody, noninstrumental worship, closed Communion, and strict sabbatarianism. By the mid-twentieth century, however, these distinctives had in large measure broken down, and since that point the church has been split between those who identify with the evangelical tradition and those who reflect mainline Protestant influences.

Historically centered in the southeastern United States, since the 1960s, the ARP Church has expanded numerically and geographically through church planting and the reception of congregations from other denominations. From 1965 to 1980, the denomination experienced a time of conflict over issues such as the authority of Scripture, the ordination of women, and the relationship between the church and its educational institutions. Some of these debates have now reemerged with vigor in the early twenty-first century.

Headquarters

1 Cleveland Street
Suite 110
Greenville, SC 29601-3696
Telephone: 864-232-8297

Core Beliefs

The Westminster Confession of Faith, the Westminster Larger Catechism, and the Westminster Shorter Catechism make up the confessional standards of the church. After 1799 revisions to remove Erastian elements from the Westminster Standards (elements that held that secular government has a certain authority over the church), the confession and catechisms remained unchanged until the mid-twentieth century, when two additional chapters ("Of the Holy Spirit" and "Of the Gospel") were added in 1959. More recently, other changes have removed confessional language deemed offensive to Roman Catholics.

Worship

As would be expected of a church in the Reformed tradition with a history of liturgical conservatism, most congregations in the ARP Church practice a traditional style of worship, though contemporary forms have made inroads in some areas. A few congregations still practice exclusive psalmody.

Controversies

With the loss of its historic praxis distinctives (such as exclusive psalmody and noninstrumental worship, which had distinguished the ARP Church from mainline Presbyterians) in the twentieth century, the ARP Church was thrown somewhat off balance. Many sought to identify with the broader evangelical tradition, while others tended toward a mainline church sensibility of genteel "culture Protestantism."

As these differences and tensions were addressed, the church experienced conflicts over a variety of issues. After more than a decade of debate over the authority of Scripture, the general synod declared in 1979 and 1980 that "the Scriptures of the Old and New Testaments are the

Word of God without error in all that it teaches" (*Minutes of the General Synod* [1980], 283). After the reemergence of similar issues, the general synod in 2008 declared that the "Bible alone, being verbally God-breathed, is the Word of God written, infallible in all it teaches, and inerrant in the original manuscripts" (*Minutes of the General Synod* [2008], 514).

Extended debates over the ordination of women resulted in the opening of the office of deacon to women in 1969. However, the offices of minister and elder continue to be reserved for males. Since the 1960s, there have also been controversies regarding the accountability of the denomination's college and seminary to the church.

Statistics

Total membership: close to 35,000
Active communicant membership: more than 23,000
Churches: 296

Largest Churches

The denomination has its greatest numerical strength in the southeastern United States, especially in North Carolina, South Carolina, Georgia, and Florida. The largest congregation is First Presbyterian Church of Columbia, South Carolina.

Missionary and Evangelistic Work

The church supports a foreign mission arm (ARP World Witness) and a domestic mission agency (Outreach North America). Foreign mission fields include Pakistan and Mexico, where indigenous ARP Church synods have long been established, as well as Russia, Germany, Great Britain, and the Middle East.

Ecumenism

Over the past century and a half, a variety of proposals for mergers with other denominations have failed to win approval. Most recently, an effort to join with the Presbyterian Church in the United States (PCUS) was defeated in 1951.

The ARP Church was a longtime member of the World Alliance of Reformed Churches and the Reformed Ecumenical Council but withdrew from those organizations in 1992 due to differences over confessional and moral issues. It currently maintains memberships in the North American Presbyterian and Reformed Council, the International Conference of Reformed

Churches, and the World Reformed Fellowship. The church also maintains a wide range of fraternal relationships with other Presbyterian and Reformed churches.

Academic Institutions

The ARP Church supports and appoints the board of trustees for Erskine College (founded in 1839) and Erskine Theological Seminary (founded in 1837), both located in Due West, South Carolina.

Publications

The ARP Church publishes a monthly magazine (the *ARP Magazine*) and an adult Sunday school curriculum (the *ARP Adult Quarterly*).

Website

http://www.arpchurch.org/

Bibliography

The Centennial History of the Associate Reformed Presbyterian Church, 1803–1903. Charleston, SC: Walker, Evans & Cogwell, 1905.

Evans, William B. "'Things Which Become Sound Doctrine': Associate Reformed Presbyterian Confessional and Theological Identity in the 20th Century." *Haddington House Journal* 8 supp. (2006): 89–116.

King, Ray A. *A History of the Associate Reformed Presbyterian Church.* Charlotte: Board of Christian Education, 1966.

Lathan, Robert. *History of the Associate Reformed Synod of the South, 1782–1882.* Harrisburg, PA: n.p., 1882.

Ruble, Randall T., ed. *The Bicentennial History of the Associate Reformed Presbyterian Church, 1950–2003.* Grand Rapids: McNaughton & Gunn, 2003.

Ware, Lowry, and James W. Gettys. *The Second Century: A History of the Associate Reformed Presbyterians, 1882–1982.* Greenville, SC: Associate Reformed Presbyterian Center, 1982.

William B. Evans

Christian Reformed Church in North America

History

The Christian Reformed Church (CRC) in North America came from the Reformed churches that flourished in the Netherlands following the Reformation in the sixteenth century. One of the key events that led to the formation of the CRC was the decision of a Reformed pastor, Albertus Van Raalte (d. 1876), to immigrate to the United States to flee religious persecution and famine in the Netherlands. In 1848, Van Raalte and his wife, his family, and some forty others established a colony in what is now Holland, Michigan. This new colony held passionately to

Calvinist doctrines, practical piety, and a strong commitment to living all of life to the glory of God. But the harsh conditions in the fledgling colony convinced Van Raalte to seek help from the Dutch Reformed Church, which had been introduced to American soil over a century earlier when Dutch Reformed merchants accompanying Peter Stuyvesant (d. 1672) settled in New York, then called New Amsterdam. That line of communication between Van Raalte's Michigan churches and the Dutch Reformed congregations of New Jersey soon developed into a complete merger.

In 1857, a small fragment of four churches, about 130 families, broke away from the new union and formed the Christian Reformed Church. Among the reasons they cited were a perceived lack of sound doctrinal preaching by American pastors; a perceived lack of piety and too much accommodation to American culture by these same pastors; the use of hymns in worship as opposed to psalm singing only; the practice by the American churches of open Communion, extending an open invitation to all believers to participate in the Lord's Supper; and the perceived lack of solidarity on the part of the Americans with the secessionist cause in the Netherlands.

On April 5, 1857, the Christian Reformed Church was born. Today, although a majority of its members are still from Dutch backgrounds, the CRC has become more and more a multicultural and multinational church.

Headquarters

2850 Kalamazoo Avenue SE
Grand Rapids, MI 49560
Telephone: 616-241-1691; 877-279-9994
Email: crcna@crcna.org

Core Beliefs

What sets the CRC apart from many other denominations is its embrace of key teachings of John Calvin. In essence, these all center on the sovereignty of God.

Salvation is by grace alone through faith and not by our own good works.
The Bible alone is the authoritative Word of God for our lives—not church tradition or what church leaders say.
All believers are priests of God, anointed in Christ to serve him always, everywhere, in all they do.
God gave us two sacraments, baptism and Communion, which are signs and seals of God's promises.

A clergy's blessing of the Communion bread and wine do not turn them into the actual body and blood of Christ.
The original sinful condition in which we are born, as well as our actual sins, are all fully washed away by Christ's sacrifice on the cross.
Prayer should be directed to God alone, not to saints or to Mary. In fact, all believers are both sinners needing God's constant forgiveness and saints whom the Holy Spirit is already remaking to be like Jesus.

Controversies

At the turn of the twentieth century, the CRC was characterized by doctrinal disagreements and cultural challenges. Among other things, in 1918, the synod rejected the dispensationalist views of Rev. Harry Bultema. In 1925, the denomination was entangled in a common grace controversy, leading to organization of the First Protesting Christian Reformed Church. But the congregation returned to denominational fellowship in 1946.

The large immigration of Dutch Calvinists to Canada in the early 1950s after the Second World War brought some significant culture clash into the CRC. While the Dutch Canadians shared a commitment to the Reformed confessions, they differed from their American cousins in life experience, mind-set, and moral and religious values. Dutch Canadians tended to focus their spiritual energies on working out the social ramifications of the gospel, not on personal piety. Yet both groups shared a genuine desire and commitment to remain obedient to God's Word—a solid foundation on which to build a binational church.

During the 1960s, changing roles for women in the larger society forced the CRC to ask whether women should be allowed to serve in ecclesiastical office. While both sides in this struggle sincerely sought to be biblically obedient and Reformed in their interpretation of Scripture, neither side was able to convince the other. The impasse led to a compromise decision that allowed individual churches (if they chose) to ordain women as elders and classes to allow their constituent congregations to ordain women as ministers of the Word. That decision spurred the departure of more than forty thousand members from the CRC.

Statistics

Total membership: 268,052 (mostly in the Midwest United States and Canada)
Churches: 1,049

Missionary and Evangelistic Work

Through Christian Reformed World Missions, the CRC participates in Spirit-led missions with churches and other Christian organizations throughout the world.

Academic Institutions

Calvin College (Grand Rapids, MI)
Calvin Theological Seminary (Grand Rapids, MI)
Dordt College (Sioux Center, IA)
Kuyper College (Grand Rapids, MI)
Trinity Christian College (Palos Heights, IL)

Electronic Media

The *Back to God Hour* is the denomination's radio and television ministry. It broadcasts the gospel in nations around the world in French, English, Arabic, Chinese, Russian, Spanish, and other languages.

Publications

Agenda for Synod
The Banner

Hymn books include *Contemporary Songs for Worship, Hymns for Worship,* and *Global Songs for Worship.*

Website

http://www.crcna.org/

Archives

Since 1962, Calvin College Archives (Grand Rapids, MI) has held archival records of local, active congregations and the CRC's minutes.

Bibliography

Borgdorff, Peter. *Manual of Christian Reformed Church Government.* Grand Rapids: Faith Alive, 2008.
The Christian Reformed Church: Who We Are and What We Believe. Grand Rapids: Faith Alive, 2009.
De Moor, Robert. *Reformed: What It Means, Why It Matters.* Grand Rapids: Faith Alive, 2001.

Kalvin Budiman

Cumberland Presbyterian Church

History

The Cumberland Presbyterian Church (CPC) was founded by three ministers in a log cabin in Dickson County, Tennessee, on February 4, 1810, to meet the needs of the frontier population in the Cumberland River Valley of middle Tennessee and southwestern Kentucky. The Cumberland Presbytery grew to a synod in 1813, and the first general assembly met in 1829. Preachers sometimes lacked formal ministerial education, so Cumberland College was founded in Princeton, Kentucky, in 1826.

After the Civil War, the denomination split along racial lines. The Colored Cumberland body organized in 1868, held its first general assembly in 1874, and eventually called itself the Cumberland Presbyterian Church in America. In 1906, about 50 percent of the Cumberland Presbyterian churches and more than twenty church-affiliated colleges joined the Presbyterian Church USA. The Cumberland Presbyterian Church celebrated its bicentennial on February 8, 2010.

Headquarters

8207 Traditional Place
Cordova, TN 38016
Telephone: 901-276-4572

Core Beliefs

The Cumberland Synod revised the Westminster Confession in 1814, removing unconditional election and enlarging human freedom. Revisions to the document were made in 1883 and again in 1984, the culmination of a seven-year study. The CPC has been seen as somewhat Arminian by some, and, indeed, the denomination does draw from Jacob Arminius. The 1984 Confession states, "Jesus Christ willingly suffered sin and death for every person." It continues, "Through the Holy Spirit, people are able to acknowledge and repent of their sin, believe in Jesus Christ as Savior, and follow Christ as Lord" (cumberland .org, "Confession of Faith").

Finances

Revenues for the CPC for fiscal year 2009 were $7,548,243. Expenses for the same period were $7,311,347, and net assets were $78,247,991.

Statistics

Members: 78,000 in the United States, Colombia, South America, Hong Kong, and Japan
Churches: over 700
Presbyteries: 23
Synods: 5

Largest Church

St. Matthew Cumberland Presbyterian Church (Burleson, TX), with a weekly attendance of about 1,200

Missionary and Evangelistic Work

The CPC has twenty-three missionaries serving in seventeen countries, including Brazil, Colombia, Guatemala, Nepal, the Philippines, Southeast Asia, South Korea, Uganda, and Zambia.

Academic Institutions

Cumberland College (now University) was founded in Princeton, Kentucky, in 1826 and later moved to Lebanon, Tennessee, but it is no longer a denominational institution. Bethel College was established in 1842 in McLemoresville, Tennessee, but thirty years later it moved ten miles north to McKenzie. The spring 2009 enrollment reached 2,626, and in August 2009, the name was changed to Bethel University. The school offers bachelor's degrees in twenty-six subject areas and has five master's programs. Bethel's graduate seminary moved from McKenzie to Memphis, Tennessee, in 1964 and became Memphis Theological Seminary. The faculty represents United Methodist, Cumberland Presbyterian, Disciples of Christ, Baptist, Jewish, Presbyterian (USA), and Roman Catholic traditions. Enrollment tops three hundred.

Parachurch Organizations

The CPC has a children's home in Denton, Texas; an orphanage in Bowling Green, Kentucky; and a publishing house in Nashville, Tennessee.

Website

http://www.cumberland.org/

Archives

Archives for both the Cumberland Presbyterian Church and the Cumberland Presbyterian Church in America are housed in the Historical Foundation in Cordova, Tennessee.

Bibliography

Campbell, Thomas H. *Good News on the Frontier: A History of the Cumberland Presbyterian Church.* Richmond, VA: CLC Press, 1965.

"Cumberland Presbyterian Church." http://www.cumberland.org. "Confession of Faith."

McDonnold, Benjamin Wilburn. *History of the Cumberland Presbyterian Church.* Nashville: Board of Publication of Cumberland Presbyterian Church, 1888.

James A. Borland

Cumberland Presbyterian Church in America

History

The Cumberland Presbyterian Church in America (CPCA) has had several previous designations. These include Colored Cumberland

Presbyterian Church and Second Cumberland Presbyterian Church. Beginning in 1868, freed slaves in the Cumberland Presbyterian Church (CPC) petitioned peacefully for a separate church denomination but without much success until meeting at Murfreesboro, Tennessee, in 1870. Their first general assembly was held in Nashville in 1874. Jno. F. Humphrey of Fayetteville was stated clerk from 1874 to 1900. He was followed by J. M. Deshong (1901), C. L. Davis (1902–10), J. M. W. Deshong (1911), James Edwards (1912–23), G. W. Sadler (1924–31), J. I. Hill (1932–60), R. Tinsley (1961–76), Robert Thomas (1977–78), Robert S. Wood (1979–97), Lynne Herring (1998–99), and Perryn Rice (2000–2002). The current stated clerk of the general assembly is Theodis Acklin (2003–10) of Huntsville, Alabama, and the moderator of the general assembly is Army Daniel Jr., also of Huntsville, Alabama.

Headquarters

226 Church Street NW
Huntsville, AL 35801
Telephone: 256-536-7481

Core Beliefs

The 1984 revision of the 1883 Confession of Faith is adhered to by both the CPC and the CPCA. This document came from an early revision of the Westminster Confession (in 1810) and is more Arminian in nature. The 1984 Confession states, "Jesus Christ willingly suffered sin and death for every person." It continues, "Through the Holy Spirit, people are able to acknowledge and repent of their sin, believe in Jesus Christ as Savior, and follow Christ as Lord" (cumberland.org, "Confession of Faith").

Website

http://www.cpcachurch.org/

Bibliography

Fuqua, Nancy, and Henry Bradford. *Built by the Hands: An Historical Account of the Love, Faith, and Determination in the Cumberland Presbyterian Church in America.* Huntsville, AL: Executive Committee of the General Assembly, 2002.

Jenkins, Jno. J. *Souvenir History of the Colored Cumberland Presbyterian Church.* Huntsville, AL: Live and Let Live, 1906.

James A. Borland

Evangelical Presbyterian Church

History

In the late 1970s and early 1980s, several churches desired to withdraw from the United

Presbyterian Church in the USA (UPCUSA) and the Presbyterian Church in the United States (PCUS) for theological reasons. Some of these churches were incompatible with other existing Presbyterian denominations such as the Presbyterian Church in America (PCA). Some had women serving as elders or were open to the exercise of charismatic gifts such as speaking in tongues, practices that many conservative Presbyterian denominations did not accept. In 1981, due in part to this dilemma, twelve churches withdrew from the UPCUSA and the PCUS and formed the Evangelical Presbyterian Church (EPC), adopting as their slogan "In essentials, unity; in non-essentials, charity; in all things, liberty."

At the first general assembly of the EPC, the denomination outlined several essentials of faith that all EPC churches must affirm. Certain issues, such as the ordination of women and the role of charismatic gifts, were not deemed essential; each individual congregation had the liberty to take its own stance on these issues. The denomination would go on to clarify its ethical convictions by publishing position papers on such issues as abortion and homosexuality, strongly opposing both.

Between 1983 and 1991, fifty-five churches left the newly formed Presbyterian Church (USA) to join the EPC. The EPC saw another influx of churches from the Presbtyerian Church (USA) at the beginning of the twenty-first century.

Headquarters

17197 N Laurel Park Drive
Suite 567
Livonia, MI 48152-7912

Core Beliefs

The EPC is Reformed in perspective, emphasizing the absolute sovereignty of God and affirming the *solas* of the Reformation: salvation is by grace alone, salvation is through faith alone, this faith is in Christ alone, and Scripture alone is the infallible authority for faith.

The EPC is guided by the Westminster Confession of Faith, and the major beliefs of the denomination are summarized in the document Essentials of Our Faith.

Worship

Because the denomination regards questions concerning the proper style of worship as nonessential, a variety of worship styles are used throughout the denomination. Some churches allow for the exercise of charismatic gifts such as tongues and prophecy during the service and have a charismatic style of worship, while others have a liturgical style of worship and still others have contemporary worship services.

Statistics

Between 2006 and 2010, the number of EPC churches grew from 185 to 287. In 2007, the EPC approved the establishment of two transitional presbyteries designed to facilitate the assimilation of existing churches into the denomination.

In addition to the continual influx of churches departing from the Presbyterian Church (USA), the EPC has grown dramatically through successful church planting and congregational growth. In 2010, the EPC had approximately 85,000 members in approximately 260 churches organized into 10 presbyteries. The denomination has many churches both in the North and in the South, although the denomination is stronger in the eastern United States than in the western.

Missionary and Evangelistic Work

The World Outreach wing of the EPC sends missionaries to twenty countries around the world. The majority of those missionaries serve in the 10/40 Window, and World Outreach gives special attention to reaching unreached people groups. Within the USA, the EPC's National Outreach wing organizes church-planting efforts and home missions.

Website

http://www.epc.org/

Bibliography

Bauswein, Jean-Jacques, and Lukas Vischer, eds. *The Reformed Family Worldwide: A Survey of Reformed Churches, Theological Schools, and International Organizations.* Grand Rapids: Eerdmans, 1999.

Heidebrecht, P. "Evangelical Presbyterian Church." In *Dictionary of the Presbyterian and Reformed Tradition in America*, edited by D. G. Hart and Mark A. Noll, 93–94. Downers Grove, IL: InterVarsity, 1999.

Jim Keener

Korean Presbyterian Church in America General Assembly

History

The Korean Presbyterian Church in America General Assembly was formed in 1976. Although primarily an ethnic church, it utilizes English as well as Korean.

Headquarters

17200 Clark Avenue
Bellflower, CA 90706
Telephone: 714-816-1100

Leadership

General secretary: Rev. Jacob Se Jang

Sarah Claudine Day

Netherlands Reformed Congregations

History

Following the Protestant Reformation in the Netherlands and the subsequent *Nadere Reformatie* (Second Reformation) in the seventeenth and eighteenth centuries there, the established Dutch Reformed Church gradually lost its commitment to Reformed doctrine and piety. In the 1830s, conservative believers within this state church began seceding from it in order to enjoy a more pure form of Calvinism without interference from King William I (reigned 1815–40). Two major denominations emerged from those who departed in this *Afscheiding* (secession): the Christian Reformed Churches of the Netherlands (1869) and the Reformed Congregations of the Netherlands (1907). The latter emerged under the leadership of Rev. Gerrit Hendrik Kersten (1882–1948), then only twenty-five.

Governmental, ecclesiastical, and societal persecution of the *Afscheiding* folk prompted many of them to emigrate to North America, where they formed independent congregations that gradually coalesced by 1910 into what came to be called the Netherlands Reformed Congregations. Early centers of ministry were in the Dutch enclaves in Paterson, New Jersey; Grand Rapids, Michigan; and northwestern Iowa. The denomination has gradually expanded geographically, although all congregations but one are located north of a line from New Jersey to Washington state.

Core Beliefs

The Netherlands Reformed Congregations hold to the great ecumenical creeds and the Three Forms of Unity: the Belgic Confession (1561), the Heidelberg Catechism (1563), and the Canons of Dordt (1618–19). Commitment to the confessional Reformed faith inherited from the fathers of the Second Reformation in the Netherlands and the British Isles is hearty and unfeigned.

Emphasis is placed on the experiential preaching of the Word of God in worship services, held twice each Sunday. One of these sermons is devoted to one of the fifty-two Lord's Days of the Heidelberg Catechism; thus, ministers cover the theological encyclopedia once per year. Singing is of the 150 psalms of the Bible in metrical form, with organ accompaniment. The King James Version of the Bible is used. The heads of women are covered in worship. The liturgy is closely based on that developed by the Dutch Reformer Petrus Dathenus (1531–88). Until 1922, worship services were conducted in Dutch; now, almost all services are in English.

Infants are baptized, but they are not presumed to be regenerate. Rather, the external call of the gospel of sovereign grace must be paired with the internal call of the Holy Spirit in each life. Sunday schools meet after morning worship for the training of covenant children. Catechism training in the teen years prepares the baptized youth to make public confession of faith. When professing faith by means of attendance at the sacrament of the Lord's Supper, each must have made a clear, threefold, personal testimony: to knowledge of the misery of sin, to faith in the redemption accomplished through the mediatorial work of Jesus Christ, and to gratitude to God for his great salvation.

Living antithetically to the world is stressed, including avoiding television, theater, movies, dancing, and card playing, and by limiting indulgence in modern fashions and sports. Dependence on divine providence leads to a predominantly negative view on contraceptives; in earlier generations, it also encouraged the refusal of insurance and vaccinations.

Bibliography

Beeke, Joel R. "Netherlands Reformed Congregations of North America." In *Dictionary of the Presbyterian and Reformed Tradition in America*, edited by D. G. Hart and Mark A. Noll, 168–69. Downers Grove, IL: InterVarsity, 1999.

Editors of *The Banner of Truth*, and A. Vergunst. "The Netherlands Reformed Congregations in North America: Centennial Commemoration." *The Banner of Truth* 73, no. 9 (September 2007): 202–13.

Kerkelijk Jaarboek, Gereformeerde Gemeenten 2010. Woerden, The Netherlands: Bureau voor Kerkelijke Administratie van de Gereformeerde Gemeenten, 2010.

Kersten, G. H., and J. Van Zweden. *A Brief Historical Survey of the Reformed Congregations in the Netherlands and the United States of America*. N.p., ca. 1948.

Thomas Reid

Orthodox Presbyterian Church

History

In 1924, a significant minority of approximately thirteen hundred (among ten thousand) Presbyterian ministers signed the liberal Auburn Affirmation, which denied the inerrancy of the Bible and declared that fundamental doctrines such as the substitutionary atonement and Christ's bodily resurrection should not be made tests for ordination or for good standing in the church. Princeton Theological Seminary was historically committed to Presbyterian orthodoxy, but in 1929, the board was reorganized and hired liberal professors for the faculty. Four conservative Princeton professors resigned in protest, and from that controversy arose the Orthodox Presbyterian Church.

The foremost opponent of liberalism in the early twentieth century was J. Gresham Machen (1881–1937). In 1933, Machen opposed the liberal theology of the Presbyterian Board of Foreign Missions and established the Independent Board for Presbyterian Foreign Missions. The presbytery reprimanded him in 1934 for his opposition to the liberal presence in the Presbyterian Church. On June 11, 1936, he founded the Presbyterian Church of America as an independent denomination with the assistance of a group of professors from Princeton Theological Seminary who also established Westminster Theological Seminary. The name was changed to the Orthodox Presbyterian Church in 1939 as a consequence of an injunction brought by the parent body, the Presbyterian Church (USA).

Membership in the Orthodox Presbyterian Church increased rapidly during the late 1950s and mid-1990s, although there were significant membership losses in 1948 and from 1989 to 1990. The former losses were the consequence of controversy with regard to statements made by Gordon H. Clark addressing the incomprehensibility of God (whether his knowledge is quantitatively or qualitatively different from humanity's knowledge), and the latter losses were the consequence of the process known as J & R (the process of joining and receiving from the Presbyterian Church in America), which resulted in the narrowly failed proposal to join the Presbyterian Church in America. In 2005, three congregations withdrew to join the Presbyterian Church in America (with one of those being a rather large congregation).

Headquarters

607 N Easton Road
Building E
PO Box P
Willow Grove, PA 19090
Telephone: 215-830-0900

Core Beliefs

As it was established in direct opposition to liberalism, the Orthodox Presbyterian Church is wholly committed to "straight" (orthodox) doctrine. The Orthodox Presbyterian Church affirms the full authority of Scripture and the virgin birth of Jesus Christ. The churches belong to the Reformed (or Calvinistic) heritage of the Protestant Reformation and therefore firmly reject Arminianism for compromising the sovereignty of God and salvation by grace alone. Frequently by means of caricature, the church has expressed opposition to dispensational teaching. Amillennialism, covenant premillennialism, and postmillennialism are regarded as compatible with church standards. The church believes the gifts of miraculous healings, prophesying, and tongues speaking ceased in the first century and therefore rejects the charismatic movement.

Officers within the Orthodox Presbyterian Church vow to "sincerely receive and adopt" the Westminster Confession of Faith and Larger and Shorter Catechisms (1647) "as containing the system of doctrine taught in the Holy Scriptures" (opc.org, "Confession and Catechisms"). The church affirms such ecumenical creeds as the Apostles' Creed and the Nicene Creed.

The church rejects hyper-Calvinism (the tendency to overemphasize divine sovereignty) and proclaims the gospel as offered freely to the lost. The 1936 general assembly concluded that Scripture does not prohibit moderate consumption of alcoholic beverages and rejected a call for total abstinence. The 1942 assembly adopted a statement that clarified the responsibility of believers in the exercise of their liberty of conscience in Christ. The same assembly concluded that masonry is a religious institution and definitely anti-Christian. Positions consistent with conservative (traditional) Christianity are held in the areas of guidance from the Holy Spirit, diaconal ministry, abortion, race relations, Sabbath observance, tongues speaking, women in office, Christian schools, homosexuality, admission to the Lord's Supper, and human origins.

Worship

Scripture is preached with high esteem. The sacraments of baptism and the Lord's Supper are given care for proper administration. Although some within the denomination have affirmed the exclusive singing of psalms (as the regulative principle of worship), the 1947 general assembly concluded that both hymns and psalms are appropriate for use in worship.

Divisions and Splits

Controversy regarding dispensational premillennialism led to division in 1937. Carl McIntire (1906–2002) formed the Bible Presbyterian Church on September 6, 1938. J. Oliver Buswell (1895–1977), whose premillennial views also were not tolerated by the Orthodox Presbyterian Church, united with McIntire and also with Allan MacRae (1902–97), who resigned from Westminster Seminary and became president of Faith Theological Seminary. The three men were covenantal theologically but adopted dispensational premillennialism in the area of eschatology.

Although Norman Shepherd was dismissed from the faculty of Westminster Seminary in 1982 for his views concerning justification (particularly that works parallel faith as an instrument of justification), his influence on the Orthodox Presbyterian Church has continued. The 2004 general assembly reaffirmed the language of the Westminster Standards concerning the doctrine of justification but did not condemn the views of some teaching and ruling elders in the denomination who were sympathetic to Shepherd's teachings. The assembly elected a special committee to study justification in response to the controversy. Division persists among those who defended Shepherd and his doctrine of justification and those who believe the denomination has tolerated teaching and ruling elders who advocate doctrines contrary to Scripture and the Westminster Standards.

Statistics

Total membership: 28,780, including 464 ministers
Membership growth rate: 0.70 percent
Average morning worship attendance: 23,429 (81.4 percent total membership)
Presbyteries and regional churches: 16
Congregations: 320
Total yearly offerings: $45.7 million

Largest Churches

The largest churches (membership exceeding three hundred) are located in California, Maryland, Massachusetts, Michigan, New Jersey, New York, Ohio, Virginia, and Wisconsin. The largest congregation is Columbia Orthodox Presbyterian Church in Maryland.

Missionary and Evangelistic Work

The denomination utilizes three ministry committees for worldwide outreach: the Committee on Foreign Missions, the Committee on Home Missions and Church Extension, and the Committee on Christian Education.

The Committee on Diaconal Ministry and the Committee on Ecumenicity and Interchurch Relations accomplish denominational work through other committees of the general assembly. Benevolence offerings for diaconal ministry, missions, and outreach represent approximately 16 percent of total contributions. The total yearly number of unorganized mission works was recently fifty-seven, with ten of the mission works organized as new and separate churches.

Publications

The original *Trinity Hymnal* was published in 1961 as a worship supplement to the Westminster Confession and was revised in 1990. *New Horizons* is a monthly magazine addressing the faith and life of the Orthodox Presbyterian Church; the August and September issues are combined for the Committee on Christian Education. *Ordained Servant* is a journal typically published as a monthly resource for church officers. The Committee on Christian Education publishes several books and pamphlets to preserve the faith of the Orthodox Presbyterian Church.

Website

http://www.opc.org/

Bibliography

Churchill, Robert K. *Lest We Forget: A Personal Reflection on the Formation of the Orthodox Presbyterian Church.* Philadelphia: Committee for the History of the Orthodox Presbyterian Church, 1986.

Dennison, Charles G., and Richard C. Gamble, eds. *Pressing toward the Mark: Essays Commemorating Fifty Years of the Orthodox Presbyterian Church.* Philadelphia: Committee for the History of the Orthodox Presbyterian Church, 1986.

Hart, D. G. *Defending the Faith: J. Gresham Machen and the Crisis of Conservative Protestantism in Modern America.* Baltimore: Johns Hopkins University Press, 1994.

Hart, D. G., and John Muether. *Fighting the Good Fight of Faith: A Brief History of the Orthodox Presbyterian Church.* Philadelphia: Committee for the History of the Orthodox Presbyterian Church, 1995.

Longfield, Bradley J. *The Presbyterian Controversy: Fundamentalists, Modernists, and Moderates.* New York: Oxford University Press, 1991.

North, Gary. *Crossed Fingers: How the Liberals Captured the Presbyterian Church.* Tyler, TX: Institute for Christian Economics, 1996.

"The Orthodox Presbyterian Church." http://www.opc.org. "Confession and Catechisms."

Robertson, O. Palmer. *The Current Justification Controversy.* Unicoi, TN: Trinity Foundation, 2003.

Ron J. Bigalke

Presbyterian Church (USA)

History

Formed June 10, 1983, the Presbyterian Church (USA) is the largest Presbyterian denomination in America. The PC(USA) was a reunion, merging the Presbyterian Church in the US (PCUS) and the United Presbyterian Church in the USA (UPCUSA). These immediate predecessors were shaped by earlier splits and reconfigurations in American Presbyterianism, placing the PC(USA) in continuity with America's first presbytery (1706, Philadelphia) and general assembly (1789).

Long-standing disputes over the Plan of Union with Congregationalists, revivals, subscriptionism, and social reform crystallized into a split between Old School and New School Presbyterians in the 1830s. The advent of the Civil War overlaid a split along regional lines and ultimately prompted reconfiguration into Northern and Southern streams. The New School divided over slavery in 1857 with a pro-slavery defection into the United Synod of the South. The Old School fractured in 1861, forming the Presbyterian Church in the Confederate States of America, which was joined by the United Synod in 1864. At the end of the war, this body became the PCUS.

An 1869 reunion of the Old School and the New School in the North established the Presbyterian Church in the United States of America (PCUSA). In 1958, it merged with the United Presbyterian Church of North America (UPCNA) to form the UPCUSA. The UPCNA was itself the product of an 1858 reunion among denominations formed in the late eighteenth century by Scottish Covenanter Presbyterians. The UPCUSA contributed over two-thirds of the subsequent PC(USA) membership.

Headquarters

100 Witherspoon Street
Louisville, KY 40202
Telephone: 800-728-7228

Leadership

The PC(USA) follows the presbyterian polity of rule by elders (Greek: *presbyteroi*) within a hierarchical system of councils: session, presbytery, synod, and general assembly. There are three ordained offices: teaching elder (ministers), ruling elder, and deacon. Ordination denotes function within the ministry of the church and is not meant to introduce distinctions of superiority. All positions of leadership and ordination are open to women. In recent years, women have comprised approximately one-third of active ministers, 50 percent of elders, and 70 percent of deacons.

Deacons serve in congregational ministries of compassion. Ruling elders and teaching elders, in addition to performing acts of ministry, constitute the denomination's four levels of governance. Elders in active service comprise the session, the governing body of local congregations. The session is ultimately responsible for the ministry, worship, finances, and personnel of the local church; only a handful of specific actions are subject to congregational vote. Ruling elders and deacons are ordained by the session. Ordination is perpetual (for life), with limitations on continuous active service in church government.

Presbyteries are geographical collections of sessions. Teaching elders are ordained by the presbytery and are members thereof. Sessions appoint representatives to the presbytery so that it is comprised of both teaching and ruling elders. While congregations vote on the call and dismissal of ministers, constitutionally these actions are petitions to the presbytery, which holds constitutional authority over ministers.

The two highest levels of church governance are the synod and the general assembly. Synods are geographical collections of presbyteries. They coordinate and support regional ministry. The general assembly is comprised of representatives from the presbyteries (with additional representation from the synods). Historically convened on an annual basis, biennial meetings were adopted by the PC(USA) in 2006. The general assembly administers national boards and affiliations with other bodies, serves as the highest court for church discipline, and provides authoritative interpretations on the Book of Order.

218

While the general assembly makes policy on its own authority, amendments to the constitution and ecumenical unions require ratification by the presbyteries. Between meetings of the general assembly, administration is conducted by staff and volunteers in a permanent Office of the General Assembly, the Presbyterian Mission Agency (renamed from the General Assembly Mission Council in 2012), standing committees and commissions, and various boards and departments.

Core Beliefs

The Constitution of the Presbyterian Church (USA) is the defining document for doctrine, polity, worship, and discipline. The constitution has two parts: the Book of Confessions and the Book of Order.

Rather than adopting a single creed, the PC(USA) adapted the UPCUSA's collection of historic confessions. The Book of Confessions contains eleven statements: Nicene Creed, Apostles' Creed, Scots Confession, Heidelberg Catechism, Second Helvetic Confession, Westminster Confession of Faith, [Westminster] Shorter Catechism, [Westminster] Larger Catechism, Theological Declaration of Barmen, Confession of 1967, and A Brief Statement of Faith—Presbyterian Church (USA). Since 2010, the PC(USA) has investigated the inclusion of the 1986 Belhar Confession from South Africa in the church's confessions.

The confessions are subordinate standards, "subject to the authority of Jesus Christ, the Word of God, as the Scriptures bear witness to him" (Book of Order, F-2.02). They are considered historically contextual affirmations of Reformed theological distinctives. Ordination to office includes affirming the confessions as authentic and reliable expositions of Scripture and assenting to being "instructed," "led," and "guided by" them. This historically contextualized approach is promoted as an example of a guiding phrase of the Reformed tradition: *ecclesia reformata, semper reformanda secundum verbum dei*, "the church reformed, always to be reformed according to the Word of God" (Book of Order, F-2.02).

The Book of Order consists of four parts: Foundations of Presbyterian Polity, Form of Government, Directory for Worship, and Rules of Discipline. The Form of Government defines church polity. The Rules for Discipline further that definition with court procedures for all four levels of governance. The Directory for Worship provides a theological exposition of Reformed

worship and directions for conducting worship. These include requirements for the administration of the sacraments (baptism and the Lord's Supper), the respective authority of teaching elders and sessions, and guidelines for specific services of worship.

Worship

Worship in the PC(USA) is frequently traditional and formal, but PC(USA) worship has been influenced by wider developments in American Protestant worship styles in the last half century. Many congregations have adopted more contemporary worship styles or added seeker sensitive services. Nevertheless, the Presbyterian penchant for doing things "decently and in order" (1 Cor. 14:40 KJV) and the deep roots of the Reformed understanding of worship are preserved by the Directory for Worship, which is expressly open to such diversity of forms enacted within theological norms.

Statistics

As of 2011, the PC(USA) consisted of 10,466 congregations, 173 presbyteries, 16 synods, 1,952,287 members, 82,714 ruling elders, 57,814 deacons (not all sessions utilize deacons), and 21,064 teaching elders, of which two-thirds were recorded as active in ministry. Over 70 percent of PC(USA) congregations have fewer than 200 members; over half have fewer than 100. PC(USA) members are predominantly middle class, college educated, and white (over 90 percent). The denomination's largest concentrations are in Pennsylvania, California, and North Carolina. In 2010, the largest congregation was Peachtree Presbyterian Church in Atlanta (9,141 members), followed by Fourth Presbyterian Church of Chicago (6,182).

Trends

Major issues in the PC(USA) reflect the liberal-conservative tension prevalent in American Presbyterianism throughout the twentieth century. The most pressing issue is twofold: ordination of noncelibate homosexuals and same-sex marriage. The issue of ordination has centered on a former requirement that ordinands "live either in fidelity within the covenant of marriage between a man and a woman, or chastity in singleness" (Book of Order, G-6.0106b, prior to 2011). An amendment approved by the 2010 general assembly struck this language from the constitution and was subsequently ratified by the presbyteries. Three previous overtures for elimination of the "fidelity and chastity clause" had failed approval or ratification since 1996.

Regarding the issue of same-sex marriage, the constitution explicitly defines marriage as between a woman and a man (Book of Order, W-4.9001). The PC(USA) previously ruled that neither church officers nor church property be involved in same-sex marriages but left open a local option for services of blessing on same-sex relationships. Recent general assemblies have seen overtures for changing the definition of marriage to support same-sex marriage. Dissatisfaction with these developments among some congregations prompted a small number to leave the PC(USA) in recent years, most often for the Evangelical Presbyterian Church.

Missionary and Evangelistic Work

The PC(USA) and its predecessor denominations maintained a long-standing commitment to missions throughout the changing dynamics of missions in the nineteenth and twentieth centuries. Denominational centralization of missions has declined across the board, with growing numbers of churches pursuing nondenominational means of commissioning and supporting missionaries. The PC(USA) is no exception to this trend. Nevertheless, in 2011, congregations reported over $301 million in expenditures associated with missions. In that same year, more than $73 million were dedicated to ministry and missions at the denominational level.

Affiliations

Upon approval of the Formula of Agreement by the general assembly in 1997, the PC(USA) joined into full communion with three other churches of Reformation heritage, namely, the Evangelical Lutheran Church in America (ELCA), the Reformed Church in America (RCA), and the United Church of Christ (UCC). The PC(USA) is a member of the following ecumenical organizations: the National Council of Churches of Christ in the United States, Churches Uniting in Christ, the World Council of Churches, and the World Communion of Reformed Churches (formerly the World Alliance of Reformed Churches).

Academic Institutions

The PC(USA) operates ten theological seminaries and is in covenant relationship with two

others. The denomination is affiliated with sixty-three colleges and universities through the Association of Presbyterian Colleges and Universities. The denomination is also affiliated with nine secondary schools.

Electronic Media

While its predecessor denominations made inroads into broadcast media in the 1950s, by 1983, nonmainline voices had come to dominate the airwaves. As a result, the PC(USA) has negligible resources in broadcast media. The PC(USA) operates a news service and otherwise focuses its media development on topical productions and educational materials rather than on broadcast media.

Publications

PC(USA) publishing interests include Westminster John Knox Press and the journals *Theology Today* and *Journal of Presbyterian History*. The PC(USA) also publishes church school curriculum, worship aids, study guides, and reports in support of the worship, witness, and mission of the church marketed primarily through websites.

Website

http://www.pcusa.org/

Bibliography

Balmer, Randall Herbert, and John R. Fitzmier. *The Presbyterians*. Denominations in America, #5. Westport, CT: Greenwood, 1993.

Bullock, Robert H., Jr., ed. *Presbyterians Being Reformed: Reflections on What the Church Needs Today*. Louisville: Geneva Press, 2006.

Coalter, Milton J., John M. Mulder, and Louis B. Weeks, eds. *The Presbyterian Presence: The Twentieth-Century Experience*. 7 vols. Louisville: Westminster John Knox, 1990–1992.

Lucas, Sean Michael. "Presbyterians in America: Denominational History and the Quest for Identity." In *American Denominational History: Perspectives on the Past, Prospects for the Future*, edited by Keith Harper, 50–70. Tuscaloosa: University of Alabama Press, 2008.

"Office of the General Assembly." http://oga.pcusa.org. "Church Statistical Reporting" and "2011 Summaries of Statistics—Comparative Summaries."

Presbyterian Church (USA). *The Constitution of the Presbyterian Church (USA) Part I: Book of Confessions*. Louisville: Office of the General Assembly, 2004.

Presbyterian Church (USA). *The Constitution of the Presbyterian Church (USA) Part II: Book of Order 2011–2013*. Louisville: Office of the General Assembly, 2011.

"Presbyterian Mission Agency." http://www.presbyterian mission.org/gamc/. "Theology, Worship, and Education,"

"Top Ten Most Frequently Asked Questions about the PC(USA)," and "2011 Annual Report."

Craig R. Clarkson

Presbyterian Church in America

History

The Presbyterian Church in America (PCA) is an evangelical and Reformed Presbyterian denomination. Concerned about the perceived theological liberalism within the mainline southern Presbyterian church, the Presbyterian Church in the United States, and a declining interest in evangelism and foreign missions, conservative southern Presbyterians established the National Presbyterian Church in 1973. The following year the denomination changed its name to the Presbyterian Church in America.

In 1982, the Reformed Presbyterian Church, Evangelical Synod, a small Presbyterian denomination found predominately in the mid-Atlantic region, merged with the Presbyterian Church in America. Following the 1983 merger of the southern Presbyterian Church (the Presbyterian Church in the United States) and the northern Presbyterian Church (the United Presbyterian Church in the United States of America), conservative congregations from both denominations joined the more conservative Presbyterian Church in America. After the Orthodox Presbyterian Church (OPC) declined an offer to merge with the PCA in 1987 because some harbored suspicions that the PCA tolerated a lax commitment to a strict confessionalist interpretation of the Westminster Standards, a number of OPC congregations merged with the PCA.

Headquarters

1700 North Brown Road
Suite 105
Lawrenceville, GA 30043
Telephone: 678-825-1000
Email: ac@pcanet.org

Core Beliefs

The Presbyterian Church in America embraces a traditionally orthodox view of the Christian faith as expressed by the Reformed tradition. The Westminster Confession of Faith, the Larger Catechism, and the Shorter Catechism serve as the denomination's confessional statements. The denomination advocates a high view of the inspiration and authority of the Bible, including its inerrancy. The PCA also confesses a belief in the Trinity, the total depravity of humanity, the sovereignty of God in the process of salvation, the penal substitutionary atonement of Christ, the covenant of grace and practice of infant baptism, the indwelling work of the Holy Spirit in the lives of believers, the future return of Christ to consummate the work begun at the first advent, and the lordship of Christ in all areas of a believer's life.

The denomination does not permit women to be ordained teaching or ruling elders.

Worship

Although the particular form of music employed in services represents a wide range, Presbyterian worship services adhere at least broadly to the "regulative principle," which holds that only those elements of worship prescribed in the Bible should be allowed in worship services. Consequently, services are comprised of prayer, confession, singing, Scripture reading, and a sermon. The denomination recognizes two sacraments, covenant baptism and the Lord's Supper.

Divisions and Splits

Although there have been some significant debates within the denomination, the denomination has not experienced any schisms.

Controversies

Although the PCA has not experienced any significant ecclesiastical schisms in its brief history, the denomination has debated a number of theological issues, including the ordination of women as deacons, paedocommunion, theonomy, new perspectives on Paul, so-called scientific creationism, the role of women in the military, and the relationship between church and state.

Statistics

Membership: more than 340,000

Although the denomination has congregations in all fifty states, it remains especially strong in the South.

Largest Churches

The largest congregation in the denomination is Redeemer Presbyterian Church in Manhattan, New York. The other largest churches are found in Florida, Maryland, Alabama, Georgia, and Tennessee.

Growth

Because of congregations joining the PCA after leaving other denominations, the PCA was one of the fastest-growing denominations during the 1980s. In recent years, growth has slowed to a rate of approximately 3 percent a year.

Trends

The PCA will likely continue to engage in an aggressive program of church planting and international missions. The denomination will continue to discuss and debate how its commitment to a high view of the authority of Scripture and adherence to Reformed confessionalism bear on the church's relationship to American society, especially involving issues related to the so-called culture wars.

Missionary and Evangelistic Work

Through its domestic mission program, Mission to North America, the PCA maintains an aggressive program of church planting. In 2010, the denomination had more than one hundred mission churches in the United States and Canada. The denomination is also deeply committed to world missions. In 2010, the church sponsored more than six hundred full-time, long-term missionaries and fifty-seven hundred short-term missionaries working in more than sixty nations.

Ecumenism

The PCA is a member of the North American Presbyterian and Reformed Council, the National Association of Evangelicals, and the World Reformed Fellowship.

Academic Institutions

The PCA has two educational institutions, Covenant College, a liberal arts college located in Lookout Mountain, Georgia, and Covenant Theological Seminary in St. Louis, Missouri. In addition, the denomination maintains Ridge Haven, a conference center located in Rosman, North Carolina.

Parachurch Organization

The denomination's mission agency, Mission to the World, oversees a Disaster Response Ministry.

Electronic Media

Covenant Theological Seminary sponsors an online daily devotional program, Living Christ 360 (livingchrist360.com), featuring Bryan Chapell, the institution's president, as well as *By Faith* magazine (byfaithonline.com), an online magazine published weekly.

Publications

The denomination publishes one magazine, *By Faith*, and Covenant Theological Seminary produces a journal, *Presbyterion*, twice a year.

Website

http://www.pcanet.org/

Bibliography

Lucas, Sean Michael. *On Being Presbyterian*. Phillipsburg, NJ: P & R, 2006.

Settle, Paul. *To God All Praise and Glory: 1973 to 1998— The First 25 Years*. Atlanta: PCA Administrative Committee, 1998.

Smith, Frank Joseph. *The History of the Presbyterian Church in America*. Lawrenceville, GA: Presbyterian Scholars Press, 1999.

Smith, Morton H. *How Is the Gold Become Dim*. Jackson, MS: Premier Printing Company, 1973.

P. C. Kemeny

Protestant Reformed Churches in America

History

The Protestant Reformed Churches in America is a denomination of Reformed churches that trace their heritage to the Protestant Reformation. The denomination began in January 1925 as a consequence of controversy concerning the doctrine of common grace among the Christian Reformed Church. On June 18, 1924, in Kalamazoo, Michigan, the synod of the Christian Reformed Church adopted the Three Points of Common Grace. The doctrine refers to God's extension of favor (or grace) through providential care to humans in general, irrespective of whether they are part of his elect.

Three consistories and the pastors of the Classis Grand Rapids East and Grand Rapids West within the Christian Reformed Church refused to subscribe to the Three Points and were either deposed or suspended from office. Herman Hoeksema (1886–1965) was the principal voice of those who believed the Three Points document was contrary to Scripture and the Reformed confessions and if adopted would lead the church to be embraced into the world and would allow worldliness into the church. As a consequence of the controversy, the objectors of common grace were deposed from the

Christian Reformed Church, and the Protestant Reformed Churches in America was organized formally.

Headquarters

4949 Ivanrest Avenue
Grandville, MI 49418
Telephone: 616-531-1490

Leadership

Church polity is presbyterian, which is distinguished by two classes organizationally. A general synod meets annually in June.

Core Beliefs

The Protestant Reformed Church is creedal and confessional. As the basis of belief in the inerrant and infallible inspiration of Scripture, congregations affirm the Three Forms of Unity: the Heidelberg Catechism (1563), the Belgic Confession (1561), and the Canons of Dort (1618–19). Protestant Reformed churches confess and proclaim the doctrines of total depravity, double predestination, limited (effectual) atonement, irresistible grace, and perseverance of the saints as essential truths of the gospel of grace. The grace of God is always particular and for the elect alone, never for the reprobate.

The gospel is not proclaimed as God's gracious offer of salvation to all humanity or as a conditional offer to all baptized infants but as an oath of God to lead his elect infallibly unto salvation and glory through faith. The doctrine of the covenant is an essential aspect of the denomination. Practical implications of the covenant include defending and promoting marriage and maintaining quality Christian schools. Congregations sing only the psalms (with organ accompaniment) and use the King James Version in public worship on the Sabbath.

Worship

Worship services are liturgical, and congregations use a Psalter (first published in 1927).

Divisions and Splits

A challenging doctrinal controversy among Protestant Reformed churches in the early 1950s concerned the unconditional nature of the covenant of grace. The denomination decreased in membership as a result of the controversy but has since maintained growth and stability.

Statistics

There are nearly seventy-five hundred members in twenty-eight congregations in Canada and the United States. The largest churches are found in the upper Midwest. The largest congregation is Georgetown Protestant Reformed Church in Hudsonville, Michigan.

Missionary and Evangelistic Work

The Protestant Reformed Church is active in missionary and evangelistic work both domestically and overseas. The Constitution of the Domestic Mission Committee states, "The Protestant Reformed Churches believe that, in obedience to the command of Christ, the King of the church, to preach the blessed gospel to all creatures, baptizing, and teaching them to observe all things which Christ has commanded, it is the explicit duty and sacred privilege of said churches to carry out this calling according to the measure of our God-given ability. We believe that this missionary activity includes the work of church extension and church reformation, as well as the task of carrying out the gospel to the unchurched and heathen. However, we are convinced that our present duty lies primarily in the field of church extension and church reformation" (prca.org, "Constitution of the Domestic Mission Committee").

Academic Institution

Protestant Reformed Theological Seminary (Grandville, MI)

Electronic Media

The *Reformed Witness Hour*, which is sponsored and supported by the entire Protestant Reformed denomination, has been broadcast for more than six decades. Herman Hoeksema was the first full-time radio pastor, and the current radio pastor is Carl Haak.

Publications

The Reformed Publishing Association publishes Reformed books in the Calvinistic tradition and the *Standard Bearer*, a bimonthly periodical of Reformed theology as communicated in the Reformed and Presbyterian creeds. The *Standard Bearer* is not an official publication, but it is representative of the Protestant Reformed churches. The Federation of Protestant Reformed Young People's Societies publishes *Beacon Lights*, a monthly periodical for young people. The Protestant Reformed Churches Teachers' Institute publishes *Perspectives in Covenant Education,* a quarterly periodical relating to Christian school training. The faculty of the Protestant Reformed Theological Seminary publishes the *Protestant Reformed Theological Journal* biyearly in April and November.

Website

http://www.prca.org/

Bibliography

Engelsma, David J. *Hyper-Calvinism and the Call of the Gospel: An Examination of the Well-Meant Offer of the Gospel.* Grand Rapids: Reformed Free Publishing Association, 1980.

Hanko, Herman C. *Notes on the Church Order.* Grand Rapids: Protestant Reformed Theological Seminary, 1973.

———. "A Study of the Relation between the Views of Prof. R. Janssen and Common Grace." ThM thesis, Calvin Theological Seminary, 1988.

Hoeksema, Gertrude. *A Watered Garden: A Brief History of the Protestant Reformed Churches in America.* Grand Rapids: Reformed Free Publishing Association, 1992.

Hoeksema, Herman. *The Protestant Reformed Churches in America: Their Origin, Early History, and Doctrine.* Grand Rapids: First Protestant Reformed Church, 1936.

"Protestant Reformed Churches in America." http://www.prca.org. "Constitution of the Domestic Mission Committee."

Ron J. Bigalke

Reformed Church in America

History

The Reformed Church in America (RCA) traces its roots to the Protestant Reformation and shares a common heritage with other Reformed movements such as Lutheranism and Presbyterianism. Its European seedbed was seventeenth-century Netherlands.

The RCA holds the distinction of being the oldest denomination with a continuous ministry within the United States. The first congregation was formed in 1628 in New Amsterdam, nineteen years after the area was settled by the Dutch.

The Christian Reformed Church in North America (CRC) was formed out of the RCA in 1857. A small group of then-RCA churches seceded due to their disagreements over three primary issues: expansion of worship to include hymns as opposed to a psalms-exclusive approach, participation in the Freemasons and other similar secretive organizations, and a lack of commitment to regular Christian education.

Having a consistently more open approach to other denominations and groups led the RCA, in direct contrast to the CRC prior to World War II,

to be a charter member of the National and World Council of Churches and the American Bible Society.

Headquarters

4500 60th Street SE
Grand Rapids, MI 49512
Telephone: 616-698-7071; 800-968-3943
Email: webservant@rca.org

Core Beliefs

The RCA draws much of its doctrinal heritage from the Protestant Reformation, specifically from John Calvin and his followers.

The RCA is a confessional church in that it embraces written expressions of core Christian belief as its doctrinal grounding. It has affirmed three historical, ecumenical creeds: the Apostles' Creed, the Nicene Creed, and the Athanasian Creed. It also holds to the Three Forms of Unity, which are distinctly Reformed in theology: the Heidelberg Catechism (1563), the Belgic Confession (1561), and the Canons of Dort (1618–19). In 2010, the general synod formally adopted the Belhar Confession (1986) as a fourth doctrinal standard.

While the RCA's foundational creeds form its doctrinal guidelines, the Book of Church Order, revised and distributed yearly by the general synod, sets the governance and judicial policies and procedures for the RCA.

Controversies

The most pressing debate within the RCA regards homosexuality. In 1978, the general synod reaffirmed its traditional approach, but the issue continued to be broached over the next two decades (1979, 1980, 1990, 1994), enough so that a moratorium was passed in 1998. The issue boiled to a head in 2006 with the trial and conviction of Rev. Norman Kansfield for presiding over a same-sex marriage. In recent years, a renewed effort at dialogue was instituted, with the 2009 general synod charging its general synod council to monitor this discussion and report its findings in 2011.

The topic of homosexuality in the RCA is geographically defined, and the ruling carries the potential to split the church into Eastern and Midwestern factions. In 2000, whereas 79 percent of those in the East agreed that practicing homosexuals should be allowed to be members of an RCA church, only 42 percent of those in the Midwest concurred. There are similar disagreements on whether a practicing homosexual can hold the office of elder or deacon or be ordained as a minister of Word and sacrament.

Finances

Total assets (2009): $69.9 million, of which $15.3 million was directed to local and global mission work

Sources (2008): 50 percent from contributions, 32 percent from assessments, and 18 percent from sales, investment income, and other sources

Statistics

Geography: 84 percent of congregations are within the larger areas of the Midwest and the East, with a full 27 percent in western Michigan alone

Ethnicity: 50 percent Dutch

Membership: 256,278

Congregations: 935

Ordained clergy: 2,053

Largest Churches

The RCA church with the most notoriety was for many years the Crystal Cathedral in Garden Grove, California, which was pastored by the late Robert Schuller. The congregation moved in 2013 and became Shepherd's Grove.

Trends

Because many RCA congregations were stagnant or declining numerically, the 2003 general synod adopted a ten-year strategic plan titled "Our Call." It stipulated several directives: revitalizing existing congregations, planting new ones, discipleship, leadership development, and missions (both local and global). In 2008, the general synod added "a multiracial future freed from racism."

Between 2003 and 2007, ninety-two new congregations were planted, with an expected pace of thirty to forty annually. Through these church starts, ten thousand new members have been added.

Missionary and Evangelistic Work

The Reformed Church World Service serves those globally who are impacted by hunger, poverty, or natural disaster. One Great Hour of Sharing is a principle way the RCWS raises awareness within congregations. The RCA's Global Mission Principles, core maxims by which it executes any missionary enterprise, are holistic mission, mission partnership, long-term commitment, mutual mission, and respectful witness. The RCA Evangelism and Church Development Service leads most denominational evangelism efforts

within the United States. A current evangelism endeavor is church planting, with recent RCA start-ups reporting that between 45 and 90 percent of all attendees have come to the church through conversion.

Academic Institutions

Central College (Pella, IA)

Hope College (Holland, MI)

New Brunswick Theological Seminary (New Brunswick, NJ)

Northwestern College (Orange City, IA)

Western Theological Seminary (Holland, MI)

Parachurch Organizations

The RCA has several large-scale denominational parachurch groups, most notably the Reformed Church World Service. Over the last decade, the RCA has become intentional about social justice issues. One example is the Friendship House at Western Theological Seminary, which allows seminarians to live with young adults who have a cognitive impairment.

Publications

The denominational magazine, the *Church Herald*, ran for 180 years, concluding with the September/October 2009 issue. The remaining denominational periodical is *RCA Today*, published nine times a year.

Website

http://www.rca.org/

Archives

The official RCA archives are housed in the Gardner A. Sage Library of New Brunswick Theological Seminary. Occupying over a half mile of shelf space, holdings date back as far as the 1630s.

Bibliography

The Book of Church Order: The Reformed Church in America. 2009 ed. New York: Reformed Church Press, 2009.

Bratt, James. *Dutch Calvinism in Modern America: A History of a Conservative Subculture.* Grand Rapids: Eerdmans, 1984.

Brouwer, Arie. *Reformed Church Roots.* New York: Reformed Church Press, 1977.

DeMoor, Robert. *Reformed: What It Means, Why It Matters.* Grand Rapids: Faith Alive, 2001.

Hageman, Howard G. *Our Reformed Church.* 12th ed. New York: Reformed Church Press, 1995.

Smidt, Corwin, Donald Luidens, James Penning, and Roger Nemeth. *Divided by a Common Heritage: The Christian Reformed Church and the Reformed Church in America at the Beginning of the New Millennium.* Grand Rapids: Eerdmans, 2006.

Worship the Lord: The Liturgy of the Reformed Church in America. New York: Reformed Church Press, 2005.

Christian R. Shearer and Mark A. Lamport

Reformed Church in the United States

History

The roots of the Reformed Church in the United States (RCUS) go back to the followers of the Swiss Reformer Ulrich Zwingli and his influence in the Palatinate following the Reformation. German Reformed churches suffered tremendously during the Thirty Years' War, and tens of thousands of Germans emigrated to America. They prospered, multiplied, and built hundreds of churches and many colleges and seminaries. Second to the English and Scottish, Germans became the dominant religious and cultural influence in what was to become the United States.

The old Eureka Classis (Eureka, South Dakota) was dismayed when, dominated by the theological perspectives of John Nevin and Phillip Schaff, the RCUS merged in the 1930s with churches that the elders of the Eureka Classis considered weakly Calvinistic or Arminian. As a result, they refused to join the mergers, and the present denomination is the continuing Reformed Church in the United States.

Core Beliefs

Deeply committed to the covenant theology of John Calvin and the European Reformation, the RCUS seeks to continue the high Calvinism of German immigrants in the United States before the War of Independence. Ministers are required to affirm the infallibility and inspiration of Scripture and the creation of the world in six sidereal days.

The RCUS confesses its faith by means of the famous Three Forms of Unity: the Heidelberg Catechism (1563), the Canons of Dort (1618–19), and the Belgic Confession (1561). Members are permitted no exceptions to the Three Forms of Unity. The RCUS does not ordain women to church office, and in many of the congregations, vote is by heads of families. Theology is covenantal, with the baptism of babies of confessing members. Government is a modified presbyterianism with some elements of congregationalism. The observance of the Sunday Sabbath is less strict outwardly than that of the Scottish Presbyterians and the Westminster Confession of Faith. Children are expected to confess their faith through confirmation after completing training in the catechism, church history, hymnology, and Christian piety. Many of the children in the denomination are homeschooled or go to Christian schools. The denomination offers regional camping for youth.

Carroll W. Powell

Reformed Presbyterian Church of North America

History

The Reformed Presbyterian Church of North America (RPCNA) traces its roots to the Covenanters of seventeenth-century Scotland: Presbyterians who insisted on firm adherence to the National Covenant of 1638 and the Solemn League and Covenant of 1643. These documents called for the thoroughgoing Presbyterianization of the national Churches of Scotland, England, and Ireland. Because the British government never fulfilled its obligations under these covenants, a minority of Covenanters steadfastly refused to acknowledge their government's legitimacy, and many fled to North America in the eighteenth and nineteenth centuries. These Covenanters, who called themselves Reformed Presbyterians, organized their first presbytery in the American colonies in 1774.

In a new nation not obviously bound by the Solemn League and Covenant, however, the vast majority of these Reformed Presbyterians abandoned their distinctive Covenanter principles and united with the Associate Presbyterians to form the Associate Reformed Presbyterian Church in 1782. A new American presbytery of Reformed Presbyterians constituted itself, nonetheless, in 1798 after that year's Irish rebellion drove Reformed Presbyterian ministers and laity to emigrate from Ireland to the United States.

Because the US Constitution acknowledged the authority of neither God nor Christ and sanctioned slavery, the new body of Reformed Presbyterians prohibited its members from voting, serving on juries, pledging allegiance to the United States government, or in any way acknowledging its legitimacy. The denomination moderated its position on this subject, however, when it endorsed United States participation in the War of 1812 and authorized its members to fight on the American side. Henceforth, Reformed Presbyterians allowed professions of loyalty to the United States but still forbade all activities, including voting, whereby one might appear to support its Constitution.

226

In 1833, dissenters from the church's political principles separated from it and formed a "New Light" body of Reformed Presbyterians, which now forms part of the Presbyterian Church in America. The original denomination, however, continued to grow rapidly because of Covenanter immigration from Northern Ireland. In 1841, a small "Steelite" faction withdrew from the church in protest of what it deemed insufficient vigilance in maintaining traditional Covenanter principles. When the Civil War began in 1861, the denomination endorsed the Union's cause and authorized its members to serve in the Union army. It swore to a new covenant in 1871. In 1939, the church's synod authorized its members to swear to uphold the Constitution as long as they prefaced their oath with an "explanatory declaration" to the effect that, as Reformed Presbyterians, they acknowledge no authority higher than Christ and intend to obey him, rather than the US Constitution, if the two come into conflict.

The denomination continued to liberalize its stance on political dissent and, in 1967, definitively granted its members the right to vote and hold political office in the United States. The church incorporated its new position on Reformed Presbyterian participation in politics into its revised Testimony of 1979.

Core Beliefs

The church subscribes to the Westminster Confession of Faith and the Westminster Larger and Shorter Catechisms, with minor exceptions stated in the denomination's Testimony.

Website

http://www.reformedpresbyterian.org/

Bibliography

Bushnell, Michael. *The Songs of Zion: A Contemporary Case for Exclusive Psalmody*. Pittsburgh: Crown & Covenant, 1980.

The Constitution of the Reformed Presbyterian Church of North America. Pittsburgh: Crown & Covenant, 2004.

Glasgow, W. Melanchthon. *History of the Reformed Presbyterian Church in America*. Baltimore: Hill & Harvey, 1888.

"Reformed Presbyterian History Archives." http://www.rparchives.org/. "Minutes of Synod."

Dennis W. Jowers

United Church of Christ

History

The United Church of Christ (UCC), one of the twenty largest American denominations, was formed on June 25, 1957, as the result of the merger of four traditions: the Congregational Church, the Christian Churches, the German Reformed Church, and the United Evangelical Church.

The Congregational Church, also known as the Congregational Way, saw itself as the first denomination in the American colonies, originating with the Puritans and the Separatists during the late sixteenth century. The Christian Churches denomination represented the eighteenth-century American Restoration movement, which viewed Christ as the only head of the church, the New Testament as the only source of faith, and "Christian" as their sole name. Finding much common ground in their beliefs, the Congregationalists and the Christian Churches merged in 1931. The German Reformed Church, which produced the Heidelberg Catechism of 1563, included the conciliatory element of the Protestant Reformation; German immigrants in the United States founded a church in 1793 and launched the Mercer movement to promote Christian unity. The United Evangelical Church was formed in Prussia in 1817 when the Lutheran and Evangelical Churches were united by royal proclamation. Its 1934 merger with the German Reformed Church gave birth to the Evangelical and Reformed Church, which joined the German Reformed Church's desire for unity with the United Evangelical Church's dedication to individual liberty.

Of the four traditions in the United Church of Christ, the dominant one is that of the Puritans, whose contradictory impulses allowed them to embrace freedom of conscience while at the same time establish a theocracy that expelled Roger Williams and Anne Hutchinson, put Baptists on trial, burned witches, and hanged Quakers. Congregationalism was a matter of polity rather than doctrine. In New England, some Congregationalists became Unitarians.

Among the early Congregationalist achievements were a commitment to higher liberal education, exemplified by the founding of Harvard University in 1636, Yale in 1707, and Dartmouth in 1769; free schools; and constitutional government. The denomination published the first catechism in the colonies in 1653 and produced two of the most notable revivalists: Jonathan Edwards and George Whitefield. After the American Revolution, Congregationalism's alliance with the state was weakened. It became a loose confederation of churches that were geographically scattered. Congregationalism helped to create many parachurch organizations seeking to combat injustice, notably slavery, to which Congregationalists were among the first Americans to voice opposition. In 1853, Congregationalists ordained Antoinette Brown, making it the first denomination to ordain a woman pastor. In 1972, they ordained the first homosexual minister, in California.

Congregationalists established one of the first global missionary programs, as the Mayhews, David Brainerd, and John Eliot began missionary work among the Native Americans shortly after the Plymouth landing. The American Board of Commissioners for Foreign Ministries, founded in 1810, sent missionaries to thirty countries—these missionaries included Adoniram Judson and Luther Rice, who went to Burma and India, respectively. Home missionaries helped to frame the 1787 Northwest Territory Ordinance and to found, in 1881, the Marietta, Ohio, Christian Endeavor, the largest Protestant youth organization, later known globally as the United Society of Christian Endeavor.

The movement to advance the care and rights of the handicapped was launched with Thomas Hopkins Gallaudet's establishment, in 1817, of the first school for the deaf in North America. Today the UCC has become one of the most liberal of the larger American Protestant churches in terms of its advocacy of gender rights and gay rights. Because of its congregational polity, in which the local churches have authority to decide doctrine, the UCC represents a variety of views. Conservative congregations expressed opposition to certain liberal positions by forming separate denominations, such as the Conservative Congregational Christian Conference and the National Association of Congregational Christian Churches.

Headquarters

700 Prospect Avenue
Cleveland, OH 44115
Telephone: 216-736-2100; 866-822-8224
Email: kelly@ucc.org

Leadership

General minister and president: Geoffrey A. Black

Blending Congregationalism and Presbyterianism, the United Church of Christ has at its core the autonomy of the local church. The constitution states, "The autonomy of the Local Church is inherent and modifiable only by its own action. Each Local Church [will] continue

to operate in the way customary to it" (ucc.org, "UCC Constitution and Bylaws"). The local church is assisted by three types of organizations; these are, in ascending order, associations, conferences, and the general synod. Associations license, install, and ordain ministers and pursue the general welfare of member churches. They are grouped into conferences, which act in an advisory capacity and operate agencies and offices. The general synod is comprised of equal numbers of clergy and laity. As the highest-ranking body, it nominates and elects church officers, including the moderator, and governs numerous boards, commissions, and other instrumentalities. These include the Board for World Ministries, Board for Homeland Ministries, Office for Church in Society, Office for Church Life and Leadership, Commission for Racial Justice, Stewardship Council, and Coordinating Center for Women in Church and Society.

Core Beliefs

The preamble to the 1957 Constitution of the United Church of Christ states:

> The United Church of Christ acknowledges as its sole Head, Jesus Christ.... It acknowledges as kindred in Christ all who share in this confession. It looks to the Word of God in the Scriptures, and to the presence and power of the Holy Spirit.... It claims... the faith of the historic Church expressed in the ancient creeds and reclaimed in the basic insights of the Protestant Reformers. It affirms the responsibility of the Church in each generation to make this faith its own in worship, in honesty of thought and expression, and in purity of heart before God.... It recognizes two sacraments: Baptism and the Lord's Supper. (ucc.org, "UCC Constitution and Bylaws")

Statistics

Churches: 5,287
Members: 1,080,199

Missionary and Evangelistic Work

The principal "covenanted" ministries of the UCC are Justice and Witness Ministries, Local Church Ministries, Office of General Ministries, and Wider Church Ministries. Founded in the 1970s, Justice and Witness Ministries works for community education and mobilization as well as for public policy about issues of social justice. It supports scholarships for ethnic students, operates a site directing women to service organization resources, and assists local churches in training community leaders to work for a just society. Its division for Media Justice Advocacy upholds UCC ideals born in the 1960s by encouraging fairer and more diverse media, especially through its annual Everett C. Parker Lecture in Ethics and Telecommunications for the media and public interest activists and its partnership with So We Might See, an ecumenical coalition seeking justice in media.

The Stillspeaking Ministry, started in 2004, joins together 2,500 churches whose members seek to share their spiritual journey and integrate relevant, contemporary ideas into the Christian faith. It portrays Jesus as a revolutionary and stresses God's love for and acceptance of everyone without reservation. With assets of more than $3.9 billion, the member ministries of the Council for Health and Human Services Ministries serve over 1 million individuals each year, operate 359 health care facilities of various sizes, and manage programs that serve children, people with disabilities, and the aging, among others. The HIV and Aids Ministry offers education, including prevention resources, and acts as a public policy advocate for those with HIV. The Council for Youth and Young Adult Ministries coordinates programs for youth.

The UCC is home to a number of special interest ministries, including several that address the needs of ethnic groups. The concerns of African American members of the UCC, including those in the more than 278 predominantly African American congregations, are represented by United Black Christians. Often working in conjunction with United Black Christians is the Ministers for Racial, Social, and Economic Justice, a clergy association that engages in political activism. The Council for Hispanic Ministries seeks not only to voice the concerns of Hispanics but also to enhance their worship experience in the church. Pacific Islanders and Asians have been represented since 1974 by Pacific Islander and Asian American Ministries. The Council for American Indian Ministry maintains Native American values as part of its practice of Christianity and seeks to increase and promote awareness of a Native American presence in the UCC. It operates five ministries in twenty-two congregations principally located in the Great Plains states, including the Eagle Butte Learning Center for clergy and lay leaders.

Ecumenism

The symbol of the UCC contains the phrase "That They May All Be One" (John 17:21 ASV),

stressing the denomination's commitment to ecumenism, which stems from the UCC's own origin as a merger of traditions. The UCC views division within the church as a result of human sin and sees it as an impediment to service to the world and to the sharing of wisdom between churches and peoples.

Full communion—a recognition of other churches' sacraments and a facilitating of the interdenominational transfer of ministers—is regarded as a means of enhancing ecumenism. The original Congregationalists, the Pilgrims, were in full communion with the French and Dutch Reformed churches. Decades ago, full communion was established with Reformed churches through the World Alliance of Reformed Churches, and it was recently created with the Union of Evangelical Churches in Germany and the Congregational Christian Church in American Samoa. The Ecumenical Partnership established full communion with the Christian Church (Disciples of Christ), as the Formula of Agreement did with the Evangelical Lutheran Church in America, the Presbyterian Church (USA), and the Reformed Church in America. Churches Uniting in Christ makes full communion an imminent reality among nine Protestant and Anglican churches. This will represent the first time that such a relationship has existed between historically African American and European American churches. There is currently a dialogue with the Baptist denomination through the Alliance of Baptists.

The UCC also engages in dialogues with non-Christian faiths, especially through the Interfaith Relations Commission of the National Council of Churches. In 1987 and 1989, the general synod declared its desire for reconciliation with the Jewish and Muslim communities.

Affiliations

A founding member of both the National Council of Churches and the World Council of Churches, the UCC participates in numerous ecumenical agencies and projects. Because of its unique historical background, the UCC is also a member of the World Alliance of Reformed Churches, which is the worldwide communion of churches in the Reformed, Presbyterian, and Congregationalist traditions.

Parachurch Organizations

Located in eastern North Carolina, the Franklin Center at Bricks (FCAB) is a conference, retreat, and educational facility staffed by the UCC's Justice and Witness Ministries. It focuses on advocacy for the poor and other disadvantaged groups. On the site of a former plantation, the FCAB was created by the merger in the 1950s of Franklinton Christian College (established in 1871) and the Congregationalist Bricks School (established in 1895).

UCC camps and retreat centers are operated by the Outdoor Ministries Association. Located at more than sixty sites of natural beauty throughout the country, they seek to strengthen faith with the display of the glory of creation and to enhance the bonds of Christian community. Camp programs are linked to the church's educational objectives of encouraging diversity and understanding. Each year guests number in the thousands, include all ages and backgrounds, and come from various nonprofit groups and business groups in addition to UCC congregations.

Publications

Common Lot
Stillspeaking
United Church News

Website

http://www.ucc.org/

Bibliography

Rohr, John V. *The Shaping of American Congregationalism, 1620–1957*. Cleveland: Pilgrim Press, 1992.
"United Church of Christ." http://www.ucc.org. "UCC Constitution and Bylaws."

George Thomas Kurian

United Reformed Churches in North America

History

The United Reformed Churches in North America (URCNA), not to be confused with the United Reformed Church of Great Britain, is a federation of North American churches established in 1996 by a group of thirty-six independent Reformed churches, most of which had formerly separated from the Christian Reformed Church (CRC) over issues related to biblical authority and interpretation. One key area of biblical interpretation at issue was the CRC's decision to admit women to the offices of pastor and elder.

Several of the independent congregations had previously become associated under the banner of the Alliance of Reformed Churches, and in 1995, most of these churches, along with others seceding

from the CRC, banded together in a federative unity called the United Reformed Churches in North America. In 2008, the URCNA voted to receive the Orthodox Christian Reformed Church, another CRC breakaway denomination, into its fellowship. In 2005, the URCNA became a member of the North American Presbyterian and Reformed Council.

Headquarters

The URCNA does not have a denominational headquarters.

Core Beliefs

The URCNA has its roots in the Protestant Reformation of the sixteenth century and particularly in the Reformed movement spawned in Geneva, Switzerland, and the Netherlands. At the heart of Reformation theology are the three *solas*: *sola scriptura* proclaims that Scripture alone, exclusive of church tradition, is the basis for Christian faith and practice; *sola gratia* expresses the belief that the sovereign grace of God, exclusive of human merits, is definitive in initiating and accomplishing salvation for lost humans; and *sola fide* contends that salvation is received by faith alone, excluding any meritorious role for human works.

Soon after its founding, the URCNA adopted the Three Forms of Unity as its doctrinal basis. These are the Belgic Confession (1561), the Heidelberg Catechism (1563), and the Canons of Dort (1618–19).

Worship

As guidelines for worship, the URCNA adopted the liturgical forms of the *Psalter Hymnal* (1976) for use in its congregations. Though not limited to psalms exclusively, the *Psalter Hymnal* reflects the strong emphasis of the Reformation on the use of psalms in worship.

Statistics

Members: 21,000
Congregations: 111
Ministers: 140 in the United States and Canada

Website

http://www.urcna.org/

Bibliography

Zekveld, Harry, and Ralph A. Pontier. "History of the United Reformed Churches in North America." http://www.bethanyurc.com/background.htm.

Mark A. House

Mar Thoma Syrian Church

History

The Mar Thoma Syrian Church is an offshoot of the Malankara Syrian Orthodox Church and is part of the community of St. Thomas Christians of India that claims apostolic succession tracing back to the apostle St. Thomas in the first century. ("Mar Thoma" is a Syriac form of "St. Thomas.") With one million members, the majority of whom live in Kerala, India, the church adheres to theologically Reformed doctrines while retaining much of the Oriental Orthodox tradition, incorporating elements of both Eastern Rite churches and Protestantism.

The church traces its origin to the nineteenth-century Reformation movement started by a teacher and cleric of the Malankara Syrian Orthodox Church, Palakunnathu Abraham Malpan (malpan is a Syrian ecclesiastical rank below a bishop). At the Mavilekara Synod of 1839, reformists encouraged by Anglican missionaries split from the Malankara Syrian Orthodox Church. The new church evolved into its present form in the years between 1830 and 1889, with formal establishment of a separate denomination taking place in 1876. Milestones of the parent church were the Synod of Diamper (1599), the Coonen Cross Oath against the Portuguese (1653), and the Synod of Mulamthuruthy (1876). A group seeking to more fully adhere to Protestant doctrines broke away from the Mar Thoma Syrian Church in 1952 to form the St. Thomas Evangelical Church.

The organization of the episcopacy reflects the Anglican model. The Mar Thoma Syrian Church is headed by a metropolitan bishop. He lays claim to the Malankara Holy Apostolic Throne of St. Thomas, although such a throne was never recognized by the early church. Laypeople make up two-thirds of the Prathinidhi Mandalam, a church assembly that elects bishops and has plenary powers to govern and organize the church. The church hierarchy is comprised of a synod of bishops headed by a metropolitan.

Active in the field of education, the church runs eight colleges, eight high schools, one training school, three technical institutions, one vocational higher secondary school, and one theological seminary. It also operates thirty-one social welfare institutions, eleven homes for the destitute, and five hospitals.

The church is in full communion with the Anglican Church and cooperates with the Church of South India and the Church of North India. The Diocese of North America was organized in 1988.

Headquarters

Sinai Mar Thoma Center
2320 S Merrick Avenue
Merrick, NY 11566
Telephone: 516-377-3311
Email: webmaster@marthomachurch.org

Leadership

The current metropolitan is Mar Chrysostom Mar Thoma, who resides near the denomination's headquarters in Tiruvalla, Kerala, India.

Core Beliefs

The church is apostolic in origin, universal in nature, biblical in faith, evangelical in principle, ecumenical in outlook, oriental in worship, democratic in function, and episcopal in character.

Statistics

Worldwide there are 1 million members, 11 dioceses, and 1,057 parishes. The Diocese of North America has a membership of 6,000 families in 68 parishes.

Publication

Mar Thoma Messenger

Website

http://www.marthoma.in/

George Thomas Kurian

Miscellaneous

American Evangelical Christian Churches

History

The American Evangelical Christian Churches (AEC) is an independent denomination founded in Chicago in 1944 that remains open to both Calvinist and Arminian doctrines. It targets Generation X and Y Christians who have grown up in a nondenominational culture and ordains both males and females.

Headquarters

PO Box 47312
Indianapolis, IN 46247-0312
Telephone: 317-788-9280
Email: aeccoffice@earthlink.net

Leadership

International coordinator: Dr. Charles Wasielewski Sr.

Core Beliefs

The AEC believes in the Bible as the written Word of God, the virgin birth, the deity of Jesus Christ, salvation through atonement, the need for evangelism, guidance through prayer, the return of the Savior, and the eternal reign of Christ. It does not require its adherents to hold to any other specific theological positions.

Website

http://www.aeccministries.com/

George Thomas Kurian

Calvary Chapel Movement

History

The Calvary Chapel Movement is an international evangelical fellowship of independent, nondenominational churches brought to prominence through the ministry of Calvary Chapel of Costa Mesa and Pastor Chuck Smith (b. 1927). The ministry took root in December 1965 when Smith, formerly a pastor with the Foursquare Gospel denomination in Costa Mesa, became pastor of the fledgling twenty-five-member Calvary Chapel of Costa Mesa.

Due to the church's rapid growth, by 1971, Calvary Chapel had purchased ten acres of land on the boundary between Costa Mesa and Santa Ana, California. Church services were initially conducted in an interim tent facility (two thousand seating capacity), which was used until 1973, when it was replaced with a permanent twenty-two-hundred-seat facility.

Calvary Chapel's outreach to those in Southern California's Jesus movement (hippies, outcasts, surfers, etc.) elevated the ministry to prominence during the early 1970s as hundreds of young people disenfranchised by traditional churches made commitments to Christ. According to some estimates, Calvary Chapel of Costa Mesa was instrumental in up to twenty thousand conversions to Christ and eight thousand baptisms during a two-year period in the mid-1970s. Several features that characterized the growing ministry and resonated with the new congregation included simple Bible teaching and verse-by-verse exposition through the Bible, reliance on the Holy Spirit, an emphasis on God's love for mankind, personal servant-like humility, and nontraditional rock worship music (e.g., Love Song, Maranatha Music, etc.).

Today, under the leadership of senior pastor Chuck Smith and associate pastor Brian Brodersen, the Calvary Chapel fellowship of churches has grown to encompass more than fourteen hundred independently operated churches worldwide. Calvary Chapel of Costa Mesa's four worship services on Sunday and various weekly ministries have combined to serve up to fifteen thousand worshipers per week, which makes the church one of the larger Protestant churches in the United States.

Headquarters

Calvary Chapel of Costa Mesa
Calvary Chapel Outreach Fellowship

3800 S Fairview Street
Santa Ana, CA 92707
Telephone: 714-979-4422

Core Beliefs

Calvary Chapel churches are trinitarian, evangelical, and conservative charismatic. Members believe in the incarnation, the virgin birth, the bodily resurrection of Christ, the universality of sin, Christ's physical second coming, salvation by grace through faith alone in Jesus Christ, and biblical infallibility.

The verse-by-verse teaching of the Bible is the main focus of Calvary Chapel ministries and church services, since it is believed that God speaks to and sanctifies each believer through the text. There is monthly observance of the Lord's Supper, and baptism is by immersion.

Worship

Worship within the vast majority of Calvary Chapel churches is instrumental, contemporary, and upbeat. Calvary Chapel of Costa Mesa often alternates contemporary worship with traditional hymns in a casual environment.

Divisions and Splits

By the early 1980s, a handful of Calvary Chapel churches influenced by John Wimber of Calvary Chapel, Yorba Linda, and Kenn Gulliksen's Vineyard congregation in Los Angeles grew closer together through their mutual desire to elevate the spiritual gifts (*charismata*) to a more prominent role in the church. As a more conservative charismatic, Smith saw the teaching of the Bible as preeminent, setting up a minor split within Calvary Chapel. The differing emphases of the two groups could be clearly seen in the ensuing years when several of the Vineyard churches embraced the signs and wonders movement, which included the manifestation of holy laughter, whereas the Calvary Chapel fellowship did not.

Statistics

In the United States, there are approximately twelve hundred Calvary Chapel churches. International churches number approximately two to three hundred.

Largest Churches

The largest churches, numbering ten thousand people or more, are found mostly in the southwestern United States, Colorado, Pennsylvania, and Florida. Among them are:

Applegate Christian Fellowship (Jacksonville, OR)
Calvary Chapel of Albuquerque (NM)
Calvary Chapel of Chino Hills (CA)
Calvary Chapel of Costa Mesa (CA)
Calvary Chapel of Downey (CA)
Calvary Chapel of Fort Lauderdale (FL)
Calvary Chapel of Golden Springs (CA)
Calvary Chapel of Old Bridge (NJ)
Calvary Chapel of Philadelphia (PA)
Crossroads Church of Denver (CO)
Harvest Christian Fellowship (Riverside, CA)
Horizon Christian Fellowship (San Diego, CA)

Growth

The Calvary Chapel Movement has experienced unprecedented growth since 1965 (from one church to fifteen hundred churches worldwide) that shows no sign of abating. The Calvary Chapel Outreach Fellowship (CCOF) estimated that seven new churches per month were either joining the Calvary Chapel fellowship of churches or were new church plants altogether. In 2012, the CCOF was dissolved, and now new Calvary Chapel church affiliations are overseen by the Calvary Chapel Association of Ministries (CCAM). The CCAM is currently comprised of a Leadership Council of nearly two dozen senior Calvary Chapel pastors and provides organizational leadership and fellowship opportunities to Calvary Chapel churches in eleven regions throughout the United States.

Missionary and Evangelistic Work

The Calvary Chapel Movement engages in extensive evangelistic and missionary outreach both in the United States and overseas, which often leads to new church plants. Pastor Brian Brodersen of Calvary Chapel of Costa Mesa has spearheaded missions and church planting in Eastern and Western Europe, the United Kingdom in particular. As a result of these outreaches, Calvary Chapel churches have been planted in England, Wales, Scotland, Spain, Germany, Austria, Hungary, Italy, and other nations.

In addition to planting new churches, Calvary Chapel utilizes evangelistic assets such as Calvary Chapel Radio UK Sky Digital 0156 (calvarychapelradio.co.uk) and events such as the Christian music festival Creation Fest (creationfest.org.uk) to reach people for Christ. Creation Fest began in 2002 in Woolacombe, North Devon, England, as a one-day outreach. By 2009, the festival had grown into a seven-day summer event at the Royal Cornwall Showground in Wadebridge, Cornwall. In the United States, various Calvary Chapel churches have developed evangelism and outreach teams to spread the gospel of Jesus Christ to unbelievers. One of the largest evangelistic venues, the Harvest Crusade, is held annually at Anaheim Stadium and is hosted by Pastor Greg Laurie of Harvest Christian Fellowship in Riverside, California.

Ecumenism

Calvary Chapel is strongly evangelical and therefore rejects any form of theologically liberal ecumenism or syncretism. Though Calvary Chapel is nondenominational, it is not *antidenominational* except when an overemphasis on secondary doctrines leads to division in the body of Christ. Alternatively, Calvary Chapel has traditionally been open to fellowship and outreach with orthodox churches outside the movement (e.g., Creation Fest encourages local churches to participate in the outreach).

Academic Institutions

Since 1975, Calvary Chapel of Costa Mesa has been operating Calvary Chapel Bible College in Murrieta, California, which offers a two-year program leading to an associate's degree in theology or a bachelor's degree in biblical studies. The majority of courses offered by the college are expositional studies of the Bible and are evangelical in their doctrinal stance. There are also two extension campuses located in Vajta, Hungary, and Costa Mesa, California. In addition to these, there are dozens of affiliate sites operated independently by local Calvary Chapel churches.

Calvary Chapel of Costa Mesa also operates Calvary Chapel High School, which offers a four-year program from a Christian perspective accredited by the Western Association of Schools and Colleges. In addition, many Calvary Chapel churches throughout the country operate their own independent elementary and high schools.

Parachurch Organizations

Calvary Chapel churches usually have their own (or support an) independent relief organization that serves the surrounding community and their congregation. Since 2000, Calvary Chapel of Costa Mesa has operated Hands of Hope, which is an umbrella organization for several relief ministries that serve the people of Santa Ana. These ministries include feeding the hungry, providing clothing, sharing the Bible in schools, alcohol and drug counseling, and caring for the homeless.

Electronic Media

Calvary Chapel of Costa Mesa owns and operates several media/resource outlets used exclusively for ministry, including Southern California's radio station KWVE 107.9, a twenty-four-hour station dedicated to evangelical Bible teaching and worship music.

Publications

Calvary Publishing is the publishing wing of Calvary Chapel, and the Word for Today Publications is the retail outlet for Calvary Chapel resource materials.

Websites

http://www.calvarychapelcostamesa.com/
http://www.calvarychapelassociation.com/

Bibliography

Smith, Chuck. *Calvary Chapel Distinctives.* Costa Mesa, CA: The Word for Today, 1993.

Smith, Chuck, and Tal Brooke. *Harvest.* Costa Mesa, CA: The Word for Today, 2005.

Joseph M. Holden

Evangelical Church Alliance

History

The Evangelical Church Alliance was founded as the World's Faith Missionary Association in 1887 in Shenandoah, Iowa, by Rev. C. S. Hanley. Its goal of harmonizing Christian leadership was shared by four hundred members, but still the association's board voted to disband the group after Hanley's death in 1925. It was reorganized as two separate entities, each claiming approval from Hanley's widow. In Minnesota, Rev. C. S. Osterhus founded one of these, while the other was established in Missouri by Dr. J. I. Montgomery, who served as its vice president, with Faye Jackson serving as president. In 1931, three years after its incorporation, the Missouri group adopted the name Fundamental Ministerial Association. The Minnesota and Missouri groups were rejoined as the Evangelical Church Alliance (ECA) in 1958.

Headquarters

PO Box 9
205 West Broadway Street
Bradley, IL 60915

Telephone: 815-937-0720; 888-855-6060
Email: info@ecainternational.org

Leadership

President and CEO: Dr. Sam Goebel

Core Beliefs

The Bible is divinely inspired and inerrant.
God exists as Father, Son, and Holy Spirit.
Jesus Christ, the Son of God, became man for the purpose of redeeming humankind.
The Holy Spirit convicts the world of sin and regenerates, sanctifies, and comforts believers.
Humankind is depraved and cannot redeem itself.
Salvation is the gift of God and is received by grace and faith in the Lord Jesus Christ, whose blood was shed on the cross for the forgiveness of sins.
Water baptism represents the union of the believer with the death and resurrection of Christ.
The Lord's Supper is a commemoration of Christ's sacrifice.
The believer's conduct must be separate from that of the world and must direct others toward Christ.
Christ will return in bodily form.

Interdenominational and nonsectarian, the ECA welcomes all individuals who embrace its Tenets of Faith, regardless of their beliefs about other, nonessential matters. It is not antidenominational, and many members simultaneously serve in denominational bodies and the ECA.

Website

http://www.ecainternational.org/

George Thomas Kurian

Grace International Churches and Ministries

History

The Colonial Tabernacle, which in 2008 became Grace International Churches and Ministries, was founded in 1934 by O. C. Harms, who also became its first president. His successor and brother, R. H. Harms, brought a great deal of organization and structure to the ministry. In 1979, he changed its name to Christian Evangelistic Assemblies (CEA). In 1982, the CEA's third president, Orvel Taylor, took over the ministry until he retired in 1997, and he continues to serve on the board of directors as president emeritus. In 1997, Steve Riggle became the fourth president of the CEA, now Grace International Churches and Ministries, and is currently the senior pastor of the multisite megachurch Grace Community

Church in Houston, Texas, with over fifteen thousand members on four campuses in Texas and California.

Headquarters

40 Cypress Creek Parkway W, PMB #391
Houston, TX 77090
Telephone: 713-363-2530
Email: graceinternational@grace.tv

Leadership

Grace International Churches and Ministries is headed by President Steve Riggle and governed by a board of directors that cares for national and international churches.

Core Beliefs

Grace International does not promote any defining doctrinal beliefs that churches must ascribe to in order to become affiliated with the ministry. Its statement of faith includes belief in all the gifts of the Holy Spirit being present today, conception as the beginning of life, and the sanctity and exclusivity of heterosexual marriage.

Core Practices

Grace International Churches and Ministries exists "to provide support, training, encouragement, and relationships for church and ministry leaders" (grace-international.tv, "Visions and Values"). It specializes in leadership development and training for church leaders and members, from which comes an emphasis on church planting worldwide.

Statistics

Grace International Churches and Ministries currently serves 7 countries and 2,400 churches and has around 165,000 members.

Website

http://www.grace-international.tv/

Bibliography

"Grace International Churches and Ministries." http://www.grace-international.tv. "Ministers," "Staff," "Statement of Faith," "Visions and Values," and "Who We Are."

Chad C. Brewer

International Council of Community Churches

History

In 1950, the International Council of Community Churches (ICCC) was founded when two nondenominational fellowships in the community church movement, the Biennial Council of the People's Church of Christ and Community Centers and the National Council of Community Churches, merged. The union of the black Biennial Council and the white National Council was historic, since it was the largest interracial merger of churches as of that time. The ICCC has expanded to include some two hundred churches in America and many churches around the world. These churches all share a conception of a community church as one that is not planted but rather develops in response to community needs; embraces the entire community, regardless of denominational affiliation; prioritizes the needs of people over the institutional needs of the church; and is ecumenical in its practice of worship.

The ICCC offers member churches consultation regarding the work of the church, assistance in clergy selection, education and counseling for clergy, pensions and other benefits for clergy and staff, conference opportunities for fellowship, matching funds for missions and charity work, opportunities for benevolence and ecumenical work, and help in establishing new churches.

Headquarters

21116 Washington Parkway
Frankfort, IL 60423
Telephone: 815-464-5690
Email: iccml@sbcglobal.net

Leadership

Executive director: Michael Livingston

Core Beliefs

The ICCC is an ardent supporter of the ecumenical movement. It seeks to unite believers of different nations, cultures, and races to honor Christ's prayer that "they all may be one" (John 17:21 KJV). By sharing truth and displaying God's love toward individuals and creation, the ICCC strives to promote peace and justice.

Finances

The ICCC requires member churches to make an annual contribution of $500 or 1 percent of their annual budget.

Statistics

According to the Association of Religion Data Archives, the ICCC had 137 congregations with almost 70,000 members as of 2009.

Affiliations

Christian Churches Together in the USA
Churches Uniting in Christ
Church World Service
Consultation on Church Union
National Council of Churches
World Council of Churches

Parachurch Organizations

Commissions include Clergy Relations; Faith, Justice, and Mission; Laity and Church Relations; and Ecumenical and Interfaith Relations.

Ten committees oversee the daily operations of the church and charitable endeavors such as the Jordan Scholarship, which assists those continuing their education past high school.

Publications

Executive Director Michael Livingston is also publisher of the Community Church Press, which has a six-member editorial board.

ICCC publications include *Christian Community*, containing news and ecumenically minded perspectives; *Inclusive Pulpit*, an annual; and *Key Lay Notes*, a clergy communique.

George Thomas Kurian

United House of Prayer for All People

History

A black Pentecostal denomination started in 1919 and incorporated in 1927, the United House of Prayer for all People (UHP, formerly Church on the Rock of the Apostolic Faith) was founded by Charles Manuel "Sweet Daddy" Grace (1881–1960). He was a young minister who began a church in 1919 in Massachusetts but found greater success in the South. He frequently traveled and preached, including in tent revivals in the 1920s. Grace traveled to Egypt in 1923 and founded a UHP church there. In 1926, he founded a UHP church in Charlotte, North Carolina, and this church would grow to become the largest UHP church in the denomination. In the 1920s through the 1940s, the UHP experienced tremendous growth and became one of the most widely known African American groups in the South.

During his life, Grace attained a near-divine status, with his role in a person's spiritual life being emphasized more than that of God. He established centers in New York; Baltimore; Washington, DC; and other major cities. After his death, his successor was known as Walter

"Sweet Daddy Grace" McCollough. Under his authority, the church moved toward a more traditional Pentecostal understanding.

The UHP plants churches by targeting an area and building a church first and then attracting a congregation.

Headquarters

601 M Street
Washington, DC 20001

Core Beliefs

The UHP has a self-generated creed:

We believe in the Almighty God, maker of Heaven and Earth. We believe in Jesus Christ, His only begotten Son who was conceived by the Holy Ghost and crucified for the redemption of the sins of the people so that all men would have a right to the tree of life. We believe in water baptism for the repentance of sins. We believe that you must be born again of the Holy Ghost. We believe in one leader as the ruler of the Kingdom of God. (tuhopfap.org, "We Believe")

The church practices Communion, speaking in tongues, and baptism, sometimes by a fire hose (a practice initiated by Grace in the 1920s). The UHP teaches that members can receive multiple baptisms in their lives for the "washing" away of sins and healing. The UHP believes in serving the community, and so the churches offer food, often weekly, to the community.

Worship

Each UHP church has a brass and drum band. The African American experience is heightened with pictures of a black Messiah and other Afrocentric art.

Division and Splits

After the death of "Sweet Daddy" Grace and the ascension of McCollough, some congregations did not acknowledge his authority and split off to form the True Grace Memorial House of Prayer.

Statistics

The UHP has 131 churches in 26 states with 50,000 members.

Website

http://www.tuhopfap.org/

Bibliography

Dallam, Marie. *Daddy Grace: A Celebrity Preacher and His House of Prayer*. New York: New York University Press, 2007.

Mark Nickens

Part 2

Ministries

Act Beyond (formerly Mission to Unreached Peoples)

History

Mission to Unreached Peoples (MUP) began in 1981 "to bridge the gap between traditional missions and Christian relief and development" (beyond.org, "History"). Initial activities were centered on fund-raising for small projects by Christians in Asia. In 1983, the first missionary family, a couple from Seattle, Washington, awaiting visas for their placement in Nepal, joined MUP. The faith and determination of this couple to work in Nepal, a country closed to traditional missionaries, shaped the vision of the new organization: to find creative strategies to enter "closed" countries, gaining access to share the good news of Jesus Christ with peoples unreached by the gospel. Unreached people groups are the world's least evangelized, with little or no access to the gospel within their own culture.

In 1986, MUP placed a fourteen-member team in China, bringing the total number of personnel in Asia to thirty-eight. In 1990, MUP added a focus on church planting and sent an increasing number of long-term missionaries.

The initial focus of MUP was the mobilization of lay Christians to use their vocational skills creatively to access closed or closing countries in order to bring the gospel. The current membership is a balance of professionally trained missionaries (including Bible school and seminary graduates), a variety of community development personnel, and vocationally trained missionaries, including tentmakers. The organization was named Act Beyond in 2013.

Headquarters

PO Box 30947
Seattle, WA 98113
Telephone: 206-781-3151
Fax: 206-781-3182

Leadership

President: Kent Parks

Act Beyond also has a sixteen-member board of directors.

Core Beliefs

We believe in one God, eternally existent in three persons, Father, Son, and Holy Spirit.

We believe in the deity of our Lord Jesus Christ, in His virgin birth, in His sinless life, in His miracles, in His vicarious death and atonement through His shed blood, in His bodily resurrection, in His ascension to "the right hand of God the Father," and in His personal return in power and glory.

We believe that for the salvation of lost and sinful man, faith in our Lord Jesus Christ and regeneration by the Holy Spirit are essential.

We believe in the present ministry of the Holy Spirit, by whose indwelling the Christian is enabled to live a godly life.

We believe all Scripture is God-breathed and is useful for teaching, rebuking, correcting and training in righteousness (2 Timothy 3:16).

We believe in the forgiveness of sins, the resurrection of the body and life eternal.

We believe in the spiritual unity of the Church, which is the body of Christ, composed of all who are regenerated through faith in our Lord Jesus Christ. (beyond.org, "Statement of Faith")

Core Practices

Act Beyond starts church-planting movements among unreached people groups. Team members spend a considerable amount of time with a people group so that when the team leaves, members are confident the new churches will plant more churches. Team members equip local leaders to carry out tasks through modeling, training, mentoring, and coaching.

Publication

The *Unreached Peoples' Advocate* is a quarterly newsletter with articles and stories from up to seventeen countries, information about recent developments of the agency, and a listing of current openings available online.

Website

http://beyond.org/

Bibliography

"Act Beyond." http://beyond.org. "Statement of Faith."

Barbara Wyman

241

Action International Ministries

History

Action International Ministries was formed in Chicago in 1974 and incorporated the following year in Washington State. The organization's roots reach back to the early 1960s, as a group of American missionaries in the Philippines consolidated and expanded their efforts. They included Will Bruce from Overseas Missionary Fellowship and Marvin Graves from New Tribes Mission, who joined with nine other individuals to create Christ for Greater Manila (CGM). CGM's success continued under the leadership of Doug and Margi Nichols. Because CGM's membership included many American-born missionaries, the group elected to move its headquarters to the United States. Today the ministry includes more than 260 members who are active in 18 countries, cooperating with churches and other groups to evangelize, shepherd believers, and assist with practical needs.

Headquarters

PO Box 398
Mountlake Terrace, WA 98043
Telephone: 425-775-4800

Core Beliefs

A doctrinal statement posted on the organization's website affirms belief in the Trinity, the deity of Christ, and biblical infallibility, among other doctrines.

Finances

In 2012, Action International Ministries had revenue of more than $6.4 million.

Website

http://www.actioninternational.org/

Bibliography

"Action International Ministries." http://www.actioninternational.org. "Our History" and "What We Believe."

"Action International Ministries." GuideStar. http://www.guidestar.org/organizations/51-0163499/action-international-ministries.aspx.

George Thomas Kurian

Acton Institute

History

Rev. Robert A. Sirico (a Roman Catholic priest) and Kris Alan Mauren founded the Acton Institute for the Study of Religion and Liberty as a nonprofit educational institution in April 1990. The institute is named in honor of Cambridge historian and moralist Lord John Emerich Edward Dalberg Acton (1834–1902) and bases its mission on his teachings and writings. Lord Acton was considered one of the most learned Englishmen of his time. Regarded as the "magistrate of history," he exhausted much of his life communicating the history of liberty and believed that political liberty is essential for religious liberty.

Headquarters

98 E Fulton Street
Grand Rapids, MI 49503
Telephone: 616-454-3080
Fax: 616-454-9454
Email: info@acton.org

Leadership

Kris Alan Mauren is executive director. Robert A. Sirico is president. A board of directors, which promotes the compatibility of faith and freedom, governs the activities of the Acton Institute.

Core Beliefs

The Acton Institute integrates Judeo-Christian truths with free market principles. The core principles of the institute include the dignity of humanity, as created in the image of God; the social nature of humanity, which allows people to interact with others and participate in moral goods; the importance of social institutions; human action that actualizes potential when a person freely chooses moral goods that fulfill one's nature; humanity as corrupted by sin and fallen in its current state but good in its created nature; the rule of law and the subsidiary role of government; the creation of wealth through protection of property rights and voluntary exchange; economic liberty; economic value; and the priority of a moral culture for liberty to flourish.

The institute affirms an objective context of moral values, and it appreciates and recognizes the subjective nature of economic value. Justice is regarded as a universal responsibility for common good and not merely for one's own desires and necessities. The institute transcends denominational convictions.

Defining Statement

"Connecting good intentions with sound economics" (acton.org, "About the Acton Institute").

Core Practices

The institute aims to promote the benefits of a limited government and a free market. As a means of promoting a more thoughtful understanding of the relationship between faith and liberty, the institute involves academic, business, and religious specialists in its various academic activities, publications, and seminars.

The mission of the Acton Institute is to uphold the vision of "a free and virtuous society characterized by individual liberty and sustained by religious principles" (acton.org, "About the Acton Institute"). The institute organizes seminars to educate academic researchers, business executives, religious leaders, and university professors. The Acton Institute promotes sound economic thinking and cognizance with regard to the foundational moral values that are necessary for a free society. The Programs and Education Department promotes the principles of a free and virtuous society through conferences and educational programs that develop relationships, facilitate discussion, equip others, promote the exchange of ideas, and provide networking opportunities.

Affiliations

The Acton Institute is an internationally recognized and respected intellectual resource. Relationships have been established with several international affiliate organizations that share the mission of the Acton Institute and seek to promote its core principles. The institute currently has four international affiliates: Centro Interdisciplinar de Etica e Economica Personalista (Brazil), Europa Institut (Austria), Institute for the Study of Human Dignity and Economic Freedom (Zambia), and Instituto Acton Argentina (Argentina).

Academic Institutions

Acton University is a unique, four-day exploration into the intellectual foundations of a free society and is guided by distinguished international faculty. The Research Department serves as the academic research facility of the Acton Institute. The department accommodates scholars in house and by extension from a variety of Christian denominations, nationalities, and international disciplines. The Calihan Academic Fellowship provides research grants and scholarships to emerging scholars and religious leaders whose academic work demonstrates exceptional potential. The Novak Award is granted to notable scholarly research into the relationship between economic freedom, the free and virtuous society, and religion.

Electronic Media

Acton Media provides an audio and video archive, in addition to the Acton Lecture Series and Radio Free Acton. *The Birth of Freedom* is a seven-session DVD curriculum that demonstrates the biblical foundation of the concept of freedom and how Christianity has positively shaped Western civilization. *The Call of the Entrepreneur* film explores how entrepreneurs impact the world. The *Effective Stewardship Curriculum* is a five-session video study that teaches biblical and critical thinking with regard to the areas of responsibility that God has entrusted to humanity.

Publications

Acton News and Commentary is a weekly email newsletter featuring book announcements, new essays, and the latest news for Acton events. *Acton Notes* is a bimonthly newsletter that features a president's message, news, and upcoming events. The quarterly newsletter *Religion and Liberty* features exclusive interviews with renowned economic and religious leaders. The semiannual academic *Journal of Markets and Morality* is devoted to examining interrelated ideas of economics, philosophy, and theology. Monographs addressing economic issues are published in the Christian Social Thought Series.

The Acton Bookshoppe provides a wide variety of products to stimulate intellectual needs. Books and DVDs are available in the categories of church and state, economics, entrepreneurship, environment, ethics, general political science, religious social thought, and welfare.

Website

http://www.acton.org/

Bibliography

"Acton Institute." http://www.acton.org. "About the Acton Institute" and "History of Acton Institute."

Beabout, Gregory R., et al. *Beyond Self-Interest: A Personalist Approach to Human Action.* Lanham, MD: Lexington Books, 2002.

Green, John, and Kevin E. Schmiesing. *The State of Economic Education in United States Seminaries.* Grand Rapids: Acton Institute, 2001.

Gregg, Samuel. *Economic Thinking for the Theologically Minded.* Lanham, MD: University Press of America, 2001.

Hill, Roland. *Lord Acton.* New Haven, CT: Yale University Press, 2000.

Santelli, Anthony L., Jr., et al. *The Free Person and the Free Economy*. Lanham, MD: Lexington Books, 2002.

White, Patricia-Donohue, et al. *Human Nature and the Discipline of Economics*. Lanham, MD: Lexington Books, 2002.

Ron J. Bigalke

ACTS International

History

The literature outreach ministry of ACTS (A Christian Teaching Service) International was commenced in 1970 in south Australia by Dick Innes with a vision to reach every family in Australia with the gospel.

To reach the two million families scattered across the vast areas of outback Australia, thousands of whom lived great distances from a local church, gospel letter kits were printed and mailed. Since it is required by law that every adult Australian register to vote, ACTS purchased printed electoral roll books, which made it possible for the organization to obtain every family's address and to reach every home via the Australia Post. Enclosed in each kit was a printed gospel booklet, a response form, and a reply envelope. From these mailings more than twenty-seven thousand people recorded a decision/response for either salvation or a recommitment of their life to Jesus Christ.

Because the Australian postage rates soared during these early years, ACTS changed from direct mail evangelism to printed leaflets (Encounter brochures) and worked with sponsoring churches across Australia to reach every family in their community with the gospel. ACTS expanded to New Zealand in the mid-1970s and to the United States in the early 1980s. Many prison and military chaplains also used the ACTS Encounter brochures to share the gospel with prisoners and military personnel in various places in the world. Due to the passing of the ACTS New Zealand director in 2008, the New Zealand board of directors decided to close the ACTS office there.

Headquarters

PO Box 73545
San Clemente, CA 92673
Telephone: 949-940-9050
Fax: 949-481-3686
Email: acts@actsweb.org

Leadership

The ACTS United States office has only two staff members, Dick Innes, director, and Joy Innes, office manager. The board of directors consists of five members.

Core Beliefs

A summary of ACTS' beliefs includes the following:

The Bible is the inspired, infallible, authoritative Word of God. There is one God, eternally existent in three persons: Father, Son, and Holy Spirit. ACTS believes in the deity of Jesus Christ, his virgin birth, his sinless life, his miracles, his vicarious and atoning death through his shed blood, his bodily resurrection, his ascension to the right hand of the Father, and his personal return in power and glory. For the salvation of lost and sinful man, regeneration by the Holy Spirit is absolutely essential. ACTS believes in the present ministry of God's Spirit (the Holy Spirit), by whose indwelling the Christian is enabled to live a godly life. ACTS believes in the resurrection of both the saved and the lost, they who are saved unto the resurrection of life, and they who are lost unto the resurrection of damnation. ACTS believes in the spiritual unity of believers in Christ (actsweb.org, "ACTS Statement of Faith/Beliefs").

Finances

ACTS International is a faith-based ministry and is funded by donor support. The board of directors has oversight of all income and expenses. ACTS is registered in the State of California as a nonprofit 501(c)(3) tax-deductible organization.

Statistics

Over 2 million families received a gospel letter kit, and over 40 million Encounter brochures were printed and distributed by several thousand churches, chaplains, organizations, businesses, and laypeople. Almost every day of the year ACTS receives salvation and recommitment responses. To date, they have come from at least 128 countries around the world.

Missionary and Evangelistic Work

ACTS literature is designed to reach people at their point of felt need and to apply the gospel to meet those needs. Articles with titles such as the following were printed and distributed: "Winning over Worry," "Turning Stress into Success," "Conquering Fear," "Failure: Never Forever," "Enrich Your Family Life," "Making

Families Strong," "Training Up Children," "The Art of Staying in Love," "Single and Satisfied," and "Resolving Conflict Creatively." Many direct salvation messages included "How to Be Sure You're a Real Christian—without Having to Be Religious," "Passport for Heaven," "Will Jesus Christ Come Again?" "Is There Life after Death?" "Is the Bible God's Word?" "Hope: The Strength to Carry On," "Love's Most Amazing Story," and many more. All told, some 250 titles are available.

Every salvation and recommitment to Jesus Christ response is followed up by both email and a special website with ten practical articles to help those recording a decision/response in their Christian life. Articles include the following: "How to Grow," "Jesus Christ: Is He God or Man?" "What a Good Church Can Do for You," and "The Importance of Baptism."

ACTS has started a People Power for Jesus movement to help even the most timid Christian become an effective witness for Jesus Christ by forwarding suitable copies of *Daily Encounter* and web articles to family, friends, and contacts.

ACTS also provides business witness cards as a way for people to witness for Christ in a nonoffensive way. Most of the cards direct the receiver to a gospel website.

To effectively use the internet to reach the unchurched, ACTS has developed Good News websites designed specifically to address the felt needs of the average person. A Good News website can be designed for any community, anywhere.

As time permits, seminars on Innes's book, *I Hate Witnessing: A Handbook for Effective Christian Communications*, are conducted.

Electronic Media

As the internet began to grow, literature sales began to diminish, so in 1998, ACTS changed from print media to electronic media via the internet and email. Today ACTS has 23 gospel websites, which are in English, Spanish, and French. ACTS also has over 380,000 worldwide email subscribers to the weekday inspirational *Daily Encounter*, almost 8,000 subscribers to the *Weekend Encounter*, and 2,600 People Power for Jesus partners.

Website

http://www.actsweb.org/

Dick Innes

Acts 29 Network

History

Founded on the belief that the Great Commission includes the planting of churches, the Acts 29 Network strives to be an interdenominational network of churches planting churches. Since its inception in 2000 by Mark Driscoll and David Nicholas, the Acts 29 Network has grown from two churches (Mars Hill Church in Seattle, WA; Spanish River Church in Boca Raton, FL) to over four hundred churches from twenty-two denominations.

Headquarters

1411 NW 50th Street
Seattle, WA 98107
Telephone: 206-816-3776
Email: info@acts29network.org

Leadership

The Acts 29 Network operates with a board of directors. Matt Chandler is the current president.

Core Beliefs

The Acts 29 Network holds to the Apostles' and Nicene Creeds and is in agreement with the doctrinal statement of the National Association of Evangelicals. The core beliefs consist of four main dogmatic stances: Christian, evangelical, missional, and reformed in soteriology.

Core Practices

"Acts 29 Network exists to build a unifying and an uncommon alliance of smaller networks to advance the mission of Jesus through church-planting churches" (acts29network.org, "Vision"). The Acts 29 Network provides support, training, and care for local churches and their pastors.

Finances

The Acts 29 Network currently has an annual budget of $250,000, funded primarily through donations from local churches and private individuals (Scott Thomas, personal email conversation).

Statistics

As of June 2010, the Acts 29 Network had a network of 321 churches with 336 Sunday worship services (Eliot Grudem, personal email conversation). As of July 2012, the network included over 400 churches, signaling extensive growth of over 20 percent in two years. The network has churches from 22 denominations in 13 countries with approximately 70,000 members.

Largest Churches

The Acts 29 Network has churches around the world. The largest church is Mars Hill Church in Seattle, Washington, with over nine thousand members meeting at eight campuses throughout the city.

Trends

The Acts 29 Network has been growing at an exponential rate since its inception in 2000. As of June 2010, the Acts 29 Network had received over five hundred new applications from church planters. The Acts 29 Network's ministerial goal is to have one thousand networked churches by 2019 (Scott Thomas, personal email conversation).

Academic Institutions

The Acts 29 Network itself does not operate a theological school. Several churches within the Acts 29 Network offer formal and informal pastoral and theological training through organizations such as the Resurgence Training Center. The center offers a yearlong graduate program for a master's in missional leadership. The school is currently pursuing accreditation, though students are able to transfer units to a number of American seminaries. Other organizations that provide training are BILD International, which offers several accredited degrees through accredited educational institutions, and the Porterbrook Network, which offers missional training.

Electronic Media

Information about the Acts 29 Network and its entire collection of media is located on its website.

Website

http://www.acts29network.org/

Bibliography

"Acts 29 Network." http://www.acts29network.org. "About," "Doctrine," "FAQ," "Leadership," and "Vision."
"BILD International." http://www.bild.org.
"Mars Hill Church." http://www.marshill.com. "About."
"Porterbrook Network." http://www.porterbrook.org.
"Resurgence Training Center." http://www.retrain.org.

Chad C. Brewer

Advent Christian World Missions

History

Organized Advent Christian missions began in 1865 when the American Advent Mission Society (AAMS) launched work among freed slaves in America's South. After brief sorties into Europe, the AAMS formed a foreign board (1882) and by 1900 had missions in Macedonia, England, the Congo, China, and Cape Verde Islands. Organized in 1897, the Advent Christian denomination's Woman's Home and Foreign Mission Society (WHFMS) was soon conducting mission work in south India. For fifty years, China and India were the chief foreign fields, but a flurry of missionary activity revived work in Japan (1945) and opened missions in South Africa (1950), the Philippines (1953), Mexico (1958), Malaysia (1960), and Nigeria (1967). The AAMS and the WHFMS merged their foreign operations in 1958 before becoming the denomination's Department of World Outreach in 1976.

Headquarters

14601 Albemarle Road
Charlotte, NC 28227
Telephone: 704-545-6161
Fax: 704-573-0712

Leadership

Director Rev. Timothy D. Fox supervises missions in the United States and in approximately 40 other countries in which 87,776 members are associated with 570 churches and/or preaching stations. Directors over three areas (Africa/Europe, Latin America, and Asia/Pacific) work through ten career missionaries. They cooperate with fully indigenous associate partners in Japan and New Zealand and have official outreach sites in Croatia, Ghana, Honduras, India, Liberia, Malaysia, Mexico, Nigeria, the Philippines, South Africa, and Thailand.

These locations may themselves be sending agencies but like traditional mission fields receive varying amounts of financial support and sometimes have cross-cultural missionaries. The department extends guidance and some financial aid to other affiliated Advent Christian ministries in Burundi, the Democratic Republic of Congo, Kenya, Malawi, Mozambique, Myanmar, Tanzania, Bosnia and Herzegovina, Cameroon, Namibia, Romania, Serbia and Montenegro, Ukraine, Zambia, and Zimbabwe.

Advent Christians assist potential affiliates and maintain ongoing contacts with outreaches in Brazil, China, Cote d'Ivoire, Indonesia, Kosovo, Papua New Guinea, Sierra Leone, and Togo.

Core Practices

Advent Christians first focused on home missions and evangelism in North America. After expanding internationally, they continued to stress evangelism and church planting. Auxiliary activities included orphanages, medical work, famine relief, day schools, printing, literature distribution, and ministerial training. Around 1960, mission leaders began to stress the creation of indigenous churches designed to reflect their national culture while propagating, governing, and supporting themselves.

As national Advent Christian churches have become more self-sufficient, the denomination's emphasis has shifted toward partnering with national Christians in evangelizing their own countries, employing more national workers and fewer career missionaries, and assisting mission churches to become sending agencies. This change has enabled more Advent Christians to serve internationally with other missions. Financial aid is now expended primarily for pastoral training, evangelism, church planting, and disaster relief.

Website

http://www.adventchristian.org/

Bibliography

Damon, Marion R. *The Thatched Hut: True Stories of India.* Charlotte, NC: Venture Books, 2008.

Dean, David A. *Who Will Go for US? People and Passion in Advent Christian World Missions, 1860–2000.* Charlotte, NC: Venture Books, 2005.

Johnson, Albert C. *Advent Christian History.* Boston: Advent Christian Publication Soc., 1912.

David A. Dean

Adventive Cross Cultural Initiatives

History

Adventive Cross Cultural Initiatives was born as New Life League, a literature effort of TEAM International, in 1954. Following their expulsion—along with all other missionaries—from China in 1949, Americans Dr. Fred Jarvis and his wife, Clara, moved to Japan. There they began to print and distribute their own literature and were joined ten years later by Arnfin Andaas, a Norwegian. Two years later, in 1961, New Life League expanded to include Cliff and Eretta Reimer and was registered as a nonprofit organization in the United States.

Andaas and the Reimers eventually helped to establish a low-cost printing facility in Sri Lanka that would come to create materials for other ministries, including the International Bible Society, Serving in Missions, Operation Mobilization, and World Evangelism Crusade. In 2002, New Life League became Adventive Cross Cultural Initiatives, and its headquarters were moved from Panoka, Alberta, to Ottawa, Ontario. While continuing to provide financial and staff support to New Life League Sri Lanka, the group has expanded to include missionary efforts around the globe.

Headquarters

United States
141 E Main Street
Rock Hill, SC 29730

Canada
89 Auriga
Nepean, Ontario K2E 7Z2
Canada

Core Beliefs

The Holy Scriptures (comprised of the Old and New Testaments) are divinely inspired, entirely trustworthy, and constitute the only supreme authority in all matters of faith and conduct.

There is one God, eternally existent in three persons: Father, Son, and Holy Spirit.

Our Lord Jesus Christ is fully God and fully human; we affirm his virgin birth, sinless humanity, divine miracles, bodily resurrection, ascension, and personal return in power and glory.

The salvation of lost and sinful humanity is possible only through the merits of the shed blood of the Lord Jesus Christ, received by faith apart from works, and is accompanied by the Holy Spirit and sincere love for Jesus.

The Holy Spirit indwells believers to enable them to live a holy life, to love others, to witness and work for the Lord Jesus Christ.

The Church, the body of Christ, consists of all those whom Christ indwells by the Holy Spirit.

Ultimately God will judge the living and the dead, those who are saved will be resurrected to eternal life with God and those who are lost will be resurrected to eternal separation from God. (adventive .ca, "Statement of Faith")

The organization's core values include:

Kingdom focused—As the kingdom is both now and not yet, it is the church that is God's agent for extending his kingdom.

Biblically based and worshipful—Scripture has full authority.

Grace oriented—Values and principles are emphasized as opposed to legalism.

A dynamic view of the Holy Spirit—They encourage the seeking of the Holy Spirit's empowering without dictating how that should occur.

Purpose centered and people minded—While remaining a mission movement with a specific purpose and vision, they aim to be that in a way that values all people.

Developmental and gift based—Each person is to be encouraged to develop his or her God-given potential.

Facilitative in leadership—Within their mission mandate and strategy, they seek to be focused but flexible.

Entrepreneurial—Things are to be done well, in faith and trust, but innovation and risk-taking are encouraged too.

Balancing the strategic and the supernatural—There is a place for both spirituality and practicality.

Authentic and transparent—Sincerity in all things is seen as vital. (adventive.ca, "Core Values")

Defining Statement

"Adventive exists for the purpose of attracting, equipping, sending, and serving the vision of passionate, effective leaders and teams who are focused on cross-culturally advancing the kingdom of Christ throughout the world" (adventive.ca, "Home").

Core Practices

The ministry seeks to serve as a conduit of sorts, connecting those interested in cross-cultural service with suitable opportunities. It describes itself as a bottom-up ministry, providing assistance to ministries that already exist.

Finances

Adventive Cross Cultural Initiatives is an interdenominational, nonsectarian, (501)(c)(3) tax-exempt, nonprofit mission organization with charity status and offices in Canada and the United States.

Statistics

Adventive Cross Cultural Initiatives produces more than three hundred tons of literature a month.

Website

http://www.adventive.ca/

Michael McMullen

Africa Inland Mission

History

The history of the Africa Inland Mission (AIM) begins with Peter Cameron Scott (1867–96), a Scottish-American missionary of the International Missionary Alliance who was sent to the Congo. After a serious illness, he went to Scotland to recover in 1892. While visiting David Livingstone's grave, Scott received a vision from God to establish a network of mission stations that would extend from the southeast coast of Africa to the interior's Lake Chad.

Unfortunately, none of the denomination churches (including his own church) had interest in his idea, though his few friends did. The first group of missionaries who would return to Africa with Scott left on August 17, 1895. This group of men and women did not have special training, just their Christian commitment, and arrived off the east African coast in Mombasa, Kenya, after a two-month journey. More missionaries came, including Scott's parents. Four Kenyan mission stations were established from Mombasa up to Lake Chad to deter the spread of Islam.

But in December 1896, barely more than a year after his arrival, Peter Scott died due to blackwater fever, and the mission almost dissolved. With the deaths of other founding members, the future of the mission was in question. But the council appointed Charles Hurlburt director of the mission, and he went to Africa with his family for the next twenty years. A strategic friend of Hurlburt, Theodore Roosevelt, intervened, and in 1912, the Belgian government allowed a new mission station in the Democratic Republic of Congo, a Belgian colony. Under Hurlburt's strong leadership, the AIM headquarters were established in Kijabe, Kenya. The AIM continued to develop its work in fourteen African countries over the next several decades.

Headquarters

37 Alexandra Park, Redland
Bristol BS6 6QB
United Kingdom
Telephone: 44 117 942 9771
Email: admin.io@aimint.net

Leadership

The International Council (IC) is the mission's final authority and sets the general direction and policy guidelines. The IC meets annually and is composed of the regional executive officers, a chairperson, and the international director. Lanny Arensen is the AIM's international director.

The executive officer of the International Council and his staff compose the International

Office, which is situated in Bristol. The International Council appoints the international director and associate director, who have to be ratified by a vote of members. Other directors are appointed by the International Council.

International Services exists to assist missionaries and the African church in their living and ministries, mainly located in Kenya.

Mobilizing Regions are composed of AIM Europe, AIM Australia, AIM Brazil, AIM Canada, AIM South Africa, and AIM United States of America. Mobilizing Regions select and send missionaries.

Core Beliefs

AIM members are God centered and acknowledge the absolute and final authority of God and his Word in all things. Members are committed disciples of the Lord Jesus Christ who embrace the essential role of individual and corporate prayer. God is considered the ultimate provider for members' spiritual and material needs. AIM members recognize the centrality of the local church in the plan of God.

The AIM is governed by and accountable to its members, whose opinions regarding ministry direction are valued by those in leadership. The AIM's decisions are made by those closest to the ministry. The AIM respects God's personal guidance in the life of individuals and the role of mission leadership and seeks to identify, equip, and empower servant leaders.

The AIM values members' families. Members commit themselves to maintaining and enhancing the well-being of their marriages and their children, and they are committed to help each member grow as they are transformed into the image of Christ.

Defining Statement

The Africa Inland Mission "is dedicated to the establishment of Christ-centered churches among all African peoples" (aimint.org, "About Our Mission").

Core Practices

AIM members are committed to making disciples of Jesus Christ and to establishing maturing churches among unreached peoples. At the same time, they are committed to developing Christlike leaders and believe that ministries are enhanced through a lifestyle consistent with the ministry context. The main tools in ministry are learning the local languages, expressing the life of Christ through teaching, and practical demonstrations of his compassion. As an autonomous, nondenominational mission organization, the AIM enters into partnerships with churches and cooperates with compatible organizations to accomplish its purpose. These tasks have to be done with integrity, both as a mission and as an individual.

Finances

The AIM's basic principle is that God supplies financial needs, as well as other needs, in answer to prayer. The supply of financial support in answer to prayer is seen as God's confirmation and seal on the call to serve overseas.

Statistics

About 930 missionaries from all parts of the world are members of the AIM. The AIM serves in more than 16 countries, primarily in southern Africa, including Chad, Central African Republic, Madagascar, Lesotho, Namibia, Southern Sudan, Kenya, and Tanzania.

Academic Institutions

The missionaries run Rift Valley Academy, a school built in Kijabe for missionary children, and Scott Theological College in Kenya, which trains African church leaders.

Website

http://www.aimint.org/

Bibliography

"Africa Inland Mission." http://www.aimint.org. "About Our Mission."

Anderson, D. We Felt Like Grasshoppers. Nottingham, UK: Crossway, 1994.

Richardson, K. Garden of Miracles: A History of the Africa Inland Mission. London: Victory, 1976.

Sywulka, M. Workers Together with Him: A Short History of Africa Inland Mission. Rethy, Irumu, Congo Belge: AIM Press, 1953.

Elena Goga and Mark A. Lamport

American Bible Society

History

The American Bible Society (ABS) began in 1816. John Jay, the United States' first chief justice, was president of the society beginning in 1821, and Francis Scott Key was vice president from 1817 to 1843.

The ABS translates, publishes, and distributes the Bible. The Good News Translation (1976) and the Contemporary English Version (1995) were produced by the ABS. The *Jesus* film (1979), viewed by over 5.6 billion people in one thousand languages, used the Good News translation of Luke for its script. The ABS provides study aids and other tools to help people engage with the Bible. Internationally, the ABS has five focus points: China, India, Sub-Saharan Africa, the Middle East, and Latin America.

Headquarters

1865 Broadway
New York, NY 10023
Telephone: 212-408-1200

Leadership

An advisory council was formed in 1916. This group continues to meet today as the National Church Leadership Council. In addition to a president and other executive officers, the ABS is governed by a board of twenty-nine members.

Core Beliefs

The ABS is a noncreedal, nondenominational, nonprofit organization. The Bible alone is its only creed.

Core Practices

The ABS partners with churches and other national Bible societies to make the Word of God and other resources available to people around the world in a language and format each can understand and afford so that all people can experience its life-changing message.

The ABS has several special units to extend its work. Global Scripture Impact provides counsel about funding worldwide projects that can impact the world for Christ. Bibles and other resources are available for purchase at bibles .com. The Nida Institute for Biblical Scholarship conducts training, education, and research. It ensures the quality of ABS products and services and develops Scripture-based educational materials. Eugene A. Nida, born in 1914, pioneered the Bible translation theory of "dynamic equivalence." Dr. Philip H. Towner serves as dean of the Nida Institute, located at the ABS headquarters in New York City.

Finances

The ABS is a member of the BBB Wise Giving Alliance and meets all twenty standards for charitable giving. For the fiscal year ending June 30, 2009, income was $54.4 million, including $8.2 million from Scripture sales and $3.8 million from other sources. Expenses for the same period were $92.7 million, leaving a deficit of $38.3 million. The deficit resulted from net investment losses. The ABS is a tax exempt 501(c)(3) organization. The ABS is also a member of Guide Star and is certified by the Independent Charities of America. After 2001, the society's revenues generally have not kept pace with spending, and about one-third of its employees were laid off after a drop in the value of its securities investments.

Statistics

In 2009, the ABS placed Scripture into the hands of 5.1 million persons through its various outreaches. The ABS has served for nearly two hundred years in over two hundred countries. Bibles are provided for servicemen, veterans, victims of natural disasters, and through almost twenty partners, such as Cru, Salvation Army, Samaritan's Purse, Prison Fellowship, and SIL International.

Publication

A digital magazine, *Record ONLINE*, appears bimonthly and features stories about placing the Bible among many people groups around the world.

Website

http://www.americanbible.org/

James A. Borland

AMG International

History

AMG International was founded in 1942, when George Georgakis and Nicholas Lambrides organized the American Committee for the Evangelization of the Greeks, with headquarters in New York, for the purpose of sending gospel literature overseas and providing aid for homeless and malnourished children in Greece. In the United States, the organization helped Greek children through the service of a nearby orphanage and published a bilingual (Greek and English) monthly magazine titled the *Voice of the Gospel* primarily as a means of evangelizing Greeks.

In 1946, Spiros Zodhiates, who was born on March 13, 1922, to Greek parents on the island of Cyprus (Nicosia), accepted an invitation to the United States from the American Committee for the Evangelization of the Greeks. Zodhiates possessed the bilingual skills and evangelical conviction that Georgikas and Lambrides sought for their publication; consequently, he became field representative for the mission and editor of the magazine. In 1947, the mission began Greek evangelism broadcasts in New York City, with Zodhiates as the speaker, and publication of evangelistic messages in the national daily Greek newspaper, *Atlantis*.

The mission's name was changed to American Mission to the Greeks (AMG) in 1958. AMG moved its headquarters to New Jersey in 1962. Due to the sudden death of Lambrides, Zodhiates became president of American Mission to the Greeks in 1966, which was renamed AMG International (for Advancing the Ministries of the Gospel) in 1974. Its international headquarters were moved to Chattanooga, Tennessee, in 1978.

Headquarters

PO Box 22000
6815 Shallowford Road
Chattanooga, TN 37421
Telephone: 423-894-6060; 800-251-7206
Fax: 423-894-6863

Leadership

Paul Jenks is president and Spiros Zodhiates is chairman emeritus. The board of trustees consists of nine members. The mission department staff includes ten members.

Core Beliefs

AMG is evangelical in its statement of faith. The mission affirms belief in the following core doctrines: the inspiration and inerrancy of Scripture in the original languages; the supreme and final authority of Scripture in all matters of faith and practice; the Trinity; the virgin birth of Jesus Christ as fully God and fully man; the creation of humans in the image of God; humanity's subsequent sin; the representative and substitutionary death of the Lord Jesus Christ; justification on the basis of his shed blood for all who receive him by repentance and faith; the bodily resurrection and ascension of Jesus; the personal and victorious "blessed hope"; and the bodily resurrection of the just unto everlasting life and the unjust unto everlasting punishment.

Statistics

AMG ministers in nearly sixty countries worldwide, including Albania, Bulgaria, Greece, Guatemala, Honduras, India, Indonesia, the Philippines, Romania, Russia, and Thailand.

Missionary and Evangelistic Work

AMG is a worldwide evangelistic and relief ministry. The mission intends to provide every person in the world at least one opportunity to hear and respond to the gospel. AMG preaches Jesus Christ as the only answer to life problems and the only hope for eternal life. The mission seeks to partner with Christians who share its passion for evangelism and discipleship. More Than Gold designated AMG as the lead agency for evangelism efforts during the 2004 Olympics in Athens.

Parachurch Organizations

AMG provides relief programs by instituting and supporting children's ministries and sponsorships, clinical ministries, daycare centers, food and clothing centers, a leprosy ministry, medical hospitals, orphanages, refugee work, and schools.

Through the cooperation of the Greek Evangelical Church, the mission established the first evangelical orphanage in Katerini, Greece, in 1953. St. Luke's Hospital in Thessaloniki, Greece, was opened as a 220-bed hospital in 1975 in memory of Lambrides. Kadyum Eye Hospital in Rajahmundry, India, opened in 1994, with ministry to blind leprosy sufferers. The Senorita Elena Medical Center in Cubulco, Guatemala, provides medical care for more than fifteen thousand patients yearly. The Peachtree Center in Smyrna, Tennessee, provides nursing and rehabilitation.

Electronic Media

In 1951, an exegetical teaching program called *New Testament Light* began daily and weekly broadcasts in Red Lion, Pennsylvania. The ministry soon expanded to stations throughout the United States and Canada. Established in 1976, Christ the Light of the World (CLW) Communications Group provides churches and ministries with affordable prices for audio and video equipment and services.

Publications

Evangelism through various forms of literature is a primary ministry of AMG. In 1959, the mission began publication of gospel messages in Greek newspapers, but in 1961, the state church prohibited newspaper evangelism. The *Voice of the Gospel* is published as an evangelical witness and encouragement to the people of God in Greek communities worldwide. *Pulpit Helps* was founded in 1975 by Zodhiates to equip readers with a greater understanding of the Bible and thereby to help them fulfill their calling adequately and effectively as Christ's ambassadors. *Pulpit Helps* provides bulletin inserts, illustrations, sermon resources, and articles on topics such as Christian living, counseling, and preaching. AMG operates four bookstores in Greece. Zodhiates has published more than two hundred books and pamphlets in English, in addition to approximately one hundred in Greek. *The Hebrew-Greek Key Word Study Bible* was first published in 1984 and has since sold more than a million copies. AMG Publishers began outreach in 1980 with the mission of teaching Scripture. The press published biblical commentaries and study guides, inspirational titles, and youth resources.

Website

http://www.amginternational.org/

Bibliography

Ward, Carol. *The Christian Sourcebook*. New York: Ballantine Books, 1986.

Ron J. Bigalke

Anglican Mission in the Americas

History

Founded as a missionary outreach of the Anglican Church of Rwanda, the Anglican Mission in the Americas (AMIA) was formally established in Amsterdam in 2000. With the consecration of the Rt. Rev. Charles (Chuck) Hunt Murphy III, missionary bishop of the Province of the Anglican Church of Rwanda, as bishop and chairman of the AMIA, and the Rt. Rev. John Hewitt Rodgers Jr., retired missionary bishop of the Province of South East Asia, the AMIA functions under the direct authority of the Province of the Anglican Church of Rwanda and its archbishop. Headquartered in Pawley's Island, South Carolina, the AMIA is organized into Mission Networks (similar in nature to districts in church denominations), each of which is unique in style but united in doctrine. Chief among the goals of the Mission Networks (currently twenty-one in number across the United States) is not only planting new churches but also developing outreach initiatives that help facilitate mission goals. While it is possible to consider South Carolina the headquarters for the AMIA, the organization has been hesitant to formalize its structure because of its mission emphasis.

Originally envisioned by the Most Reverend Emmanuel Kolini, the Anglican archbishop of Rwanda and bishop of Kigali, the AMIA came about following the devastation of Rwanda by genocide in April 1994. Called "the April that would not end," open hostilities between Hutus and Tutsis left over one million people (mostly Tutsis) dead and countless others maimed, orphaned, and displaced. Rather than becoming another displaced person and having experienced the terrible devastation brought on by genocide, Bishop Kolini turned his attention toward rebuilding his nation. Interestingly, he saw what he called an equally devastating "spiritual genocide" curable only by the gospel of Jesus Christ. To combat that "genocide," Bishop Kolini set about implementing a Scripture-based strategy for recovery in Rwanda and, at the same time, developing a similar mission strategy for reaching America with the gospel of Christ. This mission is accomplished through the ministry of local Anglican churches established on a solid biblical foundation. Bishop Kolini saw the power of the gospel at work in his own country, and he was convinced that the power of the gospel that transformed his native Rwanda could transform America as well.

Headquarters

Mailing Address
PO Box 3427
Pawleys Island, SC 29585

Street Address
297 Willbrook Boulevard
Pawleys Island, SC 29585

Core Beliefs

The Anglican Mission celebrates unity in the essential elements of Christian faith, worship, life, and ministry. It is "nourished by the three streams of Scripture, the Sacramental Life and the Holy Spirit" (theamia.org, "Our Vision of Mission"). Doctrinally, the AMIA takes positions easily recognizable in other evangelical denominations. Those positions include the following: salvation is found in Jesus Christ alone, who is the only begotten Son of the living God; the Holy Scriptures of the Old and New Testaments in their entirety is God's Word and is the standard by which we are to order our lives, express our faith, and function as a community; and we are to live our lives, to make disciples, and to grow our churches in a manner that expresses the loving and longing heart of God for those who are separated from Jesus Christ and his church.

The Anglican Mission exists to glorify God by building an alliance of congregations in North America committed to gathering, planting, and serving dynamic churches in the Anglican tradition with the primary goal of reaching the reportedly 130 million Americans and 20 million Canadians considered unchurched.

Core Practices

Relational ministry: The Anglican Mission is committed to ministry being accomplished in relationships that express the love, intimacy, and unity of God as revealed in the relationship of the Father, the Son, and the Holy Spirit.

Servant ministry: The Anglican Mission believes that every Christian is created for ministry, gifted for ministry, and needed for ministry.

Sacrificial giving: The Anglican Mission believes that we are to be generous with our time, talents, and money.

Biblical leadership: The Anglican Mission is committed to identifying and training emerging leaders who are committed to Christ and to reaching their generation with the gospel.

Expectant prayer: The Anglican Mission believes that nothing of significance happens in God's kingdom in the absence of prayer.

Worship

The Anglican Mission is committed to worship in Word and sacrament through the power of the Holy Spirit.

Controversies

The AMIA distances itself from the Episcopal Church USA (ECUSA) because of positions taken by the ECUSA on controversial issues, particularly the encouragement of practicing, noncelibate homosexual members in both laity and clergy, as well as the ordination of women. These issues are often at the heart of decisions by churches to withdraw from the ECUSA and affiliate themselves instead with the Anglican Church in Rwanda.

Website

http://www.theamia.org/

Raymond Legg

Avant Ministries

History

A group of individuals participating in a Bible study associated with the Kansas YMCA in 1889 became aware of the needs on the African continent. In 1890, the group sent six men to the Sudan and three women to Sierra Leone. Although five of them died in the first few months, this only served to fuel the group's passion for missions. They founded an organization they called World's Gospel Union in 1892 that grew throughout the 1890s, becoming increasingly influential as a missions-sending agency. In 1901, after continued growth and clarification of their purpose, they changed the name to the Gospel Missionary Union.

Throughout the twentieth century, the Gospel Missionary Union continued to expand and develop as a missions-sending and missions-training organization. The ministry's influence during this time was evident through its profound influence in such vastly distinct areas of the world as Ecuador and Morocco. In 1975, the Gospel Missionary Union merged with the Evangelical Union of South America (EUSA), further expanding its work into Argentina, Brazil, Colombia, and Bolivia, where EUSA's personnel served. In 2003, the Gospel Missionary Union changed its name to Avant Ministries.

Headquarters

United States
10000 N Oak Trafficway
Kansas City, MO 64155
Telephone: 816-734-8500

Canada
2121 Henderson Highway
Winnipeg, MB R2G 1P8
Telephone: 204-338-7831

Leadership

A board of directors consisting of business professionals and ministry personnel from the United States and Canada currently governs Avant Ministries. Avant's president manages the day-to-day operations of the organization.

Core Beliefs

Avant Ministries has six core values that define its key characteristics: the power of the gospel, the primacy of prayer, member care, vital partnerships, innovative thinking, and pervasive excellence.

Core Practices

Avant's current core ministries focus on new territories and new techniques, such as short-cycle church planting and an intentional focus on strategic partnerships with national believers.

Statistics

Avant Ministries has approximately three hundred missionaries serving in over twenty countries.

Trends

Avant Ministries continues to develop its focus on church partnerships and strategic work with national believers. A continued focus on the unevangelized and contemporary church-planting methods is central to Avant's vision for the future.

Website

http://www.avantministries.org/

Bibliography

Anderson, Gerald H. *Biographical Dictionary of Christian Missions*. Grand Rapids: Eerdmans, 1999.

Collins, George W. *Missionaries and Muslims: The Gospel Missionary Union in Morocco, 1895–1912*. Wichita: Wichita State University, 1975.

Conley, Joseph F. *Drumbeats That Changed the World*. Pasadena, CA: William Carey Library, 2000.

Frizen, Edwin L. *75 Years of IFMA, 1917–1992: The Nondenominational Missions Movement*. Pasadena, CA: William Carey Library, 1992.

Linzey, Sharon. *Christianity in Russia and Post-Communist Europe: Directory 2003*. Pasadena, CA: William Carey Library, 2003.

Maust, John. *New Song in the Andes*. Pasadena, CA: William Carey Library, 1992.

Tucker, Ruth. *From Jerusalem to Irian Jaya: A Biographical History of Christian Missions*. 2nd ed. Grand Rapids: Zondervan, 2004.

M. David Sills

Awana

History

In 1950, Art Rorheim and Lance "Doc" Latham launched the parachurch organization called the Awana Youth Association to expand the weekly children's program that the two had started nine years earlier at the North Side Gospel Center in Chicago. The word "Awana" is an acronym for the phrase "approved workmen are not ashamed" (2 Tim. 2:15 KJV). Latham served as the president, and Rorheim served as the executive director. The program sought to win over young people in order to present the gospel to them and to engage them in the study of the Bible. Using gray shirts made for the Chicago Police Department, Latham and Rorheim made uniforms for the children. These trademark gray uniforms continued to serve as a distinguishing characteristic for Awana clubbers throughout the years.

In 1951, one other church adopted the Awana program using the newly published Awana curriculum handbooks and leadership manuals. By 1955, four churches had Awana clubs, and they competed in the first Awana Olympics, known today as the Awana Games. Twelve years later Awana had its own headquarters, theme song, and missionaries, with three hundred churches participating in the annual Awana Olympics. By 1972, Awana clubs were being held in one thousand host churches across forty-six US states, Bolivia, and Canada. In 1976, Awana launched a program for younger children from kindergarten through second grade called the Sparks Club. Awana had 5,000 clubs in the United States and more than 250 worldwide by 1983. Awana had also added several more programs: Cubbies for preschoolers, a pinewood derby race, an outreach event called the Awana Grand Prix, and the Friends program for mentally disabled youth. In 1985, Latham passed away.

In 1986, the organization was renamed Awana Clubs International. Six years after this name change 62 countries had clubs, and Awana materials had been translated into 17 languages, including Arabic and braille. By 2010, Awana had clubs in 19,000 churches in 100 countries, with 1.5 million children in attendance. The growth of Awana has been particularly remarkable in India. In 2013, 1,116,918 children attended clubs outside the United States, and the number of clubs in India ballooned to 5,845, with 408,270 children attending. Awana now hosts weekly clubs for youth between 2 and 18 years of age, along with several other programs.

Headquarters

1 E Bode Road
Streamwood, IL 60107
Telephone: 630-213-2000

Leadership

Since 1999, Dr. Jack Egger has served as president, with Art Rorheim continuing as president emeritus.

Core Beliefs

Awana is not affiliated with a single denomination. As a result, its beliefs are reflective of the beliefs held in common by many conservative evangelical churches. Its statement of faith emphasizes the inerrancy of Scripture and the necessity of faith in Christ Jesus for salvation. Dispensational influences are also evident;

Awana affirms the eternal security of believers and "the personal, premillennial, and imminent coming of our Lord Jesus Christ" (awana.org, "What We Believe").

Defining Statement

The aim of Awana is to "help churches and parents raise children and youth to know, love, and serve Christ" (awana.org, "What Is Awana?").

Core Practices

Awana publishes curriculum for a broad array of weekly children's programs, each targeting a different age group. The clubs utilize an "instructional-analytical model" of children's spiritual development, with Scripture study and memorization forming key elements of all its programs (Carlson and Crupper, 103–64). A typical weekly meeting consists of a game time, Bible memorization, songs, and a Bible lesson.

There are four clubs for preschool and grade-school children: Puggles (two- and three-year-olds), Cubbies (preschool), Sparks (kindergarten through second grade), and Truth and Training (third through sixth grade). Two weekly programs, both under the umbrella of 24-7 Ministries, are geared toward middle school and high school students: Trek (seventh through ninth grade) and Journey (tenth through twelfth grade). Additional programs include Awana Lifeline, a ministry for children of prison inmates; Malachi Dads, a prison ministry training inmates to be godly parents; and the Modern Day Joseph Initiative, a campaign intended to aid parents and churches in raising children to become spiritually grounded adults. Awana hosts several annual events at local, regional, and national levels, including the Awana Grand Prix, the Awana Games (formerly Awana Olympics), the High Power Soccer sports camp, Bible quiz competitions, leadership training programs, and the national Summit meeting for high school students.

Website

http://www.awana.org/

Bibliography

"Awana." http://www.awana.org. "Around the World 3/31/13," "History," "What Is Awana?" and "What We Believe."

Carlson, Gregory C., and John K. Crupper. "Instructional-Analytical Model." In *Perspectives on Children's Spiritual Formation*, edited by Michael J. Anthony, 103–64. Nashville: Broadman & Holman, 2006.

Jim Keener

Back to the Bible

History

Back to the Bible (BTTB) is a nondenominational, international ministry whose main focus is teaching the Word of God. Using radio, television, and other media, it proclaims the Bible's message of salvation through faith in Jesus Christ to nonbelievers and endeavors to lead believers into spiritual maturity.

BTTB was born on May 1, 1939, when a young preacher named Theodore Epp aired the first *Back to the Bible* broadcast from KFOR (AM) radio in Lincoln, Nebraska. By the time Epp retired in 1981, his dream had come true, and *Back to the Bible* was being heard worldwide. Warren W. Wiersbe, former pastor of Moody Church in Chicago, succeeded Epp and served until 1989, when Woodrow Kroll, former president of Davis College, became the third president.

Headquarters

Mailing Address
PO Box 82808
Lincoln, NE 68501

Street Address
6400 Cornhusker Highway
Lincoln, NE 68507
Telephone: 800-759-6655
Fax: 402-464-7474
Email: info@backtothebible.org

Leadership

Dr. Woodrow Kroll is the president and senior Bible teacher, and Dr. Arnie Cole is the CEO.

Core Beliefs

Back to the Bible is a nondenominational, conservative, Protestant organization. It believes the Bible is the inspired, inerrant revelation of God. The ministry also affirms the following:

The Trinity of God is Father, Son, and Holy Spirit.
Jesus Christ was eternally coexistent with God.
In his incarnation, Jesus was fully man and fully God.
He lived a sinless life, was crucified on the cross for the sins of all mankind, rose from the dead, and ascended into heaven.
The Holy Spirit is the Comforter sent by Jesus Christ to indwell believers. He convicts, empowers, and seals them unto the final day of redemption.
Man was created by God in his own image.
Through man, sin came into the world.
Only by faith in Jesus Christ can a person be saved from the wages of sin.

Through obedience and the power of the Holy Spirit, believers grow in character and become increasingly conformed to Christ's image.

The church is the body of Christ, his bride. Its purpose is to glorify God and to proclaim the gospel throughout the world.

Christ's return is imminent and premillennial. He will take his people to be with him and to judge and rule the earth in righteousness. To be absent from the body is to be present with the Lord. While the resurrection of the body is for both believers and unbelievers, believers will live forever with God, but unbelievers will be judged and sentenced to eternal punishment in hell, along with Satan and his demonic angels. (backtothebible.org, "Statement of Faith")

Defining Statement

"Back to the Bible is an international Bible-teaching media ministry reaching unbelievers with the Gospel of Christ and developing spiritual maturity in believers" (backtothebible.org, "Core Values").

Core Practices

Evangelism and Bible literacy are the prime focuses of Back to the Bible.

Statistics

Back to the Bible has branches in fifteen countries. Its largest demographic is people fifty-five and older, and its second largest is people eighteen to twenty-five. The *Back to the Bible* radio broadcast goes out in twenty-five languages and can be heard by more than 50 percent of the world's population every day.

Missionary and Evangelistic Work

Back to the Bible is an international ministry with offices around the world, including Brazil, Canada, Ecuador, India, Indonesia, Jamaica, Japan, Nepal, and Sri Lanka, all of which are staffed by national Christians.

Masihi Vandana (*Christian Worship*) is a Hindi broadcast in India. KAMI is Back to the Bible's Indonesian ministry. B-Japan produces native language broadcasts on a cable radio network with over 1.3 million subscribers. *Safal Jeevanko Rahasya* (*Confident Living*) airs in India, and *Verdade Biblica* (*Truth of the Bible*) airs in Sao Paulo. Broadcasts air to more than fourteen million people in Sinhala, the major language in Sri Lanka. Since 1970, *La Biblia Dice* (*The Bible Says*) has aired across most of Latin America, in some Caribbean islands, and in Equatorial Guinea, Africa.

Affiliations

Back to the Bible International is a member of CrossGlobal Link and World By Radio, an association of international Christian broadcasting organizations. The ministry reaches out to its local community through its indoor skateboard park and concert venue. The Center for Bible Engagement is the ministry's research and development division, which seeks to address Bible illiteracy in America and offers resources and tools for Bible study.

Electronic Media

Woodrow Kroll and Tami Weissert cohost a daily twenty-five-minute radio Bible study, which is heard on more than 1,209 stations in the United States and Canada. The *Bible Minute* is a ninety-second radio message on the daily relevance of God's Word. The *Back to the Bible* television program can be seen on a variety of stations. In addition to radio and television broadcasts, Back to the Bible uses modern technology in the form of podcasts, videocasts, emails, texting, Twitter, and Facebook to send God's Word throughout the world.

Publications

Dr. Kroll has written more than fifty books on the Bible and Christian living and numerous studies of Bible books.

Website

http://www.backtothebible.org/

Bibliography

Anderson, Erin. "Back to the Bible Focuses on Relationship with God, Not Religion." *Lincoln Journal Star*, April 27, 2009. http://journalstar.com/lifestyles/article_ab6bab4c-cc91-560d-bfc8-e268326969e4.html?print=1.

"Back to the Bible." http://www.backtothebible.org. "Core Values" and "Statement of Faith."

Balmer, Randall. "The Wireless Gospel." *Christianity Today*, February 19, 2001. http://www.christianitytoday.com.au/ct/2001/february19/4.48.html.

Marlene Mankins

Baptist World Mission

History

Baptist World Mission (BWM) began as a fundamentalist and separatist Baptist missionary agency in 1961 within the Conservative Baptist Association of America (CBA). It was a direct protest to perceived new evangelical influences in the latter organization. Its original name was World Conservative Baptist Mission, but this was changed to the present designation in 1966 when all ties with the CBA were severed.

The first president was Bryce Augsburger, and Ernest Pickering was vice president. Notable initial board members were Earle Matteson, Ed Nelson, Monroe Parker, Richard Weeks, and Arno Weniger Sr. Dr. Monroe Parker of Decatur, Alabama, became the general director of BWM in 1969, and the headquarters were moved from Chicago to Decatur. Fred Moritz became the executive director upon the death of Parker in 1994.

In 1997, Baptist World Mission assimilated another mission board that had fifteen missionary families. More than four thousand churches now support missionaries through BWM. Bud Steadman became the executive director in April 2009. BWM describes itself as fundamentalist, premillennial, dispensational, noncharismatic, Baptistic, and separatist. BWM opposes neo-evangelicalism.

Headquarters

PO Box 2149
Decatur, AL 35602
Telephone: 256-353-2221
Fax: 256-353-2266

There is also a Canadian office in Milton, Ontario.

Leadership

Since 1967, BWM has had a self-perpetuating board of trustees numbering between twenty-four and thirty-two. The board normally has two annual meetings, and nine members constitute a quorum.

Core Beliefs

BWM holds to the following beliefs (the full statement can be found at baptistworldmission .org, "The Baptist World Mission Constitution"):

the inerrancy of Scripture
the Trinity
the deity of Christ
Christ's human and divine natures
the deity and personality of the Holy Spirit
the temporality of some spiritual gifts (speaking in tongues was never the common or necessary sign of the filling or the baptism of the Holy Spirit)
salvation by faith alone in Christ's atoning blood, without works
three parts of sanctification
separation from churches that walk in unbelief and practice inclusivism
separation of church and state

two ordinances—baptism by immersion and the Lord's Supper as a commemoration of Christ's death
the Great Commission as the primary program of the church
Christ's imminent coming to rapture his church prior to the seven-year tribulation period
Christ's thousand-year reign over the earth with Israel reestablished in its land while Satan is bound
the judgment of the wicked to everlasting punishment while the righteous experience "eternal conscious blessedness in the presence of the Lord"

BWM declares a fourfold purpose that characterizes its basic belief system. It is "strictly Baptistic and committed to local church ideology, biblically missionary and dedicated to the establishment of kindred Baptist churches . . . ; and unquestionably separationist in affiliation and practice; unashamedly fundamentalist in recognition of the sole authority of the Word of God" (baptistworldmission.org, "Still Standing and Striving").

The Baptist World Mission Constitution contains a preamble, followed by seven articles. It was adopted on April 18, 1995. This document outlines name, purpose, doctrine, organization, meetings, the function and duties of seven standing committees, and amendments. Members of the board of trustees must be regenerated believers in Jesus Christ, members of separatist Baptist churches, and practicing tithers.

Finances

The executive director of BWM, Bud Steadman, declined to release any information regarding mission revenues or expenditures. BWM is not a member of the Evangelical Council for Financial Accountability.

Statistics

BWM has five field administrators, including Western Europe and the Middle East, Eastern Europe and Canada, South America, Asia and the South Pacific, and the United States.

Missionary and Evangelistic Work

BWM has about three hundred missionaries working in fifty countries. The main emphasis is church planting. The primary countries for BWM work are Argentina, Brazil, Canada, France, Germany, Ireland, Japan, New Zealand, South Africa, Spain, and Uruguay. Each of these fields has at least five missionaries. Brazil has fifteen missionary families.

BWM also works in Albania, Australia, Cambodia, Cameroon, the Democratic Republic of Congo, England, Haiti, Hong Kong, Hungary, India, Indonesia, Italy, the Ivory Coast, Kenya, Lithuania, Mexico, Mongolia, Myanmar, Nicaragua, Peru, the Philippines, Poland, Puerto Rico, Romania, Russia, Scotland, South Korea, Suriname, Taiwan, Thailand, Ukraine, the United States, and Zambia. Most of these countries have only one missionary couple on the field.

Website

http://www.baptistworldmission.org/

Bibliography

"Baptist World Mission." http://www.baptistworldmission .org. "The Baptist World Mission Constitution" and "Still Standing and Striving."

Clearwaters, Richard V. *The Great Conservative Baptist Compromise*. Minneapolis: Central Seminary Press, 1973.

James A. Borland

Benedictines

History

St. Benedict of Nursia (AD 480–547), a young Roman nobleman, founded twelve monastic houses at Subiaco outside Rome. He subsequently moved the community to Monte Cassino around 529 and wrote the *Rule of Saint Benedict* as a binding constitution for this community, which it remains to this day. Other communities quickly emerged and multiplied, sharing the *Rule* as a common model. While other monastic communities preexisted St. Benedict, his *Rule* provided such a vibrant and lasting foundation for Christian monastic life that he is known as the father of Western monasticism.

Each Benedictine monk (or nun) makes three lifelong vows: stability, "conversion of manners" (*conversatio*), and obedience. The vow of stability is intended to ensure the permanence of community life and prevent itinerancy, since St. Benedict believed that a common ("coenobitic"), fraternal life under a spiritual father ("abbot") was the ideal means toward sanctity. The vow of *conversatio* entails a continuing commitment to personal conversion, including chastity (a renunciation of marriage), poverty (a renunciation of private property), and manual labor to subdue idleness, the "enemy of the soul." The vow of obedience—primarily to Christ, secondarily to the abbot, his representative—facilitates growth in humility in the struggle against pride. While the abbot is

the final authority in the monastery, decisions are made in as collaborative a manner as possible; the abbot himself is freely elected by all the monks. Despite the misleading name, the Order of St. Benedict is not an "order" in the typical sense of the term, since each monastic community is self-governed and autonomous.

The success of the *Rule* led Benedict to establish a female community near Monte Cassino led by his twin sister, St. Scholastica. Benedictine communities flourished throughout the Middle Ages, holding a near monopoly on monastic life in the West until the emergence of the Franciscans and Dominicans in the thirteenth century. Due to their autonomy, flexibility, and self-sufficiency, Benedictines played a key role in the evangelization of Europe during this time.

Core Beliefs

The Benedictines is a group of Roman Catholic monastic communities that follow the *Rule of Saint Benedict*. The central goal of all forms of monastic life in the Catholic Church is to secure "undivided devotion to the Lord" (1 Cor. 7:35 NIV) through the "evangelical counsels" of chastity, poverty, and obedience. Members are additionally characterized by their pursuit of a stable community life built on the twin pillars of *ora et labora* (work and prayer) as an indispensible means toward this end.

Statistics

It is estimated that more than twelve hundred Benedictine communities, male and female, exist today all over the world. This number includes other monastic families (e.g., the Congregation of Cluny, Cistercians, and Trappists) that follow the *Rule of Saint Benedict*. Many thousands of oblates exist as well—laypersons who do not take lifelong vows but pledge to follow the *Rule* as perfectly as possible—each affiliated with a specific Benedictine community. Benedictines today are best known for their work in education and missions.

Bibliography

Daly, Lowrie J. *Benedictine Monasticism: Its Formation and Development through the 12th Century*. New York: Sheed and Ward, 1965.

Gregory the Great. *The Life of St. Benedict*. Translated by Terrence G. Kardong. Collegeville, MN: Liturgical Press, 2009.

Grün, Anselm. *Benedict of Nursia: His Message for Today*. Translated by Linda Maloney. Collegeville, MN: Liturgical Press, 2006.

Kardong, Terrence G. *Benedict's Rule: A Translation and Commentary*. Collegeville, MN: Liturgical Press, 1996.

Jamie Blosser

Bethany International

History

Bethany International (BI) began as Bethany Fellowship in 1945 in Minneapolis, Minnesota, with five families and their pastor, Ted Hegre, who had a vision of sending out and supporting one hundred missionaries. Putting action to their faith, these five families sold their homes and together purchased a thirty-room home they named Bethany House. They soon outgrew the home and in June 1948 moved to a 62.5-acre farm in Bloomington, Minnesota, and established the Bethany College of Missions, which trained missionaries and linked them with missions-sending agencies. In 1963, Bethany International was formed as the missionary sending agency directly connected with the Bethany College of Missions. Over the years, Bethany has graduated nearly three thousand people, sent out hundreds of missionaries, planted numerous churches, distributed literature, trained church and mission leaders, and partnered with national ministries in more than fifty countries.

Headquarters

6820 Auto Club Road
Suite M
Bloomington, MN 55438
Telephone: 952-944-2121
Fax: 952-829-2753
Email: bethany@bethanyinternational.org

Leadership

The president of Bethany International is Dan Brokke, and a board of seven to fifteen trustees governs the ministry.

Core Beliefs

Bethany International is a Christian missions-training and missions-sending organization that affirms core trinitarian evangelical doctrines, as well as these identity statements (bethanyinternational.org, "Our Core Values"):

Message of the cross: "We are transformed through union with Christ who was crucified for us, as us, and in us."
Centrality of prayer: "Daily surrender, worship, ongoing prayers and intercession empower God's people and advance His Kingdom on earth."

Reach all peoples: "We take the Great Commission literally—to reach all peoples in all nations."
All-in commitment: "We abandon everything to join God in collaboration with others in the global Body of Christ."
Faith-filled initiative: "With creativity and excellence we give our best efforts in mission and business initiatives, trusting the Holy Spirit with exceptional results."

Defining Statement

"We have joined God to recruit, train, send and support mobilizing movements of Kingdom workers worldwide to reach strategically among the unreached, and the least reached, to transform people and nations for Christ wherever darkness reigns" (bethanyinternational.org, "About Bethany International").

Statistics

BI and its partners have workers in over 50 countries, reaching out along with missionaries, national partners, and ministries to share the good news of the kingdom. The college has over 135 students (90 residing on campus), with 21 more involved in the Global Internship program and another 25 working through the online Global Studies course. BI also sends short-term missions teams to various places around the world.

Missionary and Evangelistic Work

BI trains people for missions, emphasizing three characteristics: a vibrant spirituality, a godly character, and great social and intercultural skills. Formal higher education training is offered through BI's Bethany College of Missions. BI long-term missions include projects such as evangelizing and church planting, assisting national partners in establishing new missionary training schools, publishing and distributing Christian literature, establishing prayer rooms for spiritual breakthroughs, and facilitating businesses as mission initiatives.

BI short-term missions occur through STEM (Short-Term Evangelical Missions) for one-, two-, or three-week mission trips scheduled monthly.

Academic Institutions

Many of BI's long- and short-term missionaries come from the Bethany College of Missions (BCOM), located in Bloomington, Minnesota. BCOM is an applicant for accreditation with the Association for Biblical Higher Education. It offers different levels of higher education training, including a one-year certificate in Bible or missions and an associate of arts and a bachelor of arts degree in intercultural studies. The Bethany Center for Global Studies offers an online master's degree in intercultural leadership. One highlight of opportunities at BCOM is its Global Internship, through which a student serves on a team internationally for sixteen months, partnering with missionaries in evangelistic efforts, learning the culture and language, taking key academic courses, and becoming an interculturally minded Christian.

A fruit of BI outside the United States, Bethany Evangelical Bible School in Brazil is celebrating its fortieth year of operation, with over six hundred graduates going into ministry.

Electronic Media

BI is fully present on the internet, with distinct websites for its component ministries, among which are online studies through its educational units. BCOM has posted videos on YouTube that show campus life and its passion for missions. Podcasts of speakers at Bethany International are accessible through iTunes.

Publications

Bethany Press International, a unit of BI, has published Christian materials for more than sixty years. Its Bethany House Publishers contributed many titles to evangelical literature and was purchased by Baker Publishing Group in 2003. Now Bethany Press offers a full range of Christian publishing services, from design through distribution. It prints over twenty-five million books each year for Christian publishers, ministries, and self-publishing authors and has recently added Believers Press to accommodate smaller-volume publishing. Press profits go back into gospel ministry.

Website

http://www.bethanyinternational.org/

Bibliography

"Bethany International." http://www.bethanyinternational .org. "About Bethany International" and "Our Core Values."

Chris A. Ruhl

Bible League International

History

Bible League was founded in 1938 by William Chapman. Two years earlier, while hospitalized

due to a life-threatening illness, Chapman was moved by the prayer of an elder in his church who asked that Chapman's life be spared so that he could serve Christ. Chapman's initial exercise was to purchase one thousand Bibles and, on a door-to-door mission including his wife, to offer them to anyone expressing interest. Today Bible League provides Bibles and Bible-based materials that are utilized by various churches and ministries to reach several hundred language groups.

Headquarters

Mailing Address
1 Bible League Plaza
Crete, IL 60417
Telephone: 866-825-4636

Street Address
3801 Eagle Nest Drive
Crete, IL 60417

Core Beliefs

Bible League endorses the statement of faith adopted by the National Association of Evangelicals. The full statement appears on the ministry website (bibleleague.org, "Statement of Faith").

Finances

The Evangelical Council for Financial Accountability reported that in 2013 Bible League had revenue of more than $23 million.

Website

http://www.bibleleague.org/

Bibliography

"Bible League." http://www.bibleleague.org. "History" and "What We Believe."

George Thomas Kurian

Billy Graham Evangelistic Association

History

The Billy Graham Evangelistic Association (BGEA), which celebrated its sixtieth year in 2010, arose from the fruitful ministry of its namesake. Billy Graham was ordained in 1939 in the Southern Baptist Convention. He attended Florida Bible Institute (now Trinity College in Florida) and graduated from Wheaton College in 1943. After pastoring First Baptist Church in Western Springs, Illinois, he joined Youth for Christ, preaching across the United States and in post–World War II Europe. In 1949, he held an evangelistic crusade in Los Angeles that ran for eight weeks and launched him into the public eye. He continued holding crusades, many of which were extended—one crusade ran for sixteen weeks of nightly meetings.

In 1950, Graham founded the BGEA in Minneapolis, Minnesota. The headquarters later moved to their present location in Charlotte, North Carolina. The ministry continued to expand its outreaches, which included the weekly Sunday radio program *Hour of Decision*, broadcast around the world; television specials of Rev. Graham's crusades; a syndicated newspaper column called "My Answer"; *Decision* magazine, the BGEA's official publication; and World Wide Pictures, one of the top producers of evangelistic films. Rev. Graham has written twenty-seven books, counseled US presidents, and received numerous awards and honorary doctorates from around the world. The Billy Graham Library at the ministry headquarters in Charlotte was dedicated in 2008 with three US presidents present. Rev. Graham's son Franklin was appointed president and CEO of the BGEA in 2001.

Headquarters

1 Billy Graham Parkway
Charlotte, NC 28210
Telephone: 877-2GRAHAM; 704-401-2432

Core Beliefs

The BGEA believes the following (the full statement can be found at billygraham.org, "Statement of Faith"):

The Bible is the infallible, holy, and inspired Word of God, and it is of supreme and final authority.

There is one God, eternally existing in three persons—Father, Son, and Holy Spirit.

Jesus Christ was conceived by the Holy Spirit and born of the Virgin Mary. He led a sinless life, took on himself all our sins, died and rose again, and is seated at the right hand of the Father as our mediator and advocate.

All of mankind is lost and face the judgment of God and need to come to a saving knowledge of Jesus Christ through his shed blood on the cross.

Christ rose from the dead and is coming soon.

In holy Christian living, we must have concern for the hurts and social needs of our fellowmen.

We must dedicate ourselves anew to the service of our Lord and to his authority over our lives.

We must use every modern means of communication available to us to spread the gospel of Jesus Christ throughout the world.

Defining Statement

Billy Graham said, "My one purpose in life is to help people find a personal relationship with God, which, I believe, comes through knowing Christ" (billygraham.org, "Biographies").

Core Practices

Since 1950, Billy Graham has held crusades all over the world. Other outreaches include evangelism training, youth outreach, disaster response, and television and radio broadcasts. Telephone centers respond to calls for help, salvation, and comfort. The Christian Guidance Department responds to letters, telephone calls, and emails.

Statistics

Graham has preached to nearly 215 million people in more than 185 countries. Since 1948, he has been the dominant figure in the Gallup poll's "Ten Most Admired Men in the World"—with forty-four consecutive appearances and fifty-one total appearances. The films of World Wide Pictures have been translated into 38 languages and viewed by more than 250 million people worldwide.

Missionary and Evangelistic Work

Graham's son Franklin and grandson Will hold evangelistic outreaches called, respectively, Franklin Graham's Festivals and Will Graham's Celebrations.

Dare to Be a Daniel, begun in 2006, is a youth evangelism training program that trains preteens to share their faith in Jesus Christ with friends and family.

In 2002, My Hope World Evangelism Through Television began partnering with churches to train people to evangelize their families, friends, and communities using BGEA TV broadcasts and videos. Since its inception, more than 8.8 million people have come to know Christ.

The Billy Graham Rapid Response Team is a nationwide database of trained chaplains who respond to calls for assistance during times of natural and man-made disasters.

Ransom is a new project from the BGEA geared toward youth and includes a website, Facebook page, Twitter feed, and YouTube channel.

Steps to Peace with God is a free iPhone application that shows people how to have a personal relationship with God and share their faith with others.

Parachurch Organizations

The Billy Graham Schools of Evangelism train people in strategies for effective evangelism in churches and communities.

Electronic Media

Since 1950, the BGEA's weekly radio program, *Hour of Decision*, has been broadcast around the world. "Billy Graham Classics" are shown on the TBN network in the United States and Canada. BGEA's radio ministry, Blue Ridge Broadcasting, in North Carolina broadcasts twenty-four hours a day.

Publications

Decision magazine, founded in November 1960, is published eleven times a year. Rev. Graham has written twenty-seven books.

Website

http://www.billygraham.org/

Bibliography

"Billy Graham Evangelistic Association." http://www.billy graham.org. "Biographies" and "Statement of Faith."

Marlene Mankins

Brazil Gospel Fellowship Mission

History

The Brazil Gospel Fellowship Mission (BGFM) began in 1939 with the vision of sending missionaries to plant churches in northeast Brazil in Sobral, Ceará. The mission was officially organized in 1945 and incorporated in the state of Illinois in 1955.

In 1949, the Gospel Missionary Union (GMU) created the Maranatha Bible College, or the Seminário e Instituto Bíblico Maranata (SIBIMA Seminary), in Fortaleza, Ceará, Brazil. The purpose of the seminary was to train leaders for its churches in Brazil. In 1985, the GMU teamed with the BGFM to develop bachelor programs at the seminary, which now grants a BA in the pastoral sciences, Christian education, missions, and music.

The mission has also built numerous Christian grade schools in northeast Brazil, the Silver Lake Bible Camp and the Antioch Bible Institute in Ceará, and the Priscilla School, which offers one-week training seminars for women. Both missionaries and Brazilians teach in the seminary and Bible institute.

Between 1960 and 1979, the mission extended its outreach through radio and film, largely through the efforts of the ministry of the Jerry Neuman family.

Having established over seventy small churches, the mission formed the Association of Churches to unite these fellowships in Brazil and to help them collaborate in making plans and setting goals. In the 1990s, the association was turned over to Brazilians, and most of the BGFM churches were given to Brazilians to pastor instead of missionaries.

Headquarters

125 W Ash Street
Springfield, IL 62704
Telephone: 217-523-7176
Fax: 217-523-7186
Email: bgfm_office@bgfmission.com

Leadership

Larry Lipka, the executive director since 1994, leads along with a board.

Core Beliefs

Core beliefs include belief in the Triune God, the literal interpretation of the Bible, the total depravity of man, the eternal security of the believer, disciplined sanctification, millennialism, and a pretribulational and premillennial rapture.

Defining Statement

This resolution was passed on July 1963:

This body stands for the fundamentals of the faith, eschewing liberalism, modernism, neoevangelicalism and all other groups which favor ecumenism and which detract from the faith once for all delivered to the saints. (bgfmission.com, "Our Values")

Core Practices

Core practices include water baptism by immersion as a testimony of belief in salvation and Communion.

Controversies

The BGFM opposes the teaching of the modern charismatic movement, which is on the rise in Brazil. Another one of its doctrinal statements stipulates a rejection of ecumenism.

Statistics

In 2012, there were nineteen family and four single-women missionaries and seventy established churches with Brazilian pastors.

Missionary and Evangelistic Work

The work of the mission is evangelism and church planting in northeast Brazil.

Academic Institutions

Antioch Bible Institute (Ceará, Brazil)

Maranatha Bible College (Seminário e Instituto Bíblico Maranata or SIBIMA Seminary) (Fortaleza, Ceará, Brazil)

Silver Lake Bible Camp (Ceará, Brazil)

Parachurch Organization

Maranatha Multicultural Ministries sends dentists to Brazil.

Electronic Media

The BGFM conducts radio ministries with Horizonte/Coqueiro Bible Church, Planalto Bible Church, Nova Metrópole Bible Church, Sítio Boatã Bible Church, Caucaia Bible Church, and Pacajus Bible Church.

Website

http://www.bgfmission.com/

Bibliography

"Brazil Gospel Fellowship Mission." http://www.bgfmission.com. "BGFM History," "Doctrinal Statement," and "Our Values."

Holland, Clifton. *A Chronology of Protestant Beginnings: Brazil.* http://www.prolades.com/historical/bra-chron.pdf.

Brenda Ayres

Bread for the World

History

Bread for the World (BFTW) was founded in October 1972 by a group of Protestants and Catholics to combat hunger in America. The group flourished under the leadership of Rev. Arthur Simon, an ordained Lutheran minister who was the 2004 recipient of the Pacem in Terris Peace and Freedom Award. Though it started small and locally, BFTW has grown into a major national movement that mobilizes grassroots advocacy in order to influence local, state, and national policy and legislation to benefit the hungry and the poor. It is one of the eleven organizations that started the ONE campaign to end global poverty.

Headquarters

50 F Street NW
Suite 500
Washington, DC 20001
Telephone: 202-639-9400; 800-82-BREAD
Fax: 202-639-9401
Email: bread@bread.org

Leadership

In September 1991, Rev. David Beckmann succeeded Rev. Arthur Simon as the president of BFTW and the Bread for the World Institute. Beckmann came to BFTW after working at World Bank for fifteen years and received the World Food Prize in 2010, along with Jo Luck, president of Heifer International. The BFTW board of directors is chaired by David Miner.

Core Beliefs

BFTW is a Christian organization that believes the best way to end hunger is to change the laws, policies, and other conditions that allow it to persist.

Defining Statement

"Moved by God's grace in Jesus Christ, we advocate for a world without hunger" (bread.org, "History and Mission").

Core Practices

BFTW is a $501(c)(4)$ organization that seeks to end hunger in the United States and around the world by changing the laws and practices that allow hunger and poverty to happen. This involves influencing US government programs and funding for nutrition both in the United States and in developing countries.

Finances

Charity Navigator has given Bread for the World its highest rating—four stars—for financial efficiency and accountability. The American Institute of Philanthropy ranks BFTW as one of the top-rated charities in the United States. Independent Charities of America awarded BFTW the Independent Charities Seal of Excellence. BFTW makes its financial records publicly available through both Guidestar and its website. Bread for the World and Bread for the World Institute are committed to a high level of financial accountability and are audited individually each year by an independent auditor.

Statistics

In early 2009, in response to Bread for the World's letter-writing campaign, Congress approved an increase of $740 million for the development of poverty-stricken nations. In October 2008, just as the US economic downturn became more severe, a BFTW bill went into effect, providing more than $10 billion to strengthen the US food stamps program. This project is called

SNAP, or Supplemental Nutrition Assistance Program. As of 2008, BFTW membership had increased by 20 percent over the previous five years to more than sixty thousand churches and individuals.

Missionary and Evangelistic Work

BFTW focuses strictly on eliminating hunger and poverty and does not pursue traditional evangelism.

Academic Institution

The BFTW Institute, the research and educational partner of BFTW, is a 501(c)(3) organization that seeks to educate politicians, leaders, and the public about the issue of hunger in the United States and abroad. The institute reports on hunger issues and creates educational resources.

Website

http://www.bread.org/

Alycia West

Camino Global (formerly CAM International)

History

Camino Global exists "to produce and empower committed followers of Jesus Christ in Spanish-speaking areas to reach the world" (caminoglobal.org, "About Us"). Originally founded in 1890 as Central America Mission and then later known as CAM International, the ministry began with the vision and prayers of the wives of two coffee plantation owners in Costa Rica. The women, Mrs. Ross and Mrs. Lang, began to pray fervently for the Lord to raise up workers for the harvest field of Costa Rica. These prayers took root in the actions of C. I. Scofield, who was a Congregationalist minister pastoring in Dallas. While attending the Niagara Bible Conference, Scofield met and was greatly influenced by pioneer missionary and China Inland Mission founder Hudson Taylor. This friendship, coupled with learning of the needs of the people of Costa Rica, led Scofield to form a second prayer group focusing on the Central American country. It was from this prayer group that Scofield, with the help of others, founded Central America Mission in 1890.

The mission sent its first missionary within four months of its founding, and by 1894, there were seven Central America Mission missionaries in Costa Rica. Over the next five years the mission expanded its work to Honduras, El Salvador,

Guatemala, and Nicaragua. At the mission's tenth anniversary, there were twenty-five missionaries working in these five countries.

By 2012, Camino Global was reaching Spanish speakers in more than one hundred countries with a specific focus on equipping them to reach the world.

Headquarters

United States
Camino Global
8625 La Prada Drive
Dallas, TX 75228
Telephone: 214-327-8206

Canada
CAM International of Canada
PO Box 71034
Maplehurst Outlet
Burlington, Ontario L7T 4J8
Telephone: 905-689-2473

Leadership

Camino Global has a governing board for both its US and Canadian office. The appointed board members are ministers, professionals, and scholars all driven by a passion for fulfilling the Great Commission in the Spanish-speaking world.

Core Beliefs

Camino Global is undergirded by five core values: Christlikeness, community, collaboration, compassion, and creativity.

Defining Statement

"Serving the Church, Camino Global will journey with Spanish speakers everywhere to transform communities, equip believers, and reach the world" (caminoglobal.org, "Who We Are").

Missionary and Evangelistic Work

Camino Global currently provides a variety of ministry efforts, including evangelism, discipleship, church planting, leadership training and development, theological education, and global missions mobilization.

Secondary ministries include pastoral care, radio broadcasting, architecture and construction, Bible translation, Indian ministries, music ministries, Christian day schools, Awana, camps and conferences, community outreach, publishing and literature, internship programs, and summer mission programs.

Camino Global has had a ministry presence in each country of Central America. Within Central

America, the ministry currently focuses on Guatemala and Honduras. In addition, Camino Global now also focuses on Mexico, Spain, Albania, and Uruguay and serves Hispanics in the United States. A Canadian-based office serves as the global recruitment center for Camino Global.

Website

http://www.caminoglobal.org/

Bibliography

"Camino Global." http://www.caminoglobal.org. "About Us" and "Who We Are."

Dahlquist, Anna Marie. *Trailblazers for Translators: The Chichicastenango Twelve.* Pasadena, CA: William Carey Library, 1995.

Frizen, Edwin L. *75 Years of IFMA, 1917–1992: The Nondenominational Missions Movement.* Pasadena, CA: William Carey Library, 1992.

Tucker, Ruth. *From Jerusalem to Irian Jaya: A Biographical History of Christian Missions.* Grand Rapids: Zondervan, 1983.

M. David Sills

Capitol Commission

History

Capitol Commission, founded in 2009, is a charitable and religious nonprofit entity whose mission is reaching the capitol communities (legislators and their staff, capitol employees, and lobbyists) of the United States and the world with the gospel of Jesus Christ.

Headquarters

2600 Fairview Road
Suite 200
Raleigh, NC 27608
Telephone: 919-838-1200
Fax: 919-831-1122

Leadership

A national board governs the ministry, which is represented by various professions (farming, industry, missions, pastoral, and ranching). The board appoints and oversees the president of the ministry and also approves and oversees all state ministry budgets.

Core Beliefs

We believe the Bible to be the inspired, the only infallible, authoritative Word of God, profitable for doctrine, for reproof, for correction, and for instruction in righteousness.

We believe that there is one God, eternally existent in three persons: Father, Son and Holy Spirit.

We believe in the deity of our Lord Jesus Christ, in His virgin birth, in His sinless life, in His miracles,

in His vicarious and atoning death through His shed blood, in His bodily resurrection, in His ascension to the right hand of the Father, and in His personal return in power and glory.

We believe that, for the salvation of lost and sinful people, regeneration by the Holy Spirit is absolutely essential through faith in Christ alone.

We believe in the present ministry of the Holy Spirit, the third person of the holy Trinity, by whose indwelling the Christian is enabled and empowered to live a godly life.

We believe in the resurrection of both the saved and the lost; they that are saved unto the resurrection of life and they that are lost unto the resurrection of damnation.

We believe in the spiritual unity of believers in our Lord Jesus Christ. (capitolcom.org, "Statement of Faith")

Defining Statement

"Capitol Commission, in partnership with the church, is committed to making disciples of Jesus Christ and promoting the Biblical mandate to pray for those in authority in the Capitol communities throughout the United States and around the world" (capitolcom.org, "Our Mission").

Core Practices

With the Bible as its foundation and authority, Capitol Commission is committed to bringing glory to God by making disciples of Jesus Christ within the capitol communities of the world. Capitol Commission's mandate is not to reform society through political influence or legislation but to be used by God in transforming the hearts and lives of elected officials with the gospel of Jesus Christ. Those representing Capitol Commission faithfully pursue the fulfillment of their mandate by evangelizing those who have not experienced a personal relationship with Jesus Christ; establishing those who desire to grow in their faith and their knowledge of Scripture; equipping those called to spiritual leadership; and encouraging, enabling, and engaging the church to participate with Capitol Commission in this process.

Statistics

There are presently seventeen states with full-time state directors. Capitol Commission envisions eventually having a presence in all fifty states and in capitols around the world. Unofficial data indicates that the ministry currently impacts 3,400 legislators, 3,400 legislative staff, 510 other capitol employees, and 340 lobbyists.

Capitol Commission seeks to serve the 85,000 legislators, constitutional officers, staff, and lobbyists who work as leaders in the state governments throughout the country. In addition, the ministry intends to reach the more than 1,446 federally elected officials and 440,000 locally elected and appointed officials across the nation (a number extending into the millions when including staff and lobbyists).

Missionary and Evangelistic Work

Each state director teaches weekly verse-by-verse Bible studies and is charged with the responsibility of raising his own financial support through gifts and grants from businesses, churches, foundations, and individuals. All fund-raising is sent to a national accounting office, with 100 percent credited to the respective state director's account. Capitol Commission provides many opportunities for ministry to elected officials through events such as the Pastors' Commission at the Capitol, legislators' prayer breakfasts, and an election-eve prayer ministry. The national ministry provides all administrative services to establish effective ministries in every capitol community in the world where there is not an evangelical witness to the claims of Jesus Christ and where political leaders are not being discipled to the glory of God.

Publications

State directors publish weekly Bible studies for legislators, lobbyists, and staff members. The Bible studies are hand distributed to each legislative office, emailed, and made available throughout the capitol community. Ministry locations may be accessed from the national website, which includes an archive of the Bible studies in addition to providing information with regard to ministry updates and upcoming events.

Website

http://www.capitolcom.org/

Bibliography

"Capitol Commission." http://www.capitolcom.org. "Our Mission" and "Statement of Faith."

Ron J. Bigalke

Catholic Relief Services

History

Catholic Relief Services (CRS) was begun in 1943 by the Roman Catholic bishops of the United States as a humanitarian agency to help with the resettlement of the numerous World War II European refugees. The original name of the agency was War Relief Services. Today,

over seventy years later, disaster relief and work with refugees remain central to the CRS mission. However, throughout these years, Catholic Relief Services has expanded its scope to many other areas of the globe, and it responds quickly not only to people impacted by war but also to those suffering from natural disasters, such as hurricanes and earthquakes. In addition, its focus on disaster relief is combined with work to establish sustainable communities leading to just and peaceful societies, especially among the earth's most marginalized peoples.

Headquarters

228 W Lexington Street
Baltimore, MD 21201
Telephone: 888-277-7575

Leadership

Catholic Relief Services is the overseas relief agency of the United States Conference of Catholic Bishops. As such, it functions as an outreach of the Roman Catholic Church. An executive leadership team made up of seven administrators and a board of directors consisting of several bishops and other interested parties direct the extensive work of the agency.

Core Beliefs

CRS's work adheres to Catholic social teaching, which advocates for earth's most marginalized populations and follows the gospel mandates of justice and charity. In addition to international activities on behalf of the poor, CRS seeks to foster within the United States a sense of global solidarity. Part of the mission statement of CRS states, "Catholic Relief Services is the official humanitarian agency of the Catholic community in the United States. We alleviate suffering and provide assistance to people in need in more than 100 countries without regard to race, religion or nationality" (crs.org, "The Mission of Catholic Relief Services").

Core Practices

The work of CRS mostly takes place in countries outside the United States and focuses on crisis areas, areas transitioning from crisis to increased stability, and stable but needy areas. The work done in each area is necessarily different. Those in crisis areas receive direct humanitarian aid, such as food, potable water, clothing, and shelter in order to maintain life. Work in transitioning and stable areas focuses more on creating just and sustainable societies. This work is often carried out through partnerships with local Roman Catholic or other agencies and focuses on long-term needs, such as education and agriculture. The school feeding program and the microfinancing of small local businesses, especially those run by women, are examples of programs designed to foster sustainable communities.

In addition to its international work, CRS has extensive programs in the United States designed to raise awareness and funds for its humanitarian activities. These programs include the Lenten Rice Bowl initiative to alleviate hunger, Thanksgiving clothing drives, Fair Trade programs, and the Work-of-Human-Hands program, which encourages the selling of handcrafts from impoverished producers.

Policy analysis and governmental advocacy for justice are also part of the work of CRS.

Finances

Catholic Relief Services reports that ninety-five cents of every dollar donated goes directly to the poor it serves. The remaining five cents is used for fund-raising, awareness, and administration. CRS has an A rating from the Institute of Philanthropy and is currently ranked twenty-eighth in the Non-Profit Times Top 100. Its audited financial statements are available on the CRS website.

Publications

Catholic Relief Services publishes one bimonthly general interest journal, the *Wooden Bell*, which reports on recent CRS activities. Each issue is focused on a theme, such as education or children. In addition to the *Wooden Bell*, CRS has an extensive publication list of materials useful to the work of CRS representatives and others who do similar work. These publications are technical manuals, training guides, case studies, and the like on numerous topics, such as HIV/AIDS, education, and water sanitation.

Website

http://www.crs.org/

Bibliography

Archambault, Sheila. "Students Take Action as CRS Ambassadors." *National Catholic Reporter* 46, no. 2 (2009): 14a.
"Catholic Relief Services." *America* 189, no. 5, September 1, 2003.
"Catholic Relief Services." http://www.crs.org. "The Mission of Catholic Relief Services."
Egan, Eileen. *Catholic Relief Services: The Beginning Years; For the Life of the World.* New York: Catholic Relief Services, 1988.
———. *For Whom There Is No Room.* New York: Paulist Press, 1995.
Korgen, Jeffry. *Solidarity Will Transform the World: Stories of Hope from Catholic Relief Services.* New York: Maryknoll, 2007.

Sheryl O'Sullivan

Child Evangelism Fellowship

History

Child Evangelism Fellowship (CEF) is an international, evangelical, nonprofit organization founded by Jesse Overholtzer (1877–1955) in 1937. Growing up in a religious family, Jesse was convicted at the age of twelve of his own sin and sought counsel from his mother. He was told, "Son, you are too young." It was not until Overholtzer was in college that he heard the gospel and trusted Christ as his Savior.

Later, as a pastor, Overholtzer read in one of Charles Spurgeon's sermons, "A child of five, if properly instructed, can as truly believe and be regenerated as an adult." This passage, he later reckoned, led him to begin Child Evangelism Fellowship when he was sixty years old (cefonline.com, "History"). The ministry has grown into the largest evangelistic outreach to children in the world. CEF is currently ministering in over 160 countries and in every US state.

CEF is a Bible-centered organization whose purpose is to evangelize boys and girls with the gospel of the Lord Jesus Christ and to disciple them in the local church for Christian living. CEF has different types of evangelistic programs, but the two most identified with the organization are 5-Day Clubs and Good News Clubs. These ministries take place in neighborhood settings, such as homes, backyards, schools, and community centers. These one-hour programs are designed to bring the gospel to children on their level.

An auxiliary program for teenagers is Christian Youth in Action (CYIA). In June, all across the United States, hundreds of young people are trained to conduct 5-Day Clubs. Throughout the summer, they have opportunities to present the gospel to boys and girls. Two additional summer opportunities are Summer Urban Missions (SUM) and Overseas Summer Missions (OSM). College-age adults are trained to teach 5-Day Clubs in large urban centers through SUM and in foreign countries through OSM.

Headquarters

PO Box 348
Warrenton, MO 63383
Telephone: 636-456-4321

267

Leadership

Reese Kauffman is the president and Harry Robinson is the executive vice president of International Ministries. Under the direction of the executive vice president of International Ministries, the work of CEF is divided into eight regions, each led by a regional director. By charter, the CEF International board of trustees serves as the governing board over all these regions: Asia Pacific, East and Central Africa, Europe (Northwest, Southwest, Central, Eastern), Latin America (Spanish/Portuguese languages), Middle East (including North Africa), North America/Caribbean (main language other than Spanish or Portuguese), Southern Africa/Indian Ocean, and West Africa. The ministry in each country is led by a national or an expatriate missionary.

Core Beliefs

The CEF statement of faith affirms belief in the verbal inspiration of the Scriptures; one God in three persons (Father, Son, and Holy Spirit); the perfect humanity and deity of the Lord Jesus Christ; the personality and deity of the Holy Spirit; the atoning death and bodily resurrection of the Lord Jesus Christ; salvation by faith alone; the personal return of the Lord Jesus Christ; and the reality of Satan, hell, and heaven.

Defining Statement

"Reaching children worldwide" (cefonline.com, "Home").

Core Practices

Club Ministries meet once a week during the school year and are more popular than ever following the Supreme Court ruling allowing Good News Clubs to take place in public schools across America.

5-Day Clubs meet during the summer months and offer a unique opportunity for children to interact with teenagers.

Wordless Book is an evangelism tool. It is a simple book of colored pages in which the dark page represents sin, the red page represents Jesus's blood, the white page represents a clean heart, the green page represents things that grow, and the gold page represents heaven.

Through Mailbox Club, 255,000 enrolled students from 130 countries learn of evangelism and discipleship.

Camp Good News offers day camps and overnight camps.

Military Children's Ministries is a joint venture with Cadence International.

Wonderzone.com allows trained counselors with language-specific websites in fourteen countries to disciple children in a real-time, interactive environment.

In 2009, through these combined ministries, over 6.1 million children worldwide heard the gospel and over one million made a profession of faith. The Children's Ministries Institute, a modular three-month course held at CEF's headquarters in Warrenton, Missouri, is dedicated to providing quality, practical training for those called of God to take the gospel message to children. Similar training is offered in various locations around the world.

Statistics

CEF has programs established in all 50 states and in 167 countries around the world, with 750 full-time workers in the United States. There are an estimated 40,000 volunteers in the United States and Canada and over 1,200 missionaries overseas, approximately 1,000 of whom are nationals.

CEF has a staff of 188 expatriate missionaries and 2,569 national workers. In addition, 94 full-time and 22 part-time staff members plus volunteers serve at the CEF headquarters in Warrenton, Missouri.

Growth

While CEF has active ministry in 167 countries of the world, its goal is to establish active ministry in all countries by its eightieth anniversary in 2017.

Publications

To help accomplish the goals of the ministry, CEF Press produces Bible and missionary lessons for use in teaching children. Many products are translated into ninety languages.

Website

http://www.cefonline.com/

Bibliography

Balmer, Randall Herbert. *Encyclopedia of Evangelicalism.* Waco, TX: Baylor University Press, 2004.

"Child Evangelism Fellowship." http://www.cefonline.com. "History."

Myers, Brant. "The State of the World's Children: Critical Challenge to Christian Mission." *International Bulletin of Missionary Research* 18, no. 3 (July 1994): 98–104.

Overholtzer, J. Irvin. *Salvation by Grace*. Grand Rapids: Child Evangelism Fellowship Press, 1958.

Overholtzer, Ruth. *From Then Till Now: Reminiscing with Mrs. O: A Century of Memories by the Wife of the Founder of Child Evangelism Fellowship*. Grand Rapids: Child Evangelism Fellowship Press, 1990.

Pei-Yu, Fung Chin. *A Compilation of the Summer Ministries of 5-Day Club Training Conference*. Master's thesis, Western Evangelical Seminary, 1984.

Mark A. Lamport

Children International

History

Founded in 1936 as Holy Land Christian Mission, Children International is now portrayed not as a religious organization but as a humanitarian one. The religious connection was dropped in 1980 along with its initial focus, that of assisting physically handicapped children and single mothers, as it transitioned into Children International—a secular nongovernmental organization.

Children International seeks to achieve its goals primarily through the recruitment and use of individual sponsors. The organization regards this as a means of providing more targeted support to poor children, especially in the areas of health and education. Its sponsorship program currently benefits more than 335,000 children and their families in 11 countries, including Chile, Colombia, the Dominican Republic, Ecuador, Guatemala, Honduras, India, Mexico, the Philippines, the United States, and Zambia.

Headquarters

2000 E Red Bridge Road
PO Box 219055
Kansas City, MO 64121
Telephone: 800-888-3089
Fax: 816-942-3714

Core Practices

Sponsorship provides assistance in such areas as:

health: access to doctors, dentists, vaccines, and medicine

education: uniforms and other school supplies, tuition assistance, access to libraries, and tutoring

nutrition: malnutrition screenings, feeding programs, supplements, and educational programs

youth: peer education, leadership and vocational training, civic responsibility, and scholarships

community: clean-water initiatives, sanitary latrines, microenterprise programs, and grants

family: household items, income-generation programs, educational opportunities, and housing and home repair assistance

Finances

Total revenue for 2009: $146,316,901
Total expenses for 2009: $142,695,979
Net assets for 2009: $40,990,337

Charity Navigator has awarded Children International three out of four stars, and Consumers Digest has named it one of its top-rated charities. Children International has accredited status with the Better Business Bureau, meaning it has met all required standards for accountability.

Statistics

Eighty percent of income goes directly to charitable programs. The ministry has 76 community centers in 11 countries. It has over 250,000 sponsors of children. Program activities for 2009 included:

Health and Nutrition
644,646 antiparasite treatments administered
580,464 medical exams given
102,288 dental exams provided
98,483 hygiene kits distributed
17,202 given nutritional assistance

Education
379,811 school supply kits given
71,221 backpacks supplied
36,808 awarded tuition assistance
5,661 children tutored

Clothing and Shoes
767,592 clothing items provided
320,896 pairs of shoes distributed
72,861 school uniforms provided

Publications

Field Notes, a director-written annual newsletter
LiftNote, a monthly online newsletter
Journeys, a biannual magazine for donors

Website

http://www.children.org/

Michael McMullen

Children of Promise International

History

Originally known as the Bible and Literacy League, Children of Promise International was founded by Linn Haitz, a missionary in Columbia who described experiencing a distinct calling in 1968 to expand his missionary efforts. Focusing on South American jungles and slums that seemed unreachable, Haitz established four schools that taught literacy as well as the Christian message to destitute children. In the 1970s, Haitz's organization established itself in Missouri and went on to create a child sponsorship program that helped to generate funding for the physical care of needy children, as well as children's homes that addressed spiritual and material needs. In 1998, the ministry began partnering with other organizations in the operation of children's homes around the world and adopted its present name. In addition to its ministry to orphans and other children experiencing poverty, Children of Promise offers various types of assistance to Christian workers, including training for indigenous evangelists and nutrition programs that create opportunities for evangelism. A program in India offers job training for widows.

Headquarters

6844 Loop Road
Centerville, OH 45459
Telephone: 937-436-5397

Core Beliefs

The organization adheres to the statement of faith adopted by the National Association of Evangelicals.

Finances

The Evangelical Council for Financial Accountability reported that in 2013 Children of Promise International had revenue of more than $1.2 million.

Website

http://www.promise.org/

Bibliography

"Children of Promise International." http://www.promise .org. "Our History."

George Thomas Kurian

China Ministries International

History

China Ministries International (CMI) was started in 1978 by Jonathan Chao in order to train and send missionaries to mainland China. The United States office was founded in 1987, and the organization now has offices in Canada, Australia, Hong Kong, Korea, the Philippines, and the United Kingdom. In 1991, CMI began work among China's minority peoples in which it seeks to partner with churches and ministry organizations to plant churches among these groups.

Headquarters

1605 E Elizabeth Street
Pasadena, CA 91104
Telephone: 626-398-2343
Fax: 626-398-2361
Email: cmiusca@yahoo.com

Core Beliefs

CMI exists to fulfill the threefold vision of evangelizing the Chinese people, strengthening the Chinese church, and Christianizing the Chinese culture through the induction of Christian values. CMI seeks to fulfill these goals by means of research, training, publishing, and sending those who are called. The entire process is conducted "to the glory of God, under the Lordship of Christ, and in the power of the Holy Spirit" (cmiusca.org, "The Three-fold Vision and Mission").

Core Practices

CMI recognizes that the needs of China demand both a cultural and a missionary mandate. Its "long-term goal is to overcome denominationalism and self-centeredness by promoting church renewal and enabling churches worldwide to engage in a cooperative effort for the evangelization of China" (ministrywatch.com, "China Ministries International"). As a result, CMI engages in research, publication, training, and communication in order to impact Chinese culture for Christ.

To fulfill these overarching goals, CMI has established the Christianity and China Research Center, which conducts research on the history of missions in China, Chinese religious policy, Chinese church development, and missionary strategy. CMI also recruits and sends diaspora Chinese church leaders to conduct biblical training sessions for house church Christians in mainland China. In its work among China's minority groups, CMI conducts research on these groups in order to plant churches and develop training materials.

In its evangelistic work, CMI distributes what it refers to as the Twin Companion for China's evangelists: a Bible and a discipleship training resource. CMI distributes ten thousand of these sets per year. CMI also supports missionaries who are engaged in evangelistic measures within mainland China, and in 1996, CMI developed a program to evangelize mainland Chinese studying in North America.

Website

http://www.cmiusca.org/

Bibliography

"China Ministries International." http://www.cmiusca.org. "The Three-fold Vision and Mission."

William Brooks

Chosen People Ministries

History

Leopold Cohn founded the Williamsburg Mission in Brooklyn, New York, in 1894. Cohn, a Hungarian Jew, immigrated to New York in 1892 and came to Christ after hearing a Hebrew-Christian street preacher. After a move to Manhattan in 1924, the ministry name became the American Board of Missions to the Jews, but the ministry periodical had been titled the *Chosen People* since 1895. Leopold Cohn led the mission until 1937, when his son Joseph Hoffman Cohn took over.

In 1929, John Solomon opened a branch work in Pittsburgh. He led Charles Feinberg, a young Jewish rabbinic student, to Christ in 1930. In 1943, one of the mission personnel left and later founded the Friends of Israel ministry. In 1953, Joseph Cohn died, and Harry Pretlove became the mission's general secretary. In 1970, the mission transferred Moishe Rosen to San Francisco to establish a new branch, which became independent in 1973 as Jews for Jesus.

In 1988, the mission was renamed Chosen People Ministries (CPM). Its international headquarters are near the United Nations and close to the headquarters of many worldwide Jewish organizations. Daniel Fuchs became the general secretary in 1968, then the president from 1974 to 1979. Harold Sevener was the president from 1979 to 1991. Mitch Glaser is the current president.

Headquarters

International Headquarters
241 E 51st Street
New York, NY 10022

Canada
Box 897
Station B
North York, ON M2K 2R1

Great Britain
PO Box 47871
Golders Green, London NW11 1AL

Australia
Celebrate Messiah Australia
PO Box 304
Caulfield, South Vic 3162

Leadership

President: Mitch Glaser

CPM has an independent board. Missionaries plan and implement their work and are assisted by the administrative staff of the organization. The US board of directors has ten men and one woman. Members include John Holbrook Jr. (chairman), Darrell Bock of Dallas Theological Seminary, and Mitch Glaser.

Core Beliefs

CPM has a ten-point doctrinal statement, which includes belief in an inerrant Bible containing sixty-six books; one God eternally existing in three distinct and equal persons; God's sovereign creation of all things for his glory; God's creation of Adam and Eve and their fall into sin for the entire human race; God's everlasting, irrevocable, unconditional covenant with Abraham and his choice of Israel as his chosen people, with his gift of the land of Israel to them and the promises of the Messiah; Jesus as God's Messiah and the means of our salvation by belief in his atoning death and resurrection; the full deity and personality of the Holy Spirit, who regenerates believers and baptizes them into Christ; Jews and Gentiles saved by faith, not by works; Jesus's return to reign over the earth from Israel in his millennial kingdom; and saved persons experiencing eternal bliss while lost people suffer eternally and consciously in hell.

Defining Statement

"Chosen People Ministries exists to pray for, evangelize, disciple, and serve Jewish people everywhere and to help fellow believers do the same" (chosenpeople.com, "About Us").

Finances

Total revenue for 2014: $13,862,983
Total expenses for 2014: $12,080,645
Net assets for 2014: $16,100,890

CPM was a charter member of the Evangelical Council for Financial Accountability, joining on February 1, 1980.

Missionary and Evangelistic Work

Internationally, Chosen People Ministries has centers for ministry in Jerusalem, Tel Aviv, Berlin, and Buenos Aires. It has outreach programs in thirteen countries. These include evangelism and discipleship programs, Messianic Centers and congregations, equipping the local church for Jewish evangelism, print and web publications, and benevolence work. Principal countries include Argentina, Australia, Canada, France, Germany, Hong Kong, Israel, Mexico, New Zealand, Russia, Ukraine, the United Kingdom, and the United States. CPM has Messianic congregations in Manhattan and in Brooklyn, New York.

Academic Institutions

CPM offers an accredited MDiv degree at the Charles L. Feinberg Center in New York City in conjunction with Talbot School of Theology in La Mirada, California. Most classes, including Greek and Hebrew, are offered in New York City. The program is designed for those called to full-time Jewish ministry.

Publication

Chosen People Ministries produces a monthly newsletter, which is archived at chosenpeople.com and provides information about all aspects of the ministry.

Website

http://www.chosenpeople.com/

Bibliography

"Chosen People Ministries." http://www.chosenpeople.com. "About Us."

Sevener, Harold A. *A Rabbi's Vision: A Century of Proclaiming Messiah; A History of Chosen People Ministries, Inc.* Charlotte, NC: Chosen People Ministries, 1994.

James A. Borland

Christar

History

Christar, originally called the India Mission, was founded by a seventy-year-old Scotsman in 1930. In the 1950s, it changed its name to International Missions and then to Christar in 1999. Currently, the group has around three hundred laborers serving in twenty countries in North America, Europe, Africa, the Middle East, and Asia. Christar workers are serving in at least eleven creative access contexts—countries that are closed to traditional forms of mission work.

Leadership

Christar describes itself as a "field-centered, missionary-centered board." Though led by a president and headquartered near Dallas, Texas (since September 2010), Christar affirms that the headquarters staff exists to facilitate work on the field. That is, the most important decisions are left to the teams on the field. Christar highly values working in teams, and team leaders are elected democratically by team members. The Christar president is elected by the collective teams around the world.

Core Beliefs

Christar affirms a rather Baptistic evangelical statement of faith. On the one hand, the group affirms the historic doctrines of the inerrancy and authority of Scripture, the Trinity, original sin, salvation by grace through faith, the reality of Satan, the church, the return of Christ, and the final state.

On the other hand, Christar uses Baptistic language in referring to baptism and the Lord's Supper as ordinances, and, in terms of eschatology, it emphasizes the rapture of the church and a premillennial return of Christ. (For Christar's complete doctrinal statement, see christar.org, "Statement of Faith").

Core Practices

Christar's mission is "to glorify God by establishing churches among least-reached Buddhists, Hindus, Muslims, and other Asians worldwide" (christar.org, "Mission"). The group's stated vision is "to cultivate Christ-honoring transformation in communities where He is yet to be worshiped" (christar.org, "Vision"). This mission and vision are supported by the following values: godliness, the body of Christ, personal development, effectiveness, and creativity. As related in its mission statement, Christar's primary emphasis is on planting churches. With this goal in mind, the group's personnel are active in ministries such as evangelism, discipleship, theological education, teaching English as a Second Language, medical missions, translation, ethnomusicology, youth work, Business as Mission, information technology, and agricultural development.

Trends

In Christar's 2008 ministry report, the leadership shared some changes and developments in the group's overall ministry. First, while remaining committed to proclaiming the gospel message, the group is becoming more committed to transformation and holistic mission. Thus, church-planting efforts are integrated with business projects, agricultural development, and community health initiatives. Second, the group set apart eleven new mission teams in 2008 and has seen a 20 percent increase in the organization's personnel since 2000. Though most of these laborers continue to be North Americans, a training center was established in Albania to send Albanian missionaries to serve in the Muslim world. Finally, the group reported planting new churches in unreached contexts in Asia Minor and Central and South Asia, while transitioning out of one context in the Philippines that was being led by national Christians.

Website

http://www.christar.org/

Bibliography

Cate, Patrick O. "What Will It Take to Win Muslims?" *Evangelical Missions Quarterly* 28, no. 3 (1992): 230–34.

"Christar." http://www.christar.org. "Mission," "Statement of Faith," and "Vision."

Eenigenburg, Sue. *Screams in the Desert: Hope and Humor for Women in Cross-Cultural Ministry.* Pasadena, CA: William Carey Library, 2007.

Eenigenburg, Sue, and Robynn Blyss. *Expectations and Burnout: Women Surviving the Great Commission.* Pasadena, CA: William Carey Library, 2010.

Edward Smither

Christ for India

History

Christ for India was founded in 1981 by theologian and evangelist Dr. P. J. Titus and his wife, Mary, natives of India who had been ministering in the United States since 1963. Feeling a call to return to India, Titus purchased land in Bheemunipatnam, India, with the help of supporters and started a seminary and a church. Titus's ministry soon expanded to address the needs of orphans with the establishment of a school and children's home. With an objective of reaching one billion Indians for Christ, the group emphasized training Christian leaders, founding churches, and providing education and humanitarian aid. After the death of P. J. Titus in 2003, the organization was headed by Mary Titus and later by her son Johnson Titus.

Headquarters

PO Box 271086
Dallas, TX 75227
Telephone: 972-771-7221

Core Beliefs

Christ for India's statement of faith represents evangelical positions on biblical inerrancy, the deity of Christ, and the Trinity.

Finances

Christ for India is accredited by the Evangelical Council for Financial Accountability (ECFA) but requests that its financial information not be posted on the ECFA website or elsewhere online due to security concerns.

Website

http://christforindia.org/

George Thomas Kurian

Christian Broadcasting Network

History

The Christian Broadcasting Network (CBN) was founded on January 11, 1960, by Marion Gordon (Pat) Robertson, the son of the US senator Willis Robertson of Virginia and a graduate of Yale University Law School and New York Theological Seminary. CBN first aired on October 1, 1961, on WYAH-TV in Portsmouth, Virginia, the first American television station authorized by the Federal Communications Commission to devote more than half of its airtime to religious broadcasting. The $22 million International Communications Center in Virginia Beach was completed in 1979.

Despite its technological potential and television evangelism, CBN was ranked among the lowest-rated cable services. Robertson was convinced that people did not value religious programming exclusively; rather, they desired comedy, news, and sports. In 1981, the name was changed from the Christian Broadcasting Network to the CBN Cable Network to reflect a combination of family and religious programming. Robertson contended that the name change was not meant to minimize the Christian persuasion but to emphasize the professional nature of the broadcasting company. The CBN schedule included old westerns such as *The Rifleman*, *Wagon Train*, and *Wyatt Earp*, in addition to comedies such as *Bachelor Father*, *The Best of Groucho*, *Burns and Allen*, and *I Married Joan*. In only three years, CBN was tied in ranking with the USA Network after ESPN, TBS, and CNN.

The network was renamed CBN Family Channel in 1988 and sold to International Family Entertainment (IFE) in 1990. Fox Kids Worldwide acquired IFE in 1997, and the Fox Family

Channel was acquired by the Walt Disney Company and named ABC Family on November 10, 2001.

Headquarters

977 Centerville Turnpike
Virginia Beach, VA 23463
Telephone: 757-226-7000
Fax: 757-226-2017

Leadership

Pat Robertson is the chairman of CBN. Michael D. Little is the president, and Gordon Robertson is the CEO.

Core Beliefs

CBN is evangelical regarding the authority of Scripture, the Trinity, the creation and sinfulness of man, the work of Jesus Christ, the indwelling of the Holy Spirit, and the church as the body of Christ.

Robertson believes the modern nation of Israel is significant prophetically and embraces aspects of "kingdom now" theology. His worldview is most consistent with renewal theology. Robertson affirms the word of faith teaching regarding laws of God (principles of the kingdom), which will work for anyone who has faith in them, whether Christian or non-Christian, since the principles are metaphysical. He also affirms the law of reciprocity for those who give faithfully and sacrificially. Robertson believes there are eight laws of the kingdom, which are operative for those who know the "rules." Consequently, the growth of CBN was assisted by the power of God and the law of miracles.

Core Practices

Robertson will frequently look into the camera intently, as if possessing the ability to see the actual viewers, and give a description of a healing that has occurred by means of a word of knowledge. For approximately two decades, he has predicted that the United States will soon experience a religious revolution, and CBN is preparing for one of the greatest worldwide spiritual awakenings.

Lutheran minister Harald Bredesen (1918–2006) prophesied to Robertson that God had chosen him to usher in the second coming of Christ. Robertson believed Bredesen's prophecy that God wanted CBN to prepare the way for Jesus's second coming. The urgency of "faith-stretching" gifts was based on the belief that CBN

would assist in Christ's return to earth. Postmillennialism is the doctrine affirming that the coming of the Lord Jesus will be subsequent to the millennium (the thousand-year reign of Christ Jesus that is mentioned in Revelation 20:1–8). Postmillennialists assert that the millennium will be established through the moral and spiritual influence of Christian proclamation and teaching throughout the world. Robertson's practices are postmillennial in persuasion and consistent with his charismatic inclinations.

Statistics

CBN employs nearly thirteen hundred people who work primarily at the Virginia Beach headquarters, and it provides programming to over two hundred countries. The 685-acre complex includes the TV studio headquarters, the corporate support building, the Regent University campus, and the Founders Inn and Conference Center. CBN operates news bureaus in Beirut, Jerusalem, and Washington and owns commercial television stations in Boston and Dallas.

Missionary and Evangelistic Work

The twenty-four-hour telephone prayer line has more than two hundred prayer counselors. WorldReach is a global evangelism campaign for proclaiming the gospel of Jesus Christ. Domestic and international ministries are funded through donations ($90–100 million annually) and income gained from the IFE sale in 1997. CBN maintains outreaches in Asia, Europe, Hong Kong, India, Indonesia, and Latin America.

Academic Institution

In 1977, Robertson founded Regent University in Virginia Beach. The school has an enrollment of more than four thousand students, and the Commission on Colleges of the Southern Association of Colleges and Schools accredited the school to award bachelor's, master's, and doctoral degrees.

Parachurch Organizations

Robertson founded Operation Blessing International Relief and Development Corporation in 1978 as an affiliate organization. The Flying Hospital augments the medical missions of Operation Blessing. Robertson is the founder and president of the American Center for Law and Justice, a public interest law firm and educational organization that defends First Amendment rights for religious people and focuses attention on pro-family, pro-liberty, and pro-life cases nationwide.

Electronic Media

The oldest program of CBN is *The 700 Club*, which is a daily ninety-minute program with Pat Robertson, Gordon Robertson, and Terry Meeuwsen as hosts and Lee Webb as news anchor. The program, which began in 1963, combines commentary, feature stories, interviews, and religious ministry.

Publications

Robertson is the author of eighteen books. *Shout It from the Housetops* (1972) is his autobiography. In its publication year, *The Secret Kingdom* (1982) was number three on the national nonfiction bestseller list of *Time* magazine. In its publication year, *The New World Order* (1991) was number four on the *New York Times* nonfiction bestseller list. *The Secret Kingdom*, *Answers to 200 of Life's Most Probing Questions* (1984), and *The New World Order* were each the number one religious book in America when released.

Website

http://www.cbn.com/

Bibliography

Donovan, John B. *Pat Robertson: The Authorized Biography.* New York: Macmillan, 1988.

Gerbner, George, et al. *Religion and Television.* Philadelphia: Annenberg School of Communications, University of Pennsylvania, 1984.

Hadden, Jeffrey K., and Charles E. Swann. *Prime Time Preachers: The Rising Power of Televangelism.* Reading, MA: Addison-Wesley, 1981.

Harrell, David Edwin, Jr. *Pat Robertson: A Personal, Religious, and Political Portrait.* San Francisco: Harper & Row, 1987.

Marley, David John. *Pat Robertson: An American Life.* Lanham, MD: Rowman & Littlefield, 2007.

Robertson, Pat. *Answers to 200 of Life's Most Probing Questions.* Nashville: Nelson, 1984.

Straub, Gerard Thomas. *Salvation for Sale: An Insider's View of Pat Robertson.* Buffalo: Prometheus, 1988.

Wills, Garry. *Under God: The Classic Work on Religion and American Politics.* New York: Simon & Schuster, 1990.

Ron J. Bigalke

Christian Literature Crusade

History

What started off as Ken and Bessie Adams's small passion in England during World War II has now spread around the world. Their crusade to provide affordable, quality, evangelical Christian literature resulted in the establishment of six Christian Literature Crusade (CLC) centers in England by the end of the war. Today CLC serves in 58 countries—each operating autonomously but with a common vision—and is growing through the work of over 750 missionaries.

While many ministries focus on planting churches, CLC plants literature works, from publishing houses to wholesale distribution centers to itinerant bookstalls to permanent online and physical bookstores. CLC combines its commitment to its mission and core evangelical beliefs with innovation in its partnerships with workers and suppliers, as well as with its methods of establishing and operating literature works globally and online. While it continues to publish titles, it distributes and retails many more products from other publishers, serving in some places as the chief distributor of Christian products. Proceeds from product sales help the ministry expand. All CLC activity aims at providing locally affordable literature that promotes conversion to Christ and Christian maturity.

Headquarters

United States
701 Pennsylvania Avenue
PO Box 1449
Fort Washington, PA 19034
Telephone: 215-542-1242
Fax: 215-542-7580

International Office
291 Abbeydale Road
Sheffield S7 1FJ
United Kingdom
Telephone: (0)114 281 2135
Fax: (0)114 281 2136
Email: office@clcinternational.org

Leadership

Senior leadership of CLC includes the following:

Director, CLC USA: David Almack
Director, World Missions: James Pitman
Director, Americas and Caribbean: Gerardo Scalante

Core Beliefs

CLC's statement of faith expresses conservative evangelical doctrines; its core values are these (see clcusa.org, "CLC Core Values"):

Faith: "The expansion and outreach of this ministry is not determined by our visible resources but rather by the commands and promises of God."

Sacrifice: "We should be willing to face hardship, inconvenience, sickness, danger and even death if necessary, for the fulfillment of Christ's command to make known the Gospel to all people."

Fellowship: "We ... allow no national or racial prejudices or exclusive denominational or doctrinal emphases in the life and ministry of CLC. ... [W]e expect that, as we seek Him, agreement can be attained within the fellowship in making decisions."

Holiness: "We ... shall ever seek [the Holy Spirit's] power and guidance by prayer, faith, obedience, humility and holiness."

Defining Statement

"The purpose of CLC is to make evangelical Christian literature available to all nations so that people may come to faith and maturity in our Lord Jesus" (clcusa.org, "What Is CLC Ministries").

Core Practices

CLC accomplishes its mission by publishing and distributing Christian literature and using proceeds from literature sales for missions. Its own publications include classics prized by evangelicals for decades, such as *Destined for the Throne: A New Look at the Bride of Christ* by Paul E. Billheimer; *Amazing Love* by Corrie ten Boom; and *Rees Howell: Intercessor* by Norman Grubb. Recent strong-selling titles include *Fireproof Your Life* by Michael Catt and *My Enemy... My Brother: God's Grace in the Life of a Palestinian* by Hanna Shahin.

Beyond publishing books, CLC sends missionaries around the world to open book centers that distribute wholesale and sell at retail its own publications, along with other Christian books, media, and other products. CLC aims to localize its operation, using national workers and leaders, as soon as practical and to help each unit grow to support itself financially. Its innovative attitude is exemplified in the recent development of the shipping container bookstore used overseas. A metal shipping container is retrofitted with a door, windows, and electricity and then finished with fixtures, stocked with product, and placed on a small plot of land, ready for business. Such a container store, the Umoja Shop, opened in Kenya in April 2010.

CLC continues as the faith ministry the Adamses established, trusting God to provide the financial needs for the entire ministry and members. CLC members and staff live sacrificially, with many supported as missionaries by gifts from family, friends, and churches. An increasing but small number are supported by salary. The supported workforce is supplemented globally by locals who volunteer a few hours to a few days a week.

Statistics

CLC's over 750 missionaries, together with many volunteers, operate literature works in 58 countries in the regions of Europe, Asia, and the Pacific; the Middle East and Africa; and North and South America, operating 180 bookshops, 18 distribution warehouses, and 18 publishing houses. In the United States, CLC operates 4 bookstores and partners with an additional 4 church bookstores in Pennsylvania and New Jersey.

Website

http://www.clcusa.org/

Bibliography

"Christian Literature Crusade." http://www.clcusa.org. "CLC Core Values" and "What Is CLC Ministries."

Rebecca Hammes and Mark E. Roberts

Christian Missionary Fellowship International

History

Christian Missionary Fellowship (CMF) International was formed in Kansas in 1949 in response to the proliferation of American missionary agencies after the Second World War and the need to organize their efforts more efficiently. Several students at Manhattan Christian College in Kansas had envisioned a body that allowed churches to partner in sending missionaries and provided for accountability for mission field practices, as well as assurances of a biblically sound message. CMF states that its five-part strategy stresses cross-cultural endeavors, innovative ideas, a holistic approach that addresses emotional needs, partnerships with other groups, and verifiable results. Specific projects include Community Health Evangelism, which works with the urban poor; Globalscope, which conducts campus ministry; and a division created to target cultures that are less receptive to traditional mission methods. Today CMF missionaries are present in seventeen countries.

Headquarters

5525 E 82nd Street
Indianapolis, IN 46250
Telephone: 317-578-2700

Core Beliefs

CMF's statement of faith upholds belief in the Trinity, the virgin birth of Christ, the divine inspiration of Scripture, and water baptism by immersion. (The full statement can be found at cmfi.org, "Statement of Faith.")

Finances

According to the Evangelical Council for Financial Accountability, CMF had revenue of more than $16 million in 2013.

Website

http://www.cmfi.org/

Bibliography

"Christian Missionary Fellowship International." http://www.cmfi.org. "Core Values," "Our History," and "Statement of Faith."

George Thomas Kurian

Christian Reformed World Missions

History

Christian Reformed World Missions (CRWM) was founded by the Hollandsche Christelijke Gereformeerde Kerk (or the Christian Reformed Church in North America, as it is now called) on June 18, 1888. It was dedicated to support Christian Reformed Church missionaries around the world. Today over two hundred long-term and short-term missionaries are under the care of CRWM. They are working in Bangladesh, Belize, Cambodia, China, Costa Rica, Cuba, the Dominican Republic, El Salvador, France, Guatemala, Haiti, Honduras, Hungary, Japan, Liberia, Lithuania, Mexico, Nicaragua, Nigeria, the Philippines, Russia, Sierra Leone, Ukraine, and West Africa.

Headquarters

2850 Kalamazoo Avenue SE
Grand Rapids, MI 49560
Telephone: 616-224-0700; 800-346-0075

Core Beliefs

As part of the ministries of the Christian Reformed Church in North America (CRC), CRWM upholds the core beliefs of the denomination.

Core Practices

Through partnership with churches and other Christian organizations throughout the world, CRWM promotes evangelism, trains teachers in international Christian and secular schools, designs leadership training programs to equip national leaders, and works with local congregations to enhance their vision for global outreach. In January 2010, CRWM launched a project called Hope Equals, which is intended for Christian college-aged youth. Through this project they are encouraged to become actively involved in a peaceful, just, and mutually respectful resolution to the Palestinian/Israeli conflict. Together with Palestinian and Israeli organizations and individuals committed to peacemaking, CRWM began a process of discussion and discovery to help build hope in the Middle East.

With a large number of missionaries, churches, and other missionary partnerships involved, maintaining quality relationships is important. CRWM stays in touch with and encourages its missionaries through emails, missionary prayer letters in congregational prayers, and prayer chain or bulletin announcements.

Finances

The CRWM budget was $13.3 million for the 2009–10 fiscal year (July 1, 2009–June 30, 2010). Its income comes from several sources: ministry shares, churches and individuals, estates, field income, and investments. Of church-related giving to CRWM, about 60 percent is through churches and individuals who financially support a missionary or field project. Nearly 80 percent of organized CRC congregations are in partnership with at least one CRWM missionary or project. Every year CRWM encourages Christian Reformed Churches to take a special offering for the ministry in their celebration of Pentecost. Missionaries with CRWM are required to actively challenge churches and individuals to help raise at least 60 percent of their total costs. CRWM has committed to provide for the financial needs of short-term missionaries.

Website

http://www.crwm.org/

Kalvin Budiman

Christians for Biblical Equality

History

In 1987, a group of egalitarian Christian scholars started a journal called *Priscilla Papers* based on Acts 18:26: "when Priscilla and Aquila heard Apollos, they took him aside and explained the Way of God to him more accurately" (NRSV). The group, which included Gilbert Bilezikian,

W. Ward Gasque, Stanley Gundry, Gretchen Gaebelein Hull, Catherine Clark Kroeger, Jo Anne Lyon, and Roger Nicole, sought to communicate and publish their perspective on the inclusion of women in ministry.

Out of this effort, Christians for Biblical Equality (CBE) was established on January 2, 1988, as a nonprofit organization dedicated to providing leadership, education, and support regarding the issue of biblical equality between the sexes. Out of their belief that proper interpretation of the Bible teaches that all people—regardless of sex, economic status, or age—are equal, they developed a comprehensive signature statement, "Men, Women, and Biblical Equality," presenting the case for biblical equality and the need for its application. In July 1989, CBE hosted its first international conference in St. Paul, Minnesota. Catherine Clark Kroeger served as the organization's first president and was succeeded by Mimi Haddad in 2001. Christians for Biblical Equality works toward a future in which "all believers are freed to exercise their gifts for God's glory and purposes, with the full support of their Christian communities" (cbeinternational.org, "CBE's Mission").

Headquarters

122 W Franklin Avenue
Suite 218
Minneapolis, MN 55404
Telephone: 612-872-6898
Fax: 612-872-6891
Email: cbe@cbeinternational.org

Leadership

The president is Dr. Mimi Haddad. CBE has a board of directors and a board of reference.

Core Beliefs

CBE shares core doctrinal beliefs with complementarian (that is, nonegalitarian) believers, along with its distinctive conviction that all believers—male and female—have the authority and the responsibility to exercise their spiritual gifts in the home, the church, and the world. CBE believes the apostolic proclamation of equality in Christ applies not only to believers' position in Christ but also to their ability to serve in formal and informal Christian ministry functions, including ordination: "There is neither Jew nor Gentile, neither slave nor free, neither male nor female, for you are all one in Christ Jesus" (Gal. 3:28 TNIV). CBE believes humankind was created in the image of God; therefore, all persons are equal, regardless of age, class, or race, and should reflect God's image at home and in society.

Defining Statement

"We stand united in our conviction that the Bible, in its totality, is the liberating Word that provides the most effective way for women and men to exercise their gifts distributed by the Holy Spirit and thus to serve God" (cbeinternational.org, "Statement on Men, Women, and Biblical Equality").

Core Practices

Christians for Biblical Equality holds annual, international conferences. It publishes two quarterly publications and a weekly online newsletter. Its online bookstore provides resources on biblical views of gender equality. The *CBE Scroll* is a blog dedicated to CBE's core purpose to communicate the biblical truth that men and women are equally responsible to use their God-given gifts to further Christ's kingdom.

Statistics

CBE has members from over one hundred denominations and sixty-five countries.

Publications

Christians for Biblical Equality publishes two quarterly publications. *Priscilla Papers* is CBE's academic journal, with scholarly topics related to gender equality. It has received ten awards from the Evangelical Press Association. *Mutuality* magazine provides information, inspiration, and encouragement with regard to topics relating to mutuality between the sexes. *Arise* is a free weekly e-newsletter that encourages and equips egalitarians.

Website

http://www.cbeinternational.org/

Bibliography

"Christians for Biblical Equality." http://www.cbeinternational.org. "CBE's Mission" and "Statement on Men, Women, and Biblical Equality."

Marlene Mankins

Compassion International

History

Compassion International was founded in 1952 by Rev. Everett Swanson. While preaching in Korea, he was deeply moved by the desperate poverty of the war orphans he encountered.

When he returned to the United States, he created a program whereby people could help these needy children by providing food, shelter, education, medical care, and Christian training. From this foundation, the ministry grew into the Christian child advocacy ministry it is today. Its mission is twofold: (1) working through local churches to provide child development programs designed to rescue children from physical, social, and spiritual poverty and (2) speaking out on behalf of poverty-stricken children and training others to become child advocates.

Today Compassion works in twenty-six countries, including Burkina Faso, Ethiopia, Ghana, Kenya, Rwanda, Tanzania, Togo and Uganda, the Dominican Republic, El Salvador, Guatemala, Haiti, Honduras, Nicaragua, Mexico, Bolivia, Brazil, Colombia, Ecuador, Peru, Bangladesh, India, Indonesia, the Philippines, Sri Lanka, and Thailand.

Headquarters

12290 Voyager Parkway
Colorado Springs, CO 80921
Telephone: 719-487-7000; 800-336-7676

Leadership

President and chief executive officer: Santiago "Jimmy" Mellado
Senior vice president and chief financial officer: Edward W. Anderson

Core Beliefs

Compassion International is:

Christ-centered, teaching the gospel to children within their own cultures
child-focused, seeing each child as a complete person
church-based, partnering with local churches to teach and mentor children
committed to integrity

Defining Statement

"Compassion International is a child-advocacy ministry that pairs compassionate people with those who are suffering from poverty. The ministry releases children from spiritual, economic, social, and physical poverty. The goal is for each child to become a responsible and fulfilled adult" (compassion.com, "Who Is Compassion International").

Core Practices

One-to-one child sponsorship is at the heart of Compassion's operations. Monthly sponsorships enable Compassion to partner with local churches and communities to offer programs for children, ranging from feeding to education to health care, in order to break the cycle of poverty. Instruction in the gospel and Christian education is also included. The building of relationships between individual sponsors and children is encouraged through correspondence and prayer.

Through special donations, Compassion's Malaria Intervention Fund helps sponsored children and their families with mosquito nets, malaria prevention education, and medical treatment.

Compassion's AIDS Initiative offers proactive services through treatment programs administered by local churches. Children and families are offered prevention education, treatment options, and health monitoring with love and acceptance.

Finances

Compassion International is highly recognized for its financial integrity and accountability. It is a charter member of the Evangelical Council for Financial Accountability and meets the BBB Wise Giving Alliance's Standards for Charity Accountability. Charity Navigator lists it as having the most consecutive four-star ratings in its category in the nation, and it is one of Ministry Watch's "30 Brightest Shining Light Ministries."

Statistics

Compassion helps more than one million children in twenty-six countries. More than 80 percent of all expenditures goes to program activities for children.

Electronic Media

Television specials
Advocacy radio specials

Publication

Compassion Magazine

Website

http://www.compassion.com/

Bibliography

"Compassion International." http://www.compassion.com. "Who Is Compassion International."

Marlene Mankins

Congregation of the Holy Spirit (Holy Ghost Fathers or Spiritans)

History

The Spiritans of the United States Province is a Roman Catholic congregation of some three

279

thousand members. Their spiritual father is Claude des Places, born in France in 1679. Des Places came from a wealthy and generous family and while in seminary was so moved by the plight of poor students that he chose to live with them. On Pentecost Sunday in 1703, the association of friends pledged their dedication to the Holy Spirit. They promised to be laborers for the most undesirable types of ministry. The Spiritans based their program of clerical training on the exacting standards of the Society of Jesus and did so with some secrecy to circumvent policies requiring government approval for the opening of new seminaries.

A critical figure who is regarded as a second founder by many Spiritans was Francis Liebermann, who reinvigorated the Spiritan community in the mid-nineteenth century and was noted for his work addressing the needs of recently freed slaves. Born Jacob Liebermann in 1802 in the Alsace region of France, he was an orthodox Jew who intended to follow his father's path as a rabbi until he converted to Christianity after a study of the New Testament. Epilepsy interfered with his ordination to the priesthood, which took place in 1841, fifteen years after his baptism. In 1848, after offering guidance to many seminarians and ministering to people of African descent, Liebermann started a renewal movement among the Spiritans. He taught practical union with God, that is, finding the divine aspect of daily life that fosters confidence, faith, and holiness—a concept that continues to shape the Spiritan outlook. He provided needed revitalization to the Spiritans by recruiting and educating lay and clerical missionaries, reaching agreements with Rome and the French government regarding the presence of his workers, and inspiring enthusiasm for missionary work. Although he died at age forty-seven and never went overseas himself, his strategy of becoming "one with the people" made it possible for others to present the gospel in a context familiar to each group and has become a cornerstone of contemporary missionary practice.

Headquarters

6230 Brush Run Road
Bethel Park, PA 15102
Telephone: 412-831-0302
Email: information@spiritans.org

Leadership

The superior general and his council in Rome lead the Congregation of the Holy Spirit. There is a provincial or superior general and council in each country where the Spiritans serve.

Core Beliefs

The Spiritans stress openness to the leading of the Holy Spirit and a desire to be useful to God even in the most demanding situations. Guidance from the Holy Spirit is the starting point of a process that results in service to others. Spiritans see the necessity of coupling their spiritual life with tangible service to others. Priority is given to working with the young, refugees, and immigrants, as well as with groups with minimal exposure to the gospel, those who are particularly disadvantaged, and those who do not attract much attention from other outreaches. The motto of the Spiritans is "One Heart. One Spirit" (spiritans.org, "About Us").

Core Practices

Since the group's founding more than three centuries ago, the Spiritans have participated in evangelism and service to humanity, especially under circumstances that many other groups find difficult or distasteful. The earliest efforts were in France, North and South America, and the Far East. The modern Spiritans continue the historic concentration on challenging situations that do not otherwise attract much participation. Spiritan Fathers and Brothers of the United States Province seek to reflect the presence of the Holy Spirit in their activities in the fields of education, international missions, and parish ministry. They are active in worldwide missions in sixty countries on five continents, especially outreaches to the poor, often working with entire communities. Part of the success of their community-building efforts stems from the simple lifestyle embraced by the Spiritans, who are able to unite with the people they seek to help.

Financed by European provinces, Spiritans embarked on outreaches to minorities and immigrants in the United States and Canada in 1872. They worked extensively with St. Katharine Drexel in the late nineteenth and the early twentieth centuries; together they helped urban and rural blacks in the US North and South. Many Spiritan missionary provinces, including ones in Brazil and French-speaking Africa, are now engaged in evangelistic efforts on their own continents. Formal and informal education are often part of the Spiritan evangelistic mission. Spiritan educational work prepares male and female high school, university, and seminary students for charitable work and other types of service. Other programs represent a diverse range of projects, including work with orphans and in refugee camps.

The Spiritans are pioneers of lay visibility in the Catholic Church. They take vows of poverty, chastity, and obedience, but there are lay Spiritans who are not vowed brothers/sisters but are still involved in the ministry of the congregation and commit to Father Liebermann's concept of living in practical union with God. Their activities include social work, education, and missions, and their participation brings to life the "one mission, one community" approach of the congregation evident since its founding. Des Places admitted to his school lay *sodales* (associates) who handled practical tasks such as cooking and who were required to attend Mass and spiritual readings and to pray. In the 1770s, the first lay missionary associates traveled to Guiana, and their participation soon spread to other regions. Father Liebermann was instrumental in forming a unified vision of the roles of clergy and laypersons by emphasizing that both groups are members of the people of God; the laity are not merely assistants but have their own mission, and the whole church has a common objective of performing God's will. In 1968, Spiritans convened a general chapter in Rome to address the proclamations of the Second Vatican Council (1962–65), which prompted greater lay participation by making a universal call to holiness and calling the whole church "people of God." The Spiritans created the Associate Movement/Wider Spiritan Missionary Community by requiring their local communities to train laypersons for missionary work and to allow them to live with members of the congregation in some cases.

The USA East Province rededicated itself to both home and global missions in the 1970s. The informal involvement of laity (mostly relatives of East Africa missionaries who wished to teach) in missions evolved into a formal mechanism for placement of lay volunteers as associates in the 1980s. In Pittsburgh, directors of the lay workers offered orientation services to lay workers. African missions were the principal beneficiaries of the new initiative. The USA West Province stressed community-oriented programs and flexibility rather than planned projects. In 2009, the East and West Provinces in the United States merged to create the Province of the United States of the Congregation of the Holy Spirit. As the priesthood declines, the role and status of lay members is expected to increase.

Academic Institution

Duquesne University is a Catholic college founded by the Order of the Holy Spirit in Pittsburgh in 1878. Private and coeducational, Duquesne is the largest Catholic university in Pennsylvania and the world's only Spiritan institution of higher education. As part of its ongoing dedication to the Spiritan tradition, the university established the Center for Spiritan Studies in 2005 in partnership with the Congregation of the Holy Spirit. The center promotes Spiritan values and researches Spiritan history and spiritual writings. Duquesne is also home to Laval House, a Spiritan House of Formation where pre-novitiates learn and experience the Spiritan community. Other Houses of Formation include Holy Spirit Seminary in Houston; Liebermann House in New Braunfels, Texas (outside San Antonio); and St. Mary Magdelene House at Catholic Theological Union in Chicago.

Parachurch Organization

South of Pittsburgh is the Spiritan Center, a ministry of the Congregation of the Holy Spirit that offers various types of retreats, days of renewal, and spiritual direction through programs and ongoing guidance. Its forty-acre pastoral property can accommodate up to fifty guests and is utilized by individuals, families, and organizations.

Website

http://www.spiritans.org/

Sarah Claudine Day

CrossWorld

History

CrossWorld was founded in 1931 as Unevangelized Fields Mission International (UFM). The original vision was to establish self-governing, self-supporting, and self-propagating churches in the Belgian Congo and in Brazil (Amazonia). In 2004, UFM International changed its name to CrossWorld, and the organization currently has around 315 personnel serving on 80 mission teams in 40 countries.

Headquarters

10000 N Oak Trafficway
Kansas City, MO 64155
Telephone: 816-479-7300
Fax: 816-734-4601

Leadership

In September 2010, CrossWorld moved its headquarters from Bala Cynwyd, Pennsylvania, to Kansas City, Missouri. The organization also has a Canadian home office in the Toronto area. CrossWorld is led by an executive team that includes a president and four vice presidents who report to the organization's board. In addition, a team of international directors based in the US headquarters oversees all international personnel.

Core Beliefs

CrossWorld holds to an evangelical statement of faith that is rather Baptist. On the one hand, the organization affirms the inerrancy of Scripture, the Trinity, the person and work of Christ, the work of the Holy Spirit, original sin, justification by faith and the sanctification of the believer, the church, angels, last things, and the imperative to proclaim the gospel. On the other hand, CrossWorld emphasizes eternal security in salvation, uses Baptistic language by referring to baptism and the Lord's Supper as ordinances, and holds to a premillennial return of Christ. (To view CrossWorld's complete doctrinal statement, see crossworld.org, "Our Beliefs").

Core Practices

CrossWorld's core values include a commitment to passionate worship, caring community, and strategic ministry that is faithful to Scripture and relevant to the host cultures. In light of these values, CrossWorld has maintained its original mission focus of making disciples of all nations through planting churches. With this goal in mind, CrossWorld teams are presently approaching ministry from a variety of angles, including street evangelism, teaching English as a Second Language, Business as Mission, international school education, medical missions, theological training, and camping and sports ministries.

Trends

In addition to changing its name in 2004, CrossWorld has embraced some other changes in recent years. First, out of a conviction to be more deliberate about making disciples, the organization's leadership has commissioned four special teams to facilitate this task—teams devoted to disciple-making urgency, ministry innovation, international relationships, and infrastructure and decision making. Second, this renewed emphasis on making disciples has also led the organization to restructure its executive leadership team to what it is presently. Third, after moving its headquarters to Kansas City in 2010, CrossWorld began sharing office space and resources with another evangelical mission organization (Avant), a partnership that provides further services to CrossWorld personnel around the world. Finally, CrossWorld has begun to emphasize Business as Mission as a strategy for ministry, as well as an alternative to the traditional method of raising financial support through churches and individuals.

Website

http://www.crossworld.org/

Bibliography

"CrossWorld." http://www.crossworld.org. "Our Beliefs."

Dowdy, Homer. *Christ's Witchdoctor*. London: Hodder & Stoughton, 1963.

———. *Out of the Jaws of the Lion*. London: Hodder & Stoughton, 1965.

———. *Speak My Words unto Them: A History of Unevangelized Fields Mission (UFM International)*. Bala Cynwyd, PA: UFM International, 1997.

Johnson, Neal C. *Business as Mission: A Comprehensive Guide to Theory and Practice*. Downers Grove, IL: InterVarsity, 2010.

Scovill, David L. *The Amazing Danis: A Hidden Mountain Tribe Becomes a Modern People of Faith*. Longwood, FL: Xulon Press, 2007.

Edward Smither

Cru (formerly Campus Crusade for Christ)

History

Founded in 1951 by William (Bill) Bright on the campus of the University of California, Los Angeles, Cru (originally known as Campus Crusade for Christ) is an interdenominational ministry dedicated to evangelism and discipleship. It seeks to fulfill the Great Commission through the multiplication strategy of "win-build-send."

Colleges had been regarded as the seedbed of evangelism ever since the 1806 Haystack Prayer Meeting near Williams College launched the global Protestant missionary movement. The Student Volunteer Movement sent out some forty-five hundred missionaries from 1899 to 1914. After World War II, however, many American universities—even those like Harvard that were originally established to provide Christian education—became increasingly secular, and groups such as the YMCA and the YWCA lost influence. Numerous campus ministries were created to counter that trend; Cru is the largest of those ministries. Like InterVarsity Fellowship, it added a strongly evangelistic presence to mainline ministries such as the Catholic Pax Romana and Newman Club and Protestant groups such as the National Intercollegiate Christian Council and the National Student Christian Federation.

Cru stresses evangelism, devotional life, and fellowship. Its systematic approach to evangelism stems from Bill Bright's pamphlet *Have You Heard of the Four Spiritual Laws?* Cru has been successful in conducting high-profile events such as Explo '72, Explo '74, and Explo '85.

Headquarters

100 Lake Hart Drive
Orlando, FL 32832
Telephone: 888-278-7233

There are area operational offices in twelve additional locations around the world.

Leadership

President: Steve Douglass

Core Beliefs

Cru is "committed to the centrality of the cross, the truth of the Word, the power of the Holy Spirit and the global scope of the Great Commission." Its purpose is "helping to fulfill the Great Commission in the power of the Holy Spirit by winning people to faith in Jesus Christ, building them in their faith and sending them to win and build others and helping the body of Christ to do evangelism and discipleship through a variety of creative ways" (cru.org, "What We Do").

Core Practices

The following ministries represent Cru's objectives.

Campus Ministry, reaching 110 million students around the globe
Faculty Commons, working with professors
Student Venture, reaching teenagers
Athletes in Action, seeking to advance the gospel through athletics
Priority Associates, an adult ministry that has absorbed two other adult ministries: Executive Ministries, which enlists the help of influential citizens in evangelism, and the one-to-one mentoring program Life Builders
Christian Embassy, DC, seeking to reach government leaders on Capitol Hill
Christian Embassy, UN, reaching diplomats

Military Ministry, offering resources to military personnel
Josh McDowell Ministry, demonstrating the relevance and reliability of Christianity and promoting biblical values
Family Life, offering conferences, broadcasts, and other Bible-based resources for building healthy marriages and families
Here's Life Inner City, assisting churches in urban communities
The Impact Movement, targeting African Americans

Finances

Cru is a charter member of the Evangelical Council for Financial Accountability.

Statistics

Movements on more than 1,140 college campuses
Ministry presence in 191 countries
More than 50 ministries
Roughly 226,000 volunteers
Over 25,000 staff members

Academic Institutions

Cru operates the International School of Theology, New Life Training Centers, and King's College.

Publications

Cru publishes a variety of materials that assist in spiritual development.

Website

http://www.cru.org/

Bibliography

Cantelon, J. E. *A Protestant Approach to the Campus Ministry.* Philadelphia: Westminster, 1964.
"Cru." http://www.cru.org. "What We Do."
Eanshaw, G. L. *The Campus Ministry.* Valley Forge, PA: Judson, 1964.

George Thomas Kurian

Dayspring International

History

Dayspring International was founded in 1979 by John Gilman, an early participant in Pat Robertson's Christian Broadcasting Network (CBN). In Robertson's office, after a trip to India, Gilman conceived of a motion picture portraying the life of Christ with an Indian cast. His duties as a guest host and the head of programming at the CBN led to an inspiring encounter with an Indian who sought the CBN's assistance with mass media evangelism in India.

Gilman's vision for a film about the life of Christ using Indian actors had already come to fruition with *Dayasagar* (Oceans of Mercy), produced in India by actor-director Vijar Chandar. Chandar had converted to Christianity as the film's production was in progress and felt guided by God to embrace Gilman's idea of using the film as an evangelistic tool in villages across India. The choice of film as a medium capitalized on India's well-known and ample appetite for movies. Because it utilized an Indian cast, the film was able to convey the gospel message without the hindrance of cultural barriers. Professionally produced, *Dayasagar* was released in movie houses and was viewed by more than seventeen million Indians even before mobile film teams made it available to remote villages. Today ministry workers sometimes use a bed sheet hung between trees in an empty field as a screen. Where public viewing is not possible because of persecution, showings take place in private homes. The film has been dubbed into fourteen Indian languages.

Headquarters

PO Box 3309
Virginia Beach, VA 23454
Telephone: 757-428-1092
Email: info@dayspringinternational.org

Leadership

President: Rev. Dr. John Gilman
Executive vice president: Dr. David G. Mercer
Vice president of development: Norm Harvey
Director of operations: Deborah B. Darnell
Chairman: George Ivey III
Directors: Dale Berkey, John Gilman II, Timothy Persons
Treasurer: Scott Mitchell
Secretary: Deborah B. Darnell

Core Beliefs

As an organization and as individuals we strive to be a reflection of the following. These are essential matters in the life of a follower of Jesus Christ:

The Bible is God's personal introduction of Himself to all the people of the world. It is authoritative on all matters that it speaks. It exists as both a boundary and map for approaching life and its challenges.

There is only one God, the creator of heaven and earth, who exists eternally as three persons—Father, Son and Holy Spirit. Each is fully God, yet each uniquely distinct and identifiable from the other.

All people are created in God's image and matter deeply to Him. The core message of the Bible is that God loves people.

A very real part of that love is the capacity that has been given to all people to enter into an intimate relationship with God and in caring community with each other.

A caring creator offers choice in response to His expression of love and care. Sin may be a response. It separates man from God and destroys relationships.

At the heart of the Bible is the presentation of God's only Son, Jesus Christ. As He died on the Cross He was and is God's only solution to a sinful, alienated, hurting world. Through His bodily resurrection, He is also God's only salvation to human beings, individually and personally. He is the provider of forgiveness.

The Holy Spirit exists to point mankind toward Jesus Christ. He is present in all believers to enable them to live Christ-like lives and gives them spiritual gifts both to serve the Church and to reach out to a world in need.

Discipleship to Jesus Christ is the greatest opportunity human beings have in life and the only hope corporate mankind has of solving its insurmountable problems.

There is a final reckoning. It is in the eternal plan of God for mankind. There is consequence for sin and the promise of eternal fellowship with God for those followers of Jesus Christ.

A primary purpose of the church is to further God's missionary purpose in neighborhoods and nations.

The local church, at home and abroad, was established to be a reflection of God's character. It exists to draw people to Christ and enhance their lives through intentional discipleship.

Through worship, instruction, prayer and bearing with one another in community, we are to reestablish Christ as living teacher in the midst of His people. (dayspringinternational.org, "Statement of Faith")

Defining Statement

"Dayspring International's mission is to transform villages all across India by engaging each person with powerful, culturally relevant media, establishing local churches as community centers, and elevationg the individual through education, training, and relief" (dayspringinternational.org, "How It Began").

Motto: "Engage. Establish. Elevate" (dayspring international.org, "What We Do").

Core Practices

In addition to showing its evangelistic film, Dayspring International participates in church planting, literacy programs, and medical and other human services. Its approach emphasizes cultural sensitivity, an unadulterated gospel message, and a village-by-village strategy. It has fashioned a cycle of transformation in which the lives of villagers are changed and their villages are changed in turn. Dayspring International uses media to establish churches; these churches then become community centers that provide training and relief for individuals. Special attention is paid to the needs of the Dalits (formerly called "untouchables") by founding schools and providing critical humanitarian aid, such as job training and medical clinics.

Finances

As a member of the Evangelical Council for Financial Accountability since 1987, Dayspring International submits to periodic reviews of its finances. The annual report for 2013 showed income and expenses each in excess of $12,000,000.

Statistics

With dozens of film teams, Dayspring International shows *Dayasagar* 24,000 times a year. Film teams travel to 2,000 Indian villages a month, more than 115 million people have seen the film, and more than 9 million individuals have accepted Christ as Savior.

Website

http://www.dayspringinternational.org/

Bibliography

"Dayspring International." http://www.dayspringinternational.org. "How It Began," "Statement of Faith," and "What We Do."

Sarah Claudine Day

Derek Prince Ministries International

History

Derek Prince (1915–2003) was born in Bangalore, India, into a British military family. He was educated in Greek and Latin at Eton College and Cambridge University and also studied at the Hebrew University in Jerusalem. While serving in the British Medical Corps in North Africa during World War II, he began studying the Bible and experienced an evangelical conversion. Prince confessed to receiving the baptism of the Holy Spirit a few days subsequent to his conversion.

Prince immigrated to the United States in 1963 and soon identified with the emerging charismatic movement. Prince began his traveling ministry in 1967; moved to Fort Lauderdale, Florida, in 1968; and during the early 1970s

formed an alliance with Don Basham, Ern Baxter, Bob Mumford, and Charles Simpson of the Shepherding movement. David Selby established the United States office in Fort Lauderdale in May 1971, which was relocated to Charlotte, North Carolina, in 1994.

Headquarters

3930 Rose Lake Drive
Charlotte, NC 28217
Telephone: 800-448-3261
Fax: 704-357-1413

Leadership

Dick Leggatt is the president. The chairman of the nine-member board is David Selby.

Core Beliefs

Prince believed the fundamental doctrines of Christianity. He believed and taught charismatic doctrines such as the continuation of all spiritual gifts, new revelation from God, and Spirit baptism as a second work of grace. Prince believed the church needed to combat Satan and demons directly through exorcism and positive confession but rejected the extreme practices of the signs and wonders movement. He taught that generational curses were applicable to individuals, as opposed to understanding Deuteronomy 28–30 to be an expression of God's covenant with Israel. His teaching with regard to the primacy of the human will in the Christian life led to an emphasis on perseverance through focus. Prince emphasized the importance of fasting and prayer as spiritual disciplines. He believed the destinies of Israel and the church were converging in modern times.

Defining Statement

"Extending the teaching legacy of Derek Prince to the world" (derekprince.org, "Home").

Core Practices

Derek Prince adopted a nondenominational, nonsectarian approach to explaining the Bible and teaching in a manner that is both helpful and relevant to people from all racial and religious backgrounds. The ministry is dedicated to the proclamation of the gospel through distribution of Prince's teachings.

Divisions and Splits

Prince separated from the Shepherding movement in 1984.

Statistics

Derek Prince Ministries has an influence in more than 140 countries through more than 13 worldwide offices, including Australia, Canada, China, France, Germany, the Netherlands, New Zealand, Norway, Russia, South Africa, Switzerland, the United Kingdom, and the United States.

Missionary and Evangelistic Work

The ministry is especially active in economically and politically oppressed countries through distribution of its publications and radio.

Electronic Media

Prince's daily radio broadcast, *Keys to Successful Living* (now *Derek Prince Legacy Radio*), began in 1979 and is translated into Arabic, Chinese (Amoy, Cantonese, Mandarin, Shanghaiese, Swatow), Croatian, German, Malagasy, Mongolian, Russian, Samoan, Spanish, and Tongan.

The Spanish radio broadcast *Llaves Para Vivir Con Exito* began in 1985 and is aired in Argentina, Colombia, Mexico, Peru, Spain, the United States, and Venezuela and is received by shortwave radio in Cuba.

Publications

Derek Prince authored more than sixty books, six hundred audio teachings, and one hundred video teachings. Much of his teaching has been published and translated into more than one hundred languages.

Website

http://www.derekprince.org/

Bibliography

Mansfield, Stephen. *Derek Prince: A Biography.* Lake Mary, FL: Charisma House, 2005.

Prince, Derek. *Derek Prince: Man behind the Ministry.* New Kensington, PA: Whitaker House, 2005.

———. *Pages from My Life's Book.* Charlotte: Derek Prince Ministries, 1987.

———. *The Spirit-Filled Believer's Handbook.* Orlando, FL: Creation House, 1993.

Prince, Derek, and Lydia Prince. *Appointment in Jerusalem.* New Kensington, PA: Whitaker House, 2005.

Ron J. Bigalke

Dominicans (Order of Preachers)

History

The Order of Preachers is a Roman Catholic religious order with a mission "to praise, to bless and to preach." The central goal of all forms of religious life in the Catholic Church is to secure "undivided devotion to the Lord" (1 Cor. 7:35) through the "evangelical counsels" of chastity, poverty, and obedience. The Order of Preachers is additionally characterized by its embrace of evangelical poverty and the *vita apostolica* (apostolic life) of preaching and teaching, as an indispensible means toward this end.

St. Dominic de Guzman (1170–1221), a Spanish priest, started the order in 1215 in an effort to respond to the widespread urban poverty of the Middle Ages and the spread of heretical teaching by the Albigensians ("Cathars"). The central purpose of the order was to imitate the apostolic life of poverty and preaching, with the special aim of refuting Albigensian teaching by holiness of life and theological acumen. After gathering a band of like-minded followers around him, Dominic secured papal approval for the Order of Preachers in 1217, using the *Rule of St. Augustine* as a charter.

The Dominicans' commitment to preaching, and their founder's intent to refute heretical teaching, quickly put their order at the forefront of the emerging movement of scholastic theology in the Middle Ages, and some of the greatest luminaries of Medieval theology (Albert the Great, Thomas Aquinas, etc.) were Dominicans. Additionally, Dominicans frequently staffed the Inquisitions that identified members of heretical movements such as the Albigensians. The Dominicans have always had a special love for the praying of the Rosary, and a popular tradition traces this devotion back to St. Dominic himself.

Core Practices

The Order of Preachers is devoted to the particular task of preaching and teaching the Christian faith, both by engaging in theological debate and by attending to the religious education of Christians. As noted below, the Dominicans have also tended to dominate the ranks of those engaged in higher theological studies and scholarship within Catholicism. By means of public vows, Dominicans embrace the values of apostolic poverty, chastity (the renunciation of marriage), and obedience to a religious superior. These unique apostolic commitments are intended to enhance the moral witness of their preaching. Unlike more traditional monastic orders, the Dominicans are not committed to a life of withdrawal from the world and an exclusive commitment to contemplation and prayer: their central mission of preaching requires more flexibility and mobility in daily life.

The Dominican order includes several branches: friars (vowed male religious), nuns (vowed female religious who are "cloistered" or restricted to a monastery and devoted to prayer), sisters (vowed female religious who are not cloistered) and "lay Dominicans" (laity who seek to live out the ideals of the order without taking formal vows). Dominicans today are best known for their work in missions and education, especially theological instruction and inquiry.

Bibliography

Hinnebusch, William A. *History of the Dominican Order: Origins and Growth to 1500.* 2 vols. New York: Alba House, 1966.

Lehner, Francis, ed. *Saint Dominic: Biographical Documents.* Washington, DC: Thomist Press, 1964.

McGonigle, Thomas, and Phyllis Zagano. *The Dominican Tradition.* Collegeville, MN: Liturgical Press, 2006.

Vicaire, M.-H. *Saint Dominic and His Times.* Translated by Kathleen Pond. Green Bay: Alt Publishing, 1964.

Jamie Blosser

Encompass World Partners (formerly Grace Brethren International Missions)

History

The Brethren in America trace their roots to the German Pietists and Anabaptists who fled to Pennsylvania in the early 1700s to escape persecution. The Bible conference movement, dispensational fundamentalism, and a thrust toward foreign missions brought the Brethren Church into the center of American evangelicalism. The resulting missionary arm of the Brethren Church began in 1900. What became the Fellowship of Grace Brethren Churches was organized in 1939 after a split from the Brethren Church. However, Grace Brethren International Missions was the continuation of the original (1900) missionary enterprise. The name is now Encompass World Partners.

Headquarters

Mailing Address

PO Box 588
Winona Lake, IN 46590

Street Address

422 Mission Drive
Winona Lake, IN 46590
Telephone: 678-992-5313
Email: info@encompassworld.org

Leadership

The current executive director of Encompass World Partners is Dave Guiles. The executive director emeritus is Tom Julien. The staff is organized into five missional networks, which "are directed by gifted practitioners who cast vision, develop strategies, create training opportunities, allocate resources, and approve servant leaders responsible to provide strategic oversight to local teams" (encompassworldpartners.org, "Bearing More Fruit").

Core Beliefs

There are three driving forces behind Encompass World Partners. Church planting is God's plan for this age, so to mobilize members to plant churches around the world is a priority. Second, leadership training is a supreme function of the local church. Churches should teach, enlist, train, empower, and encourage new leaders. A third priority is integrated ministries to meet the personal, physical, spiritual, emotional, and economic needs of families.

The statement of faith contains twelve points, including an inerrant Bible; the Trinity, the deity of Christ, and the Holy Spirit; man's direct creation by God and his fall into sin; salvation by faith in Christ's finished, atoning work; the local and universal church; a godly Christian life; believer's baptism by trine immersion; foot washing as part of a threefold Communion; Satan's existence and final defeat; Christ's pretribulational second coming; the tribulation; Christ's visible millennial reign on the earth; and bodily resurrection, with eternal life for the saved and eternal punishment for the lost. Missionaries must subscribe to the statement, and the board of trustees endorses it annually.

Defining Statement

"To spread the knowledge and glory of God among the least reached of our world" (encompassworldpartners.org, "About Us").

Finances

Encompass World Partners has been a member of the Evangelical Council for Financial Accountability since December 4, 2001.

Total revenue for 2014: $9,153,208
Total expenses for 2014: $8,391,400
Net assets for 2014: $9,526,712

Statistics

In the United States and Canada, there are 260 Grace Brethren churches, but worldwide there are over 2,000 churches serving about 750,000 congregants.

Encompass World Partners currently serves 228 people groups in 34 countries. Over 250 missionaries work with Encompass World Partners. This includes 108 North Americans who serve long-term internationally, plus nearly 150 more individuals who cooperate with and are part of church-planting efforts in various countries.

In Europe, missionaries work in the Czech Republic, England, France, Germany, Ireland, Portugal, and Spain. Asian countries served include Cambodia, Japan, the Philippines, and Thailand. Latin American works are in Argentina, Brazil, Chile, Cuba, Guatemala, Haiti, Mexico, Paraguay, and Uruguay. African countries include Cameroon, Central African Republic, Chad, Congo, Nigeria, and others not named.

Missionary and Evangelistic Work

To win the lost, Encompass World Partners uses church planting and a host of other methodologies, including agriculture, community development, business, education, children's ministry, construction, medical work, discipleship, leadership development, teaching English, and teaching in international schools.

Website

http://www.encompassworldpartners.org/

Bibliography

"Encompass World Partners." http://www.encompassworld partners.org. "About Us" and "Bearing More Fruit."

Grace Brethren International Ministries. *2010 Global Ministries Prayer Guide.* Winona Lake, IN: GBIM, 2010.

James A. Borland

The Evangelical Alliance Mission

History

Fredrik Franson, of Swedish immigrant parentage, associated himself with D. L. Moody in Chicago and founded the Scandinavian Alliance Mission of North America in 1890. By the time of Franson's death in 1908, Scandinavian Alliance missionaries were serving in China, Japan, south and east Africa, Mongolia, India, and Venezuela.

Seven additional countries had been added by 1949, when the name of the organization was changed to the Evangelical Alliance Mission (TEAM). TEAM later merged with the Sudan United Mission (1969), the Orinoco River Mission (1979), the Japan Evangelical Mission (1983), and the Bible Christian Union (1994).

Headquarters

400 S Main Place
Carol Stream, IL 60188
Telephone: 800-343-3144

Leadership

TEAM has an international director, a fifteen-member US board of directors, and a nine-member Canadian board of trustees.

Core Beliefs

TEAM's doctrinal statement has twelve points addressing the inspiration of the Scriptures, the Trinity, the deity of Christ, his blood atonement, his bodily resurrection, his premillennial return, two ordinances of water baptism and the Lord's Supper, and the conscious eternal punishment of the lost.

Core Practices

TEAM is an evangelical, nondenominational, international mission whose purpose is to help churches send missionaries to establish reproducing churches in other nations to the glory of God. TEAM has six core values (team.org, "Our Values"):

God dependence: "we rely on God through prayer."

Church focus: "our work is focused on the church from beginning to end."

Vision: "Christian visionaries see the immediate future in light of eternity."

Passionate service: "because lost people matter to God, they matter to us."

Lifelong learners: "we increase our effectiveness and become what God already knows we can be."

Caring community: "people are our most valuable asset."

The United States and Canada have active ministry teams and provide the bulk of foreign missionary volunteers and finances. TEAM encourages laypeople, business and professional people, and missionaries to come together to meet specific needs around the world. An example of this is the ZIM Team Alliance, meant to come alongside the church in Zimbabwe so that it is inspired to lovingly and continuously provide long-term care for the HIV victims in that country in the name of Jesus Christ.

TEAM's varied work includes church planting, medical work, community development, Bible translation, evangelism, discipleship, counseling pastors and missionaries, and much more. TEAM has also been a member of CrossGlobal Link (formerly IFMA) since 1945. This

288

organization helps evangelical mission agencies to think together and implement strategies to reach the world for Christ. TEAM is active in Buddhist, Hindu, Muslim, tribal, and urban settings around the world.

Finances

TEAM joined the Evangelical Council for Financial Accountability on April 18, 2005.

Total revenue for 2014: $28,576,000
Total expenses for 2014: $31,076,000
Net assets for 2014: $84,995,000

Statistics

TEAM has over 750 missionaries in more than 40 countries on 5 continents. In Europe, these include Austria, the Czech Republic, France, Germany, Ireland, Italy, Portugal, Russia, Spain, Sweden, and Ukraine. In Asia, these include China, Indonesia, Japan, the Philippines, South Korea, Taiwan, and Thailand. In Africa, these include Chad, Mozambique, South Africa, Swaziland, and Zimbabwe. In South America these include Brazil, Colombia, Peru, and Venezuela. Missionaries are also in Mexico and Australia, including Irian Jaya.

Academic Institutions

TEAM helps staff a number of Bible colleges and institutes, Christian schools for missionary children, and international Christian schools, such as one in Hong Kong.

Website

https://www.team.org/

Bibliography

"The Evangelical Alliance Mission." https://www.team.org. "Our Values."

James A. Borland

Evangelical Friends Mission

History

The Evangelical Friends Mission (EFM) is a ministry of the Evangelical Friends Church International. Because of the differences in Quaker beliefs, the Evangelical Friends Church calls its outreach a mission instead of the standard designation of service organization. The EFM grew out of the yearly meetings of the Evangelical Friends Alliance (the original name of the Evangelical Friends Church International). In 1978, Robert Hess became the executive director of the EFM and led the mission to spread the gospel to Africa,

Central and South America, Asia, Europe, and North America. This organization has become a prominent extension of the Evangelical Friends Church International.

Leadership

In 1980, the EFM centralized its office in Denver, Colorado, where James Morris provided leadership. Today its offices are in Arvada, Colorado, and Yorba Linda, California. The organization is currently led by Chuck Mylander out of the California office.

Headquarters

5765 Olde Wadsworth Boulevard #28
Arvada, CO 80002

California Office
18639 Yorba Linda Boulevard
Yorba Linda, CA 92886

Core Beliefs

Although Quakers are noncreedal by nature, the EFM holds to a statement of faith detailing its articulation of certain Christian doctrines, including the Bible, God, Jesus Christ, the Holy Spirit, man, salvation, the church, Christian work, liberty, spiritual realities, and resurrection and judgment. (It can be viewed at friendsmission.com, "Statement of Faith.") As a mission organization, the EFM also publicizes a document on missionary lifestyle that is the basis of ethical conduct for its missionaries.

Defining Statement

"Our purpose and passion is to fuel a worldwide movement of people who seek first the kingdom of God, planting churches that live and die to carry out the Great Commission in the spirit of the Great Commandment" (friendsmission.com, "Mission Statement").

Core Practices

The EFM practices evangelical missions through preaching/teaching of the gospel, education, medical missions, and addressing social and physical concerns through local churches and other indigenous organizations.

Academic Institution

In 1982, the EFM jointly sponsored the establishment of the Bolivian Evangelical University.

Website

http://www.friendsmission.com/

289

Bibliography

"Evangelical Friends Mission." http://www.friendsmission.com. "Mission Statement" and "Statement of Faith."

Williams, Walter R. *The Rich Heritage of Quakerism.* Newberg, OR: Barclay Press, 1987.

Phuc Luu

Evangelical Mission Ministries

History

Rev. and Mrs. Walter Gomez were called to minister in Mexico in the mid-1940s. Many blessings followed, including the establishment of individual churches, a church conference, and a four-year Bible college, as well as many conversions. In 1954, Mexican Mission Ministries was founded, becoming Evangelical Mission Ministries (EMM) in May 2007 to expand the original vision to include all of the Spanish-speaking world. EMM continues to support the church conference financially and is a sending mission for United States and Canadian missionaries now serving together with those in Mexico. With fourteen missionaries, EMM describes itself as a nondenominational, Scripture-based organization.

Headquarters

415 N Sugar Road
PO Box 636
Pharr, TX 78577
Telephone: 956-787-3543

Leadership

President: Bill Yoast
Vice president: Ken Ratzlaff
Treasurer: Don Batz
Secretary: Don Schmidt

EMM also has a ten-member board.

Core Beliefs

EMM affirms the following (emm-mexico.net, "Articles of Faith"):

The Bible is the Word of God, verbally inspired, a product of men controlled of the Spirit so that it is the truth without any admixture of error for its matter and is the center of Christian union and supreme standard by which all human conduct, creeds, and opinions shall be tried. II Tim. 3:16, 17

There is one living and true God, infinite, intelligent Spirit, Maker and Supreme Ruler of heaven and earth, who is worthy of all honor, confidence and love; three persons, Father, Son and Holy Spirit in the unity of the Godhead. I Cor. 8:6; John 15:26

That Christ is the second person of the Trinity, born of a virgin, Redeemer and Mediator of man, between God and man. Luke 1:35; John 1:1, 14

The Holy Spirit is a divine person equal with God the Father and God the Son and works in perfect harmony in the Godhead in perfecting man's God-planned redemption. John 16:7–15

Satan is a person, a malignant spirit, the unholy god of this age, author of all powers of darkness, and is destined to the judgment of an eternal justice in the lake of fire. Mt. 4:1–10; Rev. 20:10

We accept the Genesis account of creation. Genesis, Chapters 1 and 2

Man was created in the image of God, by voluntary choice transgressed and fell, thus causing all mankind now to be sinners, not only by constraint but by choice, and is therefore under judgment without defense and excuse. Rom. 5:10–19

Jesus was miraculously, through the Holy Spirit, born of a virgin, that He is both the Son of God and God, the Son. Mt. 1:18–25

Man is saved wholly by grace through the mediatorial office of the Son of God who by His death made full and vicarious atonement of our sins, not exemplary but substitutionary and voluntary, the Just dying for the unjust. Eph. 2:8, 9; Rom. 3:24

By the new birth the one dead in trespasses and sins is made a partaker of the divine nature and receives eternal life solely by the power of the Holy Spirit and thus becomes obedient to the gospel which is manifested in the fruits of repentance and faith and newness of life. John 3:33; II Cor. 5:17

Justification includes the pardon of sin, the gift of eternal life on principles of God's righteousness, bestowed only through faith in the Redeemer's blood. Rom. 8:1; Rom. 5:1, 9

Faith in the Lord Jesus Christ is the only condition of salvation. Acts 16:31

A local church is a congregation of born again believers; the true church consists of all born again believers and is the bride of Christ waiting for His return and the rapture. Acts 2:42; Eph. 5:22–32; I Thess. 4:13–18

All who are truly born again are kept by God the Father for Jesus Christ. John 10:28, 29; Rom. 8:35–39

In God's sight only those who are justified through faith are truly righteous and sanctified and that all who continue in impenitence and unbelief are in His sight wicked and under the curse. Rom. 6:23; Gal. 3:10, 13

Civil government is of divine appointment and is to be prayed for and conscientiously honored and obeyed except in things opposed to the will of our Lord Jesus Christ. Rom. 13:1–7; Acts 4:18–20

We believe in
the bodily resurrection
the ascension
the high priesthood
the premillennial return of Christ

the resurrection of the righteous dead unto life
the rapture of living saints
the throne of David
the millennial reign

I Cor. 15:4; Acts 1:9–11; Heb. 5:9, 10; I Thess. 4:16;
I Cor. 15:42–44; I Thess. 4:13–18; Acts 2:29, 30;
Isa. 3:21, 22

Defining Statement

"With God's help to reach Spanish-speaking people throughout the world with the Good News of salvation through our Lord Jesus Christ and disciple them for Christian ministry" (emm -mexico.net, "FAQ").

Finances

Total revenue for 2007: $608,814
Total expenses for 2007: $543,339
Net assets for 2007: $246,315

Evangelical Mission Ministries is recognized by the IRS as a 501(c)(3) nonprofit charitable organization, and contributions are tax deductible.

Publication

EMM Messenger newsletter

Website

http://www.emm-mexico.net/

Bibliography

"Evangelical Mission Ministries." http://www.emm-mexico .net. "Articles of Faith" and "FAQ."

Michael McMullen

Evangelism Explosion International

History

Evangelism Explosion International (EE), a multidenominational, nonprofit mission organization, was started in 1962 by Dr. D. James Kennedy, the founding pastor of Coral Ridge Presbyterian Church in Fort Lauderdale, Florida. As a young pastor, Kennedy was struggling to see growth in his church. Recalling those difficult times, he said, "Extrapolation made it clear that I had two-and-a-half months of ministry left before I was preaching to only my wife—and she was threatening to go to the Baptist Church down the street!" (eeinternational.org, "History").

Kennedy visited with his friend and former pastor Rev. Kennedy Smartt. Kennedy watched his friend as he engaged people spiritually during a series of evangelistic services. By the end of the meetings, fifty-four people had made a profession of faith in Christ. This experience planted the seeds that eventually became Evangelism Explosion. By 1967, Coral Ridge Presbyterian Church was recognized as one of the fastest-growing churches in America.

The first EE Leadership Training Clinic was held in 1967 to train pastors how to teach their members to share the gospel. In 1972, EE was incorporated with its own staff and board of directors. As EE spread to other countries, its training and discipleship materials were translated into more than seventy languages. Training clinics have been held all over the world, helping to produce national leadership and establishing indigenous ministries. By 1984, more training clinics were being held overseas than in the United States.

Headquarters

PO Box 23820
Ft. Lauderdale, FL 33307
Telephone: 954-491-6100
Fax: 954-771-2256

Leadership

Dr. Kennedy passed away on September 5, 2007. He was succeeded as president by Rev. John Sorensen in March 2008. He had served on the staff of EE in a number of capacities since 1996.

Core Beliefs

Kennedy came to realize that he could not do ministry alone, so he made witness training a bedrock of his ministry utilizing the principle of on-the-job training. The key to success, Kennedy found out, was that it was not exclusively the pastor's job to share the gospel. He found the "secret" of bringing people to Christ: training laypeople to share the gospel and they, in turn, training others, with the result of developing "a mighty army" for Christ.

Statistics

By 1996, EE had been established in every nation of the world. That year a major celebration was held at Coral Ridge Presbyterian Church, with representatives from the 211 nations of the world marching down the aisle with their national flags, signifying that the gospel message had reached every nation on earth through the ministry of EE.

Growth

As ministry needs changed over the years, EE's ministry expanded to include specialized materials to reach children (Kids EE), youth and young adults (XEE), prisoners, and other segments of the population. Specialized workshops and full-length training clinics were also offered. EE remains committed to assisting local pastors in equipping their members to share the good news of Jesus Christ.

Trends

Under Rev. Sorensen the organizational structure of EE has been reformatted to give more voice to national ministries and to partner with them in developing worldwide initiatives that serve the local church in the most effective manner in each culture.

In "Vision for Our Future," Rev. Sorensen wrote, "Our vision is to be part of changing the world by being a catalyst to Christ's Church, causing it to be a witnessing, multiplying Church" (eeinternational.org, "Vision").

He reaffirmed the guiding principles that Dr. Kennedy had established for EE: love for Jesus's church, spiritual commitment, love for Jesus and his commands, love for the lost, a commitment to modeling, an open-handed nature, a biblical strategy, and spiritual multiplication.

Sorenson continued, "We will accomplish the goals [by] partnering with other ministries, increasing the number of field workers who are able to assist the local pastor, bringing creativity to the materials we produce to teach the methods of EE, and using all available means of communication to reach people, whether in a primitive people group with no written language, or in the most high-tech equipped society" (eeinternational.org, "Vision").

Website

http://www.eeinternational.org/

Bibliography

"Evangelism Explosion International." http://www.eeinternational.org. "Vision."

Dominic A. Aquila

Every Home for Christ

History

Every Home for Christ, formerly known as World Literature Crusade, was founded in 1946 by Jack McAlister, a Canadian radio minister who urged his listeners to provide literature for evangelistic use by missionaries. On a trip to Japan in 1953, McAlister and a friend realized that by distributing literature to homes, they could make

systematic and quantifiable progress. Since adopting this strategy, the ministry has brought over 3.5 billion gospel messages to over 1.6 billion homes in some 200 nations. The result has been over 139 million responses. In remote areas without any churches, new Christians receive guidance from Every Home for Christ's Christ Groups.

Headquarters

640 Chapel Hills Drive
Colorado Springs, CO 80920
Telephone: 719-260-8888

Core Beliefs

Among the doctrines included in the statement of faith are ones affirming belief in biblical infallibility, the Trinity, and the deity of Christ. (The full statement can be viewed at ehc.org, "Our Beliefs.")

Finances

The Evangelical Council for Financial Accountability reported that in 2014 Every Home for Christ had more than $35 million in revenue.

Website

http://www.ehc.org/

Bibliography

"Every Home for Christ." http://www.ehc.org. "Our Beliefs" and "Our History."

George Thomas Kurian

Far Corners Missions (formerly World Missions Far Corners)

History

J. Leonard Bell and Charles W. Turner founded World Missions Far Corners (WMFC) in 1958. Bell first worked in Mexico creating audiovisual aids for people there and in other nations. Dr. Bell guided WMFC until 2001, when his wife, Mildred Bell, took the helm. She served in this role until 2005. Patricia Murdock-Cook oversaw operations from 2005 to 2008. Gary L. Bishop, who had previously served with Mission Aviation Fellowship, became president and CEO of the organization in 2009. Ministries are in China, England, India, Kenya, Mexico, Nepal, Peru, the Philippines, and Thailand through over three hundred national workers. The missionary staff numbers twenty, and headquarters are comprised of five staff. Offices were moved from Long Beach, California, to Fort Worth, Texas, in April 2009 for cost savings. In July 2010, new offices were opened. The ministry is now known as Far Corners Missions.

Headquarters

8401 Jacksboro Highway
Suite 130
Fort Worth, TX 76135
Telephone: 817-237-3000
Fax: 817-237-3387

Leadership

President and CEO: Gary Bishop

Core Beliefs

The fifteen-point Lausanne Covenant, summarized below, is the statement of faith for Far Corners.

1. The purpose of God is to save mankind, and the church takes part through the Great Commission.
2. The divine inspiration, truthfulness, and authority of God's Word are affirmed. The Bible is "without error in all that it affirms, and the only infallible rule of faith and practice."
3. Jesus Christ is the only Savior. He is the God-man, the only ransom for sinners, and the only way to be saved is through faith in him.
4. Evangelism is to proclaim the historical, biblical Christ as Savior, and the results are incorporation into the church, obedience to Christ, and service for him.
5. Christian social responsibility includes seeking justice, liberation, and freedom from oppression for all people.
6. The church's mission is sacrificial service, taking the whole gospel to the whole world.
7. Christians "who share the same biblical faith should be closely united in fellowship, work and witness."
8. God is raising up missionaries from all parts of the globe.
9. The missionary task is urgent, with billions who have never heard the gospel.
10. Churches should not be tied to any particular culture.
11. Every church should have national leaders.
12. The church recognizes its spiritual warfare with Satan.
13. Secular governments should guarantee freedom of thought, conscience, and religion as set forth in the Universal Declaration of Human Rights.
14. The Holy Spirit is "a missionary spirit; thus evangelism should arise spontaneously from a Spirit-filled church."
15. "Jesus Christ will return personally and visibly, in power and glory, to consummate his salvation and his judgment." This promise should spur believers to further missionary service.

The conclusion states, "Therefore, in the light of this our faith and our resolve, we enter into a solemn covenant with God and with each other, to pray, to plan and to work together for the evangelization of the whole world" (fc-usa.org, "What We Believe").

Defining Statement

"Bringing life, light and hope to the far corners of the world" (fc-usa.org, "Home").

Core Practices

Far Corners is a nondenominational faith fellowship of Christian evangelists who present the claims of Jesus Christ, care for the suffering, and establish indigenous churches.

A Far Corners' chaplain ministers in a US prison. Other ministries include church planting, daycare centers, film, hospital clinics, literature, pastoral training, the rehabilitation of former prostitutes, rice kitchens, river launches, and schools for children of scavengers and slum dwellers.

Finances

Far Corners joined the Evangelical Council for Financial Accountability on May 20, 2009.

Total revenue for 2013: $947,764
Total expenses for 2013: $759,229
Net assets for 2013: $1,062,097

Statistics

One couple ministers in Croydon, England, with trips to evangelize in Poland. Four persons serve in Andhra Pradesh, India, with film evangelism, rice kitchens, and other ministries. An African pastor and his assistant train pastors in Kenya. Three couples serve in various capacities in Mexico. In Peru, a couple works with churches on the Amazon River. Ministries are also conducted in China and Thailand.

Electronic Media

Radio broadcasts share Far Corners' work on five stations in North America.

Website
http://fc-usa.org/

Bibliography
"Far Corners Missions." http://fc-usa.org. "Home" and "What We Believe."

James A. Borland

Far East Broadcasting Company

History

The Far East Broadcasting Company (FEBC) is an international religious broadcasting organization that has a potential audience of half the world's population.

The FEBC was conceived by Robert Bowman, whose work on the pioneer radio ministry of the *Haven of Rest* radio program, developed by Paul Myers, convinced Bowman of the viability of radio as an evangelistic tool. Plans for a global effort began in the late 1930s, but the intervening years of World War II cut short implementation of this strategy. Viewing radio as a key strategy for reaching vast areas of the world, Bowman and colleague John Broger, in 1945, pooled their financial resourses and funded the Far East Broadcasting Company. With additional finances provided by William J. Roberts of the Family Bible Hour, the fledgling organization established its first station in Manila, Philippines, in June 1948.

With the imminent communist takeover of mainland China, the radio efforts toward that region intensified. By 1958, the FEBC's broadcasts were covering the entirety of the Philippine archipelago from eleven stations and programs in thirty-six languages and dialects and were also being directed toward China and other Asian countries.

The growth of the FEBC was faster than any of its founders had anticipated. Despite the effectiveness of jamming efforts by communist leadership in China, the FEBC broadcasts provided a substantial resource to the millions of Chinese Christians who were suffering persecution for their faith.

The FEBC's US headquarters in La Mirada, California, were developed with offices, recording studios, and technical support. Expansion in the 1990s brought the FEBC into the Middle East and Muslim areas in Asia and West Africa.

Headquarters

15700 Imperial Highway
La Mirada, CA 90638
Telephone: 800-523-3480
Email: info@febc.org

Leadership

Gregg Harris, the president of the FEBC, has been involved in international radio ministry since 1989 and became the executive vice president of the FEBC in 2001. A board of directors, comprised of eleven members, helps guide the ministry of the FEBC in conjunction with international leaders and field directors.

Defining Statement

"We communicate the Good News among the nations by media to inspire people to follow Jesus Christ" (febc.org, "About FEBC").

Core Practices

"FEBC is an interdenominational ministry who seeks to break down these three barriers [persecution, geography, and isolation] by sharing the Good News to the world through radio, the Internet, and emerging technologies" (febc.org, "About FEBC").

The FEBC "focuses on meeting the spiritual needs of our listeners . . . , strives to reach the least reached people . . . , seeks to reach the most strategic population centers in our ministry areas . . . , is committed to the Bible as God's inspired Word and the primacy of Jesus Christ as Savior and Lord . . . , make[s] its decisions based on God's leading and principles, not on human wisdom . . . , trust[s] God to provide for all our resourcing needs . . . , [and] seek[s] to glorify God through our work" (febc.org, "About FEBC").

Statistics

The FEBC broadcasts the gospel in more than 130 languages in 50 countries from 128 transmitters located throughout the world, with broadcasting hours totaling 700 a day. Three billion people live within range of its transmitters. In 2009, the FEBC received over 850,000 responses through letters, telephone calls, emails, and text messages from listeners in Asia, Russia, Africa, and the Middle East.

Publication

REACH newsletter

Website
http://www.febc.org/

Bibliography
Bowman, Eleanor, with Susan Titus. *Eyes beyond the Horizon.* Nashville: Nelson, 1991.

Bowman, Robert. *God of Wonders.* La Mirada, CA: Far East Broadcasting Company, 2002.

"Far East Broadcasting Company." http://www.febc.org. "About FEBC."

Kaufman, Riley E. *An Account of the First Powerful Standard Band Gospel Broadcasting to Communist China.* MA project, Assemblies of God Theological Seminary, 1977.

Ledyard, Gleason H. *Sky Waves: The Incredible Far East Broadcasting Company Story.* Chicago: Moody, 1963.

Byron D. Klaus

Feed the Children

History

Feed the Children (FTC) was founded in 1979 by Larry and Frances Jones. FTC provides physical needs to children in countries affected by natural disaster, trauma, and war.

In the United States, FTC utilizes its subsidiary, FTC Transportation, to distribute food and supplies from its corporate headquarters to six of its regional distribution centers.

Headquarters

PO Box 36
Oklahoma City, OK 73101
Telephone: 800-627-4556

Leadership

Travis Arnold is the executive director and chief operations officer. FTC also has a nine-member board.

Core Beliefs

FTC challenges convention, defends dignity, champions partnership, values every donor, and drives accountability (feedthechildren.org, "About").

Defining Statement

"Our vision: Create a world where no child goes to bed hungry" (feedthechildren.org, "About").

Controversies

FTC's founder, Larry Jones, was fired from his position as president in 2009 after admitting to the bugging of three offices of FTC officials. However, he filed a wrongful termination suit in order to regain his position. FTC countersued, claiming that Jones received compensation for a three-year contract with Affiliated Media Group, gave himself and his wife unauthorized raises, and stashed pornography in his office at FTC. On January 28, 2011, Jones and Feed the Children announced a resolution of the legal dispute, and Jones is no longer associated in any way with the organization.

Finances

FTC states that it spends 92 percent of its revenues on program services, which include childcare, food, medical care, disaster relief, and community development; 5 percent on fund-raising; and 3 percent on management and supporting services. For accountability, FTC posts its 990 IRS tax form and financial report on its website.

Statistics

Internationally, FTC provides famine and poverty relief through child sponsorships and other programs to over 119 nations.

Electronic Media

FTC runs advertisements or infomercials on television and during television specials.

Website

http://www.feedthechildren.org/

Bibliography

Clay, Nolan. "'Feed the Children' Fight Rages." *Oklahoman,* March 1, 2009.

"Feed the Children." http://www.feedthechildren.org. "About."

Phuc Luu

Fellowship International Mission

History

In 1922, Irene Wenholz was sent by Calvary Baptist Church, Altoona, Pennsylvania, to serve as a missionary in North Africa. Mary Mellinger joined her in 1945. As more personnel came to the area, the need to become formally organized was strongly felt, and Mellinger's pastor, Rev. Ralph Boyer of the York Gospel Center, was asked to establish a mission board. This resulted in the establishment of the Morocco Evangelical Fellowship in 1950. When the Sahara Desert Mission expressed interest in joining the Morocco Evangelical Fellowship in 1959, the fellowship expanded its purpose and became the Fellowship of Independent Missions. A further transition occurred in 1992, when the mission relocated to Allentown, Pennsylvania, and took its present name, Fellowship International Mission (FIM).

By 1978, there were over fifty Fellowship International missionaries serving in Portugal, Sweden, Brazil, Niger, Nigeria, Venezuela, Japan, France, South Africa, and the United States. By the late 1980s, the mission was becoming much more prominent in world evangelism, with missionaries on six continents. Most were directly involved in grassroots evangelism and discipling, while others supported those ministries.

In the following decade, the FIM became a mission board in the fullest sense of the word. It no longer confined itself to missionary money matters, nor was it simply an umbrella organization for independent mission boards. In fact, many people had joined as individual missionaries over the years, quickly outnumbering the small affiliated agencies. Today almost 150 Fellowship International missionaries are involved worldwide in a wide range of ministries directly linked to the establishing of churches.

The stated purpose of the FIM is to provide "a context where churches, missionaries, and agency cooperate in the great task of missions for the glory of God" (fim.org, "Mission and Vision"). It articulates its mission and vision in three areas:

> Our passion is people trusting Christ as their personal Savior and growing in their faith.
> Our vision is a growing team of thriving missionaries who are enthusiastically fulfilling their call in accomplishing the Great Commission to the glory of God.
> Our mission is to assist local churches to fulfill their missionary vision and missionaries to fulfill their call. (fim.org, "Mission and Vision")

Headquarters

555 S 24th Street
Allentown, PA 18104
Telephone: 610-435-9099
Fax: 610-435-2641

Leadership

President and CEO: Dr. Stephen K. Wilt

Core Beliefs

The mission believes that success in living the Christian life and serving the Lord is determined largely by what someone believes. This is believed to be true generally, but it is regarded as certainly true of missionary life and service. For this reason, the FIM requires that those who serve under it indicate their acceptance of the doctrinal statement and reaffirm their agreement annually.

The FIM holds to a statement of faith consistent with the fundamentals of Christianity as historically understood. It believes that an emphasis on certain doctrinal distinctives allows its missionaries and partners to work together effectively and in harmony. It stands firmly against the ecumenical movement and other movements that it regards as contrary to the faith. Further, the FIM is dispensational in its interpretation of the Bible and in its understanding of God's unfolding plan for the ages. The mission is pretribulational and premillennial in its understanding of end-time events.

Defining Statement

"Flexibility in ministry with integrity and accountability" (fim.org, "Operational Distinctives").

Core Practices

The FIM articulates its operational distinctives by outlining three steps. Step 1 is the role of the local church: "To identify, cultivate, and launch those called by God. To prayerfully champion each missionary's ministry. To foster regular communication with the missionary. To provide ministry and personal accountability for each missionary." Step 2 is the role of the FIM: "To promote the cause of missions in every available setting. To assist missionaries to fulfill their call by supporting and reinforcing them. To assist churches in fulfilling their missionary vision." Step 3 is the role of the missionary: "To follow the leading of the Holy Spirit. To faithfully serve according to the agreed upon doctrinal and ministry statements. To communicate with supporters faithfully. To inspire others to follow in their footsteps in obedience to Christ" (fim.org, "Operational Distinctives").

Finances

Total revenue for 2008: $3,648,498
Total expenses for 2008: $3,638,273
Net assets for 2008: $629,869

Ministry Watch has awarded the Fellowship International Mission a transparency grade of A and listed the mission as a 2008 Shining Light "Top 30" Exemplary Ministry.

Website

http://www.fim.org/

Bibliography

"Fellowship International Mission." http://www.fim.org. "Mission and Vision" and "Operational Distinctives."

Michael McMullen

Fellowship of Christian Athletes

History

The Fellowship of Christian Athletes (FCA) is America's largest Christian sports organization, encouraging coaches and athletes in professional and all school levels to spread the gospel through sports. Interdenominational and international, it was founded in 1954 by Don McClanen, who was inspired by articles in which athletes discussed their faith. McClanen attempted to meet with these athletes and was finally received by the legendary Branch Rickey, then general manager of the Pittsburgh Pirates. Rickey, Paul Benedum, and other Pittsburgh businessmen provided some funding for McClanen's vision of a Christian athletic organization, and McClanen raised additional funds as he networked and promoted his idea. Among the charter members were Otto Graham, Carl Erskine, Donn Moomaw, and Rickey.

In 1956, 256 athletes and coaches attended the first national camp at Estes Park, Colorado, and headquarters were relocated from Norman, Oklahoma, to Kansas City, Missouri. Three years later the *Christian Athlete* magazine began publication. FCA camps have continually grown in popularity and included almost 47,000 participants in 2009.

Headquarters

8701 Leeds Road
Kansas City, MO 64129
Telephone: 816-921-0909
Fax: 816-923-2136
Email: fca@fca.org

Leadership

Les Steckel became the FCA's seventh president and CEO in March 2005. Donnie Dee, who has been involved with the Fellowship of Christian Athletes for nineteen years, serves as the executive director and chief operating officer. Other members of the executive team are Dan Britton, Tom Rogeberg, and Ken Williams.

Core Beliefs

The FCA's statement of faith embraces conservative evangelical beliefs. The FCA expresses its commitment to Christ and his Word through four principles (fca.org, "The FCA Values"):

Integrity—We will demonstrate Christ-like wholeness, privately and publicly. (Proverbs 11:3)
Serving—We will model Jesus's example of serving. (John 13:1–17)
Teamwork—expressing our unity in Christ in all our relationships. (Philippians 2:14)
Excellence—We will honor and glorify God in all we do. (Colossians 3:23–24)

Defining Statement

"To see the world impacted for Jesus Christ through the influence of athletes and coaches" (fca.org, "The FCA Vision").

Core Practices

The FCA's main outreach is through campus ministry led by student athletes and their coaches on middle school, high school, and university campuses. This outreach encourages Christian athletes to gather and grow in their faith. One Way 2 Play is another FCA program that confronts drug use among students, especially student athletes, through faith, commitment, and accountability. More Than Winning describes Christian salvation and life through sports metaphors for athletes. More Than Winning and other FCA Bible study programs brought more than 35,000 athletes and coaches to Christ in 2009. The FCA also sponsors camps that encourage and train athletes to be spiritual leaders.

Finances

The FCA has been a member of the Evangelical Council for Financial Accountability since August 1, 1987.

Statistics

In 2009, the FCA was present on 7,100 campuses and worked with 46,000 coaches and athletes.

Event attendance: 1,447,881
FCA events: 33,460
Number reached on campuses: 340,050
Certified campuses: 6,801
Camp attendance: 46,944
Camps: 302
Faith commitments: 35,159
One Way 2 Play drug free decisions: 34,712

Missionary and Evangelistic Work

The FCA is wholeheartedly evangelistic and pastoral, seeking to present to athletes and coaches and all whom they influence the challenge and adventure of receiving Jesus Christ as Savior and Lord, as well as serving him in their relationships and in the fellowship of the church. To achieve this, the FCA focuses on the four Cs: coaches, campus, camp, and community. The FCA seeks to minister to coaches through Bible study, prayer, and discipleship. Coaches and players gather on school campuses to support and encourage one another. The FCA sponsors camps for coaches and student athletes each year. Community Ministry connects with local churches, businesses, and parents and helps connect student athletes with their local community.

Website

http://www.fca.org/

Bibliography

"Fellowship of Christian Athletes." http://www.fca.org. "The FCA Values" and "The FCA Vision."

Alycia West

Food for the Hungry

History

Food for the Hungry was founded by Dr. Larry Ward in 1971 in Glendale, California. The ministry has since relocated to Phoenix, Arizona. From 1971 to 1980, Food for the Hungry primarily responded to natural disasters and emergencies. From 1981 to 1985, the vision grew into building trust and longer-term assistance for the poor. The present scope is meeting physical and spiritual needs worldwide. Food for the Hungry now serves in over twenty-six countries in Asia, Africa, and Latin America. Yet its emphasis remains on the importance of the individual in community. Dr. Ward is remembered to have said, "They die one at a time, and so we can help them one at a time" (fh.org, "History").

Headquarters

1224 E Washington Street
Phoenix, AZ 85034
Telephone: 480-998-3100; 800-248-6437

Leadership

Food for the Hungry is incorporated and therefore overseen by a board of directors. The Global Executive Office, which reports to the board, consists of Keith Wright, international president; Dave Evans, US president; Mary Martin, chief operating officer; and Luis Nida, field operations.

Core Beliefs

Food for the Hungry carries forward Isaiah's vision, proclaimed by Jesus, that God has good news for the poor in all nations (Luke 4:18). Jesus announced restoration to the economically destitute, the physically disabled, and the socially oppressed. Food for the Hungry strives to hold these elements together, helping communities— the backbone of developing nations—by empowering individuals to transform themselves.

Defining Statement

"To walk with churches, leaders and families in overcoming all forms of human poverty by living in healthy relationship with God and His creation" (fh.org, "Statement of Vision, Mission and Faith").

Missionary and Evangelistic Work

Food for the Hungry serves in over twenty-six countries throughout Asia, Africa, and Latin America, but also locally in Phoenix, providing food, water, sanitation, health, nutrition, child sponsorship, HIV/AIDS management, microenterprise, church development, emergency response, and public policy. The ministry also partners with local ministries and government to address child prostitution in Phoenix.

Electronic Media

Food for the Hungry utilizes several forms of media to advance its mission, including several blogs (*Disaster Relief, President's Blog, Poverty Unlocked, Artist Program*, and *Sponsor Impact*), podcasts (*GIK Mini Cast*), and Twitter, all accessible from its website.

Publication

Food for the Hungry quarterly publishes *6:8* magazine. Past issues may be viewed on its website.

Website

http://www.fh.org/

Bibliography

"Food for the Hungry." http://www.fh.org. "History" and "Statement of Vision, Mission and Faith."

John DelHousaye

Foundation for His Ministry

History

Foundation for His Ministry was founded in 1966 by Chuck and Charla Pereau from North Hollywood, California. After sensing a call to the poor children in Mexico, they purchased land and buildings and opened an orphanage, Hogar Para Ninos. By 1980, their ministry had widened to serve the many hundreds of destitute located in nearby agricultural labor camps.

The ministry continued to grow to include orchards and gardens, a modern medical center, a Bible school, a soup kitchen, print/upholstery shops, drug rehabilitation, a Christian school, literacy classes, gospel outreach, and a ministry to the disabled. In 1998 and 1999, two new mission facilities were opened in Mexico in the cities of Morelia, Michoacan, and Tlacolula, Oaxaca. Foundation for His Ministry is a Christian charitable ministry. It is a nonprofit, nondenominational organization that now has a volunteer missionary staff of over 150 and a fully volunteer board.

Headquarters

PO Box 74000
San Clemente, CA 92673
Telephone: 949-492-2200

Core Beliefs

The ministry has the following nonnegotiable ideals:

1. Always preach the Gospel.
2. Always be committed to a relationship with Christ through daily prayer, worship, and devotions.
3. Always have outreach to the poor.
4. Always give everyone the opportunity to participate in outreach.
5. Always be cross-centered (modeling Christ's example of sacrifice, obedience, and love).
6. Always be committed to fellowship with the local church.
7. Always lead through modeling by equipping, developing, and encouraging the giftedness of others.
8. Always rely on the supernatural power and provision of God.
9. Always preserve spiritual unity and accept diversity in non-essentials (those not listed in our statement of faith).
10. Always submit to the authority God has put in place.
11. Always be a good steward of God's provision.
12. Always live simply so others can simply live.
(ffhm.org, "Mission Statement")

Defining Statement

"Foundation for His Ministry is a missionary organization whose purpose is to glorify God by making disciples of Jesus Christ. To this end we share and demonstrate God's love through the power of the Holy Spirit by meeting the basic spiritual, physical and educational needs of those in Mexico and beyond" (ffhm.org, "Mission Statement").

Core Practices

Several projects illustrate the priorities of Foundation for His Ministry. Amost two hundred orphaned or abandoned children are provided the necessities of life in a loving Christian environment and an education through Christian schools at three locations.

Children receive music instruction and through participation in musical drama presentations are learning to reach others in their community with the gospel.

A students' house in Tijuana is home for those who wish to pursue a technological or university education.

Rancho de Cristo, a substance abuse center, has been opened as a rehabilitation facility for men.

Eight to ten thousand men, women, and children receive medical, dental, and maternity care each year through La Clinica del Senor (the Lord's Clinic). Services are provided free of charge, and each patient receives prayer.

A Bible Institute has been established to provide a two-year training and discipleship course for Mexican nationals called to the ministry.

A ministry to the disabled provides specially adapted wheelchairs, equipment, physical therapy, and spiritual care for shut-ins.

A government-approved school provides Christ-centered education for children in preschool through sixth grade. Older children receive apprenticeship training in construction, mechanics, printing, fire and rescue, woodworking, bicycle repair, and upholstery.

The Mission Church in Vicente Guerrero provides a place to worship for over one thousand community members. In addition, satellite churches have been established in Baja California, Michoacan, and Oaxaca.

A conference center has been established in Tlacolula, Oaxaca, to provide training and support for national pastors working in the remote and unreached areas of Mexico.

An agricultural research station specializing in fruit is a teaching tool. A macadamia nut orchard has been planted in the fertile land to supply food and finances.

The El Alcance de Dios outreach to thousands of destitute people in the area includes a food distribution center, clothing and blankets, a soup kitchen, assistance to the elderly, and a jail ministry.

Finances

Total revenue for 2013: $3,543,719
Total expenses for 2013: $3,741,406
Less than 4 percent spent on administration and fund-raising
Recipient of the Award for Integrity in Fundraising, Evangelical Development Ministries

Meets or exceeds all standards of financial accountability set by the Evangelical Counsel for Financial Accountability

Website

http://www.ffhm.org/

Bibliography

"Foundation for His Ministry." http://www.ffhm.org. "Mission Statement."

Michael McMullen

Franciscans

History

The Franciscans (the Order of Friars Minor) is a Roman Catholic religious order inspired by the life and teachings of St. Francis of Assisi. St. Francis (AD 1181–1226), the son of an Italian cloth merchant, experienced a profound conversion around 1209 after hearing Christ's words to the apostles when he sent them to preach the gospel: "Do not get any gold or silver or copper to take with you in your belts—no bag for the journey or extra shirt or sandals or a staff" (Matt. 10:9–10). He gave all his money to the poor and adopted a life of absolute poverty and preaching in imitation of the apostles. After a band of followers gathered around him, he secured from the pope formal approval for a religious order in 1210, the Order of Friars Minor (little brothers), based on the *Rule of St. Francis*, which he personally drafted.

The Franciscans led missionary efforts throughout the late medieval and early modern period, in addition to effecting widespread spiritual renewal throughout Christian Europe. Several branches of Franciscans exist today, each following the *Rule of St. Francis*. The largest are the Franciscan friars, the Capuchins, the Conventual Franciscans, and the Third Order Regular, in addition to the Order of St. Clare (Poor Clares), a female branch started by Francis himself. There are also countless smaller orders of Franciscans, along with a substantial number of laity (usually known as the Third Order) who attempt to live the ideals of the order as much as possible without taking formal religious vows.

Core Beliefs

The central goal of all forms of religious orders in the Catholic Church is to secure "undivided devotion to the Lord" (1 Cor. 7:35 NIV) through the "evangelical counsels" of chastity, poverty, and obedience. The Order of Friars Minor is additionally characterized by its embrace of the *vita apostolica* (apostolic life) of poverty, preaching, and begging, in imitation of St. Francis, as an indispensible means toward this end.

Core Practices

The Order of Friars Minor is committed to poverty and the preaching of the gospel. The commitment to poverty—which entailed begging for one's daily food, earning St. Francis's followers the name "mendicants" (beggars)—is an attempt to identify with the humble poverty of Christ, who became poor for our sakes (2 Cor. 8:9) and "had nowhere to lay his head" (Luke 9:58 RSV). The abandonment of personal property also allows a Franciscan to embrace all of creation as a gift from God and to identify with the poor to whom he ministers. In imitation of the apostolic life, the Franciscans also seek to preach the gospel, in particular repentance from sins and personal conversion. This commitment led St. Francis to abandon the vow of stability, which restricted previous generations of monks to the monasteries, since the demands of preaching required flexibility and mobility. Instead, a Franciscan takes the three vows of poverty, chastity (the voluntary renunciation of marriage), and obedience to his or her monastic superior.

Franciscans today are best known for their work in education, missions, and especially ministry to the poor and needy.

Bibliography

Armstrong, Regis, William Short, and Wayne Hellman, eds. *Francis of Assisi: Early Documents—The Saint, The Founder, The Prophet.* 4 vols. New York: New City Press, 1999, 2000, 2001.

Carmody, Maurice. *The Franciscan Story: St. Francis of Assisi and His Influence Since the Thirteenth Century.* London: Athena, 2008.

Moorman, John. *A History of the Franciscan Order from Its Origins to the Year 1517.* Oxford: Clarendon, 1968.

Short, William. *The Franciscans.* Collegeville, MN: Liturgical Press, 1989.

Jamie Blosser

Frontiers

History

Frontiers was founded in 1982 with the specific vision to plant churches among Muslim people groups. According to the organization's present leadership, at the time of Frontiers' founding, many Muslim countries did not have any deliberate church-planting efforts. Frontiers presently has sending bases in fifteen countries in

North America, Europe, Latin America, Africa, and Asia.

Headquarters

PO Box 60670
Phoenix, AZ 85082
Telephone: 800-462-8436
Email: info@frontiers.org

Core Beliefs

Frontiers missionaries affirm a general evangelical statement of faith—one that can be embraced by Christian workers from across the evangelical spectrum. It upholds such doctrines as the authority of Scripture, the Trinity, original sin, the divinity of Christ, justification by faith, the work of the Holy Spirit, the church, the return of Christ, and last things.

Frontiers makes no specific assertions about the nature of the atonement, the gifts of the Spirit, modes of baptism, or eschatology. (The doctrinal statement of Frontiers is found at frontiersusa .org, "Statement of Faith.")

Defining Statement

"With love and respect, inviting all Muslim Peoples to follow Jesus" (frontiersusa.org, "Jesus for Muslims").

Core Practices

The organization's priorities include preaching the gospel among Muslims where Christ has not been named (Rom. 15:20–21), exercising faith and humility, taking initiative and risks, embracing suffering, and pursuing the best practices for planting churches. In light of these values, the leadership structure of Frontiers is field-centered, that is, teams function effectively as their own mission organization based on their context. Each team leader is expected to develop a memo of understanding, articulating the who, what, when, where, why, and how for church planting in the leader's particular context. Upholding the principle of pursuing best practices in church planting, the international leadership holds team leaders accountable to their memo of understanding.

Controversies

A number of Frontiers authors advocate a strategy known as "insider movements." Simply put, this approach encourages Muslims to become followers of Jesus while maintaining much of their Muslim identity. For instance, Muslim followers of Jesus may continue to pray in the mosque, fast during Ramadan, and maintain other Muslim traditions that do not violate the Christian Scriptures. (For a more complete description of the strategy, see Travis, "The C1 to C6 Spectrum.") Though many missionaries in the Muslim world have appreciated this strategy, others have argued that this approach leads to syncretism and a weakened ecclesiology and ultimately proves to be deceptive to Muslims. Despite these controversies, Frontiers continues to be a catalyst within the global mission movement for planting churches among Muslims.

Statistics

In addition to having nearly 1,000 people serving on 195 mission teams in 40 countries, Frontiers has been a catalyst for other mission organizations to begin church-planting work in the Muslim world.

Trends

The original vision of Frontiers—planting churches among unreached Muslim peoples—has not changed since 1982. According to the present leadership, the priority remains reaching out to the least reached. In the forty countries where Frontiers teams are serving, there is a particular emphasis on reaching people groups in Pakistan, northern India, Chad, Sudan, Niger, and the island of Sumatra (Indonesia). Because most of these contexts are closed to conventional mission efforts, the vast majority of Frontiers workers gain entry into these countries as "tentmakers" (see Lai, *Tentmaking*).

Publications

A number of Frontiers missionaries have published books and journal articles and contributed significantly to missiological studies, especially regarding church-planting philosophies and strategies among Muslims.

Website

http://www.frontiers.org/

Bibliography

Allen, Celeste, and Lisa Seelinger, eds. *More than Some People Can Say.* Kearney, NE: Morris Publishing, 2005.

Blincoe, Robert. *Ethnic Realities and the Church: Lessons from Kurdistan.* Pasadena, CA: Presbyterian Center for Mission Studies, 1998.

"Frontiers." http://www.frontiersusa.org. "Jesus for Muslims" and "Statement of Faith."

Goldmann, David. *Islam and the Bible: Why Two Faiths Collide.* Chicago: Moody, 2004.

Lai, Patrick. *Tentmaking: Business and Missions.* Waynesboro, GA: Authentic Media, 2005.

Livingstone, Greg. *Planting Churches in Muslim Cities: A Team Approach.* Grand Rapids: Baker, 1993.

Love, Fran, and Jeleta Eckheart. *Longing to Call Them Sisters: Ministry to Muslim Women.* Pasadena, CA: William Carey Library, 2000.

Love, Rick. *Muslims, Magic, and the Kingdom of God.* Pasadena, CA: William Carey Library, 2000.

Parshall, Phil. "Danger! New Directions in Contextualization." *Evangelical Missions Quarterly* 34, no. 4 (1998): 404–6, 409–10.

Sinclair, Michael. *A Vision of the Possible.* Waynesboro, GA: Authentic Media, 2005.

Sjogren, Bob. *Unveiled at Last.* Seattle: YWAM Publishing, 1992.

Tennent, Timothy. "Followers of Jesus (Isa) in Islamic Mosques: A Closer Examination of the C-5 'High Spectrum' Contextualization." *International Journal of Frontier Missiology* 23, no. 3 (2006): 101–15.

Travis, John. "The C1 to C6 Spectrum." *Evangelical Missions Quarterly* 34, no. 3 (1998): 407–8.

Edward Smither

Frontier Ventures (formerly US Center for World Mission)

History

Ralph and Roberta Winter founded the US Center for World Mission (USCWM) in 1976. Dr. Winter, a trained engineer and linguist, spent ten years in Guatemala as a missionary, along with his wife, before accepting a teaching position at Fuller Theological Seminary in Pasadena, California. With his presentation on unreached people groups at the 1974 Lausanne Congress, Winter established himself as a leading voice in missions.

Winter, with his concern for taking the gospel to the unreached people of the world, left his teaching position at Fuller Seminary to start the US Center in 1976. The center was established to enable mission agencies to collaborate in the task of reaching the unreached for Christ. The first major challenge was to pay off the $40 million debt on their Pasadena campus, which was accomplished in eleven years. Winter began the Perspectives on the World Christian Movement course in 1974 in response to an increased interest in missions after the Urbana Conference of 1973. The course began with thirty students on the campus of Wheaton College and today has over eighty thousand alumni in the United States and many international graduates, including ten thousand from Korea. Winter provided the vision and leadership for the organization until his death in 2009. In that same year, Dave Datema

was named the general director of Frontier Mission Fellowship, the organization that oversaw the US Center for World Mission.

In March 2015, Frontier Mission Fellowship and the US Center for World Mission became Frontier Ventures, which serves "initiatives focused on increasing momentum for the breakthrough of the Gospel among the last remaining unreached people groups of the world" (frontierventures.org, "About").

Headquarters

1605 E Elizabeth Street
Pasadena, CA 91104
Telephone: 626-797-1111

Leadership

Frontier Ventures is led by three general directors, six directors, and ten program leaders.

Core Beliefs

Frontier Ventures adheres to the basic doctrines of the Christian faith and is broadly evangelical in perspective.

Defining Statement

"We are a community of dreamers and doers who long to see Jesus worshipped in the earth's darkest corners" (frontierventures.org, "Home").

Core Practices

Frontier Ventures is not a sending agency but rather an organization that serves the mission community. Its practices include publishing, educational, training, strategic, and mobilization ventures.

Publications

Global Prayer Digest (monthly prayer guide)
International Journal of Frontier Missiology (academic journal published quarterly)
Missions Frontiers (bimonthly magazine)
William Carey Library (publisher of mission books)

Website

http://www.frontierventures.org/

Bibliography

"Frontier Ventures." http://www.frontierventures.org. "About" and "Home."

Winter, Ralph D. "The Highest Priority: Cross-Cultural Evangelism." In *Let the Earth Hear His Voice*, edited by J. D. Douglas, 213–41. Minneapolis: World Wide Publications, 1975.

———. *The Twenty-Five Unbelievable Years: 1945 to 1969.* Pasadena, CA: William Carey Library, 1970.

Winter, Ralph D., and Stephen C. Hawthorne, eds. *Perspectives on the World Christian Movement: A Reader.* 4th ed. Pasadena, CA: William Carey Library, 2009.

Winter, Roberta H. *I Will Do a New Thing: The U.S. Center for World Mission, and Beyond.* Rev. ed. Pasadena, CA: William Carey Library, 2002.

Philip Bustrum and Mark A. Lamport

Gideons

History

The Gideons was organized on July 1, 1899, in Janesville, Wisconsin. The organizers were businessmen Samuel Hill, John Nicholson, and William Knights. Two of them, Hill and Nicholson, had met the year before when they had shared a double room in a crowded hotel. They desired opportunities for Christian fellowship, personal evangelism, and united service for Christ.

In 1908, members of the Gideons, a number of whom were frequent travelers and spent much time in hotels, suggested that a Bible be placed in every hotel room in the United States. A hotel Bible can potentially reach up to twenty-three hundred people during its six-year life. Hotel-industry research reveals that 25 percent of travelers read the Bibles placed in their hotel rooms. Bibles are also given to members of the United States Armed Forces and to those in Veterans Administration hospitals.

The Gideons symbol is a small lamp with two side handles and a burning flame at the top. Members are organized into thirty-two hundred "camps" across the United States. Gideons membership is available to Christian businessmen, professional men aged twenty-one or older, and those in the same categories who are retired. A Gideon must belong to a Protestant or evangelical church and have his pastor's recommendation. The wives of Gideon members were organized as the Auxiliary in 1923.

The Gideons president is elected by the membership for a two-year term. Craig Warner, an Australian, became the executive director in July 2010 after many other assignments within the upper management of the organization. The headquarters moved from Chicago to Nashville, Tennessee, in 1964. The four-story building was the former headquarters of Bridgestone Tire.

Headquarters

Mailing Address
PO Box 140800
Nashville, TN 37214

Street Address
50 Century Boulevard
Nashville, TN 37214
Telephone: 615-564-5000
Email: tgi@gideons.org

Leadership

The International Cabinet meets thrice annually and is responsible for the annual budget. Members include four officers, ten trustees from the United States, and up to eight trustees from qualified national associations outside the United States.

Core Beliefs

A Gideon must believe that the Bible is the inspired, inerrant Word of God and that the Lord Jesus Christ is the eternal Son of God. He must have received Christ as his Savior and must endeavor to follow him in his daily life. There are no other doctrinal stipulations.

Core Practices

Gideons endeavor to personally hand the Word of God to individuals, just as Jesus met people wherever they were in life. The objective is to win others to Christ through the placing of the Bible or portions thereof in hotels, hospitals, schools, and institutions.

Finances

Income is primarily through donor contributions (88 percent), membership dues (3 percent), and investment and other income (9 percent). Revenue for the fiscal years 2009 and 2010 was $122.5 million and $131.3 million, respectively. Expenses were $133.3 million and $135.4 million, leaving deficits of $10.8 million and $4 million. Net assets were $59 million on May 31, 2008, but declined to $48.1 million a year later, and to $44.1 million as of May 31, 2010. These assets are held in mutual funds, common stocks, government and corporate bonds, and annuity contracts. Fund-raising accounted for a minimal 1 percent of expenses in the 2010 fiscal year. Membership services were less than 6 percent, and administration was a mere 3.7 percent of expenses. Fully 89 percent of expenses were for Scripture purchases and distribution. Ministry Watch gives the Gideons five stars, its highest rating, based on transparency, truth claims, values, sector/functions, resourcefulness, red-flag issues, and consultation.

Statistics

Over 1 million copies of God's Word are distributed by the Gideons every week. Each copy costs about $1.32. Gideon Bibles appear in over 80 languages in over 190 countries. The ministry has spread to 4 new continents: Europe (the Netherlands, 1949), Africa (South Africa, 1950), Asia (Japan, 1950), and South America (Ecuador, 1955). Total distribution reached 100 million in 1971, 200 million in 1978, 500 million in 1991, 1 billion in 2001, and now more than 1.6 billion since a Bible was first placed in the Superior Hotel in Iron Mountain, Montana, in 1908. The KJV is the usual version, though the NKJV is distributed where a modern version is requested.

Missionary and Evangelistic Work

In addition to placing Bibles in hotel rooms, Gideons personally distribute Bibles at state and local fairgrounds; in prisons; in schools and colleges; in hospitals and convalescent homes; and to police, fire, and medical personnel.

Website

http://www.gideons.org/

Bibliography

The Gideons International 100 Years: Sharing God's Word. Nashville: Gideons International, 2008.

James A. Borland

Global Outreach International

History

Established in 1970 by a group of laypeople motivated by involvement in community development projects, Global Outreach International quickly grew and today ministers all around the globe. The initial purpose of the ministry, which is based in Tupelo, Mississippi, was to coordinate volunteers from the United States to partner with missionaries on the field by volunteering goods and services. From this initial group of lay leaders and visionaries, several arose with a broader vision for the missions-sending organization that Global Outreach International is today.

Central to this organizational leadership were Dr. and Mrs. Sammy Simpson, Owen Cooper, and Mr. and Mrs. L. D. Hancock. The Simpsons had previously served as missionaries in Ecuador with the Southern Baptists, utilizing agricultural ministry for evangelism, discipleship, and church planting. In 1976, only six years after the organization's launch of volunteer ministries, Global

Outreach employed its first two staff members and further developed its partnership ministry. Five years later Global Outreach expanded again, becoming a fully established missions-sending organization, sending out its first full-time missionaries in 1981.

Headquarters

PO Box 1

Tupelo, MS 38802

Telephone: 662-842-4615

Leadership

A board of directors made up of business professionals and ministry personnel from a host of professions and backgrounds governs Global Outreach International. The organization's president and the home office staff manage Global Outreach International's day-to-day operations.

Core Beliefs

Global Outreach International has four key values that define the organization. It is evangelism focused, discipleship driven, compassion motivated, and relationship oriented. In addition, Global Outreach is careful not to exclude candidates from missionary service on the basis of education, age, marital status, family size, or handicaps. As its website states, "If God calls you to it and you can dream it, we desire to help facilitate it" (globaloutreach.org, "About Global").

Defining Statement

Global Outreach International exists now and for the future to "form a family of career missionaries, short-term volunteers, support personnel, and partners united to promote the gospel of Jesus Christ, undergird the international indigenous church, and offer help to a hurting humanity" (globaloutreach.org, "About Global").

Core Practices

Global Outreach International has an open approach to the length of missionary service and the types of ministries pursued by its personnel. While short-term team opportunities and short-assignment mission opportunities are available for families and individuals, the key focus of Global Outreach is on career missionaries. Its missionaries serve in evangelistic ministries; indigenous discipleship; training, medical, and educational ministries; as well as other development and church roles.

Statistics

As of 2010, the organization had more than two hundred missionaries serving in nearly forty countries. Global Outreach International currently has active ministries in Argentina, Belize, Brazil, Bulgaria, Cambodia, Chile, Costa Rica, Croatia, Ecuador, Ethiopia, France, Germany, Guatemala, Guyana, Haiti, Honduras, India, Kenya, Laos, Moldova, Portugal, Romania, Rwanda, South Africa, Spain, Sudan, Thailand, Uganda, Ukraine, the United Kingdom, Uruguay, and several unspecified locations.

Website

http://www.globaloutreach.org/

Bibliography

"Global Outreach International." http://www.globalout reach.org. "About Global."

M. David Sills

Globe International

History

In addition to starting Globe Missionary Evangelism (GME) in Pensacola, Florida, Ken Sumrall began Liberty Church in Pensacola, Florida; Liberty Fellowship of Churches and Ministers in Birmingham, Alabama; Ken Sumrall Ministries in Pace, Florida; and Church Foundational Network in Valdosta, Georgia. Globe Missionary Evangelism was created in 1973 to prepare missionaries across denominations for the field. Its humanitarian arm is called Globe Hope, which sends missionaries to serve in areas hit hard by poverty, natural disaster, and war. In early 1994, Sumrall's Liberty Church donated an eleven-thousand-square-foot facility to be renovated into the GME headquarters. The name for GME has since been changed to Globe International (GI).

One of the training ministries for GI called Hawthorne Leadership Development was begun by McLean and Colleen Hawthorne in 1986. Its purpose is to prepare church and field leaders. It has trained over seven hundred leaders in India, Bangladesh, Nepal, Myanmar, Malaysia, Singapore, Cambodia, Vietnam, Indonesia, the Philippines, Uganda, Tanzania, Sudan, Ethiopia, Kenya, Nigeria, and Ghana.

In 2003, DeLynn and Gloria Hoover developed another training ministry called VidaNet, a network of short-term discipleship programs in Costa Rica. It includes PVM, a summer program that has prepared over seventeen hundred youth for mission trips; DaVida, an outreach that works with local churches and the poor; and Vida220, a ten-month discipleship program for adults over eighteen.

Global International established the Institute of Global Ministry, a six-month missions-training school that meets weekly in Pensacola, Florida. Since 2006, it has streamed live lectures by experienced missionaries via the internet. In January 2011, it launched IGM-Live, a series of online classes in mission training from Globe headquarters. In addition, the Globe School of Ministry offers online biblical studies and awards a certificate in ministerial studies. Another training agency is the Instituto Telelógico por Extensión (INST), an accredited online course taught in Spanish, English, French, Hungarian, Russian, Ukrainian, Romanian, Cebuano, Tagalog, Portuguese, Mandarin, Chinese, and Arabic. It is available in nine Latin American countries to over five thousand students, with plans to expand. INST is accredited by the Accrediting Commission of the Distance Education and Training Council in Washington, DC, and is a member of the Council on Higher Education Accreditation. Missionary Glenn Hatcher formed the Globe Edge, an online, interactive course with weekly lessons on missions. A training opportunity that is not online but on-site is NextStep. It offers an intensive cross-cultural, two-week experience in various countries throughout the world.

Headquarters

Mailing Address
PO Box 3040
Pensacola, FL 32516

Street Address
8590 Highway 98 W
Pensacola, FL 32506
Telephone: 850-453-3453
Fax: 850-456-6001
Email: info@gme.org

Leadership

In 1976, J. Robert Bishop became GI's founding director, overseeing a board of directors consisting of seven pastors and laymen. Upon his retirement in 2004, J. Douglas Gehman replaced him as president.

Core Beliefs

GI's doctrinal statement approximates the Apostles' Creed except for this point of expansion:

We believe the Holy Spirit to be the Third Person of the Trinity whose purpose in the redemption of man is to convict men of sin, regenerate the repentant believer, guide the believer into all truth, indwell and give gifts to believers as He wills, that they may minister as Christ would to men. We believe that the manifestations of the Holy Spirit recorded in 1 Corinthians 12:8–11 shall operate in present-day churches which yield to the Lord Jesus Christ. We believe in Divine Healing and the Priesthood of Believers. (globeintl.org, "Intro to Globe")

Core Practices

GI assists local churches in sending missionaries into the field. Its programs include evangelism, church planting, leadership development, and physical relief in times of crises. According to its website, GI sees itself as providing a "spiritual covering and an administrative base for missionaries. Through accountability and pastoral oversight (prayer and intercession, counseling, and field visitation), missionaries have the assurance that they are not alone on the field" (globeintl.org, "Intro to Globe").

Finances

Since 1986, GI has been a member of the Evangelical Council for Financial Accountability.

Statistics

GI services over 240 missionaries in 35 countries.

Growth

Hawthorne Leadership Development has plans to expand its teaching to prepare more leaders for India, Sri Lanka, Bangladesh, and Nepal. INST was offered to two additional Latin American countries in 2010.

Trends

The mission and vision have remained constant since the organization's inception.

Missionary and Evangelistic Work

The sole purpose of this organization is to equip those called to the mission field.

Ecumenism

Global International is an independent, charismatic agency that serves the entire body of Christ. It also oversees these ministries: Globe Nicaragua, Friends of Internationals, Arise and Shine Evangelistic Association, Challenge Farm, Globe Europe, Abundant Life Ministries,

Beacon of Hope, and Overtoun House. It is also a member of the Association of International Missions Services and the Alliance for Missions Advancement.

Academic Institutions

Globe School of Ministry

IGM-Live

Institute of Global Ministry

Instituto Telelógico por Extensión (INST)

Parachurch Organizations

GI's Globe Hope helps with orphanages, disaster relief, the Global Hope Child Sponsorship Program, Christian education, medical and dental clinics, dental campaigns and crusades, and literacy work.

Electronic Media

Radio programs and online education

Publication

Globe International Missions Update (online)

Website

http://globeintl.org/

Bibliography

Barnett, Betty. Friend Raising: Building a Missionary Support Team That Lasts. Seattle: YWAM Publishing, 2002.

Crossman, Meg. Perspectives Exposure: Discovering God's Heart for All Nations and Our Part in His Plan. Seattle: YWAM Publishing, 2003.

Cunningham, Loren. Daring to Live on the Edge: The Adventure of Faith and Finance. Seattle: YWAM Publishing, 1992.

Gehman, J. Douglas. Go to the Ripe Fields First: Focusing Outreach on Receptive People. South St. Paul: Globe Publishing, 2004.

"Globe International." http://globeintl.org. "Intro to Globe."

Hale, Thomas. On Being a Missionary. Hattiesburg, MS: William Carey Library, 2003.

Hatcher, Glenn. Why God Thinks He Can Use You. Scotts Valley, CA: CreateSpace, 2010.

Hiebert, Paul. Anthropological Insights for Missionaries. Grand Rapids: Baker, 1985.

Johnstone, Patrick, and Jason Mandryk. Operation World: When We Pray God Works. Rev. ed. Milton Keynes, UK: Paternoster, 2001.

Koehler, Paul. Telling God's Stories with Power: Storytelling in Oral Cultures. Hattiesburg, MS: William Carey Library, 2009.

Lingenfelter, Sherwood G., and Marvin K. Mayers. Ministering Cross-Culturally: An Incarnational Model for Personal Relationships. Grand Rapids: Baker Academic, 2003.

Sommer, Pete. Getting Sent: A Relational Approach to Support Raising. Nottingham, UK: Inter-Varsity, 1999.

Brenda Ayres

Gospel for Asia

History

Gospel for Asia is a Christian missionary organization that was founded in 1979 by K. P. Yohannan and his wife, Gisela. The organization was founded as an evangelistic and church-planting ministry among the unreached regions of Asia. K. P.'s mother prayed and fasted faithfully each week, asking God to call one of her six sons as a full-time missionary. Her prayer was answered in 1966 when her youngest son, K. P., volunteered to serve with Operation Mobilization in India. Yohannan studied at Criswell Bible College (Dallas) from 1974 to 1979, earning a bachelor's degree in biblical studies. During his college studies, he pastored a church in Dallas. He resigned his pastorate in 1978 to organize what is now known as Gospel for Asia.

Headquarters

1800 Golden Trail Court
Carrollton, TX 75010
Telephone: 800-946-2742
Fax: 972-300-7778

Leadership

K. P. Yohannan is the president. The board consists of four members.

Core Beliefs

Gospel for Asia is conservative theologically. The ministry affirms the verbal inspiration and inerrancy of Scripture and that it is the only authority for faith and practice. It is a trinitarian group, believing in God as the Creator of all things. Gospel for Asia affirms the deity of Jesus Christ, including his virgin birth, sinless life, substitutionary death, bodily resurrection, ascension, and imminent return. Man was created by and for God but through disobedience incurred spiritual and physical death; therefore, all humanity sins by nature and practice. All who believe in Jesus Christ are declared righteous. The Holy Spirit indwells all believers and empowers them in life and ministry. All humanity will be resurrected bodily, resulting in everlasting blessedness for the righteous and everlasting punishment for the unrighteous. Although Gospel for Asia is nondenominational, the ministry is closely affiliated with Calvary Chapel churches.

Defining Statement

"Reaching the most unreached with the love of Christ" (gfa.org, "Who We Are").

Core Practices

Native missionaries primarily engage in personal evangelism, riding bicycles or walking to villages (similar to Methodist circuit riders). Missionaries commonly practice open-air evangelism and street preaching. Other methods include tent campaigns, tract distribution, and witnessing parades. Nearly one-third of India's Dalit (untouchable) population is illiterate; therefore, gospel proclamation is typically done without the use of literature. Gospel for Asia adamantly opposes Social Gospel–oriented practices. Although the ministry does encourage Western missionaries in countries such as Afghanistan, the Maldive Islands, and Morocco, the primary emphasis is on native missionaries who are already assimilated into the local culture. Training centers utilize the inductive Bible study method.

Statistics

Gospel for Asia supports more than 16,500 national missionaries serving in the 10/40 Window amid persistent persecution. Approximately ten missionaries are abused or beaten weekly in various parts of India. Missionaries understand that many of them will die as martyrs for the Lord. The ministry has eighty-two leaders in ten Asian countries. One hundred percent of sponsorships is sent to the mission field, with nothing deducted for administration or fund-raising.

Missionary and Evangelistic Work

Gospel for Asia is intent to reach the most unreached people of Asia with the gospel, particularly the lower (Dalit) castes of northern India. The ministry recruits, trains, sends, and supports native missionaries in the work of evangelism and church planting in unreached villages of India and throughout Asia. Native missionaries are estimated to pioneer a daily average of twelve new local churches. The home-team staff serves as the connection between thousands of Christians in the West and national missionaries. There are home-team staffs at the Texas headquarters and in Canada, Germany, New Zealand, and the United Kingdom. Gospel for Asia's children's outreach ministry (Bridge of Hope) is responsible for the education and well-being of approximately forty-five thousand children.

Academic Institutions

Gospel for Asia operates missionary schools throughout areas such as Bangladesh, India, Myanmar, Nepal, and Sri Lanka, with approximately seven thousand students. The ministry operates fifty-four missionary Bible colleges, with approximately eight thousand students. Students enroll in a three-year intensive missionary training program. Founded in 1993 and located on fifty-four acres, Gospel for Asia Biblical Seminary is a mission-centered academy in Kerala, India, that is accredited by the Asia Theological Association (ATA).

Parachurch Organizations

Gospel for Asia communicates regularly with Christians in the West regarding the effectiveness, needs, and progress of the national missionaries. Churches and individuals are encouraged to partner with the ministry through donations, internships, prayer, sponsorship, and volunteer networks.

Electronic Media

Radio programs are broadcast daily in more than one hundred languages on the Indian subcontinent, resulting in villagers being more receptive to visits by native missionaries. Thousands have believed the gospel through the radio programs.

The ministry also offers four informative video productions:

Built on the Solid Rock is a fifteen-minute documentary of Gospel for Asia's church-planting ministry.

Christ's Call: "Follow My Footsteps" is a forty-one-minute video calling the church to a higher commitment to Christ.

Glad Sacrifice is a twenty-three-minute video presenting dramatic scenes of missionaries proclaiming the gospel throughout Asia.

Operation Boot Camp is a fifteen-minute video revealing the ministry's intensive training centers.

Publications

Gospel for Asia has its own printing press, which publishes around sixty to seventy million booklets, tracts, and other resources annually in eighteen languages. SEND!—Voice of Native Missions is the bimonthly news magazine of the ministry and is offered at no cost. Gospel for Asia publishes a Christmas catalog, which allows Christians in the West to send gifts that will benefit Dalits and missionaries, including unusual but valuable gifts such as chickens, goats, a water buffalo, or rabbits.

Yohannan has written more than two hundred books in India. In the United States, he has written Living in the Light of Eternity, Revolution in World Missions, Reflecting His Image, The Road to Reality, and Why the World Waits, in addition to many booklets, such as the Journey with Jesus series. Yohannan's books are sent at no cost to those who request them.

Website

http://www.gfa.org/

Bibliography

Anderson, Allan, and Edmond Tang, eds. Asian and Pentecostal: The Charismatic Face of Christianity in Asia. Waynesboro, GA: Regnum Books International, 2005.

Davis, John R. Poles Apart? Contextualizing the Gospel in Asia. Bangalore, India: Theological Book Trust, 1998.

"Gospel for Asia." http://www.gfa.org. "Who We Are."

McDonald, Mary. Even Donkeys Speak: And Other Stories of God's Miracles in Asia. Carrollton, TX: GFA Books, 2007.

Yohannan, Gisela. Dear Sister: Letters of Hope and Encouragement. Carrollton, TX: GFA Books, 2006.

Ron J. Bigalke

GoStrategic (formerly Strategic Christian Services)

History

Strategic Christian Services (SCS) was founded in February 1979 in the San Francisco Bay area. The "Jesus '79" rally held in Candlestick Park and simultaneously in other cities launched the group's major endeavors. SCS sought to train Christians in the midst of what it referred to as "Pharaoh's" culture. Regarding itself as a prophetic ministry with an international calling, SCS promoted unity among believers and encouraged them to improve their communities as they evangelized.

In the 1980s, the group created Christian activist groups targeted at state governments, as well as one directed at the national government, a project called Anatole. Rebuilder seminars were conducted in thirty-five cities from 1985 to 1991, and these gave SCS founder and president Dennis Peacocke a chance to address tens of thousands of believers, including hundreds of pastors. Peacocke also started City Action Councils, which facilitated local activism and led to many pastoral prayer fellowships. Leaders around the world benefited from seminars named "Calling the Elders to the City Gates."

The global dimension to SCS became more pronounced in the 1990s, reflected in the birth of its two global correspondence schools, Strategic Life Training and Business Leadership School, as well as in its several international conferences and its translation of the group's literature into many foreign languages. Partner offices were established in Switzerland and New Zealand. As the ministry budget grew to over one million dollars, conferences led to an important tape ministry.

In the first decade of the twenty-first century, SCS added a Latin American partner office, which serves Guatemala, Costa Rica, and Mexico. The European base runs schools in Switzerland, Germany, France, and Austria. The Austral-Asian office, which has run schools in New Zealand since 1994, covers territory all the way west to Greece. Along with Business Leadership Schools, Worldview Schools are growing in global popularity, and Strategic Christian Services provides locals with ample assistance in operating the schools after launching them.

SCS changed its name to GoStrategic in March 2014.

Headquarters

1260 N Dutton Avenue
Suite 242
Santa Rosa, CA 95401
Telephone: 707-578-7700
Fax: 707-578-1168

Leadership

Dennis Peacocke, noted speaker and author, is the founder and president.

Core Beliefs

The following is GoStrategic's statement of faith:

God. We believe in one eternal God, manifest in three distinct Persons: Father, Son, and Holy Spirit.
Creation. We believe all things were created and continue to be sustained by God.
The Bible. We believe the Bible, in its entirety, to be the inspired Word of God and the only infallible rule of faith and conduct.
Jesus Christ. We believe the Son of God, our Lord Jesus Christ, was conceived of the Holy Spirit, born of the virgin Mary, was crucified, dead, buried, resurrected; that He ascended into Heaven and is now seated at the right hand of God, the Father, and is true God and true man. He is the only mediator between God and man, and He accomplished man's redemption through His sacrificial death on the cross.
The Holy Spirit. We believe the Holy Spirit, the third Person of the Trinity, possesses all the divine attributes of the Father and Son. He baptizes all believers into Christ's body, the church, at the moment of conversion. . . .
Eternal Life. We believe in the resurrection of the dead, the eternal joy of the saved and the eternal punishment of the lost. . . .

The mission of all believers. We believe that the discipling of the nations, the Great Commission of Matthew 28:18–20, involves both personal evangelism and the addressing of whole cultures and nations. . . .
The coming age. We do not believe Jesus Christ is coming back to a perfect world, but rather He is coming back to join His bride (the church) who has prepared herself to rule with Him. . . .

GoStrategic also has a statement concerning the kingdom:

The Separation of Church and State. We believe in the explicit separation of church government and civil government. . . .
Personal Freedom. We believe that the conscience of an individual should be shaped by God's Word under the ministry of the Holy Spirit. . . .
The Separation of Powers. We believe in the biblical origin of separated spheres of government for mankind. . . .
The Place of God's Law in Society. We believe God's Old Testament laws are fulfilled in Christ, yet we also recognize . . . principles and values which carry God's heart for justice and mercy in a fallen world.
Generational Transfer. We believe that it is the privilege and responsibility of parents to shape the values and education of their children. . . .
The Centrality of God's Kingdom Reign. We believe that the gospel of the Kingdom of God is the centering point of Christ's message to the world. . . .
Christ's Return to Fulfill God's Kingdom Reign. We believe God's Kingdom has always been, now is, and is yet to be fulfilled in its entirety by Christ when He returns.
Man's Partnership with God. We believe Christ's Holy Spirit works through man to achieve God's plans for His creation. . . .
The Church and Culture. We believe that Christ came to both determine the future of mankind in eternity and to boldly influence all dimensions of human culture in every generation prior to eternity. . . .
Dominion and Voluntary Submission. We believe that in the New Testament age in which we now live, God's "cultural mandate" of Genesis 1:26–28 requires a voluntary submission of mankind to Christ's Lordship. . . . (gostrategic.org, "Beliefs")

Finances

GoStrategic is a nonprofit with 501(c)(3) status and is governed by a board who reviews its financial reports semiannually.

Website

http://www.gostrategic.org/

Bibliography

"GoStrategic." http://www.gostrategic.org. "Beliefs."

Michael McMullen

Go Ye Fellowship

History

Go Ye Fellowship (GYF) started as a Sunday school class taught by Jennie Mitchell in the early 1930s. Named after the "go ye" of Matthew 28:19, the class supported and prayed for missionaries. Then some of its members began to go. Some went to China, Borneo, and India. The mission was incorporated in 1944 under the leadership of Andrew Mitchell. Andrew and Jennie's son, Hubert Mitchell, and his wife, Helen, went to Sumatra in the 1930s. Hubert served as the president of Go Ye Fellowship from 1967 to 1993. In 1993, the mission's operations were moved to the campus of the US Center for World Mission. Bill Gustafson was the president from 1993 to 2004.

Headquarters

Mailing Address
PO Box 539
Monrovia, CA 91017

Street Address
1800 S Myrtle Avenue
Monrovia, CA 91016
Telephone: 626-386-5493
Fax: 626-386-5494
Email: info@goyefellowship.org

Leadership

Gordon F. Rohn took the helm in 2004. The ten members of the board of trustees must affirm their belief in and defense of the historic Christian faith as outlined in the organization's nine-point doctrinal statement. The board meets three or more times per year.

Core Beliefs

GYF has nine doctrinal beliefs that express the historic Christian faith. The statement is completely orthodox, holding to a verbally inspired Bible, the Trinity, the deity of Christ, the sinfulness of man, salvation by faith in Christ, the universal church commissioned to reach the world with the gospel, the personal and imminent return of Christ, and the bodily resurrection of the saved and the lost, the latter of whom will experience everlasting, conscious punishment.

GYF is interdenominational, welcoming Christians from various denominations; broadly evangelical, allowing for a variety of interpretations about the gifts of the Spirit, baptism, and eschatological issues; and international, having missionaries from various countries.

Defining Statement

"Our mission is to enable cross-cultural workers to carry out their distinct God-given vision to make reproducing disciples of Jesus among all peoples" (goyefellowship.org, "Vision and Mission").

Core Practices

Go Ye Fellowship stresses the needs of every area in the world and lists scores of opportunities for ministry where the harvest is ripe. GYF seeks to offer freedom and flexibility for missionary work within a framework of accountability.

Finances

Go Ye Fellowship joined the Evangelical Council for Financial Accountability on February 15, 2010.

Total revenue for 2014: $1,411,713
Total expenses for 2014: $1,409,853
Net assets for 2014: $463,151

Statistics

In 1993, GYF supported thirty-four missionaries. By 2010, there were sixty-five missionaries and an office staff of six. Missionaries serve in Latin America, Europe, Africa, the Middle East, Asia, and North America, including the United States. GYF reaches people in about forty countries and on all continents except Australia and Antarctica.

Missionary and Evangelistic Work

Go Ye ministries include evangelism, teaching, rallies, church planting, discipleship, literature and radio media, medical care, orphanages, correspondence courses, Bible schools, a missionary training institute, Bible translation, field visits, and tentmaking.

Website

http://www.goyefellowship.org/

Bibliography

"Go Ye Fellowship." http://www.goyefellowship.org. "Vision and Mission."

James A. Borland

Greater Europe Mission

History

Robert Evans was born in Baltimore, Maryland, in 1918 to parents who were Presbyterian missionaries to Cameroon. He served as a United States army chaplain in France during World War II, where he was wounded in action. Evans was the executive director of Youth for Christ from 1945 to 1948. In 1949, he and his wife established the European Bible Institute in Lamorlaye, France, and formed Greater Europe Mission (GEM) in 1952. During his long tenure until 1986, he started nine more Bible institutes and theological seminaries in Europe and served as the director of European operations.

The mission and urgency of GEM are driven by the unique situation in modern Europe—less than 2 percent of people actively follow Christ, Islam is growing significantly, and Christianity is in general decline.

Headquarters

18950 Base Camp Road
Monument, CO 80132
Telephone: 800-436-4488
Email: info@gemission.com

Leadership

Henry Deneen has been the president since 2007. There is an international board of directors, which governs the organization procedurally, and a GEM Leadership Team, composed of North American and European staff, which focuses on determining and implementing mission-wide strategy.

Core Beliefs

An evangelical, nondenominational organization, GEM believes the following:

We believe the Bible to be the inspired, infallible, and authoritative Word of God.

We believe that there is one God, eternally existent in three persons: the Father, Son, and Holy Spirit.

We believe in the deity of our Lord Jesus Christ, in His virgin birth, in His sinless life, in His miracles, in His vicarious and atoning death through His shed blood, in His bodily resurrection, in His ascension to the right hand of the Father, and in His personal return to power and glory.

We believe in the present ministry of the Holy Spirit by whose indwelling the Christian is enabled to live a godly life.

We believe that for the salvation of lost and sinful man, regeneration by the Holy Spirit is absolutely essential.

We believe in the resurrection of both the saved and the lost; they that are saved unto the resurrection of life and they that are lost unto the barrenness of damnation. (gemission.org, "Statement of Faith")

Defining Statement

"Disciple all peoples of Europe through rapidly reproducing churches" (gemission.org, "Our Mission").

Core Practices

Avenues of mission activity include women's ministry, technology, teaching, teaching English as a foreign language, education services, media and arts, ministry support, business, caring for immigrants, social outreach, youth ministry, counseling, discipleship, evangelism, camping ministry, and church planting.

While there are multiple roles and contexts in which GEM missionaries work, there are several values that color how they work. GEM is now primarily a relational, discipleship, and church-planting mission.

Statistics

GEM has more than 339 North American missionaries living in almost 40 countries of Europe and North Africa, and there are another 45 support staff operating in North America. There are currently 70 candidates preparing for mission service. Nearly 300 volunteers served in short-term roles (from two weeks to three months) in Europe during 2009.

Academic Institutions

Arguably the greatest contribution thus far that GEM has made in Europe is to theological education. Following are schools that GEM founded and/or participates in:

German Bible Institute (1955)
Italian Bible Institute (1956)
Free Evangelical Seminary (France, 1965)
Scandinavian Bible Institute (Sweden, 1969)
Belgian Bible Institute (1972)
Greek Bible Institute (1973)
Eastern European Bible Institute (Austria, 1974)
Free Evangelical Seminary (now German Theological Seminary, 1974)
Portuguese Bible Institute (1974)
Spanish Bible Institute and Theological Seminary (1974)
Evangelical Theological Seminary (Belgium, 1981)

Tyndale Theological Seminary (the Netherlands, 1985)
Baptist Bible College (the Czech Republic, 1991)
Evangelical Bible Institute (Croatia, 1992)
Logos Bible Institute (now United Theological Faculty, Bulgaria, 1992)
Sibiu Bible Institute (Romania, 1992)
Albanian Bible Institute (1993)
Theological and Missions Seminary (Slovakia, 1993)
College of Socium (Ukraine, 1994)
Kiev Baptist Seminary (1994)
Protestant Theological Faculty (Romania, 1994)
Zaporozhe Bible College (Ukraine, 1994)
Persip Bible Institute (Ukraine, 1995)

Further, to supplement traditional, on-site theological learning, GEM established a distance learning initiative (eDOT) in 2001.

Website

http://www.gemission.org/

Bibliography

Evans, Robert. *Transformed Europeans: Eighteen Stories of God's Power at Work in the Lives of Europeans*. Chicago: Moody, 1963.
"Greater Europe Mission." http://www.gemission.org. "About GEM," "Our Mission," and "Statement of Faith."

Mark A. Lamport

Harvest Evangelism

History

Harvest Evangelism is an evangelistic and interdenominational ministry founded in 1980 by Ed Silvoso, a native of Argentina and brother-in-law of noted evangelist Luis Palau. Silvoso, initially part of the Palau organization, resigned when he developed serious health problems, but he soon envisioned a new missionary organization and went on to launch Harvest Evangelism with a friend's encouragement. The ministry pioneered the Transformation movement, which maintains that the Great Commission involves the discipling of nations, not merely individuals, and that this discipling will result in a reduction of social ills such as poverty. Along with its sister organization, Transform Our World, Harvest works to coordinate the efforts of individuals from diverse backgrounds who seek to effect social change.

Headquarters

PO Box 20310
San Jose, CA 95160
Telephone: 408-927-9052

Core Beliefs

Harvest Evangelism advocates what it calls "Five Pivotal Paradigms for Transformation." These include responding to the Great Commission on a national level rather than an individual one, as well as recognizing that earthly labors are an act of worship. The group asserts that the eradication of poverty is a principal social indicator of a transformed consciousness and practices "prayer evangelism" to help address community needs.

Website

http://www.harvestevan.org/

Bibliography

"Ed Silvoso." http://www.edsilvoso.com. "About" and "Mission."
"Transform Our World." http://www.transformourworld.org. "About."

George Thomas Kurian

Helps Ministries

History

Helps Ministries was founded in 1976 as Helps International Ministries to provide construction services to other ministries. During the early years, architectural design, computer ministry, accounting ministry, and other technical ministries were added. In 1995, its board of directors began to reevaluate the biblical meaning of "helps" as presented by Paul in 1 Corinthians 12:28. The board decided to broaden the scope of the ministry, and its governing documents were changed to include Christian counseling, teaching and training, church planting, and other ministries deemed appropriate by the board. Since that time a new international office facility has been added, together with additional qualified staff to serve in both existing and new areas of ministry. The ministry's international opportunities have also expanded into Europe, India, Africa, Bangladesh, Nepal, and the Middle East.

The ministry is a nondenominational Christian mission that provides technical assistance to evangelical Christian mission agencies and mission-related organizations so that they might be strengthened and better equipped to reach their respective goals. In providing help or assistance, the ministry gives priority to missions affiliated with the Association of North American Missions. However, other mission ministries that subscribe to its doctrinal statement are given consideration. Since 1976, Helps Ministries has assisted many ministries by completing more than 125 projects in 22 countries.

Headquarters

1340-J Patton Avenue
Asheville, NC 28806
Telephone: 828-277-3812
Fax: 828-274-7770

Leadership

President and CEO: Dr. David Summey
Executive director: Bo Harris

Core Beliefs

Helps Ministries uses the following to express its doctrinal positions:

We believe the Holy Scriptures, consisting of Old and New Testaments, were originally given by God, divinely inspired, without error, infallible, and are entirely trustworthy and the supreme authority in all matters of faith and practice.

We believe in one God, Creator of all things, eternally existent in three persons: Father, Son and Holy Spirit.

We believe in our Lord Jesus Christ, God manifested in the flesh, His virgin birth, sinless life, divine miracles, vicarious and atoning death on the cross, bodily resurrection, ascension and exaltation, and His personal, imminent and visible return in power and glory.

We believe that Adam and Eve, created in the image of God, were tempted by Satan, the god of this world, and fell; that their sin has passed to all people, who as a result are lost, and are unable to save themselves from the wrath of God, and need to be saved.

We believe that salvation is a gift of God to those who repent and personally believe in Jesus Christ; that it is accomplished by God's grace through the shed blood of the Lord Jesus Christ and regeneration by the Holy Spirit.

We believe in God the Holy Spirit who indwells all believers enabling them to live holy lives, and to witness and work for the Lord Jesus Christ despite opposition from the world, the flesh, and Satan.

We believe in the spiritual unity of all believers, the church, as the Body of Christ and in the resurrection of eternal life with God, but they that are lost are condemned unto the resurrection of eternal separation from God.

We believe that Christ commanded the Church to go into all the world and make disciples of all peoples, baptizing them in the name of the Father, Son, and Holy Spirit, and teaching those who believe to obey all that Christ commanded. (helpsmission .org, "What We Believe")

Defining Statement

"Helps exists to 'maximize mission impact' by providing professional services that strengthen Christian ministries worldwide" (helpsmission .org, "About Us").

Core Practices

These programs demonstrate the priorities of Helps Ministries:

The Computer Ministry offers hardware, software packages, and network, web, and consulting services to other missionary organizations.

The Planning and Design Ministry is committed to helping evangelical ministries by providing professional design services at a reduced cost. Examples of completed projects are Scott Theological College in Nairobi, Kenya; TEAM Training Center in northern India; Caribbean Christian Center for the Deaf in Jamaica; Christian Memorial Hospital in Bangladesh; AEF Ministries headquarters in Fort Mill, South Carolina; and SEND International headquarters in Farmington, Michigan.

The Accounting Ministry's purpose is to provide small missions with accounting and audit support, to substantially reduce their costs, and to help them properly track and report their financial status.

The Ministry's Leadership Training, Ministry Evaluation, and Missions Mobilization programs provide short-term lecturers and teachers for overseas Bible colleges and seminaries—from two weeks to six months. They also teach and train national pastors in the development of ministries by providing encouragement and Bible, evangelism, and leadership training.

Living Free Ministries aspires to help people discover freedom and victory over strongholds, temptations, and abuse through faith in Christ. Its activities include leading individuals and groups through Steps to Freedom in Christ; training Christian counselors, missionaries, pastors, and laypeople; offering "Breaking Through to Spiritual Maturity" discipleship classes; and equipping individuals and churches with the resources they need.

The purpose of Servants Missionary Service is to provide physical support for missionaries and other Christian organizations throughout the world. Currently, approximately 250 missionaries are supported.

Finances

Ministry Watch awarded Helps Ministries a transparency grade of A for evangelism support. The ministry is a member of the Evangelical Council for Financial Accountability.

Total revenue for 2013: $1,259,657
Total expenses for 2013: $1,143,308
Net assets for 2013: $711,270

Website

http://www.helpsmission.org/

Bibliography

"Helps Ministries." http://www.helpsmission.org. "About Us" and "What We Believe."

Michael McMullen

High Adventure Ministries

History

After a powerful conversion to Christ, George Otis, who had at one time been the general manager of Learjet, founded High Adventure Ministries in 1973. The name of the ministry came from his experience of walking with Jesus, which he referred to as a "high adventure" even more thrilling than the speed or power of jet aircraft.

In 1965, Otis began Bible Voice, a book publishing business. He began the ministry primarily to lead Christian pilgrimage tours to the Holy Land. In 1979, the ministry expanded by beginning the High Adventure Broadcasting Network, with the Voice of Hope radio station being built in southern Lebanon. It was a dangerous operation, and in 1985, terrorists carried out a bombing mission on the studio, claiming five lives. Undaunted, the station was back on the air very quickly. The Voice of Hope in the Middle East now consists of AM, FM, shortwave, and satellite. These stations broadcast to many nations in various languages.

Continuing the vision to build a global network of gospel stations, the Voice of Hope for the Americas was signed on in 1986. World band station KVOH was built on Chatsworth Peak in Simi Valley, California. Broadcasts originating there are heard on shortwave in North America, the Caribbean, and Central and South America. The primary audience is Spanish-speaking people in Mexico and Cuba.

The chief methods employed by High Adventure Ministries to achieve its goals are the strategic use of mass communication, including radio; the distribution of books, films, and literature; and training. The ministry presently owns and operates its own facilities in the Holy Land, California, and Palau, as well as maintaining satellite offices in Canada, the United Kingdom, Israel, Singapore, and Australia. The ministry is also known as High Adventure Ministries Voice of Hope Global Broadcasting Network.

Headquarters

PO Box 100
Simi Valley, CA 93062
Telephone: 805-520-9460

Leadership

In September 1999, George Otis went into semiretirement, turning over control of the global ministry to Jackie Yockey, currently president and CEO.

Core Beliefs

High Adventure subscribes to the following statement of faith:

We believe the Bible to be divinely inspired, infallible, and the authoritative Word of God and source of Christian doctrine.

We believe that there is one God, eternally existent in three persons: Father, Son, and Holy Spirit.

We believe in the deity of Christ, in His virgin birth, in His sinless life, in His miracle working power, in His vicarious and atoning death through His shed Blood, in His bodily resurrection, in His ascension to the right hand of the Father, and in His personal return in power and glory.

We believe that, for the salvation of the lost and sinful man, regeneration by the Holy Spirit is essential.

We believe in the present-day ministry of the Holy Spirit and that Christians are enabled to live a godly life by the indwelling of His Spirit. We are commanded to be filled with the Spirit, empowering us to be victorious and bold witnesses unto all the world.

We believe that the outpouring of the Holy Spirit is both evident and relevant for today. Also, that the manifestation of His presence can be seen through present-day miracles in the lives of believers and non-believers alike.

We believe in the resurrection of both the saved and the lost; they that are saved unto the resurrection of life; and they that are lost unto the resurrection of damnation.

We believe in the spiritual unity of believers in Christ. We believe that the church is the body of Christ and is composed of all those who, through belief in Christ, have been spiritually regenerated by the indwelling of the Holy Spirit.

We believe in the great commission of Christ to the church. We believe that the church has a dual mission; to worldwide evangelization and to the discipleship and nurturing of Christians. (ministry watch.com, "High Adventure Ministries")

Finances

Total revenue for 2013: $119,659
Total expenses for 2013: $165,729

Electronic Media

High Adventure provides news and information through regularly scheduled radio programs. The *House of Bread* radio broadcast, for example, is broadcast from its studio in Bethlehem on FM 98.7 six hours a day. The High Adventure Broadcasting Network also began a new internet radio operation; the website is jlmnews.com.

Publication

High Adventure issues a monthly newsletter.

Website

http://www.highadventure.org/

Michael McMullen

Holt International Children's Services

History

Oregon farmers Harry and Bertha Holt began adoption placement of children orphaned by the Korean War in 1955. Holt International continues to place children of all races, religions, ethnicities, and genders in families. Holt also facilitates foster care for orphaned, abandoned, and vulnerable children overseas. Today Holt International operates in Bulgaria, China, Ethiopia, Guatemala, Haiti, India, Korea, Mongolia, the Philippines, Thailand, Uganda, the United States, and Vietnam.

Headquarters

250 Country Club Road
Eugene, OR 97401
Telephone: 541-687-2202
Fax: 541-683-6175

Leadership

Holt International was originally directed by Harry and Bertha Holt. Phillip Littleton is the president and CEO. The organization also has a fifteen-member board.

Core Beliefs

Holt's operations are based on Harry and Bertha Holt's beliefs that every child is a gift of God, the family is key in nurturing children, adoption is a valid family structure, and Christians should love others and operate their businesses with the highest standard of ethics and integrity.

In addition to adoption, Holt helps families remain together, returns children to their birth families, and places homeless children with families in their birth countries. Holt coordinates pre-adoption, long-term foster care and coordinates with government agencies to promote systemic improvements to child welfare practices.

Core Practices

Holt's website offers adoption webinars with information about the organization and its process of adoption. Holt coordinates the entire adoption process, including home study, dossier services with the adopting country, background checks, and post-placement studies. Post-adoption, Holt offers adoptee summer camps, birth country tours (Korea, China, and Thailand), recommended readings for adopting families, and a service to help adoptees connect with other adult international adoptees. Their website also includes a forum for prospective and adopting families to network with one another about their experiences. While Holt does charge for its services, the organization also solicits donations to sponsor children in overseas foster care facilities, for a special needs adoption fund, and to provide college scholarships for Holt adoptees.

Statistics

In 2009, Holt placed almost 700 children within their birth countries and over 700 with American families. Holt served over 36,000 children across its programs in 2009. Since 1956, Holt has placed nearly 40,000 children with adoptive families in the United States.

Publication

Holt International publishes *Holt International: Finding Families for Children* as a quarterly magazine. It includes stories of Holt adoptions, adoption information, country updates, and photographs of adopting families. Each year the magazine features graduating Holt adoptees. The magazine is available in print or by visiting holt international.org/magazine.

Website

http://www.holtinternational.org/

Courtney Lyons

Impact Ministries

History

While preaching on the streets of Huntsville, Alabama, in the 1970s, James B. Richards had a vision for a new church. In 1984, he began that church and called it Impact of Huntsville. People gathered together in his living room until, because of size, they relocated to a tent in Richards's front yard, where they stayed for nine months, resisting building so they could focus on missions and world evangelism. They called the global outreach Impact Ministries, which continues to offer seminars, crusades, and training throughout the world.

As the church increased in size, it met in several facilities throughout Huntsville and started building in 1988, but members felt the Lord wanted them to devote most of their resources to world evangelism. Ten years later, Richards redirected his priorities to his ministry in Huntsville. The next year Impact Ministries purchased the adjacent property and built offices, an auditorium, and a website, and Impact CyberChurch was born.

Although people can attend the live service on Friday nights, seating is limited; Impact CyberChurch is broadcast through television and streamed through the internet. Richards formed Impact Groups, which are small cells within the church where members come together in an intimate format in order to fellowship and share in personal ministry. Out of the Impact Groups came iGroups, which are similar groups but are located throughout the world.

Since the 1980s, Richards has been speaking in Canada as well. He was a frequent guest on two Canadian television Christian talk shows, *100 Huntley Street* and *It's a New Day*, as well as on several other television and radio shows.

Headquarters

3516 S Broad Place SW
Huntsville, AL 35805
Telephone: 256-536-9402
Fax: 256-217-4058
Email: cyberchurch@impactministries.com

Leadership

Dr. James B. Richards is the founder of Impact Ministries and the pastor of Impact Cyber-Church.

Core Beliefs

The group's doctrinal beliefs are consistent with most of the Apostles' Creed, expanded by these statements:

We believe all people are saved by grace through faith in the finished work of the Lord Jesus.
We believe the ministry of the Holy Spirit is to glorify the Lord Jesus, regenerate the repentant believer, to guide the believer into all truth and to manifest Himself in all believers to minister as the Lord Jesus would to men.

We believe the Holy Spirit empowers all believers to live every promise of the Bible.
We believe all New Testament manifestations of the Holy Spirit are available to all present-day believers. (impactministries.com, "Beliefs")

Defining Statement

"Changing the way the world sees God" (impactministries.com, "Home").

Controversies

Although thousands of people "attend" church via the internet instead of in a physical place, cyberchurches are controversial among many Christians. There are proponents in addition to Jim Richards, including Andrew Careag, Andrew Jones, and Patrick Dixon, but there are also those, like Drew Dyck, who have expressed dire concerns about "churchcasting" (see Dyck, "Churchcasting Kills Community").

Missionary and Evangelistic Work

Global outreach through the internet and through Impact Ministries.

Ecumenism

In 1982, Richards became burdened with the need to work with other church and business leaders and thus formed Synergistic Creative Alliance, a group encouraged to share their resources with one another so that jointly they can be more effective in kingdom service.

Academic Institution

The Impact International School of Ministry was formed in 1982 and has two educational deliveries: (1) IISOM Online with classes on the Bible, Greek, and a variety of areas of ministry and (2) a correspondence program with courses on CD. Students may earn a New Testament leadership certificate from either. IISOM also offers degrees in theology, administration, music, counseling, pastoral care, youth ministry, and other related fields.

Electronic Media

Blog
Facebook
Impact TV
Interactive CyberSeminars
Internet streaming
iPhone
Podcasts
Twitter
YouTube

Publication

Impact, a monthly print and electronic magazine

Website

http://www.impactministries.com/

Bibliography

Dixon, Patrick. *Cyberchurch*. Eastbourne, UK: Kingsway, 1995.

Dyke, Drew. "Churchcasting Kills Community." *Boundless Webzine*, November 16, 2006. http://www.boundless.org/2005/articles/a0001390.cfm.

"Impact Ministries." http://www.impactministries.com. "Beliefs."

Richards, James R. *The Gospel of Peace: No More Shame, No More Fear*. New Kensington, PA: Whitaker House, 2002.

———. *Grace: The Power to Change*. New Kensington, PA: Whitaker House, 2001.

Brenda Ayres

Independent Faith Mission

History

After visiting war-ravaged Italy in 1950 and witnessing firsthand the devastation, poverty, and spiritual need, Pastor Carl Standridge became convinced of a call to become involved in helping. Two years later a board of directors was established, and Independent Faith Mission became a reality. Bill Standridge, Carl's son, was appointed to Italy as the mission's first missionary. The ministry continues to provide service to churches through which they can send both their people and their funds for the work of world missions. The ministry oversees a number of second- and even third-generation missionaries.

Headquarters

2301 S Holden Road
Greensboro, NC 27417
Telephone: 336-292-1255
Fax: 336-292-9348
Email: info@ifmnews.com

Core Beliefs

Independent Faith Mission's doctrinal statement contains twelve points regarding Scripture, God, Christ, the Holy Spirit, the return of Christ, Satan, the lostness of man and the necessity of new birth, the resurrection of the saved and the lost, the local church and Christian ordinances, the security and priesthood of believers, ecclesiastical and personal separation, and creation.

Statistics

The mission has sixty-six missionaries.

Website

http://www.ifmnews.com/

Michael McMullen

International Children's Care

History

International Children's Care (ICC) is an orphanage program started by Christian laymen in 1978 to bring relief to children who were victims of a devastating earthquake in Guatemala. ICC sees its ministry as being holistic, providing for the mental, emotional, spiritual, and physical needs of children through a family structure instead of simply an orphanage.

Each home consists of sponsoring "parents" and ten to twelve children who live on small acreages of land. Children learn skills on this land, and older children work to farm the land in order to provide the families with food. On its own property, ICC educates children at the elementary level, and its schools are close to secondary schools for the convenience of those moving beyond an elementary education. If a person is able to attend high school or enter a college or university, ICC provides them with the support to make this possible.

Headquarters

2711 NE 134th Way
Vancouver, WA 98686
Telephone: 360-573-0429
Fax: 360-573-0491
Email: info@forhiskids.org

There are partner offices in Australia, Hong Kong, the Netherlands, Germany, and the United Kingdom.

Leadership

ICC is governed by a board of directors.

Core Beliefs

ICC's mission statement includes the following:

ICC champions the traditional Christian values of (1) the potential of each individual to reflect the image of God, (2) the dignity which is inherent in every person, and (3) the importance of quality in human life. The Bible is the basis for ICC's guiding principles. (forhiskids.org, "Expanded Mission Statement")

The organization carries out its mission without regard for a child's ethnic, political, or religious association.

Finances

In 2008, ICC reported $4,399,477 total revenue and $4,545,815 total expenses.

Website

http://www.forhiskids.org/

Bibliography

"International Children's Care." http://www.forhiskids.org. "Expanded Mission Statement."

Phuc Luu

International Christian Aid

History

The founder of International Christian Aid (ICA) was L. Joe Bass, and his story is remarkable: a high school dropout founded and built a multimillion-dollar group of organizations that have conducted activities ranging from smuggling Bibles behind the Iron Curtain to feeding the poor of the third world.

ICA regards itself as "an agent of hope, linking caring Americans with needy children, their families and communities in the developing world" (icaid.org, "About Us"). Based in a former Lutheran church building in Jerome, Pennsylvania, ICA has no paid employees. Its programs are administered both at home and abroad by local Christian organizations and staff.

The ministry provides support for the care and education of destitute children in India, Honduras, Mexico, and Nicaragua through child sponsorship. The ministry also sends shipments of material aid to Honduras to help Project Global Village and provides opportunities for volunteers to participate with work groups there.

Headquarters

1929 Penn Avenue
PO Box 395
Jerome, PA 19537
Telephone: 814-629-9279; 888-643-7555
Fax: 814-629-9279

Leadership

Executive director: John A. Blough

Defining Statement

"Loving hands supporting the world" (icaid .org, "About Us").

Finances

For many years controversy swirled around the founder of International Christian Aid, L. Joe Bass. There were many accusations of impropriety and numerous investigations, including, for example, those by the US Postal Service inspectors, a federal grand jury in Los Angeles, German tax officials, the Los Angeles Department of Social Services, and the Ventura County district attorney. In fact, the Evangelical Council for Financial Accountability refused to endorse ICA in 1979 because of its "reputation." The Council of Better Business Bureaus also declared that ICA did not meet its standards for charitable solicitations because it had declined to provide adequate information to serve as a basis for an informed decision. The National Charities Information Bureau, another private group that evaluates fund-raising organizations, also refused to endorse ICA because of inadequate financial data and Bass's veto powers over the board of directors.

Total revenue for 2008: $59,726
Total expenses for 2008: $65,135
Net assets for 2008: $33,205

Website

http://www.icaid.org/

Michael McMullen

International Lutheran Laymen's League

History

The International Lutheran Laymen's League was founded in 1917 by laypeople committed to helping meet the financial needs of the Lutheran Church—Missouri Synod. Media programming began with the North American broadcast of the *Lutheran Hour* in 1930. By 1945, the *Lutheran Hour* had become the largest regularly scheduled broadcast in the world.

The ministry of the International Lutheran Laymen's League, a volunteer organization of 100,000 members, is expressed through outreach efforts under the name Lutheran Hour Ministries, a worldwide, multimedia outreach organization. The league is itself an auxiliary of the Lutheran Church—Missouri Synod and the Lutheran Church—Canada. Utilizing the technological advances of the last century, Lutheran Hour Ministries seeks to serve Christ in all nations through its award-winning radio, television, print, and internet programming. Support for the work of Lutheran Hour Ministries is entirely by individuals and partner congregations. No denominational support is received.

Headquarters

660 Mason Ridge Center Drive
St. Louis, MO 63141
Telephone: 314-317-4100; 800-944-3450

Leadership

President and CEO: Rodger Hebermehl

Core Beliefs

About the Bible

[The Bible is] God's message of love and hope for all people. The Bible is the written Word of God, handed down to us in order to point us to the truth that we are saved from our sin and eternal death by the life, death, and resurrection of Jesus Christ. We believe that the Bible is completely reliable and without error. In it we learn everything we need to know about God's love and His gifts to us.

About God

There is only one true God—the Triune God—who exists in three separate but equal persons: Father, Son, and Holy Spirit.

God the Father is our maker and the creator of all things. By the Father's word, all things were made, and we are His most beloved creation; we are closest to His heart. The Son is Jesus Christ, who came to earth as the perfect "go-between" between God and humanity. He has redeemed us and is the voice to the Father on our behalf. The Holy Spirit calls us to believe in Jesus Christ as our Savior, keeps us in the one true faith, and equips us for living out our faith. He is the whisper in our heart's ear.

About Us

We all fall short of God's expectations because we are all born "sinful." . . . Sin can be summed up as all the things we say, think, do, and don't do, that fall outside of God's holy will for our lives and end up separating us from God.

Sin was brought into [the] world when Satan lured the first people God created (Adam and Eve) into temptation through their own free will and weakness, breaking the perfect relationship between God and us. From that point on, sin became part of our very existence. Because God also demands perfect obedience, our ultimate punishment became death.

Yet God is a loving God. . . . He sent His Son, Jesus Christ, to live the perfect life He requires and to become our substitute. . . . He took our sin upon Himself and died on the cross, on our behalf. When we believe in Jesus Christ as our Savior, He bears our sin and gives us His forgiveness.

About Being Saved

. . . In His death and resurrection, everyone who believes in Jesus as Savior has been brought back into a right relationship with God. . . .

About Faith

It is through faith in Jesus that we receive the forgiveness of sins and eternal life—by believing that He has freed us from the guilt, punishment, and power of sin. Faith is a gift worked in us by the power of the Holy Spirit. . . .

About Grace

. . . While we deserved to pay the penalty for our sins, God had a different plan. Christ paid the debt and we receive forgiveness and eternal life from Him that is offered out of unconditional love. . . . God has provided tangible ways through which He delivers His grace to those who believe, assuring us that the sins we commit are forgiven for Jesus' sake. These are . . . God's Word, holy Baptism, and the Lord's Supper (Holy Communion). . . .

About Good Works

Since there is nothing we can ever do to earn salvation, we do not do good works in order to be saved; good works are done out of praise and thanks because we are saved. . . .

About Life and Death

On Judgment Day . . . Jesus Christ is going to return. On that day, everyone who has died will be raised and those who are still alive will be bodily transformed. At that time, the final judgment will take place. Those who do not believe will go into eternal damnation in hell and all those who believe in Jesus as Savior will have eternal life in heaven. (lhm.org, "What Lutherans Believe")

Defining Statement

The mission of Lutheran Hour Ministries is "Bringing Christ to the Nations—and the Nations to the Church" (lhm.org, "About Us").

Core Practices

These programs are illustrative of the objectives of the International Lutheran Laymen's League:

By Kids . . . For Kids is a hands-on mission project in which children from North American Lutheran elementary, junior high, and Sunday and vacation Bible schools collect and package school supplies for needy children in impoverished nations.

Living for Tomorrow is a multimedia outreach program using telephone, television, radio, and print advertisements.

The Puzzle Club is an outreach program utilizing print, television, radio, and the internet to connect families with values lessons through the adventures of a group of junior detectives.

Red Boots for Christmas is an award-winning, made-for-television, animated program that shares the true meaning of Christmas and the importance of giving selflessly.

Woman to Woman is a nationally syndicated, thirty-minute radio talk show promoting the spiritual growth of its listeners.

On Main Street is a half-hour television talk show encouraging spiritual growth in viewers through candid discussions of current issues from a Christ-centered perspective.

Finances

Total revenue for 2005: $26,196,000
Total expenses for 2005: $24,399,000
Net assets for 2005: $33,248,000

Ministry Watch awarded Lutheran Hour Ministries a transparency grade of A in its financial dealings.

Website

http://www.lhm.org/

Bibliography

"Lutheran Hour Ministries." http://www.lhm.org. "About Us" and "What Lutherans Believe."

Michael McMullen

International Mission Board

History

In 1845, Southern Baptists separated from other Baptists in the United States and founded the Foreign Mission Board at their formative meeting. China was the first focus of Southern Baptist missionary work. Charlotte Digges Moon (1840–1912), the most famous Foreign Mission Board missionary, served for thirty-nine years until her death by starvation while serving the Chinese people. In 1888, Southern Baptists instituted an offering specifically to support foreign missions that in 1918 became the Lottie Moon Christmas Offering. It currently provides over half of the funding for Southern Baptist overseas mission efforts.

During a time of denominational reorganization in 1997, trustees decided to adopt the name International Mission Board (IMB) and a more concentrated focus on evangelization efforts among people groups rather than on political entities such as nation-states.

Headquarters

3806 Monument Avenue
Richmond, VA 23230
Telephone: 800-999-3113
Fax: 804-254-8986

Leadership

Senior leadership of the IMB includes the president, executive vice president, and five subsidiary vice presidents (global strategy, global personnel, finance, global logistics support, and church and partner services).

Defining Statement

The mission of the International Mission Board is "to make disciples of all peoples in fulfillment of the Great Commission" (imb.org, "About the IMB"). The IMB's vision statement and core values emphasize the lordship of Jesus Christ and the need for all peoples to hear, understand, and respond to the gospel in their own cultural contexts.

Core Practices

The IMB primarily commissions missionaries to serve unreached people groups, defined as relatively homogeneous ethnic and linguistic divisions of the world's people among whom less than 2 percent of the population are evangelical Christians. Nine general affinity groups subsume the more than one thousand unreached people groups currently engaged by IMB personnel.

Finances

Approximately 50 percent of the Southern Baptist Convention's budget and 100 percent of the denomination's Lottie Moon Christmas Offering finance the work of the IMB. Career Southern Baptist international missionary personnel receive full funding from the IMB, which Southern Baptist churches have supported since 1925 through a giving structure known as the Cooperative Program. The 2009 IMB budget was $319.8 million.

Missionary and Evangelistic Work

Approximately fifty-five hundred missionaries partner with volunteers drawn from Southern Baptist churches. All missionaries must agree with the current edition of the Baptist Faith and Message confession.

Affiliations

The IMB partners with Baptists and other "Great Commission Christians" toward the goal of birthing indigenous, reproducing Baptist churches throughout the world.

Electronic Media

The IMB produces internet-accessible videos that accent articles featured in its print edition of CommissionStories. Documentation accompanying each video typically facilitates viewer support of the highlighted mission work.

Publication

CommissionStories

320

Website

http://www.imb.org/

Bibliography

Estep, William R. *Whole Gospel, Whole World: The Foreign Mission Board of the Southern Baptist Convention 1845–1995.* Nashville: Broadman & Holman, 1994.

"International Mission Board." http://www.imb.org. "About the IMB."

McBeth, H. Leon. *The Baptist Heritage: Four Centuries of Baptist Witness.* Nashville: Broadman, 1987.

Rankin, Jerry. *Vision for Global Advance.* International Mission Board pamphlet, 2009.

Routh, E. C. "Foreign Mission Board." In *Encyclopedia of Southern Baptists*, 1:457–74. Nashville: Broadman, 1958.

Scott N. Callaham

International Students Inc.

History

International Students Inc. (ISI), founded in 1953, is an organization of Christian volunteers who want to have friendships with international students at US colleges and universities. Ministry volunteers and staff help students with such things as learning about American culture, problems needing a native speaker, finding an American Christian mentor in their academic discipline, and (if interested) learning about God and the Bible.

While ISI is a Christian organization, students need not be a Christian to participate. Those from any nationality and all religious backgrounds are welcome and encouraged to join. The ministry offers international students social services and spiritual activities. It is not necessary to participate in spiritual activities in order to receive other services. Services and friendship are offered unconditionally, and students are not pressured regarding participation in spiritual activities.

ISI works with the local church, training volunteers and providing assistance as needed, so that volunteers within the churches can have an effective ministry to international students in their own community. It also seeks to partner with other ministries working to reach international students so that the focus is on coordination, not competition.

Headquarters

PO Box C
Colorado Springs, CO 80901
Telephone: 719-576-2700; 800-474-4003

Leadership

President and CEO: Dr. Doug Shaw

Core Beliefs

International Students Inc. uses the following statement of faith:

We believe in the divine inspiration and authority of the Scriptures. By this is meant a miraculous guidance of the Holy Spirit in their original writing, extending to all parts of the Scripture equally, applying even to the choice of the words, so that the result is the very Word of God; the only infallible rule of faith and practice. Moreover, it is our conviction that God has exercised such singular care and providence through the ages in preserving the written Word, that the Scriptures as we now have them are in every essential particular as originally given, and contain all things necessary to salvation.

We believe in the one God revealed as existing in three equal Persons, the Father, the Son, and the Holy Spirit. We believe in the Deity of the Lord Jesus Christ. We believe in the Holy Spirit as a Divine Person, a personality as distinct as the Father and the Son.

We believe that as through one man sin entered the world and death through sin, so death passed unto all people, for that all have sinned.

We believe in the death of Jesus Christ, as a true substitute, and that His death was a sufficient expiation for the guilt of all people. We believe in His bodily resurrection from the dead.

We believe that those who receive Christ by faith have a new life from God given to them.

We believe that people are justified by faith alone and are counted as righteous before God only by the merit of our Lord and Savior Jesus Christ imputed to them.

We believe in the everlasting conscious blessedness of the saved, and the everlasting conscious punishment of the lost.

We believe in the personal return of our Lord.

We believe it to be the supreme responsibility of the disciples of the Lord Jesus Christ to make His Gospel known to all people. (isionline.org, "Our Statement of Faith")

Defining Statement

"International Students, Inc. exists to share Christ's love with international students and to equip them for effective service in cooperation with the local church and others" (isionline.org, "ISI's Mission Statement").

Finances

Ministry Watch has awarded ISI a transparency grade of A for its financial dealings. It is a Colorado nonprofit organization, and contributions to it are fully tax deductible. It is a member of the Evangelical Council for Financial Accountability and the National Association of Evangelicals.

Total revenue for 2014: $10,514,462
Total expenses for 2014: $10,100,852
Net assets for 2014: $3,849,580

Statistics

ISI has field staff in three hundred cities across the United States, serving more than five hundred campuses. Over twenty-two thousand ISI volunteers in three hundred US cities provide assistance and have friendships with international students.

Website

http://www.isionline.org/

Bibliography

"International Students Inc." http://www.isionline.org. "ISI's Mission Statement" and "Our Statement of Faith."

Michael McMullen

International Teams

History

International Teams was founded by Australian Kevin Dyer and his wife, Elois, in 1960 as Literature Crusades. The Dyers' vision was to send teams of missionaries to evangelize, distribute Bibles, and offer correspondence courses throughout Asia. The first team of six missionaries traveled to Calcutta, India, in 1961. International Teams has become an interdenominational Christian evangelical ministry living out worship and service to God. Through evangelism, church planting, and relief and development, International Teams seeks to assist overseas nationals in starting new churches and provides health services, medicine, food, and education for the economically disadvantaged. Currently, there are over twelve hundred workers of fifty-two nationalities serving two hundred team locations in sixty-five countries.

Headquarters

411 W River Road
Elgin, IL 60123
Telephone: 847-429-0900

Leadership

President: Scott Olson

Core Beliefs

We believe in the inspiration, authority, and power of the Scriptures in the Old and New Testaments. We affirm the mystery of the Trinity—one God in three persons: Father, Son, and Holy Spirit. We affirm the WEA statement of faith, as well as the Lausanne Covenant. . . . Things are not alright. Since Adam and Eve, all the world is broken and everyone except Jesus is separated from God. Everyone has the same need for food, freedom, and forgiveness, but our broken relationships with each other and God restrict our access to these. (iteams.us, "Statement of Faith")

Core Practices

Driven by its purpose to make Jesus Christ known and to see lives transformed by the power of God, International Teams strives to accomplish the following eight objectives: proclaim and demonstrate the gospel, equip and enable people, motivate and mobilize Christians, serve and establish churches, build and strengthen quality teams, train and equip team members, foster personal care of team members, and strive for innovation and excellence.

Finances

Total revenue for 2014: $13,432,449
Total expenses for 2014: $13,428,304
Net assets for 2014: $4,590,750

Ministry Watch awarded International Teams a transparency grade of A for its financial dealings in the area of foreign missions. The organization is a nonprofit, and contributions to it are fully tax deductible. International Teams is a charter member of the Evangelical Council for Financial Accountability.

Affiliations

International Teams is a member of the following organizations: Advancing Churches in Missions Commitment, World Evangelical Fellowship, Evangelical Missionary Alliance, Canadian Council of Christian Charities, and Philippine Missions Association.

Publications

International Teams publishes an annual ministry report, and a number of recent ones are available on its website. The ministry also publishes a bimonthly newsletter, which is also accessible on its website.

Website

http://www.iteams.org/

Bibliography

"International Teams." http://www.iteams.org. "Statement of Faith."

Michael McMullen

Interserve International

History

Interserve International began in 1852 at the initiative of two British women who were burdened for the welfare of women in India. As the group's vision grew to include biblical training and medical work, the organization became known as Zenana Bible and Medical Mission in 1887. In the 1940s, the group was renamed the Bible and Medical Missionary Fellowship, since it had begun to pursue ministry in other countries. Finally, in 1987, after relocating its international office to Cyprus, the organization became known as Interserve International. Focusing its efforts on the Arab world and Asia, Interserve presently has eight hundred workers from many nationalities serving in thirty countries.

Headquarters

7000 Ludlow Street
Upper Darby, PA 19082
Telephone: 610-352-0581
Fax: 610-352-4394
Email: ea@ludlow.net.

Leadership

The organization is led by an international director, and its international headquarters are located in Cyprus. There are eighteen national offices in countries in North America, Europe, Asia, and Latin America. Interserve teams around the world are empowered by the international office to be field led.

Core Beliefs

Interserve's statement of faith is generally inclusive of evangelicals from various traditions. The group affirms the nature of the triune Godhead and the unique work of each member, the need for conversion, the importance of the church in worship and missions, the authority of Scripture, and the person and work of Christ.

Core Practices

Interserve's stated purpose is "to make Jesus Christ known through wholistic ministry, in partnership with the global church, amongst the neediest peoples of Asia and the Arab World" (interserve.org, "Purpose"). Thus, the group is committed to evangelism and discipleship, holistic ministry, caring for the poor and needy, and partnering with Christians from all over the world.

Interserve strives to be inclusive of believers from diverse theological and cultural backgrounds, and both men and women are invited to serve in leadership roles. Other stated values include inclusivity, integrity, humility, service, and relationships—within both mission teams and the local context.

Interserve demonstrates these values by mobilizing partners who have training in theology, business, medicine, teaching, and other areas in holistic ministry. On its website, the organization maintains a list of job possibilities in the Arab world and Asia where potential partners may apply.

Trends

Since 2004, Interserve has been reflecting on ways that it can function more effectively in realizing its vision. Two particular trends are noteworthy. First, since 1993, the group has begun to emphasize Business as Mission as a viable strategy for holistic mission. Second, in light of the emergence of new mission movements from the non-Western or majority world, Interserve has enthusiastically welcomed these laborers to partner with them in mission.

Website

https://www.interserve.org/

Bibliography

"Interserve International." https://www.interserve.org. "Purpose."

Stringer, John. *Doing Mission in the Arab World*. Bangalore, India: Grassroots Mission Publications, 2008.

———. *Ministry of Reconciliation*. Bangalore, India: Grassroots Mission Publications, 2009.

Edward Smither

InterVarsity Christian Fellowship

History

The interdenominational, evangelical Christian, student-led movement known as InterVarsity Christian Fellowship (IVCF) began in Cambridge, England, in 1877 and then spread to Canada in 1928 and to America in 1938. Official US organization began in 1941 with three staff on loan from Canada. By 1950, 35 staff members were spread over 499 chapters in the United States. The number of staff members grew to more than 200 in the early 1970s and to about 1,100 in 2010.

InterVarsity ministers through small group Bible studies, large gatherings on campuses, leadership training, discipleship, and dynamic conferences and events. The large gatherings are usually weekly with a speaker. Summer camps train leaders. The leaders of the International Fellowship of Evangelical Students from 130 nations gathered in Malaysia in March 2010. Alec Hill, president of IVCF-USA, represented the United States.

Headquarters

6400 Schroeder Road
Madison, WI 53711
Telephone: 608-274-9001

Leadership

Kenneth Nielsen chairs a board of trustees numbering eighteen. Five are Presbyterian, four each are nondenominational and Evangelical Free, two are independent, and one each is Baptist, Methodist, and Episcopalian.

Core Beliefs

The doctrinal basis of IVCF was revised by its board of trustees in 2000. Prior to that time, the statement affirmed "the unique divine inspiration, entire trustworthiness and authority of the Bible. The Deity of our Lord Jesus Christ. The necessity and efficacy of the substitutionary death of Jesus Christ for the redemption of the world, and the historic fact of His bodily resurrection. The presence and power of the Holy Spirit in the work of regeneration. The expectation of the personal return of our Lord Jesus Christ" (intervarsity.org, "Our Doctrinal Basis").

The newly adopted version added more fullness. It contains an initial statement about the Trinity; adds that mankind has dignity and value, being created in God's image, but that all are alienated from God and each other by sin and guilt and thus justly subject to God's wrath; and expands on Christ, noting that he was fully human and fully divine, lived as a perfect example, and ascended to heaven after his bodily resurrection from the dead. Justification is by God's grace to all who repent and place their faith in Christ alone for salvation. The new version says that the indwelling of the Holy Spirit gives believers a new life and empowers them for obedient service and that Christ will judge all people at his return, with both justice and mercy, and that the final two states will be eternal condemnation for the unrepentant and eternal life for the redeemed.

Core Practices

IVCF's purpose is to promote witnessing communities of followers of Jesus Christ among students and faculty at colleges and universities so that they grow in love for God and his Word, in love for God's people of every ethnicity, and in love with God's purposes in the world.

Over 4,200 students made a first-time profession of faith in Christ during the 2014–15 school year, and 53,228 seekers participated in evangelistic events. InterVarsity also operates the Urbana Missions Conference, which began in 1946 and meets every three years for five days during the Christmas holiday break to challenge students with the spiritual and physical needs of the world.

Finances

IVCF is a charter member of the Evangelical Council for Financial Accountability, joining in January 1980. Revenue for the fiscal year ending June 30, 2014, included $71,714 from donations, $14,099 from book and other sales, $5,888 from conference fees, and $4,833 from investments and other income for a total of $96,534. Expenses for the same period were $93,004.

Statistics

During the 2014–15 academic year, IVCF had 985 chapters on 649 campuses. About 40,000 students and faculty were actively involved. Women comprised 59 percent, and 41 percent were men. Thirty-eight percent classified themselves as minorities. Staff members numbered 1,137. About 190 chapters are oriented primarily toward graduate and professional students and/or faculty.

Website

http://www.intervarsity.org/

Bibliography

Byassee, Jason. "Reconciliation on Campus." *Faith and Leadership*, April 27, 2010.

"InterVarsity Christian Fellowship." http://www.intervarsity.org. "Our Doctrinal Basis."

LePeau, Andrew, and Linda Doll. *Heart. Mind. Soul. Strength: An Anecdotal History of InterVarsity Press, 1947–2007*. Downers Grove, IL: InterVarsity, 2006.

Poynor, Alice. *From the Campus to the World: Stories from the First Fifty Years of Student Foreign Missions Fellowship*. Downers Grove, IL: InterVarsity, 1986.

James A. Borland

Jesuits

History

The Jesuits (the Society of Jesus) is a Roman Catholic religious order founded by St. Ignatius of Loyola (AD 1491–1556) as a missionary organization for the greater glory of God. St. Ignatius, Spanish knight and nobleman, experienced a profound conversion while convalescing from a battle wound. After several years of prayer and missionary efforts, he founded a religious order, the Society of Jesus, with a group of six friends he had made during his college studies. When prevented from evangelizing Muslims in the Holy Land, St. Ignatius asked for guidance from the pope, who formally approved the order in 1540 and asked St. Ignatius to minister within Europe instead, which was wracked by division and religious apathy.

Jesuits led Catholic missionary efforts in the modern period, including missions to South America and the Far East, while also playing a key role in revitalizing the Christian faith in Europe. While St. Ignatius did not design the order for this purpose, Jesuits ended up playing a key role in the Counter Reformation (i.e., in strengthening the faith of Catholics and countering Protestant influence in Europe). Presently, there are nearly twenty thousand Jesuits worldwide. Unique among Catholic religious orders is the fact that there are no substantial divisions or branches in the order, which remains a unity. Today Jesuits are best known for their work in higher education, especially in the foundation and governance of colleges and universities, of which there are twenty-eight in the United States alone. In addition, Jesuits carry out their ministry through mission work, parish ministry, retreats, and social justice efforts.

Core Beliefs

The central goal of all forms of religious life in the Catholic Church is to secure "undivided devotion to the Lord" (1 Cor. 7:35 NIV) through the "evangelical counsels" of chastity, poverty, and obedience. The Society of Jesus is also characterized by its focus on facilitating interior conversion of souls to Christ.

The organization and character of the Society of Jesus are determined by the group's missionary purpose. Its organization is often compared to a military structure, with a carefully delineated hierarchy headed by the superior general. In addition to the three traditional vows of poverty (renunciation of property), chastity (renunciation of marriage), and obedience (to one's religious superior), Jesuits take a fourth vow of obedience to the pope, especially in terms of missions. The missionary activity of the society is focused less on external growth (e.g., church planting) than on facilitating interior conversion, often among those who are already baptized Christians. A special role here is given to the spirituality of the founder, St. Ignatius, whose profound spiritual insights are encapsulated in his *Spiritual Exercises*. Jesuits impart this spirituality through education, preaching, hearing confessions, and especially retreats, which are typically forty days in length and are organized around the *Exercises*. Because of the centrality of preaching and hearing confessions, every professed Jesuit is a priest, and hence there is no female branch of the order.

Bibliography

Bangert, William V. *A History of the Society of Jesus.* 2nd ed. St. Louis: Institute of Jesuit Sources, 1986.

De Dalmases, Cándido. *Ignatius of Loyola, Founder of the Jesuits: His Life and Work.* Translated by Jerome Aixalá. St. Louis: Institute of Jesuit Sources, 1985.

De Guibert, Joseph. *The Jesuits, Their Spiritual Doctrine and Practice: A Historical Study.* Chicago: Institute of Jesuit Sources, 1964.

Ignatius of Loyola. *Spiritual Exercises and Selected Works.* Edited by George E. Ganss. New York: Paulist Press, 1991.

O'Malley, John W. *The First Jesuits.* Cambridge, MA: Harvard University Press, 1993.

Worcester, Thomas. *The Cambridge Companion to the Jesuits.* New York: Cambridge University Press, 2008.

Jamie Blosser

Jews for Jesus

History

Jews for Jesus is a Christian missionary organization with international headquarters located in San Francisco, California. The plaque at the headquarters reads "Jews for Jesus: EST. 32 AD Give or Take a Year." Many young Jewish people were coming to faith in Jesus when the Jesus movement was at its most intense during the late 1960s. In New York City in 1969, Martin "Moishe" Rosen created the unique style of gospel tracts known as broadsides. During the summer of 1970, Rosen moved to San Francisco to join the Jesus movement in ministering to young Jewish believers in Jesus. He officially founded the organization, which was incorporated as Hineni Ministries, in September 1973.

Headquarters

60 Haight Street
San Francisco, CA 94102
Telephone: 415-864-2600
Fax: 415-552-8325

Leadership

Executive director: David Brickner

Core Beliefs

The statement of faith for the organization includes belief in the following: the divine inspiration of the Old and New Testaments; one sovereign God who eternally exists in three persons; and Jesus as Messiah who alone is Savior of those who trust in his atoning death, burial, bodily resurrection, ascension into heaven, intercession as High Priest, and personal return (which is distinguished from a pretribulational rapture of believers) in glory and power to establish and consummate the prophecies concerning his kingdom.

Defining Statement

"We exist to make the messiahship of Jesus an unavoidable issue to our Jewish people worldwide" (jewsforjesus.org, "Our Mission Statement").

Core Practices

Recognizing the divergence among Jewish people as to what it means to "be Jewish" and "live Jewishly," members of Jews for Jesus are committed to living their Jewishness actively and view that life, as a whole, in light of their belief in Jesus as Messiah. Jews for Jesus defines Jewishness in terms of birthright and inheritance from parents. Although nearly all sects (denominations) of Judaism insist that Jews for Jesus is not truly Jewish (due to faith in Jesus), the organization insists that Jews are who they are by birth and the designation Christian indicates whom they follow. Nevertheless, Jews for Jesus and other messianic Jewish groups are thought to be antithetical to Judaism and the majority of Jewish people.

Statistics

Jews for Jesus has nine US branches (Boston, Chicago, south Florida, Los Angeles, New York [Brooklyn and Manhattan], Phoenix, San Francisco, and Washington, DC), fourteen international branches (Australia, Brazil, Canada [Montreal and Toronto], France, Germany, Israel, South Africa, the United Kingdom, Russia, and Ukraine [Dnepropetrovsk, Kharkov, Kiev, and Odessa]), and web-only branches (Hungarian, Italian, Korean, Persian, and Spanish languages).

Missionary and Evangelistic Work

All missionaries of Jews for Jesus are evangelists who proclaim Jesus as the fulfillment of all messianic prophecies in the Old Testament. The missionaries make the messiahship of Jesus a necessary matter to Jewish people worldwide. Since Jewish people have a propensity not to consider evangelistic materials and methods that are distinctly Christian in language and presuppositions, the organization is innovative in the use of evangelistic literature, internet evangelism, multimedia, music and drama, secular media outreach, and witnessing campaigns.

Parachurch Organizations

Associations and memberships include Canadian Council for Christian Charities, Cross-Global Link, Evangelical Alliance of Great Britain, Evangelical Alliance of South Africa, Evangelical Council for Financial Accountability, Fédération Évangélique de France, Lausanne Consultation on Jewish Evangelism, Mission Exchange, and World Evangelical Alliance.

Publications

Jews for Jesus publishes several collections, including book reviews, movie reviews, music reviews, recipes, poetry, and Vaysechvoos articles (Vaysechvoos is a fictitious village in nineteenth-century Russia, and the stories are typical of Jewish tales of that time). The ministry also publishes *Havurah*, a contemporary publication addressing concerns of Jewish believers, an evangelical publication (*Issues*), a monthly *Jews for Jesus Newsletter* for all Christians, and an electronic resource for Christians (*RealTime*).

Website

http://www.jewsforjesus.org/

Bibliography

Goldberg, Louis. *Our Jewish Friends*. Neptune, NJ: Loizeaux Brothers, 1983.

"Jews for Jesus." http://www.jewsforjesus.org. "Our Mission Statement."

Jews for Jesus. *Questions and Answers*. San Francisco: Purple Pomegranate, 1983.

Kaplan, Dana Evan, ed. *The Cambridge Companion to American Judaism*. New York: Cambridge University Press, 2005.

Rosen, Moishe. *Y'shua*. Chicago: Moody, 1982.

Rosen, Ruth, ed. *Testimonies*. San Francisco: Purple Pomegranate, 1987.

Telchin, Stan. *Betrayed*. Lincoln, VA: Chosen, 1981.

Ron J. Bigalke

Latin America Mission

History

Harry and Susan Strachan met in London while preparing to serve overseas and eventually served for nearly two decades in Tandil, Argentina. As Harry Strachan's sense of call to full-time evangelism deepened, the Strachans stepped out in faith to establish the Latin America Evangelization Campaign in 1921. It initially focused on a continent-wide evangelistic campaign, but the development of more permanent local institutions followed through the work of Susan Strachan. In 1938, the organization's name was changed to Latin America Mission (LAM).

Harry and Susan continued to lead the organization until Harry's death in 1945. After his death and for the next several decades, other Strachan family members led the ministry. In 1971, the LAM relinquished administrative control over the major ministries of the organization and deemed them autonomous, thus enabling them to be managed by field-based, local Christian leaders in each country. The LAM has continued to identify and develop ministries throughout Latin America, serving as a key missions-sending agency.

Headquarters

United States
PO Box 52-7900
Miami, FL 33152
Telephone: 305-884-8400

Canada
3075 Ridgeway Drive
Unit 14
Mississauga, ON L5L 5M6
Telephone: 905-569-0001

Leadership

The LAM is currently governed by a board of directors consisting of business professionals and ministry personnel from a diverse variety of professions and backgrounds. The LAM president manages the day-to-day operations of the organization.

Core Practices

The Latin America Mission has two primary purposes. The first is the promotion of evangelism as central to every aspect of ministry. The second is that all LAM missionaries partner with the Latin church.

The LAM is known for being a creative missiological enterprise that utilizes a host of ministries to reach Latin America. Intentional efforts are taken to ensure that evangelism is central to each ministry. The ministries of the LAM include theological education, church ministry, church outreach, Christian literature, mass media, leadership training, national missions, health, education, social work, youth clubs, economic development, counseling, and emergency response.

The LAM currently has missionaries working in Argentina, Bolivia, Brazil, Colombia, Costa Rica, Ecuador, Honduras, Mexico, Panama, Paraguay, Peru, Spain, Venezuela, and the United States.

Trends

In recent years, the LAM has strengthened its focus on mobilizing the Latin church, expanded a short-term mission program, and continued to make technological and communication advances so as to remain "on the cutting edge of ministry in the Latin world, garnering the respect and support of Latin evangelical leaders" (lam .org, "Vision Statement").

Website

http://www.lam.org/

Bibliography

Fahlbusch, Erwin, et al. *The Encyclopedia of Christianity*. Vol. 2. Grand Rapids: Eerdmans, 2001.

"Latin America Mission." http://www.lam.org. "Vision Statement."

"Strachan, Harry." In *Biographical Dictionary of Christian Missions*, edited by Gerald H. Anderson, 645. Grand Rapids: Eerdmans, 1999.

"Strachan, Susan Beamish." In *Biographical Dictionary of Christian Missions*, edited by Gerald H. Anderson, 645–46. Grand Rapids: Eerdmans, 1999.

Tucker, Ruth. *From Jerusalem to Irian Jaya: A Biographical History of Christian Missions*. 2nd ed. Grand Rapids: Zondervan, 2004.

M. David Sills

Liebenzell USA

History

In the late 1800s, Hudson Taylor traveled throughout Europe garnering support for the work of the China Inland Mission. In Germany, news of Taylor's work so excited Rev. Heinrich Coerper that he founded the German Support Branch of the China Inland Mission in 1899. The little society grew quickly, sending out its first missionary within a year. In 1902, the mission was given a new home in the Black Forest town of Bad Liebenzell and thus became Liebenzell Mission.

The work grew rapidly and spread to other fields in Asia and the Pacific: Manus Island and other parts of Papua New Guinea, Micronesia, Japan, and Palau. By the 1930s, over eighty missionaries were involved in full-time ministry overseas. The outbreak of World War II disrupted the work as missionaries were expelled, imprisoned, or killed.

In the late 1930s, a missionary couple returning to ministry in China became stranded in America as war broke out in Europe and Asia. Henry and Anna Zimmermann united several small groups of faithful mission supporters in the United States and founded Liebenzell USA in 1941. Within ten years, the first US missionary was sent to Manus Island, Papua New Guinea; others soon followed. The work even expanded to Taiwan when missionaries were forced to leave China in the early 1950s.

Today Liebenzell USA is an evangelical, evangelistic, interdenominational, faith-dependent Christian organization that exists to help people worldwide come to know Jesus Christ through evangelism, discipleship, education, and humanitarian aid by partnering with churches to recruit, send, and support missionaries; facilitating Christian retreats, conferences, and projects for the benefit of its ministry partners; and motivating Christians to greater mission awareness.

Liebenzell USA is a member of Liebenzell Mission International (LMI), which consists of independent offices in Austria, Canada, Germany, Hungary, Japan, the Netherlands, Switzerland, and the United States. Today about 250 career missionaries serve with LMI. Many more short-term volunteers also assist in taking the gospel to all the world. Liebenzell USA conducts two parallel ministries: Global Ministries focuses on promoting and facilitating cross-cultural evangelism and Christian discipleship around the world and in the United States through faith missionaries, and Retreat Ministries focuses on promoting missions and strengthening local churches in the US by operating a guest house and retreat center in Schooley's Mountain, New Jersey.

Headquarters

13 Heath Lane
PO Box 66
Schooley's Mountain, NJ 07870
Telephone: 908-852-3044
Fax: 908-852-4531

Leadership

President and CEO: Thomas Cooper

Core Beliefs

1. We believe that the whole Bible is inspired by the Holy Spirit and is the Divine authority and infallible rule for faith, life and doctrine.

2. We believe in one God, eternally existing in three Divine Persons, Father, Son and Holy Spirit, equal in nature, power and glory.

3. We believe in the Deity of the Lord Jesus Christ, in His virgin birth, in His sinless life, in His miracles, in His shed blood as the only atonement for sin, in His bodily resurrection and ascension to the right hand of the Father and in His personal return in power and glory.

4. We believe in the Holy Spirit who convicts of sin, testifies of Christ, enables the believer to live a victorious life, and guides into all truth.

5. We believe that man was created in the image of God, but fell into sin and is in need of regeneration through faith in Jesus Christ.

6. We believe in the resurrection of the body. The believer will arise to eternal life, the unbeliever will arise to eternal condemnation.

7. We believe in the Spiritual unity of all believers in our Lord Jesus Christ.

8. We believe in the commission of the Risen Christ ... (Matthew 28:19, 20).

9. We uphold the truths as stated in the Nicene and Apostles' Creeds. (mission.liebenzellusa.org, "Statement of Faith")

Defining Statement

First Timothy 2:4, "[God] wants all men to be saved and to come to a knowledge of the truth" (NIV 1984), has been Liebenzell's motto and challenge for over one hundred years.

Core Practices

God's great love and his desire that all hear the good news are the motivating forces for Liebenzell USA. Liebenzell seeks to help fulfill the Great Commission of the Lord by sharing the gospel of Jesus Christ and by instructing believers in obedience to the Word of God wherever God may lead around the world. The following principles help the ministry achieve that objective (mission.liebenzellusa.org, "Our Values"):

Our authority is God's Word, the Bible.

People matter to God. We reach the least, the last, and the lost. We seek to respect each person as a unique reflection of God's image.

Resources belong to God's kingdom. We are to seek first His Kingdom and trust Him to supply our needs.

Ministry depends upon God's Spirit. Without Him, we can do nothing; with Him, nothing is impossible.
Unity is in God's Son, Jesus Christ.
Integrity honors God's character.
Partnership is vital in God's work.
Excellence reflects God's nature.

Finances

Total revenue for 2013: $1,624,444
Total expenses for 2013: $1,650,388
Net assets for 2013: $1,210,340

Ministry Watch awarded the mission a transparency grade of A in its financial dealings in the area of foreign missions. It is a member of the Evangelical Council for Financial Accountability and is recognized by the IRS as a tax-exempt 501(c)(3) religious organization. Contributions are tax deductible.

Statistics

Liebenzell is at work in twenty-five countries around the world.

Website

http://www.liebenzellusa.org/

Bibliography

"Liebenzell USA." http://www.liebenzellusa.org. "Our Values" and "Statement of Faith."

Michael McMullen

Life Ministries

History

Life Ministries is actually an acronym for Literature International For Evangelism. It was begun in 1986 by Mennonites Lester and Betty Miller, who were also the founders and administrators of a Maranatha Christian school. They felt led to encourage students to participate in missions and therefore organized a trip for juniors to help in Haiti. Through this experience they realized there was a lack of Christian literature available for third world countries, so they purchased an old ski lodge in Conestoga, Pennsylvania, and began printing. Besides Bible tracts and adult instruction, Life Ministries produces children's Bible storybooks and *Pilgrim's Progress* in Creole for Haitians. The literature is paid for by donations and by five auctions held each year for Haiti. Bibles and Christian literature are also distributed to nine prisons in Haiti.
Life Ministries became incorporated in 1987. It moved to its present location in Conestoga,

Pennsylvania, in May 1997. There is also a warehouse for the literature, an office, and a guesthouse on the Blue Ridge Mission compound in Santo, Port-Au-Prince, Haiti.
The next burden the Millers felt was to educate Christians about being good stewards of their finances. Therefore, Lester Miller began counseling in this area and teaching a seminar titled "Biblical Financial Guidelines." He expanded his counseling to address other needs of married couples and individuals, and the ministry grew.
Lester Miller died on December 26, 2001, but his staff continues the ministry.

Headquarters

250 Meadow Lane
Conestoga, PA 17516
Telephone: 717-871-0540
Fax: 717-871-0547
Email: info@life-ministries.com

Leadership

Life Ministries is overseen by a seven-member executive board chaired by Titus Martin. Also in place is a nationwide twenty-five-member consulting board. The administrator of Life Ministries is Lamar Nolt of North Carolina.

Core Beliefs

The organization's doctrinal beliefs follow the 1963 Mennonite Confession of Faith. Life Ministries is Christian based and interdenominational.

Core Practices

Life Ministries has a two-pronged purpose: (1) internationally to provide literature in indigenous languages to third world countries with a concentration on Haiti and (2) domestically to provide training for counselors and counseling for needy individuals and married couples.

Growth

Life Ministries is extending its ministry to provide Spanish literature for the Dominican Republic.

Trends

Its vision has not wavered:

To be a Christ-honoring resource center for counseling, training, and "shepherding" of people from all backgrounds, providing them with skills and resources needed to live in healthy relationships in harmony with themselves, others, and God. (life-ministries.com, "About Us")

Missionary and Evangelistic Work

Life Ministries prints literature to evangelize and disciple Christians in Haiti.

Ecumenism

Life Ministries provides literature freely to any Christian mission group in Haiti, such as Hunger for Christ.

Publication

Life Ministries Newsletter (available in hardcopy and electronic form)

Website

http://www.life-ministries.com/

Bibliography

"Life Ministries." http://www.life-ministries.com. "About Us."

Brenda Ayres

Ligonier Ministries

History

Ligonier Ministries was founded as Ligonier Valley Study Center in 1971 by Christian theologian Dr. R. C. (Robert Charles) Sproul as an educational ministry designed to fill the gap between Sunday school and seminary. The theological orientation of Dr. Sproul and Ligonier Ministries is that of the Reformed churches that grew out of the Protestant Reformation. The ministry's focus is on providing advanced training in biblical teaching and Christian theology for laypeople. The goal of Ligonier's training is to enable Christians to articulate what they believe and why they believe it. A key component of Ligonier's approach is to record all the lectures offered and to provide them to people wishing to study from afar, making Ligonier a pioneer in the field of distance learning. A second component is the publication of *Table Talk*, a devotional magazine featuring articles on biblical and theological themes.

The decades of the 1980s and 1990s saw significant expansion of Ligonier's influence and work. In the 1980s, Sproul relocated the study center from its original home in Ligonier, Pennsylvania, to Orlando, Florida, and changed its name to Ligonier Ministries. The 1980s also saw the initiation of ministry-sponsored regional and national conferences at various locations throughout the United States. In the 1990s, Ligonier developed a nationally syndicated radio ministry, *Renewing Your Mind*, providing a wider forum for the presentation of the teachings of Sproul and his associates.

The first decade of the twenty-first century witnessed continued expansion as well as organizational consolidation for Ligonier Ministries. Two new publication arms were added to the ministry, Soli Deo Gloria Publications and Reformation Trust Publishing. The first, a publication enterprise dedicated to reprinting significant works of the sixteenth- and seventeenth-century Puritans, had begun in close association with Ligonier in the previous decade and now became an official part of the ministry. The second was established to offer a new imprint committed to the publication of high quality, theologically solid books. Both publication ministries would later be united under Reformation Trust Publishing.

The radio ministry was expanded by offering broadcasts by shortwave to listeners throughout the world. A music production branch, *Ligonier Music*, was also initiated, offering recordings designed to promote a sense of reverence and gravitas found in more classical forms of Christian worship. The decade also saw a significant expansion of Ligonier's internet outreach, with the organization's website featuring daily and archived radio broadcasts, information pages highlighting the various branches of the ministry, and a blog.

In the fall of 2011, the ministry launched the Ligonier Academy of Theological Studies, offering study programs on three levels: (1) an online certificate program called Ligonier Connect, (2) an undergraduate program through Reformation Bible College, and (3) a doctor of ministry program offering advanced study for pastors and other ministry leaders.

Headquarters

421 Ligonier Court
Sanford, FL 32771
Telephone: 407-333-4244; 800-435-4343
Fax: 407-333-4233

Leadership

Ligonier Ministries is overseen by a board of eight directors, with Dr. R. C. Sproul serving as chairman of the board and president of the ministry.

Core Beliefs

Ligonier Ministries is founded on the historic teachings of the Protestant Reformation and has the following statement of faith:

God and Man

We believe in one God—Father, Son, and Holy Spirit. The triune God has created man in His own image and has called him to manifest and reflect holiness through obedience to His commandments. Because man has woefully fallen in this responsibility and entered into a state of moral corruption, he has subsequently become estranged from his Creator.

Jesus Christ

Because of a profound love for His creation, God has initiated a plan of redemption which He has accomplished on behalf of His people in the realm of temporal history. The zenith of this redemption is located in the historical incarnation of God in the person of Jesus of Nazareth. We confess Jesus to be the Christ of Old Testament prophecy, being at the same time fully God and fully man. Jesus, through His substitutionary atoning death and bodily resurrection, has provided the meritorious basis of our justification, which, by God's grace, we receive by faith alone.

The Holy Spirit

Proceeding from the Father and the Son, the Holy Spirit dwells in the hearts of believers, effecting their regeneration and operating in their sanctification. The same Holy Spirit has been given to the people of God to empower them for the service of bearing witness to the kingdom of God. The Holy Spirit brings His people together to form a corporate community of believers. We believe that Christ has established a visible church which is called to live in the power of the Holy Spirit under the regulation of the authority of Holy Scripture, exercising discipline, administering the sacraments, and preaching the Gospel of Christ.

The Bible

We believe that the Bible, in its entirety, is divine revelation, and we submit to the authority of Holy Scripture, acknowledging it to be inerrantly inspired by God and carrying the full weight of His authority.

We support the work of Christian organizations and institutions that confess the Lordship of Jesus Christ. We are committed to the implementation of the social and cultural implications of God's commandments for the well-being of man and his environment. We believe our faith should be visible in concrete forms and models of personal and social behavior. We seek to be faithful disciples of Christ, enduring in love and obedience until He comes again to consummate His kingdom.

Furthermore, Ligonier Ministries adheres to the ancient statements of faith (the Apostles' Creed, the Nicene Creed, and the Creed of Chalcedon) and affirms the historic Christian faith as expressed in the five solas of the Reformation and the consensus of the historic Reformed confessions (Westminster Standards, Three Forms of Unity, and 1689 London Baptist Confession of Faith). (ligonier.org, "Our Statement of Faith")

Finances

The organization is nonprofit, and contributions to it are tax deductible. Ligonier is governed by the Standards of Responsible Stewardship of the Evangelical Council for Financial Accountability. Financial statements and president's reports are available online.

Statistics

By 2010, the several branches of Ligonier Ministries had seen significant growth, with the publication enterprises offering more than 5,000 resources, including in excess of 400 books, some 60 authored by Dr. Sproul; the daily radio broadcasts reaching 235 American outlets with an estimated audience of 2.5 million per week; and the ministry's website receiving 40,000 visitors per month. The international radio broadcast reaches 120 countries.

Ligonier Ministries' accomplishments and programs include the following: approximately 11,900 attendees of religious lectures, seminars, and programs; approximately 32,500 subscriptions to monthly publications of religious doctrine, ministry, and instruction; approximately 45,700 audiotapes distributed; approximately 14,200 videotapes distributed; and approximately 96,200 books and curriculum distributed.

Website

http://www.ligonier.org/

Bibliography

"Ligonier Ministries." http://www.ligonier.org. "Our Statement of Faith."

Mark A. House

Living Water Teaching

History

After a successful career in the construction industry, Jim and Marion Zirkle and their family moved to Broken Arrow, Oklahoma, in 1976. After a short-term mission trip to Guatemala, the Zirkles soon felt called to Central America, founding Living Water Teaching in 1979. Since then, the ministry has grown to include outreaches in eleven countries around the world. Outreach is done by way of Bible schools, evangelistic campaigns, medical clinics, Operation Shoebox, and the ministries of the graduates of the Bible institutes.

When tragedy struck in November 1998 in the form of a plane crash that killed Jim Zirkle, along with their son, son-in-law, two missionaries, and six other group members, Marion resolved to continue the work of the mission. The ministry is now active in Belize, Bolivia, Brazil, Central America, Cuba, Mexico, and Paraguay.

Living Water Teaching has graduated over twenty-nine thousand Bible school students, and more than seven hundred thousand have been converted through its mission.

Headquarters

3097 Mission Way
Caddo Mills, TX 75135
Telephone: 903-527-4160
Fax: 925-447-4524

Core Beliefs

Living Water Teaching states that its programs and activities "shall be based upon and at all times shall be consistent with the following beliefs":

A. The Bible is the mind of Christ, and it is the inspired and only infallible and authoritative Word of God. II Tim. 3:16; II Peter 1:19–21; Heb. 4:12
B. There is one God manifested in three personalities: Father, Son, and Holy Spirit. Is. 45:5, 6; I John 5:7; Mt. 28:19
C. The reality of Satan and his present control over unregenerated man does exist. I Peter 5:8; Eph. 6:11, 12; II Cor. 4:4

Christianity is based upon the following:

1. The deity of our Lord Jesus Christ. John 1:1–3; Col. 1:15–17; John 10:30
2. Born of the Virgin Mary. Luke 1:26–35; Is. 7:14; Mt. 1:23
3. His sinless life. Heb. 4:15; I Peter 2:22; II Cor. 5:21
4. His miracles. John 3:2, 11:45, 20:30
5. His vicarious and atoning death through His shed blood. Is. 53:4, 5; I Peter 2:21–24; Col. 1:14
6. His body resurrection. I Peter 1:21; Gal. 1:1; Rom. 1:4
7. His ascension to the right hand of the Father. Acts 1:19–11; Eph. 1:20; Col. 3:1
8. His personal return in power and glory as Lord of Lords and Kings of Kings. Mt. 24:30, 25:31; [II] Thess. 1:7–10
9. The fall of man and his lost of estate, which makes necessary a rebirth through confession and belief in the Lord Jesus Christ. Rom. 3:23, 5:12–21, 10:9, 10; I Cor. 15:21, 22
10. The reconciliation of man to God by substitutionary death and shed blood of our Lord Jesus Christ. Rom. 5:5–10; II Cor. 5:18
11. The resurrection of believers into everlasting life and blessing in Heaven, and the resurrection of unbelievers unto everlasting punishment in the torments of Hell. John 5:28, 19; I Thess. 4:16–18; Mark 16:16

The present supernatural ministry of the Holy Spirit, Who bestows the spiritual gifts of: the word of Wisdom, the word of knowledge, faith, gifts of healing, working of miracles, prophecy, discerning of spirits, various kinds of tongues, in and among the believers on the Earth since the day of Pentecost and continuing until our Lord's return. I Cor. 12; John 16:7, 13:15; Eph. 4:8 (livingwaterteaching .org, "Tenets of Faith")

Finances

No financial statistics are available on this ministry from standard sources. It is not a member of the Evangelical Council for Financial Accountability.

Academic Institution

Living Water Teaching Bible Institute (Quetzaltenango, Guatemala)

Website

http://www.livingwaterteaching.org/

Bibliography

"Living Water Teaching." http://www.livingwaterteaching .org. "Tenets of Faith."

Michael McMullen

LOGOI

History

Founded in 1968 by Rev. Dr. Les Thompson, LOGOI was established to equip God's people "for works of service, so that the body of Christ may be built up" (Eph. 4:12–13 NIV). The ministry has been used "to help, equip, and encourage tens of thousands of pastors and church leaders throughout the world." The ministry also reports that "thousands of churches have been planted, hundreds of churches and ministries have been revitalized, and countless lives have been brought to a saving faith in Jesus Christ," all done by national pastors and leaders (logoi.org, "Home"). LOGOI focuses on helping national Spanish-speaking pastors—those who have had little Bible training—to become effective ministers of the gospel. The ministry provides both immediate and long-term help, advice, and encouragement to pastors and teaching leaders.

Headquarters

14540 SW 136th Street
Suite 200
Miami, FL 33186
Telephone: 305-232-5880
Fax: 305-232-3592

Leadership

President: Ed Thompson

LOGOI founder and director: Dr. Les Thompson

Core Beliefs

LOGOI affirms the following:

The divine inspiration and inerrancy of the Word of God as originally given, and its supreme authority in all matters of faith and conduct.

The existence of only one God, personal, one in essence, yet existing in three persons: Father, Son, and Holy Spirit.

The sovereignty of God in creation, revelation, redemption, and the final judgment.

The universality of sin and guilt of man since the Fall, subjecting him to the wrath and damnation of God.

Redemption from guilt, sorrow, dominion, and corruption of sin only through the expiatory death of our Lord Jesus Christ, the incarnate Son of God, our representative and substitute.

The work of the Holy Spirit to make effective the redemptive death of Christ for the sinner, giving him repentance before God and faith in Jesus Christ.

The presence and power of the Holy Spirit in repentance, regeneration, and sanctification.

The indwelling work of the Holy Spirit in the believer.

Justification of the sinner only by God's mercy and grace, received through faith in Christ's substitutionary death.

The intercession of Jesus Christ, the only mediator between God and men, on behalf of His redeemed.

One Holy Universal Church, visible in the local congregations, to which all believers belong.

The certainty of our Lord Jesus Christ's second coming in his glorified body.

The resurrection of the body, life everlasting for the redeemed, and the eternal damnation of the unjust. (logoi.org, "Statement of Faith")

Finances

Total revenue for 2013: $1,314,046

Total expenses for 2013: $660,996

Net assets for 2013: $1,841,005

LOGOI is a member of the Evangelical Council for Financial Accountability.

Website

http://www.logoi.org/

Bibliography

"LOGOI." http://www.logoi.org. "Home" and "Statement of Faith."

Michael McMullen

Luis Palau Association

History

Luis Palau was born to Catholic parents in Argentina in 1934. Shortly thereafter, his parents trusted Christ, but his father died when Luis was eleven. Luis received Christ at a camp in Argentina on February 12, 1947. He spent eight years in a British boarding school in Argentina and backslid before deciding to give his life to serving Christ. Luis immigrated to Portland, Oregon, in 1960, attended Multnomah Bible College for one year, and became a United States citizen in 1962. In December 1966, Palau preached to a crowd of thirty thousand in Bogota, Colombia's capital city. In 1976, he succeeded Dick Hillis as president of Overseas Crusades. The Luis Palau Evangelistic Association was founded in 1978 in Portland and is now called the Luis Palau Association (LPA).

Headquarters

PO Box 50

Portland, OR 97207

Telephone: 503-614-1500

Fax: 503-614-1599

Leadership

The LPA has a fourteen-member United States board of directors and an eight-member United Kingdom board of directors. Palau is on each board.

Core Beliefs

The LPA affirms seven doctrinal points, including a verbally inspired inerrant Bible; the Trinity; and the deity, sinless life, and vicarious atonement of Christ. Faith in Christ is necessary for salvation, which is accomplished by the regeneration of the Holy Spirit. Christians are to live by the indwelling power of the Holy Spirit. Only Christ offers forgiveness of sins by faith. The LPA holds to the resurrection of the body and eternal life and to the unity of the church as the body of Christ. The only eschatology mentioned is that Jesus will personally "return in power and glory," a statement that can be accepted by postmillennials, amillennials, and historic premillennials (palau.org, "What We Believe").

Core Practices

The Luis Palau Association exists to proclaim the gospel, mobilize the church, and equip the next generation to evangelize the world.

Finances

The LPA is a charter member of the Evangelical Council for Financial Accountability, joining September 1, 1980.

Total revenue for 2013: $29,124,026
Total expenses for 2013: $26,541,342
Net assets for 2013: $11,000,000

Statistics

The LPA claims that Luis Palau has spoken to more than one billion people through radio and television outreach and to twenty-five million in live meetings in seventy-two countries, primarily in Central and South America. Palau has served as a Spanish interpreter for Billy Graham and has written over fifty books and booklets that appear in English and/or Spanish. A Palau book, *A Friendly Dialogue between an Atheist and a Christian*, came out of Palau's meetings with diplomat Zhao Qizheng in China in 2005. In March 2008, Palau held a CityFest-type meeting in Buenos Aires, Argentina, speaking to a crowd of one hundred thousand. Argentine president Cristina Fernandez also met with Palau in her office with government leaders present.

Missionary and Evangelistic Work

In 1998, the LPA established the Next Generation Alliance (NGA) to train and give resources to evangelists. Over two hundred evangelists work with the NGA and help with citywide and even nationwide meetings. Today the emphasis is on holding large citywide meetings called City-Fest that include neighborhood revitalization, mentoring, foster care, tutoring, and care for the homeless. In 2008, eighty thousand persons attended such a meeting in Portland, Oregon, home of the Luis Palau Association. The LPA gathered twenty-five thousand volunteers from six hundred churches and performed community service projects throughout the city. These included public school cleanups, medical and dental clinics, meals and other help for the homeless, and so forth. They worked in conjunction with Sam Adams, the self-avowed gay Portland mayor, to accomplish these projects. These meetings take place in open city squares rather than in closed arenas. Rock music concerts and inflatables for kids to play on help attract the crowd. When Luis Palau preached in Portland, about two thousand people were present.

Website

http://www.palau.org/

Bibliography

Dawdy, Philip. "Closing for Christ." *Willamette Week,* August 25, 1999.

Krattenmaker, Tom. "Evangelism 2.0." blogs.usatoday.com /oped/2009/07/evangelism-20-.html.

"Luis Palau Association." http://www.palau.org. "What We Believe."

Stafford, Tim. "Servant Evangelism." *Christianity Today,* November 2008.

Whalin, W. Terry. *Luis Palau.* Minneapolis: Bethany House, 1996.

James A. Borland

Luke Society

History

In 1964, a group of Christian physicians and dentists gathered to save a mission hospital in Rehoboth, New Mexico, just east of Gallup. Six years later Dr. Peter Boelens founded the Luke Society's first community health program in Mississippi, and in 1979, the society added international medical ministries to the domestic health care ministries the society had been working with the previous fifteen years.

The Luke Society worked with indigenous Christian leaders serving as ministry directors and with indigenous doctors, and in 1996, the society began appointing regional coordinators. These coordinators began mentoring new directors and looking for new opportunities for ministry in their regions. This practice helped the ministry grow rapidly.

In 1998, Dr. Boelens retired, and Dr. Wrede Vogel now serves as the Luke Society's executive director. With the change in leadership came a change in the location of the organization's headquarters, which are now in Sioux Falls, South Dakota. The organization has continued to expand and now serves in more than thirty countries on five continents.

Headquarters

3409 Gateway Boulevard
Sioux Falls, SD 57106
Telephone: 605-373-9686
Fax: 605-373-9711
Email: office@lukesociety.org

Leadership

Dr. Wrede Vogel is the executive director, and the ministry operates through five regional coordinators who mentor indigenous physicians and leaders as they develop their own local ministries. The work these regional coordinators do is crucial to the mission and methods of the Luke

Society because they help to expand the ministry by finding local leaders who share the vision of reaching out to their communities with health care and the gospel, providing support and guidance, and holding conferences where leaders and ministers share ideas, frustrations, solutions, and prayer requests. The regional coordinators also serve as the connection between the home office and the ministers in the mission field.

Core Beliefs

The Luke Society is a Christ-centered lay ministry of evangelism, physical and spiritual healing, and discipleship to poor and underserved communities. It seeks to reconcile mankind to God and man to man through the gospel of Jesus Christ. The Luke Society believes that these goals are best carried out through indigenous leaders, ministers, and health professionals because they know the culture and language best and because they are strengthened when they can recognize and solve their own problems with the proper resources and support.

Their seven-point statement of faith addresses the Bible, the Trinity, Christ, salvation, the Holy Spirit, the resurrection, and the unity of believers.

Defining Statement

"Touching lives in Jesus' name" (lukesociety .org, "Home").

Core Practices

The Luke Society is a Christ-centered organization focusing on medical missions: improving medical care, providing hospice care, and promoting community health care (e.g., boiling water, digging wells, building latrines, and using mosquito nets). This interdenominational ministry utilizes health and business professionals who support indigenous medical and community leaders as they bring medical care and teach disease prevention to those in their communities. Besides equipping people to take care of themselves, businesspeople with the Luke Society help locals with economic development projects (e.g., cooperatives) so that people in the communities can earn a better living for their families.

Luke Society directors are from the cultures in which they serve, an effective practice because people are more likely to accept help from and to trust indigenous directors. This practice has resulted in long-term projects, improvement in health care, protection against exploitation, and self-dependence. Although the organization may

begin a health care project as a joint project, "the ultimate aim . . . [is] to hand over management of health and development activities to the community" (lukesociety.org, "Community Health Development").

Finances

The Luke Society has been a member of the Evangelical Council for Financial Accountability (ECFA) since June 1, 1987. According to ECFA records, the Luke Society spends 88.9 percent of its total annual revenue (less than $3 million) for its primary program of health care, 8.3 percent for administrative expenses, and 2.8 percent for fund-raising. The Luke Society strives to provide support to a growing number of ministries without adding paid staff. Consequently, it makes extensive use of volunteers to keep operating expenses low and field donations high. The Luke Society is primarily supported by contributions from Christian individuals and churches worldwide.

Statistics

The Luke Society has thirty-four ministries in twenty-nine countries on five continents.

Missionary and Evangelistic Work

In addition to improving health care and sanitary conditions in a community, the Luke Society uses Partnership Ministry Teams (PMTs), which are made up of Christian health and business professionals in North America, to pray for specific society ministries, help fund projects, and provide medicine, medical supplies, and advisory services to projects in disadvantaged countries. PMTs provide a path for direct involvement that allows people to use their own skills in the development of an ongoing medical ministry.

The Luke Society formed PMTs to create partnerships between North Americans interested in missions and indigenous Christian missionaries. This strategy recognizes the global nature of missions and enables all Christians to use their gifts to help build God's kingdom.

Some team members join in part because they want to introduce their families, friends, communities, and churches to other cultures as a practical way to be involved in evangelism and ministry. Team members travel to visit their colleagues in the field each year to encourage and support their mission work, and when team members return home, they help raise funds, provide prayer support, share ministry information with their colleagues, and solicit resources for the ministries.

Website

http://www.lukesociety.org/

Bibliography

David, Brenda. "The Luke Society Reaches Out with Resources to Heal Physically and Spiritually." *Living Stones News*, August 4, 2009. http://www.livingstonesnews.com/index.php?option=com_content&task=view&id=336&Itemid=86.

"Luke Society." http://www.lukesociety.org. "Community Health Development" and "Home."

"100 Things the Church Is Doing Right." *Christianity Today*, November 17, 1997.

Zoba, Wendy. "Exit Strategy." *Christianity Today*, May 24, 1999. http://www.christianitytoday.com/ct/article_print.html?id=2297.

Linda Gray

Lutheran Bible Translators

History

Lutheran Bible Translators (LBT) is an independent mission founded in 1964 by Dr. Morris G. Watkins under the name Messengers of Christ. An educational missionary in Nigeria during the 1960s, Watkins was challenged by the linguistic diversity of Nigeria's Ogoja province. While in the United States, he retooled his skills, returning to Nigeria with the goal of translating Scripture into one of the more than five hundred Nigerian languages. Serious illness in his family and the death of his daughter cut this endeavor short. The family returned to Southern California dejected by their loss of a daughter and a calling.

Yet Watkins did not lose the vision of translating the Bible into the languages of minority people groups. Inspired and encouraged by Cameron Townsend, founder of Wycliffe Bible Translators (WBT), he began to recruit and support Lutheran workers for Bible translation. Lutheran clergy and laypersons were recruited and then sent for training and service under WBT and the Summer Institute of Linguistics in Papua New Guinea and South and Central America.

Watkins traveled extensively in Lutheran circles recruiting workers and raising funds. Lutheran Bible Translators became the organization's name to strengthen its identity as a pan-Lutheran agency. In 1969, dozens of new missionary workers were placed in Liberia. In 1974, missionaries were sent to Sierra Leone. During this period, Watkins left LBT, expanding his vision for Bible literacy in a new organization.

In 1986, the organization's headquarters moved from Orange, California, to Aurora, Illinois. By then, 120 LBT missionaries were serving in 15 countries and the first New Testaments were being completed. Seven additional New Testaments were completed by 1990.

Civil wars during the 1990s in Liberia and Sierra Leone caused LBT to close mission field operations. Work continued through partnerships with national organizations, which LBT supports and strengthens. Much work is focused on Scripture engagement—equipping communities and churches with literacy skills and facilitating the production of Scripture in audiovisual formats.

Headquarters

303 N Lake Street
PO Box 2050
Aurora, IL 60507
Telephone: 630-897-0660

Leadership

The board chair of LBT is Dr. Douglas Rutt, associate professor at Concordia Theological Seminary.

Core Beliefs

LBT pursues its ministry with an understanding of the *missio Dei* (i.e., God's mission), seeking to make the transforming power of the gospel available to those who do not have it in their heart language. LBT continues to be guided by six core values: God's Word, innovation, professionalism, dialogue, cultural sensitivity, and fiscal responsibility.

Defining Statement

"We make God's Word accessible to those who do not yet have it in the language of their hearts" (lbt.org, "Home").

Statistics

LBT has twenty-two Bible translations in process, fifty-nine Scripture engagement programs, and four language programs. It has reached seven million with completed Scriptures in fifty-one languages in fifteen countries.

Missionary and Evangelistic Work

The role of the LBT missionary has changed significantly through the years. Missionaries often played a key role in the actual writing of translation drafts. Today the emphasis is on equipping a national team to write Scripture translations in their language, faithful to the original biblical languages yet clear and natural in the host language and culture.

LBT places workers and resources through alliances and partnerships primarily in Africa, with additional projects in Asia, the Americas, and the Pacific. LBT's more than seventy projects are organized and implemented through partnerships with national Lutheran church bodies, Bible societies, national literacy organizations, and indigenous language/cultural associations. LBT was a founding member of the International Forum of Bible Agencies.

Website

http://www.lbt.org/

James Laesch

Madonna House Apostolate

History

The Madonna House Apostolate (MHA) is a Roman Catholic lay community of men and women who live under private promises of poverty, chastity, and obedience and engage in a variety of apostolic and spiritual works. It was founded in 1947 by Catherine de Hueck Doherty (1896–1985). A refugee of the Russian Revolution, Doherty had founded an earlier community, Friendship House, which served the urban poor in Toronto, Ottawa, Harlem, and Chicago. The MHA was originally known as Friendship House Canada but split from the first group in 1952.

Headquarters

2888 Dafoe Road
Combermere, ON K0J 1L0
Canada
Telephone: 613-756-3713
Fax: 613-756-0211
Email: combermere@madonnahouse.org

Leadership

The MHA consists of three branches—laymen, laywomen, and ordained priests—who each elect their own director general (DG), voting until the members reach unanimity. The three DGs decide unanimously on all matters pertaining to the entire apostolate; each unilaterally makes decisions that solely affect their own branch. The DGs appoint directors for each mission house of the apostolate who organize the daily work of the community.

Core Beliefs

The MHA is a Roman Catholic community and accepts fully all teachings of the Catholic Church. In addition, it sees the primary need of the world today as personal love and friendship: to create a community of love open to the world. The vision of the community is intensely spiritual, with prayer and service being an integral whole. The community identifies itself with the life of the holy family in Nazareth, believing that ordinary human life lived with love is a proclamation of the gospel.

Defining Statement

"What you do matters, but not much. What you are matters tremendously" (madonnahouse .org, "Field Houses").

Core Practices

Members make lifetime promises of poverty, chastity, and obedience, striving through these ancient disciplines to make themselves available to the will of God expressed through the demand of charity.

Worship

The community worships according to the rites of the Catholic Church. A Russian influence due to the group's founder can be seen in the prevalence of icons, Byzantine hymnody, and regular Eastern Rite liturgies.

Statistics

In 2010, the MHA had 203 members serving in 18 houses in 6 countries. Over half of the members reside at the main headquarters in Canada.

Trends

The community's roots are in the Depression, and its earliest works involved relieving physical poverty and promoting social justice. In the 1970s, the aridity and isolation of modern urban life shifted the focus of the community to establishing prayer-listening houses in various locales. Currently, the community sees its primary work as forming a Christian family and simply sharing this family life with those it serves, hoping thus to remedy the breakdown of family and society in the modern world.

Missionary and Evangelistic Work

The MHA runs soup kitchens and clothing rooms, teaches catechism, provides houses of prayer and listening, and so on. Hospitality is a common thread running through all the MHA's works, as is a dedication to the holiness and beauty of ordinary life and humble service.

Website

http://www.madonnahouse.org/

Denis Lemieux

Medical Ambassadors International

History

Medical Ambassadors International (MAI) is an organization that promotes what it calls the Community Health Evangelism (CHE, pronounced "chay") strategy. The goal of CHE is to "transform lives and communities from the inside out." CHE "addresses the root causes of poverty, disease, and spiritual darkness by training local leaders to share the gospel and mobilize community action" (medicalambassadors.com, "Attend a Training"). MAI sees this strategy as a way of providing stable resources, both physical and spiritual, to the communities in which it ministers.

MAI was founded by Dr. Raymond Benson in 1980. Dr. Paul Calhoun, a member of MAI's board of directors, became the executive director and implemented the CHE program, which was developed by Stan Rowand of Campus Crusade in South Africa.

Headquarters

5012 Salida Boulevard
Salida, CA 95368
Telephone: 209-543-7500
Fax: 209-543-7550
Email: info@ med-amb.org

Leadership

Dr. John Payne is the president of MAI, which is governed by a board of directors.

Core Beliefs

1. We believe that the Bible, in its entirety in the original writings, is the inspired, infallible, and authoritative Word of God. As such, we submit to it as the standard for our conduct.

2. We believe in one God, eternally existent in three persons: Father, Son, and Holy Spirit, who pre-existed all He created, and is Creator of all that exists.

3. We believe in the deity of our Lord Jesus Christ, in His virgin birth, sinless life, miracles, vicarious death as the atonement through His shed blood for all sin, His bodily resurrection and ascension to the right hand of the Father, His life in the present as sovereign Lord, and His imminent personal return in power and glory.

4. We believe humanity was made in the Image of God and that all humans lost relationship with God through sin.

5. We believe that faith in Jesus Christ as Savior and Lord provides the only grounds for forgiveness, justification, and salvation of lost and sinful human beings.

6. We believe in the Holy Spirit, and that His regenerating ministry empowers believers to live godly lives, extend mercy and agape love, and participate in God's mission to save the world.

7. We believe in the forgiveness of sins, the resurrection of the body, and life eternal with God our Father.

8. We believe in the spiritual unity of the Church, which is the Body of Christ, composed of all who are regenerated through faith in the Lord Jesus Christ.

9. We believe in the reality of heaven, hell, and Satan, the enemy of God and all that is His, which makes urgent Christ's command to reach the entire world with the Gospel. (medicalambassadors.org, "Statement of Faith")

In addition, the organization subscribes to the Lausanne Covenant, and the board and staff affirm statements made by the World Evangelical Alliance.

Core Practices

CHE's philosophy includes empowering people to do things for themselves, reaching the whole person, equipping leaders, developing community ownership, and using preventive measures instead of curative ones (medicalambassadors.org, "The CHE Philosophy").

Finances

According to the Evangelical Council for Financial Accountability, in 2013 MAI reported total revenue of $3,209,685 and total expenses of $2,799,172.

Website

http://www.medicalambassadors.org/

Bibliography

"Medical Ambassadors International." http://www.medical ambassadors.org. "Attend a Training," "The CHE Philosophy," and "Statement of Faith."

Phuc Luu

Ministries in Action

History

To mobilize Christian laity, Rev. Terry Gyger and David Cauwels founded Ministries in Action (MIA) in 1961. Operating in the Caribbean and North America, MIA relocated to

Miami, Florida, in 1967 and began evangelism training, small group studies, fellowship and discipleship ministry, and leadership training. MIA expanded into Haiti, Jamaica, and the Grenadines. In 1979, MIA began Project Ebenezer, through which local churches minister by developing free enterprise projects in their areas. MIA began offering seminary education in 1976 and doctoral-level study in 1979. The organization published the *MIA Handbook for Church Growth* in 1983, containing MIA's church growth and evangelism strategies. MIA continues to model holistic ministry through local churches in the Caribbean, North America, and Latin America.

Headquarters

PO Box 571357
Miami, FL 33257
Telephone: 305-234-7855
Fax: 305-234-7825

Leadership

MIA was originally co-led by Terry Gyger and David Cauwels. Rev. E. Walford Thompson joined MIA leadership in 1968 and became its president in 1977. Thompson has remained president emeritus since his retirement in 2009. MIA is currently led by Rev. Steve McGee. Barry Smith directs theological education.

Core Beliefs

The MIA statement of faith affirms traditional, conservative, evangelical beliefs, including biblical inerrancy. MIA also believes the church should demonstrate truth, holiness, and missions. All Christians hold responsibility for evangelism, personal holiness, and church unity. The church must be engaged in missions around the world, which is an act of service.

Core Practices

MIA's three primary ministries are strategizing for evangelism, theological training, and Project Ebenezer.

Statistics

As of 2012, MIA had thirty-two personnel working in Florida, the Dominican Republic, Grand Cayman, Brazil, Colombia, Grenada, Haiti, Jamaica, St. Vincent, and the Grenadines.

More than seven hundred local churches participate in MIA education and evangelism programs in English, French, and Creole.

Missionary and Evangelistic Work

MIA evangelizes through small groups, theological training, economic development, social relief, and medical care. MIA partners with local church leaders for training in direct evangelism, public witness, small group leadership, and discipleship.

Academic Institutions

Since 1976, MIA has offered seminary training for local pastors through IONA Centers for Theological Training. IONA schools offer a three-year curriculum in Bible, theology, and ministry, and students may work toward a certificate or diploma. IONA schools operate in Mexico, Brazil, Bolivia, Colombia, St. Vincent, the Grenadines, and Martinique in English, French, Spanish, and Portuguese. IONA graduates may enter the bachelor program at Miami International Seminary, led by MIA missionary Barry Smith.

Electronic Media

MIA president Steve McGee publishes a monthly blog, available through the MIA website. Videos of MIA's relief work are also available through their website. Various MIA personnel contribute to an MIA blog available at http://mianews.wordpress.com.

Publication

MIA publishes a bimonthly newsletter, available through the mail or on the MIA website.

Website

https://ministriesinaction.wordpress.com

Courtney Lyons

Mission Aviation Fellowship

History

Three situations occurred during World War II that produced a new opportunity for missions: international experience for the first time for many young American men and women, increased airplane technology, and an increase in the number of pilots (necessary during the war). These situations combined to produce Christian mission aviation agencies. In 1943, with the end of the war still a year and a half away, three pilots began meeting for Bible study. They realized that their new skill as pilots could serve missionaries in foreign countries in a manner not yet practiced. Therefore, on May 20, 1945, they launched a new mission organization, the Christian Airmen's Missionary Fellowship. The next year, on February 14, 1946, they purchased the first plane of the new group: a 1933 plane with a new engine. About a week later the first flight was made by Betty Greene, a member who had belonged to the Women's Air Force Service Pilots. She flew two missionaries from Wycliffe Bible Translators to a remote jungle location in Mexico. In 1947, the group changed its name to Mission Aviation Fellowship (MAF).

On January 3, 1956, MAF pilot Nate Saint and a small group of missionaries attempted to contact the Auca people, an Ecuadorian tribe known for being violent. Five days later they were martyred by members of the tribe. Eventually, many in the tribe became Christians, including seven of the nine original murderers. Saint is a central figure in the identity of MAF; his plane is on display at the MAF headquarters.

Headquarters

112 N Pilatus Lane
Nampa, ID 83687
Telephone: 208-498-0800

Defining Statement

"Sharing the love of Jesus Christ through aviation and technology so that isolated people may be physically and spiritually transformed" (maf.org, "MAF Mission").

Core Practices

While it began as an aviation support ministry, MAF has branched out to include communications, learning technology, and disaster relief. For example, MAF missionaries perform such diverse tasks as installing satellite communication systems; digging wells; operating computer centers; providing air ambulance services; ferrying missionaries, doctors, and humanitarian group workers; transporting supplies and medicine; and showing the Jesus film. Due to its unique aviation component, MAF operates in areas that would otherwise not be able to receive these services.

In the many areas of the world where electricity and local cell phone service is limited, MAF supplies and provides training for HF (high frequency) and VHF (very high frequency) radios and VSAT (high-speed internet connections via broadband satellite) cell phone service.

MAF-Learning Technologies provides distance learning tools and technology, helps establish training centers, provides consulting services, and helps produce digital Bible courses and resource materials. These include making digitized books, audio, and videos and helping produce websites. Over one hundred thousand biblical resources have been produced.

Statistics

MAF has served over 1,000 Christian and humanitarian organizations by transporting people and supplies; has a fleet of 58 aircraft (planes and helicopters); has approximately 200 missionary families who work as pilots, mechanics, communication techs, learning technology experts, support, and administrators; and serves in 42 countries in Africa, Asia, Eurasia, and Latin America. In 2009, the MAF fleet executed 34,436 flights, logged some 3 million miles, transported 104,787 passengers, and delivered 9.4 million pounds of cargo.

Affiliations

MAF in the United States is more properly known as MAF-US. It has an alliance partnership with an international body known as MAF International (MAF-I). MAF-I was established on September 2, 2006, when MAF agencies from Europe, Australia, Canada, New Zealand, and South America united to form the larger agency. While MAF-US is not a member, it participates with MAF-I in areas of mutual agreement, and vice versa.

Website

http://www.maf.org/

Bibliography

Buss, Dietrich G., and Arthur F. Glasser. *Giving Wings to the Gospel: The Remarkable Story of Mission Aviation Fellowship.* Grand Rapids: Baker, 1995.

King, Stuart S. *Hope Has Wings: The Mission Aviation Fellowship Story.* Grand Rapids: Zondervan, 1993.

"Mission Aviation Fellowship." http://www.maf.org. "MAF Mission."

Mark Nickens

Mission Generation

History

Mission Generation (MG) seeks to train students, teachers, and parents in biblical principles using textbooks. Its parent organization is Shield of Faith, founded in 1990 by Rocky and Joske Malloy, both ordained ministers who had done notable work in Honduras and

Nicaragua before founding a church in Bolivia in 1996. In 1999, Rocky was in the central park of Santa Cruz, Bolivia, when he noticed a newspaper headline about the cancellation of religion classes in school because of the scarcity of teachers. (Bolivia is officially Catholic and normally offers religious instruction in public schools.) Rocky urged his Bible school students to serve as religion teachers, and the local school superintendent authorized a pilot project that was launched that year in three schools with forty-four students. The Bolivian Senate licensed the Shield of Faith organization to produce curricula and to train teachers and parent groups.

By 2003, the project had been given access to every school in the country by executive order of the Bolivian government; its name evolved from the School Project to the Moral Orientation Project and finally to Kid FAITH in 2003. When the project was renamed Mission Generation in 2007, it was serving a quarter million students in over one thousand schools with help from more than fifteen thousand parents and teachers. It is now the largest ministry in Bolivia.

Headquarters

PO Box 327
Texas City, TX 77592
Telephone: 409-948-2633
Fax: 409-766-7955
Email: rmalloy@missiongeneration.org; jmalloy @missiongeneration.org; kdickson@mission generation.org

Shield of Faith has administrative offices in the Netherlands and Bolivia in addition to the United States.

Leadership

President and CEO: Rocky Malloy
Vice president: David Copeland
Secretary/treasurer: Kyle Dickson

Mission Generation currently has a six-member board of directors. There is no compensation for anyone working for MG administratively.

Core Beliefs

"There is only one True and Living God made up of three persons: The Father, The Son, and The Holy Spirit. All are co-equal and co-eternal. (John 1:1–5, 10–14; Matthew 28:18–20)"

(missiongeneration.org, "FAQ: What Is Your Statement of Faith").

Defining Statement

"Mission Generation exists to produce a proactive generation with purpose, principles and values" (missiongeneration.org, "Mission").

Core Practices

MG sees the network of public and private schools as a tool for fulfilling the Great Commission. Its specific strategies include utilizing government-approved textbooks to deliver the gospel and thereby reduce social ills such as teen pregnancy, drug use, truancy, and gang participation—there are thirteen colorful and captivating textbooks, K–12, using biblical principles (love, creation, purpose, work, harvest, government, marriage) to teach health, environment, economy, sexuality, gender roles, math, language, life science, nature science, and ethics; at the request of governments, holding conferences in schools—even ones not currently using the group's textbooks—on various subjects (economics, marriage, relationships, morality, self-esteem, democracy, conservation, health) and giving participants the opportunity to pray; and staging dramas that convey the gospel message.

MG requires its program beneficiaries to reciprocate in some way, believing this preserves their dignity and initiative.

Finances

Total revenue for 2013: $880,986
Total expenses for 2013: $805,919
Net assets for 2013: $179,833

Mission Generation, formally Shield of Faith Ministries Inc., is a Texas nonprofit corporation and a qualified charitable organization under section 501(c)(3) of the Internal Revenue Code. Shield of Faith is a member of the Evangelical Council for Financial Accountability.

Trends

MG's goals include one conversion for every textbook distributed, a textbook in the hands of ten million students by 2016, a continued reduction of social ills, and humanitarian aid for at-risk children. Textbooks are currently in Spanish, and there are plans to translate the books into English, Portuguese, French, and Dutch.

Website

http://www.missiongeneration.org/

Bibliography

"Mission Generation." http://www.missiongeneration.org. "FAQ: What Is Your Statement of Faith" and "Mission."

Michael McMullen

Mission Possible

History

Mission Possible (MP) was founded by Jack Snyder, who was moved by the plight of the people of Haiti while on a trip there in 1969 with his mentor, James McKeegan. Jack and Bettie Snyder raised money to build churches before creating Mission Possible in April 1979 and Mission Possible Canada the following year. In addition to MP's first school in Montrouis, Haiti, five additional schools were built. MP started work in the Dominican Republic in 1988, which led to the formation of the Ebenezer Educational Center at Batey Central in Barahona in 1992; initially only for kindergarten through third grade, the school now teaches high school students. The emphases of Mission Possible in recent years have been to develop national leaders in Haiti and the Dominican Republic, to improve the spiritual training ministry (five churches, Bible school, and discipleship classes), to improve programs in the six schools it runs, and to upgrade facilities. Mission Possible's child sponsorship program gives practical assistance. In the Dominican Republic, MP works with local churches to further their goals.

Headquarters

PO Box 1026
124 W Front Street
Findlay, OH 45839
Telephone: 419-422-3364
Fax: 419-422-3342

Leadership

President and CEO: Kurt Bishop

Core Beliefs

The ministry offers the following as its statement of faith:

We believe that there is one God, eternally existent in three persons: Father, Son and Holy Spirit.

We believe the Bible to be the inspired, the only infallible, authoritative Word of God.

We believe by His word and for His glory, God freely created everything. He made man and woman in his own image and they sinned against God and apart from grace, are incapable of returning to the right relationship with God.

We believe in the deity of our Lord Jesus Christ, in His virgin birth, in His sinless life, in His miracles, in His vicarious and atoning death through His shed blood, in His bodily resurrection, in His ascension to the right hand of the Father, and in His personal return in power and glory.

We believe Jesus Christ is the only mediator between God and humankind and by His death and resurrection, the penalty of human sin can be removed and we can be reconciled to God.

We believe the Holy Spirit is the divine agent of sanctification. By the ministry of the Holy Spirit, people are enabled to know God's grace, experience God's love in Christ, and live a Christ-centered life.

We believe in the resurrection of both the saved and the lost; they that are saved unto eternal life with God and they that are lost unto eternal separation from God.

We believe in the spiritual unity of believers in our Lord Jesus Christ, with equality across racial, gender, and class difference. (ourmissionispossible.org, "Statement of Faith")

Defining Statement

"Equipping the next generation of Christ-centered leaders" (ourmissionispossible.org, "Biblical Basis").

Core Practices

MP runs schools with over twenty-six hundred students in Haiti and the Dominican Republic, serves nutritious meals in its school feeding programs, runs a Bible school to teach pastors and lay leaders to minister effectively, runs disaster relief efforts, sends mission outreach teams to youth and adults in Haiti and the Dominican Republic, runs a vocational school for young adults to learn a trade, and runs a school nurse program to attend to the physical needs of students.

Finances

Total revenue for 2014: $1,272,449
Total expenses for 2014: $1,196,482
Net assets for 2014: $1,579,615

A member of the Evangelical Council for Financial Accountability, Mission Possible has earned an A rating from Ministry Watch. It is a nonprofit, and contributions to it are fully tax deductible.

Website

http://www.ourmissionispossible.org/

Bibliography

"Mission Possible." http://www.ourmissionispossible.org. "Biblical Basis" and "Statement of Faith."

Michael McMullen

National Association of Evangelicals

History

The National Association of Evangelicals (NAE) began in April 1942 when 147 evangelical leaders met to try to create a way to restructure evangelicalism in America. At that time, there were numerous independent ministries; however, rather than being in unity, they were in competition. At that first meeting in 1942, a constitution for the possible association was drafted. In 1943, at a constitutional convention, the constitution of the National Association of Evangelicals was confirmed by over one thousand pastors. J. Elwin Wright served as its first president.

During the 1940s, the NAE witnessed significant growth in the formulation of offshoot organizations and in media influence. In the 1950s, membership and governmental influence increased. President Eisenhower welcomed a delegation from the NAE to the White House, and *Life* magazine did a story that indirectly mentioned the NAE's growing influence.

By the 1960s and 1970s, the NAE was experiencing hard times, due in part to the cultural unrest at that point in history. Membership was barely increasing, and the NAE leadership changed frequently. Stability returned, however, toward the end of the 1970s, and under consistent leadership, the organization began to grow and prosper. In the 1980s, political influence continued to grow, and President Ronald Reagan spoke at one of the NAE conventions. The 1990s saw a shift in political party, and although the political doors were open to the NAE, many times the NAE and the party in control had differing opinions. The turn of the century brought more leadership struggles to the NAE, but now it is persistently growing under the leadership of Leith Anderson. The NAE continues to be an important organization because it helps unite evangelical churches and denominations of the United States in purpose, belief, and voice.

Headquarters

PO Box 23269
Washington, DC 20026
Telephone: 202-789-1011
Fax: 202-842-0392

Leadership

Leith Anderson is the president. In addition to the executive committee, the NAE has a large board of directors made up of influential ministry leaders and pastors of all denominations from across the country.

Core Beliefs

The NAE's statement of faith covers the association's stand on the Bible, the Trinity, Jesus, salvation, the Holy Spirit, resurrection, and unity.

Defining Statement

"The mission of the National Association of Evangelicals is to honor God by connecting and representing evangelical Christians" (nae.net, "About NAE").

Core Practices

The NAE strives for denominational effectiveness in maintaining churches and ministries, and it represents its members in bringing evangelical worries and issues to the government. The NAE works through the Chaplains Commission to encourage approval of evangelicals as chaplains in three of the military branches, as well as in the Department of Veterans Affairs. Through World Relief, the NAE affects the lives of countless people who have been affected by poverty, disaster, hunger, and persecution.

Finances

The NAE is a member of the Evangelical Council for Financial Accountability.

Statistics

The NAE is comprised of Christians from 250 organizations and roughly 40 denominations. It represents approximately 45,000 churches and 30 million people.

Missionary and Evangelistic Work

The NAE works with several organizations that are evangelically like-minded. Each of the affiliated organizations focuses on a different area of need within the evangelical world. The organizations are the Association of Evangelical Relief and Development Organizations, the Evangelical Family and Child Agency, the Mission America Coalition, the Mission Exchange, the National Hispanic Christian Leadership Conference, and the National Network of Youth Ministries.

Parachurch Organizations

The NAE is connected with thousands of local churches throughout the United States. It has an office of government affairs that mobilizes people to work in the public or political sphere. The

NAE's Chaplains Commission assists chaplains connected with the military—whether currently enlisted or veterans. Also under the cover of the NAE is World Relief, a ministry that serves the most vulnerable, from refugees to people affected by natural disasters.

Publication

The NAE publishes a seasonal newsletter called *Insight*. It may be accessed online at nae.net.

Website

http://www.nae.net/

Gretchen Knurr

Navigators

History

Dawson Trotman began the ministry later named the Navigators in the 1930s when he started teaching discipleship principles to local high school students and Sunday school classes in his area. Encouraged by the results, Trotman began to teach his discipleship methods to sailors in the United States Navy in 1933, encouraging them to memorize Scripture, pray, and study the Bible. With these, Trotman also stressed spiritual multiplication—that each sailor teach and encourage one another in the same way. Trotman's high school students began to influence people more widely in California, and in 1943, the Navigators was incorporated. Shortly thereafter, the ministry sent its first overseas missionary to China in 1949 and later moved its headquarters in 1953 to the Glen Eyrie property in Colorado Springs. The conference center there now hosts the Navigators' national and international headquarters as the organization continues Trotman's vision of encouraging, training, and discipling individuals with this driving purpose: "To know Christ and to make Him known" (navigators.org, "Home"). Building on this vision, the Navigators created NavPress in 1975, a division of its ministry that publishes books congruent with the ministry. NavPress has become a leading evangelical publisher, particularly well known for Eugene Peterson's bestselling paraphrase of Scripture, the *Message*.

Headquarters

PO Box 6000
Colorado Springs, CO 80934
Telephone: 719-598-1212
Fax: 719-260-0479

Leadership

Leaders include the president of the Navigators and a board of directors.

Core Beliefs

The Navigators embraces conservative, evangelical doctrinal beliefs (see navigators.org, "Our Statement of Faith") and these core values:

1. The passion to know, love, and become like Jesus Christ.
2. The truth and sufficiency of the Scriptures for the whole of life.
3. The transforming power of the Gospel.
4. The leading and empowering of the Holy Spirit.
5. Expectant faith and persevering prayer rooted in the promises of God.
6. The dignity and value of every person.
7. Love and grace expressed among us in community.
8. Families and relational networks in discipling the nations.
9. Interdependent relationships in the Body of Christ in advancing the Gospel. (navigators.org, "Our Core Values")

Defining Statement

"To know Christ and to make Him known" (navigators.org, "Home").

Core Practices

The Navigators has created and continues to support several ministries that target people of different ages, cultures, races, and occupations. The ministries emphasize discipleship and personal growth in Christ with a specific audience in mind. NavPress, one of the Navigators' major ministries, publishes biblical resources. NavMissions supports Navigator missionaries in 107 countries. NavVida ministers specifically to Hispanic people. The African American Network, Asian American Ministries, and American Indian Discipleship Ministries minister to African American, Asian American, and American Indian populations, respectively. The Navigators' college ministry targets college students and has ministry locations on various college campuses throughout the United States. NavYouth is for teenagers. The Navigators' military ministry seeks to support military men and women as they follow Christ and serve in the military. The Prison Discipleship Ministry works with churches and other ministries to spread God's hope to incarcerated prisoners. The Navigators runs Eagle Lake Youth Camps, as well as other ministries.

Statistics

The Navigators employs over 4,000 staff and ministers in more than 100 countries and currently has 1,100 missionaries working in 107 countries. It has over 400 long-term staff members overseas, as well as 700 people of various ethnicities around the world. The Navigators' number of workers serving overseas places it in the top 10 percent of foreign mission agencies.

Missionary and Evangelistic Work

Evangelism is central to the Navigators' approach of discipling others. The Navigators encourages people to share Christ with someone who does not yet know him and then to teach and encourage the new Christian in an intimate, one-to-one relationship of growth and discipleship.

Publications

In 1975, the Navigators created NavPress, a division of the Navigators' ministry that publishes Christian materials that propagate the purpose of the Navigators and help people grow in their relationship with Christ. Some of the publisher's bestsellers include the *Message* by Eugene Peterson and *Abba's Child* by Brennan Manning. NavPress also published *Daws*, a book about the Navigators' founder, Dawson Trotman.

Website

http://www.navigators.org/

Bibliography

"Navigators." http://www.navigators.org. "Home," "Our Core Values," and "Our Statement of Faith."

Nicole A. Pride

New Tribes Mission

History

Paul William Fleming (1910–50), an American missionary in Malaysia, founded New Tribes Mission (NTM) in 1942 to reach the primitive tribes of the world with the gospel. Minimal training (or even its absence) was required for missionaries to proclaim the gospel to the "new tribes." Fleming had a tendency to believe the task of world evangelization was simple and that John 3:16 was sufficient for communicating the gospel. Today the mission has a fuller view of world evangelization.

The mission began with Fleming, Cecil Dye, Lance Latham, and three others to disciple believers, translate the Scriptures, and provide training to reach tribal peoples. Although the mission began with little money or support, it was able to send the first missionary group to Bolivia in November 1942 (five of those sent were killed the following year). The mission converted a vacant Chicago nightclub into its headquarters, but when the ministry expanded, the organization moved to Fouts Springs, California, in 1946. Because members served as firefighters, the Forest Service granted the mission use of the vacant Fouts Springs facilities from the Civilian Conservation Corps, which closed camp as a consequence of World War II.

The first aircraft purchased by the mission crashed into a Venezuelan mountaintop on June 9, 1950, due to bad weather, killing all fifteen people aboard. Departing from Chino, California, aboard the mission's new aircraft (with plans to conduct rallies across the United States en route to South America), Fleming was killed (with other missionaries) when the plane crashed over Mount Moran in Grand Teton National Park of western Wyoming as a consequence of bad weather on November 21, 1950. Fourteen members serving as volunteer firefighters were killed in the Rattlesnake Fire in Mendocino National Forest in 1953. The mission departed from Fouts Springs shortly after the Rattlesnake Fire and moved its headquarters to the vacant Forest Lake Hotel in Sanford, Florida.

Headquarters

1000 E 1st Street
Sanford, FL 32771
Telephone: 407-323-3430

Leadership

Chairman: Oli G. Jacobsen
International coordinator for church planting and evangelism: Trevor McIlwain

Core Beliefs

Missionaries are Protestants and affirm the inspiration, sufficiency, authority, and literal interpretation of Scripture. Fleming's interpretation of Matthew 24:14 ("This gospel of the kingdom shall be preached in the whole world as a testimony to all the nations, and then the end will come" [NASB]) led him to challenge fellow missionaries to covenant with one another to reach the last tribe with the gospel in their generation. New Tribes Mission believes the Bible is the story of a missionary God seeking worshipers of every kindred, tribe, and tongue. New Tribes Mission thoroughly rejects the teachings that Christians can be demon possessed, spirits create problems by possessing houses, and territorial spirits hinder gospel work.

Defining Statement

"Reaching tribes, transforming lives" (usa.ntm .org, "Home").

Core Practices

Missionaries work among unreached people groups in the context of the tribal culture and language. Scripture is communicated foundationally by means of logical and practical methodology (the "Chronological Teaching Approach"). Biblical truth is communicated cross-culturally by means of the literary form and sequence of historically progressive revelation as expounded in Scripture. As opposed to teaching the Bible topically or simply expounding the Gospels, missionaries teach the Old Testament sequence of historical events as a unified narrative that is essential preparation for understanding the manifestation of Christ in the New Testament. Other teaching methods are implemented once there is a panoramic understanding of God's plans and purposes for humanity. The fundamental truths of the Old Testament are communicated based on the emphasis and teaching of the Holy Spirit in the New Testament.

Worship

Worship is cross-cultural, with a focus on the Creator God, who is the Redeemer.

Statistics

New Tribes Mission is among the largest North American Protestant agencies, with more than three thousand missionaries among two hundred tribal groups in more than twenty-five countries. Churches are being planted among difficult-to-access people groups in nineteen countries worldwide.

Missionary and Evangelistic Work

New Tribes Mission has sending entities in Australia, Canada, England, the Faroe Islands, Germany, Italy, the Netherlands, Norway, Singapore, and the United States.

Missionaries serve in a variety of roles, such as administration, supply purchasing, training, and translation work. Many of the missionaries suffer violent deaths in their work with primitive tribes. Churches are being planted among unreached people groups in Africa, the Asia-Pacific region, and Latin America. As co-workers of church plants, local churches send missionary pilots for ministry through New Tribes Mission Aviation. Dun Gordy established Destination SUMMIT in 1980 as a short-term program of New Tribes Mission.

Academic Institutions

Founded in 1955, the New Tribes Bible Institute is a two-year program that provides a biblical foundation for missionary training. There are nearly four hundred students currently attending classes in Jackson, Michigan, and Waukesha, Wisconsin. The Missionary Training Center teaches church-planting and teaching skills, cross-cultural ministry, and language and linguistics. Other training programs are available in Australia, Brazil, Canada, England, Germany, and Mexico.

Parachurch Organizations

NTM Homes provides affordable, attractive, economical, and efficient housing for retired NTM personnel. There are three distinct levels of care for retired missionaries: assisted living facility, independent living duplexes, and the Latham Center (for those who can no longer manage in the larger duplex apartments).

Publications

Beginning publication in 1943, *Brown Gold* challenges Christians to treasure souls in brown bodies. *Building on Firm Foundations* helps missionaries to confirm and disciple believers in the Christian faith. *NTM@work* is the quarterly magazine of New Tribes Mission. Worldwide updates are provided through *Tribal Beat, Mission News,* and *Special Reports.* Prayer updates are provided through *Daily Bulletin* and *Weekly Digest.* Destination SUMMIT has produced a video documentary of ministry among the Taliabo people in Indonesia.

Website

https://usa.ntm.org/

Bibliography

Fleming, Paul. *Early History of the New Tribes Mission and Life and Work of Paul Fleming.* Sanford, FL: Brown Gold Publications, 1962.

Johnson, Jean Dye. *God Planted Five Seeds.* San Francisco: Harper & Row, 1966.

Johnston, Kenneth J. *The Story of New Tribes Mission.* Sanford, FL: New Tribes Mission, 1985.

Lewis, Norman. *The Missionaries.* London: Secker & Warburg, 1988.

McIlwain, Trevor. *Building on Firm Foundations.* 3 vols. Sanford, FL: New Tribes Mission, 1987–1988.

———. *Notes on the Chronological Approach to Evangelism and Church Planting.* Sanford, FL: New Tribes Mission, 1981.

McIlwain, Trevor, and Nancy Everson. *Firm Foundations: Creation to Christ.* Sanford, FL: New Tribes Mission, 1991.

Pittman, Dean Lewis. *Practical Linguistics.* Cleveland: Mid-Missions, 1948.

Ron J. Bigalke

North American Mission Board

History

In 1845, Southern Baptists separated from other Baptists in the United States and immediately established a Board of Domestic Missions. Beginning in 1874, the ministry carried the name Home Mission Board, and in 1997, the North American Mission Board (NAMB) assumed responsibility for Southern Baptist mission efforts in both the United States and Canada.

Headquarters

4200 North Point Parkway
Alpharetta, GA 30022
Telephone: 770-410-6000
Fax: 770-410-6082

Leadership

The president of the North American Mission Board heads the senior leadership team, including vice presidents of the following six groups: associational strategies, church planting, evangelization, mission support, partnership missions and mobilization, and sending missionaries. Implementing specific tasks assigned to the groups are teams comprised of team leaders and their subordinate and support staff.

Core Practices

"The North American Mission Board exists to work with churches, associations, and state conventions in mobilizing Southern Baptists as a missional force to impact North America with the gospel of Jesus Christ through evangelism and church planting" (namb.net, "About NAMB"). Accordingly, three primary emphases are sharing Christ, starting churches, and sending missionaries and chaplains. These categories of action embrace a wide array of ministries, including disaster relief, hunger relief, and specialized outreach to diverse people groups, such as members of the military, college students, internationals, refugees, truck drivers, and the deaf.

Finances

Approximately 23 percent of the Southern Baptist Convention's budget and 100 percent of the denomination's Annie Armstrong Easter Offering finance the work of the NAMB. Many Southern Baptist domestic missionary personnel receive funding from both state-level Baptist conventions and the NAMB, which Southern Baptist churches have supported since 1925 through a giving structure known as the Cooperative Program. The 2010 NAMB budget was $126 million.

Missionary and Evangelistic Work

Approximately 5,300 missionaries and 2,500 endorsed chaplains partner with 450,000 mission volunteers drawn from Southern Baptist churches. All missionaries and chaplains must agree with the current edition of the Baptist Faith and Message confession.

The North American Mission Board Apologetics and Interfaith Evangelism Team "seeks to convey factual and reliable information about American and World religions and the truth of Christianity, and to equip Southern Baptists to be effective witnesses of the gospel to all people" (4Truth.net, "About Us").

Publication

On Mission

Electronic Media

As an extension of its magazine, *On Mission*, the NAMB produces a half-hour magazine format program called *On Mission Xtra* carried by the FamilyNet cable television network.

Website

http://www.namb.net/

Bibliography

Baker, Robert A. *The Southern Baptist Convention and Its People, 1607–1972.* Nashville: Broadman, 1974.

Caylor, John. "Home Mission Board of the Southern Baptist Convention." In *Encyclopedia of Southern Baptists,* 1:635–46. Nashville: Broadman, 1958.

Lawrence, John Benjamin. *History of the Home Mission Board.* Nashville: Broadman, 1958.

"North American Mission Board." http://www.namb.net. "About NAMB."

Rutledge, Arthur B., and William G. Tanner. *Mission to America: A History of Southern Baptist Home Missions.* 2nd rev. ed. Nashville: Broadman, 1983.

Scott N. Callaham

Northern Canada Evangelical Mission

History

The Northern Canada Evangelical Mission, an interdenominational faith organization bringing the gospel of Jesus Christ to the native peoples of Canada, was organized in 1946 when a group of like-minded missionaries met in Meadow Lake, Saskatchewan, and decided to join forces. These first missionaries included Stan Collie, whose calling to the mission field came after a meeting with Isaac Reine, a missionary assigned to Africa. Reine had traveled to the northern territories in 1936 and had witnessed the striking spiritual need of Canada's indigenous peoples. Reine so inspired Collie that in 1939 he sold his ranch, "loaded his family and belongings into a covered wagon pulled by four horses, and headed north. When the bush trail they traveled on came to an end, they traded the horses for a scow and sailed up Deep River to Buffalo Narrows, where they settled." After a rugged first winter, with no church behind them or any regular financial support, it was touch and go for this first missionary family. But their love for Christ and a "growing awareness of the tremendous need in the North kept their faith strong" (ncem.ca, "About Us: Our History").

In 1944, Arthur and Martha Tarry left a Saskatchewan pastorate to join the Collies in Buffalo Narrows. These missionaries' work was first associated with the Canadian Sunday School Mission (CSSM). A realization grew that their ministry to Indian people could best be performed under a separate organization. Thus, the missionaries were led, in mutual agreement with the CSSM, to establish the Northern Canada Evangelical Mission (NCEM), which would be "particularly devoted to reaching Canada's northern native people." It began with nine charter members and three mission stations. "The Mission functioned with its headquarters in the isolated village of Buffalo Narrows. An office building was constructed, and a printing press was acquired. Soon a language school was initiated for candidates applying for missionary service." By 1956, there were 80 workers in 30 stations. Currently, the NCEM has a membership of about 140 full-time missionaries (plus associate, honorary, and governing board members) in about 40 stations across the country and in specialized ministries (ncem.ca, "About Us: Our History").

With a goal to make disciples of Jesus Christ and establish indigenous churches that will propagate the gospel in their own communities and beyond, the NCEM faces the challenge of evangelizing still unreached areas, discipling native believers, and training church leaders.

Headquarters

PO Box 3030
Prince Albert, SK S6V 7V4
Canada
Telephone: 306-764-3388
Fax: 306-764-3390
Email: ncem@ncem.ca

Core Beliefs

The following is the doctrinal statement contained in the constitution of the Northern Canada Evangelical Mission:

(1) We believe that the Scriptures of the Old and New Testament are verbally inspired by God and inerrant in the original writing, and that they are of supreme and final authority in faith and life. . . .

(3) We believe in One God eternally existing in the three persons of Father, Son and Holy Spirit. . . .

(4) We believe that man was created in the image of God, that he sinned and thereby incurred not only physical death, but also spiritual death, which is separation from God; and that all human beings are born with a sinful nature, thus being sinners in thought, word and deed.

(5) We believe that Satan exists. . . .

(6) We believe that the Lord Jesus Christ died for our sins, according to the Scriptures, as a representative and substitutionary sacrifice; and that all who believe in Him are justified on the ground of His shed blood.

(7) We believe in the resurrection of the crucified body of our Lord, in His bodily ascension into Heaven, and in His present life there for us as High Priest and Advocate.

(8) We believe in the "Blessed Hope"—the personal, premillennial and imminent return of our Lord and Saviour Jesus Christ.

(9) We believe that all who accept by faith the Lord Jesus Christ are born again of the Holy Spirit and so become children of God.

(10) We believe in the present ministry of the Holy Spirit, by whose indwelling the Christian is enabled to live a godly life and bear fruit which will remain.

(11) We believe in the bodily resurrection of both the just and the unjust—the just to everlasting bliss and the unjust to everlasting punishment. (ncem .ca, "About Us: Our Statement of Faith")

Defining Statement

"NCEM exists to fulfill the Great Commission of Jesus Christ among and in partnership with the Aboriginal Peoples of Canada and related people groups" (ncem.ca; "About Us: Our Mandate and Vision").

Core Practices

To carry on a regular program of evangelism among Aboriginal Peoples of Canada.

To disciple and teach believers towards maturity in Christ.

To engage in translation and literacy work in order to provide Scriptures and related materials in the Aboriginal languages.

To use media and technology in the accomplishment of the above goals.

To encourage, support and work together with evangelical Aboriginal believers, churches and organizations.

To cooperate with other evangelicals ministering among Aboriginal Peoples.

To assist non-Aboriginal churches with outreach to the Aboriginal community.

To co-operate with "tentmakers" and Christian professionals in ministry to and with the Aboriginal community. (ncem.ca, "About Us: Our Mandate and Vision")

Missionary and Evangelistic Work

The NCEM seeks to do the following:

to provide leadership, training, counseling and care to enable NCEM staff to minister effectively in a cross-cultural environment.

To make language training available for missionaries.

To encourage and provide opportunity for Mission members to receive training to become effective leaders within NCEM. (ncem.ca, "About Us: Our Mandate and Vision")

The goals of its outreach are:

To present the ministry and needs of NCEM to the Body of Christ.

To promote increased understanding, love and acceptance for Aboriginal peoples in the Body of Christ. (ncem.ca, "About Us: Our Mandate and Vision")

The NCEM's ministries include the following:

Communication: "The mission's print shop produces full-color materials for ministry use. In the 1950s NCEM began conveying the gospel in Indian languages by radio to isolated communities and trap-lines. Though radio is still being used, NCEM now produces the weekly television program *Tribal Trails*, broadcast throughout Canada and in Alaska by satellite" (ncem.ca, "Ministries: Tribal Trails").

Bible education: "Training for Native Christians has always been a priority. From the first schools in Manitoba and Saskatchewan . . . the mission now operates the Key-Way-Tin Bible Institute in Lac La Biche, Alberta" (ncem.ca, "Ministries: Bible Schools").

Summer missions: "'Short-term' programs, once unheard of in Christian missions, have been used effectively on First Nations fields. In the early 1970s the NCEM Missionary Training Course (NMTC) was begun. . . . Since then many 'trainees' have been exposed to cross-cultural ministry, and numerous native communities have been touched with the gospel" (http://www.ncem.ca/then-now).

Bible camps: "Bible camps have proven to be an effective outreach over the years. Hundreds of native young people now attend Bible camp each summer in several locations across the country. Many family camps are also held. NCEM also runs wilderness camps, taking First Nations teens backpacking or canoe tripping, and sharing the gospel of Jesus Christ with them" (ncem.ca, "Ministries: Bible Camps").

Diverse fields: "By 1957 NCEM's fields no longer included just 'The North.' Ministry began that year among the Mi'kmaq and Malecite Indians of Canada's Maritime region. And by the end of the 1980s, outreach had been established in ten urban centers" (http://www.ncem.ca/then-now).

Publication

Northern Lights, a sixteen-page digest-size newsletter, mailed at no charge four times each year, is available from the headquarters.

Website

http://www.ncem.ca/

Bibliography

"Northern Canada Evangelical Mission." http://www.ncem.ca. "Serve," "News Stories," "Ministries," and "About Us."

Barbara Wyman

OC Ministries

History

OC Ministries is a nonprofit mission of the United Methodist Church in Minnesota. It ministers to children in developing countries through four agencies: Operation Classroom, Operation Clinic, Operation Church, and Operation Connection.

Founded in 1989 for the purpose of rebuilding UMC-related schools in Liberia and Sierra Leone, Operation Classroom added Jamaica as a field of operations in 1992. In 2000, Operation Classroom became OC Ministries, as a result of partnerships with clinics and churches, and today is regarded as the Advance Special Mission of the Minnesota United Methodist Annual Conference.

Headquarters

122 W Franklin Avenue
Suite 400
Minneapolis, MN 55404
Telephone: 612-870-0058
Email: jkzabel@aol.com

Core Practices

Operation Classroom sends funds and workers abroad to construct new schools, improve existing schools, and provide school supplies and uniforms. Operation Clinic provides medical supplies and texts to clinics abroad and sends medical teams to Sierra Leone several times a year to deliver health care. Operation Church sends Bibles and church supplies to churches overseas. Operation Connection seeks to connect students in Sierra Leone with sponsors who typically donate $150 a year to cover a student's educational expenses.

Finances

OC Ministries is a 501(c)(3) organization. All gifts are tax deductible.

Website

http://www.ocministries.com/

Michael McMullen

OMF International

History

OMF International was originally founded in Great Britain as the China Inland Mission (CIM) by Hudson Taylor (1832–1905) in 1856. The Boxer Rebellion of 1900 targeted Christian missionaries and foreigners; the China Inland Mission lost fifty-eight adults and twenty-one children. Hudson Taylor refused any reparations for the losses to demonstrate the meekness and gentleness of Christ. These events spurred missionary activity. Taylor died in 1905 in Changsha, Hunan Province.

By 1910, over six hundred churches had been established in the interior of China by CIM. Notable CIM missionaries who followed were Jim Fraser (1910); William Borden, who died in training in 1912; and John and Betty Stam, who were executed in 1934. When Christian missionaries were expelled from China in the 1950s, the mission redirected its workers to other parts of East Asia.

The name was changed to Overseas Missionary Fellowship in 1964 and to OMF International in the 1990s. With headquarters in Singapore, OMF began to reach Hong Kong, Japan, the Philippines, Malaysia, Indonesia, Thailand, Cambodia, Vietnam, and Laos. James Hudson Taylor III became general director of OMF in 1980, and in 2005, a Chinese Christian, Patrick Fung, took the position.

Today OMF has over sixteen hundred workers in sixteen countries, including Singapore and Taiwan. OMF missionaries come from thirty countries, making it a multiethnic fellowship. OMF has sending centers in over twenty countries, including Australia, Canada, New Zealand, Singapore, the United Kingdom, the United States, Germany, the Netherlands, Hong Kong, and the Philippines. The OMF-US team consists of over three hundred workers. A characteristic of Hudson Taylor still used by OMF is depending on God to meet needs by focusing on prayer.

Headquarters

10 W Dry Creek Circle
Littleton, CO 80120
Telephone: 303-730-4160; 800-422-5330
Fax: 303-730-4165

Leadership

Dr. Neil O. Thompson is the president and national director of OMF-US. The US board of trustees has ten members who are business leaders, pastors, and mission administrators.

Core Beliefs

Here is a summary of OMF's beliefs (the complete statement can be found at omf.org, "What We Believe"):

God is a Trinity, Father, Son, and Holy Spirit, who is holy, sovereign, creating, and redeeming.

The Bible is divinely inspired, entirely trustworthy, infallible, and of supreme authority in its teaching on all matters of faith and conduct and is normative in its values for all peoples, for all times, and in all places.

All people were created in God's image but are now condemned sinners in need of redemption.

Jesus Christ is the virgin-born, sinless Savior of the world who died a sacrificial death for all mankind, rose again, and ascended back to heaven.

Justification of sinners is by God's grace through faith in Jesus Christ alone.

The Holy Spirit convicts, regenerates, sanctifies, revives, guides, and empowers his church.

The one universal church experiences the unity and priesthood of believers.

Christ will visibly and personally return "in power and great glory" to judge the living and the dead.

Man's only two destinies are eternal life in the presence of God or eternal separation from God for those who have rejected him.

Core Practices

OMF exists to glorify God in urgently reaching the billions in East Asia with the gospel of Jesus Christ. OMF aims to see indigenous, biblical church-planting movements in each people group and for them to evangelize their own people and reach out in mission to others. To that end, willing, skillful workers are sent to various countries across Asia to live and work in a variety of capacities.

Finances

OMF has been a member of the Evangelical Council for Financial Accountability since May 19, 2006.

Total revenue for 2014: $16,496,153
Total expenses for 2014: $16,383,005
Net assets for 2014: $10,634,393

Statistics

OMF has more than sixteen hundred missionaries working in sixteen East Asian countries, including Brunei, Cambodia, China, Indonesia, Laos, Macau, Mongolia, the Philippines, Singapore, Taiwan, Thailand, and Vietnam.

Missionary and Evangelistic Work

In 2006, OMF asked God for 900 additional workers and by 2010 had 449. OMF still prays for the remaining workers. OMF works in Bible translation, evangelism, church planting, radio, Bible teaching, leadership training, and children/youth and student ministries. A magazine, *East Asia's Billions*, is published by OMF, as are several newsletters.

Website

http://www.omf.org/

Bibliography

Clayton, Gary. "James Hudson Taylor (1832–1905)." *East Asia's Billions*. https://omf.org/us/james-hudson-taylor-1832-1905/.

Taylor, James Hudson, III. *Christ Alone: A Pictorial Presentation of Hudson Taylor's Life and Legacy*. Hong Kong: OMF Books, 2005.

James A. Borland

One Mission Society (formerly OMS International)

History

Influenced by the challenge of Christian and Missionary Alliance founder A. B. Simpson, Charles and Lettie Cowman went to Tokyo, Japan, in 1901 as independent missionaries. The following year Ernest and Julia Kilbourne joined them. In 1908, Juji Nakada, a former student of Moody Bible Institute, was named president of the Cowman-Kilbourne mission. Two years later they renamed the mission and officially incorporated it as the Oriental Mission Society (OMS). Through the years the work of the mission expanded, first into Korea and China and later globally. In 1973, the society officially changed its name to OMS International. In January 2010, under the leadership of David Long, OMS took a new name: One Mission Society.

Headquarters

941 Fry Road
PO Box A
Greenwood, IN 46142
Telephone: 317-888-3333
Email: info@onemissionsociety.org

Leadership

One Mission Society has had nine presidents throughout its history: Charles Cowman (1911), Ernest Kilbourne (1924), Lettie Burd Cowman (1928), Eugene Erny (1949), Wesley Deuwel (1969), Everett Hunt (1982), Ed Erny (1986), J. B. Crouse Jr. (1992), and David Long (2004).

Core Beliefs

One Mission Society is evangelical in doctrine. One distinctive belief, which it retained from its Wesleyan background in the Methodist Episcopal Church and its connections with the Christian and Missionary Alliance, is a second work of grace in sanctification.

Defining Statement

"By God's grace, One Mission Society unites, inspires and equips Christians to make disciples of Jesus Christ, multiplying dynamic communities of believers around the world" (onemissionsociety.org, "Our One Mission").

Core Practices

Intentional evangelism—leading people to commit their lives "to a life-changing relationship with Jesus."

Planting churches—encouraging, empowering, and supporting new believers in Christ "to form vital, thriving and life-changing churches."

Training national leaders—training leaders in both formal and informal Bible schools and seminaries worldwide so that "the future leaders of the national churches will be from within that country."

Forming strategic partnerships—coming alongside other mission agencies, ministries, and churches in the countries it serves to show the world that Christians can work together to help spread the gospel. (onemissionsociety.org, "Our One Calling")

Missionary and Evangelistic Work

One Mission Society initiated a campaign from 1911 to 1917 called the Every Creature Crusade to reach every home in Japan with the gospel. Over the years the ministry refined its approach and renamed the ministry Every Community for Christ. The approach is for local believers to reach local inhabitants. By doing so, they present the gospel as local rather than foreign.

Electronic Media

https://onemissionsociety.org/blog/

Publication

OMS Outreach

Website

https://onemissionsociety.org/

Bibliography

Cowman, Mrs. Charles. *Charles Cowman: Missionary Warrior.* Los Angeles: Oriental Missionary Society, 1928.

———. *Streams in the Desert.* Los Angeles: Oriental Missionary Society, 1925.

Hunt, Everett N., Jr. "Cowman, Charles Elmer and Lettie (Burd)." In *Biographical Dictionary of Christian Missions,* edited by Gerald H. Anderson, 156. New York: Macmillan, 1998.

"One Mission Society." https://onemissionsociety.org. "Our One Calling" and "Our One Mission."

Tucker, Ruth. *From Jerusalem to Irian Jaya.* 2nd ed. Grand Rapids: Zondervan, 2004.

Douglas K. Wilson Jr.

Open Doors

History

Open Doors was founded by Brother Andrew in 1955. After being wounded in the course of his service in the Dutch military in Indonesia, he was inspired by the Christian love exemplified by the Franciscan sisters who cared for him in the hospital and started reading the Bible. He returned to Holland and had a conversion experience in 1950 and five years later began smuggling Bibles into communist countries in Eastern Europe. In 1956, he made the first of many "Beetle Drives," in which he traveled to the Soviet Union in a blue Volkswagen Beetle, and for the next two decades, Open Doors expanded its presence behind the Iron Curtain.

Work in the Middle East began in 1978, and in 1981, one million Bibles were delivered to a Chinese beach in a single night in Project Pearl, hailed by *Time* magazine as a "bold expedition." Project Crossfire distributed five million pieces of literature to Latin America in 1985, and 1989 saw the fruit of a seven-year prayer campaign for the communist bloc countries with the fall of the Berlin Wall and the delivery of one million New Testaments to Russia.

In 1992, other large-scale projects distributed Bibles in China and to children in remote parts of the former Soviet Union. Other notable events in the 1990s were the presentation of the first Albanian-language full Bible to the president of Albania (which at one time had described itself as the world's first atheistic state); the printing of a Chinese children's Bible storybook and an Agape study Bible in Latin America; Operation Daily Bread, providing humanitarian aid to southern Sudan; and the delivery of two million Bibles and study materials to Chinese Christians. A seven-year prayer campaign for China was launched in 2002 in anticipation of the 2008 Olympics there. Open Doors continues to seek out opportunities in countries with tyrannical regimes that have shut out or driven out many other ministries.

Using only his first name to preserve anonymity and to stress his brotherhood with all believers, Brother Andrew published a biography, *God's Smuggler,* in 1967. It became one of the bestselling books in the history of Christian literature. An ordained minister (but not a pastor) of a large evangelical denomination, he was the recipient of the World Evangelical Fellowship's Religious Liberty Award in 1997.

Headquarters

PO Box 27001
Santa Ana, CA 92799
Telephone: 949-752-6600; 888-5-BIBLE-5 (888-524-2535)
Fax: 949-752-6442
Email: usa@opendoors.org

Leadership

President and CEO: Carl Moeller

Core Beliefs

A statement of faith declares belief in the central elements of the gospel message, including Christ's virgin birth, his crucifixion and resurrection, the forgiveness of sins, everlasting life, and Christ's return to judge the world.

In defining its values, Open Doors states that it is part of the body of Christ and is "persecuted church driven," "devoted to Jesus Christ with His commission," and "motivated solely for the glory of God" (opendoors.org, "Our Values"). Its work is guided by faith, prayer, and the Bible.

Defining Statement

"Serving persecuted Christians and churches worldwide" (opendoors.org, "Home").

Core Practices

Core practices include distributing Bibles and literature to persecuted believers; training Christian leaders to minister to persecuted Christians; Christian community development, offering practical assistance to Christians who face job discrimination as a result of their faith; offering advocacy, a supportive presence, and prayers for the persecuted, including directly involved prayer teams; and compiling the World Watch List of the fifty countries in which persecution is most severe so that attention is focused on those areas.

As its name suggests, Open Doors acts on the belief that all doors are open for the purpose of proclaiming Christ. It helps facilitate the powerful and unique witness of the persecuted church by preserving its bond with the Bible and with other believers. It sees persecuted Christians as a prime resource in its wider mission of sharing the gospel and God's love with the entire world. Open Doors does not send out missionaries but supports believers so that they can reach out to their own communities. Often it is the first source of assistance to those faced with persecution.

One of Open Doors' programs urges letter writing to persecuted Christians. Open Doors welcomes the participation of youth by encouraging them to text Bibles and to participate in Locked Up, a twelve-hour simulation of a prison setting that gives them a glimpse into the hardships of persecuted Christians. Bridge Builder volunteer positions and internships have been crafted to meet a wide range of capabilities and interests, including educating the public about persecution, assisting in prayer ministry, acting as an advocate for the persecuted in public policy issues, and creating videos and blogs to expose persecution.

Through extensive relationships with indigenous individuals and churches, as well as its underground network, Open Doors obtains eyewitness field accounts of persecution in addition to accounts from certain news services and local news sources. It has constructed a four-part strategy for effectively assisting persecuted Christians, accentuating the following:

1. accessibility, meaning gaining not merely entrance to an area but also in-depth familiarity without endangering lives and staying as long as needed
2. scalability, to take large-scale steps to reach objectives
3. credibility, to speak authoritatively and without exploitation
4. invisibility, refraining from actively seeking credit for accomplishments and sharing resources for the purpose of protecting Christians

Finances

Open Doors has earned an A rating from Ministry Watch and is a charter member of the Evangelical Council for Financial Accountability. Its financial data can be viewed at ecfa.org.

Statistics

In 2008:

3.9 million Bibles and other types of literature delivered
114,400 Christian leaders trained
206,500 believers supported with vocational training
Active in 45 countries
Development offices in 20 countries

Affiliations

Among Open Doors' partners are Focus on the Family, Cru, and Child Evangelism Fellowship.

Electronic Media

Undercover with Persecuted Christians is a television docu-series.

Publication

Frontline Faith is a monthly newsletter about persecuted Christians.

Website

https://www.opendoors.org/

Sarah Claudine Day

Operation Mobilization

History

The founder of Operation Mobilization (OM) is American George Verwer. Prior to naming the chief activity enshrined in the organization's name—"mobilizing" young people and the church to world missions—Verwer was preparing for ministry as a student at Maryville College and then Moody Bible Institute. In 1958, he led a short-term mission trip to Mexico with nineteen students, which grew to forty-nine in 1959. The outcomes of these short-term trips were the first Send the Light Christian bookshop (in Mexico) and the employment of long-term, full-time staff. Verwer had not yet finished college.

Verwer, like Augustine in the fifth century, heard God's voice in relation to Bibles, Christian literature, and missions while sitting under a tree in prayer. Having just been deported from the former communist Czechoslovakia for distributing Christian literature, Verwer was watching young people mobilize and embark on a bus in Austria when the divine eureka moment arrived: Operation Mobilization. The picture of young people mobilizing to embark on a bus became a metaphor of the church getting motivated for world missions and encapsulated the early vision of OM.

Following the naming of Operation Mobilization, the first leaders drew up and signed the Madrid Manifesto while still in Spain in which they promised to give up possessions, comforts, food, and sleep and to carry on until everyone had heard the gospel. Such a commitment has defined the life, sacrifice, and impact of OM.

In 1961, Verwer was serving in Spain with his wife, Drena, and a small group of dedicated missioners. By 1963, two thousand Christians had joined summer outreach teams in Europe. At the same time, the first yearlong teams moved into the Indian subcontinent and the Muslim world. India proved to be defining in Verwer's Christian experience and development.

OM's commitment was to reach those who had never heard the gospel. Send the Light bookshops, literature distribution, and short- and long-term volunteers led to huge and rapid expansion, and with a heavy reliance on vehicles and their deployment, a group of OMers began to realize the strategic importance of coastal cities on the world map. A ship ministry was launched, and the following ships were purchased: the *Logos* in 1970 and the *Doulos* in 1977. The sinking of the *Logos* in 1988 led to the purchase of the *Logos II* and more recently the *Logos Hope* (active from February 2009).

Missionary impulses have led to banner campaigns with names such as Reach Up '74, Follow Up '75 (India), Love Europe (in the 1980s), and Go Transform (2010) in the United States.

In 1994, OM developed a strategic plan called Towards 2001 to motivate and equip people for missions and to plant churches, especially in the Middle East, South and Central Asia, and Europe.

Since 2001, OM has continued to develop new missions and initiatives, such as Sportslink, using sports as a means of providing holistic ministry, and in 2007, Emerging Mission Movements.

Headquarters

United States Office
PO Box 444
Tyrone, GA 30290
Telephone: 800-899-0432
Email: info@usa.om.org

Canada Office
84 West Street
Port Colborne, ON L3K 4C8
Telephone: 877-487-7777
Email: info@cdn.om.org

Leadership

George Verwer provided leadership for OM since its inception. However, in 1985, Verwer invited Briton Peter Maiden to join him as his associate international coordinator. Maiden took over the leadership from Verwer in 2003.

Although global and international, OM operates through a network of national offices that facilitate a region's own contribution, ownership, and emphasis toward world missions within the overall vision framework of the organization. The United States and Canada have their own offices, serving in partnership with local churches in the mobilization of Christians to world missions.

Core Beliefs

Verwer was baptized in a Brethren Assembly context, and the corporate, Bible-believing ethos of Brethrenism had an early influence on the movement. However, Verwer and the organization were from the beginning transdenominational. OM has always steered an evangelical course between competing ideas and current debates within Christendom, welcoming those from all denominations who can adhere to its evangelical statement of faith.

OM is continually birthed in the desire to serve God with a radical, New Testament Christianity, and the leadership has always searched to define what is in essence "true discipleship." In 2000, Verwer published *Out of the Comfort Zone*, delineating Christian spirituality for leaders and missioners. He wrote, "Most often, however, I find myself speaking to leaders about the need for them to work on the basics of the Christian life—their own spiritual development and walk with God" (39).

To take Christ at his word and to go, follow, and do likewise has been both the earnest endeavor of OM and arguably the reason for its impact, longevity, and continuing presence in world evangelization.

OM, as an evangelical parachurch organization, has the following statement of faith:

We believe there is one God, eternally existent in three persons, Father, Son and Holy Spirit.

We believe in the absolute deity and full humanity of our Lord Jesus Christ. We believe in His virgin birth, His sinless life, the authenticity of His miracles, His vicarious and atoning death, His bodily resurrection and His present mediatorial work in heaven.

We believe in the personality and deity of the Holy Spirit. We believe He gives life, He sanctifies, He empowers and comforts all believers.

We believe that the Scriptures, both the Old and New Testaments in their original texts, are fully inspired by the Holy Spirit, without error, and are the final authority for the Church.

We believe that man was originally created sinless. Tempted by Satan, man fell and thereby brought the whole race under the condemnation of eternal separation from God.

We believe that man is saved through repentance and faith in the finished work of Christ. Justification is through grace alone.

We believe that the Church is the body of Jesus Christ composed of all true believers. The present work of the Church is the worship of God, the perfecting of the saints and the evangelisation of the world.

We believe in the personal and bodily return of the Lord Jesus Christ to consummate our salvation and establish His glorious Kingdom. (om.org, "Statement of Faith")

Defining Statement

"Operation Mobilization works in over 110 countries, motivating and equipping people to share God's love with people all over the world" (om.org, "What We Believe").

Core Practices

Knowing and glorifying God
Living in submission to God's Word
Being people of grace and integrity
Serving sacrificially
Loving and valuing people
Evangelizing the world
Reflecting the diversity of the body of Christ
Global intercession
Esteeming the church (om.org, "Core Values")

Finances

At one stage, OM was regarded by some as being austere in its lack of concern for material possessions. A theology of giving and sacrifice translated "total dependence on God" into a spiritual muteness concerning the sharing of one's needs with others. Over time, however, this interpretation, due in part to MacDonald's influence, began to change, and a more balanced approach ensued (i.e., both total dependence on prayer and the sharing of needs are now seen as integral to the spiritual synergy of missionary work). Today OM owns property, a practice it once refused to endorse, and conducts fund-raising, such as the OM Fuel Appeal (for the ships). Potential short-term and long-term missionaries are expected to raise support through their local church, although the Emerging Mission Movements initiative provides other options for those from less-developed economies.

Statistics

OM currently supports 5,500 missionaries serving in over 110 countries worldwide. To date, it has shared the gospel with over 100 million people through a unique blend of short-term teams and long-term staff.

In 1970, the OM ship ministry was launched with the first OM vessel. Ships are useful for two reasons: many people live along the coasts, and OM can transport teams and literature to countries in this way. The ministry's four ships have visited more than 155 countries and welcomed 39 million people onboard since that time. By 2004, 33 million people had been onboard an OM ship either to visit the educational books exhibit or to benefit from ministry.

Trends

A myriad of OM ministries represents an expansion in missionary vision. These ministries include gospel literature distribution; holistic and social ministry; *Operation World*, the noted encyclopedic atlas of missionary data pertaining to every country in the world and used in prayer meetings throughout the church; Operation Mercy, a relief agency born out of ministry to the Kurdish people displaced by Saddam Hussein in the early 1990s; and AIDSlink for the current epidemic in Africa.

Opportunities for either short- or long-term missions include Haiti relief; the ship ministry; the Dalit people of India; multifaith contexts; and initiatives in Asia, Latin America, and Europe.

Website

http://www.om.org/

Bibliography

Greenlee, David, ed. *Global Passion: Marking George Verwer's Contribution to World Mission.* Waynesboro, GA: Authentic Lifestyle, 2003.

"Operation Mobilization." http://www.om.org. "Core Values," "Statement of Faith," and "What We Believe."

Randall, Ian. *Spiritual Revolution: The Story of OM.* Milton Keynes, UK: Authentic, 2008.

Rhoton, Elaine. *The Doulos Story.* Carlisle, UK: OM, 1997.

———. *The Logos Story.* Waynesboro, GA: OM, 1988.

Verwer, George. *Out of the Comfort Zone.* Minneapolis: Bethany House, 2000.

James Burnett and Mark A. Lamport

Our Daily Bread Ministries (formerly RBC Ministries)

History

Dr. M. R. DeHaan, a physician who became a pastor later in life, started a small radio program called *Detroit Bible Class* in 1938. DeHaan was renowned for his gravelly voice and impassioned Bible teaching. Listeners by the thousands quickly recognized DeHaan as a resource for biblical wisdom. The positive response to his teachings created a need for transcripts of the broadcasts to be used as study materials. The transcripts were published as Discovery Series booklets to satisfy the demand.

The program became *Radio Bible Class* in 1941 and changed its name to RBC Ministries in 1994 to reflect the increase of resources and services available worldwide. In 2015, it changed its name to Our Daily Bread Ministries after its well-known devotional *Our Daily Bread*.

Headquarters

3000 Kraft Avenue SE
Grand Rapids, MI 49512
Telephone: 616-974-2210

Leadership

Rick DeHaan is the president. The organization also has a nine-member board.

Core Beliefs

The ministry affirms belief in the inspiration and infallibility of Scripture, the Trinity, salvation by grace through faith in Christ alone, the necessity of works to express gratitude and demonstration of redemption, the resurrection of the body, the universal church, obedience to the Great Commission, the necessity of spiritual maturity through multiple means (Bible study, local church involvement, prayer, and witnessing), the imminent rapture of the church, and Christ's personal return to establish his earthly kingdom.

Defining Statement

"Our mission is to make the life-changing wisdom of the Bible understandable and accessible to all" (ourdailybread.org, "Home").

Core Practices

The mission of Our Daily Bread Ministries is to teach Scripture in a manner that will inculcate personal faith and maturity in Jesus Christ. The target audience is as diverse as the ministry methods.

Finances

Our Daily Bread Ministries has been a member of the Evangelical Council for Financial Accountability since 1987. Support is received from those who have been helped by the ministry and those who desire to uphold its purpose.

Statistics

Our Daily Bread Ministries has international offices in twenty countries, in addition to maintaining partners throughout the world who distribute the ministry's resources. *Our Daily Bread* is translated into more than fifty-five languages. The ministry supports thirty-one home and foreign missionary projects.

Missionary and Evangelistic Work

The ministry is devoted to making the transformational wisdom of Scripture both accessible and understandable to a worldwide audience. Our Daily Bread Ministries desires to help people of all nations experience a personal relationship with Christ, mature in Christlikeness, and be involved in ministry through a local church.

Academic Institution

ChristianCourses.com is a service of the ministry that offers continuing education credit (CEU), Institute of Theological Studies CEU credit, and online courses.

Electronic Media

Our Daily Bread is a radio program broadcast each day and features insights from the print version. *Radio Bible Class Daily* began in 1980 and became known as *Discover the Word* in 1998. *Sports Spectrum Radio* features discussions with athletes, coaches, and sports personalities that address relevant issues in life (faith) and sports (competition). *Words to Live By* presents stories of faith in Jesus that have impacted people worldwide and provides words of hope and wisdom as found in Scripture. Day of Discovery Television has been broadcasting since May 5, 1968, featuring programs that address biblical prophecy, the Christian faith, current and historical issues, and social issues. The documentary-style program is filmed on location in the United States and around the world, including Israel and the Middle East. The program is one of the oldest continual Christian broadcasts in United States television history.

Publications

Our Daily Bread was first published in 1956 and is currently distributed in more than fifty-five languages worldwide. The publication is distributed via email, mobile devices, podcast, print, radio, and RSS. The daily devotions are designed to help people read Scripture each day. There are also Facebook and Twitter accounts for *Our Daily Bread*.

Other devotionals provided by the ministry include *Daily Strength, My Utmost for His Highest, Our Daily Journey,* and *Wonder of Creation. Campus Journal* is published monthly as a devotional booklet for high school and college students. *Times of Discovery Newsletter* is an issue-oriented editorial from the president. Discovery House Publishers is the nonprofit publishing arm of Our Daily Bread Ministries. The intent of the publisher is to provide resources that will nourish the soul with Scripture. The Discovery Series provides topical biblical treatises. DeHaan's *The Chemistry of the Blood* (1943) was a controversial work that communicated the imperishability of Christ's blood because he believed it was sinless and divine blood.

Favorite authors and teachers for the *Radio Bible Class* include Ron Chadwick, M. R. DeHaan, Mart DeHaan, Richard W. DeHaan, Paul R. Van Gorder, Vernon Grounds, Herb Vander Lugt, Alice Matthews, Jim Pittman, and Haddon Robinson.

Website

http://ourdailybread.org/

Bibliography

Adair, James R. *M. R. DeHaan: The Life behind the Voice.* Grand Rapids: Discovery House, 2008.

———. *M. R. DeHaan: The Man and His Ministry.* Grand Rapids: Zondervan, 1969.

Bratt, James D., and Christopher H. Meehan. *Gathered at the River: Grand Rapids, Michigan, and Its People of Faith.* Grand Rapids: Eerdmans, 1993.

DeHaan, M. R. *Dear Doctor: I Have a Problem.* Grand Rapids: Zondervan, 1961.

———. *508 Answers to Bible Questions.* Grand Rapids: Lamplighter Books, 1952.

Hertel, Leona. *M. R. DeHaan, M.D., 1891–1965: Founder and Teacher, Radio Bible Class.* Grand Rapids: Radio Bible Class, 1966.

Pieters, Albertus. *Jonah, the Whale, and Dr. M. R. DeHaan.* Grand Rapids: Eerdmans, 1929.

Ron J. Bigalke

Partners International

History

Partners International was founded in 1943 as the China Native Evangelistic Crusade (CNEC). Founded on the vision that mission work could best be accomplished by national missionaries, the CNEC expanded to other parts of Asia, Africa, Europe, and Latin America between 1960 and 1985 and changed its name to the Christian Nationals Evangelism Commission (also CNEC). In 1985, after forging partnerships with like-minded agencies in Australia, Canada, and Britain, the organization became known as Partners International. Presently, the group works with 120 national workers who are serving in 58 countries.

Headquarters

1117 E Westview Court
Spokane, WA 99218
Telephone: 800-966-5515

Leadership

Partners is led by an executive team that includes a president and CEO and two vice presidents. The organization also has area leaders who give direction to nine regions of the world. Each leader possesses significant ministry experience and is regarded as an expert on his or her region of the world, enabling them to effectively come alongside national partners on the field. Finally, the executive and regional leadership is accountable to a board of directors. Aside from its national ministry partners, Partners employs around seventy support staff.

Core Beliefs

Partners International's statement of faith is deliberately inclusive of evangelicals from a variety of traditions and confessions. Borrowed from the World Evangelical Alliance, the confession is a brief document that emphasizes the authority of Scripture, the triune Godhead, the person and work of Christ, salvation by grace through faith, the work of the Holy Spirit in sanctification, the importance of the church, and the eternal state for believers and nonbelievers.

Core Practices

The organization's stated mission is "connecting the global Christian community to bring the gospel of Jesus Christ to the least reached, least resourced nations on earth" (partnersintl.org, "Our Mission"). The most distinguishing element of Partners' work is, of course, that it partners with national missionaries. Their partners are local Christians who understand the culture, speak the language, and have a passion to share God's love with their own people. The organization has a rigorous screening for potential partners; however, once a partnership is developed, Partners regards this agreement as more than mere financial support. Rather, it seeks to embrace the vision of national leaders and to help them develop sustainable ministries and infrastructures.

Finally, Partners is committed to holistic ministry. While emphasizing evangelism and church planting, it is also concerned with ministering to real, human needs by providing medical care, clean water, disaster relief, agricultural development, and other assistance to demonstrate the love of God.

Trends

At present, the group emphasizes three major areas of ministry: planting churches, transforming communities, and empowering women and children.

In 2009, 1,100 churches were planted, 17,000 church planters were trained, and 55,000 people came to faith in Christ.

When Partners speaks of community transformation, this includes digging wells, building clinics, shipping medicine, teaching nutrition, running schools and children's centers, and organizing economic cooperatives to provide small loans and vocational training. In 2009, a quarter of a million people were cared for through these efforts.

Partners also works to empower women by teaching health and hygiene and by offering vocational training. Finally, the organization coordinates a child sponsorship program that provides food, clothing, and education for children in a context in which they are able to hear the gospel and grow in the Christian faith.

Website

http://www.partnersintl.org/

Bibliography

Bush, Luis, and Lorry Lutz. *Partnering in Ministry: The Direction of World Evangelism.* Downers Grove, IL: InterVarsity, 1990.

Finley, Allen, and Lorry Lutz. *The Family Tie.* Nashville: Nelson, 1983.

Gordon-Chandler, Paul. *Pilgrims of Christ on the Muslim Road.* Lanham, MD: Rowman & Littlefield, 2008.

"Partners International." http://www.partnersintl.org. "Our Mission."

Edward Smither

Pioneers

History

Ted and Peggy Fletcher founded Pioneers in Sterling, Virginia, in 1979. Ruth Wright, the first Pioneers missionary, went to Nigeria in 1979. The Papua New Guinea field was opened in 1980. In 1992, the mission moved to Orlando, Florida, and World Outreach Fellowship merged with Pioneers in 1994. Two additional mission organizations, Asia Pacific Christian Mission and Pacific Partners, joined Pioneers in 1997. Action Partners, an Australian mission organization, merged with Pioneers in 2001. Ameritribes, a mission working with native North Americans for seventy-five years, became part of Pioneers in 2009. These mergers largely account for the rapid growth of Pioneers. The headquarters, including the Frizen Missionary Training Center with overnight accommodations and meeting rooms, is near the Orlando airport.

Headquarters

10123 William Carey Drive
Orlando, FL 32832
Telephone: 407-382-6000
Fax: 407-382-1008

Leadership

Stephen L. Richardson has been the president of Pioneers since 1999. Leaders from Pioneers' nine worldwide regions compose an international council, which meets every eighteen months. An international leadership team meets every nine months, and a separate US board meets twice a year.

Core Beliefs

Pioneers' nine-point doctrinal statement touches on God, Jesus Christ, the Holy Spirit, Scripture, man, salvation, the resurrection, the church, and the Great Commission (pioneers .org, "Statement of Faith"). A summary follows.

God is an eternal Trinity.

Christ was sinless, died for our sins, rose bodily from the dead, ascended to heaven, and is now exalted there. Christ's return will be a "personal, imminent, and visible return in power and glory."

The Holy Spirit indwells all believers.

The Old and New Testaments are "divinely inspired, without error, infallible, and are entirely trustworthy."

God created Adam and Eve, who fell into sin and passed that defilement on to the entire human race so that man is in need of salvation.

Salvation is a gift of God to all who trust Christ.

Both saved and lost will be resurrected, and the lost will experience "eternal condemnation separated from God."

The universal church is the body of Christ.

Christ commanded his church to go into the entire world to make disciples of all peoples, to baptize them, and to teach them all that Christ commanded.

Defining Statement

"Pioneers mobilizes teams to glorify God among unreached peoples by initiating church-planting movements in partnership with local churches" (pioneers.org, "About Us").

Finances

Pioneers has been a member of the Evangelical Council for Financial Accountability since August 1, 1987. The mission is also a member of CrossGlobal Link.

Total revenue for 2014: $56,512,649

Total expenses for 2014: $48,723,117

Net assets for 2014: $31,734,090

Statistics

Pioneers has "2,985 international members serving on 289 teams in 103 countries among 205 unreached people groups" (pioneers.org, "Our Story"). Over 2,000 churches partner with Pioneers in sending out missionaries. Pioneers works in the Americas, Europe, Africa, the Middle East, Central Asia, South Asia, East Asia, Southeast Asia, and the Pacific, including Australia.

Missionary and Evangelistic Work

Pioneers works among unreached people groups, and every ministry is to help plant local churches. Much of the work involves teaching English, but other types of ministry include digging wells in Chad, reaching Chinese immigrants in England, building schools in Sudan, guiding tours in India, working with orphans or a sports ministry in East Asia, living with an ethnic people in Central Asia, learning Arabic in the Middle East to establish relationships with people, and exporting products to the United States from a foreign country. Pioneers helps missionaries do their calling with as little structure as possible, though the organization helps raise support for special projects and provides insurance, a newsletter, crisis management, a retirement plan, administration, and record keeping.

Website

http://www.pioneers.org/

Bibliography

"Pioneers." http://www.pioneers.org. "About Us" and "Statement of Faith."

James A. Borland

Pocket Testament League

History

The Pocket Testament League was founded in 1893 by then twelve-year-old Helen Cadbury for the purposes of promoting interest in reading the Bible and evangelism. By the time she left school, the Pocket Testament League had over sixty members. In 1904, Helen Cadbury married Charles M. Alexander, who, along with Dr. Wilbur Chapman, officially organized the Pocket Testament League in Philadelphia, Pennsylvania, in 1908. Members of the organization committed to read the Bible daily and to practice evangelism by handing out pocket New Testaments. The Pocket Testament League has continued its mission to encourage Bible reading and evangelism throughout the world. Today the organization exists in several entities in different countries.

Headquarters

PO Box 800
Lititz, PA 17543
Telephone: 800-636-8785

Core Beliefs

The inspiration and authority of the whole Bible (Old and New Testaments) as the full revelation of God by the Holy Spirit.

The Deity of the Lord Jesus Christ, His virgin birth, His substitutionary atoning death on the cross, His bodily resurrection, and His personal return.

The necessity of the new birth for entering the Kingdom of God (as described in John 3).

The obligation upon all believers to be witnesses of the Lord Jesus Christ and to seek the salvation of others. (ptl.org, "Statement of Faith")

Core Practices

The key practices of the Pocket Testament League are Bible reading and evangelism. Membership is free. Through donations, the Pocket Testament League is able to provide free Gospels for its members to use in personal evangelism.

Electronic Media

Through its website, the Pocket Testament League provides various programs for the purpose of personal devotion and evangelism.

Publications

The Pocket Testament League provides several resources to aid its members in evangelism. It publishes editions of the Gospel of John in various cover designs for the purpose of distribution. It also publishes several booklets to aid its members in personal ministry.

Website

http://www.ptl.org/

Bibliography

Davis, George T. B. *The Pocket Testament League around the World*. Philadelphia: Pocket Testament League, 1910.

Roberts, Philip I. *"Charlie" Alexander: A Study in Personality*. New York: Revell, 1920.

"The Pocket Testament League." http://www.ptl.org. "Statement of Faith."

Bryan C. Maine

Renováré

History

Renováré is a nonprofit organization with headquarters in Colorado and an active influence worldwide. Richard J. Foster, a Quaker theologian, founded the organization in 1988. Following the publication of his *Celebration of Discipline* in 1978, Foster was invited to speak at an increasing number of churches and conferences on the subject of spiritual disciplines and formation. Encouraged by this interest, Foster withdrew from public ministry to explore how a more intentional and systematic renewal movement could be formed. Renováré is the Latin word for "renewal," and the organization seeks to promote church renewal through spiritual formation. Renováré relocated to Colorado in 1994 from its offices at Friends University in Kansas. International offices were established within the first decade of the twenty-first century.

Headquarters

8 Inverness Drive E
Suite 102
Englewood, CO 80112
Telephone: 303-792-0152
Fax: 303-792-0146

Leadership

Christopher Alan Hall is the president. A steering committee and a board of reference lead Renováré. The Renováré ministry team serves as the trustee board, and its members are available as speakers to present the vision and strategy of the organization.

Core Beliefs

Renováré affirms the Apostles' and Nicene Creeds. Scripture is one of several sources of revelation. The organization does not officially regard the Apocrypha as equal in authority with the Bible but does encourage its use for those groups who regard it as Scripture. Individuals work with God to determine life outcomes and are cocreators with God in advancing his kingdom on earth. Adam and Eve were archetypes.

Spiritual disciplines are the means to self-transformation and for receiving God's grace. "The dark night of the soul" (God's absence) is necessary for spiritual growth. Whether Scripture condemns homosexuality is regarded as a matter of contemporary debate.

Defining Statement

"Becoming like Jesus" (renovare.org, "Home").

Core Practices

The stated values of the organization include balance, change, community, integrity, relevance, and service. Renovaré is committed to being a Christian organization with an ecumenical and international outreach. The organization seeks to advocate, model, resource, and stimulate intentional living and spiritual formation among Christians and those desiring an intimate relationship with God. Renovaré promotes a practical strategy and an impartial vision for spiritual renewal and seeks to encourage individuals and churches to develop a more intimate spiritual life with God. The basic disciplines of Renovaré are fourfold: contemplation, devotional reading of spiritual masters, meditation, and prayer (*lectio divina*).

Renovaré's spiritual formation groups are modeled on spiritual renewal centers that amalgamate spiritual enlightenment techniques from the world's religions (e.g., the Shalem Institute for Spiritual Formation in Bethesda, Maryland). The format of these spiritual retreat centers is part of a strategy for integrating contemplative and meditative practices within as many local churches as possible through the development of spiritual formation groups. The groups function similar to spiritual retreat centers, with the exception that schedules are weekly and conducted in church buildings or private homes.

Renovaré encourages community groups, facilitates conferences and events, and provides training opportunities in spiritual formation. Renovaré offices are also located outside the United States in Brazil, Britain, Ireland, and Korea. The Renovaré Spiritual Formation Institute is a two-year curriculum for those dedicated to the pursuit of spiritual formation. Renovaré promotes many academic and nonacademic spiritual formation and spirituality programs.

Statistics

Renovaré has exerted a foundational impact in the spiritual formation movement for over twenty years. Hundreds of local and regional conferences are held throughout the United States. Renovaré has facilitated a series of international conferences with worldwide delegates in attendance.

Ecumenism

Ecumenism is an essential element of Renovaré, which even includes aspects of Buddhist philosophy. Spiritual "wisdom" may be pursued beyond the biblical revelation.

Publications

Renovaré offers print and video resources that communicate organizational beliefs and practices. The Apprentice Series is authored by James Bryan Smith and published by InterVarsity. The series is designed to promote apprenticeship with Jesus through the Holy Spirit, narrative transformation, soul-training exercises, and community. *The Life with God Bible* provides discipleship insights into spiritual practices. The Renovaré Spiritual Formation Guides to Scripture are designed to integrate traditional Bible study with *lectio divina*. *Conversations Journal* is published (in cooperation with Richmont Graduate University and others) semiannually to provide spiritual accompaniment and dialogue. *Explorations* (formerly *Perspective*) is the primary means of communication between Renovaré and those interested in its activities.

Website

http://www.renovare.org/

Bibliography

Foster, Richard J. *Celebration of Discipline*. San Francisco: Harper & Row, 1978.

———, ed. *The Renovaré Spiritual Formation Bible*. San Francisco: Harper, 2006.

Willard, Dallas. *The Spirit of the Disciplines*. San Francisco: HarperCollins, 1988.

Ron J. Bigalke

Samaritan's Purse

History

Traveling through post–World War II Asia with Youth for Christ, evangelist and journalist Bob Pierce saw firsthand the suffering and despair of sick and orphaned children. Through the example of some dedicated women in China who were living among lepers and orphans, Pierce received a vision for his future ministry: "to meet emergency needs in crisis areas through existing evangelical mission agencies and national churches" (samaritanspurse.org, "History"). In 1970, he founded Samaritan's Purse, named after Jesus's parable of the Good Samaritan in Luke 10. The ministry brings immediate emergency help and supplies to those in need, as well as the message of hope and eternal life through the gospel of Jesus Christ.

In 1973, Pierce met a young student named Franklin Graham. When Graham accompanied Pierce on a six-week mission to Asia in 1975, his heart too was torn by the poverty and despair they encountered, and he felt the call to work with hurting people around the world. Eighteen months after Pierce's death in 1978, Graham became the president and chairman of the board of Samaritan's Purse and to this day continues to lead the ministry in its mission of mercy and hope.

Headquarters

PO Box 3000
Boone, NC 28607
Telephone: 828-262-1980

Leadership

President and chairman of the board: Franklin Graham

Core Beliefs

Samaritan's Purse bases its ministry on eleven common evangelical affirmations of faith that include "the ministry of evangelism and discipleship is a responsibility of all followers of Jesus Christ" (samaritanspurse.org, "Statement of Faith").

Defining Statement

Following "Christ's command by going to the aid of the world's poor, sick, and suffering" (samaritanspurse.org, "About Us").

Core Practices

Samaritan's Purse sends emergency and crisis relief to areas of natural disaster, war, disease, and famine. Working with on-site ministry partners, relief teams bring food, water, medicine, and shelter to hurting people in desperate circumstances. They also provide hospital equipment and supplies; community development, educational programs, and vocational programs; and community water wells.

Finances

The ministry believes in and practices financial accountability. An independent accounting firm conducts an annual audit, and financial statements are available for public inspection.

Missionary and Evangelistic Work

Samaritan's Purse makes a conscious effort to reach the suffering people around the world by providing food, water, and medicine in the name of Jesus Christ. While meeting physical needs is core, evangelism is the heart of the ministry and is implemented through church building, evangelistic training, and support for local ministries.

When asked by people, "Why did you come?" the answer remains, "We have come to help you in the Name of the Lord Jesus Christ" (samaritans purse.org, "About Us"). Other outreaches include Operation Christmas Child, the Children's Heart Project, the Sudan Church Rebuilding Project, and the Haiti Rebuilding Program.

Parachurch Organizations

World Medical Mission coordinates short-term medical mission trips and places volunteer Christian medical and dental personnel in hospitals and clinics around the globe. It also maintains a biomedical department and warehouse that provide medical equipment and supplies to medical mission facilities.

Prescription for Hope is a comprehensive HIV/AIDS program designed to respond to the AIDS epidemic in Africa. It mobilizes private, church, corporate, and government resources; holds workshops to equip and train leaders to help prevent new HIV infections among youth and through mother-to-child transmission; offers counseling and testing; and brings the message of Jesus Christ of comfort and hope to those affected by the disease.

Electronic Media

Children's Heart, a seven-episode family television series

Publication

On Call, a quarterly publication from World Medical Mission

Website

http://www.samaritanspurse.org/

Bibliography

"Samaritan's Purse." http://www.samaritanspurse.org. "About Us," "History," and "Statement of Faith."

Marlene Mankins

SEND International

History

Philip E. Armstrong served with US forces in the Far East during World War II. Armstrong agreed to stay in the United States as the initial director of Far Eastern Gospel Crusade (FEGC) while others returned and opened outreach in Japan and the Philippines in 1948. Ministry in Taiwan was added in 1967, and in 1971, Central Alaskan Mission merged with FEGC. A decade later the name was changed to SEND

International. The mission entered Spain and Hong Kong in 1988 and moved into Eastern Europe and Russia in the 1990s and Kazakhstan in 2005. Frank Severn succeeded Armstrong as the international director of SEND in 1981 after ministering in the Philippines for fourteen years. Warren Janzen became the international director in 2004. He was previously a missionary in Japan for fifteen years.

Headquarters

PO Box 513
Farmington, MI 48332
Telephone: 248-477-4210
Fax: 248-477-4232

SEND has additional incorporated offices in Canada, Germany, Hong Kong, Japan, the Philippines, and Taiwan.

Leadership

Phillip J. Baur III is the US director of the organization. SEND has a twelve-member international council composed of eight external members, the international director, and three missionaries at large who are chosen by the directors' council, which is composed of the directors of each sending and receiving missionary area. The international council serves as the governing board. Strategy and other planning often take place at the council of area directors.

Core Beliefs

SEND has an eight-point statement of faith that includes the inerrancy of the Scriptures; the Trinity; the deity of Christ; the Holy Spirit's work of conviction, regeneration, indwelling, and empowerment; salvation for all who trust Christ; the resurrection of the dead with unbelievers receiving eternal condemnation; Christ's return for the church (time not specified); Christ's personal and visible return to reign over the earth for one thousand years with believers living in holiness and obedience.

SEND's articles of incorporation is its defining document. In addition, the SEND International Manual contains statements of principles, practices, policies, and theological positions that are affirmed and adhered to throughout the mission.

Defining Statement

"Our mission is to mobilize God's people and engage the unreached in order to establish reproducing churches" (send.org, "About").

Finances

SEND International is a member of Cross-Global Link, the Canadian Council of Christian Charities, the SOE (US Standards of Excellence in Short-Term Mission), and the Evangelical Council for Financial Accountability, joining the latter on May 1, 1985.

Total revenue for 2014: $19,514,981
Total expenses for 2014: $19,253,565
Net assets for 2014: $7,770,508

Statistics

SEND has more than 650 missionaries in over 20 countries in North America, Europe, and Asia. European countries with SEND missionaries are Albania, Bulgaria, Croatia, the Czech Republic, Hungary, Macedonia, Poland, Romania, Slovenia, and Spain.

SEND workers are in East Asia, Japan, Kazakhstan, the Philippines, Russia, Taiwan, and Ukraine. More than 20,000 churches have been started in the Philippines during the past two decades, and these churches are now prepared to send Filipino missionaries out to other parts of the world.

Missionary and Evangelistic Work

SEND International concentrates on establishing churches among unreached peoples and then discipling and educating leaders for further reproduction. Most of SEND's non–North American missionaries are from European and Latin American countries, adding to SEND's "international" flavor. Some SEND missionaries operate camps and sponsor sporting events in some countries to reach young people.

Affiliations

SEND has partnership agreements with mission agencies in Germany but does not have a sending or receiving council in that nation. Columbia International University partners with SEND and several other missionary-sending organizations by offering a tuition reduction to missionaries and dependents.

Academic Institutions

Alaska Bible College in Glennallen, Alaska, was founded by Central Alaskan Mission, now part of SEND International. Though it is independent today, some SEND missionaries teach there. FEBIAS College of Bible (originally Far Eastern Bible Institute and Seminary) in Manila, Philippines, also was founded by SEND (then

FEGC) in 1948 as its first ministry established in the Philippines. FEBIAS College of Bible is now also independent, but SEND missionaries teach there as well.

SEND has missionary personnel assigned to the independent Kiev Theological Seminary in Ukraine.

Website

http://www.send.org/

James A. Borland

Servant Partners

History

Servant Partners was founded in 1993 by Tom Pratt, a leader with InterVarsity Christian Fellowship. The goal then, as now, was to fulfill God's call to love the poor and proclaim the good news to every nation. Because of a desire to faithfully serve in a local context before working in different cultural contexts, early ministry efforts focused on inner-city ministries in the United States. Since 1995, an internship program involving living, studying, and ministering in the inner-city neighborhoods of Los Angeles has helped equip young adults for a lifetime of loving and serving the urban poor. The ministry was expanded in the late 1990s to serve the cities of the developing world. In 2003, Barnabas Ventures was started to train new missionaries to the urban poor from developing countries and to strengthen and expand the work of indigenous national leaders already working with the urban poor. Today Servant Partners has ten teams training leaders, organizing communities, and planting churches in countries from Africa, the Middle East, and Asia, as well as North and South America.

Headquarters

PO Box 92493
Pasadena, CA 91109
Telephone: 626-398-1010
Fax: 626-398-1028
Email: info@servantpartners.org

Leadership

Derek Engdahl, general director and field director, worked with InterVarsity for ten years before joining Servant Partners in 1998 to live and work in Pomona, California. Engdahl's wife, Lisa, worked with InterVarsity for fifteen years before joining Servant Partners as co-general director and director of leadership development.

Will Niewoehner, serving as executive director and Barnabas Ventures director, has frequently taken his wife and family to live with him as he has done short-term work in slum communities in Kenya, India, Honduras, and Mexico. Internships director Kevin Blue and pre-field training director Dave Palmer round out the Servant Partners leadership team.

Core Beliefs

Servant Partners is based on the knowledge that Jesus loves the urban poor. Members seek to follow Jesus's example by living among and compassionately loving the urban poor while also partnering with local Christians. Their core values include living among and sharing their lives with the people they serve (incarnation); choosing to sacrificially serve their neighbors in tangible ways (servanthood); building communities of faith with individuals who are growing in their faith and obedience to Jesus (making disciples); advocating for the poor and equipping them to become effective change agents while also helping the powerful to see opportunities for change (justice); and encouraging communities, nations, and individuals to be transformed toward God's kingdom values (transformation).

All of their efforts are based on the foundational beliefs that God is deeply concerned for the poor and oppressed and is in the process of reconciling all people to himself and to each other. They see God's Word and the Holy Spirit as their primary sources of motivation as they choose to lose their lives for the sake of the gospel and to seek justice for the oppressed.

Defining Statement

"We seek Jesus together by living and serving among the world's urban poor" (servantpartners .org, "Purpose").

Statistics

Servant Partners currently has ten teams planting churches, making disciples, and training leaders in communities from Thailand and India to North Africa, South Africa, the Middle East, Mexico, and the United States. Barnabas Ventures is working alongside indigenous leaders in East Africa, India, Brazil, and Honduras. Members are living in solidarity with the one billion people currently living in the world's urban slums.

Missionary and Evangelistic Work

Through sending teams of trained people with hearts called by God to serve the urban poor, Servant Partners works to bring spiritual and physical renewal to inner-city neighborhoods and communities. Working together with indigenous churches wherever possible, members train, evangelize, and empower people to transform their own communities in sustainable ways.

Barnabas Ventures focuses on equipping indigenous Christian leaders to minister to their own communities in culturally appropriate ways. By providing technical assistance, helping to promote fair trade projects, and developing businesses to aid local ministry partners, Barnabas Ventures comes alongside and serves the local leaders who are already working with the urban poor.

Through two-year internships, Servant Partners trains people to live among and advocate for the urban poor. While many internship alumni work directly with the poor in urban slums, all are prepared to live out God's heart for the poor and oppressed by advocating for the poor in churches and communities wherever they find themselves. Short-term internships in Los Angeles and Manila provide opportunities to live among the poor, experience the slums firsthand, and explore the possibilities of and call to further service.

Website

http://www.servantpartners.org/

Lorelle Beth Jabs

SIM International

History

SIM (Serving in Mission) is an international mission organization. SIM emerged in the late nineteenth century in North America as a union of several organizations and continues to serve with the same passion as that of its founders. The original SIM began with the ministry of Canadians Walter Gowans and Rowland Bingham and American Thomas Kent. The three founded the Sudan ("Soudan") Interior Mission (SIM) in 1893, which became SIM (Society for International Ministries) in 1982.

Martha Osborn, Andrew Murray, and Spencer Walton founded Cape General Mission in 1889, which later became the South Africa General Mission in 1894 and the Africa Evangelical Fellowship in 1963, and that merged with SIM in 1998. George and Mary (Stirling) Allan from

New Zealand founded the Bolivian Indian Mission in 1907, which later became the Andes Evangelical Mission in 1965 and joined with SIM International in 1982. Ceylon and India General Mission (founded by Scotsman Benjamin Davidson in 1893) and Poona and Indian Village Mission (founded by Australians Charles Reeves and M. E. Gavin in 1893) merged in 1968 to form the International Christian Fellowship, which united with SIM in 1989.

The slogan "Serving in Mission" was adopted in 2000, but the official name worldwide is simply SIM.

Headquarters

PO Box 7900
Charlotte, NC 28241
Telephone: 704-588-4300
Fax: 704-587-1518

Leadership

Stanley Allaby is the chairman. Steve Strauss is the president. The board consists of twenty-one members. There are nine sending offices and forty field offices.

Core Beliefs

As an interdenominational Protestant mission, SIM affirms historic, evangelical Christianity. SIM states commitment to the following doctrines: the inerrancy and inspiration of Scripture; the Trinity; the sinfulness of humanity; the virgin birth of Jesus Christ as fully God and fully man; his sacrificial death, resurrection, and ascension; justification by grace through trust alone in the Lord Jesus Christ as Savior; the work of the Holy Spirit in granting spiritual life and indwelling, empowering, gifting, and transforming all believers; the universal church of those born of the Holy Spirit; the existence of the spirit world, including holy angels and evil spirits; and the visible return of Jesus Christ to earth in glory to accomplish final triumph over evil.

Defining Statement

"Serving the church across cultures" (sim.org, "Home").

Core Practices

SIM seeks to equip churches to obey the Great Commission, evangelize unreached people groups, disciple believers through planting and partnering relationships with churches, and minister to human need through compassionate, holistic service. "Convinced that God's primary means of relating to and transforming the world is the church" (sim.org, "Who We Are") each function, responsibility, and ministry of SIM is through church-mission relationships. Because of the church-focused vision of SIM, missionaries are not likely to serve in social services for mere charity or sociological benefit. SIM works to equip, nurture, and plant churches as testimonies of Christ in their communities and to do outreach with cross-cultural missionaries to Africa, Asia, and South America. SIM missionaries primarily plant local churches and accomplish this ministry through evangelism, leadership training, and provision of resources. The highest motivation and purpose of SIM is to glorify God.

Statistics

There are more than fourteen hundred missionaries serving in more than forty countries on five continents and two islands in the Indian Ocean.

Missionary and Evangelistic Work

The primary work of SIM is church planting and evangelism. SIM supports missionary work among diverse people groups in Africa, Asia, Europe, North America, and South America. SIM missionaries serve in some of the poorest and most destitute communities and nations. As an international ministry, SIM has missionaries from thirty nationalities. Urban Ministries Serving God is based in Kenya to train local churches and theological institutions in understanding and responding to urban needs.

Academic Institutions

SIM is committed to the importance of theological education for pastors and church leaders. SIM partners with several Bible schools and seminaries overseas and is highly active in establishing educational outreaches throughout the third world. Special projects include the development and administration of student and youth centers in several communities. SIM regards educational ministries as vital to its mission because not only will workers gain experience in informal ministry opportunities and promoting literacy but also those who are discipled will be able to read the Bible for themselves.

Parachurch Organizations

The relief and development programs, which demonstrate the concern of God for humanity,

are an outgrowth of evangelistic ministries. These programs are closely related to church growth and planting. Some of SIM's ongoing and special projects include clean water projects in Ghana, HOPE for AIDS in Africa and India, literacy promotion in many regions, the Makki Health program in Ethiopia, the Prem Sewa Child Nutrition Project in India, the Spring of Life Centre in Nigeria (HIV and AIDS response), the Vocational Training Center in Bangladesh, and the Women's and Children's Health program in India.

Sports Friends is an international movement utilizing the universal language of sports for evangelism and discipleship. Sports ministries are church centered and youth focused.

Electronic Media

SIM utilizes radio broadcasts of Christian programs whenever possible. Eternal Love Winning Africa (ELWA) radio is currently rebuilding in Liberia as a consequence of brutal civil war. ELWA broadcasts in seven tribal languages, and reaches approximately two-thirds of Liberians. The *Jesus* film is used in many evangelistic outreaches. SIM websites utilize as many visual presentations as possible. SIM Kids is an online multimedia educational tool.

Publications

Serving in Mission Together is the official quarterly mission publication. *SIM Mission Connection* (formerly *SIMplicity*) is the monthly email newsletter of the mission. The *Africa Bible Commentary* (2006) was a special project of more than seventy African biblical scholars and theologians with the goal of "interpreting and applying the Bible in light of African culture and realities" (christianbook.com, "Africa Bible Commentary"). Books for Zambian Pastors is a program that provides indigenous pastors with study resources. Life Challenge Africa publishes literature and conducts outreaches to equip the church for Muslim evangelism.

Website

http://www.sim.org/

Bibliography

Allan, George. *Reminiscences: Being Incidents from Missionary Experience.* Dunedin, New Zealand: Stanton Brothers, 1936.

Carpenter, Joel A. *Revive Us Again: The Reawakening of American Fundamentalism.* New York: Oxford University Press, 1999.

Cooper, Barbara M. *Evangelical Christians in the Muslim Mahel.* Bloomington: Indiana University Press, 2006.

Corten, André, and Ruth Marshall-Fratani, eds. *Between Babel and Pentecost: Transnational Pentecostalism in Africa and Latin America*. Bloomington: Indiana University Press, 2001.

Frizen, Edwin L., Jr. *75 Years of IFMA, 1917–1992: The Nondenominational Missions Movement*. Pasadena, CA: William Carey Library, 1992.

Fuller, W. Harold. *Run While the Sun Is Hot*. Chicago: Moody, 1968.

Hudspith, Margarita A. *Ripening Fruit: A History of the Bolivian Indian Mission*. Harrington Park, NJ: Harrington Press, 1958.

Johnson, David. *Voices of Sudan*. Charleston, SC: Elevate, 2007.

Millard, E. C., and Lucy E. Guinness. *South America: The Neglected Continent*. New York: Revell, 1894.

Rawlyk, George A., and Mark A. Noll, eds. *Amazing Grace: Evangelicalism in Australia, Britain, Canada, and the United States*. Grand Rapids: Baker, 1993.

Wells, Robin. *Jesus Says Go*. Grand Rapids: Kregel, 2006.

Ron J. Bigalke

Slavic Gospel Association

History

The Slavic Gospel Association (SGA) was founded in 1934 by Rev. Peter Deyneka. Twenty years earlier, when Deyneka was fifteen years of age, his family immigrated to the United States from the former Soviet republic of Belarus. A few years later Deyneka accepted Christ as Savior during a worship service at Moody Memorial Church in Chicago.

Following his conversion, Deyneka attended and graduated from St. Paul Bible School in Minnesota. In 1925, he visited his homeland in Belarus, engaging in evangelism and establishing a strong relationship with the churches of the Union of Evangelical Christians-Baptists. However, beginning in the early 1930s, Stalin intensified persecution of churches. Committed to help the persecuted church, Deyneka, with the help of a small group of Chicago-area businessmen, founded what later came to be known as the Slavic Gospel Association.

During the Soviet era, the SGA covertly distributed millions of Bibles and Christian books to people living behind the Iron Curtain and broadcast thousands of Christian radio programs to strengthen believers. During this time, Deyneka traveled widely, holding prayer meetings for the church in the Soviet Union. He died in 1987.

The fall of the Iron Curtain in 1989 was an answer to Deyneka's longtime prayer. SGA leaders and missionaries seized the opportunities this created for reaching the people of the former USSR for Christ.

Headquarters

6151 Commonwealth Drive
Loves Park, IL 61111
Telephone: 800-242-5350

Leadership

Leadership for the SGA is provided through a board of directors. In addition, executive and operational officers include Dr. Robert Provost (president), Rosemary Gianesin (vice president of administration), and Eric Mock (vice president of ministry operations).

The SGA has grown to become an international ministry with other autonomous offices in Australia, New Zealand, Canada, and England.

Core Beliefs

An official doctrinal statement grounds the mission organization and provides direction for personnel, churches, and educational institutions. The core biblical beliefs are consistent with the fundamentals of the Christian faith and include the inerrancy and authority of Scripture and belief in the personal, premillennial, and imminent return of Jesus Christ.

Defining Statement

"SGA serves Bible-preaching churches in Russia and the Commonwealth of Independent States by helping national pastors and churches reach their own people with the Gospel of Jesus Christ" (sga.org, "Home").

Core Practices

Since the breakup of the former Soviet Union, the SGA has facilitated the training of several thousand pastors, church planters, and church workers, as well as the planting of several thousand new churches in what is now known as the Commonwealth of Independent States (CIS). Currently, the SGA serves in Armenia, Azerbaijan, Belarus, Kazakhstan, Russia, Tajikistan, Turkmenistan, Ukraine, and Uzbekistan. The SGA serves churches in these countries primarily through the provision of Russian-language Bibles and Christian literature; solid Bible training for pastors, church planters, and church workers; sponsorship of church-planting missionaries; and provision of humanitarian aid.

The SGA enjoys a special relationship with the Russian Union of Evangelical Christians-Baptists. Partnering Western churches with Russian churches to meet a tremendous spiritual need, the Antioch Initiative is a biblically structured, proactive strategy that seeks to develop key regional churches capable of training, sending, and equipping their own to produce multiplying daughter churches throughout their region.

Worship

The SGA seeks to facilitate and develop the worship ministries of local churches in the CIS. This is accomplished by partnering organizations, individuals, and congregations in the West with local churches in the CIS.

Divisions and Splits

The SGA has experienced organizational unity throughout its history.

Growth

Since the breakup of the former Soviet Union, the SGA has experienced exponential growth and is now openly partnering with educational institutions and local churches in the CIS.

Trends

Ministry is becoming more difficult in some countries—especially Russia, where state restrictions and the influence of the Russian Orthodox Church are hindering the work of the Union of Evangelical Christians-Baptists and the activities of evangelical mission organizations considered "Western" in nature.

Missionary and Evangelistic Work

The SGA targets evangelistic work in the CIS.

Ecumenism

The SGA would not be considered an ecumenical organization. Rather, the SGA focuses primarily on evangelism and discipleship, their doctrinal statement providing guidance when partnering with other organizations and denominational groups.

Academic Institutions

The SGA places a high priority on training national leadership for evangelical local churches planted across the CIS. Consequently, the SGA sponsors four seminaries and two major Bible institutes to train pastors and other individuals called to serve in Christian ministry. These schools are:

Almaty Bible Institute (Almaty, Kazakhstan)
Baku Bible Institute (Baku, Azerbaijan)
Irpen Biblical Seminary (Irpen [Kiev], Ukraine)

Minsk Theological Seminary (Minsk, Belarus)
Novosibirsk Biblical-Theological Seminary (Akademgorodok, Russia)
Odessa Theological Seminary (Odessa, Ukraine)

Parachurch Organizations

The SGA engages in a wide range of holistic ministries aimed to meet the tremendous needs of people in the CIS. Most notable are several programs targeted toward reaching children, including Immanuel's Child, Sunday school, summer camp, Orphans Reborn, and Christmas for Orphans. In this process of ministering to children, entire families are often reached with the gospel.

Website

http://www.sga.org/

Bibliography

Rohrer, Norman B., and Peter Deyneka, Jr. *Peter Dynamite: Twice Born Russian—The Captivating Story of Peter Deyneka Sr.* Grand Rapids: Baker, 1975.

Scott D. Edgar

Source of Light Ministries International

History

Founded in 1952, the Source of Light Mission (today Source of Light Ministries International) utilized free Bible correspondence courses to advance the gospel.

Rev. Charles Gilmore and Rev. Edward Steele of Madison, Georgia, participated in a Gospel-distribution campaign in Jamaica at the urging of Rev. Cameron V. Thompson, founder and director of the Pan American Testament League. The island was saturated with Gospels of John, and a program of follow-up material was planned. Inside every Gospel booklet was a coupon entitling the reader to a free Bible study course, and before long all five hundred lessons had been mailed out and additional copies were being hurriedly produced. The demand for such courses has always remained high. Today the group runs Discipleship Training Branches and Associate Discipleship Schools.

Headquarters

1011 Mission Road
Madison, GA 30650
Telephone: 706-342-0397
Fax: 706-342-9072

Leadership

General director: Dr. Bill Shade

Core Beliefs

Source of Light Ministries declares itself as "orthodox in theology and evangelistic in practice, believing in":

1. The plenary and verbal inspiration of the Bible and its inerrancy as God's Holy Word,
2. The Holy Trinity of Father, Son, and Holy Spirit; three Persons in one essence in the unity of the Godhead,
3. The creation of man by the direct act of God and man's subsequent fall as revealed in the Genesis account,
4. The Deity, Incarnation, Virgin Birth, and sinless humanity of Jesus Christ our Lord; His substitutionary death on the cross as the atonement for man's sin; His bodily resurrection from the tomb; His ascension into Heaven to sit at the Father's right hand; the imminent rapture of the Church, and the personal, visible, and premillennial return of Christ in power and great glory,
5. The power of Christ to save men eternally from the penalty of sin through faith in His shed blood, and the gift of eternal life by the grace of God,
6. The new birth of all who believe on Him through the regenerating work of the Holy Spirit,
7. The sanctification of the believer by the Holy Spirit through the Word,
8. The final judgment of the wicked and Satan's doom with the wicked in the lake of fire, and
9. The eternal happiness of the righteous in the presence of the Lord, and the ushering in of eternal righteousness in the new heaven and the new earth. (sourcelight.org, "Vision, Doctrine and Accountability")

Defining Statement

"Providing the Tools to Finish the Task" (source light.org, "Home").

Finances

Source of Light describes itself as a faith ministry, that is, it depends on God and is not endowed or backed by any organization or denomination.

Source of Light has an annual audit and is a member of the Association of North American Missions, which is an accrediting organization for doctrinal, ethical, and financial accountability and conducts five-year reviews.

Total revenue for 2008: $2,909,067
Total expenses for 2008: $2,923,592
Net assets for 2008: $1,666,248

Affiliations

The ministry is a member of the Independent Fundamental Churches of America.

Website

http://www.sourcelight.org/

Bibliography

"Source of Light Ministries International." http://www.source light.org. "Home" and "Vision, Doctrine and Accountability."

Michael McMullen

South America Mission

History

In 1914, Colorado pastor Joseph Davis moved his family to Paraguay to minister among the indigenous peoples through what was called the Paraguayan Mission. In 1902, Scotsman John Hay founded the Paraguayan Evangelistic Medical Mission, also seeking to reach the indigenous of Paraguay. After serving for two years in Paraguay, Davis met Hay, and the two recognized their shared vision and objectives. They developed a friendship and in 1919 determined to merge their two missions into what then became the Inland South America Missionary Union (ISAMU).

The Davis family needed to return to the United States for medical reasons, so in the same year of ISAMU's inception, Davis became the American director of ISAMU, officially incorporated in 1921. Within four years, the scope of the ministry had expanded to Bolivia and Peru, and as the ministry grew and expanded, so did its identification. Since the expansion included work among indigenous tribes in Colombia, the mission's name was changed to South America Indian Mission in 1934. In 1970, the mission expanded to include nationals in urban settings, in addition to its traditional indigenous focus, and the name became South America Mission (SAM).

Headquarters

United States
South America Mission
1021 Maxwell Mill Road
Suite B
Fort Mill, SC 29708
Telephone: 803-802-8580

Canada
CANSAM
336 Speedvale Avenue W
Unit H
Guelph, ON N1H 7M7
Telephone: 866-443-2250

Leadership

The authority of SAM resides in its board of directors. Board members are elected by their peers for three-year terms with the right to succeed themselves. Members are chosen for their ability to help SAM in pursuit of its purpose. They are expected to visit SAM's fields to know firsthand the people and needs. While the board functions as a policy rather than an administrative board, prospective missionaries must realize that final authority for all issues resides with the board.

Core Beliefs

SAM is undergirded by six core characteristics: evangelical, church-centered, relational, creative, accountable, and dependent.

Defining Statement

"South America Mission works for the glorification of God through planting, strengthening and serving the church of Jesus Christ in South America." It sets out to accomplish this task through "strategies of church planting, discipleship, church leadership development, redemptive outreach, mission aviation, and childhood Christian education" (southamericamission.org, "Vision/Mission").

Missionary and Evangelistic Work

SAM takes a holistic approach to ministry by focusing on several areas, all of which contribute to helping people to begin and maintain a relationship with Jesus. SAM currently focuses on leadership development and local church development, while also incorporating ministries such as a flight program, medical ministries, agriculture development, drug rehabilitation programs, and schooling for missionary kids.

SAM currently deploys missionaries in Bolivia, Brazil, Colombia, Paraguay, and Peru, and the team also includes those serving in the US-based home office and the aviation-training program.

Website

http://www.southamericamission.org/

Bibliography

Frizen, Edwin L. *75 Years of IFMA, 1917–1992: The Nonde-nominational Missions Movement.* Pasadena, CA: William Carey Library, 1992.

Records of the South America Mission, Inc. Billy Graham Center, Wheaton College. http://www.wheaton.edu/bgc/archives/GUIDES/204.htm.

"South America Mission." http://www.southamericamission.org. "About SAM."

M. David Sills

TCM and TCM International Institute

History

TCM (Training Christians for Ministry) was founded in 1957 by Gene Dulin of Toronto, Canada. Its initial mission was to assist in planting churches. Within a few years, it developed a special concern for Christians in communist Eastern Europe and worked to provide them with Christian literature and training for ministry. In 1963, TCM broke new ground by establishing a German theological seminary that would be remotely managed from the United States, and in 1970, the organization's work was expanded to reach the Soviet Union. TCM retained an emphasis on ministry education for Eastern European workers, specifically with an approach that utilized native citizens of a country to reach its population; toward that end it created a Summer Seminary in 1982, as well as the Institute for Biblical Studies, later TCM International Institute (TCMII), in 1991. The latter was designed to reflect the changing political landscape in Eastern Europe following the dissolution of the Soviet communist power structure. TCMII earned the distinction of being the only institution accredited by the Higher Learning Commission of the North Central Association of Colleges and Schools yet functioning entirely outside the United States. Today TCMII has more than twenty locations in thirteen countries.

Headquarters

PO Box 24560
Indianapolis, IN 46224
Telephone: 317-299-0333

Core Beliefs

TCM affirms its belief in biblical infallibility, the Trinity, and the deity of Christ, as well as other doctrines that are consistent with teachings of evangelical groups. At the same time, the organization stresses its nondenominational character and its intention to act "solely on Biblical authority" and to "work hand-in-hand with anyone who follows Jesus Christ as Lord in obedience to His Word" (tcmi.org, "World Christian Vision").

Finances

The Evangelical Council for Financial Accountability reports that in 2013 TCM International Institute had total revenue of $3.1 million.

Website

http://www.tcmi.org/

Bibliography

"TCM International Institute." http://www.tcmi.org. "History," "Mission," and "World Christian Vision."

George Thomas Kurian

Teen Challenge

History

Beginning with the decision of a young, rural-Pennsylvania pastor to minister to seven teens facing murder charges in Brooklyn, New York, in 1958, Teen Challenge now ministers to persons and families affected by substance abuse and other life-controlling problems through 241 units and internationally in many countries as Global Teen Challenge (GTC). That pastor, David Wilkerson, opened the first center in 1960 in New York City, where he acquired a large home and started a yearlong discipleship program reaching youths affected by drugs and gangs. Soon Teen Challenge facilities opened in major cities across America, and the national ministry was born. Global Teen Challenge was started by missionary Howard Foltz in the Hague, Netherlands, in 1969. Since then it has spread throughout Europe and now also operates in Australia, Asia, the Middle East, Africa, and Central and South America. Both Teen Challenge organizations are ministries of the Assemblies of God, a major Pentecostal denomination.

The efficacy of this explicitly Christian-conversionist approach to curing substance abuse and alleviating related social dysfunctions has been studied several times by experts independent of the ministry. These have reported a success rate of program graduates ranging from 67 to 86 percent (the latter by the National Institute on Drug Abuse in 1974). Over the years Teen Challenge has expanded its services to help not only teen drug addicts and gang members but also other "youth, adults, and families with life-controlling problems" so they can "become established in society through faith-based mentoring, counseling, education, job training, and microenterprise development" (worldmissions.ag.org, "Global Teen Challenge").

Teen Challenge's national headquarters serve the network "of autonomous local centers each with its own volunteer board of directors." It "promotes a clear and corporate definition of mission and objectives. The central office also sets uniform accrediting standards, provides leadership training and materials, offers systems support, shares best practices and assesses program performance." "The local centers generate operating funds from individuals, churches, community organizations, businesses and their own work programs. Thousands of volunteers recruited largely from churches contribute valuable time and skills, thus making it possible for Teen Challenge centers to operate with extremely low overhead" (Petersen, 4).

Headquarters

Teen Challenge
5250 N Towne Centre Drive
Ozark, MO 65721
Telephone: 417-581-2181
Fax: 417-581-2195
Email: info@teenchallengeusa.com

Global Teen Challenge
15 W 10th Street
Columbus, GA 31901
Telephone: 706-576-6555

Leadership

David Wilkerson is the founder of Teen Challenge. Early on, his brother Don Wilkerson assisted in overseeing the growing ministry and for several years served as the executive director of Global Teen Challenge. A board of eighteen members oversees Teen Challenge, and executive directors lead its regions of operation. Teen Challenge is connected to the Assemblies of God through the Assemblies of God United States Missions division. Global Teen Challenge is part of the World Missions division of the Assemblies of God.

Core Beliefs

Teen Challenge believes that the best path to freedom from substance abuse and other life-controlling problems is by turning from a self-centered life to a Christ-centered life with an ongoing relationship with Jesus Christ. A structured life in a close community saturated with devotion to Christ, Bible study, other spiritual disciplines, work, and increasing doses of service to others characterizes the Teen Challenge approach. It does not minister to clients through primarily medical or psychological approaches to therapy.

The doctrinal beliefs of Teen Challenge are evangelical and Pentecostal, mirroring those of its sponsoring church, the Assemblies of God. Participants in Teen Challenge programs are not required to adopt these beliefs.

Defining Statement

"Teen Challenge offers Christ-centered, faith-based solutions to youth, adults, and families who struggle with life-controlling problems" (teenchallengeusa.com, "About").

Core Practices

Teen Challenge operates primarily through residential programs in which residents voluntarily submit to a highly structured total-life curriculum centered on Christian discipleship. A typical day includes times of personal devotions and corporate worship; communal meals; household chores; Bible study; life-skills training; secondary education classes, as needed; work projects; and recreation.

The aim of the yearlong program is for a resident to become free from life-controlling problems and ready to reenter life beyond Teen Challenge as a stable, productive member of one's family, church, and community. While the ministry aims for residents to become disciples of Jesus Christ, profession of Christian faith is not required for entry into or graduation from Teen Challenge.

Statistics

According to a 1974 study by the National Institute on Drug Abuse, 86 percent of program graduates continued to abstain from abusing drugs and alcohol seven years after they graduated from the program. Other studies report graduate success rates of 67 percent and up.

In 2010, Teen Challenge operated over 243 centers, most of these offering residential programs. In 2009, it reported that in the previous two years, 20,000 people were inducted into Teen Challenge programs, with over 5,000 completing a one-year residential program. Teen Challenge centers "conducted over 18,000 church meetings, 4,214 school meetings, 11,360 prison meetings, over 7,000 other outreach meetings, reaching 'over 4.5 million people,' and 24,498 making 'decisions for Christ'" (2009 Biennial Report).

Internationally, Global Teen Challenge now has 455 residential rehabilitation centers and 271 evangelism outreach points in over 75 nations. GTC also partners with 312 Christian rehab coalitions in Russia and Ukraine.

Missionary and Evangelistic Work

Teen Challenge and GTC operations are, at heart, evangelistic missionary and discipleship ministries aiming to reach globally all who seek freedom from life-controlling problems through the power of Jesus Christ.

Publications

The story of founder David Wilkerson and the first five years of the ministry is known by millions through books and film. *The Cross and the Switchblade*, by Wilkerson with John and Elizabeth Sherrill, was released in 1963, followed by the film adaptation in 1970 starring Pat Boone as Wilkerson and Erik Estrada as Nicky Cruz, the former gang leader transformed by Wilkerson's ministry. Cruz's book, *Run, Baby, Run*, written with Jamie Buckingham, was released in 1968. These books (including a comic book version of the first book) have sold more than 15 million copies, the movie has been seen by over 50 million viewers in 150 countries, and both media have been translated into more than 30 languages.

Beyond these, other publications of Teen Challenge include various books, some multimedia products, program curricula, and various online and print newsletters. Many of these items are available through the Teen Challenge online store.

Websites

Teen Challenge: http://teenchallengeusa.com/
Global Teen Challenge: http://globaltc.org/

Bibliography

Dean, Jamie. "Stamped Out." *World Magazine*, August 27, 2005. http://www.worldmag.com/articles/10969.

Noonan, Kirk. "Transformed Lives: Global Teen Challenge: Portugal." *Today's Pentecostal Evangel*, September 3, 2006. http://www.pe.ag.org/2006PDFs/4817_Transformed.pdf.

Petersen, Doug. "Teen Challenge International: A White Paper." http://www.tcliberia.com/STUDIES-HTML/whitepaper.pdf.

Rebecca Hammes and Mark E. Roberts

UIM International

History

UIM International is a church-planting ministry founded in 1956 that was originally known as United Indian Missions. UIM seeks to establish indigenous churches within Native American and Hispanic communities. UIM's work began among the Navajo, Hualapais, and Havasupais communities in the United States, then spread to Native American groups in Canada and Mexico. Today UIM works with over thirty tribal groups in North America and is particularly interested in ministering to Native Americans who have moved to urban centers and tribal groups living in central Mexico, which it sees as largely unchurched.

UIM is not affiliated with any denomination and is a faith-based ministry that relies on contributions from churches and individuals to support its ministry initiatives.

Headquarters

United States
UIM International
PO Box 6429
Glendale, AZ 85312
Telephone: 623-847-9227
Email: uim@uim.org

Canada
UIM Canada Branch
PO Box 800
Houston, BC V0J 1Z0
Telephone: 250-845-2538
Email: canada@uim.org

Mexico
UIM Internacional Mexico A. C.
Calle Halcon N 10 Nextipac
Municipio Zapopan, Jalisco
Telephone: 714-865-4179
Email: mexico@uim.org

Leadership

Executive director: Daniel P. Fredericks

Core Beliefs

UIM's statement of faith situates the organization within conservative, evangelical Protestantism and includes statements affirming belief in the verbal inspiration of Scripture and the imminent rapture of the church.

Defining Statements

"The vision of UIM is to build cross-cultural relationships through committed people teaming together to accomplish our purpose" (uim .org, "Home").

"The purpose of UIM is to establish indigenous churches among Native Indian, Mexican, and Hispanic peoples of North America built on the Scriptures and functioning within their cultural orientation" (uim.org, "Home").

Core Practices

UIM International's central objective—planting self-governing and self-supporting Christian churches in areas with large Native American and Hispanic populations—is carried out by its missionaries. UIM sends both short- and long-term cross-cultural missionaries into the field who raise funds to support their work there. UIM also facilitates individuals and church groups interested in volunteering for mission trips to support the work of UIM missionaries.

In addition to church planting, UIM International has launched a variety of other ministries. It runs an aviation ministry, with one aviation center in Arizona and two in Mexico. This ministry helps support the establishment of churches in remote and isolated areas.

UIM also runs a camping ministry, with one camp located in New Mexico; one in British Columbia, Canada; and one in Oaxaca, Mexico. These sites run Bible camps for children and youth who come from tribal backgrounds.

Publication

UIM International publishes a magazine, *UIM Magazine*, that contains stories from missionary personnel about the work being carried out by UIM in various locales across North America.

Website

http://www.uim.org/

Bibliography

"UIM International." http://www.uim.org. "Home."

Joe L. Coker

United Bible Societies

History

United Bible Societies (UBS) represents a fellowship of 145 individual societies serving over 200 nations and territories. These Bible societies are not affiliated with any particular denomination and seek not only to make the Bible more widely available but also to help meet the needs of local churches and communities.

Headquarters

UBS World Service Centre
Reading Bridge House
Reading RG
1 8PJ
England

Core Practices

Some of the member societies have provided Bible translations for more than two hundred years, creating access for populations who previously had no Bible in their own language. Other activities and products include Bible distribution, literacy programs, and audio materials for the visually impaired. There are also programs to assist orphans, abused women, and prisoners. In 2004, the Good Samaritan outreach began, as combating AIDS and helping those infected became top priorities of UBS Africa.

Affiliations

United Bible Societies often works in conjunction with other Christian nongovernmental organizations. It works with the Catholic Church to produce the Word for Living website (word forliving.org), which features Gospel readings. UBS also partners with the China Christian Council and the Chinese Church to print and distribute Bibles.

Website

http://www.biblesociety.org/

Sarah Claudine Day

United World Mission

History

United World Mission (UWM) was founded in 1946 by Dr. Sidney Correll, pastor of the independent Dayton Christian Tabernacle in Dayton, Ohio. Correll emphasized missions, and his church members desired to do mission and outreach projects that exceeded their ability to support them. As a solution, Correll partnered with other churches and founded United World Mission in the hope of uniting churches around the globe for the purpose of international missions. UWM made its inaugural mission trip in 1946 to Cuba.

Today the nondenominational UWM is based in Charlotte, North Carolina. Its ministry is to work with local Christians "to form leaders, reproduce churches, and empower the poor and vulnerable" (uwm.org, "Home").

Headquarters

9401-B Southern Pine Boulevard
Charlotte, NC 28273
Telephone: 704-357-3355; 800-825-5896
Fax: 704-357-6389
Email: info@uwm.org

Leadership

President John Bernard leads United World Mission along with a thirteen-member board of directors.

Core Beliefs

UWM is committed to conservative, evangelical doctrine (expressed in seven points at uwm .org, "Statement of Faith"). In practice, UWM believes in advancing church planting throughout the world. Its mission is to "see God change lives and transform communities everywhere by partnering to equip leaders, establish churches, and engage in holistic mission" (uwm.org, "Mission and Values"). UWM carries out this mission through these values: seeking God first, serving partners well, innovating a way, living boldly, and surprising by love (uwm.org, "Mission and Values").

Core Practices

UWM's ministry practices include church multiplication, ministry training and leadership development, spiritual formation, mercy and justice, Business as Mission, mission apprenticeships, and teaching.

Statistics

UWM works in over 35 countries in South America, Europe, Africa, and Asia. In addition, UWM works in Cuba, the Dominican Republic, Nicaragua, and Costa Rica. Its website lists the location of each of its activities.

Missionary and Evangelistic Work

UWM pursues "saturation church planting," an approach that focuses on the goal of having a vital church for every one thousand persons in a region or country. UWM does not see itself as the only agency working to achieve the saturation objective, and it seeks to cooperate with all resources, including established churches and denominations, available in a region of activity.

Parachurch Organizations

Expedition 237 is UWM's two-year program that disciples and mentors students to help them discover and respond to their call to ministry.

UWM partners with the Center for Intercultural Training, a training school in North Carolina that aims to equip students for long-term intercultural missions.

Publications

UWM publishes online articles, newsletters, and brochures available on its website.

Website

http://www.uwm.org/

Bibliography

"United World Mission." http://www.uwm.org. "Home," "Ministry Focus," and "Mission and Values."

Rebekah Hardy

Voice of China and Asia

History

Voice of China and Asia (VOCA) has been ministering in Asia for over one hundred years. Throughout its history, it has sought to reach the lower classes of society by planting churches, opening schools, and starting orphanages. Its guiding principles have been to proclaim the gospel, make disciples, and establish self-sustaining churches. In recent years, it has sought to work openly and legally in China.

Headquarters

PO Box 702015
Tulsa, OK 74170
Telephone: 918-392-0560
Email: info@voiceofchinaandasia.com

Leadership

The president of VOCA is Jonathan Brooks. The board of trustees has five other members.

Defining Statement

"Raising up a new generation for Christ" (voice ofchinaandasia.com, "Home").

Core Practices

VOCA has a threefold purpose. The first is to proclaim the gospel throughout Asia and beyond. The organization's driving goal has been to make Christ known to every person in Asia and the world. The second purpose is to make disciples throughout Asia and beyond. VOCA missionaries have baptized thousands of new believers upon conversion. The final purpose is to establish self-sustaining churches throughout Asia and beyond.

Missionary and Evangelistic Work

Today VOCA is primarily focused on the distribution of Bibles in China. By working with registered churches, its missionaries are able to do so legally. In 2010, VOCA's goal was to distribute thirty thousand Bibles. Its Bible distribution work is done among the rural areas of mainland China, where Bibles are both scarce and too expensive for these believers who exist on less than $100 per year. Although thousands of people are coming to Christ each day in some of these areas, these new believers' remote location and lack of resources leave them unable to procure their own Bibles. VOCA's goal is to place God's Word into the hands of these rural Chinese Christians.

VOCA missionaries are also engaged in starting and leading schools and orphanages. In their Eric Bruce Hammond Home for Handicapped Children, they care for some ninety children who are non-adoptable due to their severe disabilities. In Pakistan and Korea, they have established schools for girls and underprivileged children.

Publication

VOCA publishes quarterly a magazine entitled *Touching Asia for Christ*, which chronicles the work of its ministry.

Website

http://www.voiceofchinaandasia.com/

William Brooks

WEC International

History

Charles Thomas (C. T.) Studd was a renowned cricketer in Great Britain who caused a great stir by surrendering to God's call to mission service. As a student at Cambridge, he became involved in the Student Volunteer Movement. He was one of the famous "Cambridge Seven" who went to China to serve with Hudson Taylor. Studd served for nine years as a missionary with the China Inland Mission, then later in India for five years prior to heading to the Belgian Congo (Zaire), Africa. In 1913, he founded the Heart of Africa mission, which Studd almost simultaneously named the Worldwide Evangelization Crusade (WEC). Today WEC is Worldwide Evangelization for Christ International.

Most notable among WEC's modern missionaries was Dr. Helen Roseveare, a medical doctor who served in the Congo from 1953 to 1973. She has since become a prolific author.

Headquarters

709 Pennsylvania Avenue
Fort Washington, PA 19034
Telephone: 215-646-2322

Leadership

Studd served as the leader of the mission until 1931. Following Studd's death, Norman Grubb, one of his sons-in-law, was appointed to serve as the general secretary, which he did until his retirement in 1965. In recent years, married couples have provided leadership as directors of the international ministry.

Core Beliefs

WEC's doctrinal statement is evangelical, holding to the inerrancy of Scripture and salvation by grace through faith in Christ alone. The following are WEC's five guiding principles:

1. Faith—"We can trust God to supply all we need to accomplish His plan for our lives and ministries. We believe God's work is best done in God's way. We seek to live a life of faith at every level, relying on God for our spiritual, physical and financial needs, and for the resources and strategies to reach the nations with the gospel."
2. Sacrifice—"The Holy Spirit enables us to willingly obey Jesus' call to mission and endure whatever hardships the journey puts in our path."
3. Holiness—"The reality of Christ in us and the power of the Holy Spirit makes it possible for us to live lives that honor God in all we think, say and do."
4. Fellowship—"Our oneness in Christ makes it possible for us to live and work together in multicultural teams as brothers and sisters, maintaining the unity of the Spirit in the bond of peace."
5. Convictions—"These include prayer as a priority, upholding biblical truth and standards, and making no appeals for funds" (wec-usa.org, "Core Values").

Core Practices

WEC's mission is to reach unreached people groups. It accomplishes this through evangelism, discipleship, church planting, Bible translation, theological education, leadership training, medical work, missions research, missions recruitment, rural development, social relief, and education.

Academic Institutions

Cornerstone Centre for Intercultural Studies (Netherlands)
EastWest College of Intercultural Studies (New Zealand)
Gateway College (Canada)

MTC Latino Americano (Brazil)
Worldview Centre for Intercultural Studies (Australia)

Electronic Media

wec.go (e-journal of WEC-USA)

Publications

InTouch newsletter
WEC information leaflets

Website

http://wec-usa.org/

Bibliography

Bonk, Jonathan J. "Studd, C(harles) T(homas)." In *Biographical Dictionary of Christian Missions*, edited by Gerald H. Anderson, 649. New York: Macmillan, 1998.

Coote, Robert T. "Grubb, Norman P(ercy)." In *Biographical Dictionary of Christian Missions*, edited by Gerald H. Anderson, 265–66. New York: Macmillan, 1998.

Grubb, Norman. *C. T. Studd: Cricketer and Pioneer.* Chicago: Moody, 1933.

Tucker, Ruth. *From Jerusalem to Irian Jaya.* 2nd ed. Grand Rapids: Zondervan, 2004.

"WEC International." http://wec-usa.org. "Core Values."

Douglas K. Wilson Jr.

Word of Life Fellowship

History

Having decided to dedicate his life to communicating the Bible, evangelist Jack Wyrtzen began preaching a weekly radio show and shortly thereafter founded Word of Life Fellowship in 1942. The fellowship sponsored religious rallies and services in the late 1940s, with some so considerable that he used Madison Square Garden and Radio City Music Hall. Word of Life Fellowship broadcasts began appearing on television by 1949. During this time, Wyrtzen purchased land in Schroon Lake in the Adirondack Mountains of New York to establish a youth camp. The fellowship eventually founded several camps and a Bible college for people of all ages. Wyrtzen died on April 17, 1996, at Glens Fall Hospital due to complications from a prior surgery to repair an aneurysm.

Headquarters

PO Box 600
Schroon Lake, NY 12870
Telephone: 518-494-6000
Fax: 518-494-6306

Leadership

Don Lough Jr. is the executive director.

Core Beliefs

Word of Life Fellowship is an evangelical and nondenominational ministry affirming the verbal inspiration of the Old and New Testaments, the inerrancy of the Word of God in the original writings, and the supreme and final authority of Scripture for faith and life. It is a trinitarian group who believes in the deity of Jesus Christ, including his virgin birth, sinless life, bodily resurrection, exaltation, and imminent and premillennial return. The sinfulness of humanity is affirmed, as is salvation for all who by faith receive Jesus Christ, who paid the penalty for sin. The Holy Spirit is active in the life of every believer. The bodily resurrection of the just and the unjust will result in the everlasting blessedness of the just and the everlasting conscious punishment of the unjust.

Statistics

Word of Life Fellowship has nearly a thousand missionaries in more than sixty countries and is always seeking to reproduce the ministry throughout the world by means of short-term and career missionary service. Word of Life Fellowship has several teenage camps, junior camps, and family camping and adult conference centers.

Missionary and Evangelistic Work

Word of Life Fellowship is a worldwide ministry devoted to evangelism and discipleship through various means consistent with Scripture for the purpose of edifying and growing the church of Jesus Christ. The fellowship seeks to reach young people in particular with the gospel of Christ to impact the current generation. The fellowship supplies Bible clubs, drama, and music ministry throughout the country. Camp and conference ministries are located in Upstate New York and Florida. The most prominent ministry of Word of Life Fellowship is the youth camps for young people ages thirteen to thirty.

Short-term and full-time missionary service opportunities are available through Word of Life Fellowship. It supports missionary work in diverse areas such as Hungary, Israel, Peru, and New Zealand. Reachout exposes teenagers to cross-cultural ministry in destinations such as Chile, Hungary, Korea, the Philippines, Russia, and Sweden. The Nehemiah Network provides opportunities to serve in the world mission process through hospitality services, professional services, providing equipment needs, and work projects. The Toolbelt Program provides volunteer opportunities to help the ministry in New York and Florida.

Academic Institutions

Word of Life Bible Institute was established in 1970 with seventy-three students. The institute is authorized by the state of New York but does not have regional accreditation. There are also campuses in Hudson, Florida, and Owen Sound, Canada; the latter is accredited by the Transnational Association of Christian Colleges and Schools. Word of Life Bible Institute is enhanced by adjunct faculty—many of whom are well known—who teach from their perspectives as college and seminary professors, college presidents, evangelists, missionaries, and pastors. Graduates receive diplomas for studies as opposed to being granted degrees. Service projects are required of all graduates. Students are expected to devote three hours each school night to quiet study time. The institute opposes social dancing but does require an aerobics program for physical wellness. Entertainment is monitored closely through the perspective of biblical separation.

Parachurch Organizations

Word of Life Local Church Ministries works with local church leaders to provide training and discipleship. Curriculum and instruction are provided for preschoolers, children, and teenagers. Word of Life Fellowship estimates that more than thirty-three thousand young people have been discipled weekly through Local Church Ministries. Word of Life Gospel Productions ministers to thirty-five thousand people annually through gospel-centered musical-drama presentations during Easter and Christmas holidays at the Harry Bollback Performing Arts Center in Hudson, Florida.

Electronic Media

Word of Life Fellowship broadcasts on more than one hundred radio stations worldwide.

Publications

Word of Life Fellowship publishes materials targeting early learners, children, and students. Resources include books, devotionals, evangelistic outreach materials, and presidential series booklets.

Website

http://www.wol.org/

Bibliography

Benson, Warren S., and Mark H. Senter III, eds. *The Complete Book of Youth Ministry*. Chicago: Moody, 1987.

Bollback, Harry. *The House That God Built: The Jack Wyrtzen "Word of Life" Story*. Schroon Lake, NY: Word of Life, 1972.

Carpenter, Joel A., ed. *The Youth for Christ Movement and Its Pioneers*. New York: Garland, 1988.

Hunter, Jack D. *Words of Life from Jack Wyrtzen*. New York: Simon & Schuster, 1976.

Reese, Edward. *The Life and Ministry of Jack Wyrtzen*. Glenwood, IL: Fundamental Publishers, 1975.

Sweeting, George. *The Jack Wyrtzen Story: The Personal Story of the Man, His Message, and His Ministry*. Grand Rapids: Zondervan, 1960.

Woodbridge, John D., ed. *More Than Conquerors*. Chicago: Moody, 1992.

Word of Life Fellowship. *Word of Life Celebration! Fifty Faithful Years*. Schroon Lake, NY: Word of Life, 1989.

Wyrtzen, Jack. *About Face!* New York: American Tract Society, n.d.

Ron J. Bigalke

World Concern

History

Wilbert Saunders, a physician, and Jim McCoy, a pharmacist, founded Medicines for Missions in 1955 to supply medicines to hospitals and clinics all over the world. When they joined the CRISTA family of ministries in 1970, the organization changed its name to World Concern. Initially a relief organization, World Concern experienced a shift in ministry focus when it realized that simply giving handouts following the 7.5 magnitude earthquake in Guatemala was not enough and was, in the long run, even detrimental to the development of a country. Beginning in 1976, World Concern shifted toward a development focus, working alongside the poor and helping them to improve their quality of life and standard of living. Over the past sixty years, World Concern, through its own projects and through partner organizations, has continued to provide both relief and development efforts in countries all over the world.

Headquarters

19303 Fremont Avenue N
Seattle, WA 98133
Telephone: 800-755-5022
Email: info@worldconcern.org

Leadership

World Concern has a president, fifteen directors of various programs, and a nineteen-member board of directors.

Core Beliefs

World Concern is a Christian organization seeking to reach the marginalized and destitute people of the world with Christ's love. Members see their work as a response to Matthew 22:37–39, where Christ reminded those who would follow him to love God and other people. Their desire is to work alongside the poor and provide them with the opportunity to change their own lives. World Concern works to relieve people's suffering, bring them out of poverty, and participate in God's transforming love in the world.

Defining Statement

"World Concern is a Christian global relief and development agency extending opportunity and hope to people facing extreme poverty" (worldconcern.org, "About").

Statistics

Of the more than one thousand field workers employed by World Concern, 95 percent of them are nationals working in their own countries. World Concern works in twenty-four of the poorest countries in the world, including Bangladesh, Bolivia, Chad, Haiti, Kenya, Laos, Myanmar, Somalia, Sri Lanka, Sudan, Thailand, Tibet, Uganda, and Vietnam.

Missionary and Evangelistic Work

World Concern's primary goal is to bring people out of poverty through targeted goals, such as providing microfinance loans to aspiring businesspeople; digging wells to provide clean water; supplying deworming medicines to children; educating people about health, personal safety, disease prevention, and farming; providing vocational training to empower people to pursue meaningful work; and many others. In terms of vocational training, World Concern is working in Laos to provide seed loans and to train local farmers to increase their yields of corn and soybeans. In Haiti, workers teach people how to make briquettes from the materials at hand—cornstalks and manure—to use for household fuel.

World Concern works primarily with underserved people living off the beaten path in places where many other organizations are unable or unwilling to go. The methods for helping people vary as their needs vary, but the consistent goal is to love people as Jesus did and to relieve their physical suffering.

World Concern continues to respond to natural disasters and provide immediate relief in crisis situations. Working primarily in places where it has ongoing development work, World Concern provides assistance in rehabilitation after the immediate crisis is over. For example, after the Port au Prince earthquake in Haiti, World Concern assisted over one hundred thousand people, providing them with food, water, tarps, and other goods to help them survive the first two months following the quake. After the initial phase, World Concern went on to help people meet longer-term needs, providing jobs, helping to rebuild homes, addressing health concerns, and assisting with ongoing food and supplies.

Website

http://www.worldconcern.org/

Lorelle Beth Jabs

World Gospel Mission

History

World Gospel Mission (WGM) began in 1910 when the National Holiness Association (now known as the Christian Holiness Association) created the Missionary Department for the Promotion of Holiness and sent four missionaries to China: Rev. and Mrs. Cecil Troxel and Rev. and Mrs. Woodford Taylor. Within a decade, fifteen missionaries and fifty Chinese workers were leading hundreds to the Lord.

In 1925, the mission established its headquarters at the Chicago Evangelistic Institute in Chicago. The next year it separated from the National Holiness Association and became incorporated in Illinois as the Missionary Society of the National Association for the Promotion of Holiness. The name changed to the National Holiness Missionary Society in 1937 and again to World Gospel Mission in 1954. The headquarters moved to the present George R. Warner Missionary Center in Marion, Indiana, in 1976.

WGM includes a variety of missionary programs that prepare and send individuals and families of different ages to the mission field. Volunteers in Action arranges for young adults to stay with missionaries abroad in order to give them exposure to a cross-cultural setting. The three-year Missionary Disciple Program prepares Christians to become full-time missionaries for WGM. Task Force allows high school and college students to work with missionaries and nationals on one- to two-week trips. A Missionary Partner

Volunteer is over thirty years of age and serves in some way in the field on a four-week to one-year mission. Other opportunities are listed on WGM's website.

WGM is a member of the Evangelical Council for Financial Accountability, Standards of Excellence in Short-Term Mission, and the Mission Exchange.

Headquarters

PO Box 948
Marion, IN 46952
Telephone: 765-671-7247
Fax: 765-671-7230
Email: wgm@wgm.org

Leadership

President and CEO: Hubert P. Harriman
The board has twenty-five members.

Core Beliefs

The doctrinal statement approximates the Apostles' Creed with this added: "The Church's purpose is to worship God, reach those without Christ, and nurture believers" (wgm.org, "Statement of Faith").

Defining Statement

"World Gospel Mission partners with individuals and churches worldwide to make disciples of Christ and encourage believers to become missions-active through ministries that reach the whole person—physically and spiritually—transforming communities" (wgm.org, "Home").

Core Practices

The ministries of World Gospel Mission are preaching, teaching, and healing ministries.

Worship

Worship is Pentecostal and includes the exercise of spiritual gifts described in 1 Corinthians 12:4–11, 27–31 and Romans 12:3–8, including singing (glossolalia) and dancing in the spirit.

Statistics

WGM has 350 missionaries and support staff serving in more than 15 countries on 5 continents.

Growth

The mission works in Argentina, Bolivia, El Salvador, Haiti, Honduras, Hungary, India, Japan, Kenya, Mexico, the Middle East, Nicaragua,

Papua New Guinea, Paraguay, Peru, Spain, Sudan, Taiwan, Uganda, Ukraine, the United States, and the West Indies.

Missionary and Evangelistic Work

WGM exists solely to evangelize.

Ecumenism

Although WGM was established by the National Holiness Association, it is now an interdenominational and international missionary organization.

Parachurch Organizations

Oaks Village Retirement Community
STEER Inc. commission community
Medical and educational ministries
Disaster relief

Publication

The Call (bimonthly, hard and electronic copies)

Website

http://www.wgm.org/

Bibliography

Applebee, Denis. *When I Tread the Verge of Jordan: An Exposition of the Crisis Experience of Entire Sanctification.* Marion, IN: World Gospel Mission, 1988.

Brown, Michael L. *Sent to the Heart: The Story of World Gospel Mission in Bolivia.* Marion, IN: World Gospel Mission, 1995.

Bushong, Burnis H. *The Best of the Story: Miraculous Answers to Prayer.* Marion, IN: World Gospel Mission, 1993.

———. *R.U.N. Reaching the Unreached Now: A Brief History of World Gospel Mission.* Marion, IN: World Gospel Mission, 1995.

Degenkolb, Joan G., and Edna M. Boroff. *Come Help Us: A Doctor in Africa.* Marion, IN: World Gospel Mission, 1998.

Heinemann, Marie H. *My Africa (Falling in Step).* Marion, IN: World Gospel Mission, 1988.

Johnson, Michael. *Making the Blind Man Lame: What Jesus Wouldn't Do.* Raleigh, NC: Higher Standard Publishers, 2006.

Brenda Ayres

World Indigenous Missions

History

World Indigenous Missions (WIM) began in 1981 as the vision of several missionaries who met in the mountains of Mexico while serving the indigenous people there. These missionaries realized they shared a common goal to "disciple the nations to reach the world" (worldim.com, "Meet WIM"). As the original missionaries' vision grew, their objective became not only to establish churches but also to help establish indigenous, or native, churches, with mission work being accomplished by the indigenous people. These principles led to the successful founding of churches that are "self-governing, self-supporting, and self-propagating" (worldim.com, "Vision and Core Values").

This first vision, now referred to as the "indigenous principle," is the heart of WIM.

Headquarters

PO Box 310627
New Braunfels, TX 78131
Telephone: 830-629-0863
Email: wim@worldim.com

Leadership

President: Chuck Hall
Director of operations: Chris Briles

The mission has a five-member board of directors.

Core Beliefs

We believe the Bible to be the inspired, the only infallible, authoritative Word of God.

We believe that there is one God, eternally existent in three persons: Father, Son, and Holy Spirit.

We believe that Jesus Christ, the Son of God, is the world's only savior. We acknowledge His incarnation, His virgin birth, His sinless life, His vicarious death, His physical burial, and His bodily resurrection.

We believe that Jesus Christ will return in a personal and visible form.

We believe in a present ministry of the Holy Spirit, whose indwelling at salvation enables the Christian to live a godly life.

We believe that man, in his natural state, is a sinner: lost, undone, without hope, and without God.

We believe that, for the salvation of lost and sinful man, repentance of sin and faith in Jesus Christ alone result in being born again by the Holy Spirit.

We believe that the baptism in the Holy Spirit is the promise of the Father that Jesus told His followers to wait for, and it was given at Pentecost. It was sent by Jesus after His ascension to empower the Church to preach the gospel throughout the whole earth.

We believe that the Holy Spirit is manifested through a variety of spiritual gifts to build and sanctify the Church, demonstrate the validity of the resurrection, and confirm the power of the gospel. . . . All believers are commanded to desire earnestly the manifestation of the gifts in their lives. These gifts always operate in harmony with the Scriptures and should never be used in violation of biblical parameters.

We believe in the spiritual unity of believers in our Lord Jesus Christ and that all true believers are members of His body the Church. It is the responsibility of the church to obey Christ's great commission to reach the whole world with the whole gospel. (worldim.com, "Statement of Faith")

Core Practices

"Evangelize the lost with the gospel of Jesus Christ. Establish indigenous churches where there are none. Equip and serve leaders" (worldim .com, "Meet WIM").

The goal of WIM, "to plant churches or works that will stand after the missionary has left," involves strong national leadership. This is accomplished by mentoring, "the model begun by Christ." "Mentoring is developing covenant relationships with people and imparting life-lived truths on which a foundation for life and ministry can be based." This relationship is key in every culture in the world. "[T]he message of the Gospel revolves around God's relationship to man and man's relationship to one another. More than a passing acquaintance, a committed relationship binds one to another with the common bond of Christ's love." It is a lifetime spent sharing. "At WIM, relationship is the foundation for ministry." This value is the basis of training both for new missionaries and national leaders.

A kingdom perspective demands that the kingdom of God is to be built first and foremost. While growth is necessary in an organization, the true desire must be for the establishment of the kingdom of God around the world. "Therefore, this core value states that [WIM is] building the Kingdom of God, not the kingdom of WIM." Networking with other organizations is necessary in order to accomplish this purpose.

Servant leadership is included in the vision statement: "to equip and serve church leaders." True greatness in God's kingdom is measured by service. With Jesus as the example who "did not come to be served, but to serve," WIM seeks to lead by example while serving one another in love (worldim.com, "Vision and Core Values").

Website

http://www.worldim.com/

Bibliography

"World Indigenous Missions." http://www.worldim.com. "Meet WIM," "Statement of Faith," and "Vision and Core Values."

Barbara Wyman

World Mission Prayer League

History

In the mid-1930s, a group of Lutherans in Minneapolis felt led to be missionaries abroad but found that the Lutheran synods had no budget to send them. In 1937, they formed the South American Mission Prayer League to make a way for laypeople to participate in missions. The league was able to send two missionaries to Bolivia the next year. Soon it was sending volunteers to Central Asia, Africa, and Eastern Europe, and thus it changed its name to the World Mission Prayer League (WMPL). In 1945, the WMPL became incorporated in the state of Minnesota. The World Mission Prayer League/Canada was formed in 1969 and incorporated in Edmonton, Alberta. Three years later the American Board of the Santal Mission merged with the league. In March 2010, an office was opened in La Paz, Bolivia.

Headquarters

232 Clifton Avenue
Minneapolis, MN 55403
Telephone: 612-871-6843
Email: wmpl@wmpl.org

Leadership

President and CEO: Rev. Charles Lindquist

Core Beliefs

Lutheran

Defining Statement

"Transforming lives through prayer" (wmpl .org, "Home").

Core Practices

Core practices include prayer; sending missionaries; and providing medicine, education, and relief. The missionaries are mobile; after they build a church, they go to another area to build more and trust God to raise up local leadership in the churches. The league does not solicit finances from any person or agency but sees God providing resources as an answer to prayer. All missionaries are nonsalaried volunteers.

Controversies

In 2009, the Evangelical Lutheran Church in America approved the ordination of practicing lesbian and homosexual pastors in leadership of the church. The WMPL does not endorse this decision.

Statistics

The league has six thousand praying members plus one hundred full-time workers in twenty countries.

Growth

Outreach and church planting have increased each year.

Trends

The WMPL prayerfully plans to minister to the unreached and to go into areas where there have been no churches. It hopes to never abandon this vision.

Missionary and Evangelistic Work

The WMPL's purpose is to evangelize and plant churches, with outreach ministries in Asia, Africa, Eastern Europe, and Latin America, as well as in the United States and Canada.

Ecumenism

The WMPL is an independent Lutheran agency.

Parachurch Organizations

The league states, "We will advocate interrelationship, interdependence, and creative partnership in the cause of mission" (wmpl.org, "Statements of Faith and Mission"). Its outreach provides medicine, education, development, and relief.

Publication

Together in Prayer (monthly printed and electronic journal)

Website

http://www.wmpl.org/

Bibliography

Handbook of the World Mission Prayer League. Minneapolis: World Mission Prayer League, 2004.
"World Mission Prayer League." http://www.wmpl.org. "Home" and "Statements of Faith and Mission."

Brenda Ayres

World Neighbors

History

World Neighbors was begun in 1951 by Dr. John L. Peters and the congregation of St. Luke's United Methodist Church in Oklahoma City. During World War II, Peters had witnessed extreme poverty and developed a strong desire to help the poor improve their condition.

After Peters delivered an inspiring sermon, the church encouraged him in his objective, and Peters opened his first mission in India. World Neighbors has influenced the lives of twenty-five million people in over forty-five countries. Dr. Peters received numerous honors because of his efforts, including two nominations for the Nobel Peace Prize, election to the Oklahoma Hall of Fame, and *Guidepost* magazine's Good Samaritan Award.

Headquarters

4127 NW 122nd Street
Oklahoma City, OK 73120
Telephone: 800-242-6387
Fax: 405-752-9393
Email: info@wn.org

Leadership

World Neighbors is governed by a board of trustees. Operations are directed by Melanie Macdonald, the president and CEO, who is assisted by senior staff members. World Neighbors is a member seal holder of the Better Business Bureau Wise Giving Alliance.

Core Beliefs

World Neighbors believes in assisting the poorest and most isolated areas of Asia, Africa, and Latin America by enabling the needy to help themselves. It seeks lasting solutions through training individuals and developing communities. World Neighbors believes that help is best offered by finding out a community's own perception of its need before aid is given.

Defining Statement

"World Neighbors inspires people and strengthens communities to find lasting solutions to hunger, poverty and disease and to promote a healthy environment" (wn.org, "Home").

Core Practices

World Neighbors emphasizes the importance of ascertaining from local individuals the needs in the mission field. When needs are determined, World Neighbors tries to meet them, endeavoring to find lasting solutions to problems rather than offering temporary help. World Neighbors typically emphasizes teaching, training, and local economic development. World Neighbors welcomes volunteers on either a short-term or long-term basis.

Statistics

World Neighbors is currently located in fifteen countries. There are eighteen team members in the United States and fifty-three abroad. World Neighbors has partnerships with over fifty organizations. According to its annual report, World Neighbors assisted about five hundred thousand individuals during the 2010–11 fiscal year. The organization has an annual budget of about $5.5 million.

Website

http://www.wn.org/

Scott Goins

World Partners

History

A ministry of the Missionary Church, the organization that would become World Partners was born in the nineteenth-century evangelical movement, which stressed not only renewal at home but also work abroad, such as the development of schools, places of worship, and hospitals in underdeveloped countries. Its missions included ones to Liberia (1890), Turkey (1898), Sierra Leone (1898), Nigeria (1901), and India (1924), and, despite harsh conditions, there was a growing number of volunteers. In 1988, the group was named World Partners and expanded its work throughout the Americas, Asia, Europe, Africa, and the Middle East, often availing itself of the talent of key local leaders to plant churches and advance world missions.

World Partners staff operates in Bulgaria, Chad, China, Cyprus, Ecuador, Egypt, France, Guinea, Hungary, Ireland, Israel, Mongolia, Morocco, Portugal, Russia, Sierra Leone, South Africa, Spain, Thailand, Turkey, the United States, Uruguay, and Vietnam.

Headquarters

PO Box 9333
Fort Wayne, IN 46899
Telephone: 260-747-9439

Leadership

There is an executive director, an associate director, and a financial director, as well as regional directors. The volunteer board of directors meets biannually.

Defining Statement

"World Partners exists to impact the world for Christ by equipping and empowering leaders to launch disciple making movements" (wpartners .org, "Home").

Core Practices

The ministry utilizes resources of the host culture and focuses on activities such as sustainable community and agricultural development, education, small business development, community health, and leadership development.

Affiliations

World Partners works in conjunction with ECHO in Fort Myers, Florida, to create lasting solutions to global hunger. Founded in 1981, ECHO helps development workers in 180 countries with expertise and access to their sizable seed bank. World Partners has lent a full-time staff member to ECHO, and two staff members trained by ECHO are serving in Asia and Africa.

World Partners has helped to create a professional interchange between Dupont Hospital in Fort Wayne, Indiana, and Kazanlak Hospital of Kazanlak, Bulgaria. Each hospital has sent three teams of professionals to the other.

Website

http://www.wpartners.org/

Michael McMullen

World Reach

History

World Reach was founded in 1982 by Timothy Prewitt, a businessman and a member of a Baptist church in Birmingham, Alabama. Prewitt envisioned an organization that would evangelize by planting churches in areas where there was limited church presence or where there was need for Christian revival. World Reach focused on creating new, Bible-based churches and training leaders who would eventually be able to direct those churches. World Reach has grown into an organization serving a dozen nations in Latin America, Africa, and Europe. It is a member of the Evangelical Council for Financial Accountability.

Headquarters

PO Box 26155
Birmingham, AL 35260
Telephone: 205-979-2400
Fax: 205-979-6289
Email: info@world-reach.org

Leadership

Timothy Prewitt, the founder of World Reach, is its general director. He is assisted by his wife, Carol, who is the administrative assistant. A board of ten directors from various denominations oversees the organization.

Core Beliefs

World Reach is an evangelical, nondenominational organization dedicated to fulfilling the Great Commission. It seeks to foster discipleship through evangelization, training, relief efforts, work with local churches, and church planting. The organization emphasizes establishing churches and training leaders, both ministers and laity. The churches that are planted are not attached to a particular denomination, and choice of denominational affiliation is left to the local church. World Reach is committed to the authority of Scriptures and believes in reliance on God's provision for finances.

Defining Statement

"Reaching the world with the Gospel of Christ through the local church" (world-reach.org, "Home").

Core Practices

World Reach has missions in Albania, Argentina, Colombia, El Salvador, Germany, Honduras, Kenya, Macedonia, Nicaragua, Peru, Romania, and Ukraine.

In areas in need of churches, World Reach has a four-phase program for creating new worship communities. First, local evangelism is begun in the target location. Second, while continuing to evangelize, World Reach seeks to disciple and train leaders through Bible study and "growth groups." Third, a pastor is chosen and trained. Fourth, as all the other phases continue, World Reach assists the local group in construction and continues to nurture the local church until it becomes self-sufficient.

Local Bible institutes for the training of new leaders are a main focal point of World Reach's ministry. The institutes train both pastors and lay leaders.

World Reach has orphanages, family counseling, and medical clinics in its various mission fields.

World Reach welcomes short-term volunteers as well as career missionaries.

Website

http://www.world-reach.org/

Scott Goins

World Servants

History

In 1986, Jack Larson, the Caribbean director of Youth for Christ's Project Serve, envisioned sending mission teams instead of individuals on short-term mission trips around the world. He believed that if a group could be sponsored by a local church, be trained and sent abroad, and then return to the local church, three groups of people would be spiritually changed in the process: the local church sponsor, the mission field, and the missionaries. Following that theory, he sent two hundred senior high school students to the Dominican Republic, where they built four churches and established a children's ministry in numerous communities. The next year approximately six hundred young people went to Mexico, the Dominican Republic, Jamaica, Belize, and a Native American reservation in the United States. The following year junior high school students were invited to participate, and they ministered in West Virginia and Ecuador.

Also in 1988, Joop van der Meer of the Netherlands recruited Europeans to participate in the mission trips. He formed World Servants Europe and served as its director. In 1989, students went into Costa Rica and Venezuela. From 1990 to 1994, they also went to Albania, Bolivia, Brazil, the Czech Republic, Egypt, French Guyana, Ghana, Hungary, Kenya, Romania, and Russia.

Later, World Servants (WS) added programs to involve adults and families. It is incorporated, became a member of the United States Standards of Excellence in Short-Term Mission in 2003, and has an impressive five-star efficiency rating from Ministry Watch.

Headquarters

7130 Portland Avenue S
Richfield, MN 55423
Telephone: 612-866-0010; 800-881-2170
Fax: 612-866-9978
Email: info@worldservants.org

Leadership

There are currently four World Servants organizations, each with its own office, board, staff, and unique mission statements. They are in the United States, Canada, the Dominican Republic, and the Netherlands. They are united under one seven-member board and one president and CEO.

Core Beliefs

Each member must adhere to the Westminster Confession.

Core Practice

WS's philosophy for bringing about spiritual transformation in any country is first to learn the culture and come to know its values. Then by demonstrating love and respect for the culture and building relationships, lives can be changed.

Statistics

26,900 participants
18,800 family participants
810 sending churches
80 churches built
6,100 decisions for Christ
40,000 have served in over 50 individual communities globally

Missionary and Evangelistic Work

WS's mission is solely evangelistic, driven to impact the world through Jesus Christ by bringing hope to the world through life-changing learning and serving experiences.

Ecumenism

WS is an independent, nondenominational organization, but it partners with American Baptist, Missouri Synod Lutheran, and Christian and Missionary Alliance churches. In addition, it often works in concert with Mission Emanuel in relief projects.

Academic Institutions

WS has no campuses but offers seminars, forums, and academic courses to teach cultural sensitivity and leadership training. World Servants Cross-Cultural Orientation, which trains in cultural sensitivity and mission leadership, is held in major cities.

Parachurch Organizations

WS partners with Compassion International, Life Touch Photography, and World Vision.

Electronic Media

WS broadcasts on various radio stations around the world, including Moody Radio Station of the Navajo Nation.

Publication

World Servants Newsletter

Website

http://www.usa.worldservants.org/

Bibliography

Alexis, Susan. *Caring Hands: Inspiring Stories of Volunteer Medical Missions*. Minneapolis: Fairview, 2003.

Kendall, Jackie. *The Mentoring Mom: 11 Ways to Model Christ for Your Child*. Birmingham, AL: New Hope Publishers, 2006.

May, Kasii. *World Servants Volunteer Department: A Change Initiative*. MA thesis, Bethel University, 2007.

Brenda Ayres

World Vision International

History

An encounter with a battered, abandoned child in China in 1947 prompted Rev. Bob Pierce to give the child's caretaker five dollars and also to seek to build an organization that would help the world's children. Thus, World Vision was born in 1950. Three years later World Vision started a child sponsorship program to support orphans from the Korean War. That program expanded over time to Eastern Europe, the Middle East, Africa, Asia, and Latin America, providing in each place necessities such as food, education, health care, and job training. In 1970, World Vision began helping with international emergencies and meeting longer-term community needs, such as water, health, sanitation, training, and education. World Vision International (WVI) now works in approximately one hundred countries and has added to its range of activities advocating for select social issues, such as child labor and sexual mistreatment of women and children.

Headquarters

800 W Chestnut Avenue
Monrovia, CA 91016
Email: worvis@wvi.org

Leadership

WVI's leadership consists of an international board of twenty-four members, as well as national boards in each participating country. Each national board consists of church and social service leaders, as well as business professionals.

Core Beliefs

Six core values are central to the organization and its actions (see wvi.org, "Vision and Values" for the complete statement):

WVI is Christian, acknowledging one God—Father, Son, and Holy Spirit—and the revelation of the love, mercy, and grace of God to all people through Jesus.

WVI is committed to the poor, both to relieving their suffering and to promoting their well-being.

WVI values people, giving priority to people and their dignity before money, structure, and systems.

WVI is a steward both of contributions entrusted to it and of God's creation.

WVI is a partner with the poor and with donors in a shared ministry.

WVI is responsive to life-threatening emergencies it can affect.

Defining Statement

"World Vision is an international partnership of Christians whose mission is to follow our Lord and Saviour Jesus Christ in working with the poor and oppressed to promote human transformation, seek justice and bear witness to the good news of the Kingdom of God" (wvi.org, "Vision and Values").

Core Practices

WVI operates in three main modes: short-term emergency relief, long-term sustainable community development, and working with policymakers and the public at the national, regional, and global level to build awareness about poverty and to address the unjust systems that help perpetuate it.

Also, WVI's projects are child-focused and patterned to provide maximum aid for children by targeting the causes (not just the symptoms) of children's suffering. One tool is WVI's child sponsorship program, which fosters relationships between sponsors and children in order to help eliminate poverty from the children's lives. In addition, WVI implements various projects and microfinance with the aim to improve adults' livelihood in order to create a community that is economically secure and can thus support its children in the future. WVI offers aid strictly on the basis of need and thus helps people regardless of whether they confess to being Christian. The organization does not proselytize and does not require that the recipients of the projects hear or convert to a religious, Christian message. WVI strives to respect the religious beliefs of the people to whom it lends assistance.

Statistics

WVI provides aid and strives to achieve social justice in almost one hundred countries spanning Eastern Europe, the Middle East, Africa, Asia, and Latin America. WVI employs approximately forty-thousand staff members.

Website

http://www.wvi.org/

Bibliography

"World Vision International." http://www.wvi.org. "Vision and Values."

Nicole A. Pride

Worldwide Discipleship Association

History

The Worldwide Discipleship Association (WDA) utilizes Christ's model of training his disciples to foster Christlike conduct in believers and to teach them to disciple others. Founded in 1974, the WDA was founded by pastor Carl Wilson, who had been Campus Crusade for Christ's director of high school ministry. Wilson wrote *With Christ in the School of Disciple Building*, and the WDA has always endeavored to model its ministry after Jesus's methods. It started on college campuses, which the group views as culturally influential, and continues an active presence there, even as it has expanded into other areas of ministry. Today the WDA sees itself as part of a worldwide network of ministries.

Headquarters

PO Box 142437
Fayetteville, GA 30214
Telephone: 770-460-6940
Fax: 770-460-1339
Email: info@disciplebuilding.org

Leadership

President and executive director: Robert D. Dukes

The WDA leadership reports to a board of directors consisting of an executive committee and three subcommittees.

Core Beliefs

The WDA embraces traditional evangelical beliefs. A statement of faith can be found at disciplebuilding.org.

Defining Statement

"WDA's mission is to serve the Church worldwide by developing Christlike character in people and equipping them to disciple others according to the pattern Jesus used to train his disciples" (disciplebuilding.org, "Home").

Core Practices

The WDA operates on the premise that disciple building is a five-phase process: establishing faith (conversion); laying foundations, that is, learning who Christ is and how to follow him; equipping for ministry; developing new leaders; and developing mature leaders. Emotional healing is seen as a critical component of spiritual growth.

The WDA believes in structure and organization in the pursuit of its goals. Its master plan, revised annually by the executive leadership team and board of directors, reflects diligent planning. The WDA has crafted a three-part approach to its mission: stressing the biblical mandate to develop mature disciples; in conjunction with partners, building disciples at training centers; and training individuals how to disciple based on Christ's model, using resources such as curricula, focused seminars, and consulting teams. Customized consulting is also offered to individual disciple builders and ministries.

On campuses and in the community, WDA teams mentor individual believers and groups by teaching about Christian growth. Five existing centers are located at DePauw University, the University of Georgia, Purdue University, the University of Tennessee, and Arusha, Tanzania.

The WDA works in partnership with churches, seminaries, mission groups, student ministries, and community groups. The WDA helped to found the Pierce Center for Disciple Building in 1999 and is actively involved in its operation. Located on all three campuses of Gordon-Conwell Theological Seminary, the center stresses the importance of spiritual growth in seminarians and the critical need for mature Christian leadership. It offers guidance to the community at large in addition to its own students. Other WDA partners include the Gathering Place (St. Simons Island, Georgia); New Hope Baptist Church—College and Career Ministry (Fayetteville, Georgia); Hong Key Chung (pastor located in Bucharest, Romania); San Pablo Seminary (Merida, Mexico); and Myanmar School of Disciple Building (Yangon, Myanmar).

Literature as well as seminars and conferences help a variety of individuals who want to mentor others or grow spiritually themselves. The theme of all of the WDA's materials is progressive process that meets people where they are and helps them reach the next stage of growth.

WDA teams travel globally to reach churches in underprivileged areas that lack resources but often experience rapid growth.

Finances

The WDA is a 501(c)(3) nonprofit organization funded primarily by tax-deductible gifts. It is a member of the Evangelical Council for Financial Accountability and has an A rating from Ministry Watch. Annual revenue is more than $1.3 million.

Trends

The WDA would like to expand its international disciple-building activities.

Website

http://www.disciplebuilding.org/

Sarah Claudine Day

Wycliffe Global Alliance (formerly Wycliffe International)

History

Wycliffe International (WI) was the child of the earlier Summer Institute of Linguistics (now SIL International), which Cameron Townsend and L. L. Legeters founded in 1934 as a summer training program on a farm in Arkansas. They, with other personnel, had worked since the 1920s among minority-language peoples of Central and South America. They had originally planned to train linguists and translators who would work under other missionary societies. But the value of a new society dedicated to Bible translation spurred the creation in 1942 of Wycliffe Bible Translators Inc. (WBTI). From small beginnings, sometimes following SIL courses offered overseas, WBTI expanded internationally through divisions incorporated in countries such as Australia, the United Kingdom, and Canada. Its Bible translation vision attracted a new workforce from Europe and Nordic countries in the 1960s, followed in the 1980s by Asian countries, led by Japan, Singapore, and South Korea. The end of the USSR opened the door to participation from Eastern and Central European countries in the 1990s, countries whose peoples had suffered without easy access to God's written Word and who were eager to help others access it in their own languages.

This internationalizing of Scripture translation prompted the incorporation in 1980 of Wycliffe Bible Translators International (WBTI), which became Wycliffe USA and finally Wycliffe International (WI). The national divisions under the old WBTI became divisions of WI. But in 1991, WI restructured, and the former national divisions became autonomous member organizations. In 2011, WI became Wycliffe Global Alliance, with headquarters in Singapore.

Today Wycliffe Global Alliance consists of more than forty-five member organizations and more than sixty partner organizations worldwide. These work in over ninety countries around the globe to provide Scripture in the over twenty-three hundred languages spoken today that still lack any portion of the Word of God. Most are minority languages, used by communities that struggle to maintain their cultural identity amid much larger majority cultures, and many of these minority languages lack a written form. Most of these peoples have never known the truth of Scripture, while others are Christians who struggle to comprehend the Bible in a language not their own. Through the initiative of Vision 2025, Wycliffe Global Alliance aims to have Bible translation underway or completed for every language in need by 2025.

Headquarters

Wycliffe Bible Translators
11221 John Wycliffe Boulevard
Orlando, FL 32832
Telephone: 407-852-3600; 800-WYCLIFF (800-992-5433)
Fax: 407-852-3601
Email: info_usa@wycliffe.org

Wycliffe Global Alliance
34 Craig Road
#02-09 Chinatown Plaza
089673 Singapore
Singapore
Telephone: (65) 62231655
Email: info@wycliffe.net

Leadership

The Global Leadership Team is led by an executive director and an associate director. The organization has a nine-member board of directors.

Core Beliefs

Wycliffe Global Alliance upholds basic evangelical doctrine, expressed in nine doctrinal affirmations (see wycliffe.net, "Doctrinal Statement"). It aspires for all people to know God by providing Scripture in their language as an expression of the church's fulfillment of the Great Commission.

In addition to its doctrinal stance, Wycliffe Global Alliance embraces the following core values: the glory of God among the nations, Christlikeness in life and work, the church as central in God's mission, the Word translated, dependence on God for everything needed, and partnership with others and service to the peoples of the earth.

Defining Statement

"Individuals, communities, and nations transformed through God's love and Word expressed in their languages and cultures" (wycliffe.net, "Mission, Vision and Values of Wycliffe Global Alliance").

Statistics

World population: over 6.5 billion

Number of languages spoken in the world: over 6,900

Languages without any part of the Bible: over 2,300

People who speak languages without the Bible: over 350 million

Translation programs working with Wycliffe in 90 countries: over 1,300

75 percent of the world's translation needs are in three areas: Central Africa and Nigeria, Mainland and Southeast Asia, and Indonesia and the Pacific Islands

Language communities with the New Testament: 1,185

Language communities with the entire Bible: 451

Missionary and Evangelistic Work

Translating the Bible into the languages of peoples is often one of the first steps toward effective evangelism. Without Scripture in indigenous languages, churches established through missionary evangelistic efforts are less effective and less enduring than those accompanied by Scripture available in the "heart" languages of the people. In this way, all of Wycliffe Global Alliance's translation activities are both missionary and evangelistic. Beyond providing translated Scripture, Wycliffe promotes literacy for those receiving new translations. Literacy, in turn, enables such communities to receive medical information, to develop marketable skills that build their economies, and to preserve their own cultures. Thus, Bible translation targets spiritual needs first but benefits other needs as a result. Wycliffe's efforts are ultimately holistic, although they focus on Scripture translation.

SIL International works with language communities around the world through research, translation, and literacy in order to advance language-based progress. It sends volunteers to lesser-known language communities to live among the people and learn their culture. Their research helps Wycliffe translate Scripture more effectively and more quickly into these languages.

Academic Institutions

Academic programs at various colleges and universities train students for specific professional translation roles, ranging from language surveyor and Bible translator to literacy worker. Such schools include Biola University, Trinity Western University (Canada), Bryan College, the University of North Dakota, and the Graduate Institute of Applied Linguistics.

Websites

Wycliffe Global Alliance: http://www.wycliffe.net/
Wycliffe Bible Translators: http://www.wycliffe.org/

Isaac Almaguer and Mark E. Roberts

Young Life

History

Young Life began in 1941 as an outgrowth of weekly youth clubs led by young Presbyterian minister and recent seminary graduate Jim Rayburn. Rayburn and four other seminarians had been leading weekly youth clubs since 1938. These men worked through these clubs to show young people that God could change lives.

By 1946, Young Life clubs had spread to several states, its staff had increased to twenty people, and its headquarters had moved from Texas to the present location in Colorado Springs, Colorado. Shortly thereafter, volunteer work for Young Life began at Wheaton College in Illinois. Young Life's international ministry began in 1953 in France through the work of Rod and Fran Johnston. Since then it has spread to more than sixty countries around the globe.

Initially, Young Life clubs focused on suburban youth, but now Young Life has over seven hundred multicultural ministries, including outreach to rural and urban areas, children with disabilities, pregnant teens and young mothers, and young people on military bases.

Headquarters

PO Box 520
Colorado Springs, CO 80901
Telephone: 877-438-9572
Fax: 719-381-1755

Leadership

In 2016, Newt Crenshaw became the president and CEO of Young Life. He is the sixth president in its history and is accountable to a board of trustees.

Core Beliefs

Young Life's statement of faith consists of eight articles that express mainstream American evangelical beliefs about Scripture, God, Jesus, the Holy Spirit, creation, redemption, sinful human nature, and the church. The statement can be accessed at younglife.org.

Core Practices

Young Life summarizes its ministry to young people in what are called the five C's. The first C, contact work, shows the kids that someone cares about them. The focus is on developing friendship and trust. The second C is club. Young Life calls the weekly clubs "a party with a purpose" because they are not only fun but also purposeful as a way to share the gospel. Before the end of every meeting, the gospel is presented, and there is an opportunity for kids to become saved. The third C is camp. Many kids who return from Young Life camps say it was the greatest week of their life; they make great friends and learn about the love of God. The fourth C is campaigners. Campaigners is an optional additional weekly meeting for students wanting to grow more in Christ through leading and serving others. Campaigners also motivates the kids to become involved in a local church. The fifth and final C is committee. The committee is made up of adults who not only invest in the kids but also support the Young Life staff morally, administratively, and financially.

Finances

Young Life is a member of the Evangelical Council for Financial Accountability and is highly rated by Charity Navigator, receiving three out of four stars on the Charity Navigator scale.

Statistics

Young Life is active in nearly one thousand communities within the United States and works with teens in more than sixty countries. Over thirty-three hundred staff members work with more than thirty-one thousand volunteer leaders in doing the work of Young Life. Young Life is a nondenominational ministry, and both Protestants and Catholics serve as staff.

Missionary and Evangelistic Work

Young Life reaches out to adolescents from junior high through high school in an effort to impact them with the good news of the gospel of Jesus Christ. Young Life's focus is on building trust through relationships that are developed during weekly time together. Young Life believes that influence is gained when trust is established. Besides weekly clubs, Young Life camps, which generally last for one week or a weekend, change the lives of many students.

Electronic Media

Young Life is present on Facebook.

Publication

The magazine *Relationships* relates stories of people's lives that have been changed through Young Life. In two issues per year, it features an article from the president of Young Life, special features for alumni, and articles about the ministry's progress.

Website

http://www.younglife.org/

Gretchen Knurr

Youth for Christ

History

Since 1944, Youth for Christ (YFC) has had a distinctive history of youth evangelism. A perceived lack of responsiveness by the church provided impetus by visionaries to create an age-specific ministry to reach neglected youth. Beginning in dozens of American cities at the end of World War II, YFC quickly organized into a national movement. Billy Graham became YFC's first full-time staff member. Other noted American evangelicals such as Torrey Johnson and Jack Wyrtzen are associated with development of the organization.

Starting with Saturday night youth rallies in the late 1940s and early 1950s, YFC's ministry turned to Bible clubs in the late 1950s and 1960s. Then in the mid-1960s and early 1970s, Campus Life and Campus Life/JV ministries to senior and junior high youth began to be the thrust of YFC ministry. Since that time, in concerted efforts to be relevant in changing youth culture, a wider variety of ministry models have emerged. Youth Guidance, for example, became an avenue in reaching at-risk and institutionalized young people. Teen Moms was started to mentor young mothers with parenting skills, as well as the love of Jesus Christ. After working primarily in suburban contexts, YFC started Urban Ministries, which focused on millions of young people in major urban communities and collaborated with the church and other organizations. Other subcategories of ministry also surfaced for deaf and military youth. In addition, YFC sponsors DCLA (meeting in Washington, DC, and Los Angeles) student evangelism conferences to equip young people to effectively impact their schools for Christ.

Headquarters

7670 S Vaughn Court
Englewood, CO 80112
Telephone: 303-843-9000

Leadership

Since 2004, the international president and CEO has been Australian David Wraight. Leadership exists at each geographical region—national, regional, and local. Area directors—for the Americas, Africa, Asia Pacific, Europe, the Middle East, and North Africa—are members of the World Leadership Team.

Core Beliefs

YFC springs from a prodigious era in the mid-twentieth century of American parachurch entrepreneurial endeavors and is decidedly evangelical in theological orientation. The statement of faith is nondenominational and states:

We believe the Bible to be the inspired, the only infallible, authoritative Word of God.

We believe that there is one God, eternally existent in three persons: Father, Son and Holy Spirit.

We believe in the deity of our Lord Jesus Christ, in His virgin birth, in His sinless life, in His miracles, in His vicarious and atoning death through His shed blood, in His bodily resurrection, in His ascension to the right hand of the Father, and in His personal return in power and glory.

We believe that for the salvation of lost and sinful people regeneration by the Holy Spirit is absolutely essential.

We believe in the present ministry of the Holy Spirit by whose indwelling the Christian is enabled to live a godly life.

We believe in the resurrection of both the saved and the lost; they that are saved unto the resurrection of life and they that are lost unto the resurrection of damnation.

We believe in the spiritual unity of believers in Christ. (yfc.net, "Our Statement of Faith")

Core Practices

The vision of YFC is to see every young person in every people group in every nation have the opportunity to make an informed decision to be a follower of Jesus Christ and become a part of a local church. An underlying strategy is working with the local church and like-minded partners to raise up lifelong followers of Jesus.

The essentials of YFC's ministry are widespread prayer, loving relationships, faithful Bible teaching, collaborative community strategy, and adults who empower.

The main programmatic elements of YFC's operating strategy are:

Campus Life High School: reaching young people on high school campuses

Campus Life Middle School: reaching young people in middle school and junior high

City Life: reaching young people in urban communities

Juvenile Justice Ministry: reaching troubled teens in juvenile institutions

Parent Life: ministering to teen mothers and fathers

Deaf Teen Quest: reaching deaf and hard of hearing young people across the nation

YFC Military Club Beyond: equipping youth workers to reach military teens

YFCamp: creating a time and a place for changed young lives

World Outreach: transforming lives through serving the world

YFC Core: training students to reach their friends for Christ

Unified Underground: reaching subculture youth with the gospel

Statistics

YFC/USA is a chartered program of Youth for Christ International. Approximately 47,000 full-time, part-time, and volunteer staff serve in 101 countries. Over 100 staff members from the United States have assignments with programs in other nations as part of YFC/USA's World Outreach Division. Over 200,000 youth responded to the gospel in 2007.

Website

http://www.yfc.net/

Bibliography

Larsen, M. *Young Man on Fire: The Story of Torrey Johnson and Youth for Christ.* Chicago: Youth Publications, 1945.

Pahl, J. *Youth Ministry in Modern America: 1930 to the Present.* Peabody, MA: Hendrickson, 2000.

Senter, M. *The Coming Revolution in Youth Ministry.* Wheaton: Victor, 1992.

"Youth for Christ." http://www.yfc.net. "Our Statement of Faith."

Mark A. Lamport

Youth With A Mission

History

Begun by Loren Cunningham when he was only twenty, Youth With A Mission (YWAM) first appeared to him as a "mental movie" in 1956. "There was a map of the world and waves were breaking all over it. The waves began to turn into young people, thousands of them, spilling on to every continent and sharing the good news about Jesus" (ywam.org, "The History of YWAM").

Four years later Cunningham founded the organization and named it after the picture he had seen. The first base was in Lausanne, Switzerland. The fiftieth anniversary of the ministry, which has grown to include 1,300 bases in 177 countries, was celebrated in 2010, and Cunningham's vision is being fulfilled through the sequence of actions YWAM training follows. Students enter YWAM through a specific base to which they have applied and been accepted and then follow the three-phase process of Start (with an entry-level Discipleship Training School that includes a cross-cultural mission component), Focus (with a second-level course specializing in an area), and Go (an extended cross-cultural mission to share the gospel with the hope that graduates will commit to long-term service).

In structure and governance, YWAM, in its own words, "has developed as a family of ministries, rather than a highly structured, centralized agency. Although we have offices that serve YWAM globally, we do not have an international administrative headquarters."

"Each YWAM location is responsible for initiating training programs, planning outreaches, recruiting staff, fund-raising and defining their objectives and activities." "All YWAM locations . . . are expected to uphold the values of YWAM" (ywam.org, "Our Leadership").

Headquarters

Highly decentralized, YWAM does not have one international headquarters from which the global ministry is administered. Instead, each YWAM base handles its own administration, with various services provided through multiple service offices. For example, YWAM's website directs inquiries about donations to a Colorado Springs location, media queries to a UK location, and generally all other questions to the appropriate bases.

Leadership

While the founders, Loren and Darlene Cunningham, reside in Hawaii near the base in Kona,

YWAM's international staff is led primarily by volunteers who are supported as missionaries by friends, family, and churches. The Global Leadership Team consists of regional and global ministry representatives and is currently led by a team of three global leaders.

Core Beliefs

YWAM's core values are these:

1. Know God
2. Make God known
3. Hear God's voice
4. Practice worship and intercessory prayer
5. Be visionary
6. Champion young people
7. Be broad-structured and decentralized
8. Be international and interdenominational
9. Have a biblical Christian worldview
10. Function in teams
11. Exhibit servant leadership
12. Do first, then teach
13. Be relationship-oriented
14. Value the individual
15. Value families
16. Practice dependence on God
17. Practice hospitality
18. Communicate with integrity (ywam.org, "YWAM Foundational Values")

YWAM's evangelical doctrinal statement is:

We of Youth With A Mission believe that the Bible is God's inspired and authoritative word, revealing that Jesus Christ is God's son; that people are created in God's image; that He created us to have eternal life through Jesus Christ; that although all people have sinned and come short of God's glory, God has made salvation possible through the death on the cross and resurrection of Jesus Christ; that repentance, faith, love and obedience are fitting responses to God's initiative of grace towards us; that God desires all people to be saved and to come to the knowledge of the truth; and that the Holy Spirit's power is demonstrated in and through us for the accomplishment of Christ's last commandment, "Go into all the world and preach the good news to all creation" (Mark 16:15). (ywam.org, "Our Beliefs")

Defining Statement

"To know God and to make Him known" (ywam.org, "Home").

Core Practices

The heart of YWAM practice is training that leads to doing. When early leaders realized that many potential participants were Christians who had progressed little in discipleship, YWAM established what has become the entry portal for all YWAMers: Discipleship Training School (DTS; Crossroads DTS for older students and those with families). DTS focuses first on discipleship—understanding and knowing God more deeply—and then transitions to training for mission service. The eleven- or twelve-week school is followed by an eight- to twelve-week outreach that crosses cultures in a firsthand experience of missions.

After successfully completing DTS, YWAMers typically enter a second-level school that trains within a specific subject area, combining classroom with hands-on experiential learning. What is offered at a given YWAM base depends on its focus and staff, but throughout the bases worldwide, these areas are taught: arts, Christian ministries, communications, counseling and health care, education, humanities and international studies, and science and technology.

Completion of a second-level school usually launches students into a longer-term period of service using their YWAM training, often in a place where students have been planning to serve.

Statistics

YWAM currently operates in more than 1,100 locations in over 180 nations. Although YWAM is primarily an organization focused on youth discipleship through missions and evangelism, its over 18,000 volunteers include people of all ages.

Missionary and Evangelistic Work

Missions evangelism is at the heart of all YWAM activities, and even in the entry DTS program, students cross cultures in an initial short-term mission. Bases, including in Haiti, Angola, Sudan, France, Brazil, and Costa Rica, offer frequent opportunities for evangelistic missions of different durations and destinations.

Academic Institutions

YWAM includes the University of the Nations (U of N), which offers studies more advanced than DTS and second-level schools, studies that may lead to associate's and bachelor's degrees, as well as to graduate diplomas.

Publications

YWAM publishes the webzine *International YWAMer*, and many bases publish their own online and print newsletters, other communications, and media resources. A more centralized publishing program exists in YWAM Publishing, located in Seattle, Washington. Its online store offers books and media in categories suited to YWAM activities, including Christian biography, fiction, true-life international adventures, missions, Christian living, and music and worship. While many products are YWAM publications, many others offered for sale are from other publishers. Some products are available in multiple languages, and all are discounted.

Website

http://www.ywam.org/

Bibliography

"Youth With A Mission." http://www.ywam.org. "The History of YWAM," "Our Beliefs," "Our Leadership," and "YWAM Foundational Values."

Rebekah Hardy and Mark E. Roberts

Appendix A

Denominational Archives

Adventist/Sabbatarian

Adventist Heritage Center
James White Library
Andrews University
Berrien Springs, MI 49104
Telephone: 269-471-3274
Fax: 269-471-2646
Email: ahc@andrews.edu
Website: http://www.andrews.edu/library/ahc/index.html

Aurora University
Charles B. Phillips Library
347 S Gladstone
Aurora, IL 60506
Telephone: 630-844-5437
Fax: 630-844-3848
Email: jhuggins@aurora.edu

Department of Archives and Special Collections
Ellen G. White Office
Loma Linda University Library
Loma Linda, CA 92350
Telephone: 909-558-4942
Fax: 909-558-0381
Email: whiteestate@llu.edu

Ellen G. White Estate
12501 Old Columbia Pike
Silver Spring, MD 20904
Telephone: 301-680-6540
Fax: 301-680-6559
Email: mail@whiteestate.org
Website: http://www.whiteestate.org/

General Conference of Seventh-Day Adventists: Archives and Statistics
12501 Old Columbia Pike
Silver Spring, MD 20904-6000
Telephone: 301-680-6022
Fax: 301-680-5022
Email: holoviakb@gc.adventist.org
Website: http://www.adventistarchives.org/

Anglican/Episcopal

Archives of the Episcopal Church
PO Box 2247
Austin, TX 78768
Telephone: 512-472-6816
Fax: 512-480-0437
Email: research@episcopalarchives.org
Website: http://www.episcopalarchives.org/

Baptist

American Baptist Historical Society
2930 Flowers Road S
Suite 150
Atlanta, GA 30341
http://abhsarchives.org/

Andover Newton Theological School
Franklin Trask Library
169 Herrick Road
Newton Centre, MA 02459
Telephone: 617-964-1100
Email: dyount@ants.edu
Website: http://www.ants.edu/

Primitive Baptist Library of Carthage
416 Main Street
Carthage, IL 62321
Telephone: 217-357-3723
Fax: 217-357-3723
Email: hwebb9@juno.com

Seventh Day Baptist Historical Society
3120 Kennedy Road
PO Box 1678
Janesville, WI 53547
Telephone: 608-752-5055
Fax: 608-752-7711
Email: sdbhist@inwave.com
Website: http://www.seventhdaybaptist.org/

Southern Baptists Historical Library and Archives
901 Commerce Street
Suite 400
Nashville, TN 37203
Telephone: 615-244-0344
Fax: 615-782-4821
Email: bill@sbhla.org
Website: http://www.sbhla.org/

Brethren

Brethren Historical Library and Archives
1451 Dundee Avenue
Elgin, IL 60120
Telephone: 847-742-5100
Fax: 847-742-6103
Email: kshaefer_gb@brethren.org

Brethren in Christ Historical Library and Archives
1 College Avenue
PO Box 3002
Grantham, PA 37027
Telephone: 717-691-6048
Fax: 717-691-6042
Email: archives@messiah.org
Website: http://www.messiah.edu/archives/

Catholic

Catholic University of America
American Catholic History Research Center and
   University Archives
101 LCI
Washington, DC 20064
Telephone: 202-319-5065
Fax: 202-619-6554
Email: meagher@cua.edu
Website: http://archives.lib.cua.edu/

Marquette University
Department of Special Collections and Archives
PO Box 3141

Milwaukee, WI 93201
Telephone: 414-288-7526
Fax: 414-288-6709
Email: charles.elston@marquette.edu
Website: http://www.marquette.edu/

Polish National Catholic Commission on History
   and Archives
1031 Cedar Avenue
Scranton, PA 18505
Telephone: 570-343-0100
Fax: 570-343-0100
Email: josephwie@aol.com

University of Notre Dame Archives
607 Hesburgh Library
Notre Dame, IN 46556
Telephone: 574-631-6448
Fax: 574-631-7980
Email: archives@nd.edu
Website: http://archives.nd.edu/

Churches of Christ/
Christian Churches

Center for Restoration Studies
Abilene Christian University
221 Brown Library
PO Box 29208
Abilene, TX 79699
Telephone: 325-674-2347
Fax: 325-674-2202
Email: churchill@acu.edu
Website: http://www.bible.acu.edu/crs/Collection
   Detail.asp?Bookmark=5

Christian Theological Seminary Library
1000 W 42nd Street
Indianapolis, IN 46208
Telephone: 317-931-2368
Fax: 317-931-2363
Email: don.haymes@cts.edu
Website: http://www.cts.edu/

Churches of God General Conference
Winebrenner Theological Seminary
701 E Melrose Avenue
Findlay, OH 45804
Telephone: 419-422-4824
Fax: 419-422-3999
Email: wts@winebrenner.edu
Website: http://www.winebrenner.edu/

Disciples of Christ Historical Society
1101 19th Avenue S
Nashville, TN 37212
Telephone: 615-327-1444
Email: mail@dishistsoc.org
Website: http://www.dishistsoc.org/

Emmanuel School of Religion Library
1 Walker Drive
Johnson City, TN 37601
Telephone: 423-926-1186
Fax: 423-926-6198
Email: library@esr.edu
Website: http://www.esr.edu/

Congregational

Archives of the Evangelical Congregational Church
Evangelical School of Theology Rostad Library
121 S College Street
Myerstown, PA 17067
Telephone: 717-866-5775
Fax: 717-866-4667
Email: theisey@evangelical.edu
Website: http://www.eccenter.com/

Friends

Friends Historical Library of Swarthmore College
Swarthmore, PA 19081
Telephone: 610-328-8946
Fax: 610-690-5728
Email: friends@swarthmore.edu
Website: http://www.swarthmore.edu/fhl.xml

Specialist Collections/Quaker Collection
Haverford College
370 Lancaster Avenue
Lancaster, PA 19041
Telephone: 610-896-1161
Fax: 610-896-1102
Email: elapsans@haverford.edu
Website: http://www.haverford.edu/library/special/

Holiness

Nazarene Archives
Church of the Nazarene
6401 The Paseo
Kansas City, MO 64131
Telephone: 816-333-7000
Fax: 816-361-4983
Email: singersol@nazarene.org
Website: http://www.nazarene.org/archives/index
.html

Salvation Army Archives and Research Center
615 Slaters Lane
Alexandria, VA 22313
Telephone: 703-684-5500
Fax: 703-299-5552
Email: archives@usn.salvationarmy.org
Website: http://www.salvationarmy.org/

Interdenominational

American Bible Society and Archives
1865 Broadway
New York, NY 10023
Telephone: 212-408-1258
Fax: 212-408-1526
Email: mcordato@americanbible.org
Website: http://www.americanbible.org/

Billy Graham Center Archives
Wheaton College
500 College Avenue
Wheaton, IL 60187
Telephone: 630-752-5910
Fax: 630-752-5916
Email: bgcarc@wheaton.edu
Website: http://www.wheaton.edu/bgc/archives

Graduate Theological Union Archives
2400 Ridge Road
Berkeley, CA 94709
Telephone: 510-649-2507
Fax: 510-649-2508
Website: http://gtu.edu/library/special-collections
/archives

Presbyterian Historical Society
425 Lombard Street
Philadelphia, PA 19147
Telephone: 215-627-1852
Fax: 215-627-0509
Email: prehist@shrsys.hslc.org
Website: http://www.history.pcusa.org/

Union Theological Seminary
Burke Library
3041 Broadway
New York, NY 10027
Telephone: 212-280-1502
Fax: 212-280-1456
Email: aw@uts.columbia.edu
Website: http://www.uts.columbia.edu/

University of Chicago
Regenstein Library
1100 E 57th Street
Chicago, IL 60537
Telephone: 773-702-8442
Email: boc7@midway.chicago.edu
Website: http://www.lib.uchicago.edu/e/su/rel/

Yale Divinity School Library
409 Prospect Street
New Haven, CT 06511
Telephone: 203-423-6374
Fax: 203-432-3906
Email: divinity.library@yale.edu
Website: http://web.library.yale.edu/divinity

Lutheran

Archives of the Evangelical Lutheran Church
in America
8765 W Higgins Road
Chicago, IL 60631
Telephone: 847-690-9410
Fax: 847-690-9502
Email: archives@elca.org
Website: http://www.elca.org/archives/

Concordia Historical Institute
Department of Archives and History
The Lutheran Church—Missouri Synod
801 De Mun Street
St. Louis, MO 63105
Telephone: 314-505-7900
Fax: 310-505-7901
Email: chi@chi.lcms.org
Website: http://www.chi.lcms.org/

Mennonite

Center for Mennonite Brethren Studies
1717 S Chestnut
Fresno, CA 93702
Telephone: 559-453-2225
Fax: 559-453-2124
Email: kennsrem@fresno.edu
Website: http://www.fresno.edu/students/hiebert
-library

Mennonite Church USA Archives
Bethel College
300 E 27th Street
North Newton, KS 67117
Telephone: 316-284-5304
Fax: 316-284-5843
Email: mla@bethelks.edu
Website: http://www.bethelks.edu/mla/

Mennonite Church USA Archives
1700 S Main
Goshen, IN 46525
Telephone: 574-535-7477
Fax: 574-535-7756
Email: johnes@goshen.edu
Website: http://www.mcusa.archives.org/

Methodist

B. L. Fisher Library
Asbury Theological Seminary
204 N Lexington Avenue
Wilmore, KY 40390
Telephone: 859-858-2235
Fax: 859-858-2350

Email: bill_kostlevy@asburyseminary.edu
Website: http://asburyseminary.edu/academics/b-l
-fisher-library/

Center for Evangelical United Brethren Heritage
United Theological Seminary
1810 Harvard Boulevard
Dayton, OH 45406
Telephone: 937-278-5817
Email: eubcenter@united.edu
Website: http://united.edu/center-for-the-evangeli
cal-united-brethren-heritage-eub/

General Commission on Archives and History
United Methodist Church
PO Box 127
Madison, NJ 07940
Telephone: 973-408-3189
Fax: 973-408-3909
Email: gcah@gcah.org
Website: http://www.gcah.org/

Heritage Hall at Livingston College
70 W Monroe Street
Salisbury, NC 28144
Telephone: 704-638-5664

Office of the Historiographer of the African Methodist
Episcopal Church
PO Box 301
Williamstown, MA 02167
Telephone: 413-597-2484
Fax: 413-597-3673
Email: denis.c.dickerson@williams.edu

Pentecostal

David du Plessis Archives
Fuller Theological Seminary
135 N Oakland
Pasadena, CA 91182
Telephone: 626-584-5311
Fax: 626-584-5644
Email: archive@fuller.edu
Website: http://libraryarchives.fuller.edu/david-du
-plessis-archives/

Flower Pentecostal Heritage Center
1445 Boonsville Avenue
Springfield, MO 65802
Telephone: 417-862-1447
Fax: 417-862-6203
Email: archives@ag.org
Website: http://www.agheritage.org/

Hal Bernard Dixon Jr. Pentecostal Research Center
260 11th Street NE
Cleveland, TN 37511

Telephone: 423-614-8576
Fax: 423-614-8555
Email: dixon_research@leeuniversity.edu

Holy Spirit Research Center
Oral Roberts University
LRC 5E02
7777 S Lewis Avenue
Tulsa, OK 74171
Telephone: 918-495-6898
Fax: 918-495-6662
Email: hsrc@oru.edu
Website: http://www.oru.edu/library/special_collect
  ions/holy_spirit_research_center/access.php

International Pentecostal Holiness Church
Archives and Research Center
PO Box 12609
Oklahoma City, OK 73157
Telephone: 405-787-7110
Fax: 405-787-3957
Email: archives@iphc.org
Website: http://iphc.org/gso/home/archives/

United Pentecostal Church
International Historical Center
8855 Dunn Road
Hazelwood, MO 63042
Telephone: 314-837-7300
Fax: 314-837-4503
Email: main@upci.org
Website: http://www.upci.org/

Pietist

Moravian Archives
Northern Province
41 W Locust Street
Bethlehem, PA 18108
Telephone: 610-866-3255
Fax: 610-866-9210
Email: morarchbeth@enter.net
Website: http://www.moravianchurcharchives.org/

Moravian Archives
Southern Province
Drawer L
Winston-Salem, NC 27108
Telephone: 336-722-1742
Fax: 336-725-4514
Email: nblum@mcsp.org
Website: http://www.moravianarchives.org/

Reformed

Andover Newton Theological School
Franklin Trask Library
16 Herrick Road

Newton Centre, MA 02459
Telephone: 617-964-1100
Email: dyount@ants.edu
Website: http://www.ants.edu/

Archives of the Evangelical Synod of North America
Eden Theological Seminary
Luhr Library
475 E Lockwood Avenue
Webster Groves, MO 63119
Telephone: 314-918-2515
Email: vdetjen@eden.edu

Congregational Library
14 Beacon Street
Boston, MA 02108
Telephone: 617-523-0470
Fax: 617-523-0491
Email: jsteyler@14beacon.org
Website: http://www.14beacon.org/

Elon University Library
PO Box 187
Elon, NC 22744
Telephone: 336-278-2000
Email: keller@elon.edu

Evangelical and Reformed Historical Society
Lancaster Theological Seminary
555 W James Street
Lancaster, PA 17603
Telephone: 717-290-8704
Fax: 717-393-4254
Email: erhs@lancasterseminary.edu
Website: http://www.erhs.info/

Heritage Hall
Calvin College
1855 Knollcrest Circle SE
Grand Rapids, MI 49546
Telephone: 616-526-6313
Fax: 616-526-6470
Email: rharms@calvin.edu
Website: http://www.calvin.edu/

Historical Foundation for the Cumberland Presby-
  terian Church
8207 Traditional Place
Cordova, TN 38016
Telephone: 901-276-8602
Fax: 901-272-3913
Email: skg@cumberland.org
Website: http://www.cumberland.org/

Presbyterian Church in America
Historical Center
12330 Conway Road
St. Louis, MO 63141

Telephone: 314-469-9077
Email: wsparkman@pcnet.org
Website: http://www.pcahistory.org/

Presbyterian Historical Society
425 Lombard Street
Philadelphia, PA 19147
Telephone: 215-627-1852
Fax: 215-627-0115
Email: refdesk@history.pcusa.org
Website: http://www.history.pcusa.org/

Princeton Theological Seminary Library
25 Library Place
Princeton, NJ 08540
Telephone: 609-497-7950
Email: william.harris@ptsem.edu
Website: http://www.ptsem.edu/library/

Reformed Church Archives
21 Seminary Place
New Brunswick, NJ 08901
Telephone: 732-246-1779
Fax: 732-249-5412
Email: rgasro@rca.org
Website: http://www.rca.org/

United Church of Christ Archives
700 Prospect Avenue
Cleveland, OH 44115
Telephone: 216-736-2106
Fax: 216-736-2203
Email: kellyb@ucc.org
Website: http://www.ucc.org/

Appendix B

Denominational Theological Seminaries and Bible Colleges

Members of the Association of Theological Schools are marked with an asterisk (*); schools that are accredited by the Transnational Association of Christian Colleges and Schools are marked with a symbol (†).

*Abilene Christian University Graduate School of Theology**
(Churches of Christ)
College of Biblical Studies
ACU Box 29422
1850 N Judge Ely Boulevard
CBS Room 297
Abilene, TX 79699
Telephone: 915-674-3700
Fax: 915-674-6180
Email: thompson@bible.acu.edu
Website: http://www.acu.edu/academics/gst/

Alaska Bible College
(Nondenominational)
PO Box 289
Glenallen, AK 99588
Telephone: 907-822-3201
Fax: 907-822-5027
Email: info@akbible.edu
Website: http://www.akbible.edu/

*Alliance Theological Seminary**
(Christian and Missionary Alliance)
350 N Highland Avenue
Nyack, NY 10960
Telephone: 845-353-2020
Fax: 845-727-3002
Website: http://www.alliance.edu/

American Baptist College
(National Baptist Convention)
1800 Baptist World Center Drive
Nashville, TN 37207
Telephone: 615-228-7877
Fax: 615-226-7855
Email: harrisfe@abcnash.edu

*American Baptist Seminary of the West**
(American Baptist Churches in the USA)
2606 Dwight Way
Berkeley, CA 94704
Telephone: 510-841-1905
Fax: 510-841-2446
Email: krussell@absw.edu
Website: http://www.absw.edu/

American Christian College and Seminary
(Nondenominational)
4300 Highline Boulevard
Suite 202
Oklahoma, OK 73108
Telephone: 405-945-0100
Fax: 405-945-0311
Email: info@accs.edu
Website: http://www.accs.edu/

*Anderson University School of Theology**
(Church of God [Anderson, Indiana])
1100 E 5th Street
Anderson, IN 46012
Telephone: 765-641-4032
Fax: 765-641-3851
Website: http://www.anderson.edu/sot/

Andover Newton Theological School*
(American Baptist Churches in the USA; United
Church of Christ)
210 Herrick Road
Newton Centre, MA 02459
Telephone: 617-964-1100
Fax: 617-558-9785
Email: admissions@ants.edu
Website: http://www.ants.edu/

Appalachian Bible College
(Nondenominational)
PO Box ABC
Bradley, WV 25818
Telephone: 304-877-6428
Fax: 304-877-5082
Email: abc@abc.edu
Website: http://www.abc.edu/

Aquinas Institute of Theology*
(Roman Catholic Church)
3642 Lindell Boulevard
St. Louis, MO 63108
Telephone: 314-977-3882
Fax: 314-977-7225
Email: aquinas@slu.edu
Website: http://www.ai.edu/

Arizona College of the Bible
(Interdenominational)
2045 W Northern Avenue
Phoenix, AZ 85021
Telephone: 602-995-2670
Fax: 602-864-8183

Arlington Baptist College
(Baptist)
3001 W Division
Arlington, TX 76012
Telephone: 817-461-8741
Fax: 817-274-1138

Asbury Theological Seminary*
(Inter/multidenominational)
204 N. Lexington Avenue
Wilmore, KY 40390
Telephone: 859-858-3581
Website: http://www.asburyseminary.edu/

Ashland Theological Seminary*
(Brethren Church [Ashland, Ohio])
910 Center Street
Ashland, OH 44805
Telephone: 419-289-5161
Fax: 419-289-5969
Email: ffinks@ashland.edu
Website: http://seminary.ashland.edu/

Assemblies of God Theological Seminary*
(Assemblies of God)
1435 N Glenstone Avenue
Springfield, MO 65802
Telephone: 417-268-1000

Fax: 417-268-1001
Email: agts@agseminary.edu
Website: http://www.agts.edu/

Associated Mennonite Biblical Seminary*
(Mennonite Church)
3003 Benham Avenue
Elkhart, IN 46517
Telephone: 574-295-3726
Fax: 574-295-0092
Email: nkraybill@ambs.edu
Website: http://www.ambs.edu/

Athenaeum of Ohio*
(Roman Catholic Church)
6616 Beechmont Avenue
Cincinnati, OH 45230
Telephone: 513-231-2223
Fax: 513-231-3254
Website: http://www.athenaeum.edu/

Atlanta Christian College
(Christian Churches; Churches of Christ)
2605 Ben Hill Road
East Point, GA 30344
Telephone: 404-761-8861
Fax: 404-669-2024
Email: admissions@acc.edu
Website: http://www.acc.edu/

Austin Presbyterian Theological Seminary*
(Presbyterian Church [USA])
100 E 27th Street
Austin, TX 78705
Telephone: 512-472-6736
Fax: 512-479-0738
Website: http://www.austinseminary.edu/

Bakke Graduate University†
(Nondenominational)
8515 Greenville Ave., S206
Dallas, TX 75243-7039
Telephone: 214-329-4447
Fax: 214-347-9367
Email: info@bgu.edu
Website: http://www.bgu.edu

Bangor Theological Seminary*
(United Church of Christ)
300 Union Street
Bangor, ME 04401
Telephone: 207-942-6781
Fax: 207-942-4914
Email: mhuddy@bts.edu
Website: http://www.bts.edu/

Baptist Bible College
(Baptist Bible Fellowship International)
628 E Kearney
Springfield, MO 65803
Telephone: 417-268-6060
Fax: 417-268-6694

Baptist Bible Seminary
(Baptist)
538 Venard Road
Clarks Summit, PA 18411
Telephone: 570-586-2400
Fax: 570-586-1753
Email: bbc@bbc.edu
Website: http://www.bbc.edu/

*Baptist Missionary Association Theological Seminary**
(Baptist Missionary Association of America)
1530 E Pine Street
Jacksonville, TX 75766
Telephone: 903-586-2501
Fax: 903-586-0378
Email: bmatsem@bmats.edu
Website: http://www.bmats.edu/

*Baptist Theological Seminary at Richmond**
(Cooperative Baptist Fellowship)
3400 Brook Road
Richmond, VA 23227
Telephone: 804-355-8135
Fax: 804-355-8182
Email: btsr@btsr.edu
Website: http://www.btsr.edu/

Barclay College
(Interdenominational)
607 N Kingman
Haviland, KS 67059
Telephone: 620-862-5252
Fax: 620-862-5403
Email: barclaycollege@havilandtalco.com

*Barry University Department of Theology and Philosophy**
(Roman Catholic Church)
11300 Northeast Second Avenue
Miami Shores, FL 33161
Telephone: 305-899-3469
Fax: 305-899-3385
Email: theology@mail.barry.edu
Website: http://www.barry.edu/theology-philos
ophy/

Bay Ridge Christian College
(Church of God [Anderson, Indiana])
PO Box 726
Kendeton, TX 77451
Telephone: 979-532-3982
Fax: 979-532-4352
Email: brcccampus@wcnet.net
Website: http://brcconline.org/

Beacon College and Graduate School†
(Nondenominational)
6003 Veterans Parkway
Columbus, GA 31909
Telephone: 706-323-5364
Fax: 706-323-3236

Email: beacon@beacon.edu
Website: http://www.beacon.edu/

*Beeson Divinity School of Samford University**
(Inter/multidenominational)
800 Lakeshore Drive
Birmingham, AL 35229
Telephone: 205-726-2991
Fax: 205-726-2260
Email: bdsadmis@samford.edu
Website: http://www.beesondivinity.com/

*Berkeley Divinity School**
(Episcopal Church)
409 Prospect Street
New Haven, CT 06511
Telephone: 203-432-9285
Fax: 203-432-9353
Website: http://berkeleydivinity.yale.edu/

Bethany Lutheran Theological Seminary
(Evangelical Lutheran Synod)
6 Browns Court
Mankato, MN 56001
Telephone: 507-344-7354
Fax: 507-344-7426
Email: gschmeli@blc.edu
Website: http://www.blts.edu/

*Bethany Theological Seminary**
(Church of the Brethren)
615 National Road W
Richmond, IN 47374
Telephone: 765-983-1800
Fax: 765-983-1840
Email: roopge@bethanyseminary.edu
Website: http://www.bethanyseminary.edu/

*Bethel Seminary of the East**
(Baptist General Conference/Converge; Conserva-
tive Baptist Association of America)
1605 N Limekiln Pike
Dresher, PA 19025
Telephone: 215-641-4801
Fax: 215-641-4804
Website: http://www.bethel.edu/

*Bethel Seminary San Diego**
(Baptist General Conference/Converge)
6116 Arosa Street
San Diego, CA 92115
Telephone: 619-582-8188
Fax: 619-583-9114
Website: http://www.bethel.edu/

*Bethel Theological Seminary**
(Baptist General Conference/Converge)
3949 Bethel Drive
St. Paul, MN 55112
Telephone: 651-638-6180
Fax: 651-638-6002
Email: webmaster@bethel.edu
Website: http://www.bethel.edu/

Beulah Heights Bible College[†]
(International Pentecostal Church of Christ)
892 Berne Street SE
Atlanta, GA 30316
Telephone: 404-627-2681
Fax: 404-627-0702
Email: bhbc@beulah.org
Website: http://www.beulah.org/

Bexley Hall Seminary[*]
(Episcopal Church)
583 Sheridan Avenue
Columbus, OH 43209
Telephone: 614-231-3095
Fax: 614-231-3236
Email: bexleyhall@bexley.edu
Website: http://www.bexley.edu/

Bible Church of Christ Theological Institute
(Nondenominational)
1358 Morris Avenue
Bronx, NY 10456-1402
Telephone: 718-588-2284
Fax: 718-992-5597
Website: http://www.thebiblechurchofchrist.org/

Biblical Theological Seminary[*]
(Inter/multidenominational)
200 N Main Street
Hatfield, PA 19440
Telephone: 215-368-5000
Fax: 215-368-7002
Email: president@biblical.edu
Website: http://www.biblical.edu/

Blessed John XXIII National Seminary[*]
(Roman Catholic Church)
558 South Avenue
Weston, MA 02493
Telephone: 781-899-5500
Fax: 781-899-9057
Website: http://www.blessedjohnxxiii.edu/

Boise Bible College
(Christian Churches; Churches of Christ)
8695 Marigold Street
Boise, ID 83714
Telephone: 208-376-7731
Fax: 208-376-7743
Email: boisebible@boisebible.edu
Website: http://www.boisebible.edu/

Boston Baptist College[†]
(Baptist)
950 Metropolitan Avenue
Boston, MA 02136
Telephone: 617-364-3510
Fax: 617-364-0723
Email: admin@boston.edu
Website: http://www.boston.edu/

Boston College Institute of Religious Education and Pastoral Ministry and Department of Theology[*]
(Roman Catholic Church)
31 Lawrence Avenue
Chestnut Hill, MA 02467
Telephone: 617-552-8440
Fax: 617-552-0811
Website: http://www.bc.edu/schools/stm/

Boston University School of Theology[*]
(United Methodist Church)
745 Commonwealth Avenue
Boston, MA 02215
Telephone: 617-353-3050
Fax: 617-353-3061
Website: http://www.bu.edu/sth/

Brite Divinity School, Texas Christian University[*]
(Christian Church [Disciples of Christ])
TCU Box 298130
Ft. Worth, TX 76129
Telephone: 817-257-7575
Fax: 817-257-7305
Email: t.palmer@tcu.edu
Website: http://www.brite.tcu.edu/

Byzantine Catholic Seminary of SS. Cyril and Methodius[*]
(Byzantine Catholic Archeparchy of Pittsburgh)
3605 Perrysville Avenue
Pittsburgh, PA 15214
Telephone: 412-321-8383
Fax: 412-321-9936

California Christian College[†]
(National Association of Free Will Baptists)
4881 E University Avenue
Fresno, CA 93703
Telephone: 559-251-4215
Fax: 559-251-4231
Email: cccfresno@aol.com
Website: http://www.calchristiancollege.org/

Calvary Bible College and Theological Seminary
(Independent Fundamental Churches of America)
15800 Calvary Road
Kansas City, MO 64147
Telephone: 800-326-3960
Fax: 816-331-4474

Calvin Theological Seminary[*]
(Christian Reformed Church in North America)
3233 Burton Street SE
Grand Rapids, MI 49546
Telephone: 616-957-6036
Fax: 616-957-8621
Email: sempres@calvin.edu
Website: http://www.calvinseminary.edu/

Campbell University Divinity School*
(Baptist State Convention of North Carolina)
116 T. T. Lanier Street
PO Drawer 4050
Buies Creek, NC 27506
Telephone: 910-893-1830
Fax: 910-893-1835
Website: http://www.campbell.edu/divinity/

Candler School of Theology of Emory University*
(United Methodist Church)
Emory University
500 Kilgo Circle NE
Atlanta, GA 30322
Telephone: 404-727-6324
Fax: 404-727-3182
Email: candler@emory.edu
Website: http://www.candler.emory.edu/

Capital Bible Seminary*
(Nondenominational)
6511 Princess Garden Parkway
Lanham, MD 20706
Telephone: 301-552-1400
Fax: 301-614-1024
Email: bfox@bible.edu
Website: http://www.bible.edu/

Carolina Evangelical Divinity School*
(Religious Society of Friends)
PO Box 5831
High Point, NC 27265
Telephone: 336-889-2262
Fax: 336-882-3370
Email: deansoffice@hgstnc.org

Catholic Theological Union at Chicago*
(Roman Catholic Church)
5401 S Cornell Avenue
Chicago, IL 60615
Telephone: 773-324-8000
Fax: 773-324-8490
Website: http://www.ctu.edu/

Catholic University of America*
(Roman Catholic Church)
620 Michigan Avenue NE
Washington, DC 20064
Telephone: 202-319-5683
Fax: 202-319-4967
Email: cua-deansrs@cua.edu
Website: http://www.religiousstudies.cua.edu/

Central Baptist College
(Baptist Missionary Association of Arkansas)
1501 College Avenue
Conway, AR 72032
Telephone: 501-329-6872
Fax: 501-329-2941
Email: cattebery@cbc.edu
Website: http://www.cbc.edu/

Central Baptist Theological Seminary*
(Baptist)
741 N 31st Street
Kansas City, KS 66102
Telephone: 913-371-5313
Fax: 913-371-8110
Email: central@cbts.edu
Website: http://www.cbts.edu/

Central Baptist Theological Seminary of Indiana
(National Baptist Convention)
1535 Avenue North
Indianapolis, IN 46202
Telephone: 317-636-6622
Email: henriettabrown@webtv.net

Central Bible College
(Assemblies of God)
3000 N Grant Avenue
Springfield, MO 65803
Telephone: 417-833-2551
Fax: 417-833-5141
Email: info@cbcag.edu
Website: http://www.cbcag.edu/

Central Christian College of the Bible
(Christian Churches; Churches of Christ)
911 E Urbandale Drive
Moberly, MO 65270
Telephone: 660-263-3900
Fax: 660-263-3936
Email: develop@cccb.edu
Website: http://www.cccb.edu/

Central Indian Bible College
(Assemblies of God)
PO Box 550
Mobridge, SD 57601
Telephone: 605-845-7801
Fax: 605-845-7744

Chapman School of Religious Studies, Oakland
City University*
(General Association of General Baptists)
143 Lucretia Street
Oakland City, IN 47660
Telephone: 812-749-4781
Fax: 812-749-1233
Email: ocuexe@oak.edu
Website: http://www.oak.edu/

Chicago Theological Seminary*
(United Church of Christ)
5757 S University Avenue
Chicago, IL 60637
Telephone: 773-752-5757
Fax: 773-752-5925
Email: sthistle@chgosem.edu
Website: http://www.ctschicago.edu/

Christian Heritage College
(Southern Baptist Convention)
2100 Greenfield Drive

El Cajon, CA 92019
Telephone: 619-441-2200
Fax: 619-440-0209
Email: chcadm@christianheritage.edu
Website: http://www.christianheritage.edu/

Christian Life College[†]
(Nondenominational)
400 E Gregory Street
Mount Prospect, IL 60056
Telephone: 847-259-1840
Fax: 847-259-3888
Email: admissions@christianlifecollege.edu
Website: http://www.christianlifecollege.edu/

Christian Theological Seminary*
(Christian Church [Disciples of Christ])
1000 W 42nd Street
Indianapolis, IN 46208
Telephone: 317-924-1331
Fax: 317-923-1961
Email: wheeler@cts.edu
Website: http://www.cts.edu/

Christian Witness Theological Seminary*
(Nondenominational)
1040 Oak Grove Road
Concord, CA 94518
Telephone: 925-676-5002
Fax: 925-676-5220
Email: admin@cwts.edu

Christ the King Seminary*
(Roman Catholic Church)
711 Knox Road
PO Box 607
East Aurora, NY 14052
Telephone: 716-652-8900
Fax: 716-652-8903
Email: rsiepka@cks.edu
Website: http://www.cks.edu/

Christ the Savior Seminary
(American Carpatho-Russian Orthodox Diocese)
225 Chandler Avenue
Johnstown, PA 15906
Telephone: 814-539-0116
Fax: 814-536-4699
Email: mrosco2@excite.com

Church Divinity School of the Pacific*
(Episcopal Church)
2451 Ridge Road
Berkeley, CA 94709
Telephone: 510-204-0700
Fax: 510-644-0712
Email: mollyanne@cdsp.edu
Website: http://www.cdsp.edu/

Church of God Theological Seminary*
(Church of God [Cleveland, Tennessee])
PO Box 3330
Cleveland, TN 37320

Telephone: 423-478-1131
Fax: 423-478-7711
Email: cogseminary@wingnet.com
Website: http://www.cogts.edu/

Cincinnati Bible Seminary*
(Christian Churches; Churches of Christ)
2700 Glenway Avenue
Cincinnati, OH 45204
Telephone: 513-244-8120
Fax: 513-244-8434
Email: info@cincybible.edu
Website: http://www.cincybible.edu/

Circleville Bible College
(Churches of Christ in Christian Union)
PO Box 458
Circleville, OH 43113
Telephone: 614-474-8896
Fax: 614-477-7755
Email: cbc@biblecollege.edu
Website: http://www.biblecollege.edu/

Claremont School of Theology*
(United Methodist)
1325 N College Avenue
Claremont, CA 91711
Telephone: 909-447-2500
Fax: 909-626-7062
Email: admission@cst.edu
Website: http://www.cst.edu/

Clear Creek Baptist Bible College
(Southern Baptist Convention)
300 Clear Creek Road
Pineville, KY 40977
Telephone: 606-337-3196
Fax: 606-337-2372
Email: ccbbc@ccbbc.edu
Website: http://www.ccbbc.edu/

Clinton Junior College[†]
(African Methodist Episcopal Zion Church)
1029 Crawford Road
Rock Hill, SC 29730
Telephone: 803-327-7402
Fax: 803-327-3261
Email: ecopeland@clintonjrcollege.org
Website: http://www.clintonjrcollege.org/

Colegio Biblico Pentecostal de Puerto Rico
(Church of God [Cleveland, Tennessee])
PO Box 901
Saint Just, PR 00978
Telephone: 787-761-0640
Fax: 787-748-9228

Colgate Rochester Crozer Divinity School*
(American Baptist Churches in the USA)
1100 S Goodman Street
Rochester, NY 14620
Telephone: 585-271-1320

Fax: 585-271-8013
Website: http://www.crcds.edu/

Colorado Christian University
(Nondenominational)
180 S Garrison Street
Lakewood, CO 80226
Telephone: 303-202-0100
Fax: 303-274-7560
Website: http://www.ccu.edu/

Columbia Biblical Seminary and School of
*Missions of Columbia International University**
(Inter/multidenominational)
PO Box 3122
Columbia, SC 29230
Telephone: 803-754-4100
Fax: 803-786-4209
Website: http://www.ciu.edu/

*Columbia Theological Seminary**
(Presbyterian Church [USA])
701 Columbia Drive
PO Box 520
Decatur, GA 30031
Telephone: 404-378-8821
Fax: 404-377-9696
Website: http://www.ctsnet.edu/

*Concordia Seminary**
(Lutheran Church—Missouri Synod)
801 DeMun Avenue
St. Louis, MO 63105
Telephone: 314-505-7010
Fax: 314-505-7002
Email: hollisterr@csl.edu
Website: http://www.csl.edu/

*Concordia Theological Seminary**
(Lutheran Church—Missouri Synod)
6600 N Clinton Street
Ft. Wayne, IN 46825
Telephone: 260-452-2100
Fax: 260-452-2121
Email: wenthedo@mail.ctsfw.edu
Website: http://www.ctsfw.edu/

*Covenant Theological Seminary**
(Presbyterian Church in America)
12330 Conway Road
St. Louis, MO 63141
Telephone: 314-434-4044
Fax: 314-434-4819
Email: admissions@covenantseminary.edu
Website: http://www.covenantseminary.edu/

Cranmer Seminary
(Anglican Rite Synod in the Americas; Episcopal
    Orthodox Church; Orthodox Anglican Church)
901 English Road
High Point, NC 27262
Telephone: 336-885-6032
Fax: 336-885-6021

Email: seminaryinfo@orthodoxanglican.net
Website: http://www.cranmerhouse.org/

Criswell Center for Biblical Studies
(Southern Baptist Convention)
4010 Gaston Avenue
Dallas, TX 75246
Telephone: 214-821-5433
Fax: 214-818-1320

Crossroads College
(Nondenominational)
920 Mayowood Road SW
Rochester, MN 55902
Telephone: 507-288-4563
Fax: 507-288-9046
Email: academic@crossroadscollege.edu
Website: http://www.crossroadscollege.edu/

Crown College
(Christian and Missionary Alliance)
8700 College View Drive
St. Bonifacius, MN 55375
Telephone: 952-446-4100
Fax: 952-446-4149
Email: crown@crown.edu
Website: http://www.crown.edu/

Cummins Theological Seminary
(Reformed Episcopal Church)
705 S Main Street
Summerville, SC 29483
Telephone: 843-873-3451
Fax: 843-875-6200
Email: jcw121@aol.com

Dallas Christian College
(Christian Churches; Churches of Christ)
2700 Christian Parkway
Dallas, TX 75234
Telephone: 972-241-3371
Fax: 972-241-8021
Email: dcc@dallas.edu
Website: http://www.dallas.edu/

*Dallas Theological Seminary**
(Inter/multidenominational)
3909 Swiss Avenue
Dallas, TX 75204
Telephone: 214-824-3094
Fax: 214-841-3625
Website: http://www.dts.edu/

Davis College
(Nondenominational)
400 Riverside Drive
Johnson City, NY 13790
Telephone: 877-949-3248
Email: askdavis@davisny.edu
Website: http://www.davisny.edu/contact-us/

*Denver Seminary**
    (Nondenominational)
    PO Box 100000
    Denver, CO 80250
    Telephone: 303-761-2482
    Fax: 303-761-8060
    Email: info@denverseminary.edu
    Website: http://www.denverseminary.edu/

*Disciples Divinity House of the University of
Chicago**
    (Christian Church [Disciples of Christ])
    1156 E 57th Street
    Chicago, IL 60637
    Telephone: 773-643-4411
    Fax: 773-643-4413
    Email: ddh.uchicago.admin@attglobal.net
    Website: http://ddh.uchicago.edu/

*Dominican House of Studies**
    (Roman Catholic Church)
    487 Michigan Avenue NE
    Washington, DC 20017
    Telephone: 202-529-5300
    Fax: 202-636-1700
    Email: assistant@dhs.edu
    Website: http://www.dhs.edu/

*Dominican School of Philosophy and Theology**
    (Roman Catholic Church)
    2401 Ridge Road
    Berkeley, CA 94709
    Telephone: 510-849-2030
    Fax: 510-849-1372
    Website: http://www.dspt.edu/

*Dominican Study Center of the Caribbean**
    (Roman Catholic Church)
    Apartado Postal 1968
    Bayamon, PR 00960
    Telephone: 787-787-1826
    Fax: 787-798-2712
    Email: fstruik@cedocpr.org
    Website: http://www.cedocpr.org/

*Drew University Theological School**
    (United Methodist Church)
    36 Madison Avenue
    Madison, NJ 07940
    Telephone: 973-408-3258
    Fax: 973-408-3534
    Email: elopezjr@drew.edu
    Website: http://www.drew.edu/theological/

*Duke University Divinity School**
    (United Methodist Church)
    Duke Box 90968
    Durham, NC 27708
    Telephone: 888-462-3853
    Fax: 919-660-3535
    Email: admissions@div.duke.edu
    Website: http://www.divinity.duke.edu/

*Earlham School of Religion**
    (Friends)
    228 College Avenue
    Richmond, IN 47374
    Telephone: 800-432-1377
    Fax: 765-983-1688
    Email: woodna@earlham.edu
    Website: http://www.esr.earlham.edu/

*Eastern Baptist Theological Seminary**
    (American Baptist Churches in the USA)
    6 Lancaster Avenue
    Wynnewood, PA 19096
    Telephone: 610-896-5000
    Fax: 610-649-3834
    Website: http://www.ebts.edu/

*Eastern Mennonite Seminary of Eastern
Mennonite University**
    (Mennonite Church)
    1200 Park Road
    Harrisonburg, VA 22802
    Telephone: 540-432-4260
    Fax: 540-432-4598
    Email: info@emu.edu
    Website: http://www.emu.edu/seminary/

*Ecumenical Theological Seminary**
    (Inter/multidenominational)
    2930 Woodward Avenue
    Detroit, MI 48201
    Telephone: 313-831-5200
    Fax: 313-831-1353
    Website: http://www.etseminary.org/

*Eden Theological Seminary**
    (United Church of Christ)
    475 E Lockwood Avenue
    St. Louis, MO 63119
    Telephone: 314-961-3627
    Fax: 314-918-2626
    Website: http://www.eden.edu/

*Emmanuel School of Religion**
    (Christian Churches; Churches of Christ)
    1 Walker Drive
    Johnson City, TN 37601
    Telephone: 423-926-1186
    Fax: 423-926-6198
    Email: wetzelc@esr.edu
    Website: http://www.esr.edu/

Emmaus Bible College
    (Christian Brethren/Plymouth Brethren)
    2570 Asbury Road
    Dubuque, IA 52001
    Telephone: 563-588-8000
    Fax: 563-588-1216
    Email: info@emmaus.edu
    Website: http://www.emmaus.edu/

Episcopal Divinity School*
(Episcopal)
99 Brattle Street
Cambridge, MA 02138
Telephone: 617-868-3450
Fax: 617-864-5385
Email: fphillips@episdivschool.org
Website: http://www.episdivschool.edu/

Episcopal Theological Seminary of the Southwest*
(Episcopal Church)
PO Box 2247
Austin, TX 78768
Telephone: 512-472-4133
Fax: 512-472-3098
Email: salexander@etss.edu
Website: http://www.etss.edu/

Erskine Theological Seminary*
(Associate Reformed Presbyterian Church)
PO Box 668
Due West, SC 29639
Telephone: 864-379-8885
Fax: 864-379-2171
Email: gore@erskine.edu
Website: http://seminary.erskine.edu/

Eugene Bible College
(Open Bible Churches)
2155 Bailey Hill Road
Eugene, OR 97405
Telephone: 503-485-1780
Fax: 503-343-5801

Evangelical School of Theology*
(Evangelical Association of Reformed and Congregational Christian Churches)
121 S College Street
Myerstown, PA 17067
Telephone: 717-866-5775
Fax: 717-866-4667
Website: http://www.evangelical.edu/

Evangelical Seminary of Puerto Rico*
(Inter/multidenominational)
Ponce de Leon Avenue 776
San Juan, PR 00925
Telephone: 787-763-6700
Fax: 787-751-0847
Website: http://www.seminarioevangelicopr.org/

Faith Baptist Bible College and Theological Seminary
(General Association of Regular Baptist Churches)
1900 NW 4th Street
Ankeny, IA 50021
Telephone: 515-964-0601
Fax: 515-964-1638
Website: http://www.faith.edu/

Faith Evangelical Lutheran Seminary
(Conservative Lutheran Association)
3504 N Pearl Street
Tacoma, WA 98407
Telephone: 253-752-2020; 888-777-7675
Fax: 206-759-1790
Email: fsinfo@faithseminary.edu
Website: http://www.faithseminary.edu/

Florida Center for Theological Studies*
(Inter/multidenominational)
111 NE First Street
Eighth Floor
Miami, FL 33132
Telephone: 305-379-3777
Fax: 305-379-1006
Website: http://www.fcfts.org/

Florida Christian College
(Christian Churches; Churches of Christ)
1011 Bill Beck Boulevard
Kissimmee, FL 34744
Telephone: 407-847-8966
Fax: 407-847-3925
Email: fcc@fcc.edu
Website: http://www.fcc.edu/

Franciscan School of Theology*
(Roman Catholic Church)
1712 Euclid Avenue
Berkeley, CA 94709
Telephone: 510-848-5232
Fax: 510-549-9466
Email: wcieslak@fst.edu
Website: http://www.fst.edu/

Free Will Baptist Bible College
(National Association of Free Will Baptists)
3606 West End Avenue
Nashville, TN 37205
Telephone: 615-383-1340
Fax: 615-269-6028
Email: president@fwbbc.edu
Website: http://www.fwbcc.edu/

Fuller Theological Seminary*
(Multidenominational)
135 N Oakland Avenue
Pasadena, CA 91182
Telephone: 626-584-5200
Fax: 626-795-8767
Email: lguernse@fuller.edu
Website: http://www.fuller.edu/

Garrett-Evangelical Theological Seminary*
(United Methodist Church)
2121 Sheridan Road
Evanston, IL 60201
Telephone: 847-866-3900
Fax: 847-866-3957
Email: seminary@garrett.edu
Website: http://www.garrett.edu/

*General Theological Seminary**
(Episcopal Church)
175 9th Avenue
New York, NY 10011
Telephone: 212-243-5150
Fax: 212-647-0294
Email: ewing@gts.edu
Website: http://www.gts.edu/

*George Fox Evangelical Seminary**
(Inter/multidenominational)
12753 SW 68th Avenue
Portland, OR 97223
Telephone: 503-554-6150
Fax: 503-554-6111
Email: seminary@georgefox.edu
Website: http://www.seminary.georgefox.edu/

George Mercer Jr. Memorial School of Theology
(Episcopal Church)
65 4th Street
Garden City, NY 11530
Telephone: 516-248-4800
Fax: 516-248-4883

*George W. Truett Theological Seminary of Baylor University**
(Baptist General Convention)
PO Box 97126
Waco, TX 76798
Telephone: 254-710-3755
Fax: 254-710-3753
Website: http://www.baylor.edu/truett/

God's Bible School and College
(Nondenominational)
1810 Young Street
Cincinnati, OH 45202
Telephone: 513-721-7944
Fax: 513-721-3971
Email: president@gbs.edu
Website: http://www.gbs.edu/

*Golden Gate Baptist Theological Seminary**
(Southern Baptist Convention)
201 Seminary Drive
Mill Valley, CA 94941
Telephone: 415-380-1300
Fax: 415-380-1302
Email: seminary@ggbts.edu
Website: http://www.ggbts.edu/

*Gonzaga University Department of Religious Studies**
(Roman Catholic Church)
502 E Boone
Spokane, WA 99258
Telephone: 509-328-6782
Fax: 509-323-5718
Website: http://www.gonzaga.edu/

*Gordon-Conwell Theological Seminary**
(Inter/multidenominational)
130 Essex Street
South Hamilton, MA 01982
Telephone: 978-468-7111
Fax: 978-468-6691
Email: info@gcts.edu
Website: http://www.gordonconwell.edu/

Grace Bible College
(Grace Gospel Fellowship)
PO Box 910
Grand Rapids, MI 49509
Telephone: 616-538-2330
Fax: 616-538-0599
Email: gbc@gbcol.edu
Website: http://www.gbcol.edu/

*Grace Theological Seminary**
(Fellowship of Grace Brethren Churches)
200 Seminary Drive
Winona Lake, IN 46590
Telephone: 574-372-5100
Fax: 574-372-5139
Website: http://www.grace.edu/

Grace University
(Independent)
1311 S 9th Street
Omaha, NE 68108
Telephone: 402-449-2809
Fax: 402-341-9587
Email: jofast@graceu.edu
Website: http://www.graceu.edu/

*Graduate Theological Union**
(Interdenominational)
2400 Ridge Road
Berkeley, CA 94709
Telephone: 510-649-2400
Fax: 510-649-1417
Email: libref@gtu.edu
Website: http://www.gtu.edu/

*Grand Rapids Theological Seminary of Cornerstone University**
(Baptist)
1001 East Beltline NE
Grand Rapids, MI 49525
Telephone: 616-222-1422
Fax: 616-222-1502
Website: http://www.cornerstone.edu/

Great Lakes Christian College
(Christian Churches; Churches of Christ)
6211 W Willow Highway
Lansing, MI 48917
Telephone: 517-321-0242
Fax: 517-321-5902

Greenville College
(Free Methodist Church of North America)
315 E College Avenue

PO Box 159
Greenville, IL 62246
Telephone: 618-664-2800
Fax: 618-664-1748
Email: rsmith@greenville.edu
Website: http://www.greenville.edu/

Harding University Graduate School of Religion
(Churches of Christ)
1000 Cherry Road
Memphis, TN 38117
Telephone: 901-761-1352
Fax: 901-761-1358
Email: dean@hugsr.edu
Website: http://www.hugsr.edu/

Hartford Seminary
(Interdenominational)
77 Sherman Street
Hartford, CT 06105
Telephone: 860-509-9500
Fax: 860-509-9509
Email: info@hartsem.edu
Website: http://www.hartsem.edu/

Harvard University Divinity School
(Inter/multidenominational)
45 Francis Avenue
Cambridge, MA 02138
Telephone: 617-495-5761
Fax: 617-495-8026
Website: http://www.hds.harvard.edu/

Heritage Bible College†
(Pentecostal Free Will Baptists)
1747 Bud Hawkins Road
PO Box 1628
Dunn, NC 28335
Telephone: 910-892-3178
Fax: 910-892-1809
Email: generalinfo@heritagebiblecollege.org
Website: http://www.heritagebiblecollege.org/

Hillsdale Free Will Baptist College†
(National Association of Free Will Baptists)
PO Box 7208
Moore, OK 73153
Telephone: 405-912-9000
Fax: 405-912-9050
Email: hillsdale@hc.edu
Website: http://www.hc.edu/

Hobe Sound Bible College
(Nondenominational)
PO Box 1065
Hobe Sound, FL 33475
Telephone: 407-546-5534
Fax: 407-545-1421

Holy Cross Greek Orthodox School of Theology
(Greek Orthodox Archdiocese)
50 Goddard Avenue
Brookline, MA 02445

Telephone: 617-731-3500
Fax: 617-850-1460
Email: admissions@hchc.edu
Website: http://www.hchc.edu/

Holy Trinity Orthodox Seminary
(Russian Orthodox Church Outside Russia)
PO Box 36
Jordanville, NY 13361
Telephone: 315-858-0945
Fax: 315-858-0945
Email: seminary@telenet.net

Hood Theological Seminary
(African Methodist Episcopal Zion Church)
800 W Thomas Street
Salisbury, NC 28144
Telephone: 704-636-7611
Fax: 704-636-7699
Email: pwells@hoodseminary.edu
Website: http://www.hoodseminary.edu/

Hope International University
(Christian Churches; Churches of Christ)
2500 E Nutwood Avenue
Fullerton, CA 92831
Telephone: 714-879-3901
Fax: 714-681-7451
Email: slcarter@hiu.edu
Website: http://www.hiu.edu/

Houston Graduate School of Theology
(Friends)
1311 Holman
Suite 200
Houston, TX 77004
Telephone: 713-942-9505
Fax: 713-942-9506
Email: hgst@hgst.edu
Website: http://www.hgst.edu/

Howard University School of Divinity
(Nondenominational)
1400 Shepherd Street NE
Washington, DC 20017
Telephone: 202-806-0500
Fax: 202-806-0711
Website: http://www.howard.edu/schooldivinity/

Huntington College Graduate School of Christian Ministries
(Church of the United Brethren in Christ)
2303 College Avenue
Huntington, IN 46750
Telephone: 260-359-4039
Fax: 260-359-4126
Email: gscm@huntington.edu
Website: https://www.huntington.edu/admissions/graduate/

Iliff School of Theology
(United Methodist Church)
2201 S University Boulevard

Denver, CO 80210
Telephone: 303-744-1287
Fax: 303-777-3387
Website: http://www.iliff.edu/

*Immaculate Conception Seminary Seton Hall University**
(Roman Catholic Church)
400 S Orange Avenue
South Orange, NJ 07079
Telephone: 973-761-9575
Fax: 973-761-9577
Email: theology@shu.edu
Website: http://www.theology.shu.edu/

*Indiana Wesleyan University**
(Wesleyan Church)
4201 S Washington
Marion, IN 46953
Telephone: 765-674-6901
Fax: 765-677-2465
Email: james.barnes@indwes.edu
Website: http://www.indwes.edu/

*Inter-American Adventist Theological Seminary**
(Seventh-Day Adventist Church)
PO Box 830518
Miami, FL 33283
Telephone: 305-403-4700
Fax: 305-403-4600
Website: http://www.interamerica.org/

*Interdenominational Theological Center**
(Interdenominational)
700 Martin Luther King Jr. Drive SW
Atlanta, GA 30314
Telephone: 404-527-7702
Fax: 404-527-7770
Email: info@itc.edu
Website: http://www.itc.edu/

International Baptist College†
(Baptist)
2150 E Southern Avenue
Tempe, AZ 85282
Telephone: 480-838-7070
Fax: 480-505-3299
Email: ibc4u@juno.com
Website: http://www.tri-citybaptist.org/

International College and Graduate School†
(Nondenominational)
20 Dowsett Avenue
Honolulu, HI 96817
Telephone: 808-595-4247
Fax: 808-595-4779
Email: icgs@hawaii.rr.com
Website: http://www.icgshawaii.org/

*International Theological Seminary**
(Nondenominational)
3215-3225 N Tyler Avenue
El Monte, CA 91731

Telephone: 626-448-0023
Fax: 626-350-6343
Website: http://www.itsla.edu/

*James and Carolyn McAfee School of Theology of Mercer University**
(Cooperative Baptist Fellowship)
3001 Mercer University Drive
Atlanta, GA 30341
Telephone: 678-547-6470
Fax: 678-547-6478
Website: http://www.theology.mercer.edu/

*Jesuit School of Theology at Berkeley**
(Roman Catholic Church)
1735 LeRoy Avenue
Berkeley, CA 94709
Telephone: 510-549-5000
Fax: 510-841-8536
Website: http://www.jstb.edu/

*John Leland Center for Theological Studies**
(Baptist)
1301 N Hartford Street
Arlington, VA 22201
Telephone: 703-812-4757
Fax: 703-812-4764
Website: http://www.leland.edu/

Johnson Bible College
(Christian Churches; Churches of Christ)
7900 Johnson Drive
Knoxville, TN 37998
Telephone: 865-573-4517
Fax: 865-251-2336
Email: jbc@jbc.edu
Website: http://www.jbc.edu/

John Wesley College
(Interdenominational)
2314 N Centennial Street
High Point, NC 27265
Telephone: 336-889-2262
Fax: 336-889-2261
Email: admissions@johnwesley.edu
Website: http://www.johnwesley.edu/

Kansas City College and Bible School
(Church of God, Holiness)
7401 Metcalf Avenue
Overland Park, KS 66204
Telephone: 913-722-0272
Fax: 913-722-2135

*Kenrick-Glennon Seminary**
(Roman Catholic Church)
5200 Glennon Drive
St. Louis, MO 63119
Telephone: 314-792-6100
Fax: 314-792-6500
Website: http://www.kenrick.edu/

Kentucky Christian College
(Christian Churches; Churches of Christ)
100 Academic Parkway
Grayson, KY 41143
Telephone: 606-474-3000
Fax: 606-474-3155
Email: knights@email.kcc.edu
Website: http://www.kcc.edu/

Kentucky Mountain Bible College
(Interdenominational)
PO Box 10
Vancleve, KY 41385
Telephone: 606-666-5000
Fax: 606-666-7744

King's College and Seminary[†]
(Nondenominational)
14800 Sherman Way
Van Nuys, CA 91405
Telephone: 818-779-8040
Fax: 818-779-8241
Email: admissions@kingsseminary.edu
Websites: http://www.kingsseminary.edu/; http://www.kingscollege.edu/

Knox Theological Seminary[*]
(Presbyterian Church in America)
5554 N Federal Highway
Fort Lauderdale, FL 33308
Telephone: 954-771-0376
Fax: 954-351-3343
Email: knox@crpc.org
Website: http://www.knoxseminary.org/

Kuyper College
(Nondenominational)
3333 East Beltline Ave NE
Grand Rapids, MI 49525
Telephone: 616-222-3000
Email: webmaster@kuyper.edu
Website: http://kuyper.edu

Lancaster Bible College
(Nondenominational)
PO Box 83403
Lancaster, PA 17601
Telephone: 717-560-8278
Fax: 717-560-8260
Email: president@lbc.edu
Website: http://www.lbc.edu/

Lancaster Theological Seminary[*]
(United Church of Christ)
555 W James Street
Lancaster, PA 17603
Telephone: 717-393-0654
Fax: 717-393-4254
Email: seminary@lancasterseminary.edu
Website: http://www.lancasterseminary.edu/

La Sierra University School of Religion[*]
(Seventh-Day Adventist Church)
4500 Riverwalk Parkway
Riverside, CA 92515
Telephone: 951-785-2000
Fax: 951-785-2901
Email: pr@lasierra.edu
Website: http://www.lasierra.edu/

Lexington Theological Seminary[*]
(Christian Church [Disciples of Christ])
631 S Limestone Street
Lexington, KY 40508
Telephone: 859-252-0361
Fax: 859-281-6042
Website: http://www.lextheo.edu/

Liberty University School of Divinity
(Baptist)
1971 University Boulevard
Lynchburg, VA 24502
Telephone: 434-592-4140

Liberty University[†]
(Baptist)
1971 University Boulevard
Lynchburg, VA 24502
Telephone: 434-582-2000
Fax: 434-582-2304
Email: admissions@liberty.edu
Website: http://www.liberty.edu/

Life Pacific College
(International Church of the Foursquare Gospel)
1100 Covina Boulevard
San Dimas, CA 91773
Telephone: 909-599-5433
Fax: 909-599-6690
Email: info@lifepacific.edu
Website: http://www.lifepacific.edu/

Lincoln Christian Seminary[*]
(Christian Churches; Churches of Christ)
100 Campus View Drive
Lincoln, IL 62656
Telephone: 217-732-3168
Fax: 217-732-1821
Email: info@lincolnchristian.edu
Website: http://www.lincolnchristian.edu/seminary/

Lipscomb University College of Bible and Ministry[*]
(Churches of Christ)
3901 Granny White Pike
Nashville, TN 37204
Telephone: 615-279-6051
Fax: 615-279-6052
Website: http://www.lipscomb.edu/

Logos Evangelical Seminary[*]
(Evangelical Formosan Church)
9358 Telstar Avenue

El Monte, CA 91731
Telephone: 626-571-5110
Fax: 626-571-5119
Email: logos@les.edu
Website: http://www.logos-seminary.edu/

*Logsdon School of Theology of Hardin-Simmons University**
(Baptist General Convention)
PO Box 16235
Abilene, TX 79698
Telephone: 325-670-1287
Fax: 325-670-1406
Website: http://www.hsutx.edu/academics
/logsdon

*Louisville Presbyterian Theological Seminary**
(Presbyterian Church [USA])
1044 Alta Vista Road
Louisville, KY 40205
Telephone: 502-895-3411
Fax: 502-895-1096
Website: http://www.lpts.edu/

*Loyola Marymount University Department of Theological Studies**
(Roman Catholic Church)
1 LMU Drive
Los Angeles, CA 90045
Telephone: 310-338-7670
Fax: 310-338-1947
Website: http://bellarmine.lmu.edu/theological-studies/

*Loyola University Chicago Institute of Pastoral Studies**
(Roman Catholic Church)
820 N Michigan Avenue
Chicago, IL 60611
Telephone: 312-915-7400
Fax: 312-915-7410
Website: http://www.luc.edu/ips/

Lutheran Bible Institute in California
(Intersynodical Lutheran)
5321 University Drive
Suite G
Irvine, CA 92612
Telephone: 949-262-9222; 800-261-5242
Fax: 949-262-0283; 877-381-4245
Email: lbicalifornia@earthlink.net
Website: http://www.lbic.org/

Lutheran Brethren Seminary
(Church of the Lutheran Brethren)
815 W Vernon
Fergus Falls, MN 56537
Telephone: 218-739-3375
Fax: 218-739-1259
Email: lbs@clba.org
Website: http://www.lbs.edu/

*Lutheran School of Theology at Chicago**
(Evangelical Lutheran Church in America)
1100 E 55th Street
Chicago, IL 60615
Telephone: 773-256-0700
Fax: 773-256-0782
Email: jechols@lstc.edu
Website: http://www.lstc.edu/

*Lutheran Theological Seminary at Gettysburg**
(Evangelical Lutheran Church in America)
61 Seminary Ridge
Gettysburg, PA 17325
Telephone: 717-334-6286
Fax: 717-334-3469
Email: info@ltsg.edu
Website: http://www.ltsg.edu/

*Lutheran Theological Seminary at Philadelphia**
(Evangelical Lutheran Church in America)
7301 Germantown Avenue
Philadelphia, PA 19119
Telephone: 215-248-4616
Fax: 215-248-4577
Email: mtairy@ltsp.edu
Website: http://www.ltsp.edu/

*Lutheran Theological Southern Seminary**
(Evangelical Lutheran Church in America)
4201 N Main Street
Columbia, SC 29203
Telephone: 803-786-5150
Fax: 803-786-6499
Email: freisz@ltss.edu
Website: http://www.ltss.edu/

Luther Rice Bible College and Seminary
(Baptist)
3038 Evans Mill Road
Lithonia, GA 30038
Telephone: 770-484-1204
Fax: 770-484-1155
Email: lrs@lrs.edu
Website: http://www.lrs.edu/

*Luther Seminary**
(Evangelical Lutheran Church in America)
2481 Como Avenue
St. Paul, MN 55108
Telephone: 651-641-3456
Fax: 651-641-3425
Email: admissions@luthersem.edu
Website: http://www.luthersem.edu/

Magnolia Bible College
(Churches of Christ)
PO Box 1109
Kosciusko, MS 39090
Telephone: 662-289-2896
Fax: 662-289-1850
Email: president@magnolia.edu
Website: http://www.magnolia.edu/

Manhattan Christian College
(Christian Churches; Churches of Christ)
1415 Anderson Avenue
Manhattan, KS 66502
Telephone: 785-539-3571
Fax: 785-539-0832
Website: http://www.mccks.edu/

Maple Springs Baptist Bible College and Seminary[†]
(Nondenominational)
4130 Belt Road
Capital Heights, MD 20743
Telephone: 301-736-3631
Fax: 301-735-6507
Email: larry.jordan@msbbcs.edu
Website: http://www.msbbcs.edu/

*McCormick Theological Seminary**
(Presbyterian Church [USA])
5460 S University Avenue
Chicago, IL 60615
Telephone: 773-947-6300
Fax: 773-288-2612
Email: ccampbell@mccormick.edu
Website: http://www.mccormick.edu/

*M. Christopher White School of Divinity of Gardner-Webb University**
(Baptist State Convention of North Carolina)
110 N Main Street
Noel Hall
Boiling Springs, NC 28017
Telephone: 704-406-4400
Fax: 704-406-3935
Website: http://www.divinity.gardner-webb.edu/

*Meadville Lombard Theological School**
(Unitarian Universalist)
701 S Woodlawn Avenue
Chicago, IL 60637
Telephone: 773-256-3000
Fax: 773-753-1323
Email: lbarker@meadville.edu
Website: http://www.meadville.edu/

*Memphis Theological Seminary**
(Cumberland Presbyterian Church)
168 E Parkway S at Union
Memphis, TN 38104
Telephone: 901-458-8232
Fax: 901-452-4051
Email: lblakeburn@mtscampus.edu
Website: http://www.mtscampus.edu/

*Mennonite Brethren Biblical Seminary**
(General Conference of Mennonite Brethren Churches)
4824 E Butler Avenue at Chestnut Avenue
Fresno, CA 93727
Telephone: 559-251-8628
Fax: 559-251-7212

Email: fresno@mbseminary.edu
Website: http://www.mbseminary.edu/

Messenger College[†]
(Pentecostal Church of God)
300 E 50th Street
Joplin, MO 64804
Telephone: 417-624-7070
Fax: 417-624-1689
Email: info@messengercollege.edu
Website: http://www.messengercollege.edu/

*Methodist Theological School in Ohio**
(United Methodist Church)
3081 Columbus Pike
PO Box 8004
Delaware, OH 43015
Telephone: 740-363-1146
Fax: 740-362-3135
Email: ndewire@mtso.edu
Website: http://www.mtso.edu/

Michigan Theological Seminary[*†]
(Nondenominational)
41550 E Ann Arbor Trail
Plymouth, MI 48170
Telephone: 734-207-9581
Fax: 734-207-9582
Email: admissions@mts.edu
Website: http://www.mts.edu/

Mid-America Christian University
(Church of God [Anderson, Indiana])
3500 SW 119th Street
Oklahoma City, OK 73170
Telephone: 405-691-3800
Fax: 405-692-3165
Email: info@macu.edu
Website: http://www.macu.edu/

*Mid-America Reformed Seminary**
(Inter/multidenominational)
229 Seminary Drive
Dyer, IN 46311
Telephone: 219-864-2400
Fax: 219-864-2410
Email: mars@jorsm.com
Website: http://www.midamerica.edu/

*Midwestern Baptist Theological Seminary**
(Southern Baptist Convention)
5001 N Oak Trafficway
Kansas City, MO 64118
Telephone: 816-414-3700
Fax: 816-414-3799
Website: http://www.mbts.edu/

*Moody Bible Institute**
(Interdenominational)
820 N La Salle Boulevard
Chicago, IL 60610
Telephone: 312-329-4000
Fax: 312-329-4109
Website: http://www.moody.edu/

*Moravian Theological Seminary**
(Moravian Church [Unitas Fratrum])
1200 Main Street
Bethlehem, PA 18018
Telephone: 610-861-1516
Fax: 610-861-1569
Email: seminary@moravian.edu
Website: http://www.moravianseminary.edu/

Moreau Seminary
(Roman Catholic Church)
PO Box 541
Notre Dame, IN 46556
Telephone: 574-631-7735
Fax: 574-631-9233

Morehouse School of Religion
(Baptist)
645 Beckwith Street SW
Atlanta, GA 30314
Telephone: 404-527-7777
Fax: 404-681-1005

*Mount Angel Seminary**
(Roman Catholic Church)
1 Abbey Drive
St. Benedict, OR 97373
Telephone: 503-845-3951
Fax: 503-845-3126
Website: http://www.mtangel.edu/

*Mt. St. Mary's Seminary**
(Roman Catholic Church)
16300 Old Emmitsburg Road
Emmitsburg, MD 21727
Telephone: 301-447-5295
Fax: 301-447-5636
Email: rhoades@msmary.edu
Website: http://www.msmary.edu/

Mt. St. Mary's Seminary of the West
(Roman Catholic Church)
6616 Beechmont Avenue
Cincinnati, OH 45230
Telephone: 513-231-2223
Fax: 513-231-3254
Email: jhaemmer@mtsm.org
Website: http://mtsm.org/

*Multnomah Biblical Seminary**
(Nondenominational)
8435 NE Glisan Street
Portland, OR 97220
Telephone: 503-255-0332
Fax: 503-251-6701
Website: http://www.multnomah.edu/

Mundelein Seminary of the University of St. Mary-of-the-Lake
(Roman Catholic Church)
1000 E Maple
Mundelein, IL 60060
Telephone: 847-566-6401

Fax: 847-566-7330
Email: syopusml@usml.edu
Website: http://www.vocations.org/

*Nashotah House Theological Seminary**
(Episcopal Church)
2777 Mission Road
Nashotah, WI 53058
Telephone: 262-646-6500
Fax: 262-646-6504
Email: nashotah@nashotah.edu
Website: http://www.nashotah.edu/

Nazarene Bible College
(Church of the Nazarene)
1111 Academy Park Loop
Colorado Springs, CO 80910
Telephone: 719-884-5000
Fax: 719-884-5199
Email: info@nbc.edu
Website: http://www.nbc.edu/

*Nazarene Theological Seminary**
(Church of the Nazarene)
1700 E Meyer Boulevard
Kansas City, MO 64131
Telephone: 816-333-6254
Fax: 816-333-6271
Email: rbenefiel@nts.edu
Website: http://www.nts.edu/

Nebraska Christian College
(Christian Churches; Churches of Christ)
1800 Syracuse Avenue
Norfolk, NE 68701
Telephone: 402-379-5000
Fax: 402-391-5100
Email: info@nechristian.edu
Website: http://www.nechristian.edu/

*New Brunswick Theological Seminary**
(Reformed Church in America)
17 Seminary Place
New Brunswick, NJ 08901
Telephone: 732-247-5241
Fax: 732-249-5412
Email: njk@nbts.edu
Website: http://www.nbts.edu/

*New Orleans Baptist Theological Seminary**
(Southern Baptist Convention)
3939 Gentilly Boulevard
New Orleans, LA 70126
Telephone: 504-282-4455
Fax: 504-816-8023
Email: nobts@nobts.edu
Website: http://www.nobts.edu/

*New York Theological Seminary**
(Inter/multidenominational)
475 Riverside Drive
Suite 500
New York, NY 10115

Telephone: 212-870-1250
Fax: 212-870-1236
Website: http://www.nyts.edu/

North American Baptist Seminary*
(North American Baptist Conference)
1525 S Grange Avenue
Sioux Falls, SD 57105
Telephone: 605-336-6588
Fax: 605-335-9090
Email: admissions@nabs.edu
Website: http://www.nabs.edu/

North Central Bible College
(Assemblies of God)
910 Elliot Avenue S
Minneapolis, MN 55404
Telephone: 612-332-3491
Fax: 612-343-4778

Northeastern Seminary at Roberts Wesleyan
College*
(Nondenominational)
2265 Westside Drive
Rochester, NY 14624
Telephone: 585-594-6800
Fax: 585-594-6801
Website: http://www.nes.edu/

Northern Baptist Theological Seminary*
(American Baptist Churches in the USA)
660 E Butterfield Road
Lombard, IL 60148
Telephone: 630-620-2100
Fax: 630-620-2194
Email: cwmoore@northern.seminary.edu
Website: http://www.seminary.edu/

North Park Theological Seminary*
(Evangelical Covenant Church)
3225 W Foster Avenue
Chicago, IL 60625
Telephone: 773-244-6214
Fax: 773-244-6244
Email: jphelan@northpark.edu
Website: http://www.northpark.edu/

Northwest Baptist Seminary†
(Baptist)
4301 N Stevens
Tacoma, WA 98407
Telephone: 253-759-6104
Fax: 253-759-3299
Email: nbs@nbs.edu
Website: http://www.nbs.edu/

Northwest College
(Assemblies of God)
5520 108th Avenue NE
PO Box 579
Kirkland, WA 98083
Telephone: 425-822-8266
Fax: 425-827-0148

Email: mail@ncag.edu
Website: http://www.nwcollege.edu/

Notre Dame Seminary*
(Roman Catholic Church)
2901 S Carrollton Avenue
New Orleans, LA 70118
Telephone: 504-866-7426
Fax: 504-866-3119
Website: http://www.nds.edu/

Oak Hills Christian College
(Interdenominational)
1600 Oak Hills Road SW
Bemidji, MN 56601
Telephone: 218-751-8670
Fax: 218-751-8825
Email: dclausen@oakhills.edu
Website: http://www.oakhills.edu/

Oblate School of Theology*
(Roman Catholic Church)
285 Oblate Drive
San Antonio, TX 78216
Telephone: 210-341-1366
Fax: 210-341-4519
Email: info@ost.edu
Website: http://www.ost.edu/

Oral Roberts University School of Theology*
(Inter/multidenominational)
7777 S Lewis Avenue
Tulsa, OK 74171
Telephone: 918-495-7016
Fax: 918-495-6259
Email: jcope@oru.edu
Website: http://www.oru.edu/

Ozark Christian College
(Christian Churches; Churches of Christ)
1111 N Main Street
Joplin, MO 64801
Telephone: 417-624-2518
Fax: 417-624-0090
Email: pres@occ.edu
Website: http://www.occ.edu/

Pacific Lutheran Theological Seminary*
(Evangelical Lutheran Church in America)
2770 Marin Avenue
Berkeley, CA 94708
Telephone: 510-524-5264
Fax: 510-524-2408
Email: president@plts.edu
Website: http://www.plts.edu/

Pacific School of Religion*
(Inter/multidenominational)
1798 Scenic Avenue
Berkeley, CA 94709
Telephone: 510-848-0528
Fax: 510-845-8948
Email: comm@psr.edu
Website: http://www.psr.edu/

Payne Theological Seminary*
(African Methodist Episcopal Church)
PO Box 474
1230 Wilberforce-Clifton Road
Wilberforce, OH 45384
Telephone: 937-376-2946
Fax: 937-376-3330
Email: lfitchue@payne.edu
Website: http://www.payne.edu/

Pepperdine University
(Churches of Christ)
24255 Pacific Coast Highway
Malibu, CA 90263
Telephone: 310-506-4352
Fax: 310-317-7271
Email: randall.chesnutt@pepperdine.edu
Website: http://www.pepperdine.edu/

Perkins School of Theology at Southern Methodist University*
(United Methodist Church)
PO Box 750133
Dallas, TX 75275
Telephone: 214-768-2293
Fax: 214-768-4245
Email: theology@smu.edu
Website: http://www.smu.edu/theology

Philadelphia Biblical University
(Nondenominational)
200 Manor Avenue
Langhorne, PA 19047
Telephone: 215-752-5800
Fax: 215-702-4341
Email: president@pbu.edu
Website: http://www.pbu.edu/

Phillips Theological Seminary*
(Christian Church [Disciples of Christ])
901 N Mingo Road
Tulsa, OK 74116
Telephone: 918-610-8303
Fax: 918-610-8404
Website: http://www.ptstulsa.edu/

Phoenix Seminary*
(Inter/multidenominational)
4222 East Thomas Road, Suite 400
Phoenix, AZ 85018
Telephone: 888-443-1020
Fax: 602-850-8080
Website: http://www.ps.edu

Piedmont Baptist College†
(Baptist)
716 Franklin Street
Winston-Salem, NC 27101
Telephone: 336-725-8344
Fax: 336-725-5522
Email: admissions@pbc.edu
Website: http://www.pbc.edu/

Pittsburgh Theological Seminary*
(Presbyterian Church [USA])
616 N Highland Avenue
Pittsburgh, PA 15206
Telephone: 412-362-5610
Fax: 412-363-3260
Email: calian@pts.edu
Website: http://www.pts.edu/

Pontifical College Josephinum*
(Roman Catholic Church)
7625 N High Street
Columbus, OH 43235
Telephone: 614-885-5585
Fax: 614-885-2307
Website: http://www.pcj.edu/

Pope John XXIII National Seminary
(Roman Catholic Church)
558 South Avenue
Weston, MA 02193
Telephone: 617-899-5500
Fax: 617-899-9057

Princeton Theological Seminary*
(Presbyterian Church [USA])
PO Box 821
Princeton, NJ 08542
Telephone: 609-921-8300
Fax: 609-924-2973
Email: comm-pub@ptsem.edu
Website: http://www.ptsem.edu/

Protestant Episcopal Theological Seminary in Virginia*
(Episcopal Church)
3737 Seminary Road
Alexandria, VA 22304
Telephone: 703-370-6600
Fax: 703-370-6234
Email: mhorne@vts.edu
Website: http://www.vts.edu/

Puget Sound Christian College
(Christian Churches; Churches of Christ)
PO Box 13108
Everett, WA 98206
Telephone: 425-257-3090
Fax: 425-258-1488
Email: president@pscc.edu
Website: http://www.pscc.edu/

Reformed Episcopal Seminary*
(Reformed Episcopal Church)
826 Second Avenue
Blue Bell, PA 19422
Telephone: 610-292-9852
Fax: 610-292-9853
Email: registrar@reseminary.edu
Website: http://www.reseminary.edu/

*Reformed Presbyterian Theological Seminary**
(Reformed Presbyterian Church of North America)
7418 Penn Avenue
Pittsburgh, PA 15208
Telephone: 412-731-8690
Fax: 412-731-4834
Email: rpseminary@aol.com
Website: http://www.rpts.edu/

*Reformed Theological Seminary**
(Inter/multidenominational)
5422 Clinton Boulevard
Jackson, MS 39209
Telephone: 601-923-1600
Fax: 601-923-1654
Email: rts.orlando@rts.edu
Website: http://www.rts.edu/

*Regent University School of Divinity**
(Nondenominational)
1000 Regent University Drive
Virginia Beach, VA 23464
Telephone: 800-723-6162
Fax: 757-226-4597
Email: vinssyn@regent.edu
Website: http://www.regent.edu/acad/schdiv/

Roanoke Bible College
(Christian Churches; Churches of Christ)
715 N Poindexter Street
Elizabeth City, NC 27909
Telephone: 252-334-2070
Fax: 252-334-2071
Email: wag@roanokebible.edu
Website: http://www.roanokebible.edu/

*Sacred Heart Major Seminary**
(Roman Catholic Church)
2701 Chicago Boulevard
Detroit, MI 48206
Telephone: 313-883-8501
Fax: 313-868-6440
Website: http://www.shmsonline.org/

*Sacred Heart School of Theology**
(Roman Catholic Church)
PO Box 429
Hales Corners, WI 53130
Telephone: 414-425-8300
Fax: 414-529-6999
Email: rector@shst.edu
Website: http://www.shst.edu/

*St. Bernard's School of Theology and Ministry**
(Roman Catholic Church)
120 French Road
Rochester, NY 14618
Telephone: 585-271-3657
Fax: 585-271-2045
Email: pschoelles@sbi.edu
Website: http://www.stbernards.edu/

*Saint Charles Borromeo Seminary**
(Roman Catholic Church)
100 E Wynnewood Road
Wynnewood, PA 19096
Telephone: 610-667-3394
Fax: 610-667-0452
Website: http://www.scs.edu/

*Saint Francis de Sales Seminary**
(Roman Catholic Church)
3257 S Lake Drive
St. Francis, WI 53235
Telephone: 414-747-6400
Fax: 414-747-6442
Email: mwitczak@sfs.edu
Website: http://www.sfs.edu/

*Saint John's Seminary**
(Roman Catholic Church)
127 Lake Street
Brighton, MA 02135
Telephone: 617-254-2610
Fax: 617-787-2336
Website: http://www.sjsboston.org/

*St. John's Seminary**
(Roman Catholic Church)
5012 Seminary Road
Camarillo, CA 93012
Telephone: 805-482-2755
Fax: 805-482-0637
Website: http://www.stjohnsem.edu/

*Saint John's School of Theology and Seminary**
(Roman Catholic Church)
PO Box 7288
Collegeville, MN 56321
Telephone: 320-363-2622
Fax: 320-363-3145
Website: http://www.csbsju.edu/sot/

*St. John Vianney Theological Seminary**
(Roman Catholic Church)
1300 S Steele Street
Denver, CO 80210
Telephone: 303-282-3427
Fax: 303-282-3453
Website: http://sjvdenver.edu/

*Saint Joseph's Seminary**
(Roman Catholic Church)
201 Seminary Avenue
Yonkers, NY 10704
Telephone: 914-968-6200
Fax: 914-968-7912
Email: sjs@dunwoodie.edu
Website: http://www.dunwoodie.edu/

St. Louis Christian College
(Christian Churches; Churches of Christ)
1360 Grandview Drive
Florissant, MO 63033

Telephone: 314-837-6777
Fax: 314-837-8291
Email: admissions@stlchristian.edu
Website: https://www.stlchristian.edu/

Saint Mary Seminary and Graduate School of Theology*
(Roman Catholic Church)
28700 Euclid Avenue
Wickliffe, OH 44092
Telephone: 440-943-7600
Fax: 440-943-7577
Website: http://www.stmarysem.edu/

St. Mary's Seminary
(Roman Catholic Church)
9845 Memorial Drive
Houston, TX 77024
Telephone: 713-686-4345
Fax: 713-681-7550
Website: http://smseminary.com/

St. Mary's Seminary and University*
(Roman Catholic Church)
5400 Roland Avenue
Baltimore, MD 21210
Telephone: 410-864-4000
Fax: 410-864-4278
Website: http://www.stmarys.edu/

Saint Meinrad Seminary and School of Theology*
(Roman Catholic Church)
200 Hill Drive
St Meinrad, IN 47577
Telephone: 812-357-6611
Fax: 812-357-6964
Email: theology@saintmeinrad.edu
Website: http://www.saintmeinrad.edu/

St. Patrick's Seminary and University*
(Roman Catholic Church)
320 Middlefield Road
Menlo Park, CA 94025
Telephone: 650-325-5621
Fax: 650-322-0997
Website: http://www.stpatricksseminary.org/

Saint Paul School of Theology*
(United Methodist Church)
5123 Truman Road
Kansas City, MO 64127
Telephone: 816-483-9600
Fax: 816-483-9605
Email: spst@spst.edu
Website: http://www.spst.edu/

Saint Paul Seminary School of Divinity of the University of St. Thomas*
(Roman Catholic Church)
2260 Summit Avenue
St. Paul, MN 55105
Telephone: 651-962-5050

Fax: 651-962-5790
Website: http://www.stthomas.edu/spssod/

St. Petersburg Theological Seminary[†]
(Inter/multidenominational)
10830 Navajo Drive
St. Petersburg, FL 33708
Telephone: 727-399-0276
Fax: 727-399-1324
Email: sptsoffice@aol.com
Website: http://www.sptseminary.edu/

SS. Cyril and Methodius Seminary*
(Roman Catholic Church)
3535 Indian Trail
Orchard Lake, MI 48324
Telephone: 248-683-0310
Fax: 248-738-6735
Email: sscms.dean@comcast.net
Website: http://www.sscms.edu/

Saint Tikhon's Orthodox Theological Seminary*
(Orthodox Church in America)
PO Box 130
St. Tikhon's Road
South Canaan, PA 18459
Telephone: 570-937-4411
Fax: 570-937-3100
Email: info@stots.edu
Website: http://www.stots.edu/

St. Vincent de Paul Regional Seminary*
(Roman Catholic Church)
10701 S Military Trail
Boynton Beach, FL 33436
Telephone: 561-732-4424
Fax: 561-737-2205
Email: cduque@svdp.edu
Website: http://www.svdp.edu/

Saint Vincent Seminary*
(Roman Catholic Church)
300 Fraser Purchase Road
Latrobe, PA 15650
Telephone: 724-537-4592
Fax: 724-532-5052
Email: kurt.belsole@email.stvincent.edu
Website: http://www.saintvincentseminary.edu/

St. Vladimir's Orthodox Theological Seminary*
(Orthodox Church in America)
575 Scarsdale Road
Crestwood, NY 10707
Telephone: 914-961-8313
Fax: 914-961-4507
Email: info@svots.edu
Website: http://www.svots.edu/

Samuel DeWitt Proctor School of Theology of Virginia Union University
(American Baptist Churches in the USA; National Baptist Convention; Progressive National Baptist Convention)

419

1500 N Lombardy Street
Richmond, VA 23220
Telephone: 804-257-5715
Fax: 804-342-3911
Website: https://www.vuu.edu/samuel_dewitt
_proctor_school_of_theology.aspx

San Francisco Theological Seminary*
(Presbyterian Church [USA])
105 Seminary Road
San Anselmo, CA 94960
Telephone: 415-451-2800
Fax: 415-451-2811
Email: sftsinfo@sfts.edu
Website: http://www.sfts.edu/

Savonarola Theological Seminary
(Polish National Catholic Church of America)
1031 Cedar Avenue
Scranton, PA 18505
Telephone: 570-343-0100
Email: pncccenter@adelphia.net

School of Theology at Azusa Pacific University*
(Interdenominational)
901 E Alosta
PO Box 7000
Azusa, CA 91702
Telephone: 845-969-3434
Fax: 845-969-7180
Website: http://www.apu.edu/theology/

Seabury-Western Theological Seminary*
(Episcopal Church)
2122 Sheridan Road
Evanston, IL 60201
Telephone: 847-328-9300
Fax: 847-328-9624
Email: seabury@seabury.edu
Website: http://www.seabury.edu/

Seattle University School of Theology and
Ministry*
(Roman Catholic Church; several mainline Protes-
tant denominations and associations)
901 12th Avenue
PO Box 222000
Seattle, WA 98122
Telephone: 206-296-5330
Fax: 206-296-5329
Email: millerdi@seattleu.edu
Website: http://www.seattleu.edu/stm/

Seminario Evangelico de Puerto Rico
(Interdenominational)
776 Ponce de León Avenue
San Juan, PR 00925
Telephone: 787-763-6700
Fax: 787-751-0847
Email: drspagan@icepr.com; jvaldes@tld.net
Website: http://www.se-pr.edu/

Seminary of the Immaculate Conception*
(Roman Catholic Church)
440 W Neck Road
Huntington, NY 11743
Telephone: 631-423-0483
Fax: 631-423-2346
Website: http://www.icseminary.edu/

Seventh-Day Adventist Theological Seminary of
Andrews University*
(Seventh-Day Adventist Church)
Andrews University
4145 E Campus Circle Drive
Berrien Springs, MI 49104
Telephone: 269-471-3537
Fax: 269-471-6202
Email: seminary@andrews.edu
Website: http://www.andrews.edu/sem/

Seventh Day Baptist School of Ministry
(Seventh Day Baptists)
3120 Kennedy Road
PO Box 1678
Janesville, WI 53547
Telephone: 608-752-5055
Fax: 608-752-7711
Email: dean@sdbministry.org
Website: http://sdbministry.org/

Sewanee: The University of the South School of
Theology*
(Episcopal Church)
335 Tennessee Avenue
Sewanee, TN 37383
Telephone: 800-722-1974
Fax: 931-598-1412
Email: theology@sewanee.edu
Website: http://theology.sewanee.edu/seminary/

Shasta Bible College and Graduate School†
(Baptist)
2951 Goodwater Avenue
Redding, CA 96002
Telephone: 530-221-4275
Fax: 530-221-6929
Email: sbcadm@shasta.edu
Website: http://www.shasta.edu/

Shaw University Divinity School*
(General Baptist State Convention, NC)
PO Box 2090
Raleigh, NC 27602
Telephone: 919-546-8569
Fax: 919-546-8571
Website: http://www.shawu.edu/SUDS/

Simpson University
(Christian and Missionary Alliance)
2211 College View Drive
Redding, CA 96003
Telephone: 916-224-5600
Fax: 916-224-5608

Southeastern Baptist College
(Baptist Missionary Association of America)
4229 Highway 15N
Laurel, MS 39440
Telephone: 601-426-6346
Fax: 601-426-6346

Southeastern Baptist Theological Seminary*
(Southern Baptist Convention)
PO Box 1889
Wake Forest, NC 27588
Telephone: 919-556-3101
Fax: 919-556-8550
Website: http://www.sebts.edu/

Southeastern Bible College
(Interdenominational)
2545 Valley Vale Road
Birmingham, AL 35244
Telephone: 205-408-7073; 205-970-9200
Fax: 205-970-9207
Email: 102064.406@compuserve.com
Website: http://www.sebc.edu/

Southeastern College of the Assemblies of God
(Assemblies of God)
1000 Longfellow Boulevard
Lakeland, FL 33801
Telephone: 863-667-5000
Fax: 863-667-5200
Email: info@secollege.edu
Website: http://www.secollege.edu/

Southern Baptist Theological Seminary*
(Southern Baptist Convention)
2825 Lexington Road
Louisville, KY 40280
Telephone: 502-897-4011
Fax: 502-899-1770
Email: communications@sbts.edu
Website: http://www.sbts.edu/

Southern California Bible College and Seminary†
(Southern Baptist Convention)
2075 E Madison Avenue
El Cajon, CA 92019
Telephone: 619-442-9841
Fax: 619-442-4510
Email: info@scbcs.edu
Website: http://www.scbcs.edu/

Southern Evangelical Seminary†
(Interdenominational)
3000 Tilley Morris Road
Matthews, NC 28104
Telephone: 704-847-5600
Fax: 704-845-1747
Email: ses@ses.edu
Website: http://www.ses.edu/

Southern Methodist College†
(Independent)
541 Broughton Street

PO Box 1027
Orangeburg, SC 29116
Telephone: 803-534-7826
Fax: 803-534-7827
Email: smced@smcollege.edu
Website: http://smcollege.edu/

Southern Wesleyan University
(Wesleyan Church)
907 Wesleyan Drive
PO Box 1020
Central, SC 29630
Telephone: 864-644-5000
Fax: 864-644-5900
Email: dspittal@swu.edu
Website: http://www.swu.edu/

Southwestern Assemblies of God University
(Assemblies of God)
1200 Sycamore Street
Waxahachie, TX 75165
Telephone: 972-937-4010
Fax: 972-923-0488
Website: http://www.sagu.edu/

Southwestern Baptist Theological Seminary*
(Southern Baptist Convention)
2001 W Seminary Drive
Fort Worth, TX 76115
Telephone: 817-923-1921
Fax: 817-923-0610
Website: http://www.swbts.edu/

Southwestern College
(Conservative Baptist Association of America)
2625 E Cactus Road
Phoenix, AZ 85032
Telephone: 602-992-6101
Fax: 602-404-2159

Starr King School for the Ministry*
(Unitarian Universalist Association)
2441 LeConte Avenue
Berkeley, CA 94709
Telephone: 510-845-6232
Fax: 510-845-6273
Website: http://www.sksm.edu/

Swedenborgian House of Studies at the Pacific School of Religion
(Swedenborgian Church)
1798 Scenic Avenue
Berkeley, CA 94709
Telephone: 510-849-8228
Fax: 510-849-8296
Email: jlawrence@shs.psr.edu

Talbot School of Theology of Biola University*
(Inter/multidenominational)
13800 Biola Avenue
La Mirada, CA 90639
Telephone: 562-903-4816
Fax: 562-903-4759

Email: talbot.receptionist@biola.edu
Website: http://www.talbot.edu/

Temple Baptist Seminary[†]
(Interdenominational)
1815 Union Avenue
Chattanooga, TN 37404
Telephone: 423-493-4221
Fax: 423-493-4471
Email: tbsinfo@templebaptistseminary.edu
Website: http://www.templebaptistseminary.edu/

Tennessee Temple University[†]
1815 Union Avenue
Chattanooga, TN 37404
Telephone: 423-493-4202
Fax: 423-493-4114
Email: ttuinfo@tntemple.edu
Website: http://www.tntemple.edu/

Theological School of the Protestant Reformed Churches
(Protestant Reformed Churches in America)
4949 Ivanrest Avenue
Grandville, MI 49418
Telephone: 616-531-1490
Fax: 616-531-3033
Email: doezema@prca.org
Website: http://www.prca.org/seminary.html

Toccoa Falls College
(Christian and Missionary Alliance)
PO Box 800777
Toccoa Falls, GA 30598
Telephone: 706-886-6831
Fax: 706-282-6005
Email: president@tfc.edu
Website: http://www.tfc.edu/

Trevecca Nazarene University
(Church of the Nazarene)
333 Murfreesboro Road
Nashville, TN 37210
Telephone: 615-248-1200
Fax: 615-248-7728
Website: http://www.trevecca.edu/

Trinity Baptist College[†]
(Baptist)
800 Hammond Boulevard
Jacksonville, FL 32221
Telephone: 904-596-2400
Fax: 904-596-2531
Email: trinity@tbc.edu
Website: http://www.tbc.edu/

Trinity Bible College
(Assemblies of God)
50 S 6th Avenue
Ellendale, ND 58436
Telephone: 701-349-3621
Fax: 701-349-5443
Website: http://www.trinitybiblecollege.edu/

Trinity College of Florida
(Nondenominational)
2430 Welbilt Boulevard
New Port Richey, FL 34655
Telephone: 727-376-6911
Fax: 727-376-0781
Email: admissions@trinitycollege.edu
Website: http://www.trinitycollege.edu/

Trinity Episcopal School for Ministry[*]
(Episcopal Church)
311 11th Street
Ambridge, PA 15003
Telephone: 724-266-3838
Fax: 724-266-4617
Email: tesm@tesm.edu
Website: http://www.tesm.edu/

Trinity Evangelical Divinity School of Trinity International University[*]
(Evangelical Free Church of America)
2065 Half Day Road
Deerfield, IL 60015
Telephone: 847-945-8800
Fax: 847-317-8141
Website: http://www.teds.edu/

Trinity Lutheran College
(Lutheran)
4221-228th Avenue SE
Issaquah, WA 98029
Telephone: 425-392-0400
Fax: 425-392-0404
Email: info@tlc.edu
Website: http://www.tlc.edu/

Trinity Lutheran Seminary[*]
(Evangelical Lutheran Church in America)
2199 E Main Street
Columbus, OH 43209
Telephone: 614-235-4136
Fax: 614-238-0263
Website: http://www.trinitylutheranseminary.edu/

Turner School of Theology of Southern Christian University[*]
(Churches of Christ)
1200 Taylor Road
Montgomery, AL 36117
Telephone: 334-387-3877
Fax: 334-387-3878
Email: southernchristian@southernchristian.edu
Website: http://www.southernchristian.edu/

Union Theological Seminary[*]
(Inter/multidenominational)
3041 Broadway at 121st Street
New York, NY 10027
Telephone: 212-662-7100
Fax: 212-280-1440
Website: http://www.uts.columbia.edu/

*Union Theological Seminary and Presbyterian School of Christian Education**
(Presbyterian Church [USA])
3401 Brook Road
Richmond, VA 23227
Telephone: 800-229-2990
Fax: 804-355-3919
Email: gbirch@union-psce.edu
Website: http://www.union-psce.edu/

*United Theological Seminary**
(United Methodist Church)
1810 Harvard Boulevard
Dayton, OH 45406
Telephone: 937-278-5817
Fax: 937-278-1218
Email: utscom@united.edu
Website: http://www.united.edu/

*United Theological Seminary of the Twin Cities**
(United Church of Christ)
3000 5th Street NW
New Brighton, MN 55112
Telephone: 651-633-4311
Fax: 651-633-4315
Email: general@unitedseminary-mn.org
Website: http://www.unitedseminary-mn.org/

*University of Chicago Divinity School**
(Interdenominational)
1025 E 58th Street
Chicago, IL 60637
Telephone: 773-702-8221
Fax: 773-702-6048
Website: http://divinity.uchicago.edu/

*University of Dubuque Theological Seminary**
(Presbyterian Church [USA])
2000 University Avenue
Dubuque, IA 52001
Telephone: 563-589-3122
Fax: 563-589-3110
Email: udtsadms@dbq.edu
Website: http://udts.dbq.edu/

*University of Notre Dame Department of Theology**
(Roman Catholic Church)
130 Malloy Hall
Notre Dame, IN 46556
Telephone: 574-631-6662
Fax: 574-631-4291
Website: https://theology.nd.edu/

*University of St. Mary of the Lake Mundelein Seminary**
(Roman Catholic Church)
1000 E Maple Avenue
Mundelein, IL 60060
Telephone: 847-566-6401
Fax: 847-566-7330
Website: http://www.usml.edu/

*University of St. Thomas School of Theology**
(Roman Catholic Church)
9845 Memorial Drive
Houston, TX 77024
Telephone: 713-686-4345
Fax: 713-683-8673
Website: http://www.stthom.edu/

*Urshan Graduate School of Theology**
(United Pentecostal Church International)
PO Box 40
Hazelwood, MO 63042
Telephone: 512-832-5433
Fax: 512-832-9108
Email: ugst@upci.org
Website: http://www.ugst.org/

Valley Forge Christian College
(Assemblies of God)
1401 Charlestown Road
Phoenixville, PA 19460
Telephone: 610-935-0450
Fax: 610-935-9353
Email: admissions@vfcc.edu
Website: http://www.vfcc.edu/

*Vanderbilt Divinity School**
(Inter/multidenominational)
411 21st Avenue S
Nashville, TN 37240
Telephone: 615-322-2776
Fax: 615-343-9957
Email: james.hudnut-beumler@vanderbilt.edu
Website: http://divinity.vanderbilt.edu/

*Wake Forest University School of Divinity**
(Inter/multidenominational)
PO Box 7719
Winston-Salem, NC 27109
Telephone: 336-758-5121
Fax: 336-758-4316
Website: http://divinity.wfu.edu/

Walla Walla University School of Theology
(Seventh-Day Adventist Church)
204 S College Avenue
College Place, WA 99324
Telephone: 509-527-2194
Fax: 509-527-2253
Email: theology@wallawalla.edu
Website: http://www.wallawalla.edu/academics
/areas-of-study/undergraduate-programs
/theology/

*Wartburg Theological Seminary**
(Evangelical Lutheran Church in America)
333 Wartburg Place
PO Box 5004
Dubuque, IA 52004
Telephone: 563-589-0200
Fax: 563-589-0333
Email: mailbox@wartburgseminary.edu
Website: http://www.wartburgseminary.edu/

Washington Baptist College and Seminary*
(Baptist)
4300 Evergreen Lane
Annandale, VA 22003
Telephone: 703-333-5904
Fax: 703-333-5906
Website: http://www.wbcs.edu/

Washington Theological Consortium
(Nondenominational)
487 Michigan Avenue NE
Washington, DC 20017
Telephone: 202-832-2675
Fax: 202-526-0818
Email: wtc@washtheocon.org
Website: http://www.washtheocon.org/

Washington Theological Union*
(Roman Catholic Church)
6896 Laurel Street NW
Washington, DC 20012
Telephone: 202-726-8800
Fax: 202-726-1716
Email: mclellan@wtu.edu
Website: http://www.wtu.edu/

Wesley Biblical Seminary*
(Interdenominational)
PO Box 9938
Jackson, MS 39286
Telephone: 601-366-8880
Fax: 601-366-8832
Website: http://www.wbs.edu/

Wesley Theological Seminary*
(United Methodist Church)
4500 Massachusetts Avenue NW
Washington, DC 20016
Telephone: 800-885-8600
Fax: 202-885-8605
Email: caldridge@wesleysem.edu
Website: http://www.wesleysem.edu/

Western Seminary*
(Conservative Baptist Association of America)
5511 SE Hawthorne Boulevard
Portland, OR 97215
Telephone: 503-517-1800
Fax: 503-517-1801
Website: http://www.westernseminary.edu/

Western Theological Seminary*
(Reformed Church in America)
101 E 13th Street
Holland, MI 49423
Telephone: 616-392-8555
Fax: 616-392-7717
Website: http://www.westernsem.edu/

Westminster Theological Seminary*
(Presbyterian Church in America)
Chestnut Hill
PO Box 27009

Philadelphia, PA 19118
Telephone: 215-887-5511
Fax: 215-887-5404
Email: slogan@wts.edu
Website: http://www.wts.edu/

Westminster Theological Seminary in California*
(Nondenominational)
1725 Bear Valley Parkway
Escondido, CA 92027
Telephone: 760-480-8474
Fax: 760-480-0252
Email: info@wscal.edu
Website: http://www.wscal.edu/

Weston Jesuit School of Theology*
(Roman Catholic Church)
3 Phillips Place
Cambridge, MA 02138
Telephone: 617-492-1960
Fax: 617-492-5833
Email: admissionsinfo@wjst.edu
Website: http://www.wjst.edu/

William Jessup University
(Christian Churches; Churches of Christ)
333 Sunset Boulevard
Rocklin, CA 95765
Telephone: 916-577-2210
Email: bjessup@jessup.edu
Website: http://www.jessup.edu/

Williamson Christian College†
(Nondenominational)
200 Seaboard Lane
Franklin, TN 37067
Telephone: 615-771-7821
Fax: 615-771-7810
Email: info@williamsoncc.edu
Website: http://www.williamsoncc.edu/

William Tyndale College
(Interdenominational)
35700 W Twelve Mile Road
Farmington Hills, MI 48331
Telephone: 248-553-7200
Fax: 248-553-5963
Website: http://www.williamtyndale.edu/

Winebrenner Theological Seminary*
(Churches of God, General Conference)
950 N Main Street
Findlay, OH 45840
Telephone: 419-434-4200
Fax: 419-434-4267
Email: wts@winebrenner.edu
Website: http://www.winebrenner.edu/

Wisconsin Lutheran Seminary
(Evangelical Lutheran Synod)
11831 N Seminary Drive 65W
Mequon, WI 53092
Telephone: 262-242-8100

Fax: 262-242-8110
Email: president@wls.wels.net
Website: http://www.wls.wels.net/

Word of Life Bible Institute[†]
(Nondenominational)
PO Box 129
4200 Glendale Road
Pottersville, NY 12860
Telephone: 518-494-4723
Fax: 518-494-7474

Email: admissions@wol.org
Website: http://www.wol.org/

*Yale Divinity School**
(Inter/multidenominational)
409 Prospect Street
New Haven, CT 06511
Telephone: 203-432-5303
Fax: 203-432-5356
Email: divinity.admissions@yale.edu
Website: http://divinity.yale.edu/

Appendix C

Denominational Periodicals

Not all the publications listed here are official publications of a particular church. The frequency of publication is indicated by W for weekly, M for monthly, Q for quarterly, Y for yearly, and I for internet. A number in front of the abbreviation indicates a modification; for example, (10/Y) indicates ten times per year, (bi-M) indicates every other month, and (bi-W) indicates every other week.

Action! (bi-M)
(Churches of Christ)
PO Box 2169
Cedar Park, TX 78630
Telephone: 800-311-2006
Fax: 512-401-8265
Website: http://www.worldbibleschool.net/news/action

Adra Today (Q)
(Seventh-Day Adventist Church)
12501 Old Columbia Pike
Silver Spring, MD 20904
Telephone: 301-680-6355
Fax: 301-680-6370

The Adult Quarterly (Q)
(Associate Reformed Presbyterian Church)
PO Box 275
Due West, SC 29639
Telephone: 864-379-8896
Email: wbevans@erskine.edu

Advent Christian News (M)
(Advent Christian General Conference)
PO Box 23152
Charlotte, NC 28227

Telephone: 704-545-6161
Fax: 704-573-0712
Email: acpub@adventchristian.org

The Adventist Chaplain (Q)
(Seventh-Day Adventist Church)
Adventist Chaplaincy Ministries
12501 Old Columbia Pike
Silver Spring, MD 20904
Telephone: 301-680-6780
Fax: 301-680-6783
Email: acm@gc.adventist.org
Website: http://www.adventistchaplains.org/

Adventist Review (W)
(Seventh-Day Adventist Church)
12501 Old Columbia Pike
Silver Spring, MD 20904
Telephone: 301-680-6560
Fax: 301-680-6638
Email: letters@adventistreview.org
Website: http://www.adventistreview.org/

Adventist Today (Q)
PO Box 1135
Sandy, OR 97055
Telephone: 503-826-8600
Email: atoday@atoday.org
Website: http://www.atoday.org/

Again Magazine (Q)
(Antiochian Orthodox Christian Archdiocese of North America)
PO Box 76
Ben Lomond, CA 95005
Telephone: 831-336-5118
Fax: 831-336-8882

Agape Magazine (bi-M)
(Coptic Orthodox Church)
PO Box 4960
Diamond Bar, CA 91765
Telephone: 909-865-8378
Fax: 909-865-8348

Alive Now (bi-M)
(United Methodist Church)
PO Box 340004
Nashville, TN 37203
Telephone: 615-340-7218
Email: alivenow@upperroom.org
Website: http://www.alivenow.org/

The Allegheny Wesleyan Methodist (M)
(Allegheny Wesleyan Methodist Connection)
PO Box 357
Salem, OH 44460
Telephone: 330-337-9376
Fax: 330-337-9700
Email: awmc@juno.com

Alliance Life (M)
(Christian and Missionary Alliance)
PO Box 35000
Colorado Springs, CO 80935
Telephone: 719-599-5999
Fax: 719-599-8234
Email: alife@cmalliance.org
Website: http://www.alliancelife.org/

The AME Christian Recorder (bi-W)
(African Methodist Episcopal Church)
1134 11th Street NW
Suite 202
Washington, DC 20001
Telephone: 202-216-4294
Fax: 202-216-4293
Email: rspain5737@aol.com
Website: http://www.the-christian-recorder.org/

American Baptist Quarterly (Q)
(American Baptist Churches in the USA)
PO Box 851
Valley Forge, PA 19482
Telephone: 610-768-2269
Fax: 610-768-2266
Email: dbvanbro@abc-usa.org
Website: http://abhsarchives.org/publications
/american-baptist-quarterly/

American Baptists in Mission (Q)
(American Baptist Churches in the USA)
PO Box 851
Valley Forge, PA 19482
Telephone: 610-768-2077
Fax: 610-768-2320

American Bible Society Record (Q)
(Nondenominational)
1865 Broadway
New York, NY 10023

Telephone: 212-408-1399
Fax: 212-408-1456
Email: absrecord@americanbible.org
Website: http://www.americanbible.org/

The Anchor of Faith (M)
(Anglican Orthodox Church)
PO Box 128
Statesville, NC 28687
Telephone: 704-873-8365
Fax: 704-873-5359

The Annual Catholic Directory (Y)
(Roman Catholic Church)
222 N 17th Street
Philadelphia, PA 19103
Telephone: 215-587-3660
Fax: 215-587-3979

El Aposento Alto (bi-M)
(United Methodist Church)
PO Box 340004
Nashville, TN 37203
Telephone: 615-340-7253
Fax: 615-340-7267
Email: elaposentoalto@upperroom.org
Website: http://www.upperroom.org/

The Armenian Church (2/Y)
(Diocese of the Armenian Church of America)
630 Second Avenue
New York, NY 10016
Telephone: 212-686-0710
Fax: 212-779-3558

The Associate Reformed Presbyterian (M)
(Associate Reformed Presbyterian Church)
1 Cleveland Street
Greenville, SC 29601
Telephone: 864-232-8297
Fax: 864-271-3729
Email: arpmaged@arpsynod.org
Website: http://www.arpmagazine.org/

The Banner (M)
(Christian Reformed Church in North America)
2850 Kalamazoo Avenue SE
Grand Rapids, MI 49560
Telephone: 616-224-0732
Fax: 616-224-0834
Email: editorial@thebanner.org
Website: http://www.thebanner.org/

The Banner of Truth (M)
(Netherlands Reformed Congregations)
1113 Bridgeview Drive
Lynden, WA 98264
Telephone: 360-354-4203
Fax: 360-354-7565

Baptist Bible Tribune (M)
(Baptist Bible Fellowship International)
PO Box 309

Springfield, MO 65801
Telephone: 417-831-3996
Fax: 417-831-1470
Email: editors@tribune.org
Website: http://www.tribune.org/

Baptist Bulletin (M)
(General Association of Regular Baptist Churches)
1300 N Meacham Road
Schaumburg, IL 60173
Telephone: 847-843-1600
Fax: 847-843-3757
Email: baptistbulletin@garbc.org
Website: http://baptistbulletin.org/

Baptist History and Heritage Journal (3/Y)
(Baptist)
PO Box 728
Brentwood, TN 37021
Telephone: 615-371-7937
Fax: 615-371-7939
Email: pdurso@tubaptist.org
Website: http://www.baptisthistory.org/

Baptist Peacemaker (Q)
(Baptist)
300 Hawthorne Lane
Suite 205
Charlotte, NC 28204
Telephone: 704-521-6051
Fax: 704-521-6053
Email: bpfna@bpfna.org
Website: http://www.bpfna.org/

The Baptist Preacher's Journal (Q)
(Baptist Bible Fellowship International)
PO Box 309
Springfield, MO 65801
Telephone: 417-831-3996
Fax: 417-831-1470

Baptist Witness (M)
(Primitive Baptists)
PO Box 17037
Cincinnati, OH 45217
Telephone: 513-821-7289
Fax: 513-821-7303
Email: bbh45217@aol.com
Website: http://www.baptistbiblehour.org
/resources/publications/

Bible Advocate (10/Y)
(Church of God, Seventh Day)
PO Box 33677
Denver, CO 80233
Telephone: 303-452-7973
Fax: 303-452-0657
Email: bibleadvocate@cog7.org
Website: http://baonline.org/

The Brethren Evangelist (5/Y)
(Brethren)
524 College Avenue

Ashland, OH 44805
Telephone: 419-289-1708
Fax: 419-281-0450
Email: brethren@brethrenchurch.org
Website: http://www.brethrenchurch.org/connec
tions/brethren-evangelist-magazine/

Brethren Journal (10/Y)
(Brethren)
6703 FM 2502
Brenham, TX 77833
Telephone: 409-830-8762
Email: manager.brethrenjournal@gmail.com
Website: http://www.unityofthebrethren.org
/organizations/brethren-journal/

Brethren Life and Thought (Q)
(Church of the Brethren)
Bethany Seminary
615 National Road W
Richmond, IN 47374
Fax: 765-983-1840
Email: gardnca@bethanyseminary.edu
Website: https://www.bethanyseminary.edu/blt/

The Burning Bush (Q)
(Wesleyan Church)
2425 W Ramsey Avenue
Milwaukee, WI 53221
Telephone: 414-282-8539
Email: metrochurchassn@wi.rr.com

ByFaith (I)
(Presbyterian Church in America)
1700 N Brown Road
Suite 105
Lawrenceville, GA 30043
Telephone: 678-825-1005
Email: info@byfaithonline.com
Website: http://byfaithonline.com/

*Call to Unity: Resourcing the Church for Ecumenical
Ministry* (bi-M)
(Christian Church [Disciples of Christ])
PO Box 1986
Indianapolis, IN 46206
Telephone: 317-713-2586
Fax: 317-713-2588
Email: rwelsh@ccu.disciples.org
Website: http://ccu.disciples.org/CalltoUnity
/tabid/1361/Default.aspx

Calvary Messenger (M)
(Beachy Amish Mennonite Churches)
7809 Soul Herren Road
Partridge, KS 67566
Telephone: 620-567-2286
Fax: 620-567-2286
Email: paullmiller@mindspring.com

Campus Life (9/Y)
(Nondenominational)
465 Gunderson Drive

Carol Stream, IL 60188
Telephone: 630-260-6200
Fax: 630-260-0114

Caring (Q)
(Assemblies of God)
1445 N Boonville Avenue
Springfield, MO 65802
Telephone: 417-862-2781
Fax: 417-862-0503

Cathedral Age (Q)
(Interdenominational)
Washington National Cathedral
3101 Wisconsin Avenue NW
Washington, DC 20016
Telephone: 202-537-5681
Fax: 202-364-6600

Catholic Chronicle (M)
(Roman Catholic Church)
PO Box 1866
Toledo, OH 43603
Telephone: 419-244-6711
Fax: 419-244-0468
Email: ccn.ews@toledodiocese.org
Website: http://www.catholicchronicle.org/

Catholic Digest (M)
(Roman Catholic Church)
185 Willow Street
Mystic, CT 06355
Telephone: 800-321-0411
Fax: 860-536-5600
Email: jkoopman@bayard-inc.com
Website: http://www.catholicdigest.org/

Catholic Herald (W)
(Roman Catholic Church)
3501 S Lake Drive
Milwaukee, WI 53235
Telephone: 414-769-3500
Fax: 414-769-3468
Email: catholicherald@archmil.org
Website: http://catholicherald.org/

The Catholic Light (bi-W)
(Roman Catholic Church)
300 Wyoming Avenue
Scranton, PA 18503
Telephone: 570-207-2229
Fax: 570-207-2271
Email: william-genello@dioceseofscranton.org
Website: http://www.dioceseofscranton.org
/media/catholic-light/

The Catholic Peace Voice (bi-M)
(Roman Catholic Church)
532 W 8th Street
Erie, PA 16502
Telephone: 814-453-4955
Fax: 814-452-4784

The Catholic Review (W)
(Roman Catholic Church)
Associate Publisher
PO Box 777
Baltimore, MD 21203
Telephone: 443-524-3150
Fax: 443-524-3155
Email: mail@catholicreview.org
Website: http://www.catholicreview.org/

Catholic Standard and Times (W)
(Roman Catholic Church)
222 N 17th Street
Philadelphia, PA 19103
Telephone: 215-587-3660
Fax: 215-587-3979

Catholic Trends (bi-W)
(Roman Catholic)
3211 4th Street NE
Washington, DC 20017
Telephone: 202-541-3250
Fax: 202-541-3255

The Catholic Worker (7/Y)
(Roman Catholic Church)
36 E 1st Street
New York, NY 10003
Telephone: 212-777-9617

Cela Biedrs (bi-M)
(Latvian Evangelical Lutheran Church in America)
14170 SW 22nd Street
Beaverton, OR 97008
Telephone: 503-781-6724
Email: celabiedrs@yahoo.com

Celebration: An Ecumenical Worship Resource (M)
(Interdenominational)
PO Box 419493
Kansas City, MO 64141
Telephone: 816-531-0538
Fax: 816-968-2291

The Challenge (Q)
(Bible Church of Christ)
1358 Morris Avenue
Bronx, NY 10456
Telephone: 718-588-2284
Fax: 718-992-5597

Charisma (M)
(Nondenominational)
600 Rinehart Road
Lake Mary, FL 32746
Telephone: 407-333-0600
Fax: 407-333-7133
Email: grady@strang.com
Website: http://www.charismamag.com/

The Children's Friend (Braille) (Q)
(Seventh-Day Adventist Church)
PO Box 6097

Lincoln, NE 68506
Telephone: 402-488-0981
Fax: 402-488-7582
Email: editorial@christianrecord.org
Website: http://www.christianrecord.org/

The Christadelphian Advocate (M)
(Christadelphians)
27 Delphian Road
Springfield, VT 05156
Telephone: 802-885-2316
Fax: 802-885-2319
Email: jimillay@vermontel.net
Website: http://www.christadelphian-advocate
.org/

Christadelphian Tidings (M)
(Christadelphians)
42076 Hartford Drive
Canton, MI 48187
Telephone: 313-844-2426
Fax: 313-844-8304

The Christian Baptist (Q)
(Primitive Baptists)
PO Box 68
Atwood, TN 38220
Telephone: 901-662-7417
Email: cbl@aeneas.net

Christian Bible Teacher (M)
(Churches of Christ)
PO Box 7385
Ft. Worth, TX 76111
Telephone: 817-838-2644
Fax: 817-838-2644

The Christian Century (bi-M)
(Nondenominational)
104 S Michigan Avenue
Suite 700
Chicago, IL 60603
Telephone: 312-263-7510
Fax: 312-263-7540
Email: main@christiancentury.org
Website: http://www.christiancentury.org/

The Christian Chronicle (M)
(Churches of Christ)
PO Box 11000
Oklahoma City, OK 73136
Telephone: 405-425-5070
Fax: 405-425-5076
Website: http://www.christianchronicle.org/

The Christian Community (8/Y)
(International Council of Community Churches)
21116 Washington Parkway
Frankfort, IL 60423
Telephone: 815-464-5690
Fax: 815-464-5692
Email: iccc60423@sbcglobal.net
Website: http://www.icccusa.com/

The Christian Contender (M)
(Mennonite Church USA)
PO Box 3
Highway 172
Crockett, KY 41413
Telephone: 606-522-4348
Fax: 606-522-4896

The Christian Index (M)
(Christian Methodist Episcopal Church)
PO Box 431
Fairfield, AL 35064
Telephone: 205-929-1410
Fax: 205-744-0010
Email: ChristianIndex@thecmechurch.org
Website: http://www.thecmechurch.org/connec
tionaldepartments/ChristianIndex.htm

Christian Journal (M)
(Churches of Christ)
PO Box 7385
Ft. Worth, TX 76111
Telephone: 817-838-2644

Christian Leader (M)
(US Conference of Mennonite Brethren Churches)
315 S Lincoln Street
Hillsboro, KS 67063
Telephone: 316-947-5543
Fax: 316-947-3266
Email: chleader@southwind.net

Christian Monthly (M)
(Apostolic Lutheran Church of America)
PO Box 2126
Battle Ground, WA 98604
Telephone: 360-687-6493
Fax: 360-687-6493
Email: christianm@apostolic-lutheran.org
Website: http://www.christianmonthlyalca.org/

Christian Record (Braille) (Q)
(Seventh-Day Adventist Church)
PO Box 6097
Lincoln, NE 68506
Telephone: 402-488-0981
Fax: 402-488-7582
Email: editorial@christianrecord.org
Website: http://www.christianrecord.org/

Christian Standard (W)
(Christian Churches; Churches of Christ)
8121 Hamilton Avenue
Cincinnati, OH 45231
Telephone: 513-931-4050
Fax: 513-931-0950
Email: christianstd@standardpub.com
Website: http://www.christianstandard.com/

The Christian Union Witness (10/Y)
(Christian Union)
PO Box 361
Greenfield, OH 45123

Telephone: 937-981-2760
Fax: 937-981-2760
Email: ohiocu@bright.net
Website: http://cuwitness.wordpress.com/

The Church Advocate (bi-M)
(Churches of God, General Conference)
PO Box 926
700 E Melrose Avenue
Findlay, OH 45839
Telephone: 419-424-1961
Fax: 419-424-3433
Email: communications@cggc.org
Website: http://www.cggc.org/resources/previous
/the-church-advocate-archives/

Church History: Studies in Christianity and Culture
(Q)
Florida State University
Department of Religion
641 University Way
PO Box 3061520
Tallahassee, FL 32306
Telephone: 850-644-1020
Fax: 850-644-7225
Email: asch@churchhistory.org
Website: http://www.churchhistory.org/church
-history-journal/

The Church Messenger (M)
(American Carpatho-Russian Orthodox Diocese)
145 Broad Street
Perth Amboy, NJ 08861
Telephone: 732-826-4442
Email: mrosco2@excite.com
Website: http://acrod.org/news/messengerl/

Church of God Evangel (M)
(Church of God [Cleveland, Tennessee]])
PO Box 2250
Cleveland, TN 37320
Telephone: 423-478-7592
Fax: 423-478-7616
Email: bill_george@pathwaypress.org
Website: http://www.pathwaybookstore.com/ev
angel/

Church of God Progress Journal (Q)
(Churches of God, General Conference)
PO Box 100000
Morrow, GA 30260
Telephone: 404-362-0052
Fax: 404-362-9307
Email: info@abc-coggc.org
Website: http://www.abc-coggc.org/

Church School Herald (Q)
(African Methodist Episcopal Zion Church)
PO Box 26769
Charlotte, NC 28221
Telephone: 704-599-4630
Fax: 704-688-2548
Email: malove@amezhqtr.org

Churchwoman (Q)
(Interdenominational)
475 Riverside Drive
Suite 500
New York, NY 10115
Telephone: 212-870-3339
Fax: 212-870-2338
Email: allamoso@churchwomen.org
Website: http://www.churchwomen.org/

Circuit Rider (bi-M)
(United Methodist Church)
201 8th Avenue S
Nashville, TN 37203
Telephone: 615-749-6538
Fax: 615-749-6061
Email: jreddig@umpublishing.org
Website: http://www.circuitrider.com/

Clarion Herald (bi-W)
(Roman Catholic Church)
PO Box 53247
1000 Howard Avenue
Suite 400
New Orleans, LA 70153
Telephone: 504-596-3035
Fax: 504-596-3020
Email: clarionherald@clarionherald.org
Website: http://www.clarionherald.org/

Clergy Communique (2/Y)
(International Council of Community Churches)
21116 Washington Parkway
Frankfort, IL 60423
Telephone: 815-464-5690
Fax: 815-464-5692

The Clergy Journal (9/Y)
(Nondenominational)
6160 Carmen Avenue E
Inver Grove Heights, MN 55076
Telephone: 800-328-0200
Fax: 651-457-4617

Club Connection (Q)
(Assemblies of God)
1445 Boonville Avenue
Springfield, MO 65802
Telephone: 417-862-2781
Fax: 417-862-0503

College and University Dialogue (3/Y)
(Seventh-Day Adventist Church)
12501 Old Columbia Pike
Silver Spring, MD 20904
Fax: 301-622-9627
Website: http://dialogue.adventist.org/

Collegiate Quarterly (Q)
(Seventh-Day Adventist Church)
12501 Old Columbia Pike
Silver Spring, MD 20904
Telephone: 301-680-6160

Fax: 301-680-6155
Website: http://www.firstsdachurch.org/resources
/members/sabbath_school_lessons.html

Columbia (M)
(Roman Catholic Church)
1 Columbus Plaza
New Haven, CT 06510
Telephone: 203-752-4398
Fax: 203-752-4109
Email: tim.hickey@kofc-supreme.com
Website: http://www.kofc.org/un/en/columbia
/index.html

The Commission (7/Y)
(Southern Baptist Convention)
PO Box 6767
Richmond, VA 23230
Telephone: 804-219-1253
Fax: 804-219-1410
Email: commission@imb.org

Common Lot (Q)
(United Church of Christ)
700 Prospect Avenue
Cleveland, OH 44115
Telephone: 216-736-2150
Fax: 216-736-2156
Website: http://www.ucc.org/women_common
-lot

Commonweal (bi-W)
(Roman Catholic Church)
475 Riverside Drive
Room 405
New York, NY 10115
Telephone: 212-662-4200
Fax: 212-662-4183
Email: editors@commonwealmagazine.org
Website: http://www.commonwealmagazine.org/

Communion (bi-M)
(Church of God [Anderson, Indiana])
PO Box 2420
1201 E 5th Street
Anderson, IN 46018
Telephone: 765-642-0256
Fax: 765-652-5652

The Congregationalist (5/Y)
(National Association of Congregational Christian
Churches)
87 Broadway
Norwich, CT 06360
Telephone: 860-889-1363
Fax: 860-887-5715
Email: jeaton@unitedcongregational.org
Website: http://www.congregationalist.org/

Connections (M)
(Alliance of Baptists)
1328 16th Street NW

Washington, DC 20036
Telephone: 202-745-7609
Fax: 202-745-0023

Conqueror (bi-M)
(United Pentecostal Church International)
8855 Dunn Road
Hazelwood, MO 63042
Telephone: 314-837-7300
Fax: 314-837-4503

Context (M)
(Nondenominational)
205 W Monroe Street
Chicago, IL 60606
Telephone: 312-236-7782
Fax: 312-236-8207

Converge Point (Q)
(Baptist General Conference/Converge)
2002 S Arlington Heights Road
Arlington Heights, IL 60005
Telephone: 800-323-4215
Website: http://www.convergeworldwide.org
/point-magazine/

Cornerstone Connections (Q)
(Seventh-Day Adventist Church)
12501 Old Columbia Pike
Silver Spring, MD 20904
Telephone: 301-680-6160
Fax: 301-680-6155
Website: http://www.cornerstoneconnections.net/

Covenant (Q)
(Presbyterian Church in America)
Covenant Theological Seminary
123330 Conway Road
St. Louis, MO 63141
Telephone: 314-434-4044
Fax: 314-434-4819
Email: eileen.ogorman@covenantseminary.edu
Website: http://www.covenantseminary.edu/

The Covenant Companion (M)
(Evangelical Covenant Church)
5101 N Francisco Avenue
Chicago, IL 60625
Telephone: 773-906-3328
Fax: 773-784-4366
Email: communication@covchurch.org
Website: http://covenantcompanion.com/

The Covenanter Witness (11/Y)
(Reformed Presbyterian Church of North America)
7408 Penn Avenue
Pittsburgh, PA 15208
Telephone: 412-241-0436
Fax: 412-731-8861
Email: info@psalms4u.com
Website: http://rparchives.org/cov_witness.html

The Covenant Home Altar (Q)
(Evangelical Covenant Church)
5101 N Francisco Avenue
Chicago, IL 60625
Telephone: 773-784-3000
Fax: 773-784-4366
Email: communication@covchurch.org
Website: http://www.covchurch.org/publications
/home-altar/

Covenant Quarterly (Q)
(Evangelical Covenant Church)
3225 W Foster Avenue
Chicago, IL 60625
Telephone: 773-244-6242
Email: pkoptak@northpark.edu

Credinta (The Faith) (Q)
(Romanian Orthodox Church)
45-03 48th Avenue
Woodside, NY 11377
Telephone: 313-893-8390

The Cumberland Presbyterian (11/Y)
(Cumberland Presbyterian Church)
1978 Union Avenue
Memphis, TN 38104
Telephone: 615-731-5556
Email: cpmag@comcast.net
Website: http://ministrycouncil.cumberland.org
/thecpmagazine

Currents in Theology and Mission (bi-M)
(Evangelical Lutheran Church in America)
1100 E 55th Street
Chicago, IL 60615
Telephone: 773-256-0751
Fax: 773-256-0782
Email: currents@lstc.edu
Website: http://www.lstc.edu/pub_peo/pub
/currents.html

Decision (11/Y)
(Nondenominational)
1 Billy Graham Parkway
Charlotte, NC 28201
Telephone: 704-401-2432
Fax: 704-401-3009
Email: decision@bgea.org
Website: http://www.decisionmag.org/

Disciples World (10/Y)
(Christian Church [Disciples of Christ])
PO Box 11469
Indianapolis, IN 46201
Telephone: 317-375-8846
Fax: 317-375-8849
Website: http://www.disciplesworld.com/

Ecu-Link (several/Y)
(Churches of Christ)
475 Riverside Drive
Suite 800

New York, NY 10115
Telephone: 212-870-2227
Fax: 212-870-2030
Email: staff@eculink.org
Website: http://eculink.org/home/

Ecumenical Trends (M)
(Nondenominational)
Graymoor Ecumenical and Interreligious Institute
PO Box 300
Garrison, NY 10524
Telephone: 845-424-3671
Fax: 845-424-2163
Email: jloughran@atonementfriars.org
Website: http://www.geii.org/ecumenical_trends
/index.html

EFCA Today (I)
(Evangelical Free Church of America)
901 E 78th Street
Minneapolis, MN 55420
Telephone: 952-854-1300
Website: http://www.efcatoday.org/

Eleventh Hour Messenger (bi-M)
(Wesleyan Holiness Association of Churches)
11411 N US Highway 27
Fountain City, IN 47341
Telephone: 317-584-3199

Elim Herald (2/Y)
(Elim Fellowship)
1703 Dalton Road
PO Box 57A
Lima, NY 14485
Telephone: 585-582-2790
Fax: 585-624-1229

Enrichment: A Journal for Pentecostal Ministry (Q)
(Assemblies of God)
1445 N Boonville Avenue
Springfield, MO 65802
Telephone: 417-862-2781
Fax: 417-862-0416
Email: gallen@ag.org
Website: http://www.enrichmentjournal.ag.org/

Episcopal Life (M)
(Episcopal Church)
815 2nd Avenue
New York, NY 10017
Telephone: 800-334-7626
Fax: 212-949-8059

The Evangel (bi-M)
(American Association of Lutheran Churches)
801 W 106th Street
Suite 203
Minneapolis, MN 55420
Telephone: 952-884-7784
Fax: 952-884-7894
Email: aa2taalc@aol.com
Website: http://www.taalc.org/

The Evangel (Q)
(Evangelical Church Alliance)
PO Box 9
Bradley, IL 60915
Telephone: 815-937-0720
Fax: 815-937-0001
Email: info@ecainternational.org
Website: http://www.ecainternational.org/

The Evangelical Advocate (M)
(Churches of Christ in Christian Union)
PO Box 30
Circleville, OH 43113
Telephone: 740-474-8856
Fax: 740-477-7766
Email: doc@cccuhq.org
Website: http://www.cccuhq.org/

The Evangelical Challenge (Q)
(Evangelical Church)
9421 W River Road
Minneapolis, MN 55444
Telephone: 763-424-2589
Fax: 763-424-9230

The Evangelist (W)
(Roman Catholic Church)
40 N Main Avenue
Albany, NY 12203
Telephone: 518-453-6688
Fax: 518-453-8448
Email: james.breig@rcda.org
Website: http://www.evangelist.org/

Explorations (Q)
(Nondenominational)
321 Chestnut Street
4th Floor
Philadelphia, PA 19106
Telephone: 215-925-2800
Fax: 215-925-3800
Email: aii@interfaith-scholars.org

Extension (M)
(Roman Catholic Church)
150 S Wacker Drive
Suite 2000
Chicago, IL 60606
Telephone: 312-236-7240
Fax: 312-236-5276
Email: info@catholicextension.org
Website: http://www.catholicextension.org/news
-media/extension-magazine

Face to Face (Q)
(Community of Christ)
1001 W Walnut Street
Independence, MO 64050
Telephone: 816-833-1000
Fax: 816-521-3043

Faith and Fellowship (M)
(Church of the Lutheran Brethren)

PO Box 655
Fergus Falls, MN 56538
Telephone: 218-736-7357
Fax: 218-736-2200
Email: ffpress@clba.org
Website: http://www.faithandfellowship.org/

Faith-Life (bi-M)
(Lutheran)
2107 N Alexander Street
Appleton, WI 54911
Telephone: 920-733-1839
Fax: 920-733-4834
Email: malbrecht@milwpc.com

Fellowship (bi-M)
(Interfaith)
PO Box 271
Nyack, NY 10960
Telephone: 845-358-4601
Fax: 845-358-4924
Email: fellowship@forusa.org
Website: http://www.forusa.org/

Fellowship Focus (bi-M)
(Fellowship of Evangelical Bible Churches)
11605 W Dodge Road
Suite 3
Omaha, NE 68164
Telephone: 402-965-3860
Fax: 402-965-3871
Email: fellowshipfocus@febcministries.org
Website: http://www.fellowshipforward.org/fellow
ship-focus.html

Fellowship News (M)
(Bible Fellowship Church)
3000 Fellowship Drive
Whitehall, PA 18052
Telephone: 717-337-3408
Fax: 215-536-2120
Email: ccsnyder@supernet.com
Website: http://www.biblefellowship.info/

Fellowship Tidings (Q)
(Full Gospel Fellowship of Churches and Ministers
International)
1000 N Belt Line Road
Suite 201
Irving, TX 75061
Telephone: 214-492-1254
Fax: 214-492-1736
Email: info@thefellowshiptoday.org
Website: http://www.thefellowshiptoday.com/

FGConnections (3/Y)
(Friends General Conference)
1216 Arch Street 2B
Philadelphia, PA 19107
Telephone: 215-561-1700
Fax: 215-561-0759
Email: connections@fgcquaker.org

Firm Foundation (M)
(Churches of Christ)
PO Box 690192
Houston, TX 77269
Telephone: 713-469-3102
Fax: 713-469-7115
Email: had@onramp.net

First Things: A Monthly Journal of Religion and Public Life (10/Y)
(Interdenominational)
156 5th Avenue
Suite 400
New York, NY 10010
Telephone: 212-627-1985
Fax: 212-627-2184
Email: ft@firstthings.com
Website: http://www.firstthings.com/

The Flaming Sword (M)
(Bible Holiness Church)
10th Street and College Avenue
Independence, KS 67301
Telephone: 316-331-2580
Fax: 316-331-2580

The Foresee (bi-M)
(Conservative Congregational Christian Conference)
8941 Highway 5
Lake Elmo, MN 55042
Telephone: 651-739-1474
Fax: 651-739-0750
Website: http://www.ccccusa.com/

Forum Letter (M)
(Lutheran)
Ruskin Heights Lutheran Church
10801 Ruskin Way
Kansas City, MO 64134
Telephone: 816-761-6815
Fax: 816-761-6523
Email: saltzman@integritynetwork.net
Website: http://www.alpb.org/

Forward (Q)
(United Pentecostal Church International)
8855 Dunn Road
Hazelwood, MO 63042
Telephone: 314-837-7300
Fax: 314-837-4503

Forward in Christ (M)
(Evangelical Lutheran Synod)
2929 N Mayfair Road
Milwaukee, WI 53222
Telephone: 414-256-3210
Fax: 414-256-3862
Email: fic@sab.wels.net
Website: http://www.wels.net/news-media/forward-in-christ/

Foursquare World Advance (Q)
(International Church of the Foursquare Gospel)
PO Box 26902
1910 W Sunset Boulevard
Suite 400
Los Angeles, CA 90026
Telephone: 213-989-4230
Fax: 213-989-4544

Free Will Baptist Gem (M)
(National Association of Free Will Baptists)
PO Box 991
Lebanon, MO 65536
Telephone: 417-532-6537
Fax: 417-588-7068
Email: gwfry@webound.com

Friends Bulletin (10/Y)
(Religious Society of Friends)
5238 Andalucia Court
Whittier, CA 90601
Telephone: 562-699-5670
Fax: 562-692-2472
Email: friendsbul@aol.com

Friends Journal (M)
(Religious Society of Friends)
1216 Arch Street
2A
Philadelphia, PA 19107
Telephone: 215-563-8629
Fax: 215-568-1377
Email: info@friendsjournal.org
Website: http://www.friendsjournal.org/

The Friends Voice (3/Y)
(Evangelical Friends Church International)
2748 E Pikes Peak Avenue
Colorado Springs, CO 80909
Telephone: 719-632-5721
Fax: 719-635-4011
Email: voicephotos@codenet.net
Website: http://www.evangelicalfriends.org/publications/

Front Line (Q)
(Conservative Baptist Association of America)
PO Box 58
Long Prairie, MN 56347
Telephone: 320-732-8072
Fax: 509-356-7112
Email: chapruss@cbamerica.org

Full Gospel Ministries Outreach Report (Q)
(Full Gospel Assemblies International)
PO Box 1230
Coatesville, PA 19320
Telephone: 610-857-2357
Fax: 610-857-3109

Gather (10/Y)
(Evangelical Lutheran Church in America)
8765 W Higgins Road

Chicago, IL 60631
Telephone: 773-380-2730
Fax: 773-380-2419
Email: women.elca@elca.org
Website: http://www.womenoftheelca.org/

The Gem (M)
(Churches of God, General Conference)
PO Box 926
700 E Melrose Avenue
Findlay, OH 45839
Telephone: 419-424-1961
Fax: 419-424-3433
Email: publications@cggc.org
Website: http://secure.cggc.org/the-gem/

General Baptist Messenger (Q)
(General Association of General Baptists)
100 Stinson Drive
Poplar Bluff, MO 63901
Telephone: 573-785-7746
Fax: 573-785-0564
Email: amy.powell@generalbaptist.com
Website: http://www.generalbaptist.com/#/con
tact-us/messenger/

God's Field (bi-W)
(Polish National Catholic Church of America)
1006 Pittston Avenue
Scranton, PA 18505
Telephone: 570-346-9131
Fax: 570-346-2188
Email: godsfield@adelphia.net
Website: http://www.pncc.org/?page_id=1354

Good News (Buna Vestire) (Q)
(Romanian Orthodox Episcopate of America)
Romanian Orthodox Deanery of Canada
2855 Helmsing Street
Regina, SK S4V 0W7
Canada
Telephone: 306-761-2379
Fax: 306-525-9650
Email: danenson@accesscomm.ca

Gospel Advocate (M)
(Churches of Christ)
1006 Elm Hill Pike
Nashville, TN 37202
Telephone: 615-254-8781
Fax: 615-254-7411
Email: info@gospeladvocate.com
Website: http://www.gospeladvocate.com/

The Gospel Herald (M)
(Church of God Mountain Assembly)
PO Box 157
Jellico, TN 37762
Telephone: 423-784-8260
Fax: 423-784-3258
Email: cgmahdq@jellico.com
Website: http://www.cgmahdq.org/id12.html

The Gospel Light (2/Y)
(Bible Church of Christ)
1358 Morris Avenue
Bronx, NY 10456
Telephone: 718-588-2284
Fax: 718-992-5597

The Gospel Messenger (M)
(Congregational Holiness Church)
3888 Fayetteville Highway
Griffin, GA 30223
Telephone: 770-228-4833
Fax: 770-228-1177
Email: chchurch@bellsouth.net
Website: http://www.chchurch.com/Gospel
_Messenger.htm

The Gospel Truth (bi-M)
(Church of the Living God)
430 Forest Avenue
Cincinnati, OH 45229
Telephone: 513-569-5660
Fax: 513-569-5661
Email: cwff430@aol.com

Grow Magazine (Q)
(Church of the Nazarene)
6401 The Paseo
Kansas City, MO 64131
Telephone: 816-333-7000
Fax: 816-523-1872

Guide (W)
(Seventh-Day Adventist Church)
55 W Oak Ridge Drive
Hagerstown, MD 21740
Telephone: 301-393-4037
Fax: 301-393-4055
Email: guide@rhpa.org
Website: http://www.guidemagazine.org/

The Handmaiden (Q)
(Antiochian Orthodox Christian Archdiocese of
North America)
PO Box 76
Ben Lomond, CA 95005-0076
Telephone: 831-336-5118
Fax: 831-336-8882

The Happy Harvester (M)
(Church of God of Prophecy)
PO Box 2910
Cleveland, TN 37320
Telephone: 423-559-5435
Fax: 423-559-5444
Email: JoDiPace@wingnet.net

Herald (M)
(Community of Christ)
1001 W Walnut Street
Independence, MO 64050
Telephone: 816-833-1000
Fax: 816-521-3043

Email: jhannah@cofchrist.org
Website: http://www.heraldhouse.org/

Heritage (Q)
(Assemblies of God)
1445 N Boonville Avenue
Springfield, MO 65802
Telephone: 417-862-1447
Fax: 417-862-6203
Website: https://ifphc.org/

High Adventure (Q)
(Assemblies of God)
1445 N Boonville Avenue
Springfield, MO 65802
Telephone: 417-862-2781
Fax: 417-831-8230

Higher Way (Q)
(Apostolic Faith Mission of Portland, Oregon)
6615 SE 52nd Avenue
Portland, OR 97206
Telephone: 503-777-1741
Fax: 503-777-1743
Email: kbarrett@apostolicfaith.org
Website: http://www.apostolicfaith.org/

Holiness Today (bi-M)
(Church of the Nazarene)
6401 The Paseo
Kansas City, MO 64131
Telephone: 816-333-7000
Fax: 816-333-1748
Email: holinesstoday@nazarene.org
Website: http://www.holinesstoday.com/

Homiletic and Pastoral Review (M)
(Roman Catholic Church)
3601 Lindell Boulevard
St. Louis, MO 63108
Website: http://www.hprweb.com/

Horizons (M)
(Christian Churches; Churches of Christ)
PO Box 13111
Knoxville, TN 37920
Telephone: 800-655-8524
Fax: 865-573-5950
Email: msa@missionservices.org
Website: http://www.missionservices.org/

Horizons (7/Y)
(Presbyterian Church [USA])
100 Witherspoon Street
Louisville, KY 40202
Telephone: 502-569-5368
Fax: 502-569-8085
Email: lbradley@ctr.pcusa.org
Website: http://www.pcusa.org/horizons

The Inclusive Pulpit (Y)
(International Council of Community Churches)
21116 Washington Parkway

Frankfort, IL 60423
Telephone: 815-464-5690
Fax: 815-464-5692
Email: iccc60423@sbcglobal.net
Website: http://www.icccusa.com/

Insight Into (bi-M)
(Netherlands Reformed Congregations)
4732 E C Avenue
Kalamazoo, MI 49004
Telephone: 269-349-9448

International Bulletin of Missionary Research (Q)
(Nondenominational)
Overseas Ministries Study Center
490 Prospect Street
New Haven, CT 06511
Telephone: 203-624-6672
Fax: 203-865-2857
Email: ibmr@omsc.org
Website: http://www.internationalbulletin.org/

Interpretation: A Journal of Bible and Theology (Q)
(Presbyterian Church [USA])
3401 Brook Road
Richmond, VA 23227
Telephone: 804-278-4296
Fax: 804-278-4208
Email: email@interpretation.org
Website: http://int.sagepub.com/

El Intérprete (bi-M)
(United Methodist Church)
PO Box 320
Nashville, TN 37202
Telephone: 615-742-5115
Fax: 615-742-5460
Email: mraber@umcom.org
Website: http://www.interpretermagazine.org/

Interpreter (8/Y)
(United Methodist Church)
PO Box 320
Nashville, TN 37202
Telephone: 615-742-5102
Fax: 615-742-5460
Email: gburton@umcom.org
Website: http://www.interpretermagazine.org/

John Three Sixteen (Q)
(Bible Holiness Church)
10th Street and College Avenue
Independence, KS 67301
Telephone: 316-331-2580
Fax: 316-331-2580

Journal from the Radical Reformation (Q)
(Churches of God, General Conference)
PO Box 100000
Morrow, GA 30260
Telephone: 404-362-0052
Fax: 404-362-9307

Email: kenthross@cs.com
Website: http://www.abc-coggc.org/

The Journal of Adventist Education (5/Y)
(Seventh-Day Adventist Church)
12501 Old Columbia Pike
Silver Spring, MD 20904
Telephone: 301-680-5075
Fax: 301-622-9627
Email: rumbleb@gc.adventist.org; goffc@gc
.adventist.org
Website: http://education.gc.adventist.org/jae

The Journal of Christian Education (Q)
(African Methodist Episcopal Church)
500 8th Avenue S
Nashville, TN 37203
Telephone: 615-242-1420
Fax: 615-726-1866
Email: ameced@edge.net
Website: http://www.ameced.com/journal.shtml

Journal of Ecumenical Studies (Q)
(Interdenominational/Interfaith)
Temple University (062-56)
1700 N Broad Street
Suite 315
Philadelphia, PA 19121
Telephone: 215-204-7525
Email: info@dialogueinstitute.org
Website: http://dialogueinstitute.org/journal-of
-ecumenical-studies/

The Journal of Pastoral Care and Counseling (Q)
(Nondenominational)
1068 Harbor Drive SW
Calabash, NC 28467
Telephone: 910-579-5084
Fax: 910-579-5084
Email: jpcp@jpcp.org
Website: http://www.jpcp.org/jpcc.htm

The Journal of Presbyterian History (2/Y)
(Presbyterian Church [USA])
425 Lombard Street
Philadelphia, PA 19147
Telephone: 215-627-1852
Fax: 215-627-0509
Email: tmanning@history.pcusa.org
Website: http://www.history.pcusa.org/history-on
line/publications/journal-presbyterian-history/

Journal of the American Academy of Religion (Q)
(Nondenominational)
Whittier College
PO Box 634
Whittier, CA 90608
Telephone: 562-907-4200
Fax: 562-907-4910
Email: gyocum@whittier.edu
Website: https://www.aarweb.org/publications
/journal-american-academy-religion/

Journal of Theology (Q)
(Church of the Lutheran Confession)
Immanuel Lutheran College
501 Grover Road
Eau Claire, WI 54701
Telephone: 715-832-9936
Fax: 715-836-6634
Email: schallers@usa.net
Website: http://clclutheran.org/online-library/

The Joyful Noiseletter (10/Y)
(Interdenominational)
PO Box 895
Portage, MI 49081
Telephone: 616-324-0990
Fax: 616-324-3984
Email: joyfulnz@aol.com
Website: http://www.joyfulnoiseletter.com/

Keeping in Touch (bi-W)
(Universal Fellowship of Metropolitan Community
Churches)
8704 Santa Monica Boulevard
2nd Floor
West Hollywood, CA 90069
Telephone: 310-360-8640
Fax: 310-360-8680

Key Lay Notes (2/Y)
(International Council of Community Churches)
21116 Washington Parkway
Frankfort, IL 60423
Telephone: 815-464-5690
Fax: 815-464-5692

The Lantern (bi-M)
(National Baptist Convention)
1320 Pierre Avenue
Shreveport, LA 71103
Telephone: 318-221-3701
Fax: 318-222-7512

Leadership: A Practical Journal for Church Leaders
(I)
(Nondenominational)
465 Gundersen Drive
Carol Stream, IL 60188
Telephone: 630-260-6200
Fax: 630-260-0114
Email: ljeditor@leadershipjournal.net
Website: http://www.leadershipjournal.net/

Learning and Living (Q)
(Netherlands Reformed Congregations)
1000 Ball NE
Grand Rapids, MI 49505
Telephone: 616-458-4367
Fax: 616-458-8532
Email: engelsma@plymouthchristian.put.k12.mi.us

Liberty (bi-M)
(Seventh-Day Adventist Church)
12501 Old Columbia Pike

Silver Spring, MD 20904
Telephone: 301-680-6691
Fax: 301-680-6695

Lifeglow (Q)
(Seventh-Day Adventist Church)
Christian Record Services Inc.
PO Box 6097
Lincoln, NE 68506
Telephone: 402-488-0981
Fax: 402-488-7582
Email: editorial@christianrecord.org
Website: http://www.christianrecord.org/

Light and Life Magazine (bi-M)
(Free Methodist Church)
PO Box 535002
Indianapolis, IN 46253
Telephone: 317-244-3660
Website: http://fmcusa.org/lightandlifemag/

Liguorian (10/Y)
(Roman Catholic Church)
1 Liguori Drive
Liguori, MO 63057
Telephone: 636-464-2500
Fax: 636-464-8449
Email: liguorianeditor@liguori.org
Website: http://www.liguorian.org/

Listen (2/Y)
(Seventh-Day Adventist Church)
55 W Oak Ridge Drive
Hagerstown, MD 21740
Telephone: 301-393-4082
Fax: 301-393-4055

Living Orthodoxy (bi-M)
(Russian Orthodox Church Outside Russia)
1180 Orthodox Way
Liberty, TN 37095
Telephone: 615-536-5239
Fax: 615-536-5945
Email: info@sjkp.org
Website: http://www.sjkp.org/

L Magazine
6160 Carmen Avenue E
Inver Grove Heights, MN 55076
Telephone: 651-451-9945
Website: http://www.lmagazine.net/?page_id=2

The Long Island Catholic (W)
(Roman Catholic Church)
PO Box 9000
200 W Centennial Avenue
Suite 201
Roosevelt, NY 11575
Telephone: 516-594-1000
Fax: 516-594-1092
Website: http://www.licatholic.org/

The Lookout (W)
(Christian Churches; Churches of Christ)
8121 Hamilton Avenue
Cincinnati, OH 45231
Telephone: 513-931-4050
Fax: 513-931-0950
Email: lookout@standardpub.com
Website: http://www.lookoutmag.com/

The Lutheran (M)
(Evangelical Lutheran Church in America)
8765 W Higgins Road
Chicago, IL 60631
Telephone: 773-380-2540
Fax: 773-380-2751
Email: lutheran@elca.org
Website: http://www.thelutheran.org/

The Lutheran Ambassador (16/Y)
(Association of Free Lutheran Congregations)
575 34th Street
Astoria, OR 97103
Telephone: 541-687-8643
Fax: 541-683-8496
Email: cjohnson@efn.org

The Lutheran Educator (Q)
(Evangelical Lutheran Synod)
Martin Luther College
1995 Luther Court
New Ulm, MN 56073
Telephone: 507-354-8221
Fax: 507-354-8225
Email: lutheraneducator@mlc-wels.edu

Lutheran Forum (Q)
(Lutheran)
207 Hillcrest Avenue
Trenton, NJ 08618
Telephone: 856-696-0417

The Lutheran Layman (bi-M)
(Lutheran Church—Missouri Synod)
660 Mason Ridge Center Drive
St. Louis, MO 63141
Telephone: 314-317-4100
Fax: 314-317-4295

Lutheran Sentinel (M)
(Evangelical Lutheran Synod)
105 Indian Avenue
Forest City, IA 50436
Telephone: 641-585-1683
Fax: 641-585-1683
Email: elsentinel@wctatel.net

Lutheran Spokesman (M)
(Church of the Lutheran Confession)
1741 E 22nd Street
Cheyenne, WY 82001
Telephone: 307-638-8006
Email: paulgf@iakes.com
Website: http://www.lutheranspokesman.org/

Lutheran Synod Quarterly (Q)
(Evangelical Lutheran Synod)
Bethany Lutheran Theological Seminary
6 Browns Court
Mankato, MN 56001
Telephone: 507-344-7855
Fax: 507-344-7426
Email: elsynod@blc.edu
Website: http://www.blts.edu/lsq/

The Lutheran Witness (M)
(Lutheran Church—Missouri Synod)
1333 S Kirkwood Road
St. Louis, MO 63122
Telephone: 314-965-9000
Fax: 314-966-1126
Email: lutheran.witness@lcms.org
Website: http://www.lcms.org/witness

Magyar Egyhaz—Magyar Church (Q)
(Hungarian Reformed Church in America)
464 Forest Avenue
Paramus, NJ 07652
Telephone: 201-262-2338
Fax: 845-359-5771

Maranatha (Q)
(Advent Christian Church)
PO Box 23152
Charlotte, NC 28227
Telephone: 704-545-6161
Fax: 704-573-0712
Email: acpub@adventchristian.org
Website: http://acgc.us/church-resources/mara
natha-2/

Marriage Partnership (Q)
(Nondenominational)
465 Gundersen Drive
Carol Stream, IL 60188
Telephone: 630-260-6200
Fax: 630-260-0114
Email: marriage@christianitytoday.com
Website: http://www.marriagepartnership.com/

Mar Thoma Messenger (Q)
(Mar Thoma Syrian Church)
2320 S Merrick Avenue
Merrick, NY 11566
Telephone: 516-377-3311
Fax: 516-377-3322
Email: marthoma@aol.com

Mature Years (Q)
(United Methodist Church)
201 8th Avenue S
Nashville, TN 37202
Telephone: 615-749-6292
Fax: 615-749-6512
Email: matureyears@umpublishing.org

The Mennonite (24/Y)
(Mennonite Church USA)
1700 S Main Street
Goshen, IN 46526
Telephone: 219-535-6051
Fax: 219-535-6050
Email: editor@themennonite.org
Website: http://www.themennonite.org/

Mennonite Historical Bulletin (Q)
(Mennonite Church USA)
1700 S Main Street
Goshen, IN 46526
Telephone: 574-535-7418
Fax: 574-535-7438
Email: mhl@goshen.edu
Website: http://mennoniteusa.org/resources/

The Mennonite Quarterly Review (Q)
(Mennonite Church USA)
1700 S Main Street
Goshen, IN 46526
Telephone: 574-535-7433
Fax: 574-535-7438
Email: mqr@goshen.edu
Website: https://www.goshen.edu/mqr/

Message (bi-M)
(Seventh-Day Adventist Church)
55 W Oak Ridge Drive
Hagerstown, MD 21740
Telephone: 301-393-4099
Fax: 301-393-4100
Email: pharris@rhpa.org; ronsmith@rhpa.org
Website: http://messagemagazine.org/

Message of the Open Bible (bi-M)
(Open Bible Standard Churches)
2020 Bell Avenue
Des Moines, IA 50315
Telephone: 515-288-6761
Fax: 515-288-2510
Email: message@openbible.org
Website: http://www.openbible.org/

Messenger (11/Y)
(Church of the Brethren)
1451 Dundee Avenue
Elgin, IL 60120
Telephone: 847-742-5100
Fax: 847-742-1407
Email: wmcfadden_gb@brethren.org
Website: http://www.brethren.org/messenger/

The Messenger (M)
(Pentecostal Free Will Baptists)
PO Box 1568
Dunn, NC 28335
Telephone: 910-892-4161
Fax: 910-892-6876

The Messenger (M)
(Swedenborgian Church)
PO Box 985
Julian, CA 92036

Telephone: 760-765-2915
Email: messenger@julianweb.com
Website: http://www.swedenborg.org/

Messenger of Truth (bi-W)
(Church of God in Christ, Mennonite)
PO Box 230
Moundridge, KS 67107
Telephone: 620-345-2532
Fax: 620-345-2582
Email: gospelpublishers@cogicm.org
Website: http://churchofgodinchristmennonite.net
/en/content/publication-agencies/

Methodist History (Q)
(United Methodist Church)
PO Box 127
Madison, NJ 07940
Telephone: 973-408-3189
Fax: 973-408-3909
Email: cyrigoyen@gcah.org
Website: http://www.gcah.org/research/method
ist-history-journal/

Ministry (M)
(Seventh-Day Adventist Church)
12501 Old Columbia Pike
Silver Spring, MD 20904
Telephone: 301-680-6000
Fax: 301-680-6502
Email: 74532.2425@compuserve.com

Mission, Adult, and Youth Children's Editions (Q)
(Seventh-Day Adventist Church)
12501 Old Columbia Pike
Silver Spring, MD 20904
Telephone: 301-680-6167
Fax: 301-680-6155
Email: 74532.2435@compuserve.com

Missionary Church Today (bi-M)
(Missionary Church)
PO Box 9127
Ft. Wayne, IN 46899
Telephone: 260-747-2027
Fax: 260-747-5331
Email: tom_murphy@mcusa.org
Website: http://www.mcusa.org/

The Missionary Messenger (bi-M)
(Christian Methodist Episcopal Church)
213 Viking Drive W
Cordova, TN 38010
Telephone: 901-757-1103
Fax: 901-751-2104
Email: doris.boyd@williams.com

The Missionary Messenger (bi-M)
(Cumberland Presbyterian Church)
1978 Union Avenue
Memphis, TN 38104
Telephone: 901-276-9988
Fax: 901-276-4578

Email: messenger@cumberland.org
Website: http://ministrycouncil.cumberland.org
/themissionarymessenger/

Missionary Seer (bi-M)
(African Methodist Episcopal Zion Church)
475 Riverside Drive
Room 1935
New York, NY 10115
Telephone: 212-870-2952
Fax: 212-870-2808
Email: domkd5@aol.com

The Missionary Signal (bi-M)
(Churches of God, General Conference)
PO Box 926
700 E Melrose Avenue
Findlay, OH 45839
Telephone: 419-424-1961
Fax: 419-424-3433
Email: communications@cggc.org
Website: http://www.cggc.org/ministries/cross
-cultural-home-page/missionary-signal/

Mission Connection (Q)
(Evangelical Lutheran Synod)
2929 N Mayfair Road
Milwaukee, WI 53222
Telephone: 414-256-3210
Fax: 414-256-3862
Email: mc@sab.wels.net

Mission Herald (bi-M)
(National Baptist Convention)
701 S 19th Street
Philadelphia, PA 19146
Telephone: 215-735-9853
Fax: 215-735-1721
Website: http://www.fmbnbc.org/missionherald
.html

Missions Ministry (Q)
(Progressive National Baptist Convention)
601 50th Street NE
Washington, DC 20019
Telephone: 202-396-0558
Fax: 202-398-4998
Email: office@pnbc.org

The Moravian (10/Y)
(Moravian Church [Unitas Fratrum])
1021 Center Street
PO Box 1245
Bethlehem, PA 18016
Telephone: 610-867-0593
Fax: 610-866-9223
Email: pubs@mcnp.org
Website: http://www.moravian.org/

The Mother Church (bi-M)
(Western Diocese of the Armenian Church of North
America)
3325 N Glenoaks Boulevard

Burbank, CA 91504
Telephone: 818-558-7474
Fax: 818-558-6333
Email: armenianchwd@earthlink.net
Website: http://www.armenianchurchwd.com/

Multiply (Q)
(Presbyterian Church in America)
1700 N Brown Road
Suite 101
Lawrenceville, GA 30044
Telephone: 678-825-1200
Fax: 678-825-1201
Email: mna@pcanet.org
Website: http://pcamna.org/communications
    /publications/multiply-archive/

NAB Today (bi-M)
(North American Baptist Conference)
1 S 210 Summit Avenue
Oakbrook Terrace, IL 60181
Telephone: 630-495-2000
Fax: 630-495-3301

NAE Insight (Q)
(Interdenominational)
PO Box 23269
Washington, DC 20026
Telephone: 202-789-1011
Email: info@nae.net
Website: http://www.evangelicalpress.com/mem
    bers/infonae-net/

National Catholic Reporter (44/Y)
(Roman Catholic Church)
PO Box 419281
Kansas City, MO 64141
Telephone: 816-531-0538
Fax: 816-968-2280
Email: editor@natcath.org
Website: http://www.ncronline.org/

Network (Q)
(Presbyterian Church in America)
1600 N Brown Road
Lawrenceville, GA 30047
Telephone: 678-823-0004
Fax: 678-823-0027
Website: http://www.pcanet.org

New Church Life (M)
(General Church of the New Jerusalem)
PO Box 277
Bryn Athyn, PA 19009
Telephone: 215-947-6225 ext. 209
Fax: 215-938-1871
Email: DonR@bacs-gc.org
Website: http://www.newchurch.org/materials
    /publications/

New Horizons in the Orthodox Presbyterian Church
(11/Y)
(Orthodox Presbyterian Church)

607 N Easton Road
Building E
PO Box P
Willow Grove, PA 19090
Telephone: 215-830-0900
Fax: 215-830-0350
Email: olinger.l@opc.org
Website: http://www.opc.org/

New Oxford Review (11/Y)
(Roman Catholic Church)
1069 Kains Avenue
Berkeley, CA 94706
Telephone: 510-526-5374
Fax: 510-526-3492
Website: http://www.newoxfordreview.org/

Newsline (M)
(Church of the Brethren)
1451 Dundee Avenue
Elgin, IL 60120-1694
Telephone: 847-742-5100
Fax: 847-742-6103
Email: cobnews@aol.com

FEConnections
(Fellowship of Evangelical Churches)
1420 Kerrway Court
Fort Wayne, IN 46805
Telephone: 260-423-3649
Fax: 260-420-1905
Email: emchdq@aol.com
Website: http://www.fecministries.org/

New World Outlook (bi-M)
(United Methodist Church)
475 Riverside Drive
Room 1476
New York, NY 10115
Telephone: 212-870-3765
Fax: 212-870-3654
Email: nwo@gbgm-umc.org
Website: http://www.umcmission.org/find-resour
    ces/new-world-outlook

North American Baptist Conference (bi-M)
(North American Baptist Conference)
S 210 Summit Avenue
Oakbrook Terrace, IL 60184
Telephone: 630-495-2000
Fax: 630-495-3300
Email: serve@nabconference.org
Website: http://www.nabconference.org/

The North American Catholic (M)
(North American Old Roman Catholic Church)
4154 W Berteau Avenue
Chicago, IL 60641
Telephone: 312-685-0461
Fax: 312-485-0461
Email: chapelhall@aol.com

The North American Challenge (M)
(United Pentecostal Church International)
8855 Dunn Road
Hazelwood, MO 63042
Telephone: 314-837-7300
Fax: 314-837-5632

NRB Magazine (9/Y)
(Nondenominational)
National Religious Broadcasters
9510 Technology Drive
Manassas, VA 20110
Telephone: 703-330-7000
Fax: 703-330-6996
Email: cpryor@nrb.org
Website: http://www.nrb.org/

On Course (bi-M)
(Assemblies of God)
1445 N Boonville Avenue
Springfield, MO 65802
Telephone: 417-862-2781
Fax: 417-862-1693
Email: oncourse@ag.org
Website: http://ag.org/

One Magazine (bi-M)
(National Association of Free Will Baptists)
PO Box 5002
Antioch, TN 37011
Telephone: 615-731-6812
Fax: 615-731-0771
Website: http://www.onemag.org/

On Mission (Q)
(Southern Baptist Convention)
4200 North Point Parkway
Alpharetta, GA 30202
Telephone: 770-410-6394
Fax: 770-410-6105
Website: http://www.onmission.com/

Orthodox America (8/Y)
(Russian Orthodox Church Outside Russia)
PO Box 383
Richfield Springs, NY 13439
Telephone: 315-858-1518
Email: info@orthodoxamerica.org
Website: http://www.orthodoxamerica.org/

The Orthodox Church (M)
(Orthodox Church in America)
1 Wheaton Center #912
Wheaton, IL 60187
Telephone: 630-668-3071
Fax: 630-668-5712
Email: tocmed@hotmail.com
Website: http://www.oca.org/

Orthodox Family (Q)
(Russian Orthodox Church Outside Russia)
PO Box 45
Beltsville, MD 20705
Email: llew@cais.com

Orthodox Life (bi-M)
(Russian Orthodox Church Outside Russia)
Holy Trinity Monastery
PO Box 36
Jordanville, NY 13361
Telephone: 315-858-0940
Fax: 315-858-0505
Email: 72204.1465@compuserve.com

The Orthodox Observer (M)
(Greek Orthodox Archdiocese)
8 E 79th Street
New York, NY 10021
Telephone: 212-570-3555
Fax: 212-774-0239
Email: observer@goarch.org
Website: http://www.observer.goarch.org/

Orthodox Russia (English translation of *Pravoslavnaya Rus*) (24/Y)
(Russian Orthodox Church Outside Russia)
Holy Trinity Monastery
PO Box 36
Jordanville, NY 13361
Telephone: 315-858-0940
Fax: 315-858-0505
Email: orthrus@telenet.net

The Other Side (bi-M)
(Interdenominational)
300 W Apsley Street
Philadelphia, PA 19144
Telephone: 215-849-2178
Fax: 215-849-3755

Our Daily Bread (M)
(Swedenborgian Church)
PO Box 396
Bridgewater, MA 02324
Telephone: 508-946-1767
Fax: 508-946-1757
Email: odb@swedenborg.org
Website: http://www.swedenborg.org/odb/index
.cfm

Our Little Friend (W)
(Seventh-Day Adventist Church)
PO Box 5353
Nampa, ID 83653
Telephone: 208-465-2500
Fax: 208-465-2531
Email: ailsox@pacificpress.com
Website: http://www.pacificpress.com/

Our Sunday Visitor (W)
(Roman Catholic Church)
200 Noll Plaza
Huntington, IN 46750
Telephone: 219-356-8400
Email: oursunvis@osv.com
Website: http://www.osv.com/

Outreach (bi-M)
(Armenian Apostolic Church)
138 E 39th Street
New York, NY 10016
Telephone: 212-689-7810
Fax: 212-689-7168
Email: info@armenianprelacy.org
Website: http://www.armenianprelacy.org/

Pastoral Life (M)
(Roman Catholic Church)
9531 Akron-Canfield Road
Canfield, OH 44406
Telephone: 330-533-5503
Email: plmagazine@hotmail.com
Website: http://www.albahouse.org/plcenter.htm

Pastor Talk (Q)
(General Association of General Baptists)
100 Stinson Drive
Poplar Bluff, MO 63901
Fax: 573-785-0564
Email: pmdir@generalbaptist.com

The Path of Orthodoxy (M)
(Serbian Orthodox Church in the USA and Canada)
300 Striker Avenue
Joliet, IL 60436
Telephone: 815-741-1023
Fax: 815-741-1883
Email: nedlunich300@comcast.net

Paul (Q)
(Netherlands Reformed Congregations)
47 Main Street E
Norwich, ON N0J 1P0
Canada
Telephone: 519-863-3306
Fax: 519-863-2793

Pentecostal Evangel, World Missions Edition (M)
(Assemblies of God)
Gospel Publishing House
1445 N Boonville Avenue
Springfield, MO 65802
Telephone: 417-862-2781
Fax: 417-862-0416
Email: pe@ag.org
Website: http://www.pe.ag.org/

The Pentecostal Herald (M)
(United Pentecostal Church International)
8855 Dunn Road
Hazelwood, MO 63042
Telephone: 314-837-7300
Fax: 314-837-4503
Email: pbuford@upci.org
Website: https://www.pentecostalherald.com/

The Pentecostal Leader (bi-M)
(International Pentecostal Church of Christ)
PO Box 439
London, OH 43140

Telephone: 740-852-4722
Fax: 740-852-0348
Email: editor@ipcc.cc
Website: http://www.ipcc.cc/Pent.%20Leader.htm

The Pentecostal Messenger (M)
(Pentecostal Church of God)
PO Box 850
Joplin, MO 64802
Telephone: 417-624-7050
Fax: 417-624-7102
Email: johnm@pcg.org
Website: http://www.pcg.org/#!pentecostal
-messenger/c1980

Perspectives (10/Y)
(Reformed Church in America)
PO Box 1196
Holland, MI 49422
Telephone: 616-392-8555
Fax: 616-392-7717
Email: perspectives@hotmail.com
Website: http://www.perspectivesjournal.org/

Perspectives on Science and Christian Faith (Q)
(Nondenominational)
4956 Singers Glen Road
Harrisonburg, VA 22802
Telephone: 540-432-4412
Fax: 540-432-4488
Email: millerrj@rica.net
Website: http://www.asa3.org/?page=PSCF

The Pilot—America's Oldest Catholic Newspaper (W)
(Roman Catholic Archdiocese of Boston)
2121 Commonwealth Avenue
Brighton, MA 02135
Telephone: 617-746-5889
Fax: 617-783-2684
Email: editorial@bostonpilot.org
Website: http://www.rcab.org/

Pockets (11/Y)
(United Methodist Church)
PO Box 340004
Nashville, TN 37203
Telephone: 615-340-7333
Fax: 615-340-7267
Email: pockets@upperroom.org
Website: http://pockets.upperroom.org/

Polka (Q)
(Polish National Catholic Church of America)
1127 Frieda Street
Dickson City, PA 18519
Telephone: 570-489-4364
Fax: 570-346-2188

Pravoslavnaya Rus (Russian) (24/Y)
(Russian Orthodox Church Outside Russia)
Holy Trinity Monastery
PO Box 36

Jordanville, NY 13361
Telephone: 315-858-0940
Fax: 315-858-0505
Email: orthrus@telenet.net

Pravoslavnaya Zhisn (monthly supplement to *Pravoslavnaya Rus*) (M)
(Russian Orthodox Church Outside Russia)
Holy Trinity Monastery
PO Box 36
Jordanville, NY 13361
Telephone: 315-858-0940
Fax: 315-858-0505
Email: orthrus@telenet.net

Preacher's Magazine (bi-M)
(Church of the Nazarene)
6401 Paseo Boulevard
Kansas City, MO 64131

Presbyterian News Service (bi-M)
(Presbyterian Church [USA])
100 Witherspoon Street
Room 5418
Louisville, KY 40202
Telephone: 502-569-5493
Fax: 502-569-8073
Email: jvanmart@ctr.pcusa.org
Website: http://www.pcusa.org/pcnews

The Presbyterian Outlook (43/Y)
(Presbyterian Church [USA])
PO Box 85623
Richmond, VA 23285
Telephone: 804-359-8442
Fax: 804-353-6369
Email: rbullock@pres-outlook.com
Website: http://pres-outlook.org/

Presbyterians Today (10/Y)
(Presbyterian Church [USA])
100 Witherspoon Street
Louisville, KY 40202
Telephone: 502-569-5637
Fax: 502-569-8632
Website: http://www.presbyterianmission.org
/ministries/today/

Primary Source (Q)
(American Baptist Historical Society)
PO Box 851
Valley Forge, PA 19482
Email: dbvanbro@abc-usa.org
Website: http://abhsarchives.org/publications
/newsletter/

Primary Treasure (W)
(Seventh-Day Adventist Church)
PO Box 5353
Nampa, ID 83653
Telephone: 208-465-2500
Fax: 208-465-2531
Email: ailsox@pacificpress.com
Website: http://www.primarytreasure.com/

Priority (M)
(Missionary Church)
PO Box 9127
Ft. Wayne, IN 46899
Telephone: 260-747-2027
Fax: 260-747-5331
Email: mcdenomusa@aol.com
Website: http://mcusa.org/

The Progressive Voice (bi-M)
(United Methodist Church)
212 E Capitol Street NE
Washington, DC 20003
Telephone: 202-546-8806
Fax: 202-546-6811
Email: mfsa@olg.com
Website: http://mfsaweb.org/?page_id=208

Pulse (M)
(Church of God, Seventh Day)
PO Box 33677
330 W 152nd Avenue
Denver, CO 80233
Telephone: 303-452-7973
Fax: 303-452-0657
Email: offices@cog7.org
Website: http://cog7.org/

Purpose (M)
(Mennonite Church USA)
616 Walnut Avenue
Scottdale, PA 15683
Telephone: 724-887-8500
Fax: 724-887-3111
Email: horsch@mph.org
Website: http://www.faithandliferesources.org
/periodicals/purpose/

PYM Today (2/Y)
(Philadelphia Yearly Meeting of the Friends)
1515 Cherry Street
Philadelphia, PA 19102
Telephone: 800-220-0796
Fax: 215-241-7045
Email: info@pym.org
Website: http://www.pym.org/publications/pym
-today/

Quaker Life (bi-M)
(Friends United Meeting)
101 Quaker Hill Drive
Richmond, IN 47374
Telephone: 765-962-7573
Fax: 765-966-1293
Email: quakerlife@fum.org
Website: http://www.fum.org/quaker-life/

Quarterly Review (Q)
(United Methodist Church)
PO Box 340007
Nashville, TN 37203

Telephone: 615-340-7334
Fax: 615-340-7048
Email: hpieterse@gbhem.org
Website: http://www.quarterlyreview.org/

Quarterly Review, A.M.E. Zion (Q)
(African Methodist Episcopal Zion Church)
PO Box 33247
Charlotte, NC 28233
Telephone: 704-599-4630
Fax: 704-688-2544
Email: jaarmstrong@amezhqtr.org

RCA Today (11/Y)
(Reformed Church in America)
4500 60th Street SE
Grand Rapids, MI 49512
Telephone: 616-698-7071
Fax: 616-698-6606
Email: webservant@rca.org
Website: https://www.rca.org/rca-today/

Reflections (bi-M)
(United Pentecostal Church International)
8855 Dunn Road
Hazelwood, MO 63042
Telephone: 918-371-2659
Fax: 918-371-6320
Email: manderson@tums.org
Website: http://www.ladiesministries.org/reflec
tions.asp

Reformed Worship (Q)
(Christian Reformed Church in North America)
2850 Kalamazoo Avenue SE
Grand Rapids, MI 49560
Telephone: 800-777-7270
Fax: 616-224-0834
Email: info@reformedworship.org
Website: http://www.reformedworship.org/

Rejoice! (Q)
(Mennonite Church)
600 Shaftesbury Boulevard
Winnipeg, MB R3P 0M4
Canada
Telephone: 204-888-6781
Fax: 204-831-5675
Email: byronrb@mph.org
Website: http://www.mph.org/rejoice

Reporter (M)
(Lutheran Church—Missouri Synod)
1333 S Kirkwood Road
St. Louis, MO 63122
Telephone: 314-996-9000
Fax: 314-966-1126
Email: reporter@lcms.org
Website: http://reporter.lcms.org/

Report from the Capital (10/Y)
(Baptist)
200 Maryland Avenue NE

Washington, DC 20002
Telephone: 202-544-4226
Fax: 202-544-2094
Email: lchesser@bjcpa.org
Website: http://www.bjcpa.org/

The Rescue Herald (3/Y)
(American Rescue Workers)
National Field Office
1209 Hamilton Boulevard
Hagerstown, MD 21742
Telephone: 301-797-0061
Fax: 301-797-1480
Email: chiefcoles@aol.com
Website: http://www.arwnational.org/rescue
-herald/

Response (M)
(United Methodist Church)
475 Riverside Drive
Room 1356
New York, NY 10115
Telephone: 212-870-3755
Fax: 212-870-3940

The Restitution Herald (bi-M)
(Church of God, General Conference)
Box 100000
Morrow, GA 30260
Telephone: 404-362-0052
Fax: 404-362-9307
Website: http://www.abc-coggc.org/

Restoration Herald (M)
(Christian Churches; Churches of Christ)
7133 Central Parks Boulevard
Mason, OH 45040
Telephone: 513-229-8000
Fax: 513-229-8003
Email: thecra@aol.com
Website: http://www.thecra.org/restoration
_herald/

Restoration Quarterly (Q)
(Churches of Christ)
PO Box 28227
Abilene, TX 79699
Telephone: 915-674-3781
Fax: 915-674-3776
Email: rq@bible.acu.edu
Website: http://www.acu.edu/sponsored/restora
tion_quarterly/index.html

Review for Religious (Q)
(Roman Catholic Church)
3601 Lindell Boulevard
St. Louis, MO 63108
Telephone: 314-977-7363
Fax: 314-977-7362
Email: review@slu.edu
Website: http://www.reviewforreligious.org/

Review of Religious Research (Q)
(Nondenominational)
618 SW 2nd Avenue
Galva, IL 61434
Telephone: 309-932-2727
Fax: 309-932-2282
Email: William_Swatos@baylor.edu
Website: http://www.rraweb.org/journal-review
-of-religious-research/

Road to Emmaus (Q)
(Orthodox Christian)
1516 N Delaware
Indianapolis, IN 46202
Telephone: 317-637-1897
Fax: 317-631-1334
Email: csb@indy.net
Website: http://www.roadtoemmaus.net/

Rocky Mountain Christian (M)
(Churches of Christ)
PO Box 26620
Colorado Springs, CO 80936
Telephone: 719-598-4197
Fax: 719-528-1549
Email: 76102.2461@compuserve.com

Sabbath Recorder (M)
(Seventh Day Baptists)
3120 Kennedy Road
PO Box 1678
Janesville, WI 53547
Telephone: 608-752-5055
Fax: 608-752-7711
Email: sdbmedia@charter.net
Website: http://seventhdaybaptist.org/category
/sabbath-recorder/

Sabbath School Leadership (M)
(Seventh-Day Adventist Church)
Review and Herald Publishing Association
55 W Oak Ridge Drive
Hagerstown, MD 21740
Telephone: 301-393-4090
Fax: 301-393-4055

Saint Anthony Messenger (M)
(Roman Catholic Church)
28 W Liberty Street
Cincinnati, OH 45202
Telephone: 513-241-5616
Fax: 513-241-0399
Email: stanthony@americancatholic.org
Website: http://www.americancatholic.org/

Saint Willibrord Journal (Q)
(Christ Catholic Church)
PO Box 271751
Houston, TX 77277
Telephone: 713-515-8206
Fax: 713-622-5311
Website: http://www.christcatholic.org/

SBC Life (10/Y)
(Southern Baptist Church)
901 Commerce Street
Nashville, TN 37203
Telephone: 615-244-2355
Fax: 615-782-8684
Email: jrevell@sbc.net
Website: http://www.sbclife.net/

The Schwenkfeldian (3/Y)
(Schwenkfelder Church)
105 Seminary Street
Pennsburg, PA 18073
Telephone: 215-679-3103
Fax: 215-679-8175
Email: info@schwenkfelder.com
Website: http://www.schwenkfelder.com/

Searching Together (Q)
(Sovereign Grace Believers)
PO Box 548
St. Croix Falls, WI 54024
Telephone: 651-465-6516
Fax: 651-465-5101
Email: jzens@searchingtogether.org
Website: http://www.searchingtogether.org/

The Secret Place (Q)
(American Baptist Churches in the USA)
PO Box 851
Valley Forge, PA 19482
Telephone: 610-768-2240
Fax: 610-768-2441
Email: thesecretplace@abc-usa.org

Seeds for the Parish (bi-M)
(Evangelical Lutheran Church in America)
8765 W Higgins Road
Chicago, IL 60631
Telephone: 773-380-2949
Fax: 773-380-1465
Email: kelliott@elca.org
Website: http://www.elca.org/co/seeds/index
.html

Shalom! (Q)
(Brethren in Christ Church)
127 Holly Drive
Mechanicsburg, PA 17055
Telephone: 717-795-9151
Email: bickhouse@aol.com
Website: http://www.bic-church.org/connect
/publications/Shalom/

Signs of the Times (M)
(Seventh-Day Adventist Church)
PO Box 5353
Nampa, ID 83653
Telephone: 208-465-2577
Fax: 208-465-2531
Website: http://www.signstimes.com/

The Silver Lining (M)
(Apostolic Christian Churches of America)
RR 2 Box 50
Roanoke, IL 61561
Telephone: 309-923-7777
Fax: 309-923-7359

Sojourners (bi-M)
(Nondenominational)
2401 15th Street NW
Washington, DC 20009
Telephone: 202-328-8842
Fax: 202-328-8757
Email: sojourners@sojo.net
Website: http://www.sojo.net/magazine

Solia Calendar Almanac (Y)
(Romanian Orthodox Episcopate)
PO Box 185
Grass Lake, MI 49240
Telephone: 517-522-4800
Fax: 517-522-5907
Email: solia@roea.org
Website: http://www.roea.org/soliacalendar.html

Solia: The Herald (M)
(Romanian Orthodox Episcopate)
PO Box 185
Grass Lake, MI 49240
Telephone: 517-522-3656
Fax: 517-522-5907
Email: solia@roea.org
Website: http://www.roea.org/soliatheherald.html

Sound of Grace (Q)
(Sovereign Grace Believers)
5317 Wye Creek Drive
Frederick, MD 21703

The Southern Methodist (bi-M)
(Southern Methodist Church)
PO Box 39
Orangeburg, SC 29116
Telephone: 803-534-9853
Fax: 803-535-3881
Email: foundry@bellsouth.net

Spirit (Q)
(Volunteers of America)
1809 Carrollton Avenue
New Orleans, LA 70118
Telephone: 504-897-1731

The Spiritual Sword (Q)
(Churches of Christ)
1511 Getwell Road
Memphis, TN 38111
Telephone: 901-743-0464
Fax: 901-743-2197
Email: getwellcc@aol.com
Website: http://www.getwellchurchofchrist.org
/the-spiritual-sword/

The Standard Bearer (21/Y)
(Protestant Reformed Churches in America)
4949 Ivanrest Avenue
Grandville, MI 49418
Telephone: 616-531-1490
Fax: 616-531-3033
Email: engelsma@prca.org
Website: http://sb.rfpa.org/

Star of Zion (bi-W)
(African Methodist Episcopal Zion Church)
PO Box 26770
Charlotte, NC 28221
Telephone: 704-599-4630
Fax: 704-688-2546
Email: editor@thestarofzion.org
Website: http://thestarofzion.com/

Stewardship USA (Q)
(Nondenominational)
4818 Quartoii Road
Bloomfield Hills, MI 48302
Telephone: 248-737-0895
Fax: 248-737-0895

Story Friends (24/Y)
(Mennonite Church USA)
616 Walnut Avenue
Scottdale, PA 15683
Telephone: 574-887-8500
Fax: 574-887-3111

The Student (Braille and Cassette) (M)
(Seventh-Day Adventist Church)
PO Box 6097
Lincoln, NE 68506
Telephone: 402-488-0981
Fax: 402-488-7582
Email: info@christianrecord.org
Website: http://www.christianrecord.org/

Sunday (Q)
(Interdenominational)
2930 Flowers Road S
Atlanta, GA 30341
Telephone: 770-936-5376
Fax: 770-936-5385

The Tablet (W)
(Roman Catholic Church)
653 Hicks Street
Brooklyn, NY 11231
Telephone: 718-858-3838
Fax: 718-858-2112

Theology Digest (Q)
(Roman Catholic Church)
3800 Lindell Boulevard
St. Louis, MO 63108
Telephone: 314-977-3410
Fax: 314-977-3704
Email: thdigest@slu.edu

Theology Today (Q)
(Nondenominational)
PO Box 821
Princeton, NJ 08542
Telephone: 609-497-7714
Fax: 609-497-1826
Email: theology.today@ptsem.edu
Website: http://theologytoday.ptsem.edu/

These Days (Q)
(Interdenominational)
100 Witherspoon Street
Louisville, KY 40202
Telephone: 502-569-5080
Fax: 502-569-5113
Website: http://www.ppcbooks.com/thesedays.asp

The Three-Fold Vision (M)
(Apostolic Faith Mission Church of God)
156 Walker Street
Munford, AL 36268
Telephone: 256-358-9763
Email: alicemtwalkerl56@aol.com

Timbrel (bi-M)
(Mennonite Church USA)
420 SE Richland Avenue
Corvallis, OR 97333
Telephone: 541-752-0444
Email: timbrel@mennonitewomenusa.org
Website: http://www.mennonitewomenusa.org
/publications/timbrel/

Today's Christian (bi-M)
(Nondenominational)
465 Gundersen Drive
Carol Stream, IL 60188
Telephone: 630-260-6200
Fax: 630-260-0114

Today's Christian Woman (bi-M)
(Nondenominational)
465 Gundersen Drive
Carol Stream, IL 60188
Telephone: 630-260-6200
Fax: 630-260-0114
Email: tcwedit@christianitytoday.com
Website: http://www.todayschristianwoman.com/

Tomorrow Magazine (Q)
(American Baptist Churches in the USA)
475 Riverside Drive
Room 1700
New York, NY 10115
Telephone: 800-986-6222
Fax: 800-986-6782

The Tover of St. Cassian (2/Y)
(Apostolic Episcopal Church/Order of Corporate
Reunion)
US Council-Society of St. Cassian
80-46 234th Street
Jamaica, NY 11427
Telephone: 718-740-4134

Treasure (Q)
(National Association of Free Will Baptists)
PO Box 5002
Antioch, TN 37011
Telephone: 615-731-6812
Fax: 615-731-0771
Email: wnac@nafwb.org
Website: http://www.wnac.org/treasure/

Truth (Q)
(Grace Gospel Fellowship)
2125 Martindale SW
Grand Rapids, MI 49509
Telephone: 616-247-1999
Fax: 616-241-2542
Email: ggfinc@aol.com
Website: http://ggfusa.org/truth-magazine/

Truth Magazine (bi-W)
(Churches of Christ)
PO Box 9670
Bowling Green, KY 42102
Telephone: 800-428-0121
Website: http://www.truthmagazine.com/

Turnings (bi-M)
(Conservative Baptist Association of America)
1501 W Mineral Avenue
Suite B
Littleton, CO 80120
Telephone: 720-283-3030 ext. 1830
Fax: 720-283-3333

21st Century Christian (M)
(Churches of Christ)
PO Box 40304
Nashville, TN 37204
Telephone: 800-331-5991
Fax: 615-385-5915

Ubique (Q)
(Liberal Catholic Church)
2033 22nd Avenue
#302
Greeley, CO 80631

Ukrainian Orthodox Herald (Q)
(Ukrainian Orthodox Church)
PO Box 774
Allentown, PA 18105

UC News (10/Y)
(United Church of Christ)
700 Prospect Avenue
Cleveland, OH 44115
Telephone: 216-736-2218
Fax: 216-736-2223
Email: goldere@ucc.org
Website: http://www.ucc.org/ucnews/

The United Methodist Reporter (W)
(United Methodist Church)
PO Box 246

Wichita Falls, TX 76307
Telephone: 615-673-4236
Website: http://unitedmethodistreporter.com/

The Upper Room (bi-M)
(United Methodist Church)
PO Box 340004
Nashville, TN 37203
Telephone: 877-899-2780
Fax: 615-340-7289
Email: sbryant@upperroom.org
Website: http://www.upperroom.org/

U.S. Catholic (M)
(Roman Catholic Church)
205 W Monroe Street
Chicago, IL 60606
Telephone: 312-236-7782
Fax: 312-236-8207
Email: editors@uscatholic.org
Website: http://www.uscatholic.org/

UU World (bi-M)
(Unitarian Universalist Association of Congregations)
25 Beacon Street
Boston, MA 02108
Telephone: 617-948-6518
Fax: 617-742-7025
Email: world@uua.org
Website: http://www.uuworld.org/

Vibrant Life (bi-M)
(Seventh-Day Adventist Church)
55 W Oak Ridge Drive
Hagerstown, MD 21740
Telephone: 301-393-4019
Fax: 301-393-4055
Email: vibrantlife@rhpa.org
Website: http://www.vibrantlife.com/

Victory (Q)
(Church of God of Prophecy)
PO Box 2910
Cleveland, TN 37320
Telephone: 423-559-5321
Fax: 423-559-5461

The Vindicator (M)
(Old German Baptist Brethren Church)
6952 N Montgomery County Line Road
Englewood, OH 45322
Telephone: 937-884-7531
Fax: 937-884-7531

Vira (Q)
(Ukrainian Orthodox Church)
PO Box 495
South Bound Brook, NJ 08880
Telephone: 732-356-0090
Fax: 732-356-9437
Email: virafaith@aol.com

Vista (Q)
(Christian Church of North America)
1294 Rutledge Road
Transfer, PA 16154
Telephone: 412-962-3501
Fax: 412-962-1766

The Voice (bi-M)
(IFCA International Inc.)
PO Box 810
Grandville, MI 49468
Telephone: 616-531-1840
Fax: 616-531-1814
Email: voice@ifca.org
Website: http://www.ifca.org/

The Voice (Q)
(Bible Church of Christ)
1358 Morris Avenue
Bronx, NY 10456
Telephone: 718-588-2284
Fax: 718-992-5597

Voice of Missions (Q)
(African Methodist Episcopal Church)
1587 Savannah Highway
Suite A
Charleston, SC 29407
Telephone: 843-852-2645
Fax: 843-852-2648

War Cry (bi-M)
(Salvation Army)
615 Slaters Lane
Alexandria, VA 22314
Telephone: 703-684-5500
Fax: 703-684-5539
Email: warcry@usn.salvationarmy.org
Website: http://www.thewarcry.org/

Weavings: A Journal of the Christian Spiritual Life (bi-M)
(United Methodist Church)
1908 Grand Avenue
Nashville, TN 37212
Telephone: 615-340-7254
Fax: 615-340-7267
Email: weavings@upperroom.org
Website: http://weavings.upperroom.org/

Wesleyan Life (Q)
(Wesleyan Church)
PO Box 50434
Indianapolis, IN 46250
Telephone: 317-774-7909
Fax: 317-774-7913
Email: wilsonn@wesleyan.org
Website: https://www.wesleyan.org/wesleyanlife online

Wesleyan World (Q)
(Wesleyan Church)
PO Box 50434

Indianapolis, IN 46250
Telephone: 317-774-7950
Fax: 317-774-7958

White Wing Messenger (bi-W)
(Church of God of Prophecy)
PO Box 3000
Cleveland, TN 37320
Telephone: 423-559-5413
Fax: 423-559-5444
Email: jenny@wingnet.net
Website: http://www.whitewingmessenger.net/

Window on the World (3/Y)
(Evangelical Congregational Church)
100 W Park Avenue
Myerstown, PA 17067
Telephone: 717-866-7584
Fax: 717-866-7383
Email: ecglobalministries@eccenter.com
Website: http://www.eccenter.com/

Wineskins (bi-M)
(Churches of Christ)
PO Box 41028
Nashville, TN 37024
Telephone: 615-373-5004
Fax: 615-373-5006
Email: wineskinsmagazine@msn.com
Website: http://www.wineskins.org/

Wisconsin Lutheran Quarterly (Q)
(Evangelical Lutheran Synod)
11831 N Seminary Drive
Mequon, WI 53092
Telephone: 262-242-8139
Fax: 262-242-8110
Email: brugj@wls.wels.net
Website: http://www.wls.wels.net/library/wis
consin-lutheran-quarterly/

With: The Magazine for Radical Christian Youth
(bi-M)
(Mennonite Church USA)
722 Main Street
Newton, KS 67114
Telephone: 316-283-5100
Fax: 316-283-0454
Email: deliag@gcmc.org
Website: http://with.mennonite.net/

The Witness (10/Y)
(Nondenominational)
7000 Michigan Avenue
Detroit, MI 48210
Telephone: 313-841-1967
Fax: 313-841-1956

Woman's Touch (bi-M)
(Assemblies of God)
1445 N Boonville Avenue
Springfield, MO 65802

Telephone: 417-862-2781
Fax: 417-862-0503
Email: womanstouch@ag.org
Website: http://www.womanstouch.ag.org/

Woman to Woman (M)
(General Association of General Baptists)
100 Stinson Drive
Poplar Bluff, MO 63901
Telephone: 573-785-7746
Fax: 573-785-0564
Email: wmdir@generalbaptist.com

Women's Missionary Magazine (9/Y)
(African Methodist Episcopal Church)
17129 Bennett Drive
South Holland, IL 60473
Telephone: 708-339-5997
Fax: 708-339-5987
Email: bettyel901@aol.com

The Word (10/Y)
(Antiochian Orthodox Christian Archdiocese of
North America)
PO Box 5238
Englewood, NJ 07631
Telephone: 201-871-1355
Fax: 201-871-7954
Email: frjpa@aol.com
Website: http://www.antiochian.org/theword

Word and Work (11/Y)
(Churches of Christ)
2518 Portland Avenue
Louisville, KY 40212
Telephone: 502-897-2831

The Worker (Q)
(Progressive National Baptist Convention)
601 50th Street NE
Washington, DC 20019
Telephone: 202-398-5343
Fax: 202-398-4998
Email: office@pnbc.org
Website: http://www.pnbc.org/The-Worker
-Magazine

World Harvest Today (Q)
(United Pentecostal Church International)
8855 Dunn Road
Hazelwood, MO 63042
Telephone: 314-837-7300
Fax: 314-837-2387

Worldorama (M)
(Pentecostal Holiness Church)
PO Box 12609
Oklahoma City, OK 73157
Telephone: 405-787-7110
Fax: 405-787-7729
Email: donald@iphc.org

World Parish: International Organ of the World Methodist Council (M)
(Methodist)
PO Box 518
545 N Lakeshore Drive
Lake Junaluska, NC 28745
Telephone: 828-456-9432
Fax: 828-456-9433
Website: http://www.worldmethodistcouncil.org/

Worship (bi-M)
(Roman Catholic Church)
St. John's Abbey
2900 Abbey Plaza
PO Box 2015
Collegeville, MN 56321
Telephone: 320-363-2011
Fax: 320-363-3039
Email: sjainfo@csbsju.edu
Website: http://www.saintjohnsabbey.org/our
-work/publishing/worship-articles/

Worship Arts (bi-M)
(Nondenominational)
PO Box 6247
Grand Rapids, MI 49516
Telephone: 616-459-4503
Fax: 616-459-1051
Email: graphics@iserv.net

Young and Alive (Q)
(Seventh-Day Adventist Church)
PO Box 6097

Lincoln, NE 68506
Telephone: 402-488-0981
Fax: 402-488-7582
Email: editorial@christianrecord.org
Website: http://www.christianrecord.org/

Youth Ministry Accent (Q)
(Seventh-Day Adventist Church)
12501 Old Columbia Pike
Silver Spring, MD 20904
Telephone: 301-680-6180
Fax: 301-680-6155
Email: 74532.1426@compuserve.com

YPD Newsletter (3/M)
(African Methodist Episcopal Church)
327 Washington Avenue
Wyoming, OH 45215
Telephone: 513-821-1481
Fax: 513-821-3073

Zion's Advocate (M)
(Church of Christ)
PO Box 472
Independence, MO 64051
Telephone: 816-206-0147
Website: http://www.churchofchrist-tl.org/zions
advocate.cfm

Contributors

Dominic A. Aquila is president of New Geneva Seminary in Colorado Springs, Colorado. He received a BA from Belhaven College, an MDiv from Reformed Theological Seminary, and a DMin from Westminster Theological Seminary. Dr. Aquila is a minister of the Presbyterian Church in America, most recently serving for twelve years as senior pastor of Kendall Presbyterian Church in Miami, Florida. He has taught courses at Reformed Theological Seminary in Jackson, Mississippi; Trinity Evangelical Divinity School in Miami, Florida; and Knox Theological Seminary in Ft. Lauderdale, Florida. Dr. Aquila has served on numerous boards for Christian schools, a college, and other Christian organizations.

Brenda Ayres is a full professor of English literature, a member of the graduate faculty, and an assistant director in the honors program at Liberty University in Lynchburg, Virginia. Most of her publications are in nineteenth-century English literature, which include about eighty articles and fourteen book publications to date. She was converted in 1972, became charismatic in 1973, was a part of the Shepherding or Discipleship movement for ten years, worked for *New Wine* magazine (the journal for the movement), and knew several Christians who belonged to Maranatha Campus Ministries.

David K. Bernard is the general superintendent of the United Pentecostal Church International, the largest Oneness Pentecostal organization, and president of Urshan Graduate School of Theology. He founded New Life United Pentecostal Church of Austin, Texas, out of which sixteen additional churches were started under his leadership. He holds a BA with high honors (Rice University), a MTh (University of South Africa), and a JD with honors (University of Texas) and is a DTh candidate in New Testament at the University of South Africa. His thirty books have been published in thirty-six languages.

Ron J. Bigalke (BS, Moody Bible Institute; MApol, Columbia Evangelical Seminary; MDiv [with honors], Luther Rice University; MTS, PhD, Tyndale Theological Seminary; PhD [ABD], University of Pretoria) is the Georgia state director for the Capitol Commission, an author and lecturer for Eternal Ministries Inc., and a missionary for Biblical Ministries Worldwide. He teaches theology and apologetics at Tyndale Theological Seminary and is a member of several Christian professional societies. He has served in Christian ministry for over a decade, and his current work is concentrated on apologetics, biblical studies, ecclesiastical literature and thought, historiography, and theology. As an educator, he has served as a Bible institute, college, and seminary professor and as a Christian school administrator and teacher.

Jamie Blosser is a professor of theology at Benedictine College in Atchison, Kansas. He holds a PhD in historical theology from the Catholic University of America, where his thesis was on the theological anthropology of Origen of Alexandria. He regularly offers courses in church history, Pauline Letters, and ecclesiology. His main interest is patristics, especially Origen and St. Augustine of Hippo.

James A. Borland, born in Santa Monica, California, attended UCLA and completed his BA (summa) at Los Angeles Baptist College. His MDiv (magna) is from LA Baptist Theological Seminary; his ThM (summa) is from Talbot Theological Seminary; and his ThD is from Grace Theological Seminary. He has pastored three churches, taught in three seminaries and universities, and is currently in his thirty-fourth year at Liberty University. He is a past president of the Evangelical Theological Society and has written eight books and nearly one hundred articles and reviews. He has six married children and resides with his wife, Linda, in Lynchburg, Virginia.

Mark Braun is a professor of religious studies at Wisconsin Lutheran College, Milwaukee. He completed his PhD in historical theology at Concordia Seminary, St. Louis. He is the author of *A Tale of Two Synods: Events That Led to the Split between Wisconsin and Missouri* (Northwestern, 2003) and articles on American Lutheran history.

Todd M. Brenneman is a visiting instructor in the department of philosophy at the University of Central Florida. He received his PhD in American religious history from Florida State University in 2009. His dissertation discussed the role of emotion in the writings of bestselling author Max Lucado. He has also written about children and religion in the United States.

Chad C. Brewer (BA, University of California San Diego; MATS and MABS candidate, Westminster Seminary California) plans to study patristics in a doctoral program and is currently pursuing ministerial ordination in Sovereign Grace Ministries. He has published on continuity of the prophetic function throughout the Bible, as well as numerous articles for reference works.

William Brooks is the pastor of Thompsonville Baptist Church in Springfield, Kentucky. He is a former missionary to East Asia and is currently working toward a PhD at Southern Baptist Theological Seminary.

Malcolm R. Brubaker is a professor of Bible at Valley Forge Christian College. He is a candidate for a PhD in renewal studies at Regent University, as well as an ordained minister in the Assemblies of God denomination. He is a member of the Evangelical Theological Society and the Society of Pentecostal Studies and holds a student membership in the American Society of Missiology.

Kalvin Budiman is a PhD candidate in theology at Baylor University. A native of Indonesia, Mr. Budiman is now a lawful permanent resident of the United States. In 2003, he received a master's degree in theology from Calvin Theological Seminary, Grand Rapids, Michigan. In 2005, he graduated from the same seminary with a master's degree in moral theology. He has presented academic papers at several national and regional theological conferences. His book reviews and academic articles have appeared in *Calvin Theological Journal* and *Stulos Journal*. He is married and blessed with a son. He and his family live in Waco, Texas.

James Burnett (MA, Oxford University; MPhil, Cambridge University) is an ordained minister with the Presbyterian Church in Ireland. Having lived for a year in Malawi, Central Africa, James is a frequent visitor to missionary projects in Nigeria and currently serves as the senior pastor of Lowe Memorial Presbyterian Church (Belfast, Northern Ireland). He is also a "Recognised Teacher" within Queen's University and teaches theology part-time at Belfast Bible College. He is married to Hazel.

Philip Bustrum (PhD, Talbot School of Theology) spent fourteen years as a missionary in Kenya serving at Moffat College of Bible as professor and academic dean. He is a professor of Christian education and past chair of the Bible division at Cornerstone University (Grand Rapids, MI). Philip and his wife, Bonnie, have four grown children and nine grandchildren.

Scott N. Callaham holds a BS from the United States Naval Academy, an MDiv from Southwestern Baptist Theological Seminary, and a PhD from Southwestern Baptist Theological Seminary. Callaham is an Old Testament scholar, and his current areas of research include Hebrew linguistics, Old Testament narrative, and Old Testament intertextuality. His first book is *Modality and the Biblical Hebrew Infinitive Absolute* (Harrassowitz, 2010). He is currently serving as a chaplain in the United States Navy.

Craig R. Clarkson received his MDiv from Princeton Theological Seminary in 2006 and is pursuing ordination in the Presbyterian Church (USA). Clarkson is also completing his doctoral studies in church history at Baylor University in Waco, Texas, where he and his family are active contributors in the life and ministry of their local church.

Joe L. Coker is a lecturer in the religion department at Baylor University. He holds an MDiv from Emory University and received his PhD in American church history from Princeton Theological Seminary. He is the author of *Liquor in the Land of the Lost Cause: Southern White Evangelicals and the Prohibition Movement, 1880–1920* (University Press of Kentucky, 2007) and a number of articles dealing with American religion, Baptist history, and the history of Christian missions. He and his wife, Amy, a nurse, live in Waco, Texas, with their two ten-year-old boys, Layton and Connor.

David Cole is vice president for student development and pastoral care and an assistant professor of theology at Briercrest College and Seminary in Caronport, Saskatchewan, Canada. He is an ordained minister with Open Bible Churches, having served for twelve years as president of Eugene Bible College (now New Hope Christian College) in Eugene, Oregon. He currently serves on the steering committee of the International Roman Catholic–Pentecostal Dialogue and previously served as chair of the Ecumenical Studies Interest Group in the Society for Pentecostal Studies.

Derek Cooper is a visiting professor of church history and New Testament at Biblical Seminary in Hatfield, Pennsylvania. He is the author of *So You're Thinking about Going to Seminary* (Brazos, 2008) and *Thomas Manton: A Guide to the Life and Thought of a Puritan Pastor* (P & R, 2011). He also serves on the pastoral staff at Immanuel Church of the Nazarene in Lansdale, Pennsylvania.

Floyd Cunningham holds a PhD from Johns Hopkins University. He is president and professor of the history of Christianity at Asia-Pacific Nazarene Theological Seminary, Taytay, Rizal, Philippines. He is the author of *Holiness Abroad: Nazarene Missions in Asia* (Scarecrow, 2003) and coauthor of *Our Watchword and Song: The Centennial History of the Church of the Nazarene* (Beacon Hill, 2009).

Ernest M. Day Jr. is a mechanical design engineer. He has served as an assistant fire chief in Conesus, New York, and as president of the Rotary in Lima, New York, where he has lived for more than twenty years on a property neighboring Elim Fellowship. He and his wife, Sarah, enjoy getting to know believers of many different church backgrounds.

David A. Dean holds emeritus professorships at Berkshire Christian College and Gordon-Conwell Theological Seminary. He has served as an Advent Christian pastor, educator, author, and overseas missionary. Educated at McGill University, Hartford (CT) Seminary, and Westminster Theological Seminary (ThD), Dean has written extensively on his denomination's history, including two volumes on its mission to the world.

John DelHousaye (PhD, Fuller Theological Seminary) is an assistant professor of New Testament at Phoenix Seminary. He contributed to the *ESV Study Bible* (Crossway, 2008) and the *Baker Illustrated Bible Dictionary* (Baker Books, 2013).

Scott D. Edgar is an ordained minister with the Evangelical Free Church and has served churches in Illinois, Kansas, and South Carolina. He and his family resided in Kiev, Ukraine, where he served as a professor and academic dean at Kiev Theological Seminary. Scott is a graduate of Trinity Evangelical Divinity School (MDiv), Fuller Theological Seminary (DMin), and the University of Wales (PhD). He is currently lead professor of religious studies at the University of Phoenix (Columbia, SC) and teaches leadership, theology, intercultural studies, and ethics at several other schools. Dr. Edgar resides with his family in Columbia, South Carolina.

Alyssa Lehr Evans received her BA in biblical studies and theology from Southeastern Bible College (Birmingham, AL) and her MA in historical and systematic theology from Wheaton College Graduate School (Wheaton, IL). She is currently an intern at College Church in Wheaton and is happily married to her husband, Peter.

William B. Evans holds degrees from Taylor University (BA), Westminster Theological Seminary in Philadelphia (MAR, ThM), and Vanderbilt University (MA, PhD). He is an ordained minister in the Associate Reformed Presbyterian Church (ARP) and served as moderator of the ARP general synod in 2005. Dr. Evans joined the faculty of Erskine College in 1993, and he currently serves as the Younts Professor of Bible and Religion and chair of the department of Bible, religion, and philosophy. In addition to writing various articles and book reviews, he is the author of *Imputation and Impartation: Union with Christ in American Reformed Theology* (Paternoster, 2008).

Elena Goga, born in Romania, graduated from university with a degree in electromechanical engineering. Called to serve, she was involved with Africa Inland Mission for two years. Currently, she is taking a two-year study leave at Belfast Bible College (Northern Ireland) before returning to Africa for long-term ministry.

Scott Goins is professor of classics and director of the honors college at McNeese State University in Lake Charles, Louisiana. He has published articles on Virgil, Boethius, and other authors, and he contributed several entries on Eastern Christian writers for the *Encyclopedia of Christian Literature* (Scarecrow, 2010). He is currently field editor in religion for *ECCB: Eighteenth-Century Current Bibliography* (AMS Press).

Linda Gray is a professor of English at Oral Roberts University, where she has taught full-time since 1985. She teaches linguistics, English education, technical writing, and early Christian literature courses and serves as the university's technical editor. She frequently presents academic papers at professional conferences and has contributed essays and entries to multiple publications. She holds a doctoral degree from Vanderbilt University and an MA in theology from Fuller Theological Seminary in Pasadena, California. Her BA in linguistics is from California State University in Fullerton. She has also been a pastor's wife (Evangelical Presbyterian Church) since 1979 and has taught numerous Bible-related classes over the years.

Bracy V. Hill II (PhD) has earned degrees in history, theology, and the history of Christianity from Missouri State University, the University of Notre Dame, and Baylor University. He teaches courses on American history, Christianity, and interdisciplinary studies. His research and publications address topics in the history of seventeenth- and eighteenth-century English dissent, Wycliffite studies, and American Pentecostalism. His most recent work explored the histories and theology of the Congregational minister Daniel Neal (1678–1743) and the Presbyterian and later antitrinitarian James Peirce (1674–1726).

Joseph M. Holden holds a BA from Western Illinois University; a BBS from Calvary Chapel Bible College; an MDiv from Southern Evangelical Seminary; and a PhD from the University of Wales, Lampeter (UK). He is cofounder and president of Veritas Evangelical Seminary in Murrieta, California; coauthor of *The Popular Handbook of Archaeology and the Bible* (Harvest House, 2013); associate editor of the *Apologetics Study Bible for Students* (Broadman & Holman, 2010); coauthor of *Charts of Apologetics and Christian Evidences* (Zondervan, 2006); coauthor of the high school apologetics textbook *Living Loud: Defending Your Faith* (Broadman & Holman, 2002); and contributor to *Dictionary of World Religions* (Baker, forthcoming).

Bill Hossler has pastored for over thirty years, including twenty-five at Colonial Woods Missionary Church (Port Huron, MI). He also served as a district superintendent for three years and is currently president of the Missionary Church (since 2001). Dr. Hossler is the director and voice for *Today's Key to Confident Living*, a radio program aired on more than 125 radio stations in the United States, and has authored two books: *Radical Promises for Desperate Times: How God Gets Us Through* (Key, 1997) and *Keys to Open Your Heart* (Key, 1999). He and his wife, Margaret, have four grown children and eleven grandchildren.

Mark A. House is professor of biblical studies and registrar at New Geneva Theological Seminary in Colorado Springs, Colorado. He also serves as the director of the online Greek program for Reformed Theological Seminary's virtual campus in Charlotte, North Carolina. He received a BA from Biola University, an MDiv from Westminster Theological Seminary, and a PhD from Fuller Theological Seminary. Dr. House formerly served as an academic editor of New Testament and Greek books for Hendrickson Publishers in Peabody, Massachusetts. He also taught courses at Talbot School of Theology in La Mirada, California; Fuller Theological Seminary in Pasadena, California; and Zaporozhye Bible College in Ukraine.

Clyde M. Hughes has been the bishop/general overseer of the International Pentecostal Church of Christ since 1990. A veteran, Hughes holds a BA from Cedarville University, an MA from the Methodist Theological School in Ohio, and an honorary DD from Heritage Bible College. He is secretary of the Pentecostal/Charismatic Churches of North America and first vice president of the International Pentecostal Press Association. He serves on the board of the National Association of Evangelicals and other organizations and is editor of the *Pentecostal Leader*. He and his wife, Linda, reside in London, Ohio, near their eight children and sixteen grandchildren.

Dick Innes, founder/director of ACTS International since 1970, grew up in Australia and has been a pastor in Michigan and the South Australian director of Youth for Christ. He has lived in California since 1981. Besides being the author of *Daily Encounter*, the weekday email devotional of ACTS International, Innes has authored three books: the bestseller *I Hate Witnessing: A Handbook for Effective Christian Communications; How to Mend a Broken Heart;* and *You Can't Fly with a Broken Wing*. He has written 250 *Encounter* brochure articles and has spoken in many churches in the United States, Australia, and New Zealand.

Lorelle Beth Jabs is an associate professor in the department of communication and journalism at Seattle Pacific University. Her professional career has been broad; Jabs worked several years as an industrial engineer before pursuing a doctorate emphasizing organizational communication. She has traveled widely and published several articles on conflict management and peacemaking in Karamoja, Uganda. She received her PhD from the University of Washington as a Vigfusson fellow and her BS and MS from Oregon State University.

Dennis W. Jowers is an associate professor of theology and apologetics at Faith Evangelical College and Seminary in Tacoma, Washington. He holds an AB in philosophy from the University of Chicago (1999) and an MTh (2001) and a PhD (2004) in systematic theology from the University of Edinburgh. Besides authoring *The Trinitarian Axiom of Karl Rahner: The Economic Trinity Is the Immanent Trinity and Vice Versa* (Edwin Mellen, 2006) and coauthoring with H. Wayne House *Reasons for Our Hope: An Introduction to Christian Apologetics* (Broadman & Holman, 2010), he has contributed articles to various scholarly publications.

Brent Juliot is pastor of Stavanger Lutheran Church and teaches at Hillcrest Lutheran Academy in Fergus Falls, Minnesota. He serves as an editor for both *Faith and Fellowship* magazine and other writing projects for the Church of the Lutheran Brethren.

Paul L. Kaufman, PhD, has taught church history at Ashland Theological Seminary for over twenty years. He served as academic dean at Allegheny Wesleyan College for twenty years and currently chairs the department of Bible and theology at Hobe Sound Bible College, Hobe Sound, Florida. He holds graduate degrees

from Hebrew University, Lutheran Theological Seminary (Gettysburg), Antietam Seminary, and Kent State University. He is retired from twenty years as pastor in the Allegheny Wesleyan Methodist Connection. In addition to publishing *"Logical" Luther Lee and the Methodist War against Slavery* (Scarecrow, 2000), he serves as a conference speaker throughout the United States.

Robert Keay, ThM (Gordon-Conwell Theological Seminary) and PhD (St. Andrews), is a lecturer in theology at the Institute of Theology, Queen's University, Belfast (Northern Ireland).

Hubert James ("Jim") Keener holds a PhD in Christian religion from Baylor University, an MDiv from Pittsburgh Theological Seminary, a graduate certificate from Knox Theological Seminary, and a BA in international ministries from Moody Bible Institute. He is also licensed for ministry by the Southwestern District of the Christian and Missionary Alliance. Keener's research interests focus on a theological interpretation of the Bible, with a special emphasis on the book of Psalms. His dissertation, titled "A Canonical Exegesis of the Eighth Psalm," was written under the supervision of Dr. William H. Bellinger.

P. C. Kemeny is a professor of religion and humanities at Grove City College. He is the author of *Princeton in the Nation's Service: Religious Ideals and Educational Practice, 1868–1928* (Oxford University Press, 1998), editor of *Church, State, and Social Justice: Five Views* (InterVarsity, 2007), and coeditor with Henry Warner Bowden of *American Church History: A Reader* (Abingdon, 1998).

Nicholas J. Kersten is the librarian-historian for the Seventh Day Baptist Historical Society (SDBHS), a position he has held since mid-2005. He graduated with a BSE in English secondary education from the University of Wisconsin–Whitewater in 2003. After that he spent two years at Denver Seminary before joining the SDBHS. In addition to his work for the SDBHS, he is continuing his studies at Trinity Evangelical Divinity School in Deerfield, Illinois, in their MDiv program. He and his wife, Brittany, live in Janesville, Wisconsin.

Paul L. King, an ordained minister of the Christian and Missionary Alliance and an associate professor at Oral Roberts University, holds a DMin from Oral Roberts University and a DTh from the University of South Africa. Specializing in nineteenth- and twentieth-century healing, Holiness, and Pentecostal movements, King is the author of more than fifty articles and nine books, including *Only Believe: Examining the Origin and Development of Classic and Contemporary Word of Faith Theologies* (Word and Spirit, 2008) and *Genuine Gold: The Cautiously Charismatic Story of the Early Christian and Missionary Alliance* (Word and Spirit, 2006). He was the 2006 Oral Roberts University Scholar of the Year.

Byron D. Klaus has served as president and professor of intercultural leadership at the Assemblies of God Theological Seminary since July 1999. Previously, he served as a local church pastor in California, Texas, and Illinois. He was also vice president of Latin America Child Care, a Christian child development agency serving twenty nations in Latin America and the Caribbean, and a faculty member and administrator at Vanguard University of Southern California. His commitment to leadership development in growing churches globally has taken him to fifty nations. His scholarly work has been published by Moody, Logion, Regal, Hendrickson, Baker Academic, Regnum, and Routledge.

James Laesch currently serves as Lutheran Bible Translators' (LBT) associate director for language programs based in Aurora, Illinois. Laesch holds an MA in linguistics from Northeastern Illinois University. He began his mission career in Liberia as a linguist and translation advisor for the Northern Grebo people, and he helped put the language into writing and began the Scripture translation effort; the New Testament was published in 1989. Laesch next served as the language program coordinator for LBT's work in Liberia, followed by a move to LBT's Service Center in 1986, where he gives guidance and support to LBT missionaries and Scripture projects worldwide. Laesch and his wife, Laura, are active in local and international mission work of their congregation, Cross Lutheran Church, Yorkville, Illinois.

Mark A. Lamport (PhD, Michigan State University; ThM, Princeton Theological Seminary) has been a professor at Christian universities and seminaries for more than twenty-five years in the United States and Europe. Currently, he serves on the faculty of London School of Theology (Northwood, England), Evangelische Theologische Faculteit (Leuven, Belgium), and Instituto Biblico Portuges (Lisbon, Portugal). He is the

author of over one hundred articles, chapters, essays, and reviews in over thirty academic journals, periodicals, and books. He is married to Therese and is the father of four grown children and the grandfather of four girls. He has been enriched by several of the denominations and ministries herein.

Robert Leach is an ordained PC(USA) minister of Word and Sacrament and a graduate of Gordon-Conwell Theological Seminary, where he wrote his master's thesis on the ecclesiology of Edward Farley and Karl Barth. He has done postgraduate studies at the University of Aberdeen (Scotland) on the ecclesiology of Thomas F. Torrance. In addition to sailing and woodworking, Leach has published numerous theological and biblical articles, including contributions to Westminster/John Knox Press's *Feasting on the Word*.

Raymond Legg, originally from Charleston, West Virginia, received a doctor of arts in English from Middle Tennessee State University. He holds undergraduate diplomas in Bible/theology and American intercultural ministries from Moody Bible Institute and a BA in anthropology from Northeastern Illinois University. In addition, Dr. Legg earned an MDiv at Trinity Evangelical Divinity School and an MA at the University of Tennessee at Chattanooga. His areas of special interest are American and African American literature, film studies, and pop culture. He has been involved in higher education both in the classroom and as an administrator since 1987 and is presently professor of English and chairman of the English department, chairman of the division of literature and modern languages, and advisor for liberal arts at Bryan College in Dayton, Tennessee. Dr. Legg has extensive experience in church ministry and currently serves as pulpit supply at area churches, preaching in place of ministers who are out of town. He has been a pastor of congregations in Illinois and North Dakota, and he has ministry experience in Europe and Africa. An honorably discharged United States Navy Vietnam veteran, Dr. Legg and Margie, his wife, have one child, a married son, Joshua.

Denis Lemieux is a priest member of the Madonna House Apostolate (MHA). He was born in Trois Rivieres, Canada, in 1966, the youngest of six children. Belonging to the MHA for twenty years, he was ordained a Catholic priest in 2004. Lemieux has a licentiate in sacred theology and is the author of two books on Catholic spirituality. Residing in Combermere, Canada, he divides his time among writing, teaching, and offering personal spiritual direction.

Phuc Luu is an adjunct lecturer in New Testament at Houston Baptist University and a graduate student at the Center for Thomistic Studies at the University of St. Thomas, Houston, Texas. He has published articles on pastoral care, church and culture, biblical studies, and philosophy. His most recent article is "Speaking about Transcendence: Three Medieval Theologians" in the posthumous Festschrift *Thriving in Babylon* (Pickwick, 2011) for the late Baptist theologian A. J. Conyers.

Courtney Lyons is a PhD student in church history at Baylor University and an ordained Baptist minister. Her research interests include the religious aspects of the African American civil rights movement and the religious leadership of women. She is particularly interested in equipping pastors to use church history in their preaching and discipleship ministries. She and her husband, Victor, live in Waco, Texas, and serve a Baptist congregation in Crawford, Texas.

Bryan C. Maine (BA, Williams Baptist College; MDiv, George W. Truett Theological Seminary) is a doctoral student in religion at Baylor University. His research interests focus on religious dissent in sixteenth- and seventeenth-century England.

Robert Martin is the presiding general superintendent of the Assemblies of the Lord Jesus Christ. Rev. Martin, elected general superintendent in 2007, previously served the organization as general youth president and assistant general superintendent. He also pastors the Voice of Pentecost in Baton Rouge, Louisiana.

James R. McConnell, a native of Indianapolis, Indiana, earned a BS degree in electrical engineering at North Carolina State University, after which he was active in the research and development areas of this field for several years. He then went on to earn an MDiv degree from Gordon-Conwell Theological Seminary in Charlotte, North Carolina, followed by a PhD from Baylor University. In 2009, he joined the faculty of the School of Divinity at Gardner-Webb University, where he teaches New Testament and Greek. He is married to Susan, and they have three children, Luke, Evan, and Molly.

Michael McMullen, PhD, has authored several books, including *Hearts Aflame* (Triangle/SPCK, 1995), *Clouds of Heaven* (Triangle/SPCK, 1996), *The Passionate Preacher* (Christian Focus, 1999), *The Prayers and Meditations of Susanna Wesley* (MPH, London, 2000), *God's Polished Arrow* (Christian Focus, 2000), *The Unpublished Sermons of McCheyne* (3 volumes, Banner of Truth, 1999), and *The Glory and Honor of God* (Broadman & Holman, 2004). He was the associate editor (church history) for Oxford University's award-winning *New Dictionary of National Biography*. Born in England, he won, over stiff competition, a major British government scholarship for his doctoral work on Jonathan Edwards, which he carried out at the University of Aberdeen (Scotland) and Yale University. He is currently a professor of church history at Midwestern Baptist Theological Seminary in Kansas City, Missouri.

Martin Monacell holds a BA in religious studies from the University of Virginia. He is an MDiv candidate (August 2010) at the Assemblies of God Theological Seminary in Springfield, Missouri. His short history of the Church of God of the Apostolic Faith was published in the book *Servants of the Spirit: Portraits of Pentecostal/Charismatic Pioneers* (OBC Publishing, 2010).

Philip G. Monroe, PsyD, is an associate professor of counseling and psychology at Biblical Seminary, Hatfield, Pennsylvania. He maintains a small private practice ministering primarily to pastors and other ministry workers.

William J. Monroe is a retired ordained minister in the Advent Christian General Conference, having served churches for forty-five years in New England and Canada. He is a board member of the Advent Christian Retirement Communities and the Maine State Advent Christian Conference. He resides in E. Waterboro, Maine.

Ryan A. Neal (PhD, University of Edinburgh, Scotland) is chair of undergraduate programs, College of Christian Studies, Anderson University (SC). He is the author of *Theology as Hope: On the Ground and Implications of Jürgen Moltmann's Doctrine of Hope* (Pickwick, 2008). His primary areas of research include theology and hermeneutics, especially soteriology and eschatology.

Mark Nickens is an associate professor of church history at the Carolina Evangelical Divinity School in Greensboro, North Carolina.

William R. Osborne is a PhD student and intern to the president at Midwestern Baptist Theological Seminary. He formerly served on the faculty of the Cameroon Baptist Theological Seminary and later as the senior pastor of the First Baptist Church of Smithville, Missouri. He and his wife, Sara, have three children and live in Kansas City, Missouri, where he is currently serving with a new church plant.

Sheryl O'Sullivan is chair of the division of teacher education at Gordon College in Barnesville, Georgia. She teaches courses in reading education and educational foundations. She has a doctorate in education and a master's degree in theology. She is a practicing Roman Catholic.

Michael Padgett has pastored the Church of God Mountain Assembly in Middlesboro, Kentucky, for the past eighteen years. From 2000 to 2004, he served on the executive board of his denomination as assistant general secretary and treasurer and as editor of the *Gospel Herald*. He is a charter member of the Historical Society of Church of God Movements and recently concluded a term as its president. Padgett authored and published *A Goodly Heritage: A History of the Church of God Mountain Assembly* in 1995. He holds an MA in history from Eastern Kentucky University and is currently pursuing his PhD in history from the University of Kentucky.

Kurt W. Peterson is an associate professor of history at North Park University in Chicago, Illinois.

J. Matthew Pinson is president of Free Will Baptist Bible College in Nashville, Tennessee. Prior to his position there, he served as a pastor of churches in Alabama, Connecticut, and Georgia. He received bachelor's and master's degrees from the University of West Florida, a master's degree from Yale, and a doctorate from Vanderbilt. His primary interests are historical theology, the intersection of ecclesiology and cultural studies, higher education, and leadership. He lives with his wife, Melinda, and their children, Anna and Matthew, in Nashville.

T. C. Porter (MDiv, Bethel Seminary San Diego) is the founding director of Adams Avenue Crossing, an organic/missional church movement in the Normal Heights section of urban San Diego.

Carroll W. Powell is academic dean and professor of historical and systematic theology at New Geneva Seminary in Colorado Springs, Colorado. He received a BA from Bob Jones University, a ThB from Sacramento Baptist Theological Seminary, and a PhD from Baptist Christian University. Dr. Powell is an ordained minister in the Reformed Church in the United States and pastor of Trinity Covenant Church, Colorado Springs. Dr. Powell has lectured extensively on Christian education and has served as an instructor at Evangelical Christian Academy in Colorado Springs. Previously, he served as founder and headmaster of Northstate Schools and University in Anderson, California.

Ray Reid (MDiv, Assemblies of God Theological Seminary; BA, Messenger College) currently serves as a chaplain for St. John's Health Center in Springfield, Missouri.

Thomas Reid has been librarian and registrar at the Reformed Presbyterian Theological Seminary in Pittsburgh, Pennsylvania, since 1996. He is a graduate of Westmont College (BA), Westminster Theological Seminary (MDiv), La Faculté de Théologie Réformée in Aix-en-Provence, France (ThM), Reformed Presbyterian Theological Hall in Belfast, Northern Ireland (DipTh), and the University of Pittsburgh (MLS). A minister in the Reformed Presbyterian Church of North America, he has served as pastor of congregations in Ireland, Kansas, and Canada. He contributed to the *Twentieth Century Dictionary of Christian Biography* (Baker, 1995) and *Worship in the Presence of God* (Greenville Seminary Press, 1992).

Dee Renner received her BSN from Anguin College and her MDiv from Claremont School of Theology. The Renners have been active in the formation of the Anglican Church in North America and the Diocese of Western Anglicans, where Dee serves on the executive council. They live in Temecula, California, and are on staff at Christ Church Anglican in Fallbrook, California.

Mark E. Roberts directs the Holy Spirit Research Center at Oral Roberts University, where he is associate professor, reference librarian, occasional teacher of New Testament and other courses, and past chair of ORU's Faculty Christian Worldview Committee. He is publisher of Word & Spirit Press, executive director of Tulsa's SilverTop Brass, and an ordained minister. He earned his BA from Mississippi College, an MA from The Ohio State University, and an MA and PhD from Vanderbilt University. He and his wife of nearly forty years, Carol, have four adult children and three grandchildren.

R. Philip Roberts is the fourth president of Midwestern Baptist Theological Seminary, a position he has held since 2001. He previously served as vice president of the North American Mission Board. In addition to being involved in theological education and international ministry, Roberts has authored two books (*Mormonism Unmasked* [Broadman & Holman, 1998] and *The Counterfeit Gospel of Mormonism* [Harvest House, 1998]), contributed to a number of Christian and evangelical journals and publications, and assisted in the production of two videos, *The Cross and the Crescent* (2001) and *The Mormon Puzzle* (1997). Roberts received his PhD from Free University of Amsterdam, did postgraduate research at Oxford University, and earned an MDiv from Southern Baptist Theological Seminary. He and his wife, Anja, have two grown children.

Warren C. Robertson is an assistant professor of biblical studies at Gardner-Webb University's School of Divinity. A native of South Carolina, he has pastoral experience in the Baptist Church and holds MDiv, MTh, MPhil, and PhD degrees. He and his family live in North Carolina.

Darrin J. Rodgers, MA, JD, is director of the Flower Pentecostal Heritage Center (Springfield, MO) and editor of *Assemblies of God Heritage*.

Scott Rushing is a teaching fellow in the religion department of Baylor University, where he is also completing his PhD in historical theology. His dissertation, under the guidance of D. H. Williams, addresses the development of the apostolic tradition in the ecclesiastical histories of Socrates, Sozomen, and Theodoret. Mr. Rushing earned an MTS in church history from Vanderbilt University and a BA in history and religion from Belmont University.

Douglas Salsbury of Ithaca, Michigan, a minister since 1984, is an avid student of Mennonite history and a member of the denomination's Historical Doctrinal Writing and Proving Committee.

Matthew Shaw, MLIS, is a librarian at Ball State University in Muncie, Indiana, where he also teaches English. He is a historian with the United Pentecostal Church International, the largest Oneness Pentecostal organization, and a regular contributor to the *Indiana Apostolic Trumpet* and the *Pentecostal Herald*. His research and writing interests center on early Pentecostal ecclesiology and theology. Additionally, Mr. Shaw is an independent scholar of British novelist

and philosopher Iris Murdoch and has presented research on her fiction and moral philosophy at various literary and academic conferences. He lives in Muncie, Indiana, with his wife and four sons.

Christian R. Shearer (PhD, Trinity Theological Seminary/University of Wales; ThM, Dallas Theological Seminary) is the senior pastor of RiverTree Community Church in Wyoming, Michigan, a member of the South Grand Rapids Classis of the Reformed Church in America. He has served in professional ministry for twenty-two years, the last eleven as a senior pastor. He is married to Heather and is the father of two children.

M. David Sills, DMiss, PhD, is a professor of Christian missions and cultural anthropology at Southern Baptist Theological Seminary in Louisville, Kentucky. Having served as a missionary to South America, a pastor in both the United States and Ecuador, and a professor, Dr. Sills is the author of several books in Spanish as well as his most recent English-language releases *Reaching and Teaching: A Call to Great Commission Obedience* (Moody, 2010) and *The Missionary Call: Find Your Place in God's Plan for the World* (Moody, 2008). David and his wife, Mary, have been married for over thirty years and currently reside in Louisville.

James D. Smith III is a professor of church history at Bethel Seminary (San Diego) and has lectured at the University of San Diego since 1993. He has been a visiting scholar at Oxford and taught at Daystar University, Nairobi. Having pastored Baptist General Conference churches in Boston, Minneapolis, and San Diego, he currently serves at Fletcher Hills Presbyterian Church. He coedited *The Fabric of Early Christianity* (Pickwick, 2007), *The Subjective Eye* (Pickwick, 2006), *Encyclopedia of Christian Literature* (Scarecrow, 2010), and *Dictionary of Christian Spirituality* (Zondervan, 2011). A longtime editorial advisor to *Christian History and Biography*, he received a ThD and a ThM from Harvard University, an MDiv from Bethel Seminary, and an AB from San Diego State University.

Edward Smither is an associate professor of church history and intercultural studies at Liberty Baptist Theological Seminary (Liberty University) and directs the master's in intercultural studies program there. He holds a PhD in historical theology (University of Wales–Lampeter) and is a PhD candidate in missiology (University of Pretoria). The author of *Augustine as Mentor: A Model for Preparing Spiritual Leaders* (B & H Academic, 2008) and the translator of François Decret's *Early Christianity in North Africa* (Cascade, 2009), Smither has also contributed scholarly articles in history and missiology. Smither served for thirteen years in transcultural ministry in the United States, France, and North Africa.

Alexander C. Stewart, BSMT, University of Kansas–Lawrence, is a graduate student at Regent University, Virginia Beach, Virginia. He is involved with the Alexander and Shirlene Stewart Pentecostal Collection, the Schomburg Center for Black Research, and the New York Public Library and is a collector and historian for the Church of Our Lord Jesus Christ of the Apostolic Faith, New York City.

Michael K. Turner is an assistant professor of religious studies at Misericordia University in Pennsylvania. He holds an MDiv from Emory University in Atlanta, Georgia, and an MA and PhD from Vanderbilt University in Nashville, Tennessee. Dr. Turner is a specialist in the history of religion in North America. At the present time, his research interests include religion in the early American republic, denominationalism, the history of American Methodism, and death and the afterlife in the American imagination.

Rustin J. Umstattd is an associate academic dean and assistant professor of theology at Midwestern Baptist Theological Seminary in Kansas City. He earned his doctorate and an MDiv from Southwestern Baptist Theological Seminary. He also holds an MBA from Georgia Southern University and a BBA from Georgia Southwestern University. Before joining the faculty at Midwestern, Dr. Umstattd served for more than fifteen years in student ministry. His research interests include the theology of both the Trinity and the Holy Spirit.

Myles Werntz is a PhD candidate in theology at Baylor University who writes on war and peace in the Christian tradition, ecclesiology, and contemporary theology.

Benjamin J. Wetzel is a graduate student in the history department at Baylor University. He received his BA in history from Grove City College in 2009. His home is in Lancaster, Pennsylvania.

David M. Wilmington has a BA from Washington and Lee University and an MTS from Duke University Divinity School. He is a PhD candidate in religion (theology) at Baylor University, and his areas of research include contemporary theology, theological ethics and politics, and theology and the arts. He is currently writing on the appropriation of the apophatic theological tradition for modern virtues ethics.

Douglas K. Wilson Jr. serves as an associate professor of Christian studies at the University of Mobile. He writes about and teaches biblical and intercultural studies locally, nationally, and internationally. He is also a member of University Educators for Global Engagement.

Barbara Wyman, MA, MFA, is an instructor of English and Latin at McNeese State University in Lake Charles, Louisiana. She has published on George Herbert and Boethius, among others. She contributed seven entries to *Encyclopedia of Christian Literature* (Scarecrow, 2010) and was cotranslator and coeditor of the Ignatius Critical Edition of Boethius's *Consolation of Philosophy* (Ignatius Press, 2011). Barbara and her husband, Bruce, also a McNeese professor, are the parents of two grown children and worship in the Extraordinary Form of the Roman Rite (Tridentine Latin Mass). In her spare time, Barbara teaches Latin to priests in order that they may learn and offer the Tridentine Latin Mass.

Additional contributors include Isaac Almaguer, Rebecca Hammes, Rebekah Hardy, Gretchen Knurr, Marlene Mankins, Glenn Miller, Nicole A. Pride, Chris A. Ruhl, and Alycia West.

About the Editors

George Thomas Kurian (1931–2015) was the founder and president of the Encyclopedia Society and the editor of sixty-one books, including twenty-seven encyclopedias. Among his books are four major Christian reference works: *World Christian Encyclopedia* (2 volumes, Oxford University Press, 2000), *Nelson's Dictionary of Christianity* (Thomas Nelson, 2001), *Encyclopedia of Christian Civilization* (4 volumes, Wiley-Blackwell, 2008), and *Encyclopedia of Christian Literature* (2 volumes, Scarecrow, 2010).

Sarah Claudine Day is the managing editor of the Encyclopedia Society. She has worked on a number of multivolume reference works, including, most recently, *Encyclopedia of Christian Literature* (2 volumes, Scarecrow, 2010), *Encyclopedia of Christian Civilization* (4 volumes, Wiley-Blackwell, 2008), *Encyclopedia of Political Science* (5 volumes, CQ Press, 2010), *Encyclopedia of the Democratic Party* (2 volumes, Sharpe Reference, 1996), and *Encyclopedia of the Republican Party* (2 volumes, Sharpe Reference, 1996). She is a graduate of Vassar College and lives in Lima, New York, with her husband, Ernie.

Bring the Bible to life with these
full-color resources

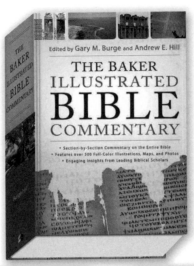

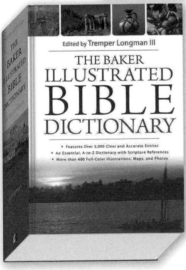

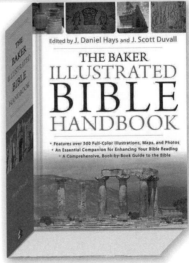